HOW BUSINESS WORKS

MAKING PROFITS, TAKING RISKS, AND CREATING VALUE IN A GLOBAL ECONOMY

By Robert S. Kemp, Adam Kemp, And Kelley Kemp

cognella® | ACADEMIC PUBLISHING

Bassim Hamadeh, CEO and Publisher
Kassie Graves, Director of Acquisitions
Jamie Giganti, Senior Managing Editor
Jess Busch, Senior Graphic Designer
Natalie Lakosil, Senior Licensing Manager
Kathryn Ragudos, Interior Designer

Cover image copyright © Depositphotos/tongdang.
Copyright © Depositphotos/sergeypykhonin.

Printed in the United States of America

ISBN: 978-1-5165-1070-2 (pbk) / 978-1-5165-1071-9 (br)

I dedicate this book to my beloved wife, Pam. She is the person who believed in me, inspired me, and ultimately empowered me to live my dream.

Professor Robert Kemp

CONTENTS

CONTENTS

CHAPTER 18: OPPORTUNITIES AND CHALLENGES IN MANAGING ASSETS 381

CHAPTER 19: OPPORTUNITIES AND CHALLENGES IN MANAGING FINANCIAL CAPITAL (DEBT AND EQUITY) 405

APPENDIX A: FINANCIAL ANALYSIS 425

AUTHORS

Robert S. Kemp, DBA, CPA is the Ramon W. Breeden, Sr. Research Professor at the McIntire School of Commerce, University of Virginia. During his 30 years at the school, he has taught numerous undergraduate and graduate courses, as well as executives around the world. His scholarly works include over 70 completed projects, including books, monographs, articles, cases, and working papers. He has worked with and taught for organizations such as Navigant, Bank of America, Wellington Management, Ernst & Young, the Russian Bankers Association, and other prestigious organizations. He is a Certified Public Accountant and possesses a baccalaureate, masters, and doctorate in business administration.

Adam Kemp, CPA has worked over 15 years in the fields of accounting and taxation in the private and public sectors. His experience covers state, local, federal, and international taxation of corporations, flow-through entities, and non-profits. Mr. Kemp has worked with some of the largest organizations in the United States, including Sallie Mae, MCI, and the PCAOB. He has drafted guidance and provided instruction on various topics, such as nexus standards, alternative tax systems, and deductible versus capital expenditures. Mr. Kemp is a Certified Public Accountant and holds a bachelor's of science in accounting from the University of Virginia and master of professional accounting in taxation from the University of Texas at Austin.

Kelley M. Kemp, JD, Esq. is a practicing attorney in central Virginia, assisting clients in criminal and civil matters. She also serves as an adjunct instructor at various colleges, teaching courses on a variety of legal topics. Prior to becoming an attorney, Ms. Kemp worked in the field of securities regulation at FINRA (formerly NASD). Ms. Kemp received her bachelor's degree from the University of Virginia and attended law school at the Washington College of Law at American University.

PREFACE

Dear Reader,

Welcome. Welcome to the world of business. We're excited that you are beginning your journey with our text, *How Business Works: Making Profits, Taking Risks, and Creating Value in a Global Economy.*

As you use our text, please realize that the text is intended for a serious student of business. The text provides a comprehensive and integrated view of the world of business. It is comprehensive in that introduces all the major elements of a successful business. It does not avoid important yet challenging topics such as law and taxation, risk management, the impact of time, accounting and financial management, or ethics. Although an introductory text, it examines all the major elements of business.

This text also uses an integrated framework based on contemporary practice and theory. That framework is stakeholder value. The framework is based on the belief that a successful business creates value for all of its stakeholders. These stakeholders include customers, employees, and owners. Think about it. If customers do not receive value, then customers will not buy a business's product. To create a valued product, a business needs good employees. Employees will not work for a business without receiving value. Last, without a sale, a business will not survive. Owners will lose. This text examines business in a competitive world where businesses compete for customers, assets, people, and money. To be successful, all the stakeholders of a business must win and receive value.

So what is value? Think how many times you ask the question: "Is it worth it?" You are embracing value when you ask this question. We'll explore the concept of value throughout the book. To do so, the text is organized in five major sections.

We'll start in Section 01 by building an appreciation of and framework for business. There are three chapters in this section. Chapter 01 examines the nature of business. Chapter 02 examines the process of creating value. Chapter 03 examines managing a business for value.

We'll then move to Section 02, looking at the environment in which business operates. There are four chapters in this section. Chapter 04 examines economics, both microeconomics and macroeconomics. Chapter 05 examines globalization and how globalization impacts business. Chapter 06 examines the forms and taxation of business. Chapter 07 examines the legal and ethical nature of business.

Next is Section 08, dealing with the tools of business. There are four chapters in this section. Chapter 08 examines financial reporting and accounting. Chapter 09 examines valuation and the time value of money.

Chapter 10 examines the relationship of a business's financing and investing decisions. Chapter 11 examines risk and risk management.

The fourth section of the text deals with how businesses meet the needs of customers. In this section are four chapters. Chapter 12 examines marketing. Chapter 13 examines the marketing mix: product, place, promotion, and pricing. Chapter 14 examines entrepreneurship and small business. Chapter 15 examines producing products and value chains.

The fifth and last section deals with managing economic resources, including people, assets, information, and financial capital. There are four chapters in this section. Chapter 16 examines the opportunities and challenges in managing information, technology, and e-business. Chapter 17 examines the opportunities and challenges in managing employees. Chapter 18 examines the opportunities and challenges in managing assets. Chapter 19 examines the opportunities and challenges in managing financial capital, both debt and owners' equity.

Last, at the end of the text, are resources including an appendix on financial analysis, a glossary, and an index.

So welcome. Welcome to the world of business.

Best wishes,

Robert S. Kemp, DBA, CPA
Adam S. Kemp, BS, MS in Taxation, CPA
Kelley M. Kemp, BA and JD

SECTION 1

A FRAMEWORK FOR BUSINESS

In this section, you will read and review the following chapters:

CHAPTER

01

THE NATURE OF BUSINESS

Introduction: Let's Talk About Business

So you want to understand business. Maybe you want to start your own business and be an entrepreneur. Maybe you want to work for a business. Maybe as a customer or other stakeholder you want to understand how business works. What you know is you're surrounded by businesses everywhere you go. But have you ever really thought about what a business truly is or what motivates businesses to do the things they do? Why are businesses so important?

In this chapter, we'll begin our exploration of the world of business. We'll start by establishing a framework for understanding why businesses exist and how businesses operate. We'll then look at how people create and operate a business that tries to make the whole greater than the simple sum of its parts. We'll begin to explore "How Business Works."

1

Customers making purchases at a Target. Today, shoppers enjoy the convenience and vast selection large retail chains provide.

WHY BUSINESS MATTERS

Over the last ten years, millions of businesses have been formed in the United States and around the world. From the creation and operation of businesses, millions of new products have been introduced. With most of these products, people's incomes and quality of life, referred to as their **standard of living**, have improved.

Think about how business has affected how we travel, our health, how we communicate, and how we shop. Can you imagine traveling to work on a horse, washing dishes without detergent, communicating with distant friends only with written letters, or going shopping in a small store with limited selection? Now think about your world with cars built by companies like Hyundai, consumer products produced by companies like Procter & Gamble (P&G), information services delivered by companies like Google, and shopping experiences provided by companies such as Target.

Today, most people live longer and better because of business. Did you know that in 1900, the average life expectancy for a person in the United States was 47 years?[1] In 2011, people in the United States are expected live 78.8 years.[2] Why are people living longer? A big part of that answer is business. Walk into a pharmacy and look at all the health care products that are created, produced, and sold by that business. Walk into a grocery store and look at the assortment of safe, tasty, and convenient food products. Walk into a hospital and see the sophisticated health care equipment that saves and enhances lives. Who provides these products? Of course the answer is businesses.

President Barack Obama and Warren Buffett in the Oval Office, July 14, 2010

PROFILE

WARREN BUFFETT, THE ORACLE OF OMAHA

Warren Buffett, often referred to as the "Oracle of Omaha," was born in Omaha, Nebraska, in 1930. His entrepreneurial drive began early and has lasted a lifetime. At the age of 6, Buffett bought a six-pack of cola for $1.50 ($.25 per bottle) and sold each bottle for $.35, netting a $.10 profit per bottle. At age 11, he began working in his father's business. At age 35, Buffett and a group of investors purchased the textile firm Berkshire Hathaway and turned it into an investment powerhouse, owning companies such as GEICO insurance, Burlington Northern Railroad, and the Washington Post newspaper. If you had invested $1,000 in Berkshire Hathaway in 1965, your investment would have been worth $10 million in 2000. What is his secret? His secret is looking for companies where managers focus on creating value for customers, owners, and other stakeholders. Today Warren Buffett is considered one of the richest people in the world, with wealth approximately $65.8 billion. He has created a great deal of value by seeing businesses that focus on it.[3]

"price is what you pay. value is what you get." —Warren Buffett

THE NATURE AND PURPOSE OF BUSINESS

To start the study of business, we need to first understand what business is. Then we'll look at the purpose of business. This purpose will become the foundation of how business operates.

WHAT IS A BUSINESS?

A **business** is an organization, recognized under the law, which attempts to create value by exchanging products with customers for money or money substitutes (such as a credit card). Looking closely at this definition, we can see that an organization must have four critical elements to be called a business:

1. Businesses are *legal entities*. That is, businesses are permitted by law to conduct transactions such as buying and selling products.

2. A business must offer *a product*, often referred to as either a *good* or *service*.
   - **Goods** are physical items that we can touch and feel. Examples include food, cars, and clothing.

   - **Services** are intangible activities that we know exist but *cannot* touch and feel. Examples include haircuts and education.

American Red Cross volunteers work tirelessly to help victims recover from disasters.

IT'S ALL ABOUT YOU

Why does business matter, and why should you study business? The answers to these questions are important for everyone in society. We all have wants, needs, and dreams. The fulfillment of many of your desires depends on business.

Think about it. You want a job. Who is going to hire you? Either a for-profit business (such as a retail store) or a not-for-profit business (such as the Red Cross or the government). Think about your need to understand why that business exists and how you should help operate that business. Now think about where you want to be in twenty years. What type of life do you want to live in the future? How are you going to get there? Business will probably play a major role in your success.

So why does business matter to you? The answer is business is everywhere and affects almost every aspect of your life. And when business works well, you and the world prosper.

Habitat for Humanity, a not-for-profit organization, relies on volunteers as well as donations of both money and materials to build affordable homes for low-income families. Since its founding in 1976, Habitat for Humanity has helped more than 6.8 million people obtain a safer place to sleep at night, along with the strength, stability and independence to build better lives.

Note that some businesses offer both goods and services. For example, a car repair shop provides the service of repairing your car along with goods such as necessary replacement parts.

3.   A business must *exchange* these products for money or money substitutes (such as a credit card) with customers. **Customers** are people or organizations that buy a business's products. A business must create an exchange, commonly referred to as a **sale**, with a customer. The business must provide the customer with a product the customer wants and for which the customer is willing to pay. Economists often say that products provide customers with **utility**, which is a measure of satisfaction or benefits gained from the purchase of a product.

4.   Finally, businesses attempt to create *value*, which we'll discuss more in a bit. Customers get value from the utility of products they buy when they use, consume, or enjoy them. However, other stakeholders in a business—those who are affected by its success or failure, including owners, employees, suppliers, and lenders—should also receive value. In just a minute we'll discuss how businesses should provide all stakeholders with such value.

FOR-PROFIT VS. NOT-FOR-PROFIT BUSINESS

Given this definition, businesses can be separated into two broad categories. First are **for-profit businesses**, which attempt to create an exchange between the business and a customer that results in a profit. A business makes a **profit** when the *revenue* (the money or money substitutes a business receives) from the exchange exceeds the **cost** (or expense) incurred in the exchange. Costs include the price of materials, labor, and services (e.g., marketing) the business incurs in generating the revenue. Procter & Gamble, Target, Google, and Hyundai are all examples of for-profit businesses. Each attempts to make a profit by offering products (goods and/or services) to customers.

Not-for-profit businesses attempt to balance revenue and costs. Such businesses attempt to create an exchange in which profit is not the objective. The focus of not-for-profit businesses is on meeting the special needs of society. Examples of not-for-profit businesses include charities such as the American Diabetes Association, religious organizations, and governments. Although this text will focus mainly on for-profit businesses, many of the principles used in creating and operating a not-for-profit business are the same as a for-profit business.

LEARNING OBJECTIVE 2
. . . .

THE FOUNDATIONS OF VALUE AND HOW BUSINESSES STRIVE TO CREATE VALUE

As we touched on earlier, the purpose of any business is to create, and ideally maximize, value. In a for-profit business, this value is often measured as the market price of the business, or what you'd pay for the business if you wanted to buy it. All too often people assume that a business exists to create a product, profit, jobs, and so on. Of course all of these things are extremely important. However, the *purpose* of a business is really to create *value*. So what is value? How do we measure value? How does value differ from profit?

THE GENERAL CONCEPT OF VALUE

When anyone enters into an exchange, he or she engages in a process of valuation. We do it so much in our society that we often don't even think about it. We go to the store and buy clothes. We go to a doctor to pay for his or her services. We go to a college and pay for an education. In doing so, we seek an exchange in which the value we receive exceeds the value that we give up. For example, if we need a new shirt, we go to a store, find a shirt we want, and then look at the price of that shirt. If we believe the value we'll receive from owning the shirt is greater than the value of the money we must pay for it, we buy it. If we believe the value of the shirt is less than the value of the money we must pay, we keep our money and don't buy the shirt. We're basically comparing the value of the shirt and the value of the money, seeking the greatest value for ourselves.

A young woman shopping for a handbag in Arlington, Virginia. What is the opportunity cost related to the purchase?

Therefore, when we estimate the value of something, we focus on the benefits we'll expect to receive if we own that item. In doing so, we consider the following three things:

- **The quantity or *amount* of the benefits we expect to receive.** The greater the benefits we expect we'll receive, the higher the value we perceive. That's why higher-quality clothing costs more than lower-quality clothing. The higher-quality clothing will last longer and provide us with more benefits than the lower-quality clothing.

How does the seasonality of fashion affect the retail pricing? What risks does a buyer face when buying clothing out of season?

- **The expected *timing* of the benefits we expect to receive.** The old adage that "time is money" is true. The quicker we expect to receive something, the more value we perceive it has. Have you ever bought summer clothing in the fall? Stores know that customers will only purchase such items if they are priced low. Why? Because customers are going to have to wait a long time before they can wear summer clothing. Time erodes the value of most products.

- **The *opportunity cost and risk* involved.** We have many different opportunities for using our money. Therefore, we compare opportunities to determine which one gives us the greatest value. So we assess an **opportunity cost**, often called a *required rate of return*. This required rate of return is related to the risk involved in our choices. **Risk** is the uncertainty of receiving benefits that are lower in amount and/or later in time than we expect. We do not like risk. Value decreases as risk increases. Value increases as risk decreases. To take risk, we require higher benefits or return. For example, one of the reasons we don't buy summer clothes for full price in the fall is we don't know what our summer needs will be next year. Our size may change. The styles and colors we want may change. The clothes currently available may not meet our needs. To get us to take that risk, the price of summer clothes sold in the fall must be low.

EXHIBIT 1.1: The Elements of Value

We see risk in every aspect of our lives. The recent crisis in the business world is an example of how value can be destroyed by focusing only on benefits without considering risks. Businesses sought higher profits (benefits) for their owners. To accomplish this, businesses took on higher levels of risk. Banks lent money to customers who were too risky. Real estate developers made investments in properties that were too risky. Companies produced products that were not adequately tested and thus risky.

The three main elements of **value**—quantity, timing, opportunity cost/risk—are depicted in Exhibit 1.1.

SUMMARIZING VALUE

In summary, the value of something is a function of the benefits we expect to receive from its ownership. Specifically, we want to know:

1. What benefits do I expect to receive if I own this item (that is, what is the quantity of expected benefits)? The greater the benefits we expect to receive, the greater the value. The lower the benefits we expect to receive, the lower the value.

2. When do I expect to get these benefits (that is, what is the timing of the expected benefits)? The quicker we expect to receive the benefits, the greater the value. The longer we expect to wait to receive the benefits, the lower the value.

3. What is the chance that I would get lower benefits than I expect or would need to wait longer than I expect? This is risk. The greater the risk, the lower the value. The lower the risk, the greater the value. To take risk, we should require higher benefits or return. We should have a higher opportunity cost.

What role did the focus on benefits play in the 2008–2010 housing market bubble burst?

Note that a key principle regarding value is the "present and future." Value is a function of what the owner expects to receive now and in the future, not the past. The benefits received in the past are gone. We look at, learn from, and appreciate the past. However, it is the expectation of *present and future* benefits that ultimately determines the value of something. Would you buy a can of soda expecting it to be empty? How much is an old car worth that can no longer be driven? The bottom line is simple: Value is about the present and future.

HOW DO BUSINESSES CREATE VALUE?

Now let's look at these principles and apply them to business. Businesses act in the same way as you do when you buy items such as a shirt. Businesses want to create an exchange where the business receives value greater than it gives up. They buy or make products that have one value—that is, a **cost**. They want to sell these products to customers at a higher value—that is, a **revenue**. Businesses want to create an exchange where revenue exceeds costs, earning a **profit**.

Let's look at the clothing store example again. If the store buys a shirt at one price and sells it to you at a higher price, this exchange creates a profit for the business. Making a profit is very important in for-profit business and drives the value of the business to its owners. But creating value is more than just generating a profit. Owners' value is also a function of *when* the profit is earned and the *risk* associated with that profit.

Let's go deeper into our clothing store example. The store buys clothing. It believes it can sell that clothing at a profit. But how certain is the business that it can sell the clothing at a profit? What happens if the clothing does not meet the rapidly changing needs of customers? It may take a long time to sell the clothing, or the business may need to reduce the price of the clothing to sell it. The business may even need to sell the clothing for a **loss** where the revenue the business receives is less than the cost of the purchased clothing. Although the business bought the clothes believing it would sell them and make a timely profit, it doesn't know this will happen for sure. The business must acknowledge that it is accepting risk.

How do discount retailers manage timing and risk? How do they benefit from other retailers' purchasing mistakes?

Therefore, a business's value is a function of the amount of *profit it expects to earn*, but it is also a function of the *timing* and *risk* of the expected profits. The greater the expected profit from a business, the greater the value of the business. The quicker owners expect to receive the profit from a business, the greater the value of the business. The less risk associated with the business, the greater the value of the business.

Thus, the trick of creating business value is to create a profit but to do it in a timely fashion and with low risk. The challenge is that the amount of the profit, the timing of the profit, and the risk in generating the profit are not independent. Greater profit often means greater risk. Managing for value is all about balancing the drive for profit with an appreciation of timing and risk.

FOR WHOM DO BUSINESSES CREATE VALUE?

The objective of a business is to create value for its owners. There are a number of different legal forms of business and forms of ownership, such as sole proprietorships, partnerships, and corporations. (Note: The forms of business will be discussed in Chapter 06. For example, owners of corporations are called **stockholders**, who buy shares of stock that represent their ownership.)

If a business does not create value for owners, owners will not provide the money needed to operate the business. Owners expect to receive value that compensates them for the use of their money over time and for taking risk. There is an old saying that goes, "It takes money to make money." It takes money to form and operate a business. To attract that money, businesses must convince the providers of that money that they will receive value. The providers of the money must believe that the value they will receive exceeds the value they are giving up.

However, owners must appreciate that in order to create value, businesses must ensure that other stakeholders, not just owners, receive value too. We noted earlier that a business has many **stakeholders**, including owners, employees, suppliers, customers, lenders, and even society at large (see Exhibit 1.2). Ideally, all stakeholders believe that the value they receive exceeds the value they give up. Let's look at some examples:

EXHIBIT 1.2: Stakeholders in a Business

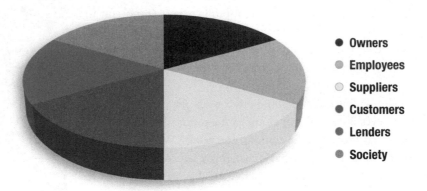

- Owners
- Employees
- Suppliers
- Customers
- Lenders
- Society

· Employees give a business their time and efforts (labor) in exchange for a paycheck.

· Suppliers sell products to a business, ideally at a profit.

· Customers buy a product from a business at a price they feel has value for them.

· Lenders, such as banks, provide money to a business and expect value in the form of the return of their money plus interest.

· Society benefits from the existence of a business through jobs, taxes, and a higher standard of living. Often the value society receives is protected by government and regulators appointed by government.

Why does focusing on *all* stakeholders matter to companies? In a **free market economy** like the one in the United States, buyers and sellers are free to buy and sell what they want, at the price they choose.

BUSINESS SENSE

RISK

Picture this: It's a hot day and you need a drink. You walk into the school cafeteria and see two drink machines. Both machines hold 12-ounce cans of soda. One machine contains a brand you recognize (such as Coke or Pepsi). The other machine is full of drinks that look similar to the brands you recognize but are sold under unknown (unbranded) names (such as cola or lemon drink). Which one do you buy? Both drinks profess to immediately quench your thirst. However, the branded drinks cost a dollar, and the unbranded drinks cost 50 cents. Why the different price? The answer is risk. You know exactly what you'll get when you buy a branded product. You, therefore, take little risk when buying the branded drink. But you're not sure you'll like the taste of the unbranded product. You take on more risk when buying the unbranded drink. To entice you to buy the unbranded drink, the seller must offer it at a lower price. The unbranded drink bears more risk, and risk lowers value.

Nobody makes an employee come to work. Nobody forces a supplier to sell its product. Nobody forces a customer to buy a product. In a free market economy, the providers of money (lenders) are also free to provide their money as they deem appropriate. Nobody forces a bank to make a loan to a business. Nobody forces an owner to put money into a business. Likewise, society is not required to permit a business to operate. Therefore, *all* stakeholders are important to a business's success—they should all feel that they are receiving value greater than the value they are giving.

So if the purpose or objective of a business is to create value, and we need to focus on value for owners and other stakeholders, how does a business create value? How does a business generate profits, over time, at a level of risk?

HOW IS VALUE CREATED?

Businesses create value by first seeing needs and opportunities and then meeting these needs and opportunities with products that are valued by customers. Look around you and see that entrepreneurship and innovation are alive. For example, Google did not exist in the year 2000. In 2000, Hyundai did not sell Kia automobiles in the United States. In 2000, there were fewer than 1,000 Target stores. Today that number is approaching 2,000. The spirit of creativity, improving the lives of customers, making profits, and creating value is everywhere.

2015 Kia Sportage photographed in Montreal, Quebec, Canada at the 2015 Montreal International Auto Show.

But for entrepreneurship to succeed in a free market economy, businesses must compete for everything, including customers, assets, employees, and money. To attract customers, businesses must have the best products. To have the best products, businesses must have the best employees and assets. To have the best employees and assets, businesses must compete for money. To compete for money, businesses must have the best use of money, which goes back to having the best products, customers, employees, and assets. Managing a business and creating value is not easy. Yet when done right, a successful business is special. It's exciting to see people, assets, and money come together to create value for customers, employees, suppliers, owners, lenders, and society.

Today, the opportunities to compete are everywhere. Great business leaders dream about change. They see things that could be. They embrace a world that is rapidly changing and the opportunities that change presents. New markets, new products, new ways of thinking and living are everywhere. Technology is changing the way we live. Globalization is opening up new markets and opportunities. Population demographics are changing, with people living longer, becoming more educated, and reevaluating their lifestyles and priorities. Change is everywhere, thus the opportunities for business to create value are everywhere as well.

And yet, these same opportunities create challenges and risks for business. For example, Google has experienced a number of challenges regarding censorship in countries such as China. Procter & Gamble also faces challenges and risks as it creates, produces, and sells new cosmetics. Likewise, Hyundai faces a number of challenges, including producing an automobile that is lighter, more fuel efficient, and also affordable. In the coming chapters we'll discuss the many ways in which businesses create value and overcome challenges.

CREATING VALUE BY ACQUIRING AND INVESTING MONEY

Creating business value begins with acquiring and investing money. A business acquires money by either borrowing money or getting owners to provide money. Borrowed money is often called **debt** or **liabilities**. Owners' money is often called **equity**. When owners put their money into a business, it is often said that owners are investing their equity money in a business.

The business then takes the money and invests it in assets and hires people. An **asset** is an economic resource (such as a building, equipment, and cash) that a business owns and can use to operate the business. The business also hires people, called **employees**, to manage and operate the business. With these assets and people, the business operates in the hope of generating an **operating profit**. Operating profit is the money a business has left after deducting the expense of operating the business (such as the cost of products it sells and the cost of employee salaries) from its revenue. The equation is as follows:

EQUATION 1.1: Operating Profit

$$Revenue - Operating\ Expenses = Operating\ Profit$$

The business then uses this operating profit to compensate the providers of the money for the use of that money. First, lenders such as banks receive interest. **Interest** is the cost or expense businesses must pay to borrow money. Then, owners get what remains, referred to as **net income** (or **net profit**). Net income is operating profit less interest expense. (Note, we'll look at taxes in Chapter 06.) The equation is as follows:

EQUATION 1.2: Net Income

$$Operating\ Profit - Interest\ Expense = Net\ Income$$

The question that lenders and owners must ask is whether or not the interest or net income they receive is worth the time and risk involved. Lenders and owners have many alternative uses for their money. They, like everyone else, seek the greatest value.

ACQUIRING AND INVESTING MONEY: AN EXAMPLE

Let's look at a simple example. Say you want to start and operate a business for one year. As the owner, you put in $100,000. To compensate for your time and risk, you expect a net income of $10,000. Thus, in one year, you *expect* to receive your original $100,000 plus $10,000 net income, or a total of $110,000. You then go to a bank and ask to borrow $100,000 for one year. The bank looks at your loan application and agrees to lend you the money. However, for the time and risk associated with your loan, the bank *requires* you to pay interest of 6 percent at the end of the year. Thus, in one year, you are required to repay the bank the $100,000 loan plus pay the bank $6,000 (6%) interest, or a total of $106,000.

You now have a total of $200,000 (your $100,000 investment plus the $100,000 bank loan). Your business now has an asset called cash of $200,000. Your business hires people and uses the cash to acquire other assets such as products to sell, called inventory. You then operate your business. After a year, you close the business and sell its assets for $205,000. You are proud of your business because you sold a product and in doing so made an operating profit of $5,000 (that is, the revenue from your

BOLD CITY BREWERY

Susan Miller and her son, Brian, founded a small brewery in October 2008 after stepping away from information-technology positions in the health-care industry. Susan and her husband, John, agreed to pull equity from their home in order to finance the business.

With Brian acting as head brewer and Susan as president and CEO, Bold City is truly a family affair. Brian's wife works in the tap room, and his sister and younger brother handle restaurant and bar relations. As Jacksonville, Florida, natives, they want the brewery to be recognized as a responsible and respected member of the local community.

The small company produced approximately 800 barrels (one barrel is 31 gallons) its first year, 3,000 barrels its second year, and 5,000 barrels its third year. It is currently producing over 40,000 barrels a year and growing.

The company and product have developed a loyal following, and many of its ten signature beers can be found at more than two hundred establishments throughout Northeast Florida.

sales exceeded the cost of these sales by $5,000). You now have the original $200,000 you invested and borrowed plus the $5,000 profit from operating the business (for a total of $205,000).

You then go to the bank to repay the $100,000 loan. However, the bank also requires you to pay the $6,000 interest. After repaying the loan plus interest ($106,000), all that remains of your $205,000 is $99,000. What has happened? You expected to receive your original $100,000 plus net income of $10,000. Instead of increasing your wealth by $10,000, you have destroyed $1,000 of wealth. You did not create value, you destroyed value.

We noted earlier that businesses get money by either borrowing it or having owners provide it. As noted above, *interest* is the cost of borrowed money. However, owners' money also has a cost. Owners are not going to provide their money without expecting to receive a benefit or net income over time. Why would an owner of a business put money in a business for no net income when he or she could deposit his or her money in a bank and earn interest? Money, whether borrowed or provided by owners, has a cost. That cost of the money is related to the time period the business will use the money. The cost of the money is also related to the risk the lender or owner is taking.

In summary, when we acquire money, we are acquiring **financial capital**. Our money or financial capital comes from borrowed funds (debt) or from owners (equity). Financial capital has a cost. What we do with that money is invest it in assets and hire people. Assets are often called **real capital**, and people are called **human capital**. We then use the real and human capital to create operating profit. Ideally, the operating profit from investing in real and human capital will exceed the cost of the financial capital. When it does, value is created. When it does not, value is destroyed.[4] Exhibit 1.3 depicts the three forms of capital.

EXHIBIT 1.3: Three Forms of Capital

What Are the Inputs Needed to Create Value?

| Real Capital | Human Capital | Financial Capital |

LEARNING OBJECTIVE 4

MANAGING A BUSINESS: CREATING VALUE

To be successful and create value, businesses require managers who work hard and work smart. Such managers must constantly look for better ways to do things and forecast opportunities and challenges in the future. But what does it really mean to be a manager? What do managers do? Such questions are at the center of creating value.

A **manager** is someone who is responsible for looking after the interests of the business's owners and other stakeholders. **Managing** or **management** is the process of making decisions that affect the value of the business. Management can be defined in many different ways, and the understanding and practice of management has evolved over time. However, the focus of successful managers is always on creating value. To create value effectively, managers must do three things:

EXHIBIT 1.4: The Management Process

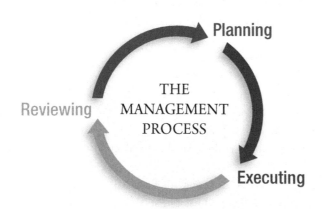

Planning

THE MANAGEMENT PROCESS

Reviewing

Executing

1. **Plan: Planning** involves envisioning the future, finding opportunities, setting goals, determining the best alternative(s) to achieve these goals, and developing systems that will enable the business to execute the selected alternatives.

2. **Execute: Executing** involves using systems to operate the business, according to plans, to achieve the desired goals.

3. **Review: Reviewing** involves using systems to compare the desired outcomes to the actual results.

We'll look at all of these aspects of management in more detail in Chapter 03. For now, it's important that you understand that the process of management is circular and ongoing. Managers envision the future and decide how to create value in the future. This is planning. Managers must then execute their plans in the present. This involves creating, producing, and selling products. However, in doing so, managers must also control the processes used to execute the plans. Finally, managers must compare the actual results with the desired results. From that review process, managers adjust and revise their plans and execution strategies.

EXHIBIT 1.5: Management Levels

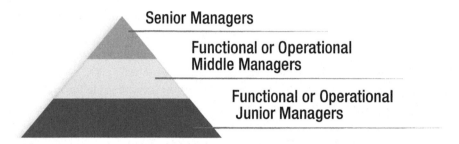

MANAGEMENT LEVELS AND BUSINESS DEPARTMENTS

A business is a team, and every player on the team must understand her or his role in making the whole team successful. To be successful, managers need to focus on their particular role in the business team. Some managers help direct and coordinate the overall organization. These managers are referred to as **senior managers**. An example of a senior manager is the president or chief executive officer (CEO) of a corporation like Procter & Gamble.

Other managers specialize in a functional area and are called **functional** or **operational managers**. An example of a functional or operational manager is a plant manager for Hyundai. Developing a product requires expertise different from accounting for that product. Selling a product requires expertise different from making that product. Having good senior managers is critical, and having good functional or operational managers, both middle managers and junior managers, is also critical.

Businesses, their managers, and other employees are organized or departmentalized in many ways. In Chapter 03 we'll look at the different ways to organize a business. However, certain basic functions are found in most businesses. These departments or functions are often referred to as *research and development, marketing, production or operations, finance, accounting, information technology,* and *human resources.*

The **research and development (R&D) department** or function is responsible for acquiring and applying new knowledge in creating new products, refining existing products, and deciding whether or not existing products can create value. The R&D department adds value by helping the business create products that customers want and will buy. For example, take the Google Android phone. Someone had to envision the phone. Someone also had to figure out there was a market for the phone. Then someone had to determine

Apple's Steve Jobs (now deceased) and Microsoft's Bill Gates have defined the way we use software and computers today. As managers they have led their respective organizations to extraordinary value and industry prominence. How did Jobs and Gates (pictured above) use the three aspects of management to successfully launch their companies' products?

The 2015 Hyundai Sonata Hybrid.

how to meet the needs of the market and develop the phone. Google's R&D department was responsible for this.

The **marketing department** or function is responsible for understanding the market (potential customers and competitors), making sure the product will meet customer needs, pricing the product, trying to show customers why the product adds superior value, and distributing the product. The marketing department adds value to a business by helping the business to identify, distribute, and sell products that customers want and will buy. Let's look at Hyundai's car called the Sonata. Working with Hyundai's R&D department, someone had to determine what the market wanted. Then someone had to determine how much customers would pay (or set the price) for the Sonata, how to promote the Sonata, and how to distribute the Sonata. Hyundai's marketing department was responsible for this.

The **production** or **operations department** or function is responsible for making the product. The production or operations department adds value by producing products customers want and will buy at a cost that creates net income for the business. For example, Procter & Gamble (P&G) manufactures and sells Crest toothpaste. To manufacture Crest toothpaste, P&G needs a system to provide a consistent product at its projected cost. Someone has to acquire and manage the facilities, equipment, materials, and people needed to make Crest toothpaste. Someone must also be responsible for producing the correct quantity and quality of Crest toothpaste. P&G's production or operations department is responsible for this.

The **finance (or treasury) department** or function is responsible for acquiring and managing financial resources (money). The finance department works with lenders and owners to acquire money and to make sure that money is wisely invested in assets and people. For example, Google needed money to develop, produce, and sell the Android phone. Working with the other departments in the company, the finance department needed to demonstrate that the operating profits from the Android phone would be sufficient to reward the lenders and owners for the use of their money.

The **accounting department** or function is responsible for recognizing, measuring, recording, and reporting the value of assets, borrowed money, money provided by owners, revenue, and costs. For example, managers at P&G need accurate and timely financial information to operate the business. Managers of P&G also need to be accountable to the providers of that money. P&G's accounting department adds value to the organization by meeting these needs.

The **information technology (IT) department** or function is responsible for managing the technology used throughout the business. Imagine the amount of information Target needs to operate. It's critical that R&D, marketing, operations, human resources, finance, and accounting have effective technology. The IT department provides value to a business by managing the data, computer hardware, and computer software the company needs to operate, staying on top of current technology, and educating the user of the technology.

The **human resource (HR) department** or function is responsible for a company's employees. This includes understanding the organization's needs for employees, finding the right employees, and motivating, training, evaluating, rewarding, and compensating them. For example, Hyundai needs good managers and employees to do the work in its R&D, marketing, production or operations, finance, accounting, and IT departments. Hyundai's HR department is responsible for this.

Exhibit 1.6 illustrates how the different departments of an organization work together to create value.

EXHIBIT 1.6: Common Business Departments or Functions

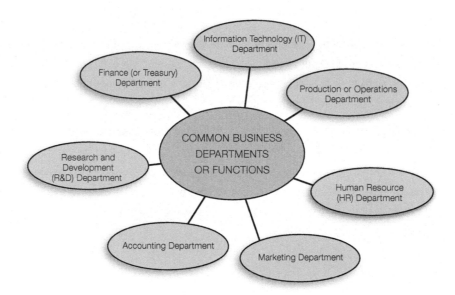

HOW MANAGERS CREATE VALUE: ETHICS AND SOCIAL RESPONSIBILITY

We've touched on the various departments present in many organizations. However, it is important to understand that a truly successful manager in *any* department must appreciate that her or his job is to convert inputs into outputs that make all stakeholders—customers, employees, and society as a whole—better. That is, effective managers focus on creating value. This requires behavior that is legal, ethical, and good for society. Merely making a short-term profit does not maximize the long-term value of the business. For example, consider a manager who makes the decision to use a misleading advertisement to promote his or her company's product. Or consider a manager who knowingly sells a defective product or asks employees to work in an unsafe environment. These actions may produce short-term profits, but ultimately, the business will lose customers, employees, and other stakeholders. In the end, these actions will hurt the business's long-term value. We'll come back to the topic of ethics and social responsibility and its relationship to value throughout this book.

LEARNING OBJECTIVE 5

THE IMPORTANCE OF BUSINESS

Can you imagine your life without your cell phone, without your computer, or without your iPod? And can you imagine a world in which there were no drugs to make you well when you were sick? Can you imagine a world with no grocery stores to collect the food you need all in one place? As we touched on earlier and as these examples show, businesses provide goods and services that change the world and improve our standard of living. How is this accomplished in a free market economy? It's done by businesses competing. Indeed, business is important in almost every aspect of life. But why?

A farmer's market in New Orleans. Selling direct to consumers presents logistical, scalable, and various financial challenges.

BUSINESS SENSE

COMPETING TO WIN

Have you ever competed in a sports event? Whether the event is individual (golf) or team (basketball), the objective is to win. In order to win, you must compete. If the event is fair, the winner is the best player or team. Great athletes love to compete and will tell you that competition makes them better and stronger. Business is like an athletic competition.

The business that is able to convince the customer it has the best product at the best price wins the race for the customer. The prize is the sale. The business that is able to create, produce, and distribute the best product at the lowest cost wins the race for operating efficiency. The prize is a high operating profit. The business that is able to attract the needed financing at the lowest cost wins the financing race. The prize is a safe, sound, and productive financial structure. The business that wins all three races wins the grand prize: creating value. Value, in a free market, is the prize for making a business work better than any other business.

The answer to this question lies in people's need to work together. People need exchanges that make them and their world better. None of us have the ability to create a prosperous world by ourselves. We each specialize in something. Some of us build and create things, some of us account for things, some of us sell things, and so on. We provide value to society and then exchange our valued output for things we need and want. Business helps with this exchange process. Remember our definition of business? A business is an organization, recognized under the law, that attempts to create value by exchanging products with customers for money or money substitutes.

BUSINESSES CONNECTING THE WORLD: INTERMEDIARIES

So business is the primary mechanism that helps us exchange goods and services. As such, businesses serve as **intermediaries** between the providers and consumers of products. An intermediary is a person or organization that facilitates an exchange.

Let's look at an example of an intermediary. Most of us do not grow our own food. We need to get food from a farmer. Enter food-processing companies and grocery stores. Both are intermediaries. The farmer sells food to a company that processes the food. That company resells the food to a grocery store. The grocery store then sells food to you.

So why do we have intermediaries? Intermediaries provide efficiency and ideally lower the cost of goods and services in our society. Imagine searching all over for a farmer who grows the various foods you want and need. It would take a lot of time and money to do so. Thus, there is a need for businesses that specialize in processing and selling food. Now imagine a farmer searching for enough customers to buy his or her products. That also would take a lot of time and money. Once again, the food processing company and grocery store come to the rescue. Simply put, the food processing company and grocery store are both intermediaries that create efficiency, lower the *overall* cost to society, and add value.

This brings us to the notion of competition. Competition makes business strive to create the best products at the best prices. Ideally, competition enhances efficiency. What happens if a grocery store does not deliver quality products, at a fair price, in a convenient location? An opportunity exists. A competitor may figure out that it can do a better job and in the process create value. The intermediary who delivers the best value wins. The intermediary who does not provide the best value loses and fails to survive.

THE STATE OF BUSINESS

So how has business done? Has it created value for stakeholders? In the United States, non-government businesses create approximately over 95 percent of all jobs.[5] Business has also changed dramatically over time because the needs and capabilities of society have changed. Exhibit 1.7 shows how US employment has evolved over recent years. Note how the non-government jobs have moved away from manufacturing into non-manufacturing jobs. Non-manufacturing jobs include services such as legal and consulting but also include jobs in information (such as in telephone companies), trade (such as in retail stores), transportation (such as in airlines), utilities (such as in electricity companies), leisure and hospitality (such as in hotels), education (such as in colleges), health (such as in hospitals), and financial (such as in banks). (Note that often, all non-manufacturing jobs are referred to as *services* for simplicity.) As you can see, the world is changing, and US business has adjusted.

EXHIBIT 1.7: US Employment by Sector (Jobs in Thousands)

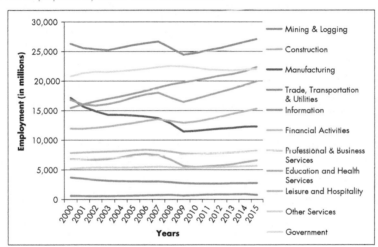

What about income? Exhibit 1.8 shows how the output or income of the US economy has grown over the last ten years. The most common measure of an economy's output and income is *gross domestic product (GDP)*, the value of goods and services produced and sold in an economy. Note that government jobs account for only 13% of the US GDP during the 2000–2013 period. That means 89% are in profit and not-for-profit businesses.

But how has the average person in the United States fared? How about income per person, called *income per capita*? Exhibit 1.9 illustrates that the average income per person in the United States has increased over time. Why has it grown? The significant factor in this growth is business.

What about the benefits to owners of business? How has business fared regarding creating net income? Exhibit 1.9 shows how business profits for corporations have grown over time.

In summary, business is a very important part of our society. It is the primary employer and driver of income in the United States. And if properly conducted, it makes the quality of our lives better with better goods and services.

EXHIBIT 1.8: United States Gross Domestic Product (in Billions Using Current Prices)

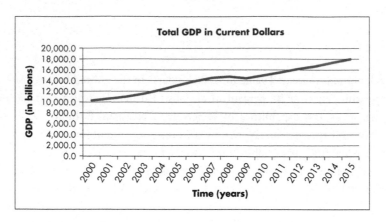

EXHIBIT 1.9: Average Income per Person in the United States

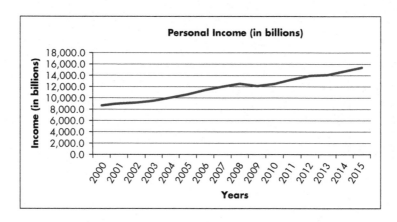

EXHIBIT 1.10: Business Profits for Corporations

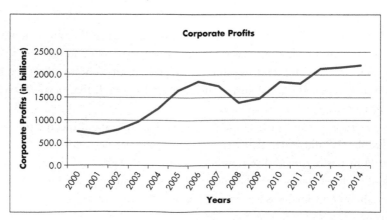

CHAPTER SUMMARY

In this chapter we introduced and began to explore the nature and purpose of business, a framework for understanding and managing business, and an appreciation of the importance of business. After reading this chapter, you should be able to:

1. Appreciate the nature and purpose of business (Learning Objective 1): A business is an organization, recognized under the law, that attempts to create value by exchanging products with customers for money or money substitutes.

2. Appreciate the foundations of value and how businesses strive to create value (Learning Objective 2): A business exists to create value for its stakeholders, including customers, employees, owners, lenders, and society. The value of a business is a function of the quantity, timing, and risks of a business's benefits. In a competitive, free market, it's important that each stakeholder receives value. The value of a business to its owners is dependent on the quantity, timing, and risk of a business's profits.

3. Appreciate how businesses create value by acquiring and investing money (Learning Objective 3): A business creates value by acquiring money and investing money. Businesses acquire money by borrowing the money or having owners provide the money. Businesses use the acquired money to invest in assets and hire employees. Employees then use the assets to create and sell a product at a cost. When the product is sold, hopefully the business earns an operating profit where revenue exceeds operating costs. This operating profit is then used to pay the cost of the borrowed money, called interest. What remains, operating profit less interest, is net income. Net income is the benefit that belongs to owners.

4. Appreciate how managers manage a business to create value (Learning Objective 4): Managing is the process of making decisions that affects the value of the business. Managing is the process of planning, executing, and reviewing. To achieve this, businesses have many functions, including research and development, marketing, production or operations, finance, accounting, information technology, and human resources.

5. Appreciate the importance of business (Learning Objective 5): Business is the primary mechanism that helps us exchange goods and services. As such, businesses are intermediaries between the ultimate provider and consumer of products. Business is at the heart of meeting the needs of our society, including creating jobs and generating income.

We've begun to look at "Making Business Work." The next question is how do we make business work so it creates value? We'll look at this topic in the next chapter.

KEYWORDS

accounting department 14

asset 10

business 3

cost 4

customers 4

debt 10

employees 10

equity 10

execute 12

finance department 14

financial capital 11

for-profit businesses 4

free market economy 8

functional managers 13

goods 3

human capital 11

human resource department
    (HR) 14

information technology (IT) 14

interest 10

intermediaries 16

liabilities 10

loss 7

management 12

manager 12

managing 12

marketing department 14

net income 10

net profit 10

not-for-profit businesses 4

operating profit 10

operational managers 13

operations department 14

opportunity cost 5

planning 12

product 3

production department 14

profit 4

real capital 11

research and development (R&D)
    department 13

revenue 6

review 12

risk 5

sale 4

senior managers 13

services 3

stakeholders 7

standard of living 2

stockholders 7

utility 4

value 5

SHORT-ANSWER QUESTIONS

1. What is the difference between profit and value?

2. What is risk?

3. Define the following terms:
   a. Asset
   b. Liability
   c. Equity
   d. Revenue
   e. Expense or Cost
   f. Operating Profit
   g. Net Income
   h. Employee
   i. Manager and Management

4. Briefly describe what the following business functions entail:
   a. Research and Development
   b. Marketing
   c. Production or Operations
   d. Finance
   e. Accounting
   f. Information Technology
   g. Human Resources

5. What do managers do?

6. How has business changed the US economy in the last ten years?

CRITICAL-THINKING QUESTIONS

1. Look around your world and think of the businesses in your community. Think of a business that is owned and operated by people who live in your community. Ask the owner of that business if you can talk with her or him. Ask the following questions:
   a. Why do you own and operate your business?
   b. How did you decide to buy or create your business?
   c. If you had the chance to do it again, would you have bought or created your business?
   d. What have been the greatest joys and challenges of owning your business?

2. Think about the businesses in your community. Think of businesses that have been successful and businesses that have failed. Ask yourself, "What made the successful business successful and the unsuccessful businesses fail?"

3. Think about the businesses in your community. Which businesses accept a lot of risk and which businesses do not? Where does the risk these businesses accept come from?

4. Look around your world and find a manager you think is successful. Talk with him or her. Ask the manager, "What do you do and why do you do it?" Now think about what he or she tells you. How do his or her answers relate to planning, executing, and reviewing?

5. Look around your world and find an older manager whom you think is successful. Talk with him or her. Ask the manager, "What is the most important thing you have learned from being a manager?" Now what do you think?

EXPLORING REAL BUSINESS

Go to the websites of Google, Target, Hyundai, and Procter & Gamble. The websites are:

Google:	http://investor.google.com
Target:	http://www.target.com
Hyundai:	http://worldwide.hyundai.com/company-overview
Procter & Gamble:	http://www.pg.com

For each company, answer the following questions:

1. What products does the company produce and/or sell?
2. Where does the company produce and/or sell its products?
3. What do you think makes these companies successful in a competitive world?

ENDNOTES

1. http://www.census.gov/statab/hist/HS-16.pdf

2. http://news.nationalgeographic.com/news/2013/04/life-expectancy-map/

3. http://www.biography.com/people/Warren-Buffett-9230729 and http://www.who2.com

4. Often people talk about the "factors of production" in describing the inputs to the process of creating profits and value. These factors include people, assets, money, and knowledge.

5. US Department of Labor: Bureau of Labor Statistics. https://www.scribd.com/document/38317858/Ftp-bls-Gov-Pub-Suppl-Empsit-ceseeb1

CHAPTER

UNDERSTANDING THE PROCESS OF CREATING VALUE

LEARNING OBJECTIVES

After reading Chapter 02, you should be able to meet the following learning objectives:

1. Appreciate how value is measured and created
2. Appreciate the principles used to operate a business and create business value
3. Appreciate how businesses use these principles to win in a competitive world
4. Appreciate how businesses use systems to operate
5. Appreciate the future of business

Introduction: Let's Talk About Value

In Chapter 01, we learned that the goal of any business is to create value for customers, owners, and other stakeholders. But there are many different types of businesses, each of which is trying to stand out from the competition. What are the important principles that *all* businesses need to follow to create value? What does a business do to differentiate itself and to be looked at as special in the eyes of customers? Why do some businesses succeed in creating value and others fail?

In this chapter, we'll extend the value framework we developed in Chapter 01 to answer these and other questions. After reading this chapter, you should understand how a business tries to create value by developing business models and strategies that give it a **sustainable competitive advantage**.[1] In this chapter, we'll look deeper at the process of creating and operating an organization that tries to make the whole greater than the simple sum of its parts.

WHY CREATING VALUE MATTERS

Every business tries to be unique. It needs to create a competitive advantage to win. Yet successful businesses do share certain characteristics, such as the ability to create operating profits that exceed their financing costs, over time, on a risk-adjusted basis. So how do businesses do it? Think about the businesses in your life—the grocery store, the telephone company, the gas station, your physician. Why do you prefer to shop with one business and not another? Why would you like to work for or even own one of those businesses and not another? Why do you feel good about one business and not another? Does it matter how those businesses operate? The answer is, of course, "yes." Understanding why creating value matters is a key component of success in any career you plan to pursue.

LEARNING OBJECTIVE 1
. . . .
THE NATURE AND PURPOSE OF BUSINESS

In Chapter 01 we discussed how, in a free market economy, prices are set by markets. A market is defined as a place, sometimes physical and sometimes not, where people and organizations exchange products or other things of value, such as money. In a free market economy, buyers and sellers are free to determine what is sold and at what price.

So how does a market, in a free market economy, work? It works by individuals and organizations demanding and supplying items. Those people or organizations who demand or want an item are willing to pay a certain price for it. Those people or organizations who supply an item are willing to sell it at a certain price. An exchange or *sale* occurs when the buyers and sellers agree on the price. Buyers will not buy an item unless they believe the value they will receive is equal to or exceeds the price they must pay. Likewise, sellers won't sell an item unless they believe the price they will receive is equal to or greater than the value they will give up. When the buyer and seller both believe they will receive more than they are giving up—when they agree that the price is a fair one—the sale occurs. Therefore, in a free market economy, we let the market determine the value of an item by setting its price.

So how can we determine what a business is worth, what its value is? In a free market, a business is worth what it would cost to buy it. That is, the value of the business is the price set by the market to buy it. Values for businesses differ because buyers and sellers have different perceptions about the quantity of expected benefits, the expected timing of the benefits, and the risk associated with the benefits of purchasing the business. Some business owners believe they can generate more profits, quicker, with less risk than other owners. But why are some owners able to create more value than others? The answer lies in investing, financing, and operating decisions.

CREATING VALUE: INVESTING, FINANCING, AND OPERATING A BUSINESS

A customer checking out at a grocery store. How does free market demand and supply influence price setting?

Let's look at an example. Say you plan to start and run a business for one year. You need just $100,000. You withdraw $50,000 from your savings account that is currently earning 6% interest each year (or $3,000 a year). You plan to put the $50,000 in your business and increase it to $54,000 by earning a

$4,000 profit by the end of one year. You then borrow $50,000 from a friend. In one year, you promise to pay your friend her original $50,000 plus 8% interest ($4,000), or $54,000. In total, you plan to invest $100,000 and in one year make it become $108,000.

You invest the $100,000 and operate your business for one year. You earn an operating profit of $6,000. At the end of the year, you liquidate the business (sell all its **assets**) and now have $106,000. You pay your friend the promised $54,000 ($50,000 loan plus $4,000 interest). All you have left is $52,000 ($106,000 − $54,000). Although you have $2,000 more than you had at the beginning of the year, you feel cheated. Why? If you had left your money in the bank, you would have earned 6%, or $3,000 in interest on your $50,000. You took a lot of risk and only earned $2,000. Was this a bad investment decision?

The answer is, maybe and maybe not. The benefit from investing your $50,000 was less than you expected. You expected $54,000 from your business. You would have had $53,000 by merely leaving your money in the bank. You only got $52,000 from operating your business. But was it a bad investment decision? It may have been a good investment decision and a bad *financing* decision. What would have happened if you did not borrow the $50,000 from your friend at an interest rate of 8%? Instead, let's assume you borrowed the $50,000 from a bank at 4%. You would have had to repay the bank $52,000 ($50,000 borrowed plus $2,000 interest). After you ended your business, you had $106,000. You would have then paid the bank $52,000, leaving you $54,000. That would have met your expectations and been more than you would have earned by leaving your $50,000 in the bank.

The trick of creating value is making sure the *net results* of the investment and financing (money) decisions make sense. Businesses want the operating profit they receive from investing in assets and hiring employees to exceed the cost of the money they use to finance the operations. As the above example shows, owners expect an adequate compensation or return for the use of their money. But generating that return is about acquiring money at the lowest possible cost, then investing that money wisely, and last operating the business in such a way that the operating profit adequately rewards both the lender and owner. Failing to do this can be a result of bad financing decisions, investing decisions, and/or operating decisions.

CREATING VALUE: MANAGING A BUSINESS

Managing a business is, therefore, really all about putting the pieces of a business together in the right combination. As we learned in Chapter 01, first, the business acquires money either from owners or lenders such as a bank. The business then uses this pool of money to hire employees and invest in assets. The owners, or their management team, then operate the business to create and sell a product.

A business is made up of a **portfolio**—a mix or pool—of different resources. A business has a portfolio of financial resources composed of the money provided by lenders and owners. Businesses then use this money to hire employees and invest in a portfolio of operating resources, its assets. Assets

Financing Portfolios Consist of Money

- Money from Lenders
- Money from Owners

Investing Portfolios Consist of Assets

- Cash
- Inventory
- Buildings
- Equipment

Managers Combine Money, Employees, and Assets to Operate the Business and Create Value

- Money
- Employees
- Assets

include **cash**, inventory, buildings, and equipment. Managers must put all these resources (money, employees, and assets) together to create value. Think of a business as a sports team or a musical group. To win or create something special, members of a sports team or musical group must work together. Likewise, managers in a business must get all the parts of the business—its money, employees, and assets—to work together to create value. Managers are like the coaches of sports teams or conductors of orchestras. What do coaches and conductors do? They get all the parts to work together effectively.

So why do some businesses win and create more value than others? Some owners and managers do a better job than others. They know how to attract money at its lowest cost. They then know how to use this money to hire the best employees and acquire the best assets. After hiring the employees and acquiring the assets, they know how to get these resources to work together in the best way possible.

LEARNING OBJECTIVE 2

OPERATING A BUSINESS FOR VALUE

To create an operating profit, a business must first have a product to sell. Creating and developing new products is the result of good research and development. Consider these examples:

- The automobile manufacturer Hyundai realized that Americans were looking for a reliable and low-cost automobile. It researched the market and developed the Kia line of automobiles.

- Likewise, Google realized that consumers wanted a cell phone that could do more than just send and receive phone calls, text messages, and email. It researched the market and developed the Android phone.

- Target realized that customers wanted to minimize the number of trips they had to take to buy their everyday needs. It researched the market and added grocery items to its line of household products.

- Finally, consider all the products that Procter & Gamble (P&G) offers, such as Crest toothpaste and Cover Girl cosmetics. P&G researched the market and developed these products in order to meet the needs of the market.

After deciding what product to sell, businesses must then produce, market, and ultimately sell the product. Ideally, a business does this at a cost that is below the price it will charge its customers. This will result in an operating profit. As you'll recall from Chapter 01, *operating profit* is the money a business has left after deducting the expense of operating the business from its revenue.

What does a business need in order to produce, market, and sell a product? It takes assets and people. You've learned that an asset is an economic resource that the business owns or controls. Let's look at some examples:

- **Cash** is an asset as it allows a business to pay its bills. Cash is the currency a business has in its cash register or its bank accounts.

- However, the business may not receive cash when it sells the product. The business may instead accept a customer's promise to pay in the future. The promise is an **accounts receivable**, which is also an asset.

- If the business sells a good, then it needs a supply of goods to sell. Such goods are **inventory**, which are also considered assets.

- The business may need a place and/or equipment to conduct business. If the business owns this place or equipment versus renting it, this place or equipment is called a **fixed asset** (or **property, plant, and equipment**).

Of course, assets do not create an operating profit without employees. The business needs people to conduct and manage the processes of producing, marketing, and selling the product. Likewise, the business needs people to account for the product, to manage the business's finances, and to direct and coordinate the different parts of the business. Assets plus people are, therefore, the resources that create operating profit. The operating profit is used to reward those who provide the money: lenders and owners.

Now why would a lender or an owner provide money to a business? The answer to this question is simply *return*, or a benefit that rewards them for letting the business use their money. The providers of money want a benefit or return for the use of their money over time. Over time, they want to receive more money than they provided.

BUSINESS SENSE

PEOPLE AND ASSETS

Ask yourself the following question: Where do operating profit and value come from? Say you drive by a factory such as one that P&G operates. You see buildings and products being made. You consider P&G to be a valuable business because it has valuable tangible assets. Likewise, you go to a store like Target and see products being sold there. You think Target is a valuable business because it has valuable assets it is selling to customers. So much of our perception of value is about the assets we or others own. Yet are these the critical element of value? It is true that assets are often necessary for creating a profit and value. Businesses need buildings, equipment, inventory, cash, and so on. But people are the most important economic resource a business has. This is because business is really about people. Assets do not create an exchange. People create an exchange. Assets do not manage. People manage. Only people can plan, execute, and review. Ultimately people create and market products that meet the needs of customers. People, not assets or money, innovate and compete. Now think again about what makes businesses such as P&G and Target special. Assets and money are important, but making business work is all about people.

THE IMPACT OF TIME ON VALUE

As we learned in Chapter 01, the quicker we receive something, the more valuable it is. The longer we wait to receive something, the less valuable it is. That's true with operating profits as well. The quicker an operating profit is earned, the more valuable the profit is to the providers of the money.

But how does time impact value? Ask yourself the following question: Would you rather have $100 today (option 1) or $100 in one year (option 2)? If you received $100 today, you could deposit it in a bank and earn interest. Let's assume you earn a 4% interest rate for one year. At the end of the year,

Supermarket staff have greatly improved their inventory accuracy and counting efficiency by using a handheld barcode scanner to track stock levels.

your $100 would grow to be $104 ($100 plus $4 in interest). So the question above is really about choosing $104 in one year or $100 in one year. Being value "maximizers," we would prefer the $104 in one year (option 1).

Now let's look at our example in a different way. Instead of comparing the $104 versus $100 values in one year, let's look at the values *today*. We have two options. Option 1 is to receive $100 today. Option 2 is to receive $100 in one year. So what is $100, if we are to receive it in one year, worth today?

In option 1, we'd receive $104 in one year for investing $100 today, assuming a 4% rate of return. We are saying that $100 today is equal to $104 in one year. The value today of $104, to be received in one year, at a 4% rate of return, is $100.

Now let's look at option 2 with the same logic. We're going to receive $100 in one year. We want to see how much we would need to invest today to have $100 in one year. We'd need to invest a little more than $96 today to have $100 in one year, assuming the 4% rate of return. This means that if we invest a little more than $96 today, it will grow at a 4% rate to become $100 in one year. We are saying that our $96 today is equal to $100 in one year.

If we compare values as of today, the original question becomes "Do you want $100 today (option 1) or something worth $96 today (option 2)?" Once again, being value "maximizers," we'll choose option 1.

As you can see, time has a major impact on value, and value is what business attempts to create. Businesses create value by acquiring and investing money today in the belief that they will generate future operating profits. These operating profits will provide the needed profit, or *return*, that lenders and owners expect and require. So the next question becomes how much profit, or return, do the providers of money expect or require?

RECOGNIZING AND UNDERSTANDING OPPORTUNITY COST OR REQUIRED RETURN

You've learned that in a free market economy, lenders do not have to lend money to a business. Likewise, owners do not have to put their money in a business. Both groups have other opportunities to use their money. So businesses, therefore, must compete for this money. So why do lenders lend money and owners put their money in one particular business and not another? They expect that money to be used to create an operating profit. That operating profit will then provide a *return* to the lenders and owners.

Returns

A **return** is defined as a percentage, relating what the lender or owner received from the business to what he or she puts in the business during a given period. Mathematically stated, return for a given period is shown as follows:

EQUATION 2.1: Return

$$R = (P_1 - P_0)/P_0$$

Where R Return
       P_1 The amount of money received during or at the end of a period
       P_0 The amount of money provided at the beginning of the period

Lenders receive their return first in the form of interest. Owners receive their return last in the form of net income, or operating profit less interest.

Required Returns

The **required rate of return** (or **expected return**) is the price of the money and creates the value sought by lenders and owners. In our example earlier in the chapter, your friend required you to pay an 8% return when she lent you $50,000. This meant you owed her interest of $4,000 (.08 x $50,000). As the owner of the business, you expected a 4% return on your money of $4,000 net income (operating profit less interest). Remember how upset you were when you did not receive the $4,000 net income or 4% return? If the providers of money do not expect they will receive their required rate of return, they will not provide the money to a business.

So how does a lender or owner determine how much return to require? Think about it. Why would you forgo the use of your money for a period of time? The answer is you want to have more money at the end of the time period than at the beginning. You want to be compensated with a return. You first want compensation to reward you for your time. Second, you want compensation for taking risk.

Lenders and owners use the same logic. Their required rate of return has two components.

First is a **risk-free return**. The risk-free return is the cost of money over time assuming no risk. It's like rent charged for letting someone else use your money. However, the rent you charge on your money assumes you are certain that you will get back the money you provided, plus the rent.

Second is a **risk premium**. The higher the risk, the higher the return required by the providers of money. As the chance of bad things happening to your money increases, you'll want to receive more return. We don't like risk, and we expect to be compensated for taking risk.

When added together, the risk-free return plus the risk premium total the required rate of return. Mathematically stated, the required rate of return for a given period is as follows:

EQUATION 2.2: Required Rate of Return

$$R = R_f + \text{Risk Premium}$$

Where

R	The required or expected rate of return
R_f	The **risk-free rate of return** in the economy
Risk Premium	The additional required return to compensate for risk

Exhibit 2.1 demonstrates how these two components come together to produce the required rate of return.

EXHIBIT 2.1: Risk and Return

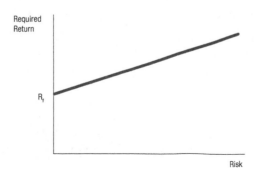

RISK AND TIME

Let's say you're a senior manager for a pharmaceutical company. A research scientist comes into your office and tells you she may be able to develop a drug that cures cancer. You're excited. Who wouldn't be? Customers need the drug, your company could stand to make a great deal of profit from it, and society will look on your company positively. However, in talking with the scientist, you learn that it will take over $1 billion to research the drug. If a drug is developed, it will take millions of dollars to test it under the careful eye of the government. In addition, you learn that your competitors are also researching a drug to cure cancer. Finally, you know that all this will take time. Your best hope is to have an approved drug ready to sell in ten years.

Do you or don't you invest over $1 billion today? There are many benefits for creating this drug, but it will take a long time to realize these benefits, and there are also many risks. What's the answer? The answer is return. To compensate for your company's time and risk, you need to believe the drug will generate a very large operating profit and return.

Managers have a challenging job. Their goal is to maximize value. But to maximize value, they must also balance the drive for more operating profits against time and risk. Sometimes higher operating profits take longer to realize or come with more risk. This can result in lower value. This can be seen when a business tries to acquire money. When the providers of money sense that the use of their money is risky, these providers will require higher returns. So how does a business compete for money, assets, people, and customers in a competitive market? How do managers create successful businesses? We'll look at these topics next.

LEARNING OBJECTIVE 3

. . . .

WINNING IN A COMPETITIVE WORLD

We've learned that businesses compete for people, assets, and money. But first, businesses must compete for the *customer*. Businesses must have a product that a customer wants and will buy. Without a product that the customer desires, a business will fail. That is not to say businesses with good products will always succeed. There are many examples of businesses failing, not for lack of a good product but because of mismanaging other aspects of the value-creating process. However, without a product the customer desires, there will be no sales, which means everything else that management does is useless. There is an old adage that says, "The customer is king." That is true for without the customer, all businesses ultimately fail.

So how does a business win customers? Although some businesses resemble each other and compete in the same market (think McDonald's and Burger King, or Coke and Pepsi), all businesses strive to *differentiate* themselves. In doing so, they want to win the competition for customers and value. They do this by forming a winning business model and strategy.

BUSINESS MODELS

A **business model** is a description of how a business creates and delivers value. A business model focuses on a business's customers and what a business does to meet its customers' needs. A business model describes a business's inputs, processes, and outputs that create value. Exhibit 2.2 depicts a business model. Simply, a business model describes a business's system that creates value. As we'll discuss later in this chapter, this system is called a business's **value chain**.

EXHIBIT 2.2: A Business Model

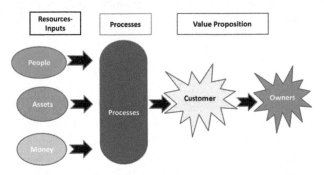

Let's consider the business models of a few companies. For example, Hyundai and Ford have the same business models. Hyundai and Ford first hire people. They then buy materials such as steel, plastic, and other automotive parts. The two companies then use these inputs to manufacture automobiles in factories. They then try to sell their automobiles to the same customers. Likewise, Target and Walmart have the same business model. Both companies hire people and buy general merchandise such as clothing, food, and household products. The two companies then place these products in stores and try to sell the products to the same customers. Yet Hyundai is different from Ford, and Target is different from Walmart. And it is this difference that makes one business more valuable than another.

BUSINESS STRATEGY

So what is this difference? How does a business differentiate itself from other businesses? The answer is strategy. A business's strategy is different from its business model. A **business strategy** is how a business tries to compete against businesses with similar business models and win the competition to create value. It is how a business attempts to be different from businesses competing for the same customers and how it attempts to deliver more value to its stakeholders, starting with customers. A business strategy is all about creating a competitive advantage that ideally is sustainable over time.

Let's consider Hyundai. Did you know that Hyundai is the fastest-growing major automobile company in the world? It has been very profitable when other automobile companies have been unprofitable. How did Hyundai achieve this? After all, its business model is similar to its competitors. It manufactures automobiles and sells these automobiles to customers who also look at automobiles produced by companies such as General Motors, Ford, Chrysler, Mercedes, Toyota, and Nissan. Why is Hyundai winning the competition? The answer lies in Hyundai's products (such as

Procter & Gamble has made its brands last over generations. It promotes its products in a variety of formats from print and television advertising to the stadium naming rights it acquired for Gillette Stadium, home of the New England Patriots.

the Kia), and how those products meet customer needs. The answer lies in Hyundai's business strategy and *competitive advantage*.

Now let's consider Target. Walmart and Target have the same business model. Although Walmart is the largest retailer in the world, Target is very successful in a tough market dominated by Walmart. How does Target achieve success? Target does it with strategy. Next time you walk into Target, ask yourself: Why am I here instead of Walmart? What's different about Target? The answer lies in Target's business strategy and *competitive advantage*.

COMPETITIVE ADVANTAGE

A business has a **competitive advantage** when it can do something that allows it to outperform its competitors. Of course, being competitive in the short term is important, but truly successful companies seek to *sustain* their competitive advantage over the long term. This is not easy, but let's consider some companies that are able to win the competition.

What makes P&G's products such as Febreze air fresheners, Gillette deodorant, and Max Factor cosmetics successful? Why do customers prefer these products over competitors' products? The answer is competitive advantage. P&G has worked hard to research the market, to understand customers, to create and produce products that customers perceive as more valuable, and to use this competitive advantage to add value to its other stakeholders such as owners. In short, P&G has created a business strategy that permits it to achieve a long-term *competitive advantage* over its rivals who have similar business models.

Now let's look at Google. Google is not the only company that produces an Internet search engine. Its competitors include giants such as Microsoft. Yet it has succeeded to such a level that people prefer Google's search engine over its competitors. In fact, Google has been so successful in being the preferred provider of this service that people often say when they need to search the Internet, "Just Google it." Google has worked hard to research the market, to understand customers, to create and produce a product that customers perceive as more valuable, and to use this *competitive advantage* to add value to its other stakeholders such as owners. Google has created a business strategy that permits it to achieve a long-term competitive advantage over its rivals who have similar business models.

How does a business create a competitive advantage? How does a business convince customers to buy its product and not the product of its competitors? Today, more than any other time, *competing* must be the focus of creating value. In a free market, competition determines which businesses succeed and which businesses fail. Although competition is not kind to losing businesses, over time, it has shown to be the most efficient process for creating value or wealth for the winning businesses and society. Think about the emergence of China as an economic power and the success of Chinese businesses such as Lenovo. When China's government planned and controlled every aspect of its economy, China suffered. As China began to embrace free market economics and competition, China prospered and grew.

So how does a business compete in today's world? It starts with *meeting customer wants and needs*. Being focused on the customer may seem a simple principle, but it is not. The world is constantly changing. Businesses that fail to recognize the changing market will fail. Businesses that embrace change succeed. Given that the world is constantly changing, successful businesses constantly *innovate* to compete.

Innovation can be defined as finding new ways to think and do things. The intent of innovation is to create value for both the customer and business. Hyundai created great value for its customers, owners, and other stakeholders with its Kia automobiles. So did P&G with its Gillette Fusion razor, Google with its Android phone, and Target with its addition of food products. These companies also recognize that their markets and customers' needs are constantly changing. To survive and prosper, these companies understand the need to evolve through innovation.

It is not just products that must evolve. Business models and strategies must also grow and change. For example, consider the evolution of the retail business model depicted in Exhibit 2.3. Selling merchandise has evolved from small shops owned by local merchants to large department stores owned by global companies to Internet retailers that sell any time, any place.

EXHIBIT 2.3: The Evolution of the Retail Business Model

Small Local Merchants → Late 1800s → Dept Stores → Early 1900s → Catalog Retailers → Early 1960s → Discount Dept Stores → Late 1990s → Internet Retailers

Sears · LL Bean · Target · Amazon

Innovation is also at the heart of a business's having a *sustainable* competitive advantage. Value starts with meeting the needs of the customer with a superior product, at a superior price, sold and delivered in a superior way. To create sustained value, a business must sustain its competitive advantage. To do this in an ever-changing world, businesses must constantly innovate. Strategy is about being different. Innovation is the key to being different over time.

PUTTING IT ALL TOGETHER: THE MISSION STATEMENT

So how do we figure out a business's model, strategy, and competitive advantage? How can we figure out how a business views itself, visions its strengths, and believes it will create value? A good place to start is to read the business's mission statement. A company's **mission statement** describes its business model, strategy, and operating values. A mission statement tells why a business exists and how it operates. Every business should have a mission statement. Large businesses often publish this mission for all stakeholders to see. This mission statement reflects what a business does, how it will operate, and why it is special. For example, here is the mission statement of Target:

> We fulfill the needs and fuel the potential of our guests. That means making Target your preferred shopping destination in all channels by delivering outstanding value, continuous innovation and exceptional experiences—consistently fulfilling our Expect More. Pay Less.® brand promise.[2]

Looking at this mission statement, you begin to see what Target does and values.

So how does a business fulfill its mission statement? How does a business operate its business model and strategy? How does a business achieve a competitive advantage? The answer to these questions is through *systems*, which we discuss next.

LEARNING OBJECTIVE 4
· ·
LOOKING AT BUSINESS AS A SYSTEM

Business systems are the processes that a business uses to operate. A business is often composed of numerous systems and subsystems. Using people, data, and processes, businesses create, produce, and sell a product.

For example, consider the functions of management: there are systems in place to plan, execute, and review. Likewise, there are systems used to create a competitive advantage, to research customer needs, develop products, and sell and deliver products. Systems are also involved when a business creates value by obtaining money, hiring employees, acquiring assets, and operating.

VALUE CHAINS

A business's systems and subsystems create its value chain. A **value chain** is a mapping of how a business converts inputs (people, assets, and money) into outputs that create value for customers, owners, and other stakeholders. As such, a value chain describes a business's model and strategy as one system composed of many subsystems. Remember how a business model and strategy are all about inputs and outputs? Well a business's value chain is a description of the systems that comprise the business's model and strategy. Exhibit 2.4 shows an example of a value chain.

EXHIBIT 2.4: The Value Chain

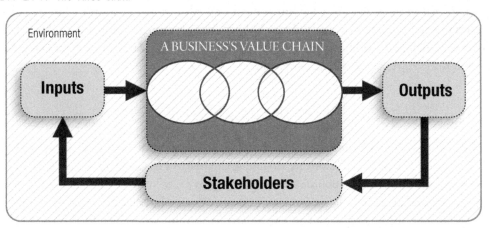

Let's look at P&G. The company's mission statement reads: "We will provide branded products and services of superior quality and value that improve the lives of the world's consumers. As a result, consumers will reward us with leadership sales, profit and value creation, allowing our people, our shareholders, and the communities in which we live and work to prosper."[3]

P&G's business model is about creating, producing, and selling consumer products such as Crest toothpaste, Max Factor cosmetics, Febreze air fresheners, and Ivory soap. But there are other companies that create, produce, and sell consumer products. Unilever produces similar products, such as Dove soap and Pond's cosmetics. P&G and Unilever have similar business models. So how does P&G successfully compete? Procter & Gamble's strategy centers on producing quality products that customers will recognize and desire for many years. It does not sell the cheapest products. It does not try to sell products that are fads and have temporary appeal. Procter & Gamble tries to be the best in creating, producing, and selling quality consumer products.

How does P&G execute its business model and strategy? Through its value chain. Exhibit 2.5 depicts a value chain for P&G. P&G's products move through a system of being created (research and development), produced (manufacturing), sold (marketing/branding and consumer purchase), and delivered.

EXHIBIT 2.5: A Value Chain for Procter & Gamble

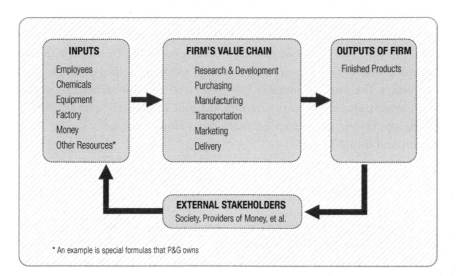

INPUTS
Employees
Chemicals
Equipment
Factory
Money
Other Resources*

FIRM'S VALUE CHAIN
Research & Development
Purchasing
Manufacturing
Transportation
Marketing
Delivery

OUTPUTS OF FIRM
Finished Products

EXTERNAL STAKEHOLDERS
Society, Providers of Money, et al.

* An example is special formulas that P&G owns

Top (left to right): Henry Ford, Thomas Alva Edison, and Harvey Samuel Firestone; Center: Ford and his wife driving his first automobile; Bottom: Ford assembly line.

THE IMPORTANCE OF BUSINESS SYSTEMS

As the world of business has evolved, the use of a systems approach has become critical to competing and creating value. Henry Ford realized this when he developed the assembly line to build cars in the early twentieth century. He made automobiles affordable by using systems to lower the cost of an automobile. In the latter twentieth century, Bill Gates and others realized that information would revolutionize the way people live. Information systems are the heart of the information revolution. Today, almost every business from fast-food restaurants to doctor's offices uses systems to compete in the ever-changing and complex business world.

So why is the business world complex and rapidly changing? Three major factors include globalization, the spread of information, and technology, which we discuss next.

MANAGING WITH SYSTEMS

You've probably been to a fast-food restaurant like McDonald's. Why do you go? The typical answer is that we want good food, delivered fast, at a low price. So how does the restaurant produce good, fast, inexpensive food? Look around you and you'll see that the restaurant is designed to efficiently facilitate each function of preparing and serving food. There are places to store the food and places to prepare it. There are places to take the orders and places to deliver the food. Then look at the people operating the restaurant. Some take orders and receive payment, some prepare the food, some move the inventory from the storage to the preparation area, and some oversee the operation.

A good fast-food restaurant reaches its objectives through systems. Every part of the restaurant operates as a subsystem fitting into the overall system. If done right, the overall system provides you with good, fast, and low-cost food.

. . . .
THE STATE OF BUSINESS—PAST, PRESENT, AND FUTURE

So we know that customer wants, needs, and values are constantly changing and that a business employs strategies, innovation, and systems to focus on customer satisfaction and to create value. But to do this, managers must be able to forecast change and understand the changing desires of the business environment and their customers. The world of business has never stood still. Innovation has always been a part of a successful business. But today, more than ever, the pace of innovation and change is increasing. The reason for the rapid increase in change has many roots. However, three of the key roots are globalization, information, and technology.

GLOBALIZATION

A woman shopping in the menswear department at a mall in Jakarta, Indonesia. Western companies are finding lucrative business opportunities in new markets. The business landscape has become much more global.

One of the major factors creating a changing business landscape is **globalization**. As author Tom Friedman put it, "The World Is Flat."[4] Friedman uses the analogy of a flat world to emphasize that many of the barriers to global trade no longer exist. These barriers include geography, language, and cultural misunderstandings. Businesses today compete in global markets more than ever. The rate of this globalization is ever increasing. It was unthinkable ten years ago that China would become one of the United States' and Europe's major trading partners. The barriers that separated people around the world are coming down. Trade between peoples and nations of the world is on the rise. This rise creates enormous opportunities and challenges. The opportunities lie in new markets. The challenges lie in new competitors. We'll explore this topic in more detail later in the book. There is no debating the fact that globalization has changed and will continue to change how business is conducted.

THE INFORMATION REVOLUTION

Another factor contributing to our changing business landscape is the spread of information. In the past, businesses could create value by relying on a *lack* of knowledge by customers. For example, businesses could generate significant profits by knowing things that other businesses and/or customers did not know. The **information revolution** has changed all that. Today, thanks to the Internet, telecommunications technologies, and other information innovations, knowledge is more accessible to everyone. When someone doesn't know something, all he or she does is go to search engines like Google. Think about all the knowledge you can quickly access about medical or legal issues. Think about how you can research car defects, customer comments, and search for the best prices online. The world has become much more transparent, and such transparency creates many opportunities and challenges, which we'll discuss later in the book.

TECHNOLOGY

Another factor contributing to our changing business landscape is the spread of technology. **Technology** refers to the devices and systems used in businesses and society. For example, consider all the recent technological advances in transportation, health care, entertainment, computing, and communication. Such technological advances are changing the way we live, work, and do business. We are more efficient. We are more connected. We are living longer. Yet we are more dependent on technology than ever. There is little debate that technology, and our dependency on technology, creates enormous opportunities and challenges for business. We'll discuss these opportunities and challenges in more detail later in the book.

The world of business is changing and will continue to change. To compete, businesses must innovate. Business models and business strategies must change to keep pace. The systems businesses use to create value must evolve. But with this change and evolution come enormous opportunities to create value. The future is bright for those who can see it, know what to do with it, and have the courage to do it.

CHAPTER SUMMARY

The market determines the value of a business in a free market economy. As such, values may go up or down based on the perceptions of the market. However, the market is focusing on the future operating profit of the business, the timing of the business's operating profit, and a required rate of return that is based on the business's risk. The market likes operating profit but also likes it sooner versus later, with less risk versus more risk.

Successful managers understand this. They compete for customers, assets, people, and money. They seek to take a business model and differentiate it with winning strategy. To win, a strategy starts by creating a sustainable competitive advantage. Successful managers understand the business world is constantly changing. Such change can create challenges, but it can also create opportunities. In this chapter we've gained insights into successful value creation with competition. After reading this chapter, you should be able to:

1. Appreciate how value is measured and created (Learning Objective 1): In a free market economy, the value of a business is measured by the market. The value of a business is what someone is willing to pay to own the business. A business creates value by obtaining money and using that money to hire employees and invest in assets.
2. Appreciate the principles used to operate a business and create business value (Learning Objective 2): A business creates value by acquiring money, hiring employees, investing in assets, and operating in such a way that the return from investing is greater than the cost of the money. The cost of the money is a function of time and risk associated with the use of the money.
3. Appreciate how businesses use these principles to win in a competitive world (Learning Objective 3): Businesses develop models and strategies to create a competitive advantage. This competitive advantage is the basis for creating value for all stakeholders.
4. Appreciate how businesses use systems to operate (Learning Objective 4): Business systems are the processes a business uses to operate. A business's systems and subsystems create a business's value chain.
5. Appreciate the future of business (Learning Objective 5): The world of business is constantly changing, creating new opportunities and challenges. Globalization, information, and technology are three major forces that are transforming the business world.

Competing and creating value are challenging. However, successful managers love these challenges. Successful managers know these challenges are the heart of "how business works." Which brings us to the question, "What do managers do?" What are some of the things that managers need to understand and do to be successful? We'll answer these and other questions in the next chapter.

KEYWORDS

accounts receivable 26

assets 25

business model 30

business strategy 31

business systems 33

cash 26

competitive advantage 32

expected return 29

fixed asset 27

free market 24

globalization 36

information revolution 36

innovation 32

inventory 27

markets 24

mission statement 33

portfolio 25

property, plant, and equipment 27

required rate of return 29

return 28

risk-free return 29

risk premium 29

sustainable competitive advantage 33

technology 36

value chain 31

SHORT-ANSWER QUESTIONS

1. For whom does a business create an operating profit and who gets that operating profit?
2. How do time and risk affect the decision to provide money to a business?
3. Define the following terms:
   a. Cash
   b. Accounts Receivable
   c. Inventory
   d. Property, Plant, and Equipment
   e. Business Model
   f. Business Strategy
   g. Competitive Advantage
   h. Market
   i. Value Chain
   j. Risk Premium
   k. Free Market

4. Briefly describe the following concepts:
   a. How time affects value
   b. How risk affects value

5. John buys an investment for $100,000 at the beginning of the year. During the year John receives $10,000 from his investment. At the end of the year John sells his investment for $120,000. What is John's return during this year?

CRITICAL-THINKING QUESTIONS

1. Look around your world and think of the businesses in your community. Think of a business that is owned and operated by people who live in your community. Ask the owner of that business if you can talk with him or her. Ask the following questions:
   a. What is the competitive advantage of this business?
   b. Is that competitive advantage sustainable for a long time? What makes it sustainable or unsustainable?

2. Close your eyes and ask yourself the following questions:
   a. What products will exist in ten years that do not exist today?
   b. What products exist today that will not be needed in ten years?
   c. How will your answers to parts A and B above create opportunities and challenges for business?

EXPLORING REAL BUSINESS

Go to the websites of Google, Target, Hyundai, and Procter & Gamble. The websites are:

Google:	http://investor.google.com
Target:	http://www.target.com
Hyundai:	http://worldwide.hyundai.com/company-overview
Procter & Gamble:	http://www.pg.com

For each company, answer the following questions:

1. What is the mission statement of each business?
2. What is the business model of each business?
3. What is the business strategy of each business?
4. What is the business value chain of each business?

ENDNOTES

1. The term "sustainable competitive advantage" is attributed to Michael Porter. See Porter, Michael, *Competitive Advantage: Creating and Sustaining Superior Performance*. New York: Free Press, 1998. Print.
2. http://sites.target.com/site/en/company/page.jsp?contentId=WCMP04-031699
3. http//www.pg.com
4. Friedman, Tom, *The World Is Flat: A Brief History of the Twenty-First Century*. New York: Farrar, Straus, and Giroux, 2005.

03

MANAGING BUSINESSES FOR VALUE

Introduction: Let's Talk About Managing

Close your eyes and think of a business. Now think about the people operating the business and their responsibilities. What do you see? You see people making and selling products. But you also see other people, sometimes in the background, orchestrating the business. These people are the *managers* of the business. What is a manager, and how do they differ from other employees? How does a manager organize a business for success? What **traits** do successful managers possess? In this chapter, we'll examine *how business works* and the role of managers in creating value and making business work.

LEARNING OBJECTIVES

After reading Chapter 03, you should be able to meet the following learning objectives:

1. Appreciate the nature and role of management
2. Appreciate how managers assess a business's environment
3. Appreciate the types of organizational structures and behaviors
4. Appreciate the traits of successful managers, including leadership
5. Appreciate the need for and challenges of teamwork and leadership

WHY LEARNING ABOUT MANAGEMENT MATTERS

Say you're a salesperson who has worked for the same company for five years. This year you made record sales and was declared Salesperson of the Year. Shortly thereafter, the vice president of marketing calls you into her office and offers you a job as regional sales manager. You'll manage thirty salespeople like yourself, and if you can motivate your sales force to achieve like you did you'll earn significantly more income. The VP gives you a week to decide whether you will stay in your current position or accept the promotion. After your initial excitement, you begin to worry. You know you have the skills it takes to be a successful salesperson, but do you have the skills needed to be a successful manager? You look around at successful managers who reach their goals and see that they create value for the business. You compare these successful managers with people who tried and failed at being a manager. You begin to understand that all employees should add value, but how managers add value from other employees is different. The skills each needs are different. Managers must plan, execute, and review. Managers achieve their goals through their employees, and their job satisfaction often comes through these employees. Non-management employees often get job satisfaction from doing and seeing the immediate results of their actions. Now ask yourself two important questions: First, do you know what skills you'll need to be a manager and do you have these skills? Second, do you want to make the leap to management?

Even if you're not planning on a career in management, learning what managers do, what they are responsible for, and how they organize a business can help you make better decisions in your own professional life.

POWER VERSUS AUTHORITY

President Theodore (Teddy) Roosevelt was noted for many things. When he became President of the United States in 1901, he was the youngest President to that date. He achieved a lot, including building the Panama Canal, fighting monopolies, advancing the US National Park Service, and receiving the 1906 Nobel Peace Prize. However did you know he was also a colonel in the US Army, serving in the Spanish-American War? In fact, he led a very famous charge at the battle of San Juan Heights (Hill) in 1898.

Now think about being Colonel Roosevelt. His general commanded him to take San Juan Hill. His general gave him the authority to lead his troops up San Juan Hill. He has the responsibility to conquer the enemy's position. However can he do it? He looks at his troops, explains the objective, and yells "Charge." Can he take San Juan Hill by himself? The answer is "no." He needs the support of his troops. The power to take San Juan Hill rests in his subordinates, his troops. If his troops do not respect and believe in their leader, they will not follow Colonel Roosevelt. Colonel Roosevelt will fail. To succeed and reach his objective, Colonel Roosevelt's troops must empower him. The power to fulfill his responsibility rests in his subordinates. Think about it. Authority comes from your boss. Power comes from your employees. Successful managers understand there is a difference between authority and power. Successful managers understand the importance of power.

LEARNING OBJECTIVE 1
. . . .
THE NATURE AND ROLE OF MANAGEMENT

In Chapter 01, we defined a manager as someone who is responsible for looking after the interests of the business owners and other stakeholders. So how are managers different from other employees? All employees should add value to a business. However, managers are strategic decision makers who often also supervise the implementation of their decisions. These decisions deal with the people, assets, and money of the business. Non-management employees then implement the decisions of managers.

Let's look at an example. Say you walk into a store such as Target. A manager has made strategic decisions such as what will be sold, the price of each item, how many sales staff will be employed, and what each employee will be paid. That manager is making strategic decisions and managing. Each salesperson will then implement the manager's decisions. Although the understanding and practice of management has evolved over time, the focus of successful managers is always on making and implementing strategic decisions that create value.

LEVELS OF MANAGEMENT

There are many ways to classify managers. Exhibit 3.1 depicts a management pyramid, or hierarchy, found in many companies. At the top of the pyramid are the owners of the business.
A business's owners are the ultimate decision makers. They own the business and all decision makers

EXHIBIT 3.1: The Management Hierarchy

should follow their directives. When a business gets large, owners are typically unable to make all the decisions. Owners then elect representatives to make critical decisions on their behalf. In a corporation these representatives are called directors and serve on a business's governing body called a **Board of Directors** (the **Board**). (Note: A corporation is a form of business. The forms of business are explored in Chapter 06.) The Board of Directors then hires the business's senior managers. **Senior managers** are responsible for decisions regarding the total business and coordinating all areas of the business. The highest senior manager is often called the **President** or **Chief Executive Officer (CEO)**. Reporting to the President are Vice Presidents and other senior managers. Exhibit 3.2 depicts some common titles and responsibilities of senior management.

EXHIBIT 3.2: The Jobs of Senior Managers

CEO	**Chief Executive Officer** (often the President of the company)
CFO	**Chief Financial Officer** (often called the Treasurer or Vice President of Finance)
COO	**Chief Operating Officer** (often called the Vice President of Operations)
CIO	**Chief Information Officer** (often called the Vice President of Technology)
CMO	**Chief Marketing Officer** (often called the Vice President of Marketing)
Controller	**The Chief Accountant**

Senior managers select middle- and junior-level managers, often called **functional or divisional managers**, to run the functional areas or divisions of the business. So what is a functional area? Most businesses define a functional area as a type of work, such as marketing, production, or finance. What is a division? Businesses typically define a division according to geography, such as Hyundai's North America division, or product, such as the hair care division of Procter & Gamble. As managers move up the management hierarchy from junior to senior levels, their span of influence and responsibilities increase from functional areas to the total business. A manager's **span of influence** relates to the scope of her or his responsibilities. An example is when the manager of the grocery function in a Target store is promoted to be the manager of the entire store. Another example is when a business's vice president, such as VP of marketing, is promoted to president.

THE MANAGEMENT PROCESS

So how are the decisions of management framed to focus on value? As we discussed in Chapter 01, to create value effectively, managers focus on three activities: planning, executing, and reviewing. Each of these activities can be broken down into many parts, including organizing, directing, leading, controlling (or monitoring), and reporting. However, all such activities are ultimately a part of *planning* for the future, *executing* in the present, and *reviewing* the past to learn from experiences to enhance the future. Exhibit 3.3 depicts the management process. As you can see, managing a business is constant and circular, with planning, executing, and reviewing occurring constantly. Let's look at each of these activities in a bit more detail.

EXHIBIT 3.3: The Management Process

Planning

It is often said that the hardest and most neglected part of managing is planning. **Planning** involves forecasting and envisioning the future and deciding what actions the business will take. Remember that creating business value is about successful investing, financing, and operating. It's about creating a business model and winning with strategy. Planning is a critical part of all these activities. The challenge for many managers is that it takes time to receive the rewards from planning. Planning is also full of risks because of the uncertainty inherent in working with the future. It's a challenge to think what will or could happen in the future. This is why many managers avoid planning. However, most successful managers will tell you that planning is a key to creating value.

Specifically, planning involves envisioning the future, finding opportunities, setting goals, finding and analyzing alternatives, selecting the best alternative(s) to achieve these goals, and developing systems that will enable the business to execute the selected alternatives.

Visioning, Finding Opportunities, and Setting Goals

First, planning starts with visioning. **Visioning** is the process of looking at the past and present, embracing the forces of change, and forecasting the future. Visioning the overall direction of a business is typically the responsibility of senior management. However, functional managers should also vision. This is because functional managers often have more contact with customers, production processes, and other critical functions of the business. As such, functional managers often see the needs and opportunities for a business to change. Remember that the value of the business depends on its ability to generate profits in the present and future. To do so, all managers must envision the opportunities and challenges that will occur in the future. In a competitive world, managers must constantly ask questions like:

· What will my customers want in the future?

· Is there a better way to produce or sell my product in the future?

Great managers understand that the world is constantly changing and that to create value they must work hard to understand why and how things are changing. Great managers also understand that if they fail to vision, they will lose because their competitors will vision and create a sustainable competitive advantage. Great managers work hard to understand the present, but they also work hard to try to see how the future will be different. With that insight, they can then build a better future for their business. Later in this chapter, we'll look at tools like SWOT analysis. Managers use such tools to help vision the future.

Let's use Google as an example. In 1996, two students, Larry Page and Sergey Brin, had an idea. They envisioned a world in which people's productivity was enhanced through easy access to knowledge. At the time, the Internet was just beginning to be used as a tool to locate information. However, it was difficult

for people to do so as there was no effective means to search all the information the Internet had to offer. Page and Brin found an opportunity by visioning. They set a goal of empowering people to use the Internet and, in the process, also creating value. From that process, they recognized and analyzed different alternatives. They created a search engine that would transform the way people used the Internet. Through such visioning, Google was born, a company that was worthless in 1996 but is now valued at billions of dollars.

Now close your eyes and think about where today's trends might lead us in ten years. That's visioning. But visioning without action does not create value. After visioning comes figuring out how to use vision to create value.

Google founders Sergey Brin and Larry Page envisioned and delivered a better way to perform searches on the Internet.

Determining and Analyzing Alternatives

After managers identify an opportunity or challenge and set their goals, they must figure out what to do next. This phase of planning starts by recognizing all feasible alternatives for action. In doing so, managers must not only focus on actions they can take, they must also realize that doing nothing is an action and an alternative they must evaluate.

PROFILE

JONATHAN MARINER

When you think of Major League Baseball, you probably think of pitchers, hitters, and big stadiums. But baseball is a billion dollar business. It takes hard-working, knowledgeable, and passionate business managers to make baseball work. The managers of Major League Baseball must create value for the fans (customers), players (employees), and owners. So who are these professionals that make Major League Baseball a success? One of the top people is Jonathan Mariner.

Throughout the world of professional sports, Jonathan is recognized as a great manager and leader. He is currently the Executive Vice President and Chief Investment Officer (CIO) of Major League Baseball. Jonathan is a Certified Public Accountant (CPA). He serves on various boards (Boards of Directors) of global organizations. During his career he served as Executive Vice President and CFO of the Florida Marlins Baseball Club, Vice President and CFO of the Florida Panthers Hockey Club, and Vice President and CFO of Pro Player Stadium (now SunLife Stadium).

Jonathan Mariner is a great businessman. He understands that successful managers create value for all the stakeholders of a business. It's about teamwork. He understands that winning in the world of baseball means winning on the field of play and in the management suite.

After managers list all feasible alternatives, managers then must gather information about each alternative and be thorough in recognizing the benefits and costs of each alternative. This is a challenging task. Because of time and other restrictions, managers need to make assumptions about the costs and benefits of each alternative. They must realize that their job is to make decisions, and that many decisions must be made with imperfect information. This lack of perfect information creates risk. For this reason, good managers try to be open, objective, and focused on creating value.

Let's take Target as an example. If Target managers believe (envision) that a community or market will be growing in the future, they have two main options: (1) build a new store, or (2) do nothing (not build a new store). Both options present risks. If they build a store and the market does not grow, the new store may not sell enough products to generate an operating profit sufficient to reward the providers of the financial capital. However, if Target waits and does not build a store, the company may also face problems. If the market grows, competitors such as Walmart may build a store first. Target may then lose out on the profit and resulting value of being the first store in the area to meet the needs of the new customers. So what to do? The answer is that managers must gather as much information as possible and make informed choices. But Target's managers must realize that both of their alternatives have risk. Target's managers are never sure of the future. Which brings us to the next step in planning: deciding among alternatives and how to execute them.

Selecting Which Alternative Creates the Most Value and Executing the Best Alternative

After determining what their alternatives are and evaluating each one, managers must next decide which alternative to choose. In doing so, managers must weigh the benefits and costs of each alternative. Managers must recognize the assumptions being used and the operating profit, timing, and risk associated with each alternative.

Value is the ultimate criteria for deciding which alternative to select and execute. The question becomes, "Which alternative will create the greatest value in the future?" Often managers fall into the trap of focusing on the present rather than the future. However, our world is constantly changing. The present is not the relevant benchmark. Managers must focus on the future.

An example is instant pudding, that dessert product you find in grocery stores. Years ago, before instant pudding was something consumers had heard about, Kraft Foods had a tough decision to make: Should or shouldn't the company introduce instant pudding? The company realized that this new pudding product would hurt sales of the company's existing Jell-O product. As such, the company almost decided not to introduce instant pudding. But Kraft managers realized that they would lose the Jell-O sales in the future *whether they introduced instant pudding or not*. They realized that in their ever-changing market, their competitors would quickly introduce a product like instant pudding. Their only choice was whether they would create value with an instant pudding product or their competitors would. They forgot the present and focused on the future. In doing so, they created significant value for Kraft.

After deciding which alternative will create the most value in the future, managers must communicate how they intend to execute the alternative through various types of plans:

- · Senior management may use a **strategic plan** to set and communicate the business's broad goals and long-term objectives. These plans are broad in scope and do not provide details. An example is Hyundai creating a strategic plan to enter the US market within ten years with automobiles that meet the evolving needs of the American consumer.

· Functional managers may use these broad goals and long-term objectives to create tactical plans. **Tactical plans** break down the broad goals and long-term objectives into more precise goals and actions. An example is Hyundai's functional managers doing research and determining the best way to implement the strategic plan is to develop a low-cost, quality automobile, such as the Kia.

· Middle and junior managers may break down the tactical plans into operational plans. An example is Hyundai's middle managers deciding how and when to produce and sell Kia automobiles. **Operational plans** are very specific about activities and standards. Operational plans show the details of how actions are to be performed and goals reached.

· Last, all plans are based on assumptions. As such, all plans involve risk. Good managers are always preparing for the unexpected. **Contingency plans** are plans that detail what course of action the company should take in case the unexpected occurs. Can you imagine Hyundai promising dealers a new automobile and not having backup or contingency plans?

Mark Zuckerberg, founder, chairman, and CEO of Facebook, shows off the company's new messaging system. Strategic, tactical, and operational planning are essential to successful product development.

EXHIBIT 3.4: Planning

Executing

Execution involves using systems to operate the business, according to plans, to create value and achieve the desired goals. In short, it is about implementing decisions and getting the job done. As such, execution is the most visible sign of creating value.

So how does a business execute for value? It starts by creating a system that helps managers organize, implement, and monitor the execution of their plans. Remember from Chapter Two that business systems are the processes that a business uses to operate. Systems help a business acquire, train, and monitor the best people. They help a business acquire the best assets and use these assets in the most efficient manner. They help a business execute by acquiring the right amount of money.

However, execution is more than merely putting a plan into action and reaping the benefits. Good managers realize that plans are based on assumptions that may or may not become reality. Have you ever been in a fast-food restaurant when an unexpectedly large number of customers show up? Have you ever gone to a store because of an advertised special, only to find the store has run out of the item? Have you ever seen an organization be challenged when a key employee was sick and could not come to work? Good managers know that executing a plan means they must monitor the business and make changes when needed. Flexibility and adapting to change is critical. This is when the contingency plans we discussed earlier come into play. Businesses use such contingency plans to adapt and alter execution as needed.

Think about why businesses fail. Many such businesses have great products but fail because of poor execution. Many fail to meet the changing needs of their customers or control costs. Often businesses have great plans but fail to execute. So how do managers stay on top of execution? The trick is to review and adapt their execution constantly.

Reviewing

Reviewing involves using systems to compare the desired outcomes from planning to the actual results of execution. Part of reviewing is monitoring how plans are being executed and holding managers accountable for their decisions. However, review is also about learning from the present and past and making timely decisions to enhance the future. As such, the review process has many dimensions.

First is control. **Control** is using systems to monitor execution and attempt to ensure that execution meets the goals of planning. The control process starts with managers setting clear and reasonable standards. That process extends to managers monitoring how the business is or is not achieving those standards. Let's take Hyundai as an example. The car manufacturer must first determine how many automobiles it should produce on an assembly line and what the quality of those vehicles must be. Then it must monitor the production process to make sure the correct number is produced and that quality standards are maintained. But what happens with the output or insight gained from the control process? Managers must be held accountable.

Accountability is about holding managers responsible for meeting standards. If managers meet or exceed standards, they should be rewarded. For example, what happens when a sales manager for P&G motivates his or her sales force to exceed a sales quota/target? Often that sales manager is rewarded with a bonus. However, if a manager fails to meet standards, corrective action must be taken. What happens when a sales manager at P&G fails to sell an agreed-upon sales quota/target? First, managers need to determine what caused the standards to not be met. If the failure is correctable, such actions need to be taken. However, if the failure is due to the manager and the manager cannot change, a new manager must be placed in charge.

Ideally, accountability leads to learning. In fact, one of the most critical dimensions of the review process is learning. Successful managers constantly review their successes and failures. They want to understand why they succeeded so they can replicate that success in the future. They want to understand why they failed so they can avoid such problems in the future. Review is about learning from the past to make the future better. Good managers are continuously trying to improve.

LEARNING OBJECTIVE 2

ASSESSING A BUSINESS'S ENVIRONMENT

So we've learned that the process of management is circular and constant. Managers vision the future and decide how to create value in the future. This is called planning. Managers must then execute their plans in the present. Finally, managers must review. They must constantly learn by comparing the actual results from the past and present with the desired results. From that review process, managers adjust and revise their plans and execution strategies.

LEARNING AND IMPROVING

Can you ride a bicycle? If so, why did you learn? Most likely, you wanted to learn to ride a bike because doing so provided you with some benefits. Knowing how to ride a bicycle enabled you to go new places and do new things. However, these benefits had a cost. That cost was failure. You realized learning to ride a bicycle also meant taking risks. You could fall and hurt yourself. So what to do? After comparing the benefits and costs, you decided to take the risk and learn to ride a bicycle. But success never comes easy. The trick to riding a bike is maintaining balance—not leaning too far to the left or the right. And how do you learn to balance? By leaning too far to the left or right, falling off, and experiencing pain. Is this a bad thing? Not as long as you learn from your mistakes and grow from them. If you don't get back on the bike and keep riding, you'll never learn.

Businesses are the same. Businesses take risk and often experience pain. However, great managers learn from their mistakes and improve. They improve as managers and improve the businesses they manage. The trick to being a successful manager is to continuously improve by learning.

So if that is what managers do, what is the best way to facilitate planning, executing, and reviewing? How do managers create and sustain a competitive advantage that creates value? Part of doing so is understanding the environment in which the business exists. First, the business needs to recognize the nature of the forces outside the business. That is, the business needs to understand its *external environment* and the opportunities and threats that exist outside the business. Next the business needs to evolve this external analysis by recognizing its internal capabilities. The business needs to recognize its internal strengths and weaknesses. After recognizing these realities, managers then must create an organizational structure that will optimize value for the company.

A worker assembling a vehicle (right) at the Alabama Hyundai plant (left).

PORTER'S FIVE FORCES

First is the task of analyzing a business's external environment. A business's **external environment** is composed of those important factors that the business does not directly control. Examples include the overall economy, customer wants, and competitor actions. A business's **internal environment** is composed of those factors that the business can control. Examples include what products a business will sell, where it will conduct business, and how it will manage its employees. To manage, managers must first understand a business's external environment and then focus on its internal environment.

In understanding a business's external environment, the ultimate question a business needs to answer is, "Who has the power?" Michael Porter of Harvard Business School frames this challenge by recognizing five external forces that affect a business and how much power of each.[1] **Porter's Five Forces** are as follows and are depicted in Exhibit 3.5:

1. **Supplier power** refers to the power that suppliers have in a business's value chain. Can the supplier dictate the terms of the relationship (e.g., price)? Does the business have alternative suppliers? For example, suppliers of oil have a lot of power over gasoline retailers.

2. **Barriers to entry** refers to the difficulty new businesses may have in entering the market. Barriers to entry include government policy, overcoming customer preferences, and financial requirements. For example, there are significant barriers to entry when starting a bank or airline because government approval is required.

3. **Customer power** refers to the power customers have in the business's value chain. Does the customer have choices? Do the business and its competitors supply more products than the market demands? Can the customer dictate the price and terms of the sale? For example, customers of fast-food restaurants have many choices and, therefore, a lot of power over such restaurants. Such restaurants must provide customers exactly what they want, how they want it, and at the price they are willing to pay.

4. **Threat of substitute products** refers to the availability of products that the customer can substitute for the business's product. If customers are dissatisfied with the business's product, can they find alternative products that will meet their needs? For example, if an airline's customers get upset over its flight schedules, pricing, or service, they may decide to travel by car or train or take another airline.

5. **Rivalry** relates to the intensity of the competition in the industry. How fiercely do competitors respond to each other's initiatives? For example, the capacity of the automobile industry is greater than the demand for automobiles. Automobile manufacturers, therefore, fiercely try to differentiate their products with advertising, pricing, guarantees, service, and so on.

EXHIBIT 3.5: Porter's Five Forces

An Example: Target

Let's look at how all of these five external forces affect Target.

1. **Supplier Power:** In order to compete, Target needs good suppliers with good products. However, good suppliers have numerous alternative outlets for their products, such as Walmart, Costco, and Kmart. Target must convince its suppliers that it is the best outlet for the suppliers' products. However, there are many suppliers with products. In addition, Target buys a lot of products, so suppliers compete for Target's business. Thus, the power of Target's suppliers is balanced. With this, the degree of supplier power for Target is moderate.

2. **Barriers to Entry:** In the mass retailing industry in which Target operates, barriers to entry are relatively high. It takes a lot of money to operate a retail store located throughout a country or even the world. Another barrier to entry is the difficulty of creating a national or global network of suppliers. It typically takes years to create such a network. Therefore, the barriers to entry protect Target and help Target balance the power of suppliers and customers.

3. **Customer Power:** Because buyers have many options in the mass retail industry, customer power is high. According to a recent survey, Target's typical customer is a 40-year-old, college educated female with children.[2] Target's customers are perceived to be sophisticated, knowledgeable, and affluent. Target's customers have a lot of options and know it. Target's customers have power, which impacts Targets decisions on what it sells, the prices it charges, and where its stores are located.

4. **Threat of Substitute Products:** Target's business model is to provide a convenient way of purchasing general merchandise such as clothing, groceries, and electronics. Target is a mass merchandiser that uses large buildings to sell a wide selection of products. It has many direct competitors, such as Walmart. But Target also faces substitutes. Think about buying clothing or electronics using the Internet. Think about buying milk from a convenience store. There are alternatives to mass merchandisers such as Target and Walmart. These alternatives are substitutes.

   The high rate of substitutes for products is, therefore, considered a significant threat for Target.

5. **Rivalry/Competition:** Competition is intense in the mass retail industry. Target's main rivals include Walmart, Kmart, and Costco. All of these are direct competitors and sell similar products, at similar prices, delivered in similar ways. Target's direct competition is fierce and limits Target's power regarding what it sells and what price it charges.

How can Target overcome its internal weaknesses and improve its overall business?

In summary, when Target's management decides what it will sell, the price it will charge, and where it will build its stores, it finds itself balancing the power held by external forces with the power it possesses. Target cannot dictate to its customers. Customers are very powerful because they have many options with both substitute products and direct competitors. Likewise, Target needs its suppliers. However, because of barriers to entry, Target's suppliers have limited outlets for their products and need Target. Target and its suppliers share power. In summary, Target must recognize its customers, and suppliers create threats and opportunities. Next, Target must look inside and recognize its internal strengths and weaknesses.

SWOT: STRENGTHS, WEAKNESSES, OPPORTUNITIES, AND THREATS

After examining the external environment, a business must analyze its ability to compete in that environment. If the first question managers ask is, "Who has the power?," the next question becomes, "What does that mean with regard to managing the business?" To answer that question, managers must recognize their company's strengths, weaknesses, opportunities, and threats. This process is often called a **SWOT analysis**[3]. Exhibit 3.6 depicts a SWOT analysis.

EXHIBIT 3.6: SWOT Analysis

In a SWOT analysis, **strengths** and **weaknesses** are internal to the business, meaning that they are things that the business can control. An example of a strength is the legal right to be the exclusive producer of a product (e.g., holding a patent). An example of a weakness is a lack of trained employees.

Opportunities and **threats** are external to the business, meaning they are things that the business cannot control. Examples of external opportunities include entering a new market, acquiring new technology, and improving economic conditions. Examples of external threats include a new competitor in the market, deteriorating economic conditions, and changing tastes of customers.

A Second Example: Target

Let's look at Target as an example.

Target's internal strengths include:

- Its name and brand are well recognized

- It offers many products

- Its products are perceived to be fashionable and of good quality

- It has good locations

- Its operations are efficient and consistent regardless of location

Target's internal weaknesses include:

- It operates only in North America. Note: This limits Target's negotiations with suppliers and makes it 100% dependent on the prosperity of one economic area.

- It experiences high employee turnover at the store level

- The profitability of food items is lower than general merchandise such as clothing

- Stores vary little by region and may lose regional opportunities

Target's external opportunities include:

- It needs to improve pricing perception as Target is typically perceived as more expensive than Walmart

- It needs to increase the number of trips to Target made by its best customers

- It needs to expand outside North America

- Although food items are less profitable, this can be offset by increasing the volume of food sales. It needs to update its store design, making the shopping experience more enjoyable and convenient.

Target's external threats include:

- Poor economic conditions may force its core shoppers to buy low-priced substitutes from competitors

- Small competitors are entering the market and focusing on regional needs

- A shortage of qualified employees, requiring Target to pay higher wages

- Dependence on select suppliers, causing concern that such suppliers can dictate prices and other important decisions.

After a business understands its external environment and internal capabilities, it's time to organize. It's time to address its threats and take advantage of its opportunities. It's time to overcome its internal weaknesses while exploiting its internal strengths. It's time to create an organization that successfully competes.

LEARNING OBJECTIVE 3

ORGANIZATIONAL BEHAVIOR AND STRUCTURE

Every organization is different. Why? The answer is that they seek to differentiate. Companies have different business models and strategies to deal with their strengths, weaknesses, opportunities, and threats. As such, you'd expect that different businesses may be organized in different ways to maximize their strengths and opportunities while minimizing their weaknesses and threats. Can you imagine organizing a technology company such as Google the same way that you'd manage a home products company such as P&G? So how do senior managers organize a business?

Networks are communication processes that bring people and organizations together for a common purpose. Networks are made up of customers, suppliers, competitors, employees, and other important groups such as the government. A business's organization is merely the **formal network** structure adopted by senior management. When a business hires an employee and purchases an item from a supplier, it is using its formal networks. However, senior management must also recognize the impact of **informal networks**, often called **social networks**. Think about what happens when one part of an organization gets a pay raise and another part does not. Employees quickly pass the word through informal networks. What happens when a product's price differs in different markets? Customers quickly figure it out because of informal networks. What happens is that the informal networks take hold of the business and create opportunities or challenges. Managers must organize the business with a formal structure, or network, which recognizes the informal networks of a business environment.

An example is organizing a **team** to research a new product at a company such as Procter & Gamble. Procter & Gamble must recognize that the members of the team may have colleagues outside the team whom they respect and trust. These trusted colleagues form an informal network for the members of the team. The team members may seek information and advice from these colleagues that could help or hurt the project. A business, to create the best possible product, must carefully organize the formal team in such a way as to enhance the use of this informal network.

CENTRALIZED VS. DECENTRALIZED ORGANIZATIONS

In creating the formal structure of a business, senior managers must answer two critical questions:

1. Where will the authority and thus responsibility rest for making decisions?

2. How should the areas of the business be organized to maximize productivity?

Procter & Gamble headquarters.

Let's look at the first question: the location of decision-making authority and responsibility. Some businesses create a very centralized organization. A **centralized organization** is one in which the authority to make decisions rests in a few senior managers. Organizations that adopt a centralized structure often seek consistency and standardization. An example of a centralized organization is a bank. Often loans must be approved by senior managers and loan committees. This enhances consistency but inhibits loan officers from taking initiative. Businesses may lose opportunities because employees lack authority to make decisions.

Other businesses create a decentralized organization. A **decentralized organization** is one in which authority to make and implement decisions rests in many managers, often junior or middle managers. Organizations that adopt a decentralized structure often seek flexibility and creativity and need managers to quickly adapt to changing conditions. An example of a decentralized organization is a hospital where the needs of patients are diverse and constantly changing. Doctors and nurses must be able to make quick decisions. A decentralized organization fosters initiative and takes advantage of opportunities when opportunities arise. However, a decentralized organization can also cause problems because it can create inconsistencies.

In reality, the choice of centralized or decentralized structure is not an either/or decision. Often businesses are a combination of centralized and decentralized decision making. In a bank, senior loan officers may be organized in a flexible decentralized structure while inexperienced loan officers may be organized in an inflexible centralized structure. Likewise, a hospital may organize its medical staff in a decentralized structure while its accounting department may be organized in a centralized structure.

DIVISIONAL VS. FUNCTIONAL ORGANIZATIONS

Now let's look at the second question managers must address: how the areas of the business should be organized to maximize productivity. There are two basic models for organizing a business: *divisional and functional*. A **divisional organization** is one in which the business is divided into divisions. A division is usually defined as a certain market (or geographical area) or a certain product. Exhibit 3.7 shows an example of a divisional organization based on geographic region. Exhibit 3.8 shows an example of a divisional organization based on a product-based structure.

The divisional model helps organizations focus on a particular market (region) or product. A divisional model focuses on the product and the customer who buys the product. Think about Hyundai designing, producing, and selling automobiles for North America and Europe. In North America, gasoline is less expensive than in Europe. Drivers in North America drive longer distances using straighter roads than drivers in Europe. Customers in North America and Europe have different needs. Here a divisional model would work best. The disadvantage is that each division must be self-contained and thus have its own research and development, production, marketing, accounting, information systems, and finance areas. This may prove expensive and inefficient.

EXHIBIT 3.7: Organization Structure Based on Geography

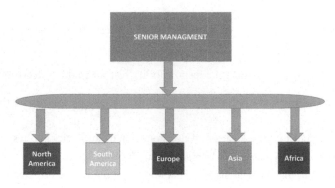

EXHIBIT 3.8: Organization Structure Based on Product

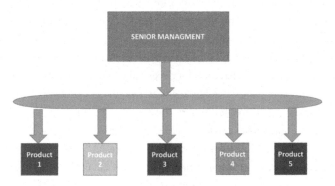

A **functional organization** is one in which the business is organized based on functions. Exhibit 3.9 shows an example of a functional organization. Often these functions are classified as **line** or **staff functions**.

EXHIBIT 3.9: Organization Structure Based on Function

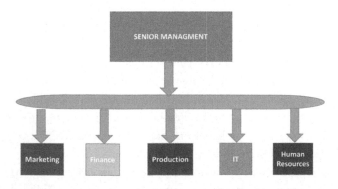

- **Line functions** include those functions that are directly involved in a company's value chain, specifically the inputs, the process(es) used to convert the inputs into outputs, and the outputs sold to customers. Examples of line functions include purchasing, production, and marketing.

- **Staff functions** are those functions that are indirectly *involved* in the company's value chain. Staff functions support the activities of the line functions. Examples of staff functions include accounting, finance, and information systems.

A functional model focuses the business's expertise according to functions. This often gains efficiency and lowers costs. However, the challenge is the organization may not recognize the unique needs of different markets. Functional models work best when customers seek consistency. Think about Target. Every Target store has a similar look, similar inventory, and provides the customer a similar shopping experience. This has many benefits. However, it can create challenges when individual stores cannot adapt to the unique needs of its market.

MATRIX ORGANIZATIONS

From the Oval Office (left) to an average business's conference room (right), successful managers and leaders continuously strive to improve.

In reality, many businesses blend divisional and functional models. An example of this blending is a matrix organization. A **matrix organization** is a combination of a divisional model and a functional model. Exhibit 3.10 depicts a matrix structure. Note the parts of the business report to two bosses, a functional boss and a divisional boss. The goal of a matrix organization is to achieve the benefits of both a divisional and a functional structure. One challenge with matrix organizations is coordinating the parts of the business. Matrix organizations can become inefficient and ineffective without strong leadership, communication, and acceptance of responsibility.

Let's look at an example. You want to create an organization that focuses on the customer. The challenge is your customers are very different. You create a divisional organization where each division is responsible for a specific product or geographic area. Within each division are people who purchase or produce the product, market the product, and manage

EXHIBIT 3.10: Matrix Organization

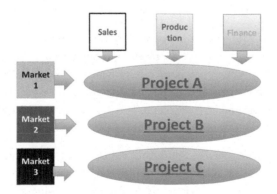

the financing of the product. You have problems. Your company does not want the different divisions to individually go to banks or approach owners for money. The company wants the finance function to be centralized for consistency and efficiency. How does the business deal with this challenge? The answer is a matrix organization. The company would combine divisional and functional models. A matrix organization would have a central core of people doing finance within each division and reporting to the top manager of that division. The finance personnel would also report to a separate functional area that coordinates all finance functions within the company. Sound good? The challenge is the finance people now have two bosses, the head of the division and the head of the finance function. Problems will occur if the two bosses do not coordinate their activities.

Choosing the right structure for a business is important. Without the right organizational structure, a company will find it difficult to deal with its external opportunities and threats, or minimize its weaknesses and use its strengths. The right organization structure is very important in maximizing value.

LEARNING OBJECTIVE 4
. . . .
THE TRAITS OF SUCCESSFUL MANAGERS

We've learned that different organizations need different structures to create value. Regardless of structure, the success of all organizations rests on their having good managers. So what makes some managers more successful than others? Successful managers often have the following **traits**:

1. *An ability and willingness to understand the company's business model and strategy.* Successful managers understand the business and how it creates value. They grasp what differentiates the business from its competitors and have an understanding of the company's ability or inability to generate a sustainable competitive advantage.

2. *Honesty and integrity, with a desire to be accountable and responsible.* Successful managers are honest, act with integrity, and behave ethically. From this honesty, integrity, and ethical behavior comes a sense of responsibility and accountability. Successful managers also expect others to be honest, ethical, accountable, and responsible.

3. *An ability and desire to constantly compete by learning and improving and helping others learn and improve.* Successful managers are always learning and helping others learn. They ask questions, learn from their mistakes, and are persistent. They take their knowledge and use it to continuously improve the business.

4. *The ability to be focused and organized.* Successful managers know what is important and what is not. They are, therefore, able to prioritize, stay focused, and get the job done. They are results-oriented people who realize that value is the reward for results, not effort.

5. *The ability to empathize with customers, suppliers, competitors, employees, and fellow managers.* Successful managers understand that people are the most important part of any business. For people to enter an exchange and create value, they must receive benefits. Successful managers understand that people are complex and often challenging and that different people seek different benefits. They try to understand people and be empathetic. They try to create a situation where all stakeholders feel they are understood, appreciated, and receive fair value for their work or other inputs.

6. *The ability to effectively deal with time.* Successful managers know how to manage their time. They understand there are times to be patient and times to be impatient. They know that time is a critical element of value and a precious commodity in the business world.

7. *The ability to deal with change in an effective and positive manner.* Change is everywhere. Successful managers try to embrace change and understand the opportunities and challenges that change presents. In embracing change, they sense when to be flexible and when not to be flexible. This aspect of managing is often called **change management**.

8. *The ability to grasp the future and manage uncertainty.* Successful managers seek to recognize and understand that the future is the company's source of profits, risks, and value. They are prudent but are also proactive and not scared of taking risks. However, successful managers also demand to be compensated for taking risk and producing greater profits.

9. *The ability to communicate with all parties involved in the business's value chain.* Successful managers are good communicators across the entire value chain. They understand that failing to communicate creates problems. They also understand that communication includes both verbal and nonverbal communication and that good communication starts with listening and understanding.

10. *The ability to build and lead teams.* Business is about **teamwork**. Great teams have great leaders. An effective manager may or may not be a great leader. However, great managers seek to be leaders. Leaders are people who help others achieve by challenging the status quo, enabling, empowering, and inspiring others.

LEARNING OBJECTIVE 5
. . . .

BUSINESS SENSE

TEAMWORK

Let's take a trip to a performance of an orchestra. Have you ever wondered how each member of the orchestra got there? Why, when auditioning, was each member selected to be a part of that orchestra or musical team? Ask these questions to the conductor and he or she would say that first the team needs a given number of violinists, a given number of percussionists, and so on. Second, each of the musicians must have a certain level of musical skill. Third, each musician plays a certain role. The orchestra does not need everyone to be soloists. Some musicians must play back-up. The conductor, therefore, selects those individuals whom he or she believes will contribute the most to the overall success of the team.

A successful business is like a fine orchestra. When everyone works together and fills needed roles, great things happen. For an orchestra, the result is wonderful music. For a business, the result is value.

TEAMWORK AND LEADERSHIP

In Chapter 02 we learned that a business is made up of a portfolio—a mix or pool—of different resources, including assets and people. Another way to describe a portfolio of people is to call it a team. **Teams** are cohesive groups of people who focus on an objective. **Teamwork** is what members of a team do to achieve that objective. Teams and teamwork are at the heart of making business work. Businesses that create value understand this.

Think about all the employees who worked together to create the Google search engine that people use to explore the Internet. It takes people to research customer needs, to develop products to meet customers needs, and to market advertising and other services. It takes people to construct and operate the systems and to provide customer support at all times. It takes people to acquire the needed money and account for the business's activities. It takes a team of people who each have expertise in his or her particular field and come together to produce an effective team that creates value for all stakeholders.

So how do managers form and motivate teams who create value? First, managers pick team members who have 1) the needed skills (such as marketing, technical, or other skills) and 2) the ability to work with other team members. Second, managers find leaders to help the team reach its objective.

FORMAL VS. INFORMAL LEADERS

You may be inclined to think of managers and leaders being one and the same, but this is not always true. *Managers* are people who have the authority to do something. This authority comes from owners and higher-level managers. For example, the CEO of a company is its top manager. She or he is authorized to run the business by the company's Board of Directors or owners. **Leaders**, on the other hand, are people who are empowered by a team. Leaders motivate team members to collectively achieve a goal and may or may not be managers. Managers who are leaders are often called formal leaders. **Formal leaders** have formal authority based on the position they hold in the company and also are empowered by team members. **Informal leaders** do not have formal authority within the company but are empowered by team members.

Let's look at an example. Have you ever been a part of a sports team? Teams all have coaches who direct the players during the contest. These coaches are considered the managers of the team. Sometimes these people have the ability to motivate the team to achieve. If they do, the managers are also the formal leaders of the team. However, sometimes other members of the team are empowered by the team to lead. Sometimes you find individual players on the team motivating their fellow teammates to achieve. These individuals are the informal leaders of the team. They have no direct authority but are empowered by team members.

A coach shares last-minute instructions before his player enters the field. What are the key differences between managing and leading?

TYPES, TRAITS, AND STYLES OF LEADERS

So what is the role of a leader? What do we need leaders to do? What do we expect leaders to do? The answer depends on the situation. Some leaders help their team reach a clearly defined, desired objective. We call these leaders **transactional leaders**. George Washington was a transactional leader when he led the Continental Army to victory in the US Revolution. The US Continental Congress gave George Washington a clear task. That task was to defeat the British army.

However, some leaders help their team envision possibilities and the need to change. We call these leaders **transformational leaders**. Thomas Jefferson was a transformational leader when he envisioned and helped create a new and radical form of democratic government in the United States. Thomas Jefferson saw the need for change. Thomas Jefferson envisioned a government of the people, by the people, and for the people. He then led his colleagues to create a government that could operate with those principles.

So what makes a great leader? Many studies have tried to answer this question, but no definitive list of traits has been proven. It is believed that successful leaders possess many of the traits discussed earlier for successful managers. Two traits are often viewed as especially critical. The first is honesty and integrity. For leaders to be successful, people must trust and respect them. Successful leaders must earn this trust and respect through honesty and integrity. The second is the ability to communicate. Motivation starts with understanding. Understanding starts with communicating. To lead a team, team members must believe in their leader. That belief requires effective communication.

Now think about George Washington leading his troops to victory. Those troops trusted and respected Washington. Why? The answer is that Washington communicated with his troops. Now also think of Thomas Jefferson being entrusted with drafting the US Declaration of Independence. Why? The answer is Jefferson's colleagues trusted and respected him and believed him to be a great communicator.

John Trumbull's painting, *Declaration of Independence*, depicting the five-man drafting committee of the Declaration of Independence presenting their work to the Congress. Thomas Jefferson is pictured at center wearing a red waistcoat. The painting can be found on the back of the US $2 bill. The original hangs in the US Capitol rotunda.

Given that it's sometimes hard to define the traits that make successful leaders, what about leadership style? Is there one particular style that helps someone be an effective leader? The answer once again is that it depends on the situation. Typically, leadership styles are classified as autocratic, participative, or laissez-faire.

- **Autocratic leaders** make decisions without seeking the input of others. They often dictate. Such a style can create problems in some instances and success in other instances. Do you want a leader in a jury to be autocratic? Probably not. Would you want the leader of a police team to take charge, instill confidence, and direct his or her team members in a time of crisis? Probably yes.

- **Participative leaders**, or *democratic leaders*, attempt to involve as many people as possible in decision making. A participative leader would be very effective in a jury hearing a court case. However a participative leader may be a disaster in a police crisis.

- A **laissez-faire leader** is one who sets the overall direction and guidelines but permits others to make the decisions about implementation. An example of such a leader is a judge overseeing a jury trial in our court system. A judge may direct the jury to follow certain rules, but the jury may be free to apply those rules as they desire.

MANAGERS AND LEADERS: REALITY OF SUCCESS

Leading and managing are challenging tasks that can mean the success or failure of a business. Why? The answer is business is first about people, and leaders and managers are the key people in creating a successful business. It is often said that great leaders and managers are born. Research has shown that many of the traits that make people effective leaders and managers can be learned. Great leaders and managers have a passion for learning. They evolve, embrace change, and stay focused on creating value.

PROFILE

KATHARINE GRAHAM, A LEADER WITH COURAGE

Katharine Graham was the wife of the CEO and owner of the Washington Post. In 1963 her husband died. She inherited the *Post*. She admitted to being a socialite and falling under the control of her husband. However she quickly evolved, became her own person, and transformed the *Post* from a regional newspaper to a national and international force. She established that she and her newspaper would lead the charge for openness, inclusiveness, and honesty. Although principles are not always easy to live, Katharine Graham decided to live her principles. Under threats of harm and prosecution, she decided that the *Post* would publish the secret "Pentagon Papers." These documents revealed US government deceptions about the Vietnam War. Later she supported her reporters Woodward and Bernstein in investigating the Watergate scandal that caused US President Richard Nixon to resign. James Collins, the famous writer for *Fortune* magazine, called Katharine Graham one of the 10 greatest business leaders of all time. Katharine Graham had more than conviction; she had courage.

CHAPTER SUMMARY

Managing is about planning, executing, and reviewing. Being a good manager takes a lot of skills, hard work, and dedication. It's about making, organizing, and operating a business that creates value. The bottom line is managing and leading a business is challenging. But when done right, the reward of creating and operating a business is enormous. It is special to see the inputs come into a business, to see the business transform those inputs, and to ultimately see outputs or products that create value. In this chapter, we have begun to explore the nature of managing a business. Specifically you should be able to:

1. Appreciate the nature and role of management (Learning Objective 1): A manager is someone who is responsible for looking after the interests of the business owners and other stakeholders. Managers plan, execute, and review.
2. Appreciate how managers assess a business's environment (Learning Objective 2): Successful managers understand a business's internal and external environments. They use tools such as Porter's Five Forces and SWOT analysis to help them understand a business's environment.
3. Appreciate the types of organizational structures and behavior (Learning Objective 3): Businesses are organized differently because businesses attempt to be different, or differentiate themselves from competitors. Different businesses have different models and strategies, requiring them to be organized differently.
4. Appreciate the traits of successful managers, including leadership (Learning Objective 4): Being a successful manager requires many traits centered on understanding, communicating, adapting, and leading.
5. Appreciate the need for and challenges of teamwork and leadership (Learning Objective 5): Managers are people who have the authority to do something. This authority comes from owners or higher-level managers. Leaders, on the other hand, are people who are empowered by a team. Teams are cohesive groups of people who focus on an objective.

So given that the objective of business is to create value, the next step is to understand the environment in which business operates. We need to explore economics, the forces of globalization, the different forms of business, and the laws affecting business. It's time to get deeper into "How Business Works."

KEYWORDS

accountability 49

autocratic leaders 61

barriers to entry 51

board 43

board of directors 43

centralized organization 55

change management 59

chief executive officer (ceo) 43

contingency plans 48

control 49

customer power 51

decentralized organization 55

determining and analyzing
   alternatives 46

divisional managers 44

divisional organization 55

execution 48

external environment 50

formal leaders 60

formal network 54

functional or divisional
   managers 44

functional organization 56

Informal leaders 60

informal networks 55

internal environment 51

laissez-faire leader 61

leaders 60

line functions 56

matrix organization 57

networks 54

operational plans 48

opportunities 53

participative leaders 61

planning 45

Porter's Five Forces 51

president 43

review 49

rivalry 51

senior managers 43

social networks 54

span of influence 44

staff functions 56

strategic plan 47

strengths 53

supplier power 51

SWOT analysis 53

tactical plans 48

team 54

teamwork 59

threat of substitute products 51

threats 53

traits 41

transactional leaders 60

transformational leaders 60

visioning 45

weaknesses 53

SHORT-ANSWER QUESTIONS

1. What is a manager? What does a manager do? How are managers different from other employees?
2. What are the traits of a successful manager?
3. Define the following terms:
   a. Accountability
   b. Autocratic Leader
   c. Board of Directors (the Board)
   d. Chairperson of the Board of Directors
   e. Change Management
   f. Chief Executive Officer (CEO)
   g. Chief Financial Officer (CFO)
   h. Chief Information Officer (CIO)
   i. Chief Marketing Officer (CMO)
   j. Chief Operating Officer (COO)
   k. Contingency Plans
   l. Control
   m. Formal Leader
   n. Formal Networks
   o. Functional or Divisional Managers
   p. Informal Leader
   q. Informal Networks
   r. Laissez-Faire Leader
   s. Networks
   t. Operational Plans
   u. Participative Leader
   v. President
   w. Senior Managers
   x. Social Networks
   y. Staff Functions
   z. Strategic Plans
   aa. Tactical Plans
   ab. Team
   ac. Transactional Leader
   ad. Transformational Leader
   ae. Vice Presidents
   af. Visioning
4. Briefly describe how leadership and management are different.

CRITICAL-THINKING QUESTIONS

1. Look around your world and think of the businesses in your community. Ask a senior manager in that business the following questions:
   a. What is the biggest challenge you face as a manager?
   b. What do you do regarding the functions of planning, executing, and reviewing? Ask for examples of these functions.
2. Ask yourself the following questions:
   a. When would you use a centralized form of organization versus a decentralized form of organization? Can you give some examples of businesses that are organized in a centralized manner? Can you give some examples of organizations that are organized in a decentralized manner?
   b. What are the strengths and challenges of using the following forms of organization structure?
      i. Divisional
      ii. Functional
      iii. Matrix
   c. Think of a situation where a team failed to reach the desired outcome. Ask yourself why the team failed. Is it because the individual members of the team did not have the skills needed, or is it because the team members did not work well together?

EXPLORING REAL BUSINESS

Go to the websites of Google, Target, Hyundai, and Proctor and Gamble. The websites are

Google:	http://investor.google.com
Target:	http://www.target.com
Hyundai:	http://worldwide.hyundai.com/company-overview
Procter & Gamble:	http://www.pg.com

For each company, try to prepare the following:

1. A diagram depicting and detailing *Porter's Five Forces.*
2. A SWOT analysis.

ENDNOTES

1. Michael E. Porter, "How Competitive Forces Shape Strategy," *Harvard Business Review*, March/April 1975.
2. Per Target, "Our guests are young, well-educated, moderate-to-better income families who live active lifestyles. The median age of our guests is 42, the youngest of major discount retailers. They have a median annual income of $60,000, 51 percent have completed college and 33 percent have children at home." http://pressroom.target.com/news/fastfacts. 2009.
3. Creation of SWOT analysis is attributed to Albert Humphrey, a Stanford Research Institute Professor, in the 1960s and 1970s.

SECTION 2

THE ENVIRONMENT

In this section, you will read and review the following chapters:

04

UNDERSTANDING ECONOMICS

Introduction: Let's Talk About Economics

SLook around you and you see people working and earning income. Yet you also see people struggling because they want to work but can't find a job. You walk into stores and see prices of products going up and down. You see some businesses growing and some going out of business. You ask why. People say it's the economy. But what is an *economy*? What do we mean when we say *economics*? What are the major forces that operate in and affect an economy? Have you ever wondered how these economic forces affect you and business? In this chapter, we'll explore these questions. We'll also explore why business owners and managers must understand and be concerned with the state of the economy and how it affects how their business works.

LEARNING OBJECTIVES

After reading Chapter 04, you should be able to meet the following learning objectives:

1. Appreciate the nature of economics, including microeconomics and macroeconomics
2. Appreciate different macroeconomic theories and systems
3. Appreciate economic cycles
4. Appreciate how government impacts economic cycles
5. Appreciate how economic cycles affect the management of business

WHY ECONOMICS MATTERS

Say you walk into a store that has a product you want to buy, such as a television. You look at the TV, weigh its costs and its benefits, and ask yourself, "Can I afford it?" You decide you have the money to spend on a TV and that it's worth your investment, so you buy it. Yet there are other times you don't buy a product you want because you decide you can't afford it. Why?

The answer is we experience good times and bad times. In good times, we believe we have a lot of capacity to buy products. We have good jobs paying us good salaries. We feel confident that we can afford to purchase items such as TVs. Yet other times we do not believe we have the capacity to buy such products. We may not have a job or are scared we may lose our job.

Now let's look at business. When you buy the television, you create a sale and ideally a profit for the store. When you do not buy the television, the store suffers. Why do customers, like you, and businesses have good times and bad times? A big part of the answer is the economy. Understanding the economy—how you affect it and how it affects you and the world around you—will play a large role in your making good decisions, both as a potential employee or manager and as a consumer.

LEARNING OBJECTIVE 1

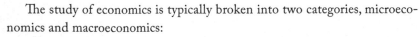

UNDERSTANDING HOW PEOPLE WORK TOGETHER IN AN ECONOMY

Over the last few years, you've no doubt heard people talk about the economy—bad economic times, uncertain economic times, and hopefully better economic times. But what exactly is an *economy*? You can think of an economy as a way of describing a society. Societies are the people and organizations, including businesses, that exist together in a given geographic area. We talk about the US economy, the Chinese economy, even the world economy. So why do we use the word *economy* instead of *society*? Usually people use the word **economy** to talk about the economic or financial state of a society. Do people have jobs and income? What are people doing with that income? Are they spending it or saving it? Do people have enough income to acquire the products they want and need?

Economics is the study of the financial welfare of an economy and how an economy operates. We refer to those individuals who study the economy as **economists**. Studying economics is complex because it involves how people and organizations, individually and collectively, create and spend income. As we've seen in earlier chapters, it takes financial capital (money), real capital (assets), and human capital (people) to create income. Thus, economics is the study of how a society acquires and uses its financial capital, real capital, and human capital.

The study of economics is typically broken into two categories, microeconomics and macroeconomics:

ATM users accessing their personal bank accounts in England.

- **Microeconomics** is the study of how individual people and organizations behave financially—how they work, earn money, and spend money. It answers such questions as: If your income doubled, what would you do with the extra income? How would you react if the price of a product doubled? Would you still buy it? What would you do if the government took more out of your paycheck (in the form of taxes) to build roads? How would a business react to a change in tax law? What would a business do if a new competitor entered its market?

- **Macroeconomics** is the study of how an overall society behaves financially. It looks at a society's total income and where that society gets and spends that income. It answers such questions as: How are the members of a society financially dependent on each other? When a person makes income or loses her or his job, how does it affect the other members of their economy? What do all the businesses within an economy collectively produce? People make products. Do people, within a country and outside a country, want those products? What is a society's competitive advantage? Are the products produced within an economy the best?

The New York Stock Exchange as seen from Federal Hall, New York City. How does the stock exchange reflect macroeconomic behavior?

So microeconomics studies the economic behavior of individuals and organizations. Macroeconomics looks at how individuals and organizations come together to operate as an economy. But what is the goal of all this insight? Why is studying economics important?

BUSINESS SENSE

THE ART OF ECONOMICS

It is often said that if you put ten economists in a room, you'll get ten different opinions of where the economy is and where the economy is going. Why? Economics is a social science. It deals with human behavior. Like physical scientists such as chemists and physicists, economists know their work deals with relationships. However, unlike physical scientists, economists have a hard time predicting the magnitude and timing of these relationships. This lack of precision is due to human behavior.

Say you want to buy a new car. You just got a raise, so you know you can afford it. Your old car is adequate, but you want something better. You start looking at new cars. However, something happens. You get sick or have other personal challenges. You become worried about the future. You decide not to buy a new car. Why? Because something unpredictable occurred. Because economics is the study of human behavior, which is hard to understand and predict, it often looks less like a science and more like an art.

WHAT MATTERS IN AN ECONOMY

Everything in an economy works together. Thus, everything in an economy matters. But to grasp the overall nature of an economy, let's look at four major components of any economy: income, employment, capacity, and prices.

Income

Groceries for sale at a Los Angeles supermarket chain.

From a microeconomic standpoint, income is what individuals or businesses receive in exchange for their labor or for producing something that others want. Income is an incentive and reward for *doing* something right and adding value. The harder or smarter we work, for example, the more income we expect to earn. Junior managers aspire to be senior managers in part because they expect more income. However, their employer also expects them to take on more responsibilities and add more value in exchange for that additional income. We want and need income to enhance our standard of living—to buy food, clothing, housing, and so on. The more income we have, the better we can meet our needs and wants.

From a macroeconomic standpoint, income is a measure of the total products produced and sold by a society. It's a measure of what we as a society have earned. As a society, we want everyone to be able to buy the things they need and want. We want everyone to have housing and to be able to pay for food, health care, education, transportation, and so on. We want society to create enough income for people to achieve an adequate standard of living. Thus, the goal is for society to provide individuals with the opportunity to make income that adequately compensates their ability and hard work. If done right, individuals and organizations prosper and income grows.

Employment

Income is created through *employment*. We want everyone who wants and needs a job to have a job. This is referred to as **full employment**. So how are jobs created? The answer is based on supply and demand. For example, we all need food. When you buy food at a grocery store, you create jobs for the farmer, the company that supplies the farmer with fertilizer, the employees of the grocery store, and the employees of the utility company that provides the electricity to the grocery store. When you demand products, you create jobs for those who supply the products. So people, buying products from other people and businesses, create income. When you buy something from your neighbor, you are providing him or her wih a job and ability to make an income. With that income, your neighbor can then buy something from you. That, in turn, makes you income. In this way everyone in an economy affects everyone else.

So employment benefits everyone in society. However, full employment is not something we see often. People leave one job for another because they or their employer decide that a change is needed. When

EXHIBIT 4.1: Unemployment Rates

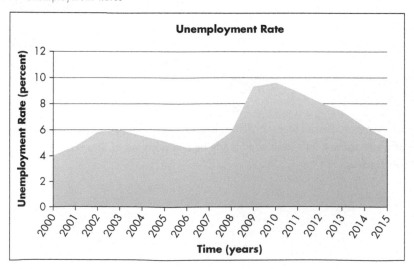

full employment does not occur, we experience **unemployment**. Exhibit 4.1 illustrates historical unemployment figures in the United States. Such unemployment is often classified as one of the following four types:

People queue to apply for unemployment benefits at a state employment and development office.

- **Cyclical unemployment** occurs when the market for a person's labor is temporarily low. The person produces a valued and desired product, but customers just can't afford the product at the time. This type of unemployment is affected by downturns in the economy. When the economy begins to grow again, the product is once again in demand. For example, consider Hyundai, which manufactures cars. When the economy is growing, people can afford new cars, and so Hyundai employs a lot of people. However, when the economy is in trouble, people cannot afford new cars and so Hyundai does not need to employ as many people.

- **Seasonal unemployment** occurs when the demand for employees varies depending on the time of year. For example, a shop that sells water skis in Minnesota will most likely not employ many people in the winter months. Large retailers can affect seasonal unemployment too. For example, Target needs many employees during the October to December holiday period. However, after the holiday period, it needs fewer employees, and so it hires these employees only temporarily or lays off employees when the busy period is over.

- **Structural unemployment** occurs when there are structural barriers that prevent employers and employees from coming together. An example of a structural barrier is geography. For example, Google's headquarters is in California. Say Google wants employees in its California location. However, what happens if there are not enough qualified people in California but there is an abundance of qualified people in Florida? The people in Florida must move to California. Another structural barrier may be education. In our Google example, there may be an abundance of people who would like to work at Google in California, but perhaps these people do not have the required computer skills.

- **Transitional unemployment** occurs when an employee or employer desires to make a change. This change is not due to cyclical, seasonal, or structural issues. For example, employees may leave one job to search for another job that better uses their abilities and pays more. Likewise, an employer may dismiss an employee because the employer believes it can find a better employee.

We've discussed various types of unemployment. However, we also want everyone to have a job that meets her or his abilities and desires. Have you ever seen someone working at a job she or he is overqualified to do? This is called **underemployment**.

EXHIBIT 4.2: Factors of Production

Capacity

Capacity deals with the resources that an economy processes, or its ability to acquire those resources. The use of the resources to create income is called **productivity**. Productivity deals with getting the most output from the resources in an economy. The resources that an economy needs to operate and prosper are often called the **factors of production** (see Exhibit 4.2).

- **Labor**: Labor refers to the people in an economy or organization. For example, Procter & Gamble hires many people to operate its business.

- **Natural resources**: Natural resources include minerals, water, land, and other elements found in nature. For example, the land that Target uses to locate its stores is considered a natural resource.

- **Money**: Money, often called financial capital, is the medium of exchange we use to buy and sell products, pay bills, and operate the economy. For example, Hyundai uses money to buy supplies and pay employees, and Hyundai receives money when it sells automobiles.

- **Knowledge**: Knowledge is the insights and expertise of the people. For example, Google acquires knowledge by researching the needs of customers and uses this knowledge in developing and delivering products.

To prosper, an economy must be able to (that is, have the capacity to) access the needed factors of production. Without the right amount and blend of the factors of production, an economy cannot prosper.

Prices

Say you go into Target to buy a product. You find the product and look at the price. It cost you $1 last year. The new price is $1.25. You ask yourself the question, "Why did the price of the product change?" When the prices of items go up, we say we are experiencing **inflation**. When the prices of items go down, we say we are experiencing **deflation**. Exhibit 4.3 illustrates historical inflation rates in the United States. First, let's look at the *consequences* of inflation and deflation. Then, let's look at the *causes* of inflation and deflation.

EXHIBIT 4.3: US Inflation Rate (Consumer Price Index)

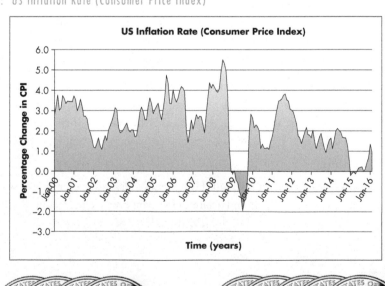

Last year

This year

When we consider the consequences of price changes, we must first ask, "Are price changes always a bad thing? Is it fair for prices to change?" The answer is sometimes yes and sometimes no. Price changes are a positive thing when they reflect the changing value of an item. For example, when the price of a car goes up because it requires less fuel to operate, the increase in the car's price could be offset by the decrease in the cost of operating the car. The total cost of traveling a mile may actually go down even when the price of the car increases.

However, what happens when prices go up or down, not because the product is better or worse, but because of activity in the overall economy? Such price changes, particularly major price changes, can create problems. Why? First, price changes can artificially and unfairly redistribute wealth. Second, price changes can create uncertainty and thus affect how people behave. Sometimes people do things in the short term that cause problems in the long term because they are scared or concerned.

For example, say your grandfather stops at a gas station to buy ten gallons of gas. He sees that the price of gas has shot up to $5 a gallon. He is retired and has a limited income, so he may become scared and uncertain. He can't afford to spend more money on gas. If the price continues to increase, he may need to stop driving or limit his driving drastically. So, he decides to buy twenty gallons of gas today instead of the ten he originally planned to buy because he is scared that the price may be $6 tomorrow. In doing so, he is increasing the demand for gas. If enough people behave in the same way and if the supply of gas does not increase, the gas station will increase the price of the gasoline. Why did the price of gas go up? Because your grandfather and others were scared and uncertain.

Let's look at the causes of price changes. There are two types of inflation, each caused by different forces:

- **Demand-pull inflation** occurs when *demand* for a product exceeds the available *supply* of the product. (Note that *deflation* would occur when the *supply* for a product exceeds the *demand* for the product.) An example of demand-pull inflation would be if Hyundai can only produce a given number of cars a year. Its manufacturing capacity is fixed in the short term. If more people want Hyundai's cars than Hyundai can produce, Hyundai will increase the price of its cars. As we'll see later in this chapter, prices typically go up when demand exceeds supply, and prices go down when supply exceeds demand.

- **Cost-push inflation** occurs when the cost of an item goes up without an increase in demand. This typically happens when supply is artificially and suddenly limited. For example, say a hurricane destroys an oil refinery. The price the oil company charges for petroleum products, therefore, increases, so the cost of energy increases. Because the cost of energy increases, companies like Target must pay higher utility bills and, therefore, may increase the prices of their products to compensate for these higher costs.

Whether from demand-pull or cost-push forces, the impact of changing prices on *income* can be hard to measure. Economists look at two forms of income: *nominal income* and *real income*. With **nominal income**, we measure the income of individuals, businesses, and nations in current-year dollars and do not adjust for changing prices caused by inflation or deflation. With **real income**, we adjust nominal income for inflation or deflation.

How do we do this adjustment? We use economic indices. An **economic index** measures the relative change of an economic factor over time. Earlier we presented an example. You paid Target $1 for a product last year that costs you $1.25 this year. The price of your product has gone up 25 percent. If we set the price from last year as 100 percent, this year's price would be 125 percent. The most common economic indices used to measure price changes are the *Consumer Price Index (CPI)*, the *Producers Price index (PPI)*, and the *GDP deflator*.

- The **Consumer Price Index (CPI)** estimates how the average price of consumer goods has changed in a given period. Such prices are often called **retail prices**. The government estimates the CPI by looking at the prices of such items as food, medical services, and housing throughout the country.

- The **Producers Price Index (PPI)** estimates how the prices of products sold between businesses have changed in a given period. Such prices are often called **wholesale prices**. The government estimates the PPI by looking at the price of items such as minerals, labor, and energy throughout the country.

- The **GDP deflator** estimates how the prices of all items have changed in a given period. As we'll see later, the gross domestic product (GDP) of a country is a measure of the total income produced in a given period. The government estimates the GDP deflator by looking at the price of all items within the economy, including the prices paid by consumers and producers.

In summary, changing prices are good when the new price reflects the increase or decrease in the value an item produces. However changing prices, inflation or deflation, can be bad and cause problems when they are artificial and do not reflect an increase or decrease in the value an item produces. An example of such undesirable behavior and consequences is deflation in the real estate market. Say you buy a home for $200,000. To purchase the home, you use $20,000 of your money and borrow $180,000. You are counting on your home appreciating, or increasing in value. However, the overall economy begins to have problems. People buying homes are reluctant to buy homes because they are uncertain and scared. Housing prices drop, or deflate. You go to sell your house and the best price you are offered is $160,000. That's not enough to repay your loan. You have lost $40,000 in value.

LEARNING OBJECTIVE 2
. . . .
MACROECONOMIC THEORIES AND SYSTEMS

In a perfect world, we want a lot of income and income that grows every day. We'd have full employment. Everyone would work to his or her ability and desires. We'd have all the resources we need to make our economy work. And last, we'd have price stability where prices only change to reflect the increase or decrease in the value an item produces. But we live in an imperfect world. Governments, representing the welfare of their citizens, often try to make their economies work better. What can a government do to help an economy prosper?

Over the years the actions of government have evolved because economic theory has evolved. Years ago, economics was called "the dismal science" because economists saw the world as a give-and-take proposition. If you prospered, another person could not prosper. Economies were perceived as a zero-sum game where there are people with things and people without things. Economics was a process of either winning or losing. The capacity to generate income was fixed. There were not enough resources to meet the needs of everyone. However, over time, economic thinking has evolved.

FREE MARKETS

In 1776, Scottish philosopher **Adam Smith** wrote *An Inquiry into the Nature and Causes of the Wealth of Nations*.[1] Smith did not see economies as a zero-sum game, and in his book, he proposed that economics was not a dismal science. He argued that economies, if permitted to be free, could be a win-win game. An economy would best prosper if people were free to own property such as a business, businesses were free to compete for customers, and customers were free to choose between competing products and businesses. Smith believed in competition. He believed competition made an economy better through an *invisible hand*. Today we call this notion the *multiplier effect*. The **multiplier effect** states that when you spend money, you create income for someone else. That person now has income to spend. When that other person spends her or his income, she or he creates income for you. You win and the other person also wins.

A critical element underpinning Smith's philosophy was freedom to own property, to make and keep profits, to sell your labor to whomever you desire, and to be free to choose what products you will buy or sell. Smith said for such an economic system to work, it must be a **free market system**. Today we call free market economies **capitalistic economies**. In capitalistic economies, individuals and businesses are free to compete. They also are free to receive the benefits from winning the competition.

An engraving of Adam Smith, dated 1790

SUPPLY AND DEMAND

A major foundation of a free market system is that the markets are free to set the price for any given product. The price of a product is what the market determines that product is worth at that time. Price is, therefore, the market's assessment of an item's value. It is what the sellers and buyers in a market agree the product is worth. As such, prices are a function of supply and demand.

Let's look at supply. When we discuss **supply**, we are referring to those individuals and businesses that have something they want to sell, or supply, to buyers. Sellers want to get as high a price as possible for their items. Higher prices mean higher profits. If suppliers are able to charge higher prices for their products, they will have an incentive to provide more. Conversely, lower prices give the suppliers less incentive, or disincentive, to supply products. Exhibit 4.4 depicts a **supply curve** that shows this relationship. As you can see, higher prices create higher supply. Lower prices create lower supply.

Think about it. Would you be motivated to sell your car if someone offered you a higher price? Price matters to suppliers.

Now let's look at demand. **Demand** refers to those individuals and businesses that buy products. Demand reflects the behavior of customers. When prices are lower, buyers have an incentive to demand more products. Higher prices give buyers less incentive, or disincentives, to buy products. Exhibit 4.5 depicts a **demand curve**

EXHIBIT 4.4: Supply

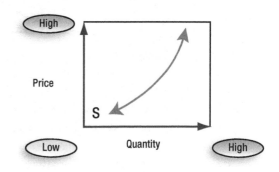

EXHIBIT 4.5: Demand

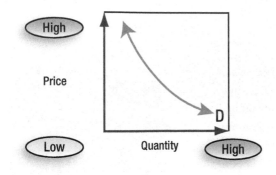

EXHIBIT 4.6: Demand and Supply

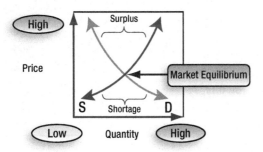

that shows this relationship. As you can see, higher prices create lower demand. Lower prices create higher demand.

Think about that car you want but can't afford. Would you buy it if the price dropped and you could now afford it? Probably yes.

Let's put our demand and supply curves together. Exhibit 4.6 shows where demand and supply meet. That point is called the **equilibrium point**. It is the price where buyers (demand) and sellers (supply) agree to make an exchange. It is also called the **market price**. That point tells us the quantity and price of products that will be bought and sold in the market.

Think about buying a car. You go to the car dealer and find a car you want. The dealer tells you the price it wants for the car, or the "suggested retail price." You tell the car dealer what you want to pay for the car. The dealer's price is too high for you and your price is too low for the dealer. You begin to negotiate, ultimately agreeing on a price. Your demand and the car dealer's supply have met. The buyer and seller have reached an equilibrium point or market price.

Now what happens when demand exceeds supply? What happens when customers increase their demand for a product and suppliers cannot meet this demand? As Exhibit 4.7 shows, prices go up in a free market. Conversely, when demand is below supply, prices fall in a free market.

What happens when sellers increase the supply of products and supply exceeds demand? What happens when suppliers create more product than buyers want? As Exhibit 4.8 shows, prices fall in a free market. Conversely, when supply is below demand, prices go up in a free market.

The question becomes, "Does the quantity of products demanded and supplied always react to prices?" The answer is sometimes yes and sometimes no. When demand and supply react to price changes, we say the demand

EXHIBIT 4.7: Increasing Demand

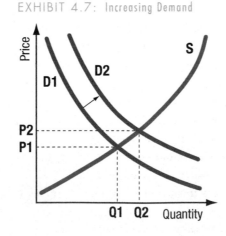

EXHIBIT 4.8: Increasing Supply

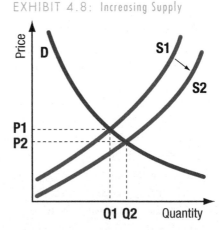

and supply functions are **price-elastic**. Typically prices are elastic when customers have alternatives or choices—either they can defer the purchase to another time or there are plenty of other competing products. When demand and supply do not react to price changes, we say the demand and supply functions are **price-inelastic**. Typically prices are inelastic when customers must have the product now and do not have alternatives or choices.

Let's look at two examples. First, you want to buy a car from Hyundai. However, the price of your initial selection goes up. You have many options from which to choose. You decide that the value you will receive from buying that particular car is less than the value you must pay, so you choose an alternative. You do not buy your initial selection from Hyundai. Your demand for that car is *price-elastic*. The higher price diminished your demand for the car you originally wanted.

Now let's look at a second example. You need to buy gas for your car. The price of all gas goes up in your market. You need the gas and you have no other options. Do you stop buying gas? If so, you stop going to work, so you pay the higher gas prices. You do not significantly cut your demand for gasoline. Where do you get the extra money to pay for the gas? You cut other expenditures, such as entertainment. Your demand for gasoline is *price-inelastic*.

So the supply and demand for different products react to price changes differently. Why? What are the consequences? The answer lies in economic power.

ECONOMIC POWER

In a free market, it is assumed that buyers and sellers share economic power equally. We say the market has **perfect competition**. In perfect competition, there are numerous buyers and sellers. Buyers have alternatives and choices and sellers must supply the buyer with the best product at the lowest price. Sellers compete for buyers. An example is the automobile industry. People and business need and buy cars. However, there are many different companies that produce cars. Thus, buyers need sellers and sellers need buyers.

However, sometimes buyers and sellers do not share economic power equally. Sometimes *monopolies* and *oligopolies* are created that give suppliers significant power over the market and buyers.

A **monopoly** happens when one business controls the entire supply of a product. If that product is essential to the buyer, the supplier has enormous power. The demand for the product is price-inelastic, so the supplier can set the price as high or as low as it desires. The seller knows the customer has no alternatives. The customer must have the product and will pay whatever the seller requires. Utility companies are often monopolies. We'd have a hard time living without electricity and clean water. Our utility companies could set the price for their product as high as they want. So what does government do to balance this economic power? Government encourages other companies to compete. If that fails, then government regulates the utility company. In regulation, government dictates a fair price that the utility company can charge its customers. That fair price should compensate the utility company for its operating costs, the cost of its borrowed money (interest), and an adequate net income to reward owners for providing the company money.

An **oligopoly** occurs when a few businesses control the supply of a product. The challenge is when these competing businesses get together and set prices. This is called **collusion**. If the product is essential to the welfare of society, the oligopoly has a great deal of power. Given the product is price-inelastic, the oligopoly can set the price as high or as low as it desires. An example is companies that produce gasoline. Because of the large amount of money oil companies must invest in equipment and other assets, there are high barriers to entering the business. This means only a few companies produce gasoline, including Exxon, Royal Dutch Shell, and British Petroleum (BP). These companies form an oligopoly. So what can be done? Later in the book we'll look at laws that regulate business, specifically antitrust laws. If government finds that firms are colluding, it can force the companies to stop, pay fines, and correct the situation.

EXHIBIT 4.9: Economic Power

TYPE OF POWER	CHARACTERISTICS	COMPETITION BETWEEN SELLERS	POTENTIAL NEED FOR GOVERNMENT REGULATION
PERFECT COMPETITION	Numerous buyers and sellers share power. Nobody controls the market.	High	Low, as market forces determine prices and quantity of products sold.
OLIGOPOLY	Numerous buyers and few sellers. Sellers hold the power. Buyers lack power. Sellers control the market.	Low	Moderate, as regulation may be needed to prevent sellers from colluding to fix prices and quantities sold.
MONOPOLY	Numerous buyers and one seller. Seller holds the power. Buyers lack power. The single seller controls the market.	None	High, as regulation may be needed regarding the prices and quantity sold.

ALTERNATIVES TO FREE MARKETS

As noted in Chapter 01, free market economies have produced enormous wealth and prosperity. Free markets, however, are not without challenges when economic power is not shared between buyers and sellers. It is often said that economic power is more dominating than any military power. For example, when there is too much labor and high unemployment, people may not have enough money to buy food. Employers can, therefore, have enormous power over labor. In the United States, labor relations and labor laws have evolved to protect workers who find themselves in such positions (we'll explore this issue later in Chapter 16).

As alternatives to free markets, governments have adopted more controlled systems, including:

· Socialism

· Communism

· Controlled or regulated economies

· Mixed economies

Socialism

Socialism is an economic system in which the government owns selected businesses. Typically, the government owns businesses that are more critical to the welfare of the society. In these businesses, the government decides what will be produced, the price of the products, and who can or cannot purchase these products. Examples of such businesses are banks, transportation companies, utilities, and natural resources such as oil. When the government owns a business, the business is said to be **nationalized**. Private individuals and organizations are permitted to own businesses that are less critical to the welfare of the society and are not nationalized. These businesses use the free market to decide what to produce and what price to charge. Thus, the economy is a blend of government-owned and privately owned businesses. Venezuela is an example of a country that uses socialism.

In socialism, the government uses taxes and the profits from nationalized businesses to pay for education, health care, transportation, and other services for its citizens. Socialism, therefore, attempts to create social equity—eliminating the disparity between the wealthy and not wealthy—regarding important services. Although admirable in numerous ways, the challenge with socialism is that it can take away the incentives of a free market economy. Private businesses and individuals are highly taxed and regulated. Tax rates often exceed 50 percent. There are lower rewards for innovation and lower incentives to create better products at better prices.

Communism

Communism is a political and economic system formulated by **Karl Marx** and others in the late 1800s and early 1900s.[2] There is no private ownership in a communist society. All things, including businesses, are owned by everyone. Because the government represents everyone in society, the government owns everything. The government decides what will be produced and what prices will be paid. The government decides what jobs each citizen will do as well as what each citizen will be paid. In short, the government decides everything: there is no free market. An example of a communist country is North Korea.

Karl Marx

The goals of communism are similar to socialism—providing social equity. Ideally, everyone works to his or her capacity and receives according to his or her needs. The challenge with communism is once again based on incentive. Without private ownership, communism provides little incentive to work hard and innovate. Competition and often innovation do not exist.

Controlled or Regulated Economies

A **controlled or regulated economy** is an economy in which businesses are privately owned but heavily regulated by government. In such an economy, the government tells businesses what they can and cannot do. However, the profits from the business belong to the owners of the business, not the government. Remember the earlier example of the utility company that operated as a monopoly? The utility company was a *regulated* business. The goal of a controlled or regulated economy is to eliminate some of the abuses that the free market can create. However, regulation can inhibit innovation with government bureaucracy and added costs. An example of an economy that is heavily controlled or regulated is Russia.

Mixed Economies

All economic systems have strengths and challenges. However, over the years, the free market system has produced more prosperity than any other system. But to say that a perfectly free market economy exists is rather naïve. As we discussed above, free markets have produced abuses, and in order to manage such abuses, economies have often modified free markets with regulation and socialism. Such economies are called **mixed economies**. Some mixed economies are dominated by free markets and selectively use socialism or regulation. Some mixed economies are dominated by socialism and selectively use free markets and regulation.

The United States is often called a free market economy, and the US economy is often used as an example of capitalism. However, the United States is really a mixed economy. The US economy is

dominated by free markets but also has some elements of socialism and regulation. Let's look at two companies in the United States, the passenger train service company Amtrak and Bank of America.

Amtrak is owned and operated by the US government. In the mid-1900s, railroads realized that their passenger train service was unprofitable. It was easier and cheaper for customers to use cars and airplanes to travel. The number of people using railroads to travel was decreasing, so railroads wanted to stop providing passenger service. The US government felt passenger service was still important, particularly between major cities such as New York, Boston, Washington DC, Chicago, Los Angeles, and San Francisco. The government, therefore, formed a company called Amtrak and started to provide passenger service to critical cities.

Bank of America, on the other hand, is not owned by the government. However, because banks are a very important part of the US economy, the US government *regulates* banks such as Bank of America to ensure banks are operated safely and soundly. For example, the Federal Deposit Insurance Corporation (FDIC) and other government agencies regulate Bank of America and other financial institutions to ensure they comply with government policies.

EXHIBIT 4.10: Economic Systems

SYSTEM	OWNERSHIP OF BUSINESS	ROLE OF GOVERNMENT	BUSINESS PROFITS
FREE MARKET OR CAPITALISTIC ECONOMIES	Private citizens own all businesses. Governments do not own business.	To regulate business to ensure fair practices.	Go to private citizens who own business.
SOCIALISTIC ECONOMIES	Private citizens and government own businesses.	To operate critical businesses such as banks, and to regulate private businesses to ensure fair practices.	Go to private citizens and government, depending on who owns the business.
COMMUNISTIC ECONOMIES	Private citizens own no businesses. Governments own all business.	To manage all aspects of business.	Go to government.
CONTROLLED OR REGULATED ECONOMIES	Private citizens own all business.	To control and regulate major aspects of business, including the quantity and price of products sold.	Go to private citizens who own business.
MIXED ECONOMIES	Private citizens own most businesses. Governments own selected business.	To regulate business to ensure fair practices. To operate selected businesses when necessary.	Go to private citizens and government, depending on who owns the business.

The economics of a society are complex from both a microeconomic and macroeconomic perspective. Economies go up and go down. The goal is to have a prosperous economy that meets the income, employment, capacity, and price goals set forth earlier. But how do we measure these goals? How do we know that our chosen economy is meeting those goals? What can the government do when the goals are not being met?

LEARNING OBJECTIVE 3
. . . .
ECONOMIC CYCLES

All economies have good times and bad times. In a free market economy, sometimes people spend money and the multiplier effect works in a positive way, providing jobs and income for others. When people buy products from stores such as Target, jobs are created, income is created, and the economy prospers. However other times people don't spend and the multiplier effect works in reverse. Customers don't buy products from Target. Target has less revenue so it does not hire employees to work in the store. These unemployed people have no income to purchase things. And so goes the multiplier effect in reverse and the economy suffers.

As an economy goes through these ups and downs, we say the economy is going through an **economic cycle**, often referred to as a **business cycle**. Exhibit 4.11 depicts an economic cycle. As you can see, economies hit peaks, contract, hit troughs, and expand.

EXHIBIT 4.11: Macroeconomic Cycles

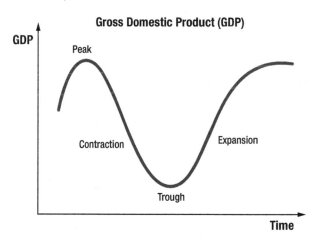

A peak occurs when the income in an economy is at its highest level. Income, employment, prices, and the utilization of capacity are high. For various reasons noted later, the economy begins to contract. Income, employment, prices, and the utilization of capacity drop. When the economy stops contracting, the economy is now in an economic trough where income, employment, prices, and utilization of capacity are low. From a trough, the economy then begins to expand. As the economy expands, income, employment, prices, and utilization of capacity increase until the economy reaches another peak.[4]

So how do we measure such economic cycles? The answer is income. And we measure an economy's or nation's income by its *Gross Domestic Product (GDP)*.

GROSS DOMESTIC PRODUCT

The **gross domestic product (GDP)** of an economy is the value of the goods and services produced in an economy in a given year. In effect, it is a country's income.

EQUATION 4.1: GDP

$$GDP = Q * P$$

Where   GDP   Gross Domestic Product
          Q   Quantity of Goods and Services Produced
          P   Price of Goods and Services Produced

As you'll recall from our price discussion earlier in the chapter, income can be divided into *nominal income* and *real income*. GDP can also be measured in two different ways. **Nominal GDP** defines the price component of GDP as the *current* price of goods and services produced. **Real GDP** is nominal GDP with one adjustment. The impact of price changes are eliminated with an adjustment: the GDP deflator. As we discussed earlier, the GDP deflator tries to eliminate the impact of price changes so we can focus on the quantity of goods and services produced.

So if that's what GDP is, where does GDP come from and where does it go to? What are the sources and uses of GDP?

THE SOURCES OF INCOME (GDP)

Let's begin with the four sources of GDP:

- Consumption

- Investment

- Government spending

- Exports

Mathematically stated, GDP is

EQUATION 4.2: The Sources of GDP

$$GDP = C + I + G + E$$

Where   GDP   Gross Domestic Product
          C   Consumption
          I   Investment
          G   Government spending
          E   Exports

Consumption occurs when individuals buy products (goods and services) that are manufactured in their home country. As noted above, we create income for others when we buy products. These products can be broken into two main groups:

- **Goods** include *durable* and *nondurable goods*. **Durable goods** are goods that have long lives such as cars, washing machines, and computers. **Nondurable goods** are goods that have relatively short lives such as food and clothing.

- **Services** are intangible products that we buy, such as doctor's visits, a haircut, or a college education.

In the United States, approximately 70 percent of GDP comes from consumption. People in the United States love to buy things.

Investment occurs when individuals or businesses spend money on capital items, such as buildings and equipment. Investment can be broken into three groups:

- Residential structures are new houses built for individuals.

- Business structures and equipment include new factories, machinery, and computer software.

- "Change in business inventories" is the difference between the goods produced by business versus the goods sold by business. Businesses produce inventory in hope of quickly selling it. When the inventory does not sell quickly, it is considered a long-term investment.

Government spending occurs when governments spend money. Government expenditures include national defense, roads, and services. Government spending can be divided into spending by the federal government and spending by state and local governments. The majority of government spending in the United States is done by state and local governments.

US soldiers on patrol in Baghdad is an example of government spending.

Exports are goods and services that are produced in a home country but sold to buyers in another country. For example, US wheat sold to countries around the world is a US export.

Consumption, investment, government spending, and exports all create income for the producing country. So if that's where income comes from, where does it go? How is income used?

THE USES OF INCOME (GDP)

So we get income or GDP from consumption, investment, government spending, and exports. But what do we do with it? How do we spend or use it? The sources of GDP must equal the uses of GDP. Like the sources of GDP, we can break the uses of GDP into four parts: consumption, savings, taxes, and imports. Mathematically stated, GDP is

EQUATION 4.3: The Uses of GDP

$$GDP = C + S + T + Imp$$

Where   GDP   Gross Domestic Product
         C   Consumption
         S   Savings
         T   Taxes
         Imp   Imports

Italian vineyards grow grapes for wineries to produce world-renowned wines. These wines are imported by the United States and other countries of the world.

Consumption here refers to the same consumption we discussed above. It refers to our buying products that are produced in our home country. When we buy or consume a product, that consumption creates income for someone else.

Savings refers to the money we set aside for the future. We may deposit it in a bank, put it in a retirement fund, or invest it in the stock market. However we do not spend it to buy products or pay taxes.

Taxes are the required payments we make to the government and reflect the cost we pay to live in a society. Taxes pay for our roads, public servants, our military, and all the other things our government does.

Imports relate to the products we buy from sources outside our country. In the United States, we import a lot of products from Japan (such as automobiles), China (such as toys), India (such as computer services), and Europe (such as wines).

PUTTING GDP INTO PERSPECTIVE

Now let's pull our discussion together by looking at how we get and spend our income. People get a paycheck for working for a business or government. People have jobs that produce products, both goods and services. Where do these jobs come from? Jobs come from individuals within a country consuming products, individuals and businesses making investments, governments making expenditures, and foreigners purchasing products.

Now what do we do with that income? Think about going to work. You get a paycheck. What do you do with the money you earned? First, you pay taxes. Your paycheck reflects your gross earnings, less your taxes, which equals your net paycheck. This is often called **disposable income**. Disposable income is what we individually, and collectively, have to spend on other things. So what do we do with disposable income? We can either 1) spend our disposable income on products produced within our country or outside our country (imports) or 2) save it. Our tendency to spend our disposable income is called the **marginal propensity to consume**. Our tendency to save our disposable income is called our **marginal propensity to save**.

A country's GDP, whether measured by the source or use, is the same. Typically GDP is measured by looking at its sources. Economists sometime make one adjustment: They look at a country's *net income* or *net GDP*. This *net GDP* is composed of consumption, investment, government spending, and *net exports*. Net exports are exports minus imports. Mathematically stated, Net GDP is

EQUATION 4.4: Net Gross Domestic Product (GDP)

$$GDP = C + I + G + NE$$

Where	GDP	Gross Domestic Product
	C	Consumption
	I	Investment
	G	Government spending
	NE	Exports less imports

Exhibit 4.12 on the following page summarizes the nominal US gross domestic product.

Now think about what you see in Exhibit 4.12. Ask yourself "Where does the US get its income and jobs?" Think about what you hear on television and other media about Americans consuming a lot, the US importing a lot, and the US becoming an economy that relies on services to create jobs. So what does Exhibit 4.12 say about these questions and concerns? The US economy is big and complicated. Consumption is the biggest part of the US GDP. Services are more important than goods. Americans

EXHIBIT 4.12: US Nominal Gross Domestic Product (in Billions)

Line		2010	2011	2012	2013	2014	2015
1	**Gross domestic product**	14964.4	15517.9	16155.3	16663.2	17348.1	17947
2	**Personal consumption expenditures**	10202.2	10689.3	11050.6	11392.3	11865.9	12271.9
3	Goods	3362.8	3596.5	3739.1	3836.8	3948.4	3978.8
6	Services	6839.4	7092.8	7311.5	7555.5	7917.5	8293.1
7	**Gross private domestic investment**	2100.8	2239.9	2511.7	2665	2860	3020.6
8	Fixed investment	2039.3	2198.1	2449.9	2593.2	2782.9	2911.4
14	Change in private inventories	61.5	41.8	61.8	71.8	77.1	109.2
15	**Net exports of goods and services**	−512.7	−580	−565.7	−508.4	−530	−528.9
16	Exports	1852.3	2106.4	2198.2	2263.3	2341.9	2253.4
19	Imports	2365	2686.4	2763.8	2771.7	2871.9	2782.3
22	**Government consumption expenditures and gross investment**	3174	3168.7	3158.6	3114.2	3152.1	3183.4
23	Federal	1303.9	1303.5	1292.5	1230.6	1219.9	1224.6
26	State and local	1870.2	1865.3	1866.1	1883.6	1932.3	1958.8

still produce and consume a lot of goods made in the US, but more and more Americans are buying products made in other countries.

GDP AND ECONOMIC CYCLES

We've looked at the sources and uses of GDP, but what causes a country's GDP to go up and down? Why do we experience economic cycles (or business cycles)? To answer these questions, let's imagine an economy that is growing and doing very well. People have jobs and money. They feel secure and good. Because they feel good, they spend their money and buy the things they need and want. Businesses are prospering. Customers who buy products create jobs for others, who in turn spend their money and buy things. The multiplier effect is working positively.

But all of a sudden, people and businesses get scared. Maybe the economy is shocked by an unexpected event such as a terrorist attack. Maybe people are worried about losing their jobs. Maybe all the buying created so much demand that demand exceeds supply of products, causing high rates of inflation. What do you think the people and businesses will do? They stop buying things they want (such as entertainment) and only buy things they need (such as food). People use less of their disposable income to buy things (that is, they lower their consumption) and start saving more. Businesses see the demand for their products decreasing and do not invest in new jobs and facilities.

What does this do? It reverses the multiplier effect. The economy begins to contract or shrink. The economy goes into a recession or even a depression. A **recession** is defined as two consecutive quarters of negative growth in real GDP. (A quarter is a quarter of a year, or three months. Quarters end on March 31, June 30, September 30, and December 31.) A **depression** is a very long and severe recession. So what stops an economy from declining? People and businesses must feel confident again. So is there anything a government can do to help?

This Great Depression-era image has become an icon of resilience in the face of adversity. This 1936 photograph by Dorothea Lange is known as *Migrant Mother*. The photograph depicts the 32-year-old Florence Owens Thompson with three of her children in Nipomo, California.

EXHIBIT 4.13: Nominal Gross Domestic Product Timeline

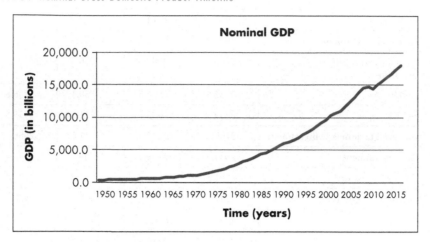

BUSINESS SENSE

MEASURING GDP

Have you ever tried to measure something that is massive or is moving? These are the challenges that economists face in measuring economic flows such as GDP. So how do they do it? They do it by taking samples and using those samples to make estimates about the overall economy. However, this is a challenge.

Let's look at inflation as an example. When we want to understand inflation, we want to understand how the average price of products changes over time. We also want to understand how this price change affects the average consumer. But what is an average price? The price of gas is different in different places. And what is an average consumer? An increase or decrease in the price of gas does not affect everyone the same way. Economists are forced to make assumptions.

Let's look at another example: unemployment figures. We want to understand who does not have a job. But how do we figure out who wants a job but does not have a job? Economists look at people collecting unemployment compensation and other sources of information. (Note: US unemployment compensation is discussed later in this chapter.) But what about people who want a job but have given up searching for one? How do you count those people?

Measuring economic activity is hard and based on samples and numerous assumptions. As time passes, economists have better insights and measurements of what actually happened. It is easy to understand why economists often must revise their estimates of GDP, inflation, employment, and other economic statistics.

THE ROLE OF GOVERNMENT IN ECONOMIC CYCLES

Often citizens look to their government to enhance the welfare of society. Governments may regulate business, nationalize business, or take other steps to control the economy. In a free market, the government also has tools to help an economy through troubled times. Troubled times could be when the economy is growing too fast. Demand exceeds supply. High rates of inflation occur. Troubled times could also be when the economy is in recession. There are not enough jobs. People feel insecure. So what can a government do besides regulating and nationalizing? Government has two sets of tools to use: *fiscal policy* and *monetary policy*.

FISCAL POLICY

Fiscal policy relates to government spending and taxation. As you'll recall from our earlier discussion, both government spending and taxes are components of GDP. When the economy is in a recession, the government can choose to spend more. In doing so, it will create jobs and income that ripples through the economy. An example is the recession in 2007–2009. The government spent billions of dollars to encourage consumers to spend money, save floundering businesses (such as General Motors), and create jobs. In fact, the administration proclaimed that the stimulus created or saved over 3 million jobs. Conversely, when the economy is expanding too fast, government can slow the economy down by spending less.[5]

Government can also use taxes to influence the state of the economy. For example, in a recession, the government may choose to decrease taxes. During the recent recession the government provided one-time tax rebates and cut taxes for people who bought fuel-efficient cars and energy-conserving devices. When consumers pay less in taxes, they have more disposable income to spend. If consumers spend the extra disposable income and not save it, the spending creates jobs through the multiplier effect. However, note that decreasing taxes works to stimulate the economy only if consumers spend the money they normally would have paid in taxes. If they opt to save it, the saved money does not

KEYNESIAN ECONOMICS

In the early 1900s, John Keynes developed the Keynesian approach to economics.[3] Keynesian economics states that governments should rely on free markets to dominate an economy. However, when free markets temporarily fail to provide adequate income to a society, governments should step in with fiscal policy. If needed, governments should be willing to borrow money to finance new government spending or lower taxes. According to Keynesian economics, it's okay for a government to have a deficit. Likewise, if an economy is expanding too fast, governments should spend less and tax more. According to Keynesian economics, it's also okay for a government to run a surplus.

Keynes envisioned a world where governments would run a deficit in bad times and a surplus in good times. Governments would use the surplus to pay back the loans incurred by deficit spending. The challenge is that governments have a hard time spending less and taxing more. The result is large and growing deficits. There is much debate about running consistently large deficits immediately stimulate the economy. As in the case of government spending, when the economy is expanding too fast, government can slow the economy down by taxing more.

MONETARY POLICY

Monetary policy refers to the government's management of the supply of money to help an economy grow faster or slower. Money can be defined in numerous ways, from paper and coin currency, to checking accounts, to savings accounts, and beyond. GDP can be measured as the amount of money in an economy (**money supply**) times how many times the money is used (**velocity**) in a given period.

EQUATION 4.5: GDP and Money

$$GDP = M_S * V$$

Where GDP   Gross Domestic Product
       M_S Money Supply
       V   Velocity

If an economy is in recession, the government can attempt to stimulate the economy by supplying it with more money. If the velocity stays the same, GDP will increase. In other words, people will use the increase in money to buy products and the economy will grow. If an economy is growing too fast, the government can use monetary policy to slow down the economy by decreasing the supply of money.

So who determines the amount of money supplied within an economy? That responsibility typically rests with a country's central bank. In the United States, the central bank is called the **Federal Reserve (or the Fed)**. The Fed controls the money supply in three ways:

1. It can print and circulate more or less money.

2. It can regulate how much money a bank can lend and how much money a bank must hold in reserve. (We'll explore this topic in more depth in Chapter 19.)

3. It can influence interest rates.

Let's look further at the third way. Interest is the price of borrowed money. The higher the interest rate, the less people and businesses typically borrow and spend. The lower the interest rates, the more people and businesses typically borrow and spend.

The Federal Reserve influences interest rates by 1) changing the interest rate it charges banks and 2) buying and selling financial securities in the market. When banks borrow from the Federal Reserve, the interest rate the Fed charges is called the *discount rate*. When the Federal Reserve buys financial securities, such as government debt, it supplies money to the market. When the Federal

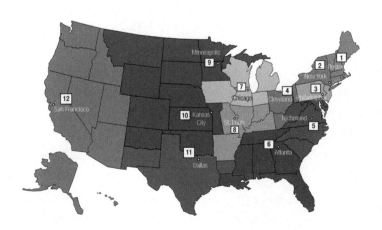

EXHIBIT 4.14: The US Federal Reserve Districts

Reserve sells financial instruments in the market, it takes money out of the market. This buying and selling financial securities is called *open market operations.*

In summary, when an economy is in a recession, governments may spend more, tax less, or increase the money supply. When the economy is growing too fast, governments may spend less, tax more, and decrease the money supply. In the 2007–2009 recession, the government used both fiscal and monetary policy to stop the economy from sliding into a deeper recession and ultimately help it expand. The US government increased spending, cut taxes, and expanded the money supply to create jobs and encourage spending.

REALITIES OF GOVERNMENT POLICY

As we've noted earlier in this chapter, economies are complex because the behavior of individuals and businesses are complex. However, the effectiveness of fiscal and monetary policy rests in how people and businesses react. Will people buy more products if the government increases the money supply or reduces taxes? Will businesses hire more people and invest in assets? Will people take the extra money and save it instead of spending it?

U.S. NATIONAL DEBT CLOCK

$19,359,832,551,843

The national debt clock as of July 24, 2016, www.usdebtclock.org

Government policy can also have long-term implications. Let's look at fiscal policy. If a government spends more and taxes less, it may run a deficit. A **deficit** happens when government spending is greater than tax revenue. If this occurs, the government must borrow the extra funds it needs. Borrowing means the government will incur interest costs in the future to repay those funds. This may serve to help the economy in the present but the future state of the economy may be hurt. Exhibit 4.15 depicts the US debt over time. As you can see, it has increased drastically over the past 60 years. The ultimate question is how much debt can an economy afford? Where is a society going to get the money to pay the interest and principal on its debt? Does that mean increasing taxes in the future?

EXHIBIT 4.15: US Debt over Time

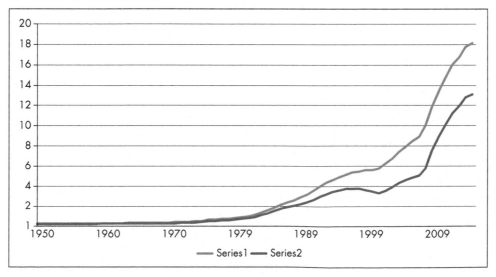

Now let's consider monetary policy. Economists want to understand and stimulate the buying of products. Monetary policy looks at the means we use to pay for these purchases. Let's look at two challenges with monetary policy. First, economists have a hard time defining money. Is money cash and the funds in your checking account? Economists call that *M1 money supply*. Or is money M1 plus funds in your savings account? Economists call that *M2 money*. In fact, economists have a hard time defining exactly what we use to buy things. There are numerous measures of money supply, including money market funds, credit cards, and other means used to pay for purchases.

Second, economists have a hard time determining how much money an economy *needs*. If the government expands the supply of money, the economy may grow faster. However, this growth may also cause demand to exceed supply, causing inflation. But what happens when a government does not increase the money supply adequately? Without enough money, an economy will not grow and prosper.

Third, economists have a hard time forecasting how we use money (velocity). Understanding when and why people spend money is a challenge.

LEARNING OBJECTIVE 5
. . . .
THE IMPACT OF ECONOMIC CYCLES ON MANAGING BUSINESS

You've learned that managing a business is about planning, executing, and reviewing. Managers must constantly ask, "What will customers want and need, and how much will they pay for those wants and needs?" A business does not operate in a vacuum. Understanding the overall state of the economy is. therefore. critical in answering this question. The business must understand where the economy is and where it is going. This, given the complexity of an economy, is a challenge. However there are some *leading indicators* that help managers understand the direction of the economy and make good decisions.

LEADING INDICATORS

We've discussed how the economy flows through cycles of peaks, contractions, troughs, and expansions. Measures of these peaks, contractions, troughs, and expansions are called economic indicators. GDP, unemployment rates, and inflation are some of those economic indicators. When a change in an economic indicator precedes a peak, contraction, trough, or expansion, managers can use it to predict the future state of the economy, and upon this they can base their decisions. Such events are called **leading economic indicators.** Examples of such leading indicators include:

- Consumer sentiment
- Claims for unemployment benefits
- Housing starts
- Inventories
- Interest rates
- Prices of products

Consumer sentiment is a measure that tells managers how consumers feel. Are they optimistic or pessimistic about the future? If they are optimistic, they will most likely spend more. If they are pessimistic, they will most likely spend less. A common measure of consumer sentiment is the University of Michigan's Consumer Sentiment Index. A group of economists at the University of Michigan surveys consumers through the United States to learn how they feel.

Claims for unemployment benefits foretell future employment levels. In the United States, employees who lose their job can apply to the government for unemployment benefits. The US government has a program that pays unemployed people a modest amount, for a number of weeks, while they search for new jobs. The number of new people claiming this benefit indicates whether employment is increasing or decreasing.

Housing starts are measured by the number of permits issued to construction companies to build new houses. Construction companies are not going to build new houses unless they believe that customers feel good enough to buy these houses. Building a house also creates jobs.

Inventories are the store of products that businesses have on hand to sell in the future. If businesses feel future sales will be good, they will increase their inventories. If businesses feel future sales will not be good, they will decrease their inventories.

Interest rates are the price of borrowed money. Interest rates are determined by the demand and supply for money. The higher the interest rate, the higher the cost of money. The higher the cost of money, the fewer individuals and businesses demand the money. Individuals and businesses cannot spend money they do not have.

Prices are the cost of products. Remember the CPI and PPI? The Consumer Price Index (CPI) attempts to measure the cost of average products consumed by individuals. The Producer Price Index (PPI) tries to measure the cost of products used in the creation of products by business. When demand is strong and exceeds supply, prices go up. When prices increase, we have inflation, which causes problems noted earlier. Likewise when demand drops and is below supply, prices go down. When prices go down (deflation), this can cause uncertainty and other problems.

MANAGING FOR VALUE

How does all of this affect managers in a business? How do they use this information to create value for their organization? Let's say you are a manager of Hyundai in the United States. Your decisions have a big impact on the future and on Hyundai's value. You are concerned about whether or not people will buy your cars. You do not want to acquire money, hire people, invest in a factory, and build cars that nobody will buy. You think you have the best cars in the market. But will customers feel good enough to buy your cars? It's a matter of forecasting the future. You look at consumer sentiment and other measures that provide you insight. Businesses operate within an economy, and the state of the economy affects most businesses.

ELIZABETH DUKE

Elizabeth Duke graduated from college with a degree in dramatic art and no idea of the path her career would follow. The aspiring actress took a job as a part time teller to supplement the uneven income from jobs in the theater. She later moved to a start-up bank to get full time work. That's where she met her mentor, the bank's president. Under his tutelage she discovered a talent for finance. She began to pursue financial education with a vengeance, completing numerous industry education programs and an MBA. Fifteen years later, her mentor suddenly died. She was ready to take over as the bank's chief executive officer (CEO). Several years later, the Virginia Bankers Association elected her as its first female chairman. She then became the first woman to chair the American Bankers Association. In 2008, President George Bush appointed her to the Board of Governors of the Federal Reserve System. She joined the Board just as a major financial panic was getting underway. During her five years of service she worked with her colleagues to first stem a financial crisis and then restore a badly damaged economy to health. With her banking expertise, she was able to make significant contributions in the areas of credit availability and housing issues. Ms. Duke credits her success to lifelong learning.

CHAPTER SUMMARY

So understanding economics is important. The flows within an economic cycle are hard to measure, often requiring estimates. Being a successful manager requires you to understand the flows within an economy and how those flows affect your business.

All too often businesses have failed because they failed to understand macroeconomics. Businesses were positioned for an economic expansion when the economy contracted. Or businesses were positioned for an economic downturn when the economy expanded. On the other hand, many successful businesses create value by understanding macroeconomics. Successful businesses understand economic ups and downs. Successful businesses know how to take advantage of the opportunities in economic good and bad times.

After reading this chapter, you should be able to:

1. Appreciate the nature of economics, including microeconomics and macroeconomics (Learning Objective 1): Economics is the study of the financial welfare of an economy and how an economy operates. The study of economics is broken into two categories, microeconomics and macroeconomics.
2. Appreciate different macroeconomic theories and systems (Learning Objective 2): There are numerous economic theories and systems that attempt to explain and help manage economies. These include free markets, socialism, communism, and mixed economies.
3. Appreciate economic cycles (Learning Objective 3): Economies go through cycles, including good and bad times. These cycles include peaks, contractions, troughs, and expansions and are defined in terms of and influenced by several factors.
4. Appreciate how government impacts economic cycles (Learning Objective 4): Governments have various tools to help economies avoid the potential problems associated with the peaks and troughs of such cycles. These tools include fiscal policy and monetary policy.
5. Appreciate how economic cycles affect the management of business (Learning Objective 5): Successful managers take into consideration not only where the economy is but also where the economy is going in the future. Managers often look at leading economic indicators to help them in this task.

In this chapter we looked at the inner workings of an economy. Now it's time to expand these insights beyond an economy. In the next chapter we'll look at how one country's economy interfaces with another country's economy. We'll see how globalization affects "How Business Works."

KEYWORDS

business cycle 94

capitalistic economies 75

claims for unemployment benefits 91

collusion 77

Communism 79

consumer price index (CPI) 74

consumer sentiment 90

consumption 82

controlled or regulated economy 79

cost-push inflation 73

cyclical unemployment 71

deficit 89

deflation 72

demand 75

demand curve 75

demand-pull inflation 73

depression 85

disposable income 84

durable goods 83

economic index 73

economic cycle 81

economics 68

economists 68

economy 68

equilibrium point 76

exports 83

factors of production 71

Federal Reserve (or the Fed) 88

fiscal policy 87

free market system 75

full employment 70

GDP deflator 74

goods 83

government spending 83

gross domestic product (GDP) 82

housing starts 91

imports 84

inflation 72

interest rates 91

inventories 91

investment 83

knowledge 72

labor 72

leading economic indicators 90

macroeconomics 69

marginal propensity to consume 84

marginal propensity to save 84

market price 76

Marx, Karl 79

microeconomics 68

mixed economies 80

monetary policy 88

money 72

money supply 88

monopoly 77

multiplier effect 75

nationalized 79

natural resources 72

nominal GDP 82

nominal income 73

nondurable goods 83

oligopoly 77

perfect competition 77

price-elastic 76

price-inelastic 76

prices 91

producers price index (PPI) 74

productivity 71

real GDP 82

real income 73

recession 85

retail prices 74

savings 84

seasonal unemployment 71

services 83

Smith, Adam 75

Socialism 78

structural unemployment 71

supply 75

supply curve 75

taxes 84

transitional unemployment 71

underemployment 71

unemployment 71

velocity 88

wholesale prices 74

SHORT-ANSWER QUESTIONS

1. What are economic cycles? What impact do economic cycles have on business?

2. What is the multiplier effect? Explain how it works.

3. Define the following terms:

   d. Capitalism

   e. Communism

   f. Consumer Price Index (CPI)

   g. Consumer Sentiment

   h. Consumption

   i. Controlled or Regulated Economies

   j. Cost-Push Inflation

   k. Cyclical Unemployment

   l. Deficit

   m. Deflation

   n. Demand Curve

   o. Demand-Pull Inflation

   p. Depression

   q. Disposable Income

   r. Economic Cycle (Business Cycle)

s.   Economic Indices
t.   Economics
u.   Equilibrium or Market Price
v.   Exports
w.   Factors of Production
x.   Federal Reserve (the Fed)
y.   Fiscal Policy
z.   Free Market Economy or System
aa. Full Employment
ab. GDP Deflator
ac. Government Spending
ad. Gross Domestic Product (GDP)
ae. Housing Starts
af. Imports
ag. Inflation
ah. Interest Rates
ai. Investment
aj. Macroeconomics
ak. Marginal Propensity to Consume
al. Marginal Propensity to Save
am. Microeconomics
an. Mixed Economies
ao. Monetary Policy
ap. Money Supply
aq. Monopoly

ar. Multiplier Effect
as. Nominal GDP
at. Nominal Income
au. Oligopoly
av. Perfect Competition
aw. Producer Price Index (PPI)
ax. Productivity
ay. Real GDP
az. Real Income
ba. Recession
bb. Savings
bc. Seasonal Unemployment
bd. Socialism
be. Structural Unemployment
bf. Supply Curve
bg. Taxes
bh. Transitional Unemployment
bi. Underemployment
bj. Unemployment
bk. Velocity

4. Briefly describe how Adam Smith changed the study of economics.

CRITICAL-THINKING QUESTIONS

1. What are the benefits and challenges of:
    a. Economies built on free markets,
    b. Economies built on socialism,
    c. Economies built on communism,
    d. Economies that are a mixture of free markets and socialism?

2. Think of products that are price-elastic and price-inelastic. What happens to demand when price increases or decreases for these products?

3. What are the good and bad things that happen in economic expansions and economic contractions regarding the following:
    a. Employment
    b. Prices
    c. Income
    d. Utilization of capacity?

4. What can a government do to deal with the bad things that happen in economic peaks and troughs?

EXPLORING REAL BUSINESS

Go to the websites of Google, Target, Hyundai, and Proctor and Gamble. The websites are

Google:	http://investor.google.com
Target:	http://www.target.com
Hyundai:	http://worldwide.hyundai.com/company-overview
Procter & Gamble:	http://www.pg.com

For each company, try to prepare the following:

1. How is the business affected by economic cycles?
2. What should the business do differently in economic expansions, peaks, contractions, and troughs? Provide examples.

ENDNOTES

1. Smith, Adam, *An Inquiry into Nature and Causes of the Wealth of Nations*; 1776.
2. Karl Marx and Freidrich Engels, *The Manifesto of the Communist Party*, 1848.
3. John M. Keynes, *General Theory of Employment, Interest, and Money*, 1936.
4. Sometimes an economy can contract and still have increasing prices. This is called stagflation and occurred in the US during the 1970s due in part to increasing energy prices.
5. http://www.bloomberg.com/news/articles/2010-08-25/obama-s-economic-stimulus-program-created-up-to-3-3-million-jobs-cbo-says

CHAPTER

05

CREATING VALUE IN A GLOBAL ECONOMY

LEARNING OBJECTIVES

After reading Chapter 05, you should be able to meet the following learning objectives:

1. Appreciate the nature, opportunities, and challenges of doing business around the world
2. Appreciate the methods used to conduct global business
3. Appreciate the nature and impact of foreign exchange rates
4. Appreciate the arguments and organizations that foster global business

Introduction: Let's Talk About Globalization

Have you ever walked into a Target store and wondered where all the products you can buy there come from? How do the products travel from the country where they were manufactured to your shopping cart, ready to be put into your car? And speaking of your car, where was it made? Is it a Hyundai? Hyundai is headquartered in South Korea, but does that mean the car and all its parts were manufactured in South Korea? In fact, over half the cars Hyundai sells in the US are made in the US. Hyundai has manufacturing facilities in Alabama, engineering facilities in Michigan, plus design, research, and testing facilities in California. Hyundai provides around 5,000 jobs for US automotive workers, 32,000 jobs at US Hyundai dealerships, and 6,000 jobs at various US suppliers.[1] What's happening? It's called *globalization*.

Today, more than ever, creating value is about embracing the opportunities and challenges of doing business not just in your home country but also throughout the world. Markets that were closed ten years ago are now open. New competitors from around the globe are forcing businesses to rethink how they do business. Better, lower-cost products are coming to customers, enhancing their lives and increasing their standard of living. Innovation and change are everywhere. Business models and strategies are adapting to global forces. Businesses in every corner of the world find it almost impossible to exist and compete without networking around the world. To create value, businesses must embrace the evolutionary forces of globalization.

So what is *globalization*? How do businesses operate in different parts of the world? Why do some businesses succeed and others fail in reaching beyond their home borders? After reading this chapter, you should be able to appreciate the nature, opportunities, and challenges of doing business around the world. In this chapter, we'll explore how and why the practice of business is evolving throughout the world. We'll begin to see that "how business works" is about working in the global marketplace.

WHY GLOBALIZATION MATTERS

Hyundai corporate headquarters, Seoul, South Korea.

Hyundai is the fastest-growing automobile company in the United States, yet it is not a US company. It is a South Korean company. So why are so many Americans buying Hyundai automobiles? Because customers perceive that Hyundai automobiles provide value. Hyundai competes in the United States and provides US customers an alternative that many like (example: Kia automobiles). Now think of a French person walking into a Paris store and asking for detergent. He is directed down an aisle and sees numerous alternatives. However, he chooses Procter & Gamble's (P&G's) Tide detergent. When asked why he chose Tide, he says it's the best value for his money.

What's happening? Hyundai and P&G are competing around the world. In doing so, they are creating value for their owners, lenders, and employees. But they are also making the world of their customers better. Can you imagine a world where you can only buy products made within your country? Can you imagine a world where you could only sell products to customers within your country? Trade between countries matters. It's about creating a better and more prosperous world. And understanding globalization and your place in it—from a consumer, manager, employee, or other standpoint—is a building block toward your future success.

LEARNING OBJECTIVE 1
. . . .
THE NATURE OF DOING BUSINESS AROUND THE WORLD

So products are coming from and going to places all over the world. Globalization of business is a fact. But what exactly is meant by globalization? When business leaders talk about **globalization** they are talking about the evolution of business from operating in a single country to operating in many countries.

THE EVOLVING WORLD OF BUSINESS

Where and how businesses operate is evolving. New opportunities are everywhere. The global business landscape is incredibly varied, with businesses operating as domestic businesses, international businesses, and global businesses. What are the differences between these business forms?

It's all about a business's value chain. Businesses that have a value chain that is totally domestic are considered **domestic businesses.** All inputs come from domestic or home country sources. All processes are in the home country. All outputs are sold and consumed by domestic customers. Let's consider an example. A US oil refinery only buys oil from a US oil company that extracts the oil only from oil fields found in the United States. It then only sells to US gas stations. It's a domestic business. A US gas station that only buys gas from this US oil refinery and only hires US employees and only sells to US customers would also be considered a domestic business. In domestic businesses, all inputs and outputs come from and go to domestic sources. All processes are also domestic.

International businesses are businesses whose value chains have evolved to include selected international inputs, processes, and outputs. For example, a US company that makes its products in the

United States but sells these products in markets outside the US would be considered an international business. A US company that sells products in the United States made from inputs acquired from outside the US would also be considered an international business. Going back to our oil example, an international business may buy oil produced in a foreign country and sell it in the United States.

Global businesses are businesses where the inputs, processes, and outputs come from, are in, and go to markets throughout the world. These inputs and processes involve assets, people, and money. The outputs are products. It is often said that a truly global business is a business without a home country. A global business views the entire world as its home. Exhibit 5.1 lists the ten largest companies in the world.

A Hyundai dealership in Kobe, Japan.

EXHIBIT 5.1: Ten Largest Companies in the World: 2015 (in Billions of US Dollars)

Company	Business	Home Country	Revenues (in billions)	Profits (in billions)
Wal-Mart Stores	Retail Stores	United States	485.7	16.4
Sinopec Group	Energy	China	446.8	5.2
Royal Dutch Shell	Energy	Netherlands	431.3	14.9
China National Petroleum	Energy	China	428.6	16.4
Exxon Mobil	Energy	United States	382.6	32.5
BP	Energy	United Kingdom	358.7	3.8
State Grid	Energy	China	339.4	9.8
Volkswagen	Automotive	German	268.6	14.6
Toyota Motor	Automotive	Japan	247.7	19.8
Glencore	Commodities	Switzerland	221.0	2.3

Today, it is very hard to find a totally domestic firm in the major economies of the world. Domestic businesses are often small in size. Most businesses are **multinational businesses**, meaning they are international or global. The evolution from international business to global business is in full force. Businesses are acquiring money from lenders and owners throughout the world and are investing in assets around the world. Businesses are employing people around the world and are selling their products around the world. Business models and strategies are becoming global. Think about Hyundai investing billions of US dollars into US facilities, hiring thousands of people in the US, and selling millions of cars in the US. Now think about P&G, which has operations in approximately 70 countries and sells its products in more than 180 countries and territories around the world, including Australia, Brazil, Canada, China, France, Japan, Kazakhstan, Kenya, Mexico, Russia, Saudi Arabia, South Africa, Turkey, and the United States. So why is this evolution occurring? How is it occurring? And where's the value coming from?

THE RISE OF FREE MARKETS THROUGHOUT THE WORLD

After years of governments trying to control the supply and demand of goods and services, many countries have begun to believe that free markets are the most efficient way to produce and distribute products. The term **free trade** refers to buying and selling of products in markets that are free from government intervention. In Chapter 04, we explored different economic systems, including socialism, communism, and mixed-market economies. Many countries now believe that markets free from government control produce a higher standard of living for their citizens. Competition for people, assets, money, and customers has increased. How businesses work has therefore become a global affair.

Remember, however, that competition through free markets rewards the winner of the competition. Competition through free markets typically makes the greater population better. In a global marketplace, that greater population is the citizens of the world. However, competition in free markets is not kind to those who compete and fail. Although many countries are embracing competition and free markets, some countries still hold onto the belief that government, not the free market, should ultimately decide how a business operates.

So why do businesses in different countries trade with one another? How does such trade enhance value? The answer is comparative advantage. The theory of **comparative advantage** holds that businesses in different countries have an advantage in producing certain products over others. This advantage should be used by countries to produce superior products at lower costs than other countries. This comparative advantage permits these businesses to successfully compete. This advantage typically comes from the inputs in the value chain. These inputs are people and assets, both tangible (such as natural resources) and intangible (such as knowledge). An example is Saudi Arabia, which has a comparative advantage in producing oil. Why? Saudi Arabia and a few other countries form an oligopoly regarding oil. Only a few countries have large reserves of oil. Saudi Arabia has such reserves of oil and thus has a comparative advantage over most other countries. Another example is China, which has become a major manufacturer of products for the world. Why? China has a comparative advantage because it has a large pool of hard-working, inexpensive labor.

So how does comparative advantage reveal itself in the process of creating value?

OUTSOURCING AND OFF-SHORING BUSINESS

An oil drilling platform in Abu Dhabi.

You've no doubt heard the term outsourcing. **Outsourcing** occurs when a business uses another business to build or service all or part of its product. Businesses do so because they find the business with which they contract, or to which they outsource, can create or deliver something better or at a lower cost. An example is *contract manufacturing*, where a business enters into an agreement to buy goods manufactured by another business. **Off-shoring** occurs when a business uses *foreign factors* of production instead of or in addition to domestic factors of production. For example, when a US business closes a US factory and produces the product in a factory located in another country, it is engaging in off-shoring.

When a business uses outsourcing and/or off-shoring, it often hurts the employees who are replaced if they are unable to find work in other companies or industries. But businesses outsource and use off-shoring based on competition and comparative advantage. For a business to survive, it must produce the best product at the lowest price. If a business's costs are too high, it must charge a price above its competitors. Customers will not buy the business's products. In turn, the business will lose money, and lenders and owners will not provide it with money. All the stakeholders of the business will suffer, including employees. Competition, therefore, produces great economic benefits although it has its costs.

INCREASING VALUE THROUGH GLOBALIZATION

Globalization hopefully produces better products and choices for customers and thus enhances their standard of living. However globalization can also increase business value in numerous ways:

· By creating new markets and customers for products

- By lowering costs

- By lowering risk by diversifying markets and products

Let's look at each of these in a bit more detail.

Creating New Markets and Customers

Businesses are constantly looking for new customers for existing products. With over 7 billion people in the world, the world is full of potential customers. For example, China's GDP has grown so much over the last ten years that it has surpassed Japan to be the second-largest GDP in the world. As China's GDP grows, more Chinese citizens can afford US automobiles, French wine,

Workers making blue jeans for a US company in a maquiladora-factory in Mexico.

and Belgian chocolates. In fact, China is one the fastest-growing markets for products produced by P&G. Conversely, the US is a new market for Chinese products. Go into a Target and look at toys, clothing, and other products. Look at the labels and packaging. Where are these products made? Many are made in China.

Lowering Costs

To compete effectively, businesses must produce their products at the lowest costs possible. Businesses, therefore, look around the world for people and assets that cost less. They seek the best quality of inputs, but they also seek to be the lowest-cost producer. Lower costs give businesses a competitive edge or comparative advantage. For example, consider buying a television. Most televisions bought in the United States are manufactured outside the US. Why? Do these countries have better technology? No. Do these countries have better materials? No. Do these countries have better skilled and unskilled labor? No. What these countries have is lower costs for technology, materials, and labor.

Lowering Risk

When businesses make and sell their products around the world, they are relying on many markets instead of just one domestic one. When markets expand and contract at different times, selling or producing in these different markets helps lower the overall volatility a business experiences. This lower volatility or variability lowers risk. For example, consider the 2008–2009 recession in the United States. During this period, General Motors was selling fewer automobiles in the United States, but because China's economy was still expanding, the company was selling more automobiles in China. Selling and producing products in different markets around the world can smooth the ups and downs that businesses experience.

So, if done right, globalization increases value. Doing it right increases sales, lowers costs, and lowers risk. But what's the right way to do business around the world?

LEARNING OBJECTIVE 2
· · · · · · · · · · · · · · · · · · · ·
THE METHODS OF GLOBAL BUSINESS

Going global produces many opportunities to increase value. However if done wrong, globalization can decrease value. It can hurt sales, increase costs, and increase risk. Managers of successful global businesses will tell you that going global is difficult. Businesses must, therefore, be careful in choosing the right form or way to conduct global business.

THE FORMS OF GLOBAL BUSINESS

There are many forms businesses use to operate throughout the world. Some businesses prefer to make products in their home country and sell or export those products to another country. Some businesses prefer to buy or import their products for sale in their country from another country. However, as businesses evolve in the pursuit of global opportunities, they often find the need for more complex investment strategies and business relationships. These strategies and relationships include:

- **Licensing:** In licensing, a company that owns intellectual property, called the *licensor*, grants another company, called the *licensee*, the right to use that property, typically for a fee. For example, an entertainment company in one country, such as Disney, may license a company in another country to use its entertainment products (e.g., motion pictures). The company that owns the property gets the fee without significant investment in the other country. This lowers the risk to the licensor. However, the fee limits the profits to the licensor as well.

- **Joint ventures:** Joint ventures occur when two or more parties, typically businesses, enter into a business relationship for a single enterprise or transaction. For example, the US company Novartis entered into a joint venture with the European company Bayer to produce a new drug. Joint ventures require each party to make significant investments. However, the investment is lower than if a single company conducted the business. Each party receives its portion of the profit or loss, as specified in the joint-venture agreement. Although the potential profit is lower, the risk is also lower.

Kentucky Fried Chicken, China.

- **Franchising:** Franchising occurs when a business, called a *franchisor*, sells the right to use its name, processes, and products to another business. The *franchisee* pays the franchisor a fee and royalties based on sales. For example, when McDonald's, Wendy's, and Kentucky Fried Chicken entered many international markets, they often did not own the restaurants. Rather, they sold a franchise to companies in those countries. Franchising reduces the investment a company must make to enter into a market. This reduces the risk to the franchisor. However, franchising also limits the profits a franchisor can earn.

- **Strategic alliance:** A strategic alliance occurs when businesses in different countries agree to help each other produce and/or sell multiple products over time. For example, the US company General Motors and the Chinese company Shanghai Motor Works formed a strategic alliance to produce and sell numerous automobiles in China. Strategic alliances often center on the marketing of a company's product by another foreign company. This diminishes the risk of entering an unknown market, but it also reduces potential profit.

- **Direct foreign investment (DFI):** Direct foreign investment is when a business directly invests money in assets to conduct business in a different country. Direct foreign investment can include starting a new business, expanding a business's current business, or buying an existing business. For example, Procter & Gamble has participated in DFI by building distribution centers in Europe, including Germany, Russia, and the United Kingdom. DFI is the riskiest form of global business, but it has the greatest potential for profit.

With so many alternative methods, what is the right way to do business around the world?

FACTORS IN CHOOSING THE RIGHT WAY TO OPERATE AROUND THE WORLD

There are many factors in choosing the way to conduct business and create value around the world. However, two major factors are *culture* and *government regulation*.

Culture

Culture refers to the beliefs and norms of a society. The success of a business depends on understanding the culture in a chosen country. The soft drink industry must understand the culture before expanding into new markets. In the United States, consumers like cold drinks. However, in Asia and other parts of the world, many consumers do not like cold drinks. It is often felt that pouring a cold drink into a warm body shocks and hurts the body.

Culture is complicated. It is a function of numerous factors such as geography, religion, social values, standard of living, and education level. Have you ever thought about the culture of the United States? Think about being from another country trying to understand the US culture. As an example, ask yourself, "Why in many places in the US is it lawful to bring a gun into a restaurant but unlawful to bring a lighted cigarette?" Culture is not easy to understand.

Not understanding culture creates risk. When a business faces such risks, it may decide to use licensing, joint ventures, or franchising. It needs another business, located in the new country, to help.

A GLOBAL MINDSET

Being global is about embracing opportunities and challenges throughout the world. It's about understanding that everything and everyone in the world are tied together. It's about creating a global mindset. Success in the world of business is all about embracing differences. Differences create opportunities, not just threats.

So why do different people see the same thing differently? The answer is culture. To be successful, a business must understand the different perspectives of all its stakeholders. Let's look at several examples. First, think about words and the meaning of words. Years ago Chevrolet introduced a car named "Nova" in Latin American. "Nova" in Spanish means "no go." Chevrolet learned the hard way that words matter. Second, think about symbols. In the US, the color pink is considered the most feminine color. Yellow is considered the most feminine color in most of the world. Color matters in designing and marketing products in different countries. Last, think about actions. A firm handshake is preferred in Latin America. In Japan, a firm handshake is often seen as rude and inconsiderate. Not understanding this can create relationship challenges.

So how does a business turn differences from challenges into opportunities? It's about having a global mindset. Let's look at an example. The religion of Islam teaches that it is not right to exploit the misfortunes of others. Think about conducting business in a country such as Saudi Arabia, Turkey, or Pakistan. Think about banking and charging interest to people that need money. However from this challenge has come a whole specialty called "Islamic finance." Billions of dollars are being managed under the principles of Islamic finance. Instead of interest, lenders are rewarded with fees, profit sharing, and other benefits. It's all about having a global mindset. It's about creating value by seeing differences as opportunities.

It needs a partner who understands the culture. Doing business in a new culture using direct foreign investment, for example, may be too risky.

Government Regulation

Government regulation also plays a major part in selecting the method of doing business in different countries. Governments, hoping to protect domestic businesses, have a wide range of options to limit the operations of foreign businesses. These options are often called **trade barriers** and this use is called **protectionism**. For example, governments often place restrictions on importing and selling products or direct foreign investment. When a government imposes an **embargo**, it does not permit the importing and/or exporting of a product within its borders. When a government imposes a **quota**, it permits selected products to be imported and/or exported but limits the amount. Governments may also tax foreign businesses at higher rates than domestic businesses. These taxes are often called **tariffs**. Licensing, joint ventures, and franchising with foreign partners are often the best alternatives to address these government regulations.

As you can see, business managers must consider numerous factors before deciding to do business in another country. The decisions are complex and often deal with risk. For example, when businesses are certain that foreign customers will buy their product, they often use direct foreign investment. When businesses are less certain that foreign customers will buy their product, they often avoid direct foreign

BUSINESS SENSE

THE CHALLENGE OF ETHICS AND CULTURE

Different people think differently about the same thing. Why? In part, this difference is based on culture. Culture refers to the beliefs and norms of a society. It is a function of such things as geography, history, and religion. We see it in the products businesses buy and sell. We see it in how businesses buy and sell products. But we also see it in the beliefs people have about ethics.

Some cultures are more individualistic whereas others are more communal. Individualistic cultures have no problem in individuals owning things. Private property is very important in such cultures. The United States is such a culture. However, communal cultures believe certain things belong to the society and not individuals. Many countries in Asia and Africa have such a culture. Individualistic and communal cultures sometimes clash regarding personal property laws and ethics regarding such things as patents, copyrights, and trademarks.

Let's consider an example. Say you're the manager of a successful pharmaceutical company that has created a drug that cures a dreaded disease. Your company has spent a lot of money developing the drug, and your country has granted you a patent to protect your investment. You begin to produce and sell the drug, demanding a high price because of your large investment. The first year, sales of the drug are strong. However, sales begin to fall in the second year, and you soon find out that the drug is being pirated in a developing country. Without the large investment to develop the drug, the pirating company can charge a significantly lower price for your drug than you can. You go to the government of the developing country and demand action.

However, the government refuses to act. You claim illegal and unethical business practices. The country of the pirating businesses asks you two simple questions: First, why should it protect your investment when it will mean the poor people of its country will die from the dreaded disease? Second, how can one group, your business, claim ownership of knowledge that affects all people? This is the challenge of culture.

investment and choose less risky alternatives. Because each situation is different, deciding which method to use is often made on a country-by-country basis. As we'll see in the next section, another major factor that managers consider when making global business decisions is the value or price of different currencies.

EXHIBIT 5.2: Selected Currencies of the World

Country	Currency
Argentina	Argentine peso
Australia	Australian dollar
Brazil	Real
Canada	Canadian dollar
China	Yuan
Colombia	Colombian peso
France	Euro (formerly French franc)
Germany	Euro (formerly deutsch mark)
India	Rupee
Italy	Euro (formerly Italian Lira)
Japan	Yen
Kenya	Kenyan shilling
Mexico	Mexican peso
Russia	Ruble
Rwanda	Rwanda franc
Saudi Arabia	Riyal
South Africa	Rand
Spain	Euro (formerly Spanish peseta)
Sweden	Krona
Turkey	Turkish lira
United Kingdom	Pound sterling
United States	US Dollar

LEARNING OBJECTIVE 3

THE NATURE AND IMPACT OF FOREIGN EXCHANGE RATES

Of course, countries must pay one another for all these products flowing across the world in the wake of globalization. **Foreign exchange**, or **FX**, refers to the act of exchanging one country's currency for another. Exhibit 5.2 lists many of the world's currencies. The rate used to convert one currency into another currency is called the **foreign exchange rate**.

When businesses operate around the world, they use the foreign exchange market. Foreign exchange permits efficient exchanges, the heart of business. Can you imagine a world without currencies? We'd end up exchanging one product for another product, or **bartering** for goods.

Let's look at how foreign exchange rates can affect a business. Let's assume that the price of a currency in relation to another currency (the foreign exchange rate) is free to rise or fall based on market forces (demand and supply). We call such a system a *floating exchange rate system*. Say you are a US business that imports Belgian chocolates. You agree to buy 1,000 cases of Belgian chocolates for 100 euros each, for a total of 100,000 euros. You know that the current exchange rate between the US dollar and the euro is $1 = 1 euro. Thus, you believe you will pay $100,000 for the chocolates. You sign the contract with the Belgian chocolate company and

A chocolate shop in Belgium.

agree to take delivery of the chocolates in three months. You then agree to sell the 1,000 cases of chocolates to a US company for $150 each. You agree to deliver the chocolates to the US company in three months. You smile because in three months, you believe that you will take 100,000 US dollars and convert them to 100,000 euros to pay for the Belgian chocolates. You'll then sell the chocolates for 150,000 US dollars, thus producing 50,000 US dollars in profit. Our example seems simple. Right? Wrong. If currencies are traded in a free market, we may have problems.

That's because in three months, the value of the US dollar and the euro could change. Let's look at one possible scenario in our example. Let's say, after three months, it now takes two US dollars to buy one euro. This means it takes more US dollars to buy a euro, so you get fewer euros for your dollar. The US dollar has declined in value, or **depreciated**. The euro has increased in value, or **appreciated**. So what's the problem? You just lost money. Note that the price of the chocolates in euros did not change. It is still 100,000 euros. You lost money because the value of the US dollar depreciated. When you go to pay for the chocolates, you must pay the Belgian chocolate company the 100,000 euros, which is equal to 200,000 US dollars. When you fulfill your contract and sell the chocolates for 150,000 US dollars, you lose 50,000 US dollars.

Exhibit 5.3 depicts the value of the US dollar versus the European currency (the euro) and the Japanese currency (the yen) over the last ten years. As you can see, a great deal of fluctuation occurs. So what causes a currency to increase and decrease in value? In a free market, a currency's value or price changes when the demand and supply for that currency changes. To understand why the demand and supply of a currency changes, we need to look at the balance of payments.

EXHIBIT 5.3: The US Dollar (USD) versus the Euro (EUR) and Japanese Yen (JPY)

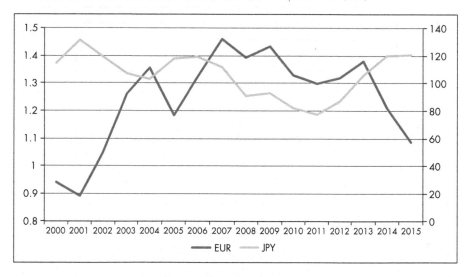

THE BALANCE OF PAYMENTS

Let's look at economic flows between countries. In Chapter 04 we discussed GDP and noted that a country's GDP was affected by its exports and imports. A country's exports and imports are also a part of its balance of payments. A country's **balance of payments** is a summary of the economic transactions, in a period, between that country and other countries. It is divided into three parts or accounts: the *current account*, the *capital account*, and the *financial account*.

1. The **current account** is composed of three elements: 1) exports and imports, 2) **factor payments**, and 3) transfer payments. Exports less imports is often called the **balance of trade** or **trade account**. *Factor payments* include the payment of interest and dividends. (A dividend is when a

corporation distributes its profits to its owners.) *Transfer payments* include aid and gifts from one country to another country.

2. The **capital account** is composed of two elements. First the capital account includes financial assets (debt and stock) transferred from one country to another because the owner moves from one country to another. Second the capital account includes the transfer of ownership from one country to another of intangible assets such as patents, trademarks, and copyrights. (Note: Chapter 07 explores patents, trademarks, and copyrights in more depth.)

3. The **financial account** is composed of three elements. First, the financial account includes direct foreign investment. Second, the financial account includes buying and selling long-term financial assets (debt and stock). (When business people say long-term, they typically mean the item has a life

Various currencies of the world (from top to bottom, left to right: China, Egypt, Euro zone, South Korea, Brazil, and Mexico)

greater than one year.) Third, the financial account includes buying and selling short-term financial assets (debt). (Short-term items have a life of one year or less.)

Exhibit 5.4 on the following page depicts the balance of payments for the United States.

SO WHY IS THE BALANCE OF PAYMENTS IMPORTANT FOR FOREIGN EXCHANGE?

Think about your budget. You start with a list of things you need. Then you figure out how to pay for these things. How do you pay for products you want? The answer is money. The economic flows between countries represent where a country's money is going to and coming from outside its borders.

Let's look at an example. Say you decide to buy a new BMW car produced in Germany. This transaction is a part of the current or trade account. When you buy the German automobile, you pay for it in US dollars. However, BMW must pay for its inputs (labor, materials, etc.) using the German currency, the *euro*. Germany exports the car to the United States. The US imports the car from Germany. This creates a trade imbalance between the two countries. US dollars must be exchanged for euros. The supply of US dollars goes up and the demand for euros goes up. What happens? As we discussed in Chapter 04, when demand and supply shift in a free market, prices change. The supply of US dollars is increasing and the demand for euros is increasing. Therefore, the value of the US dollar would go down and the value of the euro would go up.

EXHIBIT 5.4a: US International Trade in Goods and Services

Period	Balance			Exports			Imports		
	Total	Goods (1)	Services	Total	Goods (1)	Services	Total	Goods (1)	Services
2013									
Jan. - Dec.	-478,394	-702,587	224,193	2,279,937	1,592,043	687,894	2,758,331	2,294,630	463,700
January	-41,589	-60,517	18,928	188,110	131,228	56,883	229,699	191,745	37,955
February	-42,754	-61,647	18,893	188,913	132,084	56,828	231,666	193,731	37,935
March	-37,524	-56,233	18,708	186,740	130,093	56,647	224,264	186,326	37,938
April	-39,764	-58,039	18,275	188,060	131,468	56,592	227,824	189,507	38,318
May	-43,864	-62,257	18,392	187,476	130,553	56,922	231,340	192,810	38,530
June	-37,628	-55,869	18,241	189,611	132,677	56,934	227,239	188,546	38,693
July	-39,764	-58,200	18,436	189,275	132,356	56,919	229,039	190,556	38,483
August	-39,960	-58,804	18,843	190,037	132,400	57,637	229,998	191,204	38,794
September	-42,430	-61,409	18,979	190,103	132,301	57,802	232,533	193,711	38,822
October	-39,904	-58,316	18,412	193,571	135,762	57,809	233,475	194,078	39,396
November	-35,764	-54,523	18,759	195,062	136,784	58,278	230,826	191,307	39,519
December	-37,449	-56,774	19,325	192,979	134,336	58,642	230,428	191,111	39,317
2014									
Jan. - Dec.	-508,324	-741,462	233,138	2,343,205	1,632,639	710,565	2,851,529	2,374,101	477,428
January	-39,462	-59,968	20,506	192,879	133,738	59,141	232,341	193,706	38,635
February	-42,835	-61,292	18,457	189,495	131,768	57,726	232,330	193,060	39,270
March	-43,121	-63,050	19,929	194,759	135,923	58,837	237,881	198,973	38,908
April	-44,271	-64,321	20,051	195,024	135,556	59,468	239,295	199,877	39,417
May	-42,070	-62,091	20,021	197,269	137,314	59,955	239,340	199,405	39,934
June	-42,371	-61,700	19,330	195,579	136,282	59,298	237,950	197,982	39,968
July	-41,411	-60,177	18,767	196,907	138,406	58,500	238,317	198,584	39,734
August	-41,275	-60,824	19,549	197,303	138,155	59,148	238,578	198,979	39,599
September	-43,186	-62,075	18,889	195,053	136,371	58,682	238,239	198,446	39,793
October	-42,753	-61,917	19,163	197,759	138,107	59,652	240,513	200,024	40,489
November	-40,021	-59,331	19,309	196,201	136,474	59,726	236,222	195,805	40,417
December	-45,549	-64,716	19,167	194,975	134,544	60,431	240,524	199,260	41,264
2015									
Jan. - Dec.	-531,503	-758,934	227,431	2,230,317	1,513,888	716,429	2,761,820	2,272,821	488,999
January (R)	-43,616	-62,978	19,362	188,999	129,266	59,733	232,615	192,244	40,371
February (R)	-38,565	-58,068	19,504	185,863	126,303	59,560	224,428	184,372	40,057
March (R)	-52,191	-71,192	19,002	186,739	127,157	59,583	238,930	198,349	40,581
April (R)	-43,395	-62,027	18,631	188,404	129,320	59,084	231,800	191,347	40,453
May (R)	-43,473	-62,105	18,632	187,063	127,808	59,255	230,536	189,913	40,623
June (R)	-46,287	-65,143	18,855	186,903	127,499	59,404	233,191	192,642	40,548
July (R)	-42,460	-61,307	18,847	188,209	128,653	59,557	230,670	189,960	40,710
August (R)	-48,839	-67,765	18,926	184,137	124,348	59,790	232,976	192,112	40,864
September (R)	-42,484	-60,995	18,511	186,739	126,856	59,884	229,224	187,851	41,373
October (R)	-44,610	-63,598	18,989	183,751	123,584	60,167	228,361	187,182	41,178
November (R)	-42,226	-61,241	19,015	182,010	121,940	60,071	224,237	183,181	41,056
December	-43,357	-62,514	19,157	181,497	121,155	60,343	224,854	183,669	41,185
November data as published last month:									
	-42,374	-61,284	18,910	182,212	122,192	60,021	224,587	183,476	41,111

In millions of dollars. Details may not equal totals due to seasonal adjustment and rounding. (R) - Revised.

(1) Data are presented on a balance of payments (BOP) basis.

NOTE: For information on data sources and methodology, see the information section on page A-1 of this release or at www.census.gov/ft900 or www.bea.gov/newsreleases/international/trade/tradnewsrelease.htm.

EXHIBIT 5.4b: US International Trade in Goods and Services: Three-Month Moving Averages

In millions of dollars. Details may not equal totals due to seasonal adjustment and rounding. (R) - Revised.

Month of Moving Average	Balance			Exports			Imports		
	Total	Goods (1)	Services	Total	Goods (1)	Services	Total	Goods (1)	Services
2013									
January	-42,109	-60,646	18,538	187,816	131,316	56,500	229,925	191,962	37,962
February	-40,804	-59,621	18,817	188,871	132,130	56,741	229,676	191,751	37,924
March	-40,622	-59,465	18,843	187,921	131,135	56,786	228,543	190,601	37,943
April	-40,014	-58,640	18,625	187,904	131,215	56,689	227,918	189,855	38,064
May	-40,384	-58,843	18,458	187,425	130,705	56,720	227,809	189,547	38,262
June	-40,419	-58,722	18,303	188,382	131,566	56,816	228,801	190,287	38,513
July	-40,419	-58,775	18,357	188,787	131,862	56,925	229,206	190,637	38,569
August	-39,117	-57,624	18,507	189,641	132,478	57,164	228,758	190,102	38,657
September	-40,718	-59,471	18,753	189,805	132,353	57,453	230,523	191,823	38,700
October	-40,765	-59,510	18,745	191,237	133,488	57,749	232,002	192,997	39,004
November	-39,366	-58,083	18,717	192,912	134,949	57,963	232,278	193,032	39,246
December	-37,706	-56,538	18,832	193,870	135,628	58,243	231,576	192,165	39,411
2014									
January	-37,558	-57,088	19,530	193,640	134,953	58,687	231,198	192,041	39,157
February	-39,915	-59,345	19,429	191,784	133,281	58,503	231,699	192,626	39,074
March	-41,806	-61,437	19,631	192,378	133,810	58,568	234,184	195,246	38,937
April	-43,409	-62,888	19,479	193,093	134,416	58,677	236,502	197,303	39,198
May	-43,154	-63,154	20,000	195,684	136,264	59,420	238,838	199,419	39,420
June	-42,904	-62,704	19,800	195,958	136,384	59,574	238,862	199,088	39,773
July	-41,951	-61,323	19,372	196,585	137,334	59,251	238,536	198,657	39,879
August	-41,685	-60,901	19,215	196,597	137,614	58,982	238,282	198,515	39,767
September	-41,957	-61,025	19,068	196,421	137,644	58,777	238,378	198,670	39,709
October	-42,405	-61,605	19,200	196,705	137,545	59,161	239,110	199,150	39,960
November	-41,987	-61,107	19,121	196,338	136,984	59,353	238,324	198,092	40,233
December	-42,774	-61,988	19,213	196,312	136,375	59,937	239,086	198,363	40,723
2015									
January (R)	-43,062	-62,342	19,280	193,392	133,428	59,964	236,454	195,769	40,684
February (R)	-42,576	-61,921	19,344	189,946	130,038	59,908	232,522	191,958	40,564
March (R)	-44,790	-64,080	19,289	187,201	127,575	59,625	231,991	191,655	40,336
April (R)	-44,717	-63,762	19,045	187,002	127,593	59,409	231,719	191,356	40,364
May (R)	-46,353	-65,108	18,755	187,402	128,095	59,307	233,755	193,203	40,552
June (R)	-44,385	-63,091	18,706	187,457	128,209	59,248	231,842	191,301	40,541
July (R)	-44,074	-62,852	18,778	187,392	127,987	59,405	231,465	190,838	40,627
August (R)	-45,862	-64,738	18,876	186,417	126,833	59,583	232,279	191,572	40,707
September (R)	-44,595	-63,356	18,761	186,362	126,619	59,743	230,957	189,975	40,982
October (R)	-45,311	-64,119	18,808	184,876	124,929	59,947	230,187	189,048	41,138
November (R)	-43,107	-61,945	18,838	184,167	124,126	60,040	227,274	186,071	41,202
December	-43,397	-62,451	19,054	182,420	122,226	60,193	225,817	184,677	41,140

(1) Data are presented on a balance of payments (BOP) basis.

NOTES:

*The three-month moving averages shown in this exhibit are computed by summing the subject month and the two prior months, dividing by three, and showing the average at the end month of the period. A moving average is useful in smoothing the volatile trade data so that trends can better be discerned.

*For information on data sources and methodology, see the information section on page A-1 of this release or at www.census.gov/ft900 or www.bea.gov/newsreleases/international/trade/tradnewsrelease.htm.

Now let's look at another example. When Germany imports US food products, it demands US dollars and supplies euros. What happens? The supply of euros and demand for US dollars increase. This causes the value of US dollars to increase and euro to decrease. So exports and imports impact the value or price of a country's currency.

Now what happens when a country imports more than it exports? The country is said to have a **negative trade balance**, often called a **trade deficit**. A negative trade balance indicates that a country is supplying more of its currency and demanding more of other currencies. That puts downward pressure on that country's currency. The currency, in a free market, will depreciate. What happens when a country exports than it imports? The country is said to have a **positive trade balance**, often called a **trade surplus**. A positive trade balance indicates that a country is supplying less of its currency and demanding less of other currencies. That puts upward pressure on that country's currency. The currency, in a free market, will appreciate.

Now think about the US economy and the US dollar over the last several years. What has been happening? The US has a large negative trade balance, or trade deficit, with countries such as China. Because of that trade deficit, the value of the US dollar has decreased against currencies such as the Chinese yuan. It takes more US dollars to buy a Chinese yuan. Now think about the Chinese economy and the Chinese currency, the yuan. China has a positive trade balance, or trade surplus, with the US. Because of that trade surplus, the value of Chinese yuan has increased. It takes fewer Chinese yuans to buy a US dollar.

But is the trade account all that determines a foreign exchange rate in a free market? The answer is no. Remember the capital and financial accounts in the balance of payments? These flows also affect the value of a currency. Let's use the United States as an example. The US has had a negative trade balance for years. Yet the value of the US dollar has not depreciated as much as the trade account would predict. Why? The answer is in the capital and financial accounts of the balance of payments. Although the US has a negative current account balance, it has a positive financial account balance. Countries around the world have used their excess US dollars to buy the debt of the US government. In doing so, these countries demanded dollars and supplied their countries' currencies. This demand for the US dollar placed upward pressure on the US dollar, counterbalancing the downward pressure from the negative current account. The result is the negative trade balance was offset by the positive balance in the financial account.

A good example of foreign governments buying US government debt is China and Japan. In 2015, China owned $1.24 trillion and Japan owned $1.23 trillion in US government debt. In fact, China and Japan are the largest owners of US government debt outside the US. As China and Japan received US dollars from selling products to the US, they used those dollars to purchase US government debt. This increased the demand for US dollars, slowing the US dollar's decline.

In summary, the balance of payments reflects a country's economic flows with other countries. It captures the forces that create the demand for and supply of a country's currency. In a free market, those forces set the price of that country's currency. That price in turn affects how businesses operate around the world.

EXHIBIT 5.5: Ten Largest Trading Partners for the United States, 2015

RANK	COUNTRY	US EXPORTS TO	US IMPORTS FROM	TRADE GAP
1	China	116,186.3	481,880.8	(365,694.5)
2	Canada	280,326.5	295,190.3	(14,863.8)
3	Mexico	236,377.4	294,741.1	(58,363.7)

4	Japan	62,471.8	131,119.7	(68,647.9)
5	Germany	49,946.7	124,139.2	(74,192.5)
6	Korea South	43,498.7	71,827.4	(28,328.7)
7	United Kingdom	56,352.9	57,805.2	(1,452.3)
8	France	30,077.2	47,644.2	(17,567.0)
9	Italy	16,429.2	44,004.9	(27,575.7)
10	Taiwan	25,928.7	40,708.1	(14,779.4)

THE DETERMINANTS OF FOREIGN EXCHANGE

So the balance of payments reflects a country's transactions with other countries. What determines the demand and supply of currency used to conduct such transactions? Why do foreigners buy a country's products and financial securities? The major determinants are:

· Income level

· Price level

· Interest rates

· Government actions

Let's look at each of these in more detail.

Income Level

We discussed earlier that when people have income, they like to spend that income. When people have more income, they can buy more products or financial securities from other countries. As a country's income increases, so does its demand for imported products and ability to buy foreign securities. These transactions show up in the balance of payments and affect exchange rates. How a country's income affects exchange rates depends on how much the country imports and exports products and buys and sells foreign securities.

Price Level: Purchasing Power Parity

Price level relates to inflation. A theory called **purchasing power parity** holds that inflation in a country hurts the value of that country's currency. The theory holds that the same item in two different countries should have the same "real" cost, where real cost adjusts for inflation. If the price is not the same, we buy the lower-cost alternative.

Let's use a 16-ounce bottle of Coke as an example. Let's say the US dollar is equal to one Canadian dollar. A bottle of Coke costs 1 US dollar in the US and 1 Canadian dollar in Canada. Let's say Canada experiences 25 percent inflation. The bottle of Coke in Canada now increases to 1.25 Canadian dollars. Without a change in the exchange rate between the US and Canada, the bottle of Coke produced in Canada now costs someone in the US 1.25 US dollars. But does that make sense? Someone in the US can buy a bottle of Coke produced in the US for 1 US dollar versus a bottle of Coke produced in Canada for 1.25 US dollars. The bottles of Coke are the same and should have the same price. So what will happen? The US dollar will increase in value and the Canadian dollar will decrease in value

Cranes unloading shipping containers in Long Beach, CA, loaded with Asian goods destined for US retail markets.

BUSINESS SENSE

DEBT AND GLOBAL ECONOMICS

In Chapter 04 we discussed fiscal policy and how the government borrows money to compensate for budget deficits. So who does the US government borrow money from? Who is the lender? Today, the US is borrowing increasingly from international sources.

For example, consider Japan and China. Both countries have large trade surpluses with the US. The US in turn has a trade deficit with Japan and China. This trade imbalance increases the value of the Japanese and Chinese currencies and decreases the value of the US dollar. What does this do? It makes goods and services imported by the US from Japan and China more expensive. This causes US consumers to buy fewer Japanese and Chinese products, which hurts the Japanese and Chinese economies. To counter this imbalance, Japan and China use their excess dollars to buy US government debt. That is, they lend the US government money. Japan and China lend money to the US in part to keep the value of the US dollar high. This high value keeps the price of Japanese and Chinese products low for US consumers. This low price keeps US demand for Japanese and Chinese products high, which in turn creates a lot of jobs and income in Japan and China.

So the US government runs a deficit financed by foreign governments. Is this good or bad? There are many arguments for and against this. However, this borrowing and lending makes the governments involved very dependent on one another. Think of what would happen if a lender refuses to lend. The borrower is hurt. However, think what happens if a borrower refuses to pay its debt. The lender is hurt. This is just another force of globalization.

so the two bottles of Coke cost the same in US dollars. The exchange rate will change so 1 US dollar is equal to 1.25 Canadian dollars. Because of inflation in Canada, the US dollar has increased in value and the Canadian dollar has decreased in value. Once again when a US consumer buys a bottle of Coke produced in Canada, it only costs him or her 1 US dollar.

Interest Rates

As we've discussed in earlier chapters, in a free and global market, businesses and countries compete for money. If one country offers a higher interest rate, its lenders, individuals, companies, and governments will prefer to lend money to that country versus other countries. In doing so, the lenders will demand the borrower's currency, increasing the value of the borrower's currency. As noted above, an example is the United States, which offers attractive interest rates to the world. The world demands US dollars to buy US debt, increasing the value of the US dollar. This lending and borrowing shows up in the balance of payments.

Government Actions: Fixed versus Floating Exchange Rates

Governments can affect the value of their currency and the value of other currencies. How do they do it? It depends on the exchange rate system the government chooses. So far, we have assumed a government permits the price of its currency to be determined by a free market. We call this a **floating exchange rate system**. Governments often let the market determine the price of their currency in normal times. However, when the value of their currency begins to radically change, governments may step in and take action to prevent their currency from appreciating or depreciating. When a government takes these actions, the exchange rate system is often called a **managed floating exchange rate system**. The United States uses a managed floating exchange rate system to manage the value of the US dollar. There are numerous actions governments can take within a managed floating exchange rate system:

1. Governments can restrict the flow of their currency. For example, for a number of years in the 1990s, Russia declared it unlawful to take its currency, the *ruble*, outside its borders. The Russian government was attempting to increase the value of the ruble by controlling the supply of rubles.

2. Governments can buy and sell their currency and the currency of other countries. This will affect the demand and supply of the currencies. This in turn affects the value of the currencies.

3. As noted in Chapter 04, governments can also impact the level of income and interest rates within their economy. As noted earlier, this will affect the value or price of its currency.

4. Governments can impose tariffs (or taxes) on international transactions. Higher tariffs increase the cost of imported products to customers, thus decreasing the demand for such products. Decreasing imports causes a decrease in the demand for foreign currency, which decreases the value of the foreign currency.

5. As noted earlier, governments can limit the amount of imports and exports flowing into and out of their country with embargos, quotas, and other restrictions.

Governments may also choose not to use a floating exchange rate system but to instead have a **fixed exchange rate system**. In such a system, one government fixes, or pegs, the exchange rate of its currency to another country's currency. For example, Saudi Arabia fixes the value of its currency (the riyal) to the US dollar. As the US dollar appreciates, so does the Saudi Arabian riyal. As the US dollar depreciates, so does the Saudi Arabian riyal. This eliminates some of the risk in doing business between these countries, but it can cause problems. When a country fixes its exchange rate to another currency, that country guarantees that rate. That country must be willing to buy its currency at that fixed rate. How does that country pay for this currency? It pays with reserves composed of currencies of other countries or commodities such as gold. What happens when that country no longer has any reserves? It cannot guarantee the fixed rate of exchange. Nobody wants the country's currency and trade stops. For that reason, countries that fix their exchange rate to another country's currency may need to adjust the rate they guarantee over time. If the country sees that its reserves are decreasing, it knows its fixed rate of exchange for its currency is too high. It knows the guaranteed value of its currency should be decreased. If the country sees that its reserves are increasing, it knows its fixed rate of exchange for its currency is too low. It knows the guaranteed value of its currency should be increased.

It's important for managers to understand foreign exchange transactions and how these transactions affect the value or price of currencies. Currencies can go up and go down. But what is preferable?

APPRECIATING OR DEPRECIATING CURRENCIES: WHICH IS BEST?

Do countries want an appreciating currency or a depreciating currency? What is good and what is bad? The answer depends. There are good and bad aspects related to both appreciating and depreciating currencies.

An appreciating currency, like the one we discussed earlier in the Belgian chocolate example, means the price of a country's products increases for foreign consumers. This could lower the demand for exports. This in turn could force the Belgian chocolate company to reduce production and dismiss employees. This could hurt the overall Belgian economy. In addition, an appreciating currency means Belgian consumers can buy more imported products. Using the same number of euros, citizens of Belgium can buy more US chocolates. This also could hurt domestic production and employment. However, an appreciating currency has a benefit: The low price of imports keeps domestic prices and inflation low. In our example, the prices in Belgium are low.

A depreciating currency, like our US dollar example, means the price of exported goods becomes less for foreign consumers. This could increase the demand for exports. This in turn could create growth and employment in the exporting economy. As the value of the US dollar depreciates, the price of US products is cheaper for foreigners. A depreciating US dollar also means US consumers find imported products more expensive. These forces could increase domestic production and employment, which helps the overall US economy. However, a depreciating currency can have a cost: higher-priced imports may increase domestic inflation.

So what's the role of government in this challenge? Japan does not want the Japanese yen to appreciate too much. Why? Because its economy is dependent on exporting. Lower exports decrease Japan's GDP and employment. The US does not want the dollar to depreciate too much. Why? Because its economy is dependent on importing. The increasing prices of imports cause inflation.

Is this good or bad? That is decided by each country. Let's look at an example. In the United States, the majority of televisions sold are not produced in the US. The US does not have the capacity to produce enough TVs to satisfy its domestic demand for TVs. If the value of the US dollar depreciated significantly and quickly, the cost of TVs would increase significantly in the short term. US companies could not respond quickly enough to build factories to produce TVs in the US. People may not be able to afford television sets in the short term. So governments need to look at the global economy to decide what is best for their people. In choosing what to do and what not to do, governments have numerous tools. But whatever governments do, it always has an impact on business.

THE IMPACT ON BUSINESS

Foreign exchange rates obviously have a big impact on global business. First, foreign exchange rates affect the demand and supply of products through price. Foreign exchange rates also affect a business's revenue and cost. Businesses like to have their revenue in appreciating currencies and costs in depreciating currencies. The uncertainty and volatility of foreign exchange rates also causes risk. Businesses must weigh the risks against the benefits from doing business outside their country's borders.

However, doing business globally has its benefits. The multiplier effect, noted in Chapter 04, also works in global free markets. There is a definite benefit in recognizing that countries have comparative advantages that can foster prosperity for all. For that reason, governments around the world have tried to foster global business by creating trade agreements and agencies that help.

LEARNING OBJECTIVE 4

THE AGREEMENTS AND ORGANIZATIONS THAT FOSTER GLOBAL BUSINESS

Over the years, countries and businesses, individually and collectively, have entered into agreements and created organizations that foster global business. Let's look at a few of these agreements and organizations.

US ORGANIZATIONS

In the United States, three prominent organizations help foster international trade:

- The **Export-Import Bank (Ex-Im Bank)** is a US government agency that facilitates US exports. It loans money directly to foreign companies that import US products or guarantees loans from private lenders to such importers.

- The **Private Export Funding Corporation (PEFCO)** is owned by a group of private US banks that lend money to foreign companies that import US products. It works closely with the Ex-Im Bank.

- The **Overseas Private Investment Corporation (OPIC)** is a US government agency that encourages US companies to invest in foreign countries. OPIC ensures that the US company will not lose money because it insures US investments in foreign countries against 1) currency devaluation if the foreign country's currency loses value or 2) a foreign government takes control of the business's investment. OPIC also has several loan programs to help US exporters.

ORGANIZATIONS THAT FOSTER GLOBAL BUSINESS

Besides agencies and organizations created by and in a specific country, countries have joined together to create global organizations to foster understanding and economic cooperation between countries. Let's look at some of the more prominent organizations (shown in Exhibit 5.6).

After World War II, several countries began to negotiate guidelines for international trade. Those talks started the **General Agreement on Tariffs and Trades (GATT)**, founded in 1947. From GATT, the **World Trade Organization (WTO)** was created in 1995. The WTO attempts to break down economic barriers and mediate trade disagreements between member countries. The WTO is headquartered in Geneva, Switzerland, has over 160 members, and represents over 95 percent of the world's trade. The United States is a member of the WTO. Members of the WTO must agree to five principles:

1. Their trade policies must not discriminate among members. This is often called *most favored nation rule (MFN)*. A WTO country must treat all other WTO members the same.

2. Trade policies must reflect reciprocity where a country gives and receives the same consideration to and from other WTO members.

3. Trade polices must be based on binding and enforceable commitments.

4. Trade policies must be transparent and easily understood.

5. WTO members acknowledge that developing and struggling economies may need temporary relief from binding agreements.

Entrance to the World Bank building, Washington, DC.

The **World Bank,** formerly named the International Bank for Reconstruction and Development (IBRD), was created after World War II. The World Bank is owned by countries throughout the world and makes loans to countries to help develop their economies. Although not the majority owner of the World Bank, the United States is the largest shareholder in the World Bank. The World Bank's headquarters are in Washington, DC.

The **International Monetary Fund (IMF)** was created after World War II to promote international trade and help countries create and maintain stable economies. The IMF does this primarily by helping member countries with exchange-rate problems. The United States is a member of the IMF. The IMF's headquarters are in Washington, DC.

The **Bank of International Settlements (BIS)** was created after World War II to facilitate banking between member countries. Let's say you go to Germany and buy a new German car. You pay for it with a check from your bank account in a US bank. What happens to the check? The German seller deposits the check in a German bank. The German bank then presents the check to the BIS, which then presents the check to your US bank for payment. Besides facilitating financial transactions, the BIS also sets many international banking standards. The BIS is headquartered in Basel, Switzerland. The United States is a member of the BIS.

The **United Nations (UN)** was formed after World War II to foster world peace and cooperation. Such goals cannot be achieved without economic understanding and cooperation. The UN has numerous agencies within its structure that work toward economic development, understanding, and cooperation. The United States is a member of the UN, which is headquartered in New York.

TRADE ALLIANCES AND AGREEMENTS

Even with country-specific and global organizations, many countries have found the need to bond together to form special alliances and trade agreements (see Exhibit 5.7). Let's look at some of these trade alliances and agreements.

The **European Union (EU)** consists of 28 countries in Europe that have come together to form one economic trading unit. The 28 countries are shown in Exhibit 5.8. Before the EU was formed, each of the member countries had its own currencies. Each country had different tariffs and other restrictions on imports. The countries of the EU realized that together they could create an economic trading bloc comparable to the United States and Japan. The countries, except the United Kingdom, therefore agreed

EXHIBIT 5.7: Prominent Alliances and Trade Agreements

to eliminate their individual currencies for one common currency, the European Currency Unit (the euro). The countries, including the United Kingdom, also eliminated tariffs and restrictions between member countries and agreed to act as one economic unit in dealing with non-EU countries.

The **North American Free Trade Agreement (NAFTA)** is an agreement started in 1994 that joined the United States, Canada, and Mexico into an economic unit. In doing so, the countries eliminated barriers to trade such as tariffs, quotas, and other restrictions between the three member countries. The purpose of NAFTA was to enhance competition and efficiency between the United States, Canada, and Mexico. These three countries have a combined output of US$17.0 trillion per year and are home to 444.1 million people. After NAFTA was enacted, trade between the three members tripled. However, NAFTA is not without controversy, particularly in the US. It is argued that the United States lost thousands of jobs because of NAFTA. Without tariffs and other restrictions, US companies found it less expensive to produce goods in Mexico and Canada.

A number of other free trade agreements govern other areas of the world. Each is designed to eliminate tariffs and trade restrictions between members:

- The **Central American Free Trade Agreement (CAFTA)** is an economic agreement between the United States, Costa Rica, El Salvador, Guatemala, Honduras, Nicaragua, and the Dominican Republic.

- The **Association of Southeast Asian Nations (ASEAN)** is an economic agreement between Indonesia, Malaysia, the Philippines, Singapore, Thailand, Brunei, Vietnam, Cambodia, Laos, and Myanmar.

- The **Commonwealth of Independent States (CIS)** is an economic agreement between the 11 republics that formerly composed the Soviet Union—Armenia, Azerbaijan, Belarus, Georgia, Kazakhstan, Kyrgyzstan, Moldova, Russia, Tajikistan, Turkmenistan, Ukraine, and Uzbekistan.

- The **Common Market of the Southern Cone (MERCOSUR)** is an economic agreement between Argentina, Brazil, Paraguay, Uruguay, Venezuela; Columbia, Ecuador, Peru, Bolivia, and Chile are associate countries.

- The **Organization for Economic Cooperation and Development (OECD)** is an organization that promotes free trade between member countries. There are 34 member countries in North America, Europe, East Asia, and South Pacific. The US is a member of OECD.

Former Russian President, Dmitry Medvedev, meeting with Secretary General of the Organization of the Petroleum Exporting Countries (OPEC) Abdalla El-Badri.

In addition to these agreements, other agreements pertain to the trading of particular resources between countries. For example, the **Organization of Petroleum Exporting Countries (OPEC)** is an economic agreement between member countries regarding the production of crude oil. The current member countries are Algeria, Angola, Ecuador, Indonesia, Iran, Iraq, Kuwait, Libya, Nigeria, Qatar, Saudi Arabia, United Arab Emirates, and Venezuela. The agreement creates a trading bloc that impacts the pricing of crude oil.

THE NEED FOR AND CHALLENGES OF ECONOMIC COOPERATION

Today, more than ever, no country can prosper without global trade. Yet sometimes the drive to foster economic growth causes countries and businesses within countries to use tactics that are often perceived as unfair. To create employment and income, countries often use tactics that enhance exports and restrict imports. Let's look at two examples:

1. To foster exports, countries may sell products to other countries below the cost incurred to produce those products. This is called **dumping**. Countries may also try to artificially keep the value of their currency low. They can do this by keeping their interest rate low or selling their currency to create an excess supply. This is designed to foster exports and limit imports.

2. Countries may try to create artificial barriers to imports with fees, tariffs, quotas, inspections, and other actions.

There is a real need for the above organizations, agencies, and agreements to foster free and fair trade between countries. The benefits of international trade and global business are dependent on communication, understanding, and constant vigilance. Globalization is a fact. Markets for employees, assets, money, and customers are global. Such markets are becoming highly integrated and dependent on one another. Competing to create value is about competing in the global marketplace.

EXHIBIT 5.8: Map of EU Countries

CHAPTER SUMMARY

Globalization is a fact of today's business world. Each day the countries and businesses of the world become more interdependent. To be successful, managers must understand why and how business is conducted throughout the world. They must appreciate differences in culture and law. Globalization creates great opportunities to create value. However globalization also creates great risk.

After reading this chapter, you should be able to:

1. Appreciate the nature, opportunities, and challenges of doing business around the world (Learning Objective 1): Globalization is the evolution of business from operating in a single country to operating in many countries. Globalization is a reality that all businesses must face. It provides opportunities and challenges to business.

2. Appreciate the methods used to conduct global business (Learning Objective 2): Because of forces such as culture and government policies, businesses use different methods to conduct business throughout the world. These methods include licensing, joint ventures, franchising, strategic alliances, and direct foreign investment.

3. Appreciate the nature and impact of foreign exchange rates (Learning Objective 3): Foreign exchange refers to the act of exchanging one country's currency for another. The value of a country's currency determines the prices of products it buys from and sells to other countries.

4. Appreciate the agreements and organizations that foster global business (Learning Objective 4): Doing business around the world is complicated. To assist global business, countries have come together and formed organizations and alliances. These organizations include the World Trade Organization, the World Bank, and the International Monetary Fund. Alliances include the European Union and the North American Free Trade Agreement.

In this chapter we looked at globalization. Now it's time to look at the impact of the law on business. In the next chapter we'll look at the legal forms and taxation of business in the United States. We'll see how law and taxation affects "How Business Works."

KEYWORDS

SHORT-ANSWER QUESTIONS

1. What is globalization and why is it happening?
2. Describe the different methods businesses use to conduct business around the world. What are the pros and cons of each form?
3. Define the following terms:
   a. Balance of Payments
   b. Balance of Trade
   c. Barter
   d. Capital Account
   e. Current Account
   f. Direct Foreign Investment (DFI)
   g. Domestic Business
   h. Dumping
   i. Embargo
   j. Factor Payments
   k. Financial Account
   l. Fixed Exchange Rate System
   m. Floating Exchange Rate System
   n. Foreign Exchange (FX)
   o. Foreign Exchange Rate
   p. Franchising
   q. Free Trade
   r. Global Business
   s. Globalization
   t. International Business
   u. Joint Venture
   v. Licensing
   w. Managed Floating Exchange Rate System
   x. Off-Shoring
   y. Outsourcing
   z. Overseas Private Investment Corporation (OPIC)
   aa. Positive Trade Balance or Trade Surplus
   ab. Private Export Funding Corporation (PEFCO)
   ac. Protectionism
   ad. Purchasing Power Parity
   ae. Quota
   af. Strategic Alliance
   ag. Tariff
   ah. Transfer Payments

4. What is outsourcing, briefly? How is it different from off-shoring?

CRITICAL-THINKING QUESTIONS

1. What are the benefits and challenges of a:
   a. Floating exchange rate system,
   b. Fixed exchange rate system,
   c. Managed floating exchange rate system?

2. What is a country's balance of payments? What are the parts of a country's balance of payments? What makes up each part of a country's balance of payments?

3. What determines a country's foreign exchange rate?

4. What are the benefits and costs of having an appreciating exchange rate and a depreciating exchange rate?

EXPLORING REAL BUSINESS

Go to the websites of Google, Target, Hyundai, and Proctor and Gamble. The websites are

Google:	http://investor.google.com
Target:	http://www.target.com
Hyundai:	http://worldwide.hyundai.com/company-overview
Procter & Gamble:	http://www.pg.com

For each company, answer the following questions:

1. Is this business a domestic, international, or global business? Why?
2. How has globalization affected the business? Give specific examples.

ENDNOTE

1. https://www.hyundaiusa.com/about-hyundai/our-company/

06

THE FORMS AND TAXATION OF BUSINESS

Introduction: Let's Talk About Forming a Business

So you want to start a business, but how do you do this legally? In Chapter 01 a business is defined as an organization, recognized under the law, that attempts to create value by exchanging products with customers for money or money substitutes (such as a promise to pay money later). But how does the law recognize a business? What cost (tax) does the law assess on a business? What are the different forms of business and does it matter which form a business chooses?

After reading this chapter, you should be able to understand the legal forms of business and appreciate how businesses are taxed. You should also appreciate the special opportunities in forming and operating a business, such as mergers, licensing, franchising, and cooperatives.

After reading Chapter 06, you should be able to meet the following learning objectives:

1. Appreciate the legal forms of business
2. Appreciate the different types of taxes and how taxes affect business decisions
3. Appreciate the special opportunities in business formation (e.g., mergers, licensing, franchising, and cooperatives)

WHY THE FORM OF A BUSINESS MATTERS

Have you ever thought about the challenges of starting a business? One challenge in choosing the form of the business is that businesses are not all the same in the eyes of the law. Making the correct choice is not a simple matter. There are a number of things an owner must understand in forming a business, including knowing how the business forms differ on such things as taxation and the responsibilities of owners. The ramifications for choosing the wrong form of business are serious and can hurt value. Choosing the right business form does matter.

LEARNING OBJECTIVE 1.

THE LEGAL FORMS OF BUSINESS

The law recognizes three basic forms of business. The three basic forms are:

Sole Proprietorship
Partnerships
Corporations

A US highway bridge construction project on the I-95.

A sole proprietorship is the most common form that US businesses take. The least numerous form of US businesses is corporations. Although the fewest in number, the biggest businesses in the US are corporations.

The three forms differ in several ways; the primary differences are owner liability and taxes. First is owner liability. A **liability** is defined as an obligation of an individual or organization that comes about because of a transaction or event. Liabilities are debts; claims that individuals or organizations must pay. When someone or some organization is liable, it is responsible for paying money because a party has a claim on that individual or organization. Liabilities are a part of everyone's world. An example is when you buy something at Target with a credit card. You owe the credit card company money and are liable for this debt. Liabilities are money that a person or organization owes because the person or organization did something.

Next are taxes. **Taxes** are amounts governments levy on individuals or organizations. Individuals and organizations pay taxes so they can exist and operate in a society. Taxes are levied by local, state, and federal governments. Taxes have two functions. First, taxes are how governments pay for the goods and services that governments provide society (roads, schools, military, etc.). Second, taxes are also a way governments motivate behavior. An example in the US is in charitable donations. The government wants individuals and businesses to give to charities. To foster charitable giving, the US government allows individuals and businesses to reduce their taxable income, and thus taxes, when they give to charities.

As noted later in the chapter, there are many forms of taxes. But one form is a tax on taxable income. **Taxable income** is net income (revenue less costs) before taxes. Governments often tax the profit or net income earned by individuals and businesses. Taxes are a complicated cost of doing business and, as such, affect the value of a business. In an attempt to maximize value, businesses attempt to *legally* 1) minimize taxes and 2) postpone paying taxes.

There are several issues when deciding what form of business to choose. First, owners look at the ease and cost of creating and ending a business. Second, owners look at their ability to control and manage their business. Complicated forms of businesses can sometimes frustrate owners. Third, owners often worry about selling their businesses in the future. Most businesses are bought and sold in the private market, not a public market. A **private market** is a market that is not open to everyone. A **public market** is where anyone can buy all or part of a business. Organized exchanges, such as the New York Stock Exchange, are public markets. It should be noted that only certain forms of business, such as corporations, can be traded in a public market. Markets such as the New York Stock Exchange are explored in Chapter 19.

So choosing the legal form of a business is important and complex. Let's look at the different forms of business.

A SOLE PROPRIETORSHIP

Sole proprietorships are the most numerous form of US business because they are the easiest to create and end: it takes no formal legal action to start or close a sole proprietorship. A **sole proprietorship** is where one person owns and controls the business. To start a sole proprietorship, all a person needs to do is begin selling a product. An example is when someone does yard work for a neighbor for $100. Why does the law make it so easy to start or close a sole proprietorship? The answer is that the law does not recognize a difference between the business and the owner of the business. The business and its owner are viewed as one body or entity by the law.

So what does it mean for the law to view the owner and his or her business as one legal entity? First, when a sole proprietorship owns assets and owes money, the owner owns those assets and owes money. Is this good for the owner? Not necessarily so. The liabilities of a sole proprietorship are viewed as the liabilities of the owner, which means if the business gets into financial trouble, it can affect the personal finances of the owner. If the sole proprietorship can't pay its debts, then the owner is responsible for those debts. The owner is said to have "**unlimited liability**." Think about this. You start a lawn service and name it Ace Lawn Care. You accidentally cause damage to a customer's home. The customer claims that it will take $10,000 to repair the damage. If the claim is valid, then you, the sole proprietor of Ace Lawn Care, owe the $10,000. The law does not recognize that you and your business are separate entities—the law views you and your business as one.

Next are taxes. As one legal entity, the law does not recognize a difference between the income of the sole proprietorship and income of the owner. The income of the business is not taxed at the business level. The income of the sole proprietorship is assumed to flow to the owner. The tax is paid by the owner, not the business. Is this good? The answer is yes. It's good because the income is taxed once. It's called **single taxation**. We'll see later this is not always the case for other forms of business, which can be taxed multiple times. Let's look at Ace Lawn Care. You charge your neighbor $100 for your services. You incur costs of $50 for gasoline and other expenses. You make $50 in taxable income, net income before taxes. The government does not tax Ace Lawn Care. The government taxes "you" on the $50 net income. You must declare the $50 net income on your individual tax return. Let's assume your personal tax rate is 20%. You will pay a 20% tax on your $50 taxable income, or $10. You get to keep $40 ($50 − $10).

So the good thing about a sole proprietorship is it's easy to start and close. It's good in that it has single taxation and bad in that owners have unlimited liability.

PARTNERSHIPS

General Partnerships are like a sole proprietorship with one exception. A general partnership has multiple owners, each of whom is called a **general partner**. The rights and responsibilities of each general partner are typically stated in a legal document called a **partnership agreement**. Let's think about Ace Lawn Care. You decide to ask a friend to join your business and form a partnership. You agree on what each of you will do and that you will split the profits or losses equally. You have entered into a partnership agreement.

In the eyes of the law, the government does not view the partners as being different from their business. Although you have a legal agreement, that law views your business as a part of your life and the life of your partner.

The good things about a general partnership are the good things of a sole proprietorship. General partnerships are easy to start and end, and they have single taxation. If a business is formed as a general partnership, the net income is divided among the partners in accordance with the partnership agreement. The business, or partnership, pays no income taxes. The individual partners pay taxes on their share of the net income. Thus, the general partnership, like a proprietorship, has single taxation. Let's look at Ace Lawn Care's earnings of $50 in taxable income. Your partnership agreement states that you and your partner will share equally in the profits and losses. Thus, you are allocated $25 and your partner is allocated $25. The government will tax your $25 profit when you pay your personal income taxes. Let's assume your tax rate is 20%. Thus, you pay $5 in taxes ($25 * 20%) and keep the remaining $20 ($25 − $5). The government will tax your partner's $25 profit when he or she pays his or her personal income taxes. Let's assume your partner's tax rate is 40%. Your partner will pay $10 taxes ($25 * 40%) on his or her $25 profit, leaving him or her $15 ($25 − $10).

However general partnerships also have the challenge of unlimited liability. The law holds all general partners personally liable for the debts of the partnership. In addition, the law states that all general partners are responsible for all debts of the partnership. The partners are said to have "**joint and several liability**" for the debts. This joint and several liability adds complexity to becoming a partner. Let's look at Ace Lawn Care. Your business caused $10,000 in damage to your customer's property. Who owes the $10,000? You and your partner both owe the $10,000. Even though your partnership agreement states you share the profits and losses equally, you are both responsible for the debt. Let's assume your business has no assets. Your customer approaches you and your partner to pay the debt from your personal funds. Your partner indicates he or she has no personal funds to pay any or all of the debt. Guess what? You owe the $10,000. Why? The answer is you and your partner are jointly liable.

So, general partnerships are easy to create and end, which is good. General partnerships have single taxation, which is also good. General partners, however, have unlimited liability. In addition, general partners are jointly liable. Liability issues can create problems.

To help with the challenge of unlimited joint liability, the law recognizes a special type of partnership called a **Limited Liability Partnership (LLP)**. A limited liability partnership is just like a general partnership with the exception that some of the partners can be designated as **limited partners**. A limited partner puts money into the partnership and receives an agreed-upon share of the profits or losses. However a limited partner cannot actively manage the partnership. Given her or his limited involvement, the most a limited partner can lose is the amount she or he put into the business. Thus, a limited partner's liability is limited to her or his investment. Under the law, however, every limited liability partnership must have at least one general partner, and that general partner has unlimited liability and can actively manage the business.

The law has evolved in other ways regarding partnerships. Another challenge with general partnerships is most are not publicly traded. To address this, the law recognizes a **Master Limited Partnership (MLP)**. A master limited partnership is a limited partnership that can be traded in a public market.

CORPORATIONS

Any time you see the letters **Corp.** or **Inc.** behind or in the name of a company, you are looking at a **corporation**. The business has been incorporated. A group of owners has created a new entity or body in the sight of the law. Corporations are different from sole proprietorships and partnerships because they are viewed by the law as an entity that is different from its owners. This is an important distinction. When a corporation is formed in the US, it must be chartered by a state government. This **corporate charter** includes the **Articles of Incorporation**. That charter makes the corporation a separate legal entity with the ability to enter into contracts, own property, incur liabilities, and earn net income or loss in and of itself. When owners put their money in a corporation, they do so by buying shares of **stock**. Each share of stock represents part ownership in the business. The owners of the stock are called **stockholders** or **shareholders**. So what does this mean?

Owners own the corporation. However they are independent of the corporation. So how is the corporation governed? As noted in Chapter 03, owners (stockholders) meet, vote, and elect a Board of Directors. The stockholders authorize the members of the Board of Directors to act as their agents. An **agent** is a person or organization that acts for the benefit of another person, called the **principal**. The stockholders are the principals and the agents are the Board of Directors. The Board of Directors selects a chairperson, who is the head of the board, and then it elects the senior or **corporate officers** of the corporation, including the President, Vice Presidents, Treasurer, and Secretary of the corporation. The senior officers of the corporation then hire the remaining management and employees of the corporation.

Now let's look at corporations and liability. The law views the corporation and its owners as separate entities. As such, owners have **limited liability**. The most an owner can lose is the amount she or he pays for his or her stock. This is good. Let's go back to Ace Lawn Care. You decide to incorporate your business in your home state. Your business is called Ace Lawn Care, Inc. You are the only owner or stockholder of the business. You put $1,000 in your business and receive stock. Your customer contracts for services with Ace Lawn Care, Inc. When your business causes $10,000 in damages, your customer can demand Ace Lawn Care, Inc. to pay for the damages. However if Ace Lawn Care, Inc. only has $1,000 in assets, that is all your customer can receive. The customer cannot demand you, the stockholder, to pay the remaining $9,000 from your personal funds. You and Ace Lawn Care, Inc. are legally separate entities. Unless you have done something personally wrong, the most you can lose is the $1,000 you put into the business.

Now what about taxes? As a legal entity, a business is taxed on its taxable income. But guess what? When the business decides to distribute this income to its owners, it pays a **dividend**, which is taxed again. The personal tax return of the business owner (stockholder) must reflect the dividend as income. The corporation pays taxes on the income and the owner pays taxes when the income is distributed as a dividend. This is called "**double taxation**." This is not good, and it particularly hurts small businesses. Let's look at Ace Lawn Care, Inc. Your business makes taxable income of $50. Assuming a 40% corporate tax rate, Ace Lawn Care, Inc. must pay $20 in taxes ($50 * 40%). This leaves the corporation with $30 in net income after taxes ($50 – $20). As the owner of Ace Lawn Care, Inc., you decide you want to take the $30 out of the business and use it to meet personal needs. You declare a $30 dividend. Ace Lawn Care, Inc. pays you, the stockholder, $30. When you file your personal tax return, you must show this $30 dividend as income. Assuming your tax rate is 20%, you owe $6 in taxes ($30 * 20%). You get to keep only $24 ($30 – $6). From the $50 taxable income, Ace Lawn Care, Inc paid $20 in taxes and you paid $6 in taxes, leaving you the owner only $24.

So a corporation has limited liability—this is good for owners. A corporation has double taxation and is harder to start and end—this

Stock certificates represent shares of corporation stock

is bad for owners. These challenges are especially hard on small businesses. To help small business, the government has two alternatives, an S Corporation and a Limited Liability Corporation.

Most corporations are conventional corporations, or **C Corporations**. To help small businesses, the law recognizes a special type of corporation that permits a small business to incorporate so it can limit liability but be taxed as a partnership. These special corporations are called Sub Chapter S Corporations, or **S Corporations**. To be an S Corporation a business must meet the following requirements:

· Have no more than 100 stockholders

· All stockholders must be individuals or estates

· All stockholders must be permanent residents of the United Sates

· There can be only one type or class of stockholders. (Note: A company can have different classes of stockholders. This will be discussed in Chapter 19.)

· Must have at least 75% of its income from "active" activities such as selling goods and services. (Income from rents, royalties, interest, and related activities are not active income. Such activities are called "passive" income.)

The law recognizes a corporation that is called a **Limited Liability Corporation (LLC)**. A limited liability corporation has some advantages and disadvantages. It has limited liability, it can elect to be taxed as a partnership or corporation, and the restrictive ownership rules of an S Corporation (S Corp.) do not apply. Ownership in a limited liability corporation, however, cannot be sold or transferred. A limited liability corporation must have a limited life, and it cannot give employees some of the incentives that other corporations can pay (e.g., the option to buy ownership). So where do you see LLCs? Next time you visit a lawyer or doctor, look at the name of his or her business. Professionals often do business as an LLC.

CHOOSING THE RIGHT FORM OF BUSINESS

Choosing the right form is important, but complex. The choice has many dimensions, but starts in liability and tax issues. See Exhibit 6.1. Chapter 07 explores the liability issue in more depth. But what about the tax issue?

EXHIBIT 6.1: The Forms of Business

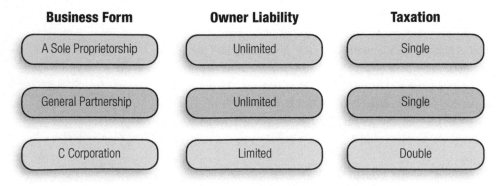

Business Form	Owner Liability	Taxation
A Sole Proprietorship	Unlimited	Single
General Partnership	Unlimited	Single
C Corporation	Limited	Double

TAXES AND BUSINESS

Taxes are a cost of doing business; they are the means by which governments raise funds and motivate behavior. In the US, taxes are assessed by various levels of government, including the federal government, state governments, and local governments.

A government needs money to pay for the goods and services it delivers. Individuals and businesses pay taxes to governments to pay for the police, firefighters, and other activities of governments.

Governments may also use taxes to motivate behavior. An example of how a government may want to motivate certain behavior is in encouraging business to invest in conservation and the environment. To do so a government may lower a business's tax if the business invests in equipment that uses wind or solar energy.

Tax laws are different in different places (e.g., countries, states, cities) because needs and values are different in different places. Tax laws also change as the needs and desires of societies change.

Taxes impact business value by affecting the amount and timing of the after-tax net income owners receive. However, changing tax policy also creates uncertainty and risk for a business. So understanding taxes is important.

Taxes come in many different forms. Three of the most common forms of taxes are: income taxes, excise or sales taxes, and property taxes.

TAXABLE EVENTS AND TAX RATES

The amount of tax a business pays is a function of the amount of the taxable event and the tax rate. The most common taxable events are earning income, transacting a sale, or holding property that has value. The taxable event is first measured. Then, in accordance with law, a tax rate, which can be a percentage or a specified amount, is assessed. Last, the tax due is computed by multiplying the amount of the taxable event times the tax rate. See Equation 6.1.

EQUATION 6.1: Tax Due

$$\text{Taxable Event} \ * \ \text{Tax Rate} = \text{Tax Due}$$

Let's look at three examples. First are income taxes where the taxable event is earning income. Your business earns taxable income, net income before taxes, of $100,000. The laws state you should pay 20% of your pre-tax net income. You would pay $20,000 to the government in taxes ($100,000 * 20%). Second are sales taxes, where the taxable event is a sale. You buy something for $20,000. The law states you should pay a sales tax of 5% of the sales amount. You would pay $1,000 to the government in taxes ($20,000 * 5%). Third are property taxes, where the taxable event is holding property. You own real estate valued at $1,000,000. The law states you should pay a property tax of 1% of the value of the property. You would pay the government $10,000 in property taxes ($1,000,000 * 1%).

INCOME TAXES

Income taxes are taxes a government assesses on a business's net income before taxes, or taxable income. Different governments have different rules for recognizing taxable income. Income taxes can be assessed as 1) a constant or flat rate or 2) a graduated rate. A flat tax is where the tax rate does not vary. A **graduated tax** rate is where the tax rate varies depending on the level of income. If the rate goes up as the level of income goes up, the tax is said to be a "**progressive tax.**" In the US, we currently have a progressive graduated tax rate structure for income taxes paid to the federal government. Exhibit 6.2 show these rates.

EXHIBIT 6.2: 2015 US Federal Income Tax Rates for Business

Taxable Income Over	But Not Over	Tax is	Of the Amount Over
$ 0.00	$ 50,000.00	$ 0 +15%	$ 0.00
$ 50,000.00	$ 75,000.00	$ 7,500 + 25%	$ 50,000.00
$ 75,000.00	$ 100,000.00	$ 13,750 + 34%	$ 75,000.00
$ 100,000.00	$ 335,000.00	$ 22,250 + 39%	$ 100,000.00
$ 335,000.00	$ 10,000,000.00	$ 113,900 + 34%	$ 335,000.00
$ 10,000,000.00	$ 15,000,000.00	$ 3,400,000 + 35%	$ 10,000,000.00
$ 15,000,000.00	$ 18,333,333.00	$ 5,150,000 + 38%	$ 15,000,000.00
$ 18,333,333.00	and over	35%	$ 0.00

Let's look at an example using the tax rates in Exhibit 6.2. You have sales less costs, resulting in a taxable income of $15,000,000. How much tax would you owe the US government? You'd owe 15% on the first $50,000, or $7,500 ($50,000 * 15%). You'd then owe 25% of the amount between $50,000 and $75,000, or $6,250 ($25,000 * 25%). Next you'd owe 34% of the amount between $75,000 and $100,000, or $8,500 ($25,000 * 34%). Next you'd owe 39% of the amount between $100,000 and $335,000, or $91,650 ($235,000 * 35%). Next, you would owe 34% of the amount between $335,000 and $10,000,000, or $3,286,100 ($9,665,000 * 34%). Last, you would owe 35% of the amount between $10,000,000 and $15,000,000, or $1,750,000 ($5,000,000 * .35). The total amount of US taxes you would owe on your $15,000,000 is $5,150,000 ($7,500 + $6,250 + $8,500 + $91,650 + $3,286,100 + $1,750,000).

Some state and local governments in the US use a flat income tax rate, some use a graduated income tax rate, and some have no income taxes, choosing to raise revenue with excise (sales) and property taxes. Exhibit 6.3 shows the maximum tax rate selected states assess on business income.

When income is taxed using a graduated rate, people often talk about the average tax rate and the marginal tax rate. The **average tax rate** is the total tax divided by the total taxable income. See Equation 6.2.

EQUATION 6.2: Average Tax Rate

Total Taxes / Total Taxable Income = Average Tax Rate

In the case of our example, the average tax rate is 33.33% ($5,150,000/$15,000,000). The **marginal tax rate** is the tax rate the business will pay on the next dollar of taxable income. In the case of our example, the marginal tax rate would be the tax rate applied to the taxable income earned between $15,000,000 and $15,000,001. Per Exhibit 6.2, the extra dollar of taxable income would be taxed at a 38% tax rate; the business would pay the government $.38 and keep $.62. Thus, the marginal tax rate is 38%.

EXHIBIT 6.3: 2015 US State Income Tax Rates of Selected States

STATE	(percent)	STATE	(percent)	STATE	(percent)
ALABAMA	6.50	LOUISIANA	8.00	OHIO	N/A
ALASKA	9.40	MAINE	8.93	OKLAHOMA	6.00
ARIZONA	6.00	MARYLAND	8.25	OREGON	7.60
ARKANSAS	6.50	MASSACHUSETTS	8.00	PENNSYLVANIA	9.99
CALIFORNIA	8.84	MICHIGAN	6.00	RHODE ISLAND	7.00
COLORADO	4.63	MINNESOTA	9.80	SOUTH CAROLINA	5.00
CONNECTICUT	7.50	MISSISSIPPI	5.00	SOUTH DAKOTA	N/A
DELAWARE	8.70	MISSOURI	6.25	TENNESSEE	6.50
FLORIDA	5.50	MONTANA	6.75	TEXAS	N/A
GEORGIA	6.00	NEBRASKA	7.81	UTAH	5.00
HAWAII	6.40	NEVADA	N/A	VERMONT	8.50
IDAHO	7.40	NEW HAMPSHIRE	8.50	VIRGINIA	6.00
ILLINOIS	7.75	NEW JERSEY	9.00	WASHINGTON	N/A
INDIANA	7.00	NEW MEXICO	6.90	WEST VIRGINIA	6.50
IOWA	12.00	NEW YORK	7.10	WISCONSIN	7.90
KANSAS	4.00	NORTH CAROLINA	5.00	WYOMING	N/A
KENTUCKY	6.00	NORTH DAKOTA	4.53	DIST. OF COLUMBIA	9.40

EXCISE TAXES

An **excise tax** is a tax that a government assesses on the manufacture, sale, or consumption of a product. Let's look at an example of an excise tax. In the US, the federal government currently assesses a $.184 excise tax per gallon of gasoline. States also assess varying amounts of excise taxes on gasoline. In 2014, the average state excise tax on gasoline was $.265. That means that a US customer paid excise taxes on gasoline that averaged $.45 per gallon. What do governments do with these funds? These funds are used to build roads and pay for other transportation needs.

There are many forms of excise taxes. A **sales tax** is an excise tax on the purchase, sale, and consumption of a product. When individuals or businesses buy something for consumption, it pays a sales tax. In Chicago, Illinois, you would pay a sales tax of 10.25% if you purchased products

Foundry workers in Louisiana pour molten steel, salvaged from the World Trade Center site, into a mold to form the bow stem of the Amphibious Transport Dock ship USS New York.

such as clothing, furniture, and entertainment. The 10.25% tax is composed of a 6.25% state sales tax, 1.25% Chicago city sales tax, 1.75% Cook County sales tax, and 1.00% regional transportation sales tax. If you purchased a meal at a restaurant in Chicago, you'd pay an additional 2.25% sales tax assessed on restaurant sales, bringing the total tax to 12.50%. (Soft drinks sold via grocery stores are taxed at an even higher rate.) In contrast, if you bought similar items in Baton Rouge, Louisiana, you would pay a sales tax of 9%. The 9% tax is composed of a 4% state tax and 5% local tax. There is no special tax on restaurant sales in Baton Rouge.

Another form of excise tax is called a **value-added tax (VAT)**. A value-added tax is an imbedded tax ultimately paid by the consumer. However the tax is not assessed at the point of consumption. The tax is assessed at each stage of converting the inputs into outputs as a product moves through its value chain. As

TAXING THE INTERNET

You go to the toy store to buy a birthday gift for your best friend's child. You find the perfect toy at a local store, but it's expensive. You think about alternatives. You cannot find a better toy, so you start looking for alternative places to buy the toy. You think about surfing the Internet, looking for toy vendors that will sell you the same toy at a lower price. You find a vendor in another state that will sell you the toy at a slightly lower price. The vendor will also ship you the toy at no additional costs. You begin to think how much you can afford to pay for the toy. All of a sudden you realize that taxes will play a part of your decision. Your decision is a function of the total cost of the toy, including taxes. You realize that Internet sales have no or low sales taxes.

First, is this fair? Should you pay sales tax on this Internet purchase? You'd pay a sales tax if you bought the toy from the local store. Second, if you are going to pay a sales tax for your Internet purchase, where should you pay the tax? Should the sale be taxed in your state or the vendor's state? Where did the sale occur? These questions are being asked by governments.

The world of business is constantly changing. Governments must constantly change their approaches to taxation. States are beginning to address the Internet question and tax Internet transactions. But there are many challenges with such taxes. Business is complex, which means taxes are complex.

this value is added, a government assesses a tax based on the valued added. Thus, as the product progresses through the value chain, its costs are increased by the additional taxes. The person or organization that purchases and consumes the product must ultimately pay the tax. An example is manufacturing an automobile. Iron ore is mined. Value is created and a tax assessed. Iron ore is transformed into steel. Value is added and a tax is assessed. Steel is used to create an automobile. Value is added and more tax is assessed. You buy the automobile. The taxes have added costs to the automobile that the seller must recover. Thus, the price you pay for the automobile is higher because of the imbedded value-added taxes. The US does not have a value-added tax. However, many countries do (e.g., Canada, Mexico, and many European countries).

PROPERTY TAXES

Property taxes are periodic taxes assessed by governments on the value of property. Governments can tax the value of buildings, equipment, and intellectual property (e.g., patents). Although the US federal government does not use property taxes to raise funds, many state and local governments do.

OTHER TYPES OF TAXES

Governments can assess other taxes in addition to income taxes, sales taxes, and property taxes. Such taxes include licenses, fees, and tariffs for selected items or transactions. Examples include a license to do business in a specific location; a fee to transport products through a location; a tariff, where one country taxes products imported from another country; and employment taxes such as unemployment tax or social security tax. Such taxes are explored in the different chapters of this text.

TAX PLANNING AND STRATEGY

So taxes have a big impact on business operations and business value. But how do businesses deal with taxes?

First, a business must understand the tax law and always comply. Taxes are complex, but ignorance is not a legal defense for not complying with tax law. Paying multiple types of taxes in multiple locations is challenging. For that reason many businesses have employees who deal strictly with taxes. Staffers in compliance departments fill out tax returns and pay taxes. If a business does not have the tax expertise, it often hires an accounting, law, or consulting firm to help with tax issues.

Second, taxes impact the value of a business. Taxes impact the quantity of net income, after tax, available to distribute to owners. Taxes also affect the timing of the net income and risk associated with net income. Practically all management decisions have tax implications. A business needs tax professionals to help plan, execute, and review. Businesses need to conduct **tax planning and strategy**. Such strategy is designed to 1) ensure the business complies with the law and 2) minimize or defer the payment of taxes.

BUSINESS SENSE

TAXING MYTHS

Taxes are often misunderstood. Two major myths about taxes relate to 1) tax planning and 2) losing money.

Myth number one is about is tax planning. Often people think that tax planning or strategy is about eliminating or reducing taxes. Sometimes this is feasible under the tax law. Often it is not. What is more feasible is determining the time that sales and costs are recognized. It is also possible to select the place the sale or costs are recognized. To do so, businesses must carefully plan each transaction.

So how do such decisions help the value of the business? First is time—remember that time impacts value. If a business must pay taxes, it would prefer to pay the taxes later than sooner. Businesses attempt to defer the payments of taxes by legally deferring the recognition of taxable income. To do so, however, the transactions must be planned carefully. Second is location. Different places have different taxes. By carefully planning transactions, businesses can recognize the taxable income in a place with the lowest taxes.

Myth number two is about losses. Often people will say a business lost money for tax purposes. Sometimes businesses can offset income in one period with losses in another period. However in the long term, businesses do not want to consistently lose money. Let's look at the logic. Let's assume your business's tax rate is 50%. Do you want to lose $100 to save $50 in taxes? Doesn't make sense, does it?

LEARNING OBJECTIVE 3.
. . . .

SPECIAL OPPORTUNITIES IN BUSINESS FORMATION

Businesses have opportunities. Businesses have challenges. Owners and managers must decide, using different strategies and business forms, how to respond to such opportunities and challenges. These strategies and forms include:

Mergers and Acquisitions
Joint Ventures
Franchising
Licensing
Cooperatives

MERGERS AND ACQUISITIONS

Often businesses desire to own or influence other businesses. They may acquire a business or merge with another business. An **acquisition** is when a company buys the assets of another company. The buying company may or may not assume all or part of the debts of the other company. A **merger** is when a company buys another company. When a company is bought, the owner buys all the assets and assumes all the debts of the purchased company. All that changes is who owns the purchased company.

A company can acquire or merge with another company by paying cash, debt, or stock. When a company buys another company with cash, it gets this cash from its own cash, borrowing the cash with debt, or receiving the cash from selling its stock. In 2008, when Google bought the Swedish music and video company Global IP Solutions, Google had plenty of cash and used its own cash to purchase the stock of Global IP Solutions. Google did not need to borrow additional funds or sell additional stock.

When a company buys another company using high levels of debt, it is sometimes referred to as a **leveraged buyout (LBO)**. The purchasing company borrows the cash to pay for the stock of the purchased company. By borrowing money, it is using financial leverage. In 2005 a group of private investors bought Toys "Я" Us using the LBO strategy. The investors borrowed billions of dollars and used the cash to buy Toys "Я" Us's stock.

Often a company will acquire the stock of another company using its own stock as payment, which is called a "**stock swap.**" The purchasing company uses its own stock to pay for the stock of the purchased company. In 2004 the banking firm of JPMorgan Chase purchased the banking firm of Bank One Corp. JPMorgan Chase gave each stockholder of Bank One Corp. 1.32 shares of JPMorgan Chase stock in exchange for each share of Bank One Corp. This was a stock swap. (Chapter Ten explores the use of debt, owner's funds, and financial leverage.)

Google China headquarters in the Tsinghua Science Park, Beijing.

After a company is purchased, it may be dissolved into the purchasing company. JPMorgan Chase combined the operations of Bank One Corp. into its own operations. It then dissolved Bank One Corp. However, the purchased company may remain a separate entity. If it remains a separate entity, it is called a **subsidiary** of the company that owns it. The company that owns it is called the **parent company**. When Wells Fargo Bank purchased Wachovia Bank in 2009, Wells Fargo did not immediately dissolve Wachovia Bank. Wells Fargo was the parent company and Wachovia was the subsidiary.

Sometimes companies buy all (100%) of another company. If the company buys all of another company, the purchased company is said to be a "**wholly owned**" subsidiary and **consolidated** with the parent. When a company is consolidated, it is combined with the parent company and the group of entities is viewed as a single company.

Sometimes companies buy part of another company (less than 100%). If the purchasing company does not buy all of the purchased company, the purchased company may or may not be considered to be a part of the purchased company. The purchased company may or may not be consolidated into the parent. So when is it consolidated? It depends. If the purchasing company owns enough of the purchased company to control the purchased company, the purchased company is consolidated into the purchasing company. Control usually means owning the majority of the stock (e.g., 51% of the ownership). The purchasing company is called the **majority stockholder** and owns a **majority interest**. The part of the company not owned by the majority shareholder is called the **minority interest** or **minority stockholder**. If the purchasing company does not control the purchased company, the purchased company is viewed as a separate and independent entity. The company is not consolidated into the purchasing company. The purchasing company is the minority stockholder.

So why would a company acquire or merge with another company? Hopefully such moves are designed to create value. But how is value created?

There are three basic reasons for a business to buy another business. See Exhibit 6.4. These three reasons are:

Horizontal integration

Vertical integration

Conglomeration

Horizontal Integration

Horizontal integration occurs when a business buys another business that is a competitor or similar company. A manufacturer of beer buys another manufacturer of beer. Did you know that InBev, the European company that manufactures Beck's and Bass beers, bought and owns Anheuser-Busch, the US company that manufactures Budweiser and Michelob? A retail department store buys another retail department store chain. Did you know that Sears bought and owns Kmart? These are examples of

EXHIBIT 6.4: Why Businesses Buy Each Other

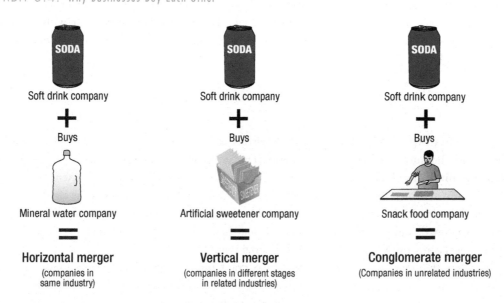

Soft drink company	Soft drink company	Soft drink company
+	**+**	**+**
Buys	Buys	Buys
Mineral water company	Artificial sweetener company	Snack food company
=	**=**	**=**
Horizontal merger	**Vertical merger**	**Conglomerate merger**
(companies in same industry)	(companies in different stages in related industries)	(Companies in unrelated industries)

horizontal integration. Horizontal integration is designed to create value by increasing sales, reducing costs, and reducing risk from competition.

Vertical Integration

Vertical integration occurs when a business buys another business that is a part of the business's value chain. A soft drink manufacturer buys a restaurant chain to create an outlet for the soft drink. Did you know that Pepsi once owned Taco Bell? A manufacturer of automobiles buys a supplier of auto parts. Did you know that General Motors once owned Delphi, a supplier of auto parts? A retail department store buys a supplier of clothing. Did you know that Sears owns Lands' End? These are examples of vertical integration. Vertical integration is designed to create value by increasing sales, reducing costs, and lowering risk caused by buyers and suppliers.

Conglomerate

A **conglomerate** is a combination of unrelated businesses. An example of a conglomerate is Tyco International. Tyco once owned businesses that manufactured industrial tape, medical supplies, and security systems. Firms like Tyco exist because managers seek to diversify. **Diversification** occurs when unrelated businesses come together in such a way that the overall risk of the company is reduced. It's like the old saying, "Don't put all your eggs in one basket." The hope is that when one part of the business is having challenges, the other parts are doing well enough to sustain it. The business's overall risk is reduced and value created. (Chapter Eleven explores diversification and risk.)

JOINT VENTURES

Joint ventures (JV) are when two or more businesses enter into a legal relationship similar to a partnership. The difference between joint ventures and partnerships is that JVs are created for a single enterprise or transaction. When that enterprise or transaction is complete, the JV is dissolved. Partnerships are created as continuing businesses. An example of a JV is when a real estate company and a construction company agree to buy a piece of land and build a shopping center, with the plan to sell the shopping center when it's completed. When the shopping center is finished and sold, the joint venture is dissolved.

LICENSING

Businesses often own **intellectual property**. Such property is an "**intangible asset**" of the business and is an asset because it is valuable. (Chapter Seventeen explores intangible assets.) It helps create an operating profit. Examples of intellectual property are copyrights, trademarks, and patents.

A company may own the right to publish a book, or **copyright**. Cognella owns the rights to publish this book. A business may own a **trademark**. McDonald's owns the trademark of its golden arches. A company may own a unique process or product. It may hold a **patent** on such a process or product. The pharmaceutical company Merck owns patents of certain drugs.

A company that owns intellectual property may grant another company the right to use that property. When it does, the businesses enter into a legal agreement called a **license**. **Licensing** is granting, typically for a fee, the right to use the intellectual property. The business that owns the intellectual

MERGERS AND ACQUISITIONS

Time Warner Center

When two companies are combined, there are opportunities and challenges. It's like a marriage between two people. Some marriages work out, some do not. So what determines a good marriage and a marriage that fails in business? There are many reasons, but two are often cited. First, businesses that come together often do not understand each other's business model and strategy. Second, businesses that come together often do not understand each other's culture.

First is the challenge of understanding different business models and strategies. When the German firm Daimler bought the US firm Chrysler, Daimler viewed it as a horizontal merger: both companies manufactured automobiles and Daimler thought both companies had the same business model and strategy. Daimler was creating a global company and was using the acquisition of Chrysler to enter new markets. The challenge was Daimler and Chrysler did not have the same business model. (Refer back to Chapter 02 for the definition of a business model.) Daimler did not appreciate that customers of Daimler and Chrysler were different. Daimler was a premier and dominant brand in Germany; Chrysler was struggling against General Motors and Ford for brand identity and customers in the United States. Daimler was competing on quality while Chrysler had to compete on price. So what happened? Daimler, after buying Chrysler to increase its value, realized the Chrysler acquisition was destroying its value; it sold Chrysler. The marriage of Daimler and Chrysler failed.

Second is culture. Different businesses have different ways of doing business. As noted in Chapter 03, businesses have different business models and strategies. Thus, businesses need to be organized differently. Each business has a different culture or different ways of operating. Some businesses need to be centralized and some decentralized. Some businesses need to inspire creativity and some need to require consistency. Each business has a culture and that culture is critical to its success. To have a successful merger or acquisition, businesses must understand and appreciate each other's culture. When businesses do not understand and appreciate each other's culture, problems occur.

An example is the AOL-Time Warner merger. America Online (AOL) and Time Warner agreed to merge because they felt this vertical merger would create value. Time Warner had a large inventory of creative materials (movies, books, etc.) and AOL was a leader in the Internet, the new and growing way consumers were receiving information, entertainment, etc. This seemingly perfect marriage of AOL and Time Warner failed because the two businesses did not understand and appreciate their different cultures: running a company that creates new material and running a company that consistently distributes information is different. Time Warner was an older, more mature firm. AOL was a newer business that was growing very fast. Management could not successfully operate a combined company because the distinct cultures didn't blend.

property and grants or sells the license is called the **licensor**. The business that buys the license is called the **licensee**. An example of licensing is when your college or university licenses computer software for a specific use and period.

FRANCHISING

Sometimes businesses develop a product that it needs help in selling or distributing. McDonald's is a good example. Ray Kroc saw something special years ago when he came across a small hamburger chain. He bought the chain, further developed the systems and products, and then wanted to unleash his products and systems on the world. He dreamed of thousands of restaurants around the world selling hamburgers, French fries, and sodas in clean and efficient restaurants. He proved his concept with a few restaurants but did not have the financial and human capital needed to build and operate all the restaurants he envisioned. So he used franchising to make his dream come true.

Franchising is where a business sells the right to use its name, processes, and products to another business. The **franchisor** is the business that owns and sells the rights to use its name, processes, and products. Those rights are called a **franchise**. The **franchisee** is the business that buys the rights to use the franchisor's name, processes, and products. The franchisee often pays an initial fee to the franchisor and then a percentage of sales over time. The agreement between the franchisor and franchisee is called the **franchise agreement**. The franchise agreement specifies rights and responsibilities of the franchisor and franchisee and what will happen if the franchisor or franchisee fails to meet his or her commitments.

COOPERATIVES

Cooperatives are everywhere. Examples of cooperatives can be seen in health care, financial services (credit unions), and housing. So what are cooperatives? Why do they exist?

Sometimes individuals and businesses have trouble conducting business because they are small and uncompetitive. Let's look at some examples. Small farms have difficulty because they purchase seeds, fertilizer, and other essential things in smaller quantities than large farming companies. So what do these small farmers do? They often form a cooperative. Another example is where rural businesses need electricity. Large utility companies must charge high rates to such customers because it is expensive to deliver electricity to distant places in small quantities. So what do these rural, small businesses do? They often form a cooperative.

A **cooperative** is a business, formed either as a partnership or corporation, for the benefit of its customers. In fact, the customers of a cooperative are often its owners. By bonding together, the owners create a cooperative that is big enough to buy products at a lower price, to get better service, and lower risk.

CHAPTER SUMMARY

So choosing a business form is complex and challenging. However it is very important. The choice of business form can affect its ability to create value: the amount and timing of the operating profit, the cost of financing, and the risk of the business. Choosing the right form for a business is not easy but it does matter. The ramifications for choosing the wrong form of business are serious and can hurt value.

In this chapter we've explored the forms and taxation of business. Specifically you should be able to:

1. Appreciate the legal forms of business (Learning Objective 1): There are three basic legal forms of businesses: sole proprietorship, partnership, and corporation. The primary differences between the three forms are owner liability and taxes.
2. Appreciate the different types of taxes and how taxes affect business decisions (Learning Objective 2): Taxes are a cost of doing business. There are many types of taxes. Businesses need to understand, comply with, and plan for taxes.
3. Appreciate the special opportunities in business formation (Learning Objective 3): Businesses face many opportunities and challenges in their drive to create value. Mergers, acquisitions, joint ventures, licensing, franchising, and cooperatives are means of addressing some of these opportunities and challenges.

In this chapter we examined different forms of businesses. Special attention was paid to taxes. In doing so, we began to explore the legal aspects of business. Chapter 07 extends this challenge and looks at the legal environment in "How Business Works."

KEYWORDS

acquisition 134

agent 127

Articles of Incorporation 127

average tax rate 130

C Corporations 128

conglomerate 137

consolidated 134

cooperative 138

copyright 136

Corp. 126

corporate charter 127

corporate officers 127

corporation 126

diversification 136

dividend 127

double taxation 127

excise tax 131

flat tax 129

franchise 138

franchise agreement 138

franchisee 138

franchising 138

franchisor 138

general partner 125

general partnerships 125

graduated tax 129

horizontal integration 135

Inc. 126

income taxes 129

intangible asset 136

intellectual property 136

joint and several liability 126

joint ventures (JV) 136

leveraged buyout (LBO) 134

liability 124

license 136

licensee 138

licensing 136

licensor 138

limited liability 127

Limited Liability Corporation (LLC) 128

Limited Liability Partnership (LLP) 126

limited partners 126

majority interest 135

majority stockholder 135

marginal tax rate 130

Master Limited Partnership (MLP) 126

merger 134

minority interest 135

minority stockholder 135

parent company 134

partnership agreement 125

patent 136

principal 127

private market 125

progressive tax 130

property taxes 132

public market 125

sales tax 131

S Corporations 128

shareholders 127

single taxation 125

sole proprietorship 125

stock 127

stockholders 127

stock swap 134

subsidiary 134

taxable income 124

taxes 124

tax planning and strategy 133

trademark 136

unlimited liability 125

value-added tax (VAT) 131

vertical integration 136

wholly owned 134

SHORT-ANSWER QUESTIONS

1. Define the pros and cons of forming a business as a:
   a. Sole proprietorship,
   b. General partnership, or
   c. Corporation.

2. What is the difference between the following forms of taxes:
   a. Graduated income tax
   b. Flat income tax
   c. Excise tax
   d. Sales tax
   e. Value-added tax
   f. Property tax

3. Explain the difference between a business's average and marginal tax rates.

4. Define the following terms:
   a. Sole proprietorship
   b. Unlimited liability
   c. Single taxation
   d. General partnership
   e. General partner
   f. Joint and several liability
   g. Limited liability partnership (LLP)
   h. Limited partner
   i. Master limited partnership (MLP)
   j. Corporation
   k. Corporate charter
   l. Articles of incorporation
   m. Stock
   n. Stockholder or shareholder
   o. Agent
   p. Principal
   q. Limited liability
   r. Dividend
   s. Double taxation
   t. C Corp.
   u. S Corp.
   v. Limited liability corporation (LLC)
   w. Income tax
   x. Taxable income
   y. Flat tax
   z. Graduated tax
   aa. Progressive tax
   ab. Average tax rate
   ac. Marginal tax rate
   ad. Excise tax
   ae. Sales tax
   af. Value-added tax (VAT)
   ag. Acquisition
   ah. Merger
   ai. Stock swap
   aj. Leveraged buyout (LBO)
   ak. Subsidiary
   al. Parent company
   am. Wholly owned
   an. Consolidated
   ao. Majority interest or majority stockholder
   ap. Minority interest or minority stockholder
   aq. Vertical integration
   ar. Horizontal integration
   as. Conglomerate
   at. Diversification
   au. Joint venture (JV)
   av. Intellectual property
   aw. Intangible asset
   ax. Copyright
   ay. Trademark
   az. Patent
   ba. License
   bb. Licensor
   bc. Licensee
   bd. Franchising
   be. Franchisor
   bf. Franchisee
   bg. Franchise agreement
   bh. Cooperative

5. What is the difference between a C Corporation, an S Corporation, and a LLC?

CRITICAL-THINKING QUESTIONS

1. What are the benefits and challenges of a:
    a. Floating exchange rate system,
    b. Fixed exchange rate system,
    c. Managed floating exchange rate system?

2. What is a country's balance of payments? What are the parts of a country's balance of payments? What makes up each part of a country's balance of payments?

3. What determines a country's foreign exchange rate?

4. What are the benefits and costs of having an appreciating exchange rate and a depreciating exchange rate?

EXPLORING REAL BUSINESS

Go to the websites of Google, Target, Hyundai, and Proctor and Gamble. The websites are

Google:	http://investor.google.com
Target:	http://www.target.com
Hyundai:	http://worldwide.hyundai.com/company-overview
Procter & Gamble:	http://www.pg.com

07

CHAPTER

THE LEGAL AND ETHICAL NATURE OF BUSINESS

LEARNING OBJECTIVES

After reading Chapter 07, you should be able to meet the following learning objectives:

1. Appreciate the US legal system
2. Appreciate the laws that affect business
3. Appreciate the nature and challenges of business ethics and social responsibility

Introduction: Let's Talk About Business, the Law, and Ethics

You want to operate a business. Society has a lot to say about what you can and should do. Think about it. What is the law? Where does the law come from? How is the law administered? What are business ethics and social responsibility?

The law influences almost everything that any business does. The law affects hiring protocol, tax strategies, compliance with the environmental laws, where the business is located, how contracts are written, and even the signs that have to be placed in the employee break room. Many people only think of calling a lawyer when they have committed a criminal act or are being sued. However, businesses must be proactive and have good legal counsel in order to comply with all state, local, and federal laws.

After reading this chapter you should be able to answer the above questions. You should appreciate the US legal system and the types of laws that affect business. You should also appreciate how business should operate ethically and be socially responsible.

WHY THE LAW, ETHICS, AND SOCIAL RESPONSIBILITY MATTER TO BUSINESS

Remember from Chapter 01 that a business is a legal organization. For society to recognize a business as legal, society must believe that the business adds value to society. As such, society creates rules, or laws, which define what it requires of the business to be an accepted and valuable part of society. If a business fails to abide by these rules, society will not permit the business to exist and operate. Not understanding the law can be costly and destroy value for businesses. But should businesses' decisions only be governed by the law? Should corporate governance include a sense of ethics and social responsibility? These are challenging issues and questions. These issues matter.

LEARNING OBJECTIVE 1

THE LAW AND BUSINESS

A crowded prison.

In society, people and organizations must exist and relate to one another. To do so, there must be agreed-upon principles that govern these actions, because without them, chaos would reign. Society needs rules to exist, function, and prosper. Likewise society needs to establish penalties for not abiding by such rules: people and organizations must be accountable for their actions.

From the onset we need to recognize four realities. First, societies are complex. Thus, the rules or laws that govern societies must be complex. Laws reflect values and value systems that are never simple in theory or application.

Second, different societies have different values. As such, laws will differ between societies. In the US, different states have different laws. Why? The answer is that people in different states have different values. An example is the death penalty. Some states have the death penalty and other states do not. Likewise the difference in laws can be seen between countries. Different countries view the same events in different ways and thus have different laws.

Third, laws change over time. Why? The answer is that societies and their values change over time. Change is everywhere. An example is Internet crime, which did not exist thirty years ago. Today Internet crime is a large and growing challenge.

Fourth, legal systems are not perfect. Mistakes are made. In the US, a person or business accused of breaking the law is assumed to be innocent until proven guilty. The burden of proof is on the party accusing, not the party accused. Sometimes the guilty are not punished, and sometimes the innocent are punished. Legal systems, including those of the US, do not guarantee the correct action. The best a legal system can hope to provide is a fair and just process (justice).

It is also important to understand that legal matters can be costly for businesses. Businesses either have in-house legal teams or they hire outside legal teams. Both options can be very expensive. Litigation costs businesses millions of dollars each year. Understanding the law and having a good team of legal advisors can help businesses create value. However, the opposite is also true.

So laws and legal systems are complex, different places have different laws, laws are constantly changing, and legal systems are not perfect. But what are laws? What happens in the US legal system?

THE US LEGAL SYSTEM AND THE CREATION OF LAWS

Laws are the rules that a society accepts as its minimum acceptable behavior; they are the rules that society has created to govern what is acceptable and not acceptable behavior. **Business laws** are the rules that society has created to govern what is accepted and not acceptable behavior for businesses. In the US legal system, laws are created in the following three ways:

1. Laws enacted by votes of the people or by representatives elected by the people (**statutory law**).

2. Laws developed by individuals or agencies, empowered by the government (**administrative rules and decisions**).

3. Laws created through the court system by interpreting other laws or settling disputes (**common law**).

EXHIBIT 7.1: Statutory Law, Administrative Rules and Decisions, Common Law

THE TYPES OF LAW: CRIMINAL VERSUS CIVIL

EXHIBIT 7.2:
The Balance Between
Criminal and Civil Law

Laws can be divided into two categories, criminal and civil law. **Criminal law** deals with breaches of duty to society. The penalties for breaking a criminal law are designed to punish the lawbreaker. Examples of criminal offenses are theft, murder, and other offenses clearly stated as criminal by the law. An example of a business crime is when a company deliberately disregards environmental law and pollutes the water. The penalties for breaking a criminal law are imprisonment and/or fines. Fines are paid to the government or parties designated by the court. When there is adequate evidence that a crime has occurred, government lawyers called **prosecutors** charge the accused (**defendant**) with the crime and bring the accused to court. In criminal cases, the prosecutor has the burden of proving the case "beyond a reasonable doubt" (the highest standard of proof).

Civil law deals with breaches of duty between two parties, such as businesses or people. When one party believes the other party has harmed or wronged him or her (physically, monetarily, or emotionally), the harmed party (**plaintiff**) can file a lawsuit against the accused party (**defendant**) in the appropriate court. Both parties use private lawyers. The **lawsuit** will be brought to the court for settlement. The burden of proof varies depending on the type of civil cases, but it is less than the criminal standard of beyond a reasonable doubt. The intent of the law is typically not to punish the defendant, but to compensate the plaintiff for damages incurred; these **compensatory damages** relate to the value lost by the plaintiff. If the court finds that the act is outrageous, however, then **punitive** or **exemplary damages** can also be assessed. Let's look at an example. You buy a product from a company. The company gives you a one-year warranty. After six months the product fails and needs repair. The company refuses to repair the product and honor the warranty. What can you do? You can sue the company for the cost of repairing the product.

Sometimes an action can create both a criminal and civil action. An example is when management is grossly negligent and that negligence causes the death of an employee or customer.

A courtroom in the Federal Building and US Courthouse, Providence, Rhode Island.

RESOLVING DISPUTES IN THE US LEGAL SYSTEM— THE COURTS

What happens if a business believes it has been harmed? What happens if a business is accused of harming a person or another business? Lawyers will assess the evidence and statutory requirements and determine whether a claim can or cannot be proven, or the act occurred too far in the past. The law often prescribes what type of evidence is permissible to prove a claim. The law also requires that certain wrongful acts must be proven within a stated period of time (**statute of limitations**). Second, in a civil case the parties may ask a **mediator** to help negotiate a settlement (**mediation**). Sometimes the parties agree to **arbitration**, where an independent party (**arbitrator**) reviews the facts and makes a decision. Third, if needed, the lawyers will take the disagreement to a court for resolution.

So what is a court? A **court** is a place, designated by the government, where it is decided if an illegal or wrongful act occurred. **Judges** oversee and manage courts. Some judges are elected and some judges are appointed by elected officials. In some courts, judges decide guilt, and in other courts, **juries** decide guilt. Juries are a group of citizens selected to decide guilt or innocence.

EXHIBIT 7.3: Federal and State Court Systems

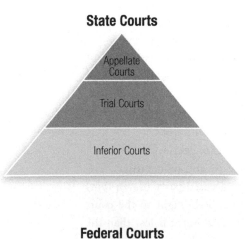

So if a dispute goes to court, what court does it go to? The answer deals with jurisdiction. A court must have the authority to resolve the dispute—it must have **jurisdiction**. Certain courts decide certain cases: some courts deal with certain types of disputes such as patents and copyrights, and some courts deal with claims based on the amount in controversy. For example small claims courts, may only hear cases where the damages are less than $5,000. All courts' jurisdiction is limited by geography.

An example, assume there is a car accident that occurs in Charlottesville, Virginia. Assume both drivers live in Virginia and the amount of the damages is $20,000. The plaintiff can only sue in Virginia—it is the only state that would have jurisdiction (the federal court system would not have jurisdiction). So what are the different courts and how do their jurisdictions differ? Who does what? There are two broad classes of courts, federal courts and state courts. Both federal and state courts deal with criminal and civil actions.

Federal courts deal with 1) disputes regarding federal laws or 2) disputes involving parties in multiple states (**interstate issues**) with an amount in controversy that exceeds $75,000. Within the federal court system there are multiple levels of courts. A dispute is first tried in either a **district court** or a court designated to hear special cases (**special or administrative court**). Examples of special courts are tax courts and bankruptcy courts. District courts use judges and juries to decide isputes. If either party disagrees with the judgment, he or she then can appeal the decision to a designated **court of appeals**. Courts of appeals are the second level of federal courts. The US is divided into 12 circuits, each with a court of appeal. In the US judges make decisions in courts of appeals. If either party disagrees with the judgment of the court of appeals, he or she then can petition the US Supreme Court to hear the case. The **US Supreme Court** is the third and highest level of federal courts. The US Supreme Court is the highest federal court of appeals and can choose whether or not to hear and rule on the case (the US Supreme Court receives approximately 7,000 petitions each year and only hears about 80 of those cases).[1]

State courts deal with all **intrastate** (within state) disputes not covered by federal law. State courts deal with the disputes not handled by federal courts. Each state has its own court system, but typically has three levels. The first level is often referred to as **inferior courts**. Examples of inferior courts are municipal courts, small claims courts, and justice of the peace courts. In such courts a judge hears the facts and makes a decision or judgment. The second level is **trial courts**. Trial courts have jurisdiction over the matters not covered by inferior courts. Trial courts have many names, including circuit courts, superior courts, district courts, and county courts. Trial courts use judges and juries to decide disputes. Third, each state and the District of Columbia have an appeals court. If either party does not agree with the judgment of the inferior or trial courts, he or she can appeal the decision to various **appeals** or **appellate courts**. Judges make decisions in state appeals courts. A **state supreme court** is the highest court of appeals at the state level and operates much like the US Supreme Court in federal cases.

LEARNING OBJECTIVE 2
. . . .
LAWS THAT AFFECT BUSINESS

There are many laws that affect business, however, the major categories are:

- Contract Law
- Laws Regarding Property Rights
- Tort Law
- Sales Laws
- Laws that Regulate Business
- Agency and Employment Laws
- Laws that Deal with Financial Capital
- Bankruptcy and Reorganization Laws

CONTRACT LAW

Entering into contracts is a natural and critical element of all businesses. A business buys goods and services from a supplier. To do so, a contract must exist. An employee goes to work and gives his or her labor expecting a paycheck. This is also a contract. A customer buys a product expecting it to work. This is also a contract. So what is a contract?

WHERE IN THE WORLD

You worked hard for the $2,000 you used to buy a new computer. The new computer is everything you want, and it has the power to help you become educated and achieve your dream job. You take it to school and put all your treasured documents and coursework on it. After four months of hard work, you start studying for your final exam in your most critical course. You turn on your computer and it goes blank. You take it back to the store. The store clerk examines the computer and announces, "Guess what? You have a virus on your machine. Read your warranty—this is not covered under the warranty." You check with all other sources and realize two things. First, your new machine is ruined. It's fried. Second, you have lost all your critical documents and work. No way can you pass the exam, no way can you pass the course, and no way can you get that special job without the course. You are upset. You want justice. Clearly you have been harmed. You have suffered an economic loss. Whoever caused this virus should pay. The question is whom do you sue? You start reading about the virus. Its origins are unknown. Most people think it came from a different country with different laws.

The challenge with the law is that laws evolve. Societies create new laws to help with new activities societies deem unacceptable. The law is constantly catching up with new crimes. In this case, there is a need for international laws dealing with Internet crimes. There is a need for countries to agree on such Internet laws and consistently enforce such laws.

Contracts have existed as long as people have made agreements. A modern contract is pictured above. Below it is a land sales contract from Sumeria ca. 2600 BC.

A **contract** is when two or more parties enter into an agreement. In the US, the **Uniform Commercial Code (UCC)** has been adopted by all states and governs most contract law. The UCC requires five things to be present for a contract to exist.[2] These are:

1. An agreement has been reached through a process of extending and accepting an offer.

2. The parties of the contract have the legal capacity to enter into a contract. (An example is that a child under the age of 18 cannot enter into a contract.)

3. The parties of the contract enter into the contract voluntarily.

4. The agreement deals with legal activities.

5. The contract is evidenced by the giving and receiving of consideration, where consideration is payment or promise to pay.

Contracts can be either expressed or implied. An **expressed contract** occurs when the details of the contract are clearly stated and agreed upon by all parties. An example is buying a house. The seller and buyer agree to terms in a written sales contract. An **implied contract** occurs when the circumstances and facts imply that a contract exists. An example is going to an auto mechanic to repair your car. You believe that the auto mechanic will fix your car, and the auto mechanic believes you will pay for their services. An implied contract exists.

Contracts can be oral or written. **Oral contracts** occur when the parties agree verbally without recording their agreement in a written document. You go to a restaurant, look at the menu, and order. After the food is delivered and accepted, the waiter brings you a check. Guess what? You owe that money. Why? The answer is you entered into an oral contract. A **written contract** is where the parties record their agreement in a written document. You buy a car and sign an agreement. This is a written contract. You borrow money from a bank and sign a promissory note. This is a written contract.

So we enter into oral and written contracts. But do we always have the option to choose between an oral and a written contract? Not all the time. Certain contracts, to be enforceable, must be in writing. Each state in the US has **statutes of frauds**. It is clearly stated in these statutes what contract must be in writing to be enforceable in that particular state. Examples of contracts that are typically required to be in writing are transfers of land, contracts that guarantee debt with collateral, contracts exceeding a given amount (e.g., $500), and contracts that must take over one year to complete.

LAWS REGARDING PROPERTY RIGHTS

A piece of **property** is an item of value that a person or businesses owns. The owners of property have certain rights and responsibilities, but these rights and responsibilities differ between the different types of property. An example of this is taxes. Different types of property are taxed differently. So what are the different types of property under the law? The law classifies property in three ways.

The Types of Property

First, property can be real property or personal property. **Real property** is land and items permanently attached to the land. **Personal property** is all property not classified as real property. Examples of personal property are cars, movable machines, and inventory.

Second, property can be classified as either tangible property or intangible property. **Tangible property** can be seen and touched because it physically exists. Examples of tangible property are equipment, land, and buildings. **Intangible property** is all property that is not tangible. Examples of intangible property are copyrights, patents, trademarks, and financial securities. Tangible and intangible assets will be explored in more depth in Chapter 17.

Third, property can be divided into private property and public property. **Private property** is owned by individuals and businesses. **Public property** is property owned by a government.

A storefront for lease in Hong Kong.

The Rights and Responsibilities of Owning Property

To own property means that the owner has certain rights. The owner has the right to use the property, to offer the property as collateral for a loan, and to rent or lease the property to another person or business. A **lease** is an agreement between the owner of the property and another party where the owner gives the other party the right to use the property. The owner is the **lessor**. The party renting the property is called the **lessee**. When you rent an apartment you are leasing the apartment. You are the lessee. The landlord is the lessor.

However property owners also have certain responsibilities. The owner cannot use the property to injure other parties. The owner has the responsibility to abide by state and local laws governing the property (example: pay property taxes). The owner must also surrender the property, for reasonable compensation, to a government if the government needs the property for public use. Government can do this under the doctrine of **eminent domain**.

TORT LAW

A tort is a wrongful act that injures another person. Most torts can be classified as either intentional or unintentional. Examples of an intentional tort are battery, slander, invasion of privacy, and trespass. Intentionally misrepresenting facts is also an intentional tort called **fraud**. Unintentional torts are called **negligence**. A negligent person or business is one that does not use reasonable care in the conduct of its affairs. An example of negligence is when a customer slips and hurts him or herself on a business's slippery floor.

PRODUCT LIABILITY LAWS

We go to the store and buy products. We and the store enter into a sales contract. A **sale** transfers the ownership of property. US law requires that sales be made in good faith (honesty) and be reasonable. Product liability laws are classified as torts and were designed to protect consumers from unsafe products and dishonest transactions.

Customers buying groceries at a London supermarket.

Generally product liability claims are based on either negligence, breach of warranty, or strict liability theory.

Claims of negligence might include that a manufacturer used inferior materials or an item was improperly assembled.

A **warranty** is a seller's promise or guarantee regarding the property's quantity and quality. A warranty can be expressed or implied. An **expressed warranty** occurs when the seller explicitly makes statements to the buyer that become a part of the bargaining and sales transaction. An example is when the retailer of a television promises to repair the television if it fails within 90 days of sale. An **implied warranty** is a warranty that exists but is not explicitly stated. Unless the seller explicitly states that no warranty exists, property must be fit for ordinary use.

An example of an implied warranty is when you buy a car. You expect the car to run. If the seller states the car is to be sold "as is," then the seller is saying he or she is not providing any warranty.

Another example is if you purchase a hairdryer, there is the implied warranty that the hairdryer will be fit for the ordinary purpose of drying a person's hair. If you use that hairdryer to inflate your air mattress and the motor burns out, you have not used the hairdryer for its ordinary purpose and the seller would not have to honor the implied warranty.

In addition to the issue of negligence and warranties, sellers must also be aware of the concept of strict liability. The doctrine of **strict liability** holds a seller liable for damages, incurred by the buyer or other parties, when the product was unreasonably unsafe. In a strict liability case, the plaintiff does not have to show intent or negligence by the defendant. The plaintiff simply must show that there was an injury and the defendant's actions or product caused that injury. For example, a company is hired to demolish an old building and in the explosion several cars are damaged. Regardless of how much care the demolition company took to ensure the safety of neighboring property, the demolition company would be held strictly liable for the damages because demolition is an inherently dangerous activity.

LAWS THAT REGULATE BUSINESS

Over the years, US law has evolved to address society's concerns and needs. Laws have been enacted to regulate business activities. Such regulations can be divided into the following four groups:

· Antitrust laws

· Consumer protection laws

· Environmental laws

· Laws that establish government agencies that oversee the operations of certain businesses

Antitrust Laws

In a free-market economy, the market must be free to operate. Competition must exist. In 1890, the US government passed the **Sherman Antitrust Act**. Later the Sherman Act was amended by the **Clayton Act, Robinson-Patman Act**, and **Hart-Scott-Rodino Antitrust Improvements Act**. These acts are intended to foster competition by preventing a business or businesses from restraining and thus controlling trade. In other words, a business cannot do anything that inhibits competition. Three prohibited activities are: price fixing, monopoly power, and price discrimination.

First is **price fixing**. Prices should be set by markets, not by one company or a group of companies working together. An example is when competitors meet and decide the price that will be charged for a product. This is a crime called collusion. Price fixing and collusion take away customers' power in the market. Second is monopolizing a market, as discussed in Chapter 04. Monopolies and oligopolies can inhibit competition. A **monopoly** is where one business controls the market. An **oligopoly** is where a few firms control a market. Let's look at an example. In the 1980s there was one major telephone company in the US. That company was American Telephone and Telegraph Company (AT&T). The US government charged AT&T with restraint of trade and accused it of being a monopoly. After many court battles, AT&T agreed to break into several independent companies. Today, these companies include Verizon, AT&T (formerly Cingular), and Sprint.

Third is **price discrimination**. Businesses cannot charge similar customers different prices. The law requires businesses to charge the same price to similar customers unless there is a good reason, such as transportation costs or quantity ordered. An example of price discrimination is a publisher offering to sell its books to different bookstores, at different prices, to manipulate competition.

Consumer Protection Laws

The **Federal Trade Commission (FTC)** is responsible for administering laws designed to protect consumers. The FTC operates using numerous laws, some of which have been already noted (e.g., warranties). There are two additional sets of laws that protect consumers.

First are numerous laws dealing with lending money, or extending credit. The process of borrowing money should be fair, private, and based on accurate information. **Truth-in-lending laws** require lenders to inform a borrower of all the terms of the debt, including the effective interest rate being charged. The **Equal Credit Opportunity Act** prohibits lenders from discriminating based on race, color, religion, sex, marital status, national origin, or age. The **Fair Debt Collection Practices Act** prohibits lenders from using abusive collection tactics like harassment. The **Gramm-Leach-Bliley Act** protects a borrower's privacy. The **Fair Credit Reporting Act** ensures credit information is

accurate.

Second are laws that protect buyers from unsafe products. At the federal level, the **Consumer Product Safety Act** created the **Consumer Protection Safety Commission (CPSC)**. The CPSC is a government agency that sets product safety standards. The CPSC requires the disclosure of information regarding the content, operation, and safety of products.

Environmental Laws

Businesses must always be aware of laws and regulations that society has enacted to protect the environment. In the US, the **Environmental Protection Agency (EPA)** is responsible for administering the federal laws dealing with the environment, including water quality, air quality, and waste disposal. Many states also have environmental laws.

Governmental Agencies

The FDIC: A History of Confidence and Stability

FDIC history exhibit in the lobby of the headquarters building by the White House.

The government recognizes that certain industries and transactions are critical to the welfare of society and require extra oversight. Regulators of these industries are charged with protecting the welfare of society. Governmental agencies were created to regulate selected industries or business relationships. Some of these regulatory agencies are the **Interstate Commerce Commission (ICC)**, **Federal Food and Drug Administration (FDA)**, the **Federal Deposit Insurance Corporation (FDIC)**, and the **Federal Aviation Administration (FAA)**. Can you imagine trying to do business between states without a common set of rules and regulations? What is more significant than the food we eat? Our whole economy hurts when our financial institutions don't work. Don't you think we need an agency to ensure flying is safe? We need the ICC, the FDA, the FDIC, and the FAA.

AGENCY AND EMPLOYMENT LAW

Employees are the heart of creating business value. But what can a business expect from its employees and what can employees expect from the business?

Employees are agents of a business. An **agent** is defined as a person who is empowered by another (**principal**) to represent that person or business. An employee is an agent and the business is the principal. As such, employees have certain responsibilities and rights under the law. The business is liable for the actions of its employees. The business may or may not agree to indemnify its agents or employees. When an employee is **indemnified**, the business agrees to defend the employee for any accused wrongdoing.

Regarding responsibilities, the law requires employees to be loyal, obey instructions, exercise care, communicate information, and account for funds and property assigned to them. An employee is a **fiduciary**. A fiduciary is one who is entrusted with responsibilities and expected to act in the business's best interest. An employee cannot take a business's trade secrets and sell them to a competitor. On the other hand the business is responsible for compensating the employee, reimbursing the employee for business-related expenses, and keeping good records regarding work and compensation.

It is very important that the business clearly define an employee's authority. The business must be clear on what it expects an employee to do and not do. As an agent of the business, an employee can legally bind the business through contracts and related actions. However, the employee must have the authority to do so. Employees and businesses need to make sure the authority of each employee is clearly stated and understood. Also, a business cannot expect an employee to conduct an illegal act. In fact, if the employee commits an illegal act, on behalf of the business, the employee and employer can both be charged with the crime.

In the US, there are numerous employment laws. The **Fair Labor Standards Act** requires employers to pay employees no less than a minimum wage. Other laws require businesses to pay employees injured on the job (**workers' compensation**), provide a safe workplace (**Occupational Safety and Health Act** or **OSHA**), and ensure job security for ill employees (**Family and Medical Leave Act**). There are laws that prohibit discrimination in hiring and compensating employees based on race, color, religion, sex, marital status, and age (**Civil Rights Acts** and **Equal Pay Act**). There are laws that prohibit discrimination based on physical and mental handicaps (**Americans with Disabilities Act**). Likewise, there are laws that deal with employees' pensions, freedom and ability to organize, and privacy. These laws are discussed in Chapter 16.

LAWS THAT DEAL WITH FINANCIAL CAPITAL

Money is critical for an economy to function. Chapter 04 explores this topic. We need a process where people and organizations that have extra money can channel that money to people and organizations that have value-creating opportunities. We need a way to get money (financial capital) to businesses so the businesses can create value. As we've discussed, businesses receive this money by borrowing the money or having owners put money into the business. Borrowed money is called **debt** or **liabilities** and comes in various types. Owner's money is called **owner's equity** and also comes in different types. The owners of a corporation are called stockholders.

The documents that represent debt and equity are called **financial instruments**. The documents that represent debt are called various names, including **notes**, **bonds**, and **loans**. In a corporation, owners have a document called a **stock certificate**. In a sole proprietorship and partnerships, the money an owner puts into a business is legally documented by various legal documents (example: partnership agreement).

So business needs money, or financial capital, to create value. But how does it get that debt and equity? First is debt. The business gets debt money by either using financial intermediaries or capital markets. An example of a financial intermediary is a bank. A bank borrows money from its depositors and lends money to its loan customers. A **financial intermediary** is a middleman between the ultimate provider of the money (depositor) and user of the money (loan customer). Besides financial intermediaries, businesses can also borrow money in a capital market. A **capital market** is where the provider of money lends the money directly to the borrower and does not use an intermediary. When a business does not use a financial intermediary, it issues or sells its debt in a capital market.

Government legislation mandates access for the disabled. A modified turnstile for disabled people is pictured above.

Second is owner's equity. A business gets money from owners by selling ownership interests (e.g., stock) in the capital markets. The nature and regulation of financial intermediaries and capital markets are explored in Chapter 19.

So businesses acquire money by issuing or selling financial instruments, both debt and equity. So what's the challenge? The answer is we need fair and consistent rules about information. We do not want fraud. When you go to buy an automobile, you want to clearly understand what you are buying. When someone or some organization provides money to a business, it also expects to clearly understand what it is buying. We need laws that require clear disclosures and punish fraud. We also need laws that clearly state the rights and responsibilities of those who provide and receive debt and equity funds.

Rules Regarding Debt

First, let's discuss debt. Whether a business borrows money or writes a check, it is creating commercial paper. **Commercial paper**, per the law, is considered a financial substitute for money. It's a promise to pay money at a future time under certain conditions. It is debt. The law that governs commercial paper is in the Uniform Commercial Code (UCC), which details the requirements for commercial paper to be negotiable, along with the rights and responsibilities of all parties.

Commercial paper or debt can be **negotiable** or **non-negotiable**. Negotiable means that the owner of the commercial paper can sell it without the consent of the borrower. An example of a negotiable instrument is when a business borrows money from a bank. If the loan is negotiable, the bank can sell the loan to another bank without the consent of the business. If the loan is non-negotiable, the bank cannot sell the loan to another bank without the consent of the business.

Besides being negotiable or non-negotiable, debt can also be secured or unsecured. When a business guarantees its loan with **collateral**, the debt is said to be **secured**. Collateral is an asset and can take many forms, including land, building, and intangible property. The bank has a **lien** on the collateral in case the borrower does not pay the loan as agreed. A lien is a legal document that gives the lender the right to seize and sell the collateral if the borrower does not pay the loan. When there is no collateral backing a loan, the loan is said to be **unsecured**. The lender is said to be a **general creditor**.

Let's look at two examples. First, you go to buy a house and borrow money to pay for the house. You promise to pay the loan. The lender looks at your income and believes the income is sufficient to pay off the debt. However the lender is concerned and worries about you losing your job or other events that may stop you from paying back the loan. So the lender requires you to use the house as collateral. The lender has a lien on your house. If you fail to pay the loan, the lender can seize your house and sell it. The lender can then use the proceeds from this sale to pay the loan. The loan is called a secured loan and the lender is a secured creditor. Let's look at a second example. You apply for a credit card, which is a loan. The lender approves your loan based on your income and other financial information. However you give no collateral, only your promise. The loan is said to be unsecured and the lender is a general creditor. It is more risky to be a general creditor. In a bankruptcy, general creditors get paid last and often do not get paid the full amount they are owed. This is why a general creditor may require a higher interest rate to loan money.

Now what happens if a loan is guaranteed by another party? Let's look at the credit card example. You have just been employed and the lender is concerned about the stability of your income and asks that you get someone to help. You have two alternatives. First, you can get a **surety**, someone who **cosigns** the loan. The lender is lending the money to both you and your surety (**cosigner**) and looks to you and your cosigner to pay the loan. Second, you can get someone to **guarantee** the loan. That person, or **guarantor**, is liable for the loan only if you fail to pay the loan. If you do not pay the loan, the lender can require payment from the guarantor.

Financial Instruments and Markets

Businesses often acquire money from owners and lenders by using capital markets. In a corporation, the business issues a financial instrument called stock for owners and debt for lenders. A **public capital market** is a market where anyone can buy or sell a financial instrument. The New York Stock Exchange is an example of a public market. When a company's stocks and debt are traded in a public capital market, we say the financial instruments are **publicly traded**.

A view from the Member's Gallery inside the New York Stock Exchange.

In the US, the **Securities and Exchange Commission (SEC)** regulates public markets where financial instruments are bought and sold. The SEC does so to ensure market participants are well informed and the market is not being unfairly manipulated. In an effort to prevent fraud, the SEC requires businesses using public markets to provide financial reports using specified rules, which are explored in Chapter Eight. The SEC also regulates public markets to ensure the markets are fair for all participants. An example of such regulation is the ban on insider trading. **Insider trading** occurs when someone buys or sells a financial instrument based on insider or preferential information. Insider or preferential information is information not publicly available.

The SEC regulates both primary and secondary markets that are public. So what are primary and secondary markets? A corporation sells stock, the business receives money, and the buyer of the stock (stockholder) receives stock. When this happens we say the money was raised in the **primary market**. Now the stockholder wants to resell his or her stock. He or she finds a buyer for the stock and the stockholder sells the stock at an agreed-upon price. The company is not directly involved in the transaction. The buyer gives the seller the money, the seller gives the buyer the stock, and the company does not get the money. When a stockholder sells his or her stock to anyone other than the issuing company, the stock is being sold in the **secondary market**. The issuance of stock in a public primary market must meet stringent disclosure requirements set forth by the SEC. When the stock is traded in a public secondary market, the SEC requires additional disclosures.

BANKRUPTCY LAWS

What happens when a business cannot pay its debts? What options are there for the business and its creditors? The answer is bankruptcy.

The law acknowledges that businesses can have problems that leave them unable to pay their debts. The law provides a means for addressing these problems through bankruptcy. **Bankruptcy** is defined as a regress for the honest debtor and is governed by the US federal **Bankruptcy Act**. The federal government has exclusive jurisdiction over bankruptcy, thus a claim can only be filed in Bankruptcy Court, never in a state court. The Bankruptcy Act classifies a bankruptcy as either a 1) **straight bankruptcy or liquidation** (chapter 7 of the Bankruptcy Act) or 2) **reorganization** (Chapter 11 of the Bankruptcy Act).

A bankruptcy, either a straight bankruptcy or reorganization, may be voluntary or involuntary. A **voluntary bankruptcy** occurs when the business puts itself into

Priority of Claims in Liquidation

Secured debt

↓

Unsecured debt

↓

Owners

EXHIBIT 7.4: Priority of Claims in Liquidation

bankruptcy by petitioning the bankruptcy court. An **involuntary bankruptcy** occurs when the business's creditors put the business into bankruptcy by petitioning the bankruptcy court.

Bankruptcy law is based on the priority of claims. Under the law, the **priority of claims** gives preference to different types of financial capital. First, the secured creditors should be paid. Secured creditors have security interests in assets or collateral. Security interests may have different levels, with one creditor having a more senior claim than other security interest. An example is a business that builds a factory with borrowed money. The business may use the factory as collateral on the loan. Later, however, the business may use that same factory as collateral on another loan. Now the factory is being used as collateral on two loans. The first loan has **seniority**. The second loan is **subordinated** to the first loan. If the factory had to be sold during bankruptcy, the proceeds would go first to pay off the senior debt. The remaining funds from the sale would then go to pay the subordinated loan.

After the secured creditors are paid, the priority of claims states that the unsecured or general creditors should be paid. Examples of unsecured creditors are suppliers and lenders with no collateral. After the general creditors are paid, then the owners receive any remaining funds.

It should be noted that the priority of claims is the guideline set forth by the law. However bankruptcy judges have the ability to alter the priority of claims. An example is a judge deciding to make a secured creditor an unsecured creditor.

Straight Bankruptcy (Chapter 7)

So what happens in a straight bankruptcy? After the bankruptcy court receives the petition, the judge/court takes control of the business and appoints a trustee to run the company while the court figures out what to do. Then the court seeks to understand the business, its assets, employees, debt, equity, sales, costs, customers, and competitors. It begins to figure out what went wrong and whether or not the business can be saved. If the court decides it cannot be saved, the business is liquidated. In liquidation, the trustee sells the assets of the business. The money from this sale is distributed in accordance to the priority of claims or the desires of the bankruptcy judge. The business ceases to exist.

Let's look at an example. A business fails and the judge decides to liquidate the business (chapter 7 bankruptcy). The business's assets are valued at and sold for $1,000. However there are secured creditors who claim they are owed $700 and have security interests (collateral) equal to $700. The unsecured creditors claim they are owed $500. If the judge adheres to the priority of claims, the secured creditor will receive $700, the unsecured creditors will receive $300, and the owners will receive nothing. The unsecured creditors lost $200 ($500 − $300) and the owners lost all their owner's equity.

Reorganization (Chapter 11)

A chapter 11 bankruptcy is called a reorganization. In a reorganization the court tries to figure out a way to reorganize the company so it can exist in the future. If the court believes that the business can be saved, it may direct the business to take certain actions. The court may direct the business to sell or eliminate assets, to stop selling certain products, and/or to terminate employees. Likewise, regarding the business's financial capital, the court may discharge the business from having to pay certain debts. When a debt is discharged, the business no longer owes the money. The court may also change the terms of the debt. An example of this is extending the time the business has to pay the debt. In summary, the court decides the best actions to save the business and directs such actions. The reorganized business continues.

LEARNING OBJECTIVE 3

BUSINESS ETHICS AND SOCIAL RESPONSIBILITY

The law defines the minimum level of acceptable behavior within a society. Law controls how people and businesses must act. However, that does not mean that the law is exactly how people and businesses should behave. Moral or ethical behavior is how we *expect* people and businesses to behave. Law is how we *require* people and businesses to behave.

Ethics relate to the codes and standards of behavior we live by. Ethics deal with behavior. Remember the old saying "Actions speak louder than words." Our ethics are revealed in how we act. We see ethics in how a business treats its customers, employees, lenders, suppliers, and stockholders. Look at Procter & Gamble's mission statement on www.pg.com to see if you can figure out some of the indicators of the company's ethics.

BUSINESS SENSE

EVERYDAY ETHICS

It's February. You are the senior manager of a growing and valuable business. You've worked hard for the past two years and you are proud of your accomplishments. You decide you need and deserve a vacation, so you look at your calendar. There's a conflict: you also need to meet with a group of junior managers and to lead a previously scheduled management retreat. You decide to combine your vacation with the retreat. Your administrative assistant tells you the retreat is planned for New York City. Although the most efficient place to hold your meeting, New York is cold in February. You want warm weather. You want to go to Hawaii, but meeting in Hawaii will cost three times as much as New York. But it's your decision. What do you do? It may be legal to go to Hawaii, but is it ethical? As the agent of the business's owners, is going to Hawaii in the owners' best interest?

You are torn and argue with yourself. You've worked hard and created a lot of value for the owners. The business owes you a trip to Hawaii. Besides, going to Hawaii will rest you and you'll be more productive when you return. You rationalize that going to Hawaii makes sense.

Two days later you catch your administrative assistant taking office supplies home. They are clearly for personal use. You question your administrative assistant. She tells you she has been working late and has not had time to go the store. Your assistant is stressed because her child has not been doing well in school, the child needs a good grade on a project, and the supplies are needed to finish this school project. You question your assistant's ethics. Your assistant tells you she has worked hard for the business and created a lot of value and that the business owes her the supplies. The supplies will help her child get a good grade, which will reduce the stress in your assistant's life, which will in turn make the assistant more valuable to the business in the future.

What's the difference? This is ethics in everyday business. You make the call.

ETHICAL STANDARDS

There are many ways to classify ethical standards. Some ethical standards are **principle-based ethics** because they are based on principles. An example of a principle may be "Do to others as you'd like others to do to you." Another such principle would be transparency. Ask yourself the question, "What would others think if I took this action?" The challenge with principles is they are often hard to define and apply.

Some ethical standards are **rule-based ethics** because they are communicated by rules. Rules specify what behavior is acceptable and unacceptable. A rule may be that a business cannot dump waste within a mile of any public property. Another rule would be that employees cannot use business assets (e.g., telephone) for

CASE STUDY

CREATING VALUE BY BEING GREEN: WIND ENERGY

Wind Energy Corporation was founded in 2007 by four socially responsible entrepreneurs. They saw a need to help business's eliminate waste, pollution, and dependency on fossil fuel energy. Their first target was commercial buildings such as offices, factories, and retailers. They believed every commercial building could power itself. These visionaries realized that the five million commercial buildings in the US consumed over 40% of US electricity, costing around $120 billion each year. They believed wind was part of the solution.

The need for energy conservation was not new. Solutions included building design, operating efficiency, and new technology such as solar panels. Wind, however, wasn't viewed as a viable solution because it wasn't efficient, looked bad, created vibration and noise, and threatened people and wildlife. So Wind Energy Corp. undertook a $10 million research effort to break through each of those barriers. The potential reward was a sizable financial opportunity, a $70 billion market in the US alone. But more important to the founders was the opportunity to create a sustainable business model that provided the benefits of a triple bottom line: people, planet, and profit.

The breakthrough was a unique, relatively low cost wind turbine called "Windy™." Windy has excited leaders in a wide range of businesses and governments who see the economic benefits from being socially responsible. Per Jim Fugitte, Wind Energy's CEO and one of the company's founders, "The combined economic profit generated by on-site generation from renewable sources, combined with conservation, is simply magnificent."

The founders' vision and hard work saw the company through tough times, including the international financial meltdown of 2008 and a lack of a national energy policy. However by the summer of 2012 the company was installing its first "Windys" at Ford dealerships in the Rio Grande Valley of South Texas. The value of Wind Energy Corp. has grown exponentially. The market is embracing the company's innovative product, visionary leadership, and bright future.

Wind Energy Corp. is a great example of a business creating value for society, value for customers, and value for its owners. It's a win-win-win.

personal purposes. The challenge with rules occurs when the rules do not cover a situation. Questions occur like, "Can I only do the things the rules tell me I can do? I cannot do anything else?" An alternative view of rules is, "I can do anything that the rules do not specifically prohibit."

BUSINESS ETHICS—REALITIES

There are many theories regarding ethics. Some theories focus on the means of doing business. Some theories avoid the means and focus on the result of doing business. In reality, the ethical standards of most organizations are a blend of many theories, and applied with both principles and rules. Three certain facts are evident in making business work and creating value.

1. Behavior unacceptable to society, although legal, may provide short-term benefits. However, long-term value will be hurt as society understands the behavior. Customers will stop buying products; employees will not work for such businesses; and suppliers, lenders, and even owners will turn away from such businesses.

2. For a business to have an effective code of ethics, senior management must direct and support the desired behavior. Ethical standards must be clearly stated. Everyone, particularly senior management, must embrace and act in accordance with the business's ethical standards.

3. Being ethical is never easy. All stakeholders in a business are constantly challenged. Consistent application of ethical standards is required. Constant vigilance is the rule. Ethical standards that fluctuate (e.g., situational ethics) fail.

To foster ethical behavior, many professionals and associations have ethical standards. Examples are the accounting, medical, and legal professions; all have their own clearly stated standards of behavior that their members must agree to and abide by. All Certified Public Accountants (CPAs), all doctors and nurses, and all lawyers are held to their professional standards. If accountants, lawyers and doctors do not adhere to the ethical rules set by their profession, they can be publicly reprimanded and/or lose their license. For example, each state bar has a code of ethics for attorneys to follow. Each state is different, but very similar. One tenet that is true in each state is that attorneys must not co-mingle client money with their own money. This can result in an attorney being disbarred. and thus he or she will not be allowed to practice law in that state. So where do you see ethical behavior in business? You see it in everything a business does. You see it in how the business creates an operating profit, how it acquires money, how it deals with customers. Today, however, more than ever, you see it in social responsibility. Go to Target's website, Target.com, and look at its "Business Conduct Guide." Look at what the guide covers, how it is a blend of principles and rules, and how it affects all of Target's stakeholders.

SOCIAL RESPONSIBILITY

So what do we mean when we talk about social responsibility? The answer goes back to the fact that all stakeholders in a business should receive value. **Social responsibility** is how a business relates to society, including its customers, employees, and suppliers. A socially responsible business seeks to improve the quality and quantity of life for all of its stakeholders. Social responsibility can be seen in everything a business does. Examples of social responsibility are how the business deals with the environment, hiring and training people who have challenges, and giving to charities. Social responsibility is not ethics, and companies may view their social responsibility in very different ways. For example, some companies see it as their duty to be closed on Sundays for religious reasons. This is not an ethical consideration and not even a social responsibility that most companies see as necessary.

Given the ever-growing transparency of business, social responsibility is good business. All stakeholders eventually see a business's contribution to society. Benjamin Franklin had a saying, "Do well by doing good." What that means is by doing good and being socially responsible, a business can prosper. Being socially responsible makes good business sense.

If properly done, being socially responsible can help a business create value. Look at Target's focus of "corporate responsibility," at http://sites.target.com/site/en/company/page.jsp?contentId=WCMP04-031084 and read its latest report on its corporate responsibility. Look at its programs such as giving 5% of its income to local communities for education, medical, and other needs. Look at its environmental initiatives. See how Target believes being socially responsible creates value for all stakeholders. Target had a goal of giving $1 billion and met that goal in 2015.

LAW, ETHICS, AND SOCIAL RESPONSIBILITY

When we look at the law, ethics, and even social responsibility, we are looking at the rules and standards that govern people and business. In a perfect world, responsible ethics would dominate human behavior. The need for law would be minimal. However, we live in an imperfect world where people do not agree on what constitutes responsible ethics. Thus, society needs laws to regulate the activities of individuals and businesses.

Law is the minimum behavior society requires; however, society must question how much law is needed to regulate behavior. When does regulation inhibit the good things a free market provides? How do we know when we have the right amount of law and regulation?

The debate on how to regulate business will always be with us. Why? The answer is society is constantly changing. However, what we have seen is society reacts, with additional laws, when business abuses society's trust. In a free market, society is dependent on business, but society must trust business to do the right thing. If that trust is broken, society will create new laws that regulate business.

In summary, a free market provides efficiency and value, but the participants in that free market must act responsibly. If businesses act responsibly, society will entrust its welfare to the free market and business.

CHAPTER SUMMARY

The law is very important. A business needs to constantly question whether or not its actions are legal regarding customers, assets, employees, suppliers, lenders, and owners. That's why businesses must have good legal advice before they make any major decision. Yet there is more to making good decisions than complying with the law. Decisions should also be based on ethics and appreciation for social responsibility.

In this chapter we've explored the law, ethics, and social responsibility. Specifically you should be able to:

1. Appreciate the US legal system and the types of laws (Learning Objective 1): Businesses must comply with the law. The law specifies the minimum level of behavior a society requires. Laws can be criminal or civil.
2. Appreciate the laws that affect business (Learning Objective 2): In the US, businesses are impacted by laws regarding property rights, sales, regulated activities, agency and employment, financial capital, and bankruptcy and reorganization.
3. Appreciate the nature and challenges of business ethics and social responsibility (Learning Objective 3): Businesses are expected to act ethically and with a sense of social responsibility. Ethics are how a society expects business to behave. A business that is socially responsible attempts to improve the quality and quantity of life for all of society.

The marketplace is constantly providing businesses with new opportunities and new challenges. Competing is never easy; however the rewards, when done right, are enormous. We've seen that doing it right must include abiding by the law, be founded in clear and consistent ethics, and embrace social responsibility. With that knowledge, business can embrace the economics of the market. It's now time to look at the information we use to operate a business. We need to understand the role and nature of accounting, and how financial information is critical to "How Business Works."

KEYWORDS

statutory law 145

stock certificate 153

straight bankruptcy or liquidation 155

strict liability 150

subordinated 156

surety 154

tangible property 149

tort 150

trial courts 147

truth-in-lending laws 151

Uniform Commercial Code (UCC) 148

unsecured 154

US Supreme Court 147

voluntary bankruptcy 155

warranty 150

workers' compensation 153

written contract 149

SHORT-ANSWER QUESTIONS

1. What is the difference between criminal law and civil law?
2. What is the difference between chapter 7 and chapter 11 bankruptcy?
3. What are the requirements to have a contract?
4. Define the following terms:
   a. Statutory law
   b. Administrative rules and decisions
   c. Common law
   d. Tort
   e. Fraud
   f. Negligence
   g. Prosecutor
   h. Defendant
   i. Plaintiff
   j. Lawsuit
   k. Compensatory damages
   l. Punitive or exemplary damages
   m. Statute of limitations
   n. Mediator and mediation
   o. Arbitrator and arbitration
   p. Jurisdiction
   q. Contract
   r. Uniform Commercial Code (UCC)
   s. Expressed contract
   t. Implied contract
   u. Oral contract
   v. Written contract
   w. Statute of frauds
   x. Property
   y. Real property
   z. Personal property
   aa. Tangible property
   ab. Intangible property
   ac. Private property
   ad. Public property
   ae. Lease
   af. Lessor
   ag. Lessee
   ah. Eminent domain
   ai. Warranty
   aj. Expressed warranty
   ak. Implied warranty
   al. Strict liability
   am. Sherman Act
   an. Clayton Act
   ao. Robinson-Patman Act
   ap. Hart-Scott-Rodino Antitrust Improvments Act
   aq. Price fixing
   ar. Monopoly
   as. Oligopoly
   at. Price discrimination
   au. Federal Trade Commission (FTC)
   av. Truth-in-Lending laws
   aw. Equal Opportunity Act
   ax. Fair Debt Collection Practices Act
   ay. Gramm-Leach-Bliley Act
   az. Fair Credit Reporting Act
   ba. Consumer Protection Safety Act
   bb. Consumer Protection Safety Commission (CPSC)
   bc. Environmental Protection Agency (EPA)
   bd. Interstate Commerce Commission (ICC)
   be. Federal Food and Drug Administration (FDA)
   bf. Federal Deposit Insurance Corporation (FDIC)

bg. Federal Aviation Administration (FAA)

bh. Agent

bi. Principal

bj. Indemnify

bk. Fiduciary

bl. Fair Labor Standards Act

bm. Workers' compensation

bn. Occupational Safety and Health Act (OSHA)

bo. Family and Medical Leave Act

bp. Civil Rights Act

bq. Americans with Disabilities Act

CRITICAL-THINKING QUESTIONS

1. Describe the different levels of:
   a. US federal courts
   b. State courts in your state

2. How does the "priority of claims" work?

3. What are the responsibilities of employers relating to their employees, and of employees relating to their employers?

4. What are the rights and responsibilities of owners of property?

5. Look around you. Do you think your government regulates business too much, too little, or just right? Why do you feel that way? Give examples.

EXPLORING REAL BUSINESS

Go to the websites of Google, Target, Hyundai, and Proctor and Gamble. The websites are

Google:	http://investor.google.com
Target:	http://www.target.com
Hyundai:	http://worldwide.hyundai.com/company-overview
Procter & Gamble:	http://www.pg.com

For each company:

1. Describe the ethics policies of each company.

2. How is each of these companies socially responsible?

ENDNOTE

1. http://www.supremecourt.gov
2. All states, Puerto Rico, and Guam have adopted most provisions of the UCC. Louisiana has adopted all but article II because they are based off of civil law (historically from the French).

SECTION 3

TOOLS FOR BUSINESS

In this section, you will read and review the following chapters:

08

FINANCIAL REPORTING AND ACCOUNTING

Introduction: Let's Talk About Financial Reporting and Accounting for a Business

So you want to be a decision maker, managing a business. Have you thought about the information you and others need to manage a business? Have you thought about where and how to get this information? Have you thought about the reliability or quality of information you need? Making good decisions is a big responsibility—the success or failure of your business depends on good decisions. But good decisions start with using good information.

After reading this chapter, you should be able to appreciate the nature and role of accounting, including the techniques and rules used in accounting. You should be able understand the financial statements of a business.

WHY ACCOUNTING MATTERS

We go through life constantly facing decisions. We make the best decisions we can, but on what are those decisions based? The answer is information. Have you ever made a decision that didn't work out like you wanted? Did you ever look back on that decision and wish you had more or better information before you made your decision? Good decisions are based on having the right information at the right time. That reality is particularly true for business because being a good manager starts with asking the right questions at the right time and seeking the right information on a timely basis. Planning, executing, and reviewing are all based on information, and successfully creating value is dependent on information. Accounting is at the center of providing good information—it matters to make business work.

LEARNING OBJECTIVE 1
. . . .
THE NATURE AND ROLE OF ACCOUNTING

Accounting is the function devised to provide decision makers with the financial information they need. Accounting is the function within a business that recognizes, measures, records, and reports information about a business's transactions. To do this, businesses have accounting systems that are administered by an accounting department or function. **Accountants** are people who work within the

EXHIBIT 8.1: The Accounting Function

accounting department and carry out the accounting function.

Most people look at accounting as a rather unimaginative, straightforward process. In reality accounting is a very challenging and complex process. Accounting is responsible for recognizing, measuring, recording, and reporting all the important economic events that a business experiences. But to do so, accountants must understand the events. Accountants must understand the business's model and strategy and how that model and strategy are executed. Accountants must have insight into how the business operates and is managed. Likewise managers must understand the processes and rules accountants use to recognize, measure, record, and report business transactions. Accountants are critical members of the team that operates and manages a business.

Accounting systems are composed of two elements. First are the processes used to account for the transactions. Second are the rules that specify when and how a business recognizes, measures, records, and reports business transactions. Accounting systems differ between businesses. Why? Different businesses have different models and strategies and thus need different information. Do you think a retail store such as Target needs the same information as a manufacturer of automobiles such as Hyundai? The answer is no. Target buys and sells its product, while Hyundai manufactures its product. Target sells to consumers, the ultimate users of its products. Hyundai sells to dealers, not consumers. Yet within a business, managers attempt to standardize its accounting systems. Why? Without standardization the information accountants provide would not be useful. Can you imagine Target letting its individual stores have different accounting processes and different accounting rules? That would make it hard for Target's senior managers to manage Target. Dependability and consistency are critical.

So what are the processes and rules that make up an accounting system?

ACCOUNTING PROCESSES

Accounting processes are designed to provide understandable, relevant, and reliable information. Good accounting processes are based on:

Effective internal control

Correct and consistent application of rules

Effective communication of results

First are internal controls. **Internal control** relates to the ability of the accounting system to 1) capture all business transactions and 2) detect and prevent fraud. Let's look at an example. Your neighbor comes to your home and asks for a donation to a local charity. You give your neighbor $50 cash. You trust your neighbor to send the $50 to the charity. But are you sure the charity will receive and recognize your gift? Your neighbor did not give you a receipt. Your internal control is weak. You are not sure your contribution will be recognized, measured, recorded, or reported as you intended. Internal control systems are designed to ensure all transactions are recognized correctly and to minimize the opportunity for fraud. That's why businesses have a lot of checks and balances. An example is a person who orders supplies typically does not authorize payment for the supplies. Another example is requiring receipts for all transactions.

Second is the need to correctly and consistently apply the given accounting rules. If an accounting system has good internal controls, the system should correctly recognize, measure, record, and report the business's transactions. Who defines what is correct? The answer is the user or group of users through their rules. Later in this chapter we'll look at rules and different users.

Last, accounting processes are designed to effectively communicate or report the information needed by decision makers. The information needed starts with three basic questions. The three basic questions deal with how a business creates value. These questions are:

1. What economic resources (assets) does the business have at a specific time with which it can create value?

2. Where did the business get the money (debt and owner's) to acquire these economic resources at that specific time?

3. How has the business used the economic resources to create a net income or loss in a given period? (Remember that owner's value is a function of the net income earned from a business.)

The processes used in accounting will communicate the answers to these questions with financial reports called financial statements. Accounting provides numerous financial statements to help the users answer these questions. We'll explore these statements later in this chapter, but accounting uses two basic financial statements to answer the above questions. The first two questions are answered with a financial statement called a balance sheet. A **balance sheet** tells 1) what economic resources a business owns or controls (assets) and 2) the sources of funds the business uses to finance those economic resources (debt and owner's money). The balance sheet communicates the assets, liabilities, and owner's money at a point in time (e.g., December 31, 2015). The third question is answered with a financial statement called an **income statement**. An income statement tries to answer the question "Did the business earn a net income or loss for its owners in a given period?" An income statement communicates how the business has performed during a period (e.g., for the year ending December 31, 2015).

ACCOUNTING RULES

The purpose of accounting is to provide useful information. The user or groups of users must decide what useful information is. But because different groups of decision makers have different needs, different groups of decision makers have different rules. So who are these groups? There are many, including:

Managers within the business

Lenders and owners

Customers

Regulators

Taxing authorities

As discussed later in this chapter, each of these groups can have its own set of rules to recognize, measure, record, and report business transactions. They all face the same challenges and they all ask the same three basic questions noted above. The answers for these basic questions come from a standardized set of processes.

THE FOUNDATIONS OF ACCOUNTING—USING ACCOUNTING PROCESSES AND RULES

Accounting is the function of recognizing, measuring, recording, and reporting business transactions. This looks simple, but often is not. Let's dissect each of the parts of this process.

A bicycle shop in Macau, China.

Recognizing Business Transactions

What is a business transaction? When does a business transaction occur? These are not simple questions. In theory, a business transaction is an economic event that occurred and affected the value of the business, but putting this into practice is hard. Let's look at an example. A customer comes into your bicycle shop and orders a new bicycle from your catalogue. Have you sold a bicycle? The answer is no. Why? Because you and your customer have entered into a contract to sell and buy a bicycle, but you have not fulfilled that contract. You have not delivered the customer his bicycle. The customer has not paid for the bicycle. No exchange has occurred. Something important happened: you entered into a contract. So what is the business transaction? What should the accountant recognize, measure, record, and report? Accountants follow a rule to recognize a sale only when the contract is fulfilled by all parties and the exchange is complete. In the bicycle example, this is when the business delivers the bicycle to the customer and the customer owes the business money.

Measuring Business Transactions

After an accountant recognizes a business transaction, the next step is to measure the business transaction. To do so, a monetary measure must be assigned. Once again this appears easy, but may be a challenge. Let's look at an example. A customer comes into your bicycle store, buys a bicycle, and gives you $250. You give the bicycle to the customer. An exchange occurs. You recognize a sale, which you measure as $250. This transaction is easy to measure. However there are business transactions that are not easy to measure. Let's adjust our example. Your customer comes into your store looking for a bicycle. He has no money, but he offers to pay you in three months. You agree. You give the bicycle to the customer and the customer gives you a promise of future payment or accounts receivable. An exchange occurs. You recognize a sale, but what amount do you recognize? What happens if the customer does not pay you the money in three months? We need rules for measuring business transactions.

Recording Business Transactions

How does a business record a business transaction? First, the accountant must categorize transactions into groupings called accounts. An **account** is a summary of the transactions of a particular type. An example of an account is cash. Accountants summarize all the transactions that affect a business's cash in an account called "cash." Examples of other accounts are accounts receivable, inventory, accounts payable, sales, and revenue. Many of the accounts used in businesses are explored later in this chapter.

Second, a business needs to record the complete business transaction. You buy something, but that is only half the transaction. Where did you get the money to buy it? The complete transaction is what you got and where you got the money to get it. You give up something, but that is only half the business transaction. Why did you give it up? What did you receive in return? The complete transaction is what you gave and received. Businesses need to record the complete transaction.

Let's look at the sale in your bicycle shop. You received $250 cash. Why? You made a sale. You also gave a bicycle to your customer that cost you $100. The $250 sale cost you $100. Looking at the total transaction, you sold a bicycle for $250 in cash. The cash is an asset. You gave up another asset called a bicycle that cost you $100. So you increased your total assets by $150. Why? You made a $150 profit that belongs to you, the bicycle shop owner.

Businesses record complete transactions by using journal entries, which use a technique called debits and credits. Journal entries and debits and credits are means to record the complete transaction and are a subject for more advanced courses in accounting. However it is important that the business recognize the complete transaction.

Reporting Business Transactions

Different groups have different information needs. Thus, different groups want different reports. Yet the reporting function is focused on answering the three questions all decision makers ask. Reporting starts with balance sheets and income statements. Other financial statements or reports provide detail on components of these statements.

THE RULES OF ACCOUNTING

We need rules to account for business transactions accurately and consistently. Different users have different rules. Although the business transaction is the same, it can be recognized, measured, recorded, and reported different ways.

Let's look at an example. You start your bicycle store. You put in $100,000 of your own money. You borrow another $100,000 from the bank. Your business now has $200,000 in cash—an asset of $200,000 cash. Where did you get the $200,000 cash? Your business owes the bank $100,000 and $100,000 comes from you, the owner. Now you use the $200,000 to buy a building. What has happened? You traded one asset for another asset. Your business no longer has cash but now has a building worth $200,000. Where did the business get the $200,000 for the building? The business owes the bank $100,000 and the other $100,000 belongs to you, the owner. One year later someone comes to you and offers to buy the building for $500,000. You decide not to sell, but you are happy. Your building now has increased in value. Your building has a current market value of $500,000, $300,000 more than

BUSINESS SENSE
CAUSE AND EFFECT

People will say "they bought something." But where did they get the money to buy it? People will say "they owe a certain amount." But why do they owe that amount? Accounting is a process based on balance. Balance is a principle of life. Have you ever studied physics? What did you learn? You learned, "For every action there is an equal and opposite reaction." When you study physical and social sciences, you learn that, "For every cause there is an effect." The world works on a principle of balance. Accountants use techniques such as journal entries and debits and credits to ensure this balance. Paul Harvey, a famous news reporter and radio commentator from Chicago, would always end his broadcasts with the phrase, "And now you know the rest of the story." Paul Harvey understood that sometimes people do not see the complete story. Accountants try to tell the complete story. It's life. Things balance.

The accounting process used to achieve this balance is often called "double-entry" accounting. In double-entry accounting, each transaction is recorded as a journal entry. In each journal entry, the amount of debits must equal the amount of credits. The Father of Accounting is Friar Luca Pacioli (1447–1517), an Italian mathematician, Franciscan friar, and collaborator with Leonardo da Vinci on numerous projects. Pacioli's double-entry process was first published in 1494, in Summa de arithmetica, geometrica. Proportioni et proportionalita.

you paid for it. Now ask yourself, should the accountant recognize the building has increased in value by $300,000? Should the accountant record and report this increased value by saying the building is worth $500,000? If so, where did the value come from? Who gets credit for this increased value? You still owe only $100,000 to the bank. If the business has assets worth $500,000, who has claim on that $500,000? The bank has a $100,000 claim. The remaining $400,000 must belong to the owner. By holding the building, the owner increased his or her value from $100,000 to $400,000. The owner made $300,000 in net income.

The above example demonstrates a major challenge that accountants face. Do they reflect the business's assets, liabilities, and owner's equity at their original cost or current market value? Should the accountant report that the value of the building is $200,000 (original cost) or $500,000 (current market value)? The accountant can do either. The choice is dictated by the users' rules. We've already seen that different users have different rules, so what are these different groups, and what are their rules? Let's explore each.

Managers Within the Business

Managers within a business can set their own rules. Such rules are referred to as managerial accounting. Managerial accounting attempts to meet the information needs of the business's managers by looking at the details of a business transaction. Managers must understand what is happening in a business transaction for the purpose of planning, executing, and reviewing. Managers get to specify how and when they want each business transaction to be recognized, measured, and reported. Managerial accounting is discussed later in this chapter.

Lenders and Owners Outside the Business

Lenders and owners provide money to a business. Lenders and owners, however, are often not the managers of those businesses, particularly corporations. The managers are the agents of the owners and are accountable to the owners. The accounting rules used to report to owners and lenders are referred to as financial accounting. In the US, the government created the Securities and Exchange Commission (SEC) to protect lenders and owners (stockholders) of publicly owned companies from misleading accounting practices. The SEC directs the Public Company Accounting Oversight Board (PCAOB), which oversees and approves of the rules set by the Financial Accounting Standards Board

A Wells Fargo bank branch in Napa, California.

(FASB). FASB is made up of accounting and business professionals and sets the rules, or standards, companies must follow in providing information to lenders and stockholders. These standards are called Generally Accepted Accounting Principles (GAAP). FASB, with the approval of PCAOB, is constantly reviewing and revising US GAAP. Why? The answer is that the practice of business is constantly changing.

A major underlying principle of US GAAP is conservatism. Conservatism means that accountants should not overstate the value of an asset or understate the value of a liability or debt. Let's look back at the building example. Under current US GAAP, the accountant would not recognize the building increased in value by $300,000. Why? The answer is there has been no completed, verifiable transaction. Thus, the building would be reported as being worth $200,000. The debt would be reported as $100,000, and the owner's funds would be reported as $100,000. No income would be recognized until the building was actually sold.

Why? The answer is that accountants are conservative and never want to report increased value before it is proven with a cash or similar transaction. However if the value of your building decreased, the accountant would decrease the value of your building and indicate the owners suffered a loss. Why? The answer is again conservatism. The accountant would lower the value of your building and recognize the owner's loss if there is any evidence that the value of the building decreased. But is that fair? It's conservative.

As globalization proceeds, the business world recognizes the need for a set of accounting rules or principles that are the same throughout the world. Lenders and owners desire the same standards to make companies around the world comparable. Currently FASB is working with the **International Accounting Standards Board (IASB)** to converge US GAAP with the IASB's **International Financial Reporting Standards (IFRS)**. The primary difference is IFRS is not as conservative as US GAAP. IFRS reports assets and liabilities based on current value, often called **fair value**. Under IFRS, your building could be reported at $500,000, your liabilities as $100,000, and your owner's funds as $400,000.

Customers

Customers of a business often want and need to understand the business. Would you buy an automobile from a company that does not have the financial ability to fulfill its warranty? Customers often do not have the time or expertise to understand the complex world of business and accounting, so government regulators often represent customers.

Regulators

As noted in Chapter 07, regulators are government agencies that are responsible for protecting the welfare of society. Regulators have their own set of rules and accounting standards. Regulators require the companies they regulate to file reports that conform to these regulatory rules and standards. An example is the Federal Deposit Insurance Corporation (FDIC), which requires banks to file reports that conform to the FDIC's accounting standards. Another example is the Federal Aviation Authority (FAA), which requires airlines to file reports that conform to FAA accounting standards. Regulators have standards that are typically conservative, as their objective is to protect society.

Taxing Authorities

As noted in Chapter 06, there are many different taxing authorities (e.g., federal, state, international). Each taxing authority has its own accounting standards. Each must determine how it will determine the value of an asset, liability, and owner's funds. Likewise each must determine how and when it will recognize income and expense.

LEARNING OBJECTIVE 2
· ·
FINANCIAL STATEMENTS

Accountants create financial statements to summarize and report a business's transactions. As noted earlier, the two primary financial statements are the balance sheet and income statement. Before we look at the balance sheet and income statement, we need to look at a critical concept. The concept is accrual accounting and deals with *when* we recognize a transaction.

THE BASIS OF ACCOUNTING—CASH VERSUS ACCRUAL

So what is the basis of your accounting? Is it cash or is it accrual? A **cash basis** is when a business transaction is recognized only when it affects the business's cash. A cash system only recognizes, measures, records, and reports a business transaction when cash is received or cash is paid out. What is an example of a cash system? Most people use a cash system to manage their personal finances. How many times have you walked into a store, found something you wanted, and realized you did not have the cash to pay for it? That's a cash perspective.

The trouble with a cash basis of accounting is that it does not recognize business transactions until they affect cash. You go into a store, find something you want but realize you do not have the cash to pay for it. So what do you do? You buy the item using a credit card. You're borrowing the money, not using cash. The cash basis of accounting would not recognize you bought the item or owe the money. If you used a cash basis, the business transaction would be recognized only when you pay off the debt.

An **accrual basis** recognizes business transactions when they occur, regardless of whether or not the transaction immediately affects cash. You go into a store, buy something, and use your credit card. A business transaction has occurred. Accrual accounting would recognize, measure, record, and report the transaction when you give the store's cashier your credit card. You bought something and owe money.

The challenge with accrual accounting is that accountants must make assumptions. An example is your credit card bill. You owe money to the credit card company. You have a debt or liability to the credit card company. The credit card company has a receivable from you. That receivable is an asset of the credit card company. But what is the asset worth? It is worthless if you do not pay it. The credit card company must make assumptions about your ability and willingness to pay your debt.

Cash is important. Businesses that cannot pay their bills fail. Accrual accounting, however, is the rule for most businesses. Why? The answer is time. Users of financial information want to understand a business's transactions as soon as the transaction occurs. All transactions eventually affect cash, but the users do not want to wait for that to happen. If we buy something on credit, we eventually have to pay cash for the debt. When we sell something on credit, we are owed cash. We accept the customer's promise to pay cash in the future. But users of accounting information need to know that a business transaction has occurred even though it may take time for the transaction to affect cash.

So businesses worry about cash even though most businesses use accrual accounting to recognize, measure, record, and report business transactions. Let's look at the financial statements that use accrual accounting to communicate a business's transactions.

THE BALANCE SHEET

The balance sheet answers the following two questions.

1. What economic resources (assets) does the business have at a specific time with which it can create value?

2. Where did the business get the money (debt and owner's) to acquire these economic resources at that specific time?

A balance sheet reports the assets a business owns or controls at a specific time. A balance sheet also reports the claims on those assets, or where the business got the money to invest in the assets at that specific time. Remember that the money comes either from debt, called liabilities, or from owner's funds. In accounting, the funds that come from and belong to owners are called **owner's equity**. As such, the balance sheet is a picture of the business at a specific point in time. For example, a balance sheet would report the assets, liabilities, and owner's equity as of December 31, 2015. A balance sheet is called a balance sheet because it must balance. This fact can be seen in the following equation:

EQUATION 8.1: The Accounting Equation: The Balance Sheet

$$Assets = Liabilities + Owner's\ Equity$$

Exhibit 8.2 depicts a typical balance sheet.

EXHIBIT 8.2: The Balance Sheet

Assets	Liabilities and Owner's Equity
Current Assets Cash Investments Accounts Receivable Inventories Other Current Assets	**Current Liabilites** Accounts Payable Accrued Liabilities Other Current Liabilities
Long-term Fixed Assets Land Property and Plant Less Depreciation	**Long-Term Liabilities** Long-Term Loans Other Long-Term Liabilities
Long-term Other Assets Goodwill Other Intangible Assets	**Owner's Equity** Stock Accounts Retained Earnings

Assets

An **asset** is an economic resource that a business owns or controls. Assets are categorized as either current or long-term assets. **Current assets**, often called short-term assets or working capital, are cash or assets expected to be converted to cash within the next year. Current assets include cash, accounts receivable, and inventory. **Long-term assets** are assets that are not short-term assets and have an economic life greater than one year. Long-term assets include land, buildings, equipment, and intangible assets, such as patents, copyrights, and trademarks.

There are a lot of challenges in accounting for assets. Let's look at some of the assets and challenges the accountant faces.

Current Assets

Cash is the currency a business owns. It also includes the deposits the business has in banks. Cash can be hard to control, but it is easy to measure. Either a business has cash or does not have cash.

Accounts receivable are the amounts owed to the business. The challenge accountants face with accounts receivable is they do not want to report that a business will receive money in the future when it may not. For that reason accountants measure and report accounts receivable as that amount they

WHAT'S AN ASSET?

So what is an asset? It's an economic resource. And you know what? People are the most important economic resource a business has. Look at the value of a growing and valuable company. Don't you buy from that company in part for its managers and employees? But does that business own those people? Does it control those people? People, in a free society, are free to work or not work for a business. Businesses do not own people. Thus, accountants have a problem.

Being conservative, accountants record the cost of labor (people) as a cost or expense. Is this right? The answer is maybe and maybe not. Let's look at your bicycle store. You send one of your employees to school to learn to fix bicycles and you pay the cost of her education. Why? The answer is that you expect that employee to use this new knowledge to help you earn income in the future. Your employee's new knowledge is an economic resource. When you pay for the education, do you record it as an asset? The answer is no. You are conservative. You are worried that the employee could leave you to go work for a competitor. Thus, you record the cost of the education as an expense in the period incurred. You are conservative.

believe the business will receive or collect in the future. As such, the accountant must estimate and report how much will be collected and how much will not be collected.

Inventory can be purchased or produced and represents the products the business has to sell. An example of **purchased inventory** is a store such as Target. When you walk into Target, you see clothes, electronics, food, and other items. Target purchased these items for resale. An example of **produced inventory** is an automobile manufacturer such as Hyundai. When you go to an automobile manufacturer you see a lot of different types of inventory. You see a store of materials needed to build the automobiles (steel, tires, etc.). You see automobiles in the process of being manufactured. You see the finished automobiles. The materials used to build the automobiles are called **raw materials inventory**. The partially finished automobiles are called **work-in-process inventory**. The finished automobiles are called **finished goods inventory**. Raw materials, work-in-process, and finished goods are types of produced inventory.

Accounting for inventory is a challenge. There are two primary questions an accountant must address.

- · What did the inventory cost to buy or produce?

- · Is the inventory worth at least what it cost to buy or produce it?

Accountants have different methodologies to help with these questions. Some of these methodologies are explored in Chapter 17.

Long-Term Assets

There are two types of long-term assets. First are tangible long-term assets. **Tangible assets** have a physical presence; you can touch and feel them. Second are **intangible assets**. Intangible assets are real, but you cannot directly touch or feel them.

Inside the SpaceX factory.

Tangible assets include land, buildings, and equipment. Such assets are often referred to as **property, plant, and equipment (PP&E)**. PP&E assets are sometimes called **fixed assets**. Under US GAAP, these assets are typically reported at cost, or what the business originally paid for these assets. Accountants are challenged because these long-term assets can and often do lose value as they are used.

Let's look at an example. You buy an automobile for $20,000 and drive it for a year. You go to sell the automobile after one year and realize it is only worth $15,000. In driving the automobile for the year you have used $5,000 of its value. The automobile has depreciated by $5,000. **Depreciation** is recognizing that an asset's value is decreased by the use or age of that asset and is shown as a reduction of the asset's value on the balance sheet. This reduction in a given period is also a cost of doing business (depreciation expense) and lowers net income. Land cannot be depreciated. Buildings and equipment are depreciated. Accountants must estimate how an asset depreciates over time. The accountant wants to report an asset as the value that has not been depreciated to date, which is the original cost of the asset less accumulated depreciation to date.

Let's go back to your automobile example. Your automobile originally cost $20,000. During the first year of use you incurred $5,000 in depreciation expense. Your automobile now has a value of $15,000 ($20,000 – $5,000) on the balance sheet. Your net income, which belongs to owners, also decreased by $5,000 during the year. Why? The answer is depreciation expense. You lost $5,000 in asset value and owner's equity value because you incurred $5,000 in depreciation expense.

In addition to tangible assets, a business also can have intangible assets. Although intangible assets do not have a physical presence, they can have significant value. Intangible assets include copyrights, trademarks, and patents. Like tangible assets, intangible assets can lose value over time as they are used. When an intangible asset loses value because it was used, the value is lowered with amortization. Accountants do not depreciate intangible assets, they amortize intangible assets. **Amortization** is like depreciation in that it reflects the loss of the value of the asset over time. It is an adjustment to the value of the intangible asset and an expense. The accountant reports intangible assets as the value that has not been amortized to date, which is the original cost of the assets less accumulated amortization to date. The reduction in a given period is also a cost of doing business (amortization expense) and lowers net income and owner's equity.

Let's look at an example. You buy a patent for $20,000. You believe that it will have value for four years and that it will be worthless after the four years lapse. You estimate that after one year, your patent will only be worth $15,000. In the first year your patent has decreased in value from $20,000 to $15,000. You also incurred a $5,000 amortization expense in the first year, lowering your net income and owner's equity.

There is one special intangible asset that is not amortized. That asset is goodwill. **Goodwill** is an intangible asset that reflects the special value that some businesses have created. This value may be due to marketing, research, or other factors. Accountants recognize goodwill only when it is purchased. How is it purchased? It's purchased when one company buys another company. If a company pays a purchase price that is greater than the value of the assets purchased, the accountant recognizes a new asset called goodwill. When goodwill loses its value, the accountant will reduce the value on the balance sheet and record an expense called **impairment**.

Think about goodwill. Why is a company worth more than the value of its tangible and intangible assets? The answer is the company has created and owns something special such as a brand name. Think about Procter & Gamble and its products such as Crest toothpaste. Procter & Gamble owns a brand that people trust, respect, and desire. Procter & Gamble has created something special in developing the Crest brand. So why doesn't US GAAP recognize all goodwill? The answer is goodwill is hard to measure. As such, US GAAP lets an accountant recognize goodwill only when it is purchased. It goes back to US GAAP being conservative.

Liabilities

A liability is a claim, or a debt of, the business. Liabilities are amounts owed by the business and represent amounts that individuals or organizations have lent to the business. So where do liabilities come from? The answer is from many places. An example is a business going to a bank and borrowing money. The business agrees to repay the loan at a future time; the loan is a liability. The business also pays interest for the use of the money over time. Another example of a liability is when a business buys inventory and agrees to pay for it at a later date. The business owes money to the supplier of the inventory; it has borrowed the money from the supplier to acquire the inventory. Typically the business does not pay the supplier interest. However this transaction still creates a debt or liability.

Accountants typically report liabilities either as a current liability or long-term liability. Current liabilities are short-term liabilities that are due to be repaid in one year or less. These include accounts payable, estimated liabilities called accrued liabilities, and short-term debt from banks and other lenders. Long-term liabilities are liabilities that are due to be paid in periods beyond one year.

Accountants worry about not reporting or understating liabilities. Usually liabilities are easy to recognize, measure, record, and report. The only challenge is with long-term estimated liabilities noted below.

Current Liabilities

Accounts payable are amounts a business owes its suppliers. Usually accounts payable are represented by formal documents. A clothing supplier delivers clothes to a Target. The delivery person has the manager sign a document acknowledging that Target has received the clothes and owes money for the clothes. Target has received and owns clothing inventory. It also owes the supplier and has an account payable.

Accrued liabilities are like accounts payable, except no formal document is used. An example is an employee of Google goes to work and goes home at the end of the day. Although there is no formal bill, the manager and employee agreed that the employee would receive a specified amount in the future for her or his work. After the employee works, Google owes the employee money. Google has a debt that is called an accrued liability. Other examples of accrued liabilities include rent, interest, and utilities.

An employee working at the Google offices in Germany.

Short-term borrowings include loans from banks and other lenders that a business must pay within the next year.

Long-term Liabilities

Long-term liabilities include loans that are due in a period beyond one year to banks or other lenders. Long-term liabilities also include real, but harder-to-estimate, liabilities that deal with retirement benefits promised to employees, long-term taxes, and valuing contingent debts from lawsuits and other actions. Accountants are challenged with such liabilities.

Because long-term liabilities are to be paid over periods greater than one year, the lender may require the business to pay interest. Interest is the cost of borrowing money over time.

Owner's Equity[1]

Owner's equity represents the money that owners have provided the business. Owners provide money two ways. First, owners provide money by contributing money directly to the business. In return they receive ownership rights. Second, owners provide money by leaving the profits in the business.

First is contributed money. In a sole proprietorship or partnership, this amount is represented as **owner's capital**. In a corporation, this amount is represented as **stock**. Corporations sometimes have different types of stock (e.g., common stock and preferred stock). The owners of different types of stock have different rights. Different types of stock are reported in separate accounts. The topic of stock is explored in Chapter 19. Each type of stock account can also be further subdivided, for legal purposes, into accounts labeled "par" and "additional paid-in capital." Together these two accounts represent the amount of money the original stockholder paid the company for its stock. Accountants record owners' capital or stock transactions based on the money received from the business owners.

Second are profits or losses retained in a business. When a business earns a profit or incurs a loss, it belongs to the owners. As such, it is reflected in the owner's equity section in an account called "retained earnings." **Retained earnings** represent the business's accumulated net income and losses that owners have left in the business. When owners decide they do not want to let the business retain earnings, the business pays the earnings to the owners. In a corporation, this payment is called a **cash dividend**. Thus, the amount of a company's retained earnings, at a point in time, is the sum of the company's net income, less losses, less dividends over the entire life of the company.

Let's Look at Target

Look at Exhibit 8.3, Target's balance sheet as of January 31, 2015.

What do you see? You first see a list of Target's assets. There are current assets, including cash, accounts receivable, and inventory. You also see long-term assets, including land, buildings, and

EXHIBIT 8.3: Target's Balance Sheet on January 31, (in Millions of US Dollars)

Assets	2014	2015	Liabilities	2014	2015
Current Assets					
Cash and Short-Term Investments	$695	$2,210	Accounts Payable	$7,683	$7,759
Credit Cards Receivables	$-----	$-----	Other Current Liabilities	5,094	3,977
Inventories	8,766	8,790	Total Current Liabilities	12,777	11,736
Other Current Assets	2,112	3,075			
Total Current Assets	11,573	14,075	**Long-term Liabilities**		
			Loans	12,622	12,705
			Other Long-term Liabilities	2,923	2,966
Fixed Assets			Total Long-Term Liabilities	15,545	15,671
Property and Equipment	45,780	41,064			
Less Accumulated Depreciation	(14,402)	(15,106)	Total Liabilities	28,322	27,407
Net Property	31,378	25,958	**Owner's Equity**		
			Stock Accounts	4,523	4,952
Other Assets			Retained Earnings	11,708	9,045
Other Assets	1,602	1,371	Total Shareholders' Equity	16,231	13,997
Total Assets	$44,353	$41,404		$44,553	$41,404

Source: https://corporate.target.com/annual-reports/pdf-viewer-2013?cover=6725&parts=6727

intangibles. Second you see Target's liabilities and owners' equity. There are current liabilities, including accounts payable and accrued liabilities. Then there are long-term liabilities. Last there is owners' equity. Do you see the contributed capital (par and additional paid-in capital) and the retained earnings?

Now look at Target's balance sheet in total. What does it tell you? It tells you the assets Target owns on January 31, 2015, and it tells you how Target funded these assets. The money is either coming from liabilities or owners' equity. Target's balance sheet balances because it answers the following two questions:

1. What economic resources (assets) does Target have on January 31, 2015, with which it can create value?

2. Where did Target get the money (debt versus owners) to acquire these economic resources on January 31, 2015?

Target's assets equals Target's liabilities plus owners' equity.

THE INCOME STATEMENT

An **income statement** answers the following question:

How has the business used the economic resources to create a net income or loss in a given period?

A balance sheet reports the assets a business owns or controls at a point in time. A balance sheet also reports the claims on those assets, or where the business got the money to invest in the assets (debt and owner's equity) at a point in time. An income statement reflects how the business used these assets in a given period to create sales and expenses, which combine to be net income or loss. As such, the income statement is a picture of what the business did in a given period to produce a net income or loss. For example, an income statement will report the sales and costs incurred during a given period, such as the year ending on December 31, 2015. An income statement is seen in the following equation:

EQUATION 8.2

$$\text{Sales} - \text{Expenses} = \text{Net Income (Loss)}$$

Exhibit 8.4 depicts a typical income statement.

EXHIBIT 8.4: The Income Statement

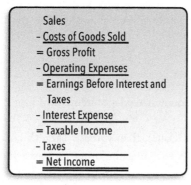

```
Sales
- Costs of Goods Sold
= Gross Profit
- Operating Expenses
= Earnings Before Interest and
  Taxes
- Interest Expense
= Taxable Income
- Taxes
= Net Income
```

Advertising in Times Square, New York City.

Now let's look at sales and expenses.

Sales

A **sale**, or revenue, occurs when there is an exchange. There are two criteria for recognizing a sale. First, the amounts exchanged must be earned. What that means is that the business has delivered the product or completed the promised work. When you sell a bicycle from your bicycle store, you deliver the bicycle to the customer. You have earned the revenue and you can recognize the sale. Second, there is a reasonable expectation that you will ultimately receive money or other value for the sale. What that means is 1) the customer has paid for the sale or 2) you believe that the customer will pay you for the sale. When a customer comes in and buys a bicycle from your bicycle store, what do you get in return? If you get a promise to pay you in the future, the customer is giving you an accounts receivable. However if there is a very high probability that the customer will never pay you, then you did not sell the bicycle—you gave the bicycle to the customer.

Expenses

Businesses incur expenses in operating a business. An **expense** is the cost or value surrendered to create a sale and operate a business during a period of time. Accountants try to match sales and the expenses incurred to generate those sales. This is called the "**matching concept.**" An example of this matching concept is matching sales with the expense of the products sold, or **cost of goods sold (COGS)**. You buy a bicycle to sell to a customer. The bicycle cost $100. You sell the bicycle to a customer for $250. You recognize a sale of $250 and a cost of goods sold of $100. This produces a gross profit of $150. A **gross profit** is computed as sales less cost of goods sold.

But there are other operating expenses. These expenses are hard to allocate to specific sales. Thus, businesses allocate these expenses to the period in which the expense is incurred. Examples of such operating expenses are employee salaries, rent, depreciation, utilities, and advertising. Gross profit less these operating expenses results in "earnings before interest and taxes." **Earnings before interest and taxes (EBIT)** are the **operating profit** earned by the business. EBIT is the return generated, in that period, from investing in assets.

So what happens to EBIT? First, the business must pay interest expense. Remember that **interest** is a cost of borrowed money, the periodic return that is owed to the providers of debt. EBIT less interest expense is **net income before taxes,** or **taxable income (or loss)**. Business must then compute the taxes it owes and record a tax expense. Taxable income less tax expense is **net income or loss**. Net income or loss belongs to the owners of the business.

So what happens to the income statement after the period ends? All the sales and costs accounts are netted. The net income or loss is put in the retained earnings account in the balance sheet. A new period begins and a new income statement is started. Accountants call this process of ending one period and starting another period as "**closing the accounting records**" or "**closing the books.**"

Let's Look at Target

Look at Exhibit 8.5, Target's income statement, called a Statement of Operations, for the year ending January 31, 2015.

What do you see? You first see Target's sales, then you see Target's cost of goods sold. Sales less cost of goods sold is called gross profit. Next come the other expenses such as selling expense and depreciation expense. Gross profit less these other operating expenses nets to earnings before interest and taxes (EBIT). From EBIT, interest expense is deducted. This leaves taxable income. When the tax expense is subtracted from taxable income, the result is net income.

EXHIBIT 8.5: Target's Income Statement through January (in Millions of US Dollars)

	2014	2015
Sales	$72,596	$72,618
− Costs of Goods Sold	(51,160)	(51,278)
= Gross Profit	21,436	21,340
− Operating Expenses	(17,207)	(16,805)
= Earnings Before Interest and Taxes	4,229	4,535
− Interest Expense	(1,126)	(882)
= Taxable Income	3,103	3,653
− Taxes	(1,132)	(1,204)
= Net Income	$1,971	$2,449

Now look at Target's income statement in total. What does it tell you? It tells you for the year ending January 31, 2015, the sales and expenses Target experienced during the twelve months ending in January 31, 2015. It tells you how these sales and expenses netted to net income, which belongs to Target's owners. Target's income statement answers the following question: How has Target used the economic resources to create a net income or loss in the year ending January 31, 2015? Target's net income equals Target's sales less expenses.

OTHER FINANCIAL STATEMENTS AND INFORMATION

Accountants provide additional information to help clarify the assumptions and procedures used to recognize, measure, record, and report business transactions. This additional information is provided by 1) notes or explanations and 2) supplemental financial statements. Two very important supplemental statements are the statement of retained earnings and the cash flow statement.

The **statement of retained earnings** shows how the retained earnings account, in the owner's equity section of the balance sheet, changed during a given period. It reflects beginning retained earnings, plus the net income earned in the period, less the net losses earned in the period, less the dividends declared during the period. (Note: The Statement of Retained Earnings is often included in a statement that reconciles the changes, in a given period, of all accounts in owner's equity.)

The **cash flow statement** shows how the cash account, in the balance sheet, changed during a given period. The cash flow statement shows a business's sources and uses of cash. It reflects beginning cash, plus sources of cash, less uses of cash, netting to ending cash. So where does a business get and use cash? A business can receive cash and use cash from operating, investing, and financing activities.

Operating activities reflect cash provided by or used in generating net income. Remember that net income is not a cash number. It is an accrual number. Let's look at an example. You sell a customer a bicycle for $250. The customer promises to pay you in 90 days. You have a receivable. Your income statement says you have revenue of $250, but you did not receive $250 in cash. When using accrual accounting standards, remember that sales, costs, and thus net income or loss are not the same as cash. **Investing activities** reflect cash provided by or used in buying and selling long-term assets. You receive cash when you sell a building. You use cash to buy a building. **Financing activities** reflect cash provided by or used to

Bicycles for rent in Paris, France.

pay for financing activities. Financing activities relate to long-term debt and owner's equity. Borrowing money from lenders and selling stock are sources of cash. Repaying debt and paying cash dividends are financing activities that use cash.

So this is the world of accounting. This is the world of recognizing, measuring, recording, and reporting business transactions to provide useful information. It's now time to look at some special insights regarding how groups use this information.

LEARNING OBJECTIVE 3

SPECIAL INSIGHTS FOR USING ACCOUNTING INFORMATION

Accounting attempts to provide useful information. As we've seen, there are many different users, all with different needs. Let's look at some special needs and issues faced by users.

MANAGERIAL ACCOUNTING

Managers have different accounting information needs than lenders and owners. Managers must understand and manage every transaction. The information provided to lenders and owners aggregates and summarizes information. The financial reports given to lenders and owners report total sales, total expenses, total assets, etc. Managers need more detailed information. They need more detail to plan, execute, and review.

Planning

Managers should plan future business transactions. To quantify these plans and look at the financial impact of those plans, managers set up a budget. A **budget** is a financial plan that shows the projected sales and costs that result from management decisions. Budgets also show the assets and people needed to produce the sales and expense, as well as the source of money to finance the decisions.

Budgets are a basis for creating standards. **Standards** are benchmarks that businesses use to determine if budgeted transactions are being achieved. Let's look at an example. Your bicycle store is budgeted to sell 100 bicycles at an average price of $250 per bicycle. Each bicycle is budgeted to cost $100. In addition to the cost of each bicycle, your store is also budgeted to have expenses for employees, rent, advertising, and utilities. These additional costs are budgeted to total $10,000. Your budgeted income statement is

Sales	$25,000 (100 bicycles at $250 each)
Cost of Goods Sold	10,000 (100 bicycles at $100 each)
Gross Profit	$15,000
Other Operating Expenses	10,000
Operating Profit	$ 5,000

Your volume or quantity standard is selling 100 bicycles. Your pricing standard is $250 per bicycle. Your expense standard is $100 per bicycle and $10,000 other expenses.

NEEDING A ROAD MAP

Have you ever gone on a long trip in your automobile? You know where you are and where you want to go. But how are you going to get to your destination? What do you do? You map out your trip. You decide how you will drive, where you will drive, and when you will drive. You create a travel plan. Part of your travel plan is thinking through the things that may happen to cause a change in plans. What happens if you have a flat tire? What happens if a road is under construction and you must detour? To be safe, you also create a backup or contingency plan.

Businesses are like you—they know where they are and where they want to go. They map out the most efficient way to achieve their goals—we call this plan a budget—but they realize that things can change. One part of budgeting is contingency planning, and another part is doing sensitivity analysis and seeing what would happen if sales, costs, or other factors change. Value is a function of the future, and business uses all types of budgets to make the future better.

Execution

You execute or operate your business and you want to monitor your operations. You compare your actual results with standards. This comparison is called variance analysis. A **variance** is the difference between actual and budgeted (standard) amounts.

Let's look at our bicycle store example. You actually sold 120 bicycles at an average price of $200. You paid $100 for each bicycle sold and incurred $8,000 in other operating costs. You had a favorable or positive variance in the quantity sold (120 bicycles actually sold versus 100 budgeted). However you have an unfavorable or negative variance in the price your customers paid ($200 average price versus $250 budgeted price). You were on budget and had a zero variance for the cost of the bicycles sold. You budgeted and paid $100 per bicycle. You had a $2,000 favorable or positive variance for other operating costs ($8,000 actual versus $10,000 budgeted). Your actual income statement looks like:

Sales	$24,000	(120 bicycles at $200 each)
Cost of Goods Sold	12,000	(120 bicycles at $100 each)
Gross Profit	$12,000	
Other Operating Expenses	8,000	
Operating Profit	$ 4,000	

Review

So what have we learned from comparing the plan or budgeted amounts with the executed or actual amounts? You made $4,000, not $5,000, or $1,000 less than you budgeted. That's bad. But how did you do it? The lost $1,000 in profit is the result of good things and bad things. It's good you sold more bicycles than you budgeted. It's good you were able to buy the bicycles at the budgeted cost. It's good you were able to save $2,000 in other operating costs. However it was bad you sold each bicycle for $50 less than you budgeted. So is there anything you can do to perpetuate the good things and correct the bad things? When managers ask such questions, they are reviewing. They are learning. They are looking to improve the future.

Pricing and Costing

In the process of planning, executing, and reviewing, managers must determine the price they will charge for their products. To do so, they also want to understand the costs the business will incur. Managers try to separate expenses into two categories, variable costs and fixed costs. **Variable costs** vary directly with the amount sold. In your bicycle store, every bike sold cost you $100. The $100 per bicycle was a variable cost. **Fixed costs** are costs that do not vary with the amount sold. You incur fixed costs whether you have sales or not. Your $8,000 of other operating expenses were fixed costs.

Managers need to know the nature of the costs they incur. We'll look more at this topic when we explore pricing products in Chapter 13.

ACCOUNTANTS AND THE ACCOUNTING PROFESSION

Representatives from the global accounting firm of KPMG are on hand for the signing of an agreement with a Saudi business.

Accounting is a critical function in any business. It requires special education to be a good accountant within a business. The chief accountant in a business is often called the business's **controller** or **comptroller**. But besides accountants within a business, there are accountants who work outside a business. These accountants work for accounting firms that help businesses with accounting, tax, and advisory services, as well as the major function of audit services.

Audits and Certified Public Accountants (CPAs)

Lenders and owners want to make sure the information management provides is reliable. To make sure that the information is reliable, businesses hire outside accounting firms to audit the business. The US government requires all companies traded in public markets have an annual audit. An **audit** is where an accounting firm (**auditors**), independent of the business, comes into the business and reviews 1) the business's internal control and 2) how the transactions are being recognized, measured, recorded, and reported. Auditors review the business transactions to make sure that the financial statements generated by management, for investors and lenders, fairly present the operations and activities of the business. Auditors attest that the financial reports conform to GAAP. Auditors do not produce the financial reports. Managers produce the financial reports. However, auditors attest to the fairness of the reports by issuing an **audit opinion**. There are **four types of audit opinions**.

1. **Unqualified or clean opinion.** Auditors believe the financial statements fairly present the business's operations and activities.

2. **Qualified or subject-to opinion.** Auditors believe the financial statements fairly present the business's operations and activities except for select items.

3. **Adverse opinion.** Auditors do not believe the financial statements fairly present the business's operations and activities.

4. **Disclaimer.** Auditors state they are not issuing an opinion on whether or not the financial statements fairly present the business's operations and activities.

In the US, audit opinions must be issued by a **Certified Public Accountant (CPA)**. CPAs are licensed by a state. Each state sets the requirements to be a CPA, but all states have stringent education and practice requirements to be licensed as a CPA. There are also strict ethical standards that CPAs must meet.

Accounting Regulation and Disclosures

US GAAP is constantly being revised as the business world evolves. The US government is also requiring more disclosures from businesses traded in public markets. The Sarbanes-Oxley law (SOX) is an example of such a requirement. **Sarbanes-Oxley (SOX)** is a law that requires management to disclose the significant risks faced by a business. SOX also places more personal responsibility on management to provide fair and complete financial statements.

FINANCIAL ANALYSIS

So financial statements answer the following questions:

1. What economic resources (assets) does the business have at a specific time with which it can create value?

2. Where did the business get the money (debt versus owner's) to acquire these economic resources at that specific time?

3. How has the business used the economic resources to create a net income or loss in a given period? (Note: Remember that owner's value is a function of the net income earned from a business.)

Now let's add a fourth question.

4. Did the business do a good or bad job? That is, did the business make sufficient net income to justify the investment of funds and assumption of risk and did the business operate in such a way as to create value?

The answer to this question is financial analysis. **Financial analysis** is the process of analyzing the business's operations to see how it creates value. As such, financial analysis looks at the operating profit produced by hiring people and investing in assets. Financial analysis also looks at how the business is financed, debt or owner's equity, and how it pays its debts. As such, financial analysis looks at every aspect of the business through the financial statements.

Let's look at some questions asked in financial analysis.

1. What return did the business generate for its owners? We call that return on equity, or ROE. **Return on Equity (ROE)** is computed as:

EQUATION 8.3: Return on Equity (ROE)

$$\text{Net Income/Total Owner's Equity} = \text{Return on Equity}$$

How did the business use its assets to generate the net income? We call that return on assets (ROA). **Return on Assets (ROA)** is defined as:

EQUATION 8.4: Return on Assets (ROA)

$$\text{Net Income/Total Assets} = \text{Return on Assets}$$

How did the business finance its assets? We call that **financial leverage**. A measure of financial leverage is:

EQUATION 8.5: Financial Leverage

$$Total\ Assets/Total\ Owner's\ Equity = Financial\ Leverage$$

In answering these questions, never forget that it is the total business that creates value, not just one aspect of the business. The objective of the business is to create net income for the owners, which drives value. To demonstrate this, put Equations 8.3, 8.4, and 8.5 together and see how a business's investing and financing decisions create a return for owners. The result is:

EQUATION 8.6: ROE Decomposed

$$Net\ Income/Total\ Owner's\ Equity = Net\ Income/Total\ Assets * Total\ Assets/Total\ Owner's\ Equity$$

$$ROE = ROA * Financial\ Leverage$$

Let's Look at Target

Look at Exhibits 8.3 (Target's Balance Sheet) and 8.5 (Target's Income Statement). What do you see for the year ending January 31, 2015? You see the needed numbers to compute Target's ROE, ROA, and financial leverage.

Target's ROE = Net Income/Owner's Equity
Target's ROE = $2,449/$13,997 = .175

(Note the net income number comes from the income statement, Exhibit 8.5, and owner's equity comes from the balance sheet, Exhibit 8.3.)

Target's ROA = Net Income/Total Assets
Target's ROA = $2,449/$41,404 = .059

(Note the net income number comes from the income statement, Exhibit 8.5, and the total asset number comes from the balance sheet, Exhibit 8.3.)

Target's Financial Leverage = Total Assets/Owner's Equity
Target's Financial Leverage = $41,404/$13,997 = 2.958

(Note the total assets and owner's equity come from the balance sheet, Exhibit 8.3.)

Now multiply Target's ROA and financial leverage. What do you get? You get Target's ROE.

By conducting financial analysis, you are beginning to get the insights you need to answer the question: Did Target do a good or bad job? Did Target make sufficient net income to justify the investment of funds and assumption of risk? Did Target operate in such a way as to create value?

(For a more in depth discussion of financial analysis, see the appendix at the end of this text, titled Financial Analysis.)

CHAPTER SUMMARY

So information is a key ingredient in the decisions of managers, owners, lenders, customers, regulators, and taxing authorities. Accounting is the function that provides that information. Because business is complex, accounting is complex.

After reading this chapter, you should now be able to:

1. Appreciate the nature and role of accounting, including the rules and techniques used in accounting (Learning Objective 1): Accounting is the function of recognizing, measuring, recording, and reporting business transactions. Good decisions start with good, complete, relevant, and reliable information.

2. Appreciate financial statements (Learning Objective 2): Businesses use accrual accounting to create financial statements that report the operations and activities of a business. These financial statements include the balance sheet, income statement, statement of retained earnings, and cash flow statement.

3. Appreciate some special insights for the use of accounting information (Learning Objective 3): Managers often ask accountants for different insights from those provided in financial statements. Such insights help managers plan, execute, and review. Businesses also ask special accountants, called Certified Public Accountants, to audit the businesses and issue opinions on their financial statements. Financial statements provide users insights they can use to conduct financial analysis. Financial analysis is the process of analyzing the business's operations to see how it creates value.

You now can look at how the business invests in assets and hires people, finances its assets, and operates to create a profit. You can look at the transactions that create value. It's time to begin exploring the principles and techniques used to value a business and "How Business Works."

KEYWORDS

SHORT-ANSWER QUESTIONS

1. Explain what the following financial statements reflect:
   a. Balance sheet
   b. Income statement
   c. Statement of retained earnings
   d. Cash flow statement

2. Why do assets equal liabilities plus owner's equity?

3. What is the difference between variable and fixed costs?

4. Explain the difference between financial and managerial accounting.

5. Explain the difference between cash basis of accounting and accrual basis of accounting.

6. Define the following terms:
   a. Accounting
   b. Internal control
   c. Account
   d. US Securities and Exchange Commission (SEC)
   e. Public Company Accounting Oversight Board (PCAOB)
   f. Financial Accounting Standards Board (FASB)
   g. Generally Accepted Accounting Principles (GAAP)
   h. Conservatism
   i. International Accounting Standards Board (IASB)
   j. International Financial Reporting Standards (IFRS)
   k. Fair value
   l. Asset
   m. Current assets
   n. Long-term assets
   o. Cash
   p. Accounts receivable
   q. Inventory
   r. Purchased inventory
   s. Produced inventory
   t. Raw material inventory
   u. Work-in-process inventory
   v. Finished goods inventory
   w. Tangible assets
   x. Property, plant, and equipment (PP&E), or fixed assets
   y. Depreciation
   z. Intangible assets
   aa. Amortization
   ab. Goodwill
   ac. Impairment
   ad. Liabilities
   ae. Current liabilities
   af. Long-term liabilities
   ag. Accounts payable
   ah. Accrued liabilities
   ai. Short-term borrowing
   aj. Owner's equity
   ak. Stock accounts
   al. Retained earnings
   am. Cash dividend
   an. Sale
   ao. Expense
   ap. Matching concept
   aq. Cost of goods sold
   ar. Gross profit
   as. Earnings before interest and taxes (EBIT)
   at. Operating profit
   au. Interest
   av. Net income before taxes, or taxable income
   aw. Net income or loss
   ax. Budget
   ay. Standards
   az. Variance
   ba. Controller or comptroller
   bb. Sarbanes-Oxley law (SOX)

CRITICAL-THINKING QUESTIONS

1. What is an audit and why do businesses have audits?
2. What is a CPA and what are the four types of audit opinions?
3. What is financial analysis?
4. Pameland, Inc. earned net income of $1,000. It had assets totaling $5,000, liabilities totaling $2,000, and owner's equity totaling $3,000. What is Pameland's
    a. ROA,
    b. Financial leverage, and
    c. ROE?

EXPLORING REAL BUSINESS

Go to the websites of Google, Target, Hyundai, and Proctor and Gamble. The websites are

Google:	http://investor.google.com
Target:	http://www.target.com
Hyundai:	http://worldwide.hyundai.com/company-overview
Procter & Gamble:	http://www.pg.com

For each company, try to identify the following:

1. Total assets
2. Total liabilities
3. Total owner's equity
4. Sales
5. Cost of goods sold
6. Gross profit
7. Earnings before interest and taxes (EBIT)
8. Net income
9. Cash flow from operations
10. Cash flow from investing
11. Cash flow from financing

ENDNOTE

1. Many businesses have a third type of account in owner's equity. This account is called "other comprehensive income" (OCI). OCI occurs in special situations where accountants recognize the value of an asset or liability changes on the balance sheet but do not recognize the change in the income statement. The change is accounted for in OCI. Such transactions are very limited and the subject for advanced accounting courses.

09

CHAPTER

VALUATION AND THE TIME VALUE OF MONEY

Introduction: Let's Talk About Value and Time

People often say, "Time is money." Why? Why is time important and how does time impact value? Why should managers worry about time?

In this chapter we'll explore these questions and issues. We'll develop tools that help in understanding and measuring the impact of time on value. We'll see why and how time is important in "How Business Works."

LEARNING OBJECTIVES

After reading Chapter 09, you should be able to meet the following learning objectives:

1. Appreciate the impact of time on value
2. Understand the mechanics of the time value of money
3. Appreciate how the time value of money is used in business decisions, particularly valuation

WHY TIME MATTERS

It is often said that time is the most precious commodity that someone owns. The reason is time, once past, can never be recaptured. Time is valuable. Think about it. You want to get a good grade in a course. You have limited time to read, study, and attend lectures, yet you also want to go out and have a good time with your friends. You do not have enough time to study and go out. How do you decide which option to choose? You value the outcomes of each option. What is the value of studying for your course and what is the value of having a good time? Which value is greatest in your mind? You are the decision maker. You are the one who receives the benefits and pays the cost of choosing. You understand that time is a precious commodity and matters greatly.

LEARNING OBJECTIVE 1
. . . .
THE IMPACT OF TIME ON VALUE

How do we measure the value of something? Value is a function of

· The quantity of the benefits we expect to receive if we own it

· The expected timing of the benefits we expect to receive if we own it

· Our opportunity cost or required rate of return we assess on it

Simply put, we value something by asking the following questions:

· What benefits do I expect to receive if I own something?

· When do I expect to get these benefits if I own something?

· What other opportunities do I have and what is the appropriate required rate of return for this opportunity?

Time is at the heart of creating value. First, time impacts the second question dealing with "when." The timing of the benefits is important by itself. Time also impacts the third question, the opportunity cost or required rate of return. The longer we have to wait for the benefits, the greater the risk. The greater the risk, the greater the required rate of return. Understanding time is critical to understanding value.

It's often said that patience is golden and that it takes time for good things to occur. These statements are true. It takes time to plan, execute, and review, and to create value. However, time is not a free good. Time is a precious commodity that managers must understand, appreciate, and use.

Let's look at an example. Ask yourself whether you'd like one dollar today or one million dollars in one thousand years. If you are like most people, the answer is one dollar today. Why? The answer is our expected life is significantly less than one thousand years. We'll never receive the one million dollars. In answering this way, however, we acknowledge that time is very important in what we do and when we do it. Time is a precious and critical element of our lives. We go through life making choices of how we'll spend our time and make those choices based on our forecast of which alternative will give us the greatest value.

Time does matter. We cannot avoid the impact of time. Time presents a challenge. When looking at alternatives, we realize that alternatives have different timing. We try to evaluate the alternatives in comparable timeframes.

Now for another more realistic and common example, look back at Chapter 02 and the discussion of time. Ask yourself the question, "Would you rather have $100 today (option 1) or $100 in one year (option 2)?" We realize that we need to evaluate the two options using a common point in time. Assuming a 4% interest rate per year, we realize that $100 today is equivalent to $104 in one year. If we use the future (one year from now) as our common reference point in time, our choice is $104 (option 1) versus $100 (option 2). We, being value "maximizers," chose the $104 in one year (option 1). If we use today (the present) as our reference point in time and a 4% interest rate, we realize that $100 in one year (option 2) is worth a little over $96 today. (We could invest $96 today at 4% and have $100 in one year.) Our choice is $100 today (option 1) or $96 today (option 2). Once again we'd choose option 1 to maximize value.

The above example shows the impact of time. But how does time impact value?

TIME AND BUSINESS VALUE

Time does matter. When a business generates an operating profit, or return, impacts value. The quicker an operating profit is earned, the more valuable that operating profit is to the providers of money. The longer it takes to earn an operating profit, the less valuable it is to the providers of the money.

Money is not free. When owners and lenders provide money to a business, they expect compensation in return for the use of their money. As noted in Chapter 02, owners and lenders expect a return.

Owners and lenders expect a return that compensates them for two things. First is compensation for time without considering risk. Second is compensation for risk. When added together, these two components equal the required rate of return. (Return, unless otherwise noted, is stated as a return per year or annual return.) As noted in Chapter 02, the required return for a given period is

EQUATION 9.1: Required Rate of Return

$$R = R_f + Risk\ Premium$$

Where

R	Required or expected rate of return
R_f	Risk-free rate of return in the economy
Risk Premium	The additional required return to compensate for risk

Exhibit 9.1 demonstrates how these two components come together to produce the required rate of return.

EXHIBIT 9.1: Risk and Return

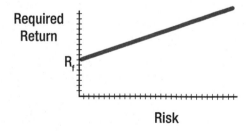

The Risk-Free Rate of Return (R$_f$)

The first component of the required rate of return is a risk-free rate. The **risk-free rate of return** is the return required to use the money for a period of time (e.g., one year), assuming that the return is certain. People often think of the risk-free rate as the rent or price charged for simply using the money. It assumes the providers of the money are certain that the actual return will be the same as their expected return. This risk-free rate is the same for everyone at a point in time. However, like all things, this rate can go up and down over time. In good times when the economy is growing, the demand for money is greater than the supply of money, and the price or required rate for the money goes up. However, when the economy is not growing, the demand for money is less than the supply of money, and the price of or required rate for the money goes down. Thus, the risk-free rate is not constant over time. Because the risk-free rate changes, the providers of the money must first look to the market to find out the current risk-free rate of return.

In the world of today, everything is risky. However, some things have very high degrees of risk and some things have very low degrees of risk. In the United States, providers of money often use the short-term rate charged on US government loans, called **Treasury Securities**, as the risk-free rate. Short-term Treasury Securities are called **Treasury Bills.** They are due in less than a year. It is assumed that loaning money for a short period of time to the US government is safer and thus less risky than loaning money to any other group, or for longer periods of time.

A manager and employee working late to meet a deadline. How do managers confront risk?

The Risk Premium

The second component of the required rate of return is the risk premium. The risk premium is the amount of return the providers of money require to compensate them for risk. Risk, as previous noted in Chapter 01, is the uncertainty that could lead to a loss or undesirable outcome. People and organizations do not like risk. To accept risk, they require more benefits or return. The more risk, the higher the required rate of return. The less risk, the lower the required rate of return. Look at Exhibit 9.1. As risk goes up, the required rate of return goes up.

So where does risk come from? Risk comes from everything a business does. Risk comes from management's decision to address opportunities and challenges within the business (e.g., better ways to produce a product) and outside the business (e.g., changing market conditions). Risk comes from decisions to invest in assets and hire people. Risk comes from creating, producing, and marketing a product to customers. Risk comes from how a business is financed.

So risk comes from everything a business does. Everything managers do is based on beliefs and expectations, not certainty. So is risk constant? The answer is "no," risk and risk premiums are constantly changing. So can we measure risk? The answer is "risk measurement is hard, but good managers try." We have different risk measures for different types of risks. Which leads us to the next question, "can we manage risk?" The answer is "risk management is hard, but good managers try." Some risks can be eliminated or managed. The risk that cannot be eliminated should be recognized and addressed in determining the risk premium. Chapter 11.

So how do time and return work together? Let's look at the mechanics.

THE MECHANICS OF THE TIME VALUE OF MONEY

To explore the impact of time, we'll first look at how single amounts of money grow from the present to the future. Then we'll look at the present value of single amounts of money received in the future. Next we'll look at the required rate of return, followed by time. We'll then extend our work from single amounts of money to money received or paid in multiple periods. Last, we'll look at some special topics.

SINGLE AMOUNTS

Let's look first at how time affects value using a single amount of money.

Future Value (FV)

Go back to our example of $100 received today. We asked the question, "How much will we have in one year if our $100 grows at a rate of 4%?" Our question has four parts. The first part is how much we have today, or **present value.** Our present value is $100. The second part is our rate of change or **rate of return.** Our expected rate of return is 4%. The third part is the **time period.** Our time period is one year. The fourth part is what we expect to receive in the future, or future value. In our example the future value is our unknown. When we use the other three parts we can compute the fourth part. The answer to our example is $104. Mathematically, our example is

$$(\$100 * 1.04)^1 = FV$$
$$\$104 = FV$$

Now let's look at our four parts without numbers. Mathematically we can state the relationship of the four parts as:

EQUATION 9.2: Future Value

$$PV * (1 + r)^t = FV$$

Where

PV	Present value
r	Rate of return
t	The number of time periods
FV	Future value

Let's go back to our example and change our question to, "How much will we have in two years if our $100 grows at a rate of 4% per year?" What are we saying? We are saying our $100 will grow at a rate of 4% for the first year. At the end of the first year we will have a new amount, which we will then let grow at 4% during the second year. Mathematically, our example is

$$\$100 * (1.04)(1.04) = \$108.16$$

EXHIBIT 9.2: Multiple Period Future Value

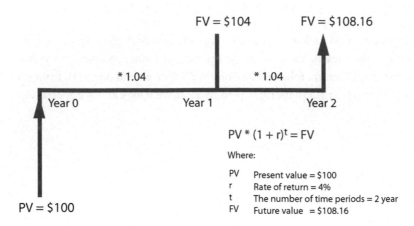

Payment In = $100

What happened? Our $100 grew to be $104 after one year. During the second year the $104 grew to be $108.16. Let's dissect what happened. First, our $100 earned a return of $4 for the first year. We now have $104 after one year. Our $104 earned a return of $4.16 the second year. The $4.16 can be decomposed into 1) the $4 return on the original $100 and 2) the $.16 return on the $4 earned during the first year. The $.16 is called **interest-on-interest** and represents **compounding.** If we put our example into Equation 9.2, we get

$$\$100(1.04)2 = FV$$
$$\$108.16 = FV$$

Present Value (PV)

If we can determine the future value of a present amount, can we determine the present value of a future amount? Using our example, the question becomes, "How much must we invest today to have $104 in one year, assuming a 4% rate of return?" Remember the four parts of our equation: the present value, the future value, the rate of return, and time? Now we know the future value, the rate of return, and the time, but we do not know the present value.

Let's take Equation 9.2 and rearrange the terms.

$$\text{If } PV\ (1\ +\ r)^t\ =\ FV,\ \text{then}$$

EQUATION 9.3: Present Value

$$PV\ =\ FV/(1\ +\ r)^t$$

Where

PV	Present value
FV	Future value
r	Rate of return
t	The number of time periods

THE RULE OF TIME — 72

Computing the impact of time can be daunting unless you have a computer or calculator. This is particularly true when you are working with long time periods. Compounding makes calculations challenging. But guess what? The finance world has a general rule that approximates how long it takes for money to double. It's called the Rule of 72. The equation is:

Time to double your money = 72/interest rate.

Let's look at an example. Assume you have $10,000. You need $20,000. You feel you can earn a 6% rate of return per year. So how long will it take you to have $20,000? Divide 72 by 6 and you get 12 years. It will take you approximately 12 years for your $10,000 to grow to be $20,000, assuming a 6% rate of return compounded annually. Now think about it and revise your question. Ask yourself how much rate of return you must earn to double your money in 12 years? How much return must you earn to grow your $10,000 into $20,000 in 12 years? To convert your $10,000 into $20,000 in 12 years, you must earn a return of 6% per year. That's the Rule of 72.

The answer to our question is $100, found using Equation 9.3 as

$$PV = \$104/(1.04)^1$$
$$PV = \$100$$

Thus, $100 today will grow into $104 in one year, assuming a 4% return.

Let's revise our question again and ask, "How much must we invest today to have $108.16 in two years, assuming a 4% rate of return per year?" The answer to our question is $100, found using Equation 9.3 as

$$PV = \$108.16/(1.04)^2$$
$$PV = \$100$$

Thus, $100 today will grow into $108.16 in two years, assuming a 4% return per year.

Rate of Return (r)

If we can determine future and present values, can we determine the rate of return of an investment? Can we determine the rate that equates a present value to a future value during a given period? Once again we have three of our four parts. We know the present value, the future value, and time. We do not know the rate of return. Using our example, the question becomes, "How much return must we earn to grow our $100 now to $104 in one year?"

Let's take Equation 9.2, rearrange the terms, and solve for "r."

$$\text{If } PV \ (1+r)^t = FV, \text{ then}$$

EQUATION 9.4: Return

$$(1 + r)^t = FV/PV$$

Where

r	Rate of return
t	The number of time periods
FV	Future value
PV	Present value

The answer to our question is 4%, found using Equation 9.4 as

$$(1.04)^1 = \$104/\$100$$

The rate that equates $100 today and $104 in one year is 4%.

Let's revise our question to ask, "How much annual return would we earn if we invested $100 today and received $108.16 in two years?" The answer to our question is 4%, found using Equation 9.4 as

$$(1 + r)^2 = \$108.16/\$100$$
$$r = .04$$

The rate that equates $100 today and $108.16 in two years is 4%.

Time (t)

If we can determine present values, future values, and rates of return, can we determine time? Can we determine how long it will take for a present value to become a future value at specified rate of return? Once again we have three of our four parts. We know the present value, the future value, and the rate of return. We do not know time. Using our example, the question becomes, "How long will it take for $100 to become $104 assuming a 4% rate of return?"

Let's use Equation 9.4 and solve for "t." The answer to our question is one year, found as

$$(1.04)^t = \$104/\$100$$
$$t = 1 \text{ year}$$

Let's revise our question to ask, "How long will it take for $100 to become $108.16, assuming a 4% rate of return?" Solving for "t," the answer to our question is two years, found as

$$(1.04)^t = \$108.16/\$100$$
$$t = 2 \text{ years}$$

Summarizing the Time Value of Money: Future Value, Present Value, Rate of Return, and Time

Let's look at Equation 9.2 again.

$$PV * (1 + r)^t = FV$$

Where

PV	Present value
r	Rate of return
t	The number of time periods
FV	Future value

Per the equation, there are four terms. We can compute any of the four terms if we know the other three terms. This is very important. The terms that equate the present and future are time and return.

MULTIPLE AMOUNTS

Now let's use our insights to consider amounts of money received or paid in multiple time periods.

Future Value Using Multiple Periods

What happens when you have more than one payment in? Let's ask the question, "How much will we have at the end of two years if we invest $100 today and $100 in one year, assuming a 4% rate of return compounded annually?" Look at Exhibit 9.3.

EXHIBIT 9.3: Future Value of Multiple Amounts

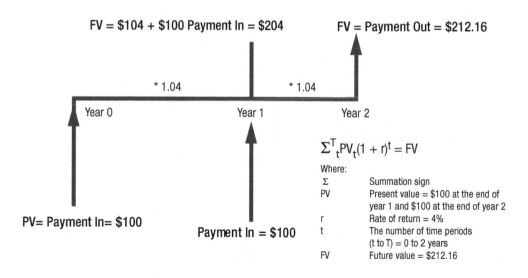

We have one question that can be broken into two parts. Let's look back at our earlier example of single amounts. First we know that the future value of $100, in two years, assuming a 4% rate of return, will be $108.16. Second, we know that the future value of $100, in one year, assuming a 4% rate of return, will be $104. If we add these two parts together, we can answer our new question. We will have a total of $212.16 in two years, assuming a 4% rate of return compounded annually ($104 + $108.16 = $212.16).

Let's analyze what happened. First, we invest $100. Our $100 then grows at a 4% rate to become $104 at the end of year one. We then invest another $100 giving us a total of $204 at the end of year one. This $204 grows at a rate of 4% during the second year, giving us $212.16 at the end of the second year. Mathematically we can state what happened as:

$$\$100 \ (1.04)^2 + \$100(1.04)1 = FV$$
$$\$212.16 = FV$$

When we adjust Equation 9.2 to include multiple future values, we get Equation 9.5.

EQUATION 9.5: Future Value of Multiple Amounts

$$\sum\nolimits^T_t PV_t(1+r)^t = FV$$

Where

$\sum$	Summation sign
PV	Present value
r	Rate of return
t	The number of time periods (t to T)
FV	Future value

Present Value Using Multiple Periods

Now let's ask the question, "How much must we invest (present value) today to receive $104 in one year and $108.16 in two years (future values), assuming a 4% rate of return compounded annually?" Look at Exhibit 9.4.

EXHIBIT 9.4: Present Value of Multiple Amounts

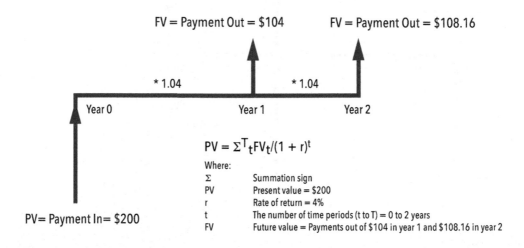

$$PV = \sum\nolimits^T_t FV_t/(1+r)^t$$

Where:

$\sum$	Summation sign
PV	Present value = $200
r	Rate of return = 4%
t	The number of time periods (t to T) = 0 to 2 years
FV	Future value = Payments out of $104 in year 1 and $108.16 in year 2

Once again we have one question that can be broken into two parts. Let's look back at our earlier example of single amounts. First we know that the present value of $104 to be received in one year, assuming a 4% rate of return compounded annually, is $100. Second, we know that the present value of $108.16 to be received in two years, assuming a 4% rate of return compounded annually, is $100. If we add these two parts together, we can answer our new question. We need to invest $200 today to receive $104 in one year and $108.16 in two years, assuming a 4% rate of return compounded annually.

Let's analyze what happened. First, we invest $200. Our $200 grows at a 4% rate to become $208 at the end of year 1. We then take out $104 at the end of year 1, leaving $104 to grow during the second year. This remaining $104 grows at a rate of 4% during the second year, leaving us $108.16 at the end of the second year. We can then take out the $108.16 at the end of year 2. Mathematically we can state what happened as:

$$PV = \$104/(1.04)^1 + \$108.16/(1.04)^2$$
$$PV = \$200$$

When we adjust Equation 9.3 to include multiple future values, we get Equation 9.6.

EQUATION 9.6

$$PV = \sum_{t}^{T} FV_t/(1 + r)^t$$

Where

$\sum$	Summation sign
PV	Present value
FV	Future value
r	Rate of return
t	The number of time periods (t to T)

Rate of Return and Time

Using Equation 9.5 or 9.6, the rate of return or time can be determined if the other terms of the equation are known.

SPECIAL TOPICS

Now let's look at the three special topics:

1. Annuities

2. The compounding period

3. Calculators

Annuities

An **annuity** is a stream of equal payments made at equal intervals of time. Let's look at two examples. First you want to save for a new auto, an asset. You decide to deposit $5,000 every year for the next four years. You expect to earn a rate of return of 4% per year. How much will you have at the end of four years? You are planning to make equal payments of $5,000 at the end of each year for the next four years. You are working with a future value of an annuity. Second, let's look at another example dealing with a liability. You borrow $20,000 to buy a car. You agree to pay 36 equal monthly payments to repay the loan plus interest. You agree to pay interest of 6% per year. You are working with an annuity.

A special note should be made about when the equal payments are made. If the annuity payments are made or received at the end of the period, the annuities are called **regular annuities.** If the payments are made or received at the beginning of the period, the annuities are called **annuities due.**

A special type of an annuity is a perpetuity, which pays a future amount forever. For example, you want to invest enough money so your favorite charity will receive $1,000 per month forever. To determine the present value of a perpetuity, use Equation 9.7.

EQUATION 9.7: *Present Value of an Annuity*

$$PV = PP/r$$

Where

PV	Present value of perpetuity
PP	Periodic perpetuity payment
r	Rate of return

Annuities are like any other present or future value problem with multiple cash flows, but these calculations are made easier by recognizing the payments are equal amounts. As noted later, these complex computations are made easier using calculators and other aids.

The Compounding Period

Rates of return are quoted in annual terms. When a rate is quoted, it is assumed that it deals with a calendar year of twelve months. When the compounding period is one year, as used in the above examples, people will say they are using **simple interest.**

The challenge is that rates of return are often computed in periods less than one year. Let's go back to our earlier future value example of investing a single amount of $100 for one year. Let's assume that we are going to compound the rate of return every three months, or quarterly. Our rate is quoted as an annual rate or 4%. But we will earn 1/4th that rate every three months. We will earn 1% every three months. Using our example, the question becomes, "How much will we have in one year if our $100 grows at a rate of 4% compounded quarterly?" What we are saying is, "How much will we have in one year if our $100 grows at a rate of 1% every three months, for twelve months?"

Let's take Equation 9.2 and adjust the terms. First, the rate of return (r) becomes 1%, or 1/4th of 4%. Second, the number of periods (t) becomes four periods, or four quarters times one year.

$$\text{If } PV\ (1 + r)^t = FV, \text{ then}$$
$$\$100(1.01)^4 = FV$$
$$\$104.06 = FV$$

Thus, $100 today will grow into $104.06 in one year, assuming a 4% return compounded quarterly. So where did the extra 6 cents come from? It came from the interest-on-interest. The quicker the rate of return is compounded, the greater the impact of the rate of return.

Now let's look at the impact of compounding periods on the present value, rate of return, and timing elements of our example.

First is present value. Let's ask the question, "How much must we invest today to have $104 in one year, assuming a 4% rate of return compounded quarterly?"

Let's take Equation 9.3 and solve for PV. The answer to our question is $99.94 found as

$$PV = \$104/(1.01)^4$$
$$PV = \$99.94$$

Thus, $99.94 today will grow into $104 in one year, assuming a 4% return compounded quarterly. Once again we see the power of compounding in periods less than one year. Our present value is 6 cents less, compared to annual compounding, because of compounding quarterly. The interest earned in growing the present value to the future value is greater because of quarterly compounding.

Next is the rate of return. Let's ask the question, "How much return will we earn if our $100 today grows to be $104 in one year, assuming quarterly compounding?"

Let's take Equation 9.4 and solve for "r."

$$(1 + r)^4 = \$104/\$100$$
$$r = .00985$$

The rate of return each quarter is not 1%, or .01. The actual rate is .985%, or .00985. Why is this quarterly rate lower than 1%? The answer is compounding quarterly versus annually.

Annual rates of return are typically stated in simple interest terms, although the actual rate of return earned can be significantly different as seen in the above example. The actual rate earned is often called the **annual percentage rate (APR)** or the **effective rate of return**. US law requires that lenders clearly disclose the actual rate so that borrowers clearly understand the cost of borrowing.

Last is the time period. Let's ask the question, "How long will it take for $100 to become $104 assuming a 4% rate of return compounded quarterly?"

Let's take Equation 9.4 and solve for "t."

$$(1 + .01)^t = \$104/\$100$$
$$t = .9973 \text{ years}$$

The time period is slightly less than a year, or approximately 364 days. Quarterly compounding created a higher effective rate of return. With this higher rate of return, it takes less time for our $100

BUSINESS SENSE
WHAT'S THE TRUE COST OF YOUR MONEY?

You need money. You go to the bank and ask for a loan. The bank agrees to loan you $1,000. The loan is to be repaid, with interest, in one year. The bank states the interest rate is 9% compounded daily. The bank also requires you to pay a 3% fee for processing the loan. So what's the cost of your loan? Is it the 9% as stated by the bank? The answer is no. Let's look at what is happening.

The bank lends you $1,000 but requires you to immediately pay it $30 for the 3% processing fee. All you receive is $970 ($1,000 – $30). Each day you are charged interest on the $1,000 at the rate of .09/365 days. This daily rate is .00024658. (In the financial world, rates of return are often quoted in basis points, or BPs. A basis point is one one-hundredth of a percentage point. Thus, our daily rate per above would be 2.4658 BPs.) That rate is charged every day, for 365 days. Because of the daily compounding, your actual rate is 9.42%. At the end of the year you'll owe the bank the original $1,000 plus $94.20 in interest, or a total of $1,094.20. So you borrowed $970 and must repay $1,094.20 in one year. Your annual percentage rate (APR) or effective interest rate is 12.8%. Now that you appreciate compounding, watch out.

to grow to be $104. The faster the compounding, the more interest on interest is earned. That means it takes less time for a present value to grow to a future value.

So the compounding period is very important. Rates are usually quoted in annual terms. However, often you'll see semiannual, quarterly, and even daily compounding. If so, the actual rate will be greater than the simple interest rate due to compounding.

Calculators, Computers, and Time Value of Money Computations

Doing the math regarding time is complicated and challenging. To assist the calculations, people often use calculators with a special function to deal with these computations. Often computers have a similar function with programs such as Excel. This function is often denoted as the *TVM or Time Value of Money function*. Remember all the above computations have four terms. These terms are:

1. Present value

2. Rate of return

3. The number of time periods

4. Future value

Calculators are designed to compute the fourth term if you enter the other three terms. Exhibit 9.5 is a listing of selected companies, with Websites, which make popular calculators that perform time value of money calculations. Note that instructions on how to operate these calculators are provided on the following Websites.

EXHIBIT 9.5: Calculators and Time Value of Money Computations

HP - Website
http://store.hp.com/us/en/pdp/accessories-88342-1/hp-12c-platinum-financial-calc-f2231aa-aba
Sharp - Website
http://sharpcalculators.com/
Texas Instruments (TI) - Website
http://education.ti.com/en/us/products/calculators/financial-calculators
Casio - Website
http://www.casio.com/products/Calculators_%26_Dictionaries/Fraction_%26_Scientific/FC-200V/

LEARNING OBJECTIVE 3
. . . .
USING THE TIME VALUE OF MONEY IN BUSINESS DECISIONS

Businesses must make decisions that have long-term implications. When making such decisions, businesses must incorporate time and an opportunity cost (required rate of return).

TYPICAL LONG-TERM BUSINESS DECISIONS

Let's look at several long-term decisions businesses face. Let's first look at buying a truck, an asset. Then let's look at borrowing money, a liability. Last let's look at funding a future need for an employee.

Buying a Truck, an Asset

Your business is growing, and if you continue to grow, you'll need a new truck for delivering your product. You begin to think about buying a new truck. But is it worth it? You begin to plan. You ask your marketing and operations team to give you forecasts for the revenue from the costs of the new truck. They tell you the truck will cost $20,000 and have an expected life of three years. During those three years the truck will provide additional operating profit of $10,000 per year. You realize that the truck needs to provide you a 10% rate of return. So is it worth it?

Let's look at the decision. The decision is whether or not the truck is worth $20,000 given a required rate of return of 10%. If the benefits from investing in the truck are worth more than $20,000, then you should buy it. Why? The answer is it adds value. If the benefits from investing in the truck are worth less than $20,000, then you should not buy it. Why? The answer is it will decrease value. So is it worth it?

The benefits from owning the truck are $10,000 in year 1, $10,000 in year 2, and $10,000 in year 3. Your required rate of return is 10%. Using Equation 9.6, this can be stated mathematically as:

$$\text{Present Value of Owning Truck} = \$10,000/(1.10)^1 + \$10,000/(1.10)^2 + \$10,000/(1.10)^3$$

$$\text{Present Value of Owning Truck} = \$9,091 + \$8,264 + \$7,513 = \$24,868$$

VALUING MANAGERS AND EMPLOYEES

Have you ever heard someone call a manager or employee "invaluable"? Have you ever seen a manager or employee ask for a raise because his or her current pay does not reflect the value he or she is adding to the business?

Valuing the contribution of a manager or employee is a challenge. However, it comes down to recognizing the benefits that the person renders to the business, the timing of those benefits, and the risk associated with those benefits. People are the most valuable asset any business has. Yet valuing the contribution of people is often a challenge. The ultimate measure is to ask the question, "What is the value of this business with and without this person?" The answer will be the person's contribution to the value of the business.

Sometimes answering the above question is easy. It's easy to measure the contribution of some salespeople. Because of that, businesses often pay such people with commissions. The more sales the person makes for the business, the higher the pay he or she receives. However, sometimes it's hard to answer the above question. What's the contribution of an accountant? What's the contribution of the president's administrative assistant? What's the contribution of the person who cleans the factory? All these jobs are important and add value, but how do you measure this value-added activity? Chapter 16 explores this issue.

So our decision is whether we want an asset of $20,000 cash or a truck worth $24,868 in present value terms. Being value maximizers, we'd choose the asset that gives us the greatest expected value in today's term. We'd choose the truck. We'd give up our $20,000 cash today to get an asset we believe is worth $24,868 today.

Borrowing Long-Term Money, a Liability

You go to the bank to borrow money. After looking over your credit application, the bank approves your loan. The bank will loan you $100,000 today, but will charge you annual interest of 8% compounded monthly. The bank requires you to pay the loan back in thirty-six equal monthly installments (an annuity). The first installment will be due at the end of the first month. The final installment will be due at the end of the thirty-sixth month.

The question you face is how much will each installment be? How much must you repay the bank at the end of each of the next thirty-six months? Let's look at the question. You are receiving $100,000 in the present. You will make thirty-six equal installments at the end of the next three years. Your annual interest rate is 8% compounded monthly or .666% (.08/12 months = .00666) every month. Using Equation 9.6, each payment is $3,133.64.

Funding a Future Need (Planning an Employee's Retirement)

You have a valued employee. You want that employee to work with you for the next five years. You and your employee sit down and discuss her needs. Your employee says that she wants to work for you, but she is planning to retire in five years. To retire in five years, your employee needs to have saved $200,000. Your employee tells you she will be happy to work for you for five years if, in addition to her regular income, you will provide her $200,000 when she retires.

You think about it and want to do this. To fund this promise, you decide to set aside an equal amount of money at the end of each year for the next five years. You believe you can invest these funds and earn a 6% return each year, compounded annually (an annuity). Your question is, "How much should each payment be to have $200,000 at the end of five years?" Using Equation 9.5, this can be state mathematically as:

$$(Payment * (1.06)^4) + (Payment * (1.06)^3) + (Payment * (1.06)^2) + (Payment * (1.06)^1) + (Payment) = \$200,000$$

Each payment should be $35,480. If you invest $35,480 at the end of each of the next five years, you will have $200,000 at the end of five years.

As the above examples show, managers must address time and return in making long-term business decisions. All decisions should create value for the business—the most important question is the value of the business itself. What is a business worth?

BUSINESS VALUATION

Remember that the objective of the business is to maximize the value of the business. The value of a business is the value of its debt plus the value of its owner's equity. We'll see in Chapter 10 that maximizing the value of owner's equity is the same as maximizing the value of the business. So how do we measure the value of ownership? The value of owners' equity is equal to the present value of the benefits owners expect to receive.

Using Equation 9.6, we see that

$$PV = \sum\nolimits_{t}^{T} \text{Future Benefits}_t / (1 + r)^t$$

Where

PV	Present value
$\sum$	Summation sign
r	Rate of return
t	The number of time periods (t to T)
FV	Future benefits from owning the business

So what are the benefits that owners expect? The answer is net income. Remember in Chapter 08 we noted that measurement rules are often different for different users. For that reason owners sometimes use net income to value a business. Sometimes owners value a business based on net income converted from an accrual basis to a cash basis. Sometimes owners value a business based on the payment of net income, or dividends. However, whatever measure owners use, it captures the net benefit that they expect to receive.

After estimating the benefits, owners must estimate when they expect to receive the benefits (time) and the required or expected rate of return. As noted in Equation 9.1, this rate of return is a function of the risk owners accept. Chapter 11 explores the topic of risk.

So how does a business create value? A business creates value by investing in assets and hiring people. Where does it get the money to invest in assets and people? A business gets the money from lenders and owners, or the financing function. It's now time to explore the investing and financing functions of a business.

VALUING BUSINESS

Valuing a business is challenging. Why? The answer is that the inputs in the equation are estimates of the future and thus subjective. For that reason people who value businesses use a lot of different techniques; however, all techniques are based on the future benefits owners expect to receive. The best technique is discounting over time the estimated benefits to be received in the future. But let's look at a commonly used technique in valuing a business called the price-earnings ratio (PE).

A PE is the current price of a share of stock divided by the business's current earnings per share. A business's earning per share is the business's net income divided by the number of shares of stock outstanding. When someone says she or he will buy the business at ten times earnings, she or he is using a PE.

So what does a PE tell us? A PE tells us about the company's future versus its present. Remember price reflects the present value of future benefits. Earnings are a measure of present benefits. A PE compares a business's future with its present.

So why are some PEs higher than others? Risk and time impact PEs. But a major reason for a company having a high or low PE is the future prospects of the business. If the business is growing and is expected to do better in the future than the present, then it will have a high PE. If the business is not growing and declining, the future will be worse than the present. The company will have a low PE.

CHAPTER SUMMARY

So time is important. Time is not free. Time has a cost called a required rate of return. Time and return are at the heart of making business decisions that create value. Managers and owners worry about time.

In this chapter we've explored the impact of time on value. After reading Chapter 09, you should be able to:

1. Appreciate the impact of time on value (Learning Objective 1): Value is a function of time. The longer we must wait for something, the less valuable it is. Time matters.
2. Understand the mechanics of the time value of money (Learning Objective 2): Time impacts value through the compounding of return. Time is an important element of computing future and present values.
3. Appreciate how the time value of money is used in business decisions, particularly valuation (Learning Objective 3): In making decisions, business uses the time value of money to determine which alternative creates the greatest value. These decisions include what assets in which to invest and how to finance the business.

Now we've seen how and why time is important in "How Business Works." Next, we need to explore how a business uses time and return to make decisions. We'll explore acquiring money with financing and using that money to invest in assets and hire people.

KEYWORDS

annual percentage rate (APR) 205

annuities due 203

annuity 203

compounding 198

effective rate of return 205

future value 197

interest-on-interest 198

present value 197

price-earnings ratio (PE) 210

rate of return 197

regular annuities 203

risk-free rate of return 196

risk premium 196

simple interest 204

time period 197

Treasury Bills 196

Treasury Securities 196

SHORT-ANSWER QUESTIONS

1. Explain why time is so important in managing a business.
2. Define the following terms:
   a. Required rate of return
   b. Risk-free rate (Rf)
   c. Treasury securities
   d. Treasury bills
   e. Risk premium
   f. Interest-on-interest
   g. Compounding
   h. Future value
   i. Present value
   j. Time
   k. Rate of return
   l. Annuity
   m. Regular annuity
   n. Annuity due
   o. Simple interest
   p. Annual percentage rate (APR)
   q. Effective rate of return
   r. Basis point (BP)
   s. Price earnings ratio (PE)

CRITICAL-THINKING QUESTIONS

1. You have $10,000 to invest today. You believe you will earn an annual return of 12% each year. Answer the following questions:
   a. How much will you have one year from now?
   b. How much will you have five years from now?
   c. How much will you have ten years from now?
   d. How much will you have twenty years from now?

2. Look back at question 1 and answer parts "a" through "d" assuming your 12% annual return will be compounded monthly?
   a. 1 year from now:
   b. 5 years from now:
   c. 10 years from now:
   d. 20 years for now:

3. You need to have $1,000 in 1 year. How much do you need to invest today under the following assumptions:
   a. An annual rate of return of 6%
   b. An annual rate of return of 8%
   c. An annual rate of return of 12%

4. Look back at question 3 and answer part "a" through "c" assuming the return will be computed quarterly.
   a. An annual rate of return of 6%
   b. An annual rate of return of 8%
   c. An annual rate of return of 12%

5. You are worrying about having enough money for your retirement. You are eighty years old and believe you will live forever. You want to receive $40,000 per year into perpetuity. How much money do you need to have now, assuming a 5% return, to be able to receive $40,000 a year forever?

6. You need to have $10,000 in the future. How long would you need to wait if you invested $5,000 today and it earned a 12% return per year? (Note: Round to the nearest year.)

7. You invest $5,000 now. You need $10,000 in 6 years. How much return must you earn per year to make your $5,000 turn into $10,000 in 5 years? (Note: Round to the nearest percent.)

8. You plan to invest $1,000 at the beginning of each of the next 5 years. You believe that your investment will earn a return of 10% per year. How much will you have at the end of year 5?

9. You are excited. You just won the lottery. You will receive $10,000 for the next 20 years. Someone offers to buy your lottery ticket from you. You ask the question, "What is this stream of income worth to me today?" You say your opportunity cost, or required return, is 10% per year. What is your lottery ticket worth? What is the present value of the stream of future payments worth today assuming a 10% discount factor?

10. You plan to go to graduate school in 3 years. Your graduate program is a two-year program that will cost you $40,000 the first year and $50,000 the second year. You need figure out how much you need to invest today to be able to pay for your graduate education. You assume an 8% annual rate of return, compound quarterly. How much do you need to invest today to afford paying $40,000 at the beginning of year 4 (end of year 3) and $50,000 at the beginning of year 5 (end of year 4)?

11. You are about to start college. You need to pay $20,000 at the beginning of each of the next four years. The first year starts now. How much do you need to have now?

EXPLORING REAL BUSINESS

Go to the websites of Google, Target, Hyundai, and Proctor and Gamble. The websites are

Google:	http://investor.google.com
Target:	http://www.target.com
Hyundai:	http://worldwide.hyundai.com/company-overview
Procter & Gamble:	http://www.pg.com

For each company, how will the following transactions affect their balance sheet and income statement?

1. Google is thinking about investing a billion dollars in new software that will make its search engine faster.
2. Target is thinking about building stores in China.
3. Hyundai is thinking about investing a billion dollars in research that could produce a solar-powered car.
4. Procter & Gamble is considering borrowing a billion dollars.

CHAPTER

10

FINANCING AND INVESTING:
MONEY

Introduction: Let's Talk About Acquiring and Using Money to Create Value

A business acquires money, which is often called financial capital. The business then hires people and invests the money in assets. If done right, value is created. But how is money acquired? What is a good investment in assets? How is value created?

In this chapter we'll explore these questions and issues. We'll explore the concepts and issues that frame the financing and investing decisions. We'll explore how financing and investing is the central focus of "How Business Works" and creating value.

LEARNING OBJECTIVES

After reading Chapter 10, you should be able to meet the following learning objectives:

1. Appreciate how the source and use of money impacts the value of a business
2. Appreciate how a business obtains money
3. Understand how a business invests money in assets
4. Understand how a business's financing and investing decisions are related

WHY UNDERSTANDING HOW FINANCING AND INVESTING WORKS MATTERS

You acquire $100. You want to invest the $100 for one year. You have two options. First you can invest the $100 in a business, operate the business for one year, earn an operating profit of $20, then end the business and receive your original $100 plus $20 profit, for a total of $120. Second you can invest the $100 in a business, operate the business for one year, earn an operating profit of $10, then end the business and receive your original $100 plus $10 profit, for a total of $110. The question is which of these two options would you prefer? Most people would initially choose the first option. The $20 operating profit appears better than the $10 operating profit. However, the first option may not be the correct answer. Option two may be the better of the two options. Why? The answer is that we have not considered the source of the $100 you invested. How would you feel if the $100 for option one came from a lender that charged you 25% interest? You would need to pay the lender $25 in interest plus the $100 you borrowed, or a total of $125. You only had $120 from your investment. You would have destroyed $5 in value. Now if the $100 for option two came from a lender that charged you 5% interest, then you'd owe that lender $105, $5 interest and the original $100. In option two you had $110. After paying the lender $105 you would have created $5 in value.

What does this show us? It matters how we acquire money and how we invest money. It's important that we compare the cost of the money to the operating profit we earn from investing the money.

LEARNING OBJECTIVE 1
· ·
USING MONEY TO CREATE VALUE

In Chapter 03 we looked at the management process. The three parts of that process are plan, execute, and review.

First a business needs a vision and plan about how it will create a competitive advantage and value. At the heart of that plan must be the people and assets it will need to create value. But to acquire these assets and hire the people, the business needs money.

Think about the management of Procter & Gamble developing its Crest toothpaste years ago. Procter & Gamble first needed to believe it could create a superior product. The idea for Crest came from people doing research. Then people had to create a plan, including estimating the money needed to develop and manufacture Crest. To create value, a business's model and strategy must make sure all parts are understood and work.

Second, a business obtains money based on this plan. A business obtains money by borrowing the money from lenders and/or receiving the money from owners. In doing so, the business must recognize that lenders and owners do not provide money without requiring and expecting a return. This return is the cost of the money. Interest is the return to lenders. If a business fails to meet this *required return*, the business fails to meet its legal obligation. The result is bankruptcy or reorganization, noted in Chapter 07. The return to owners is net income or the payment of net income called dividends. If a business fails to meet this *expected return*, the business fails economically. Owners will look for something better to do with their money. Although the business may not legally fail, it fails to create ownership value and thus it fails economically. Owners become frustrated with the business and choose to close the business.

Now think about Procter & Gamble telling its lenders and owners about its plan for Crest. Think about lenders and owners questioning whether or not Crest could create an operating profit that would meet their requirements and expectations. Think about Procter & Gamble convincing those who provide the money that Crest is a good investment and would create value.

Third, businesses hire people and invest money in assets according to the plan. In doing so, businesses must believe that these decisions and investments will provide the needed return that meets, and ideally exceeds, the requirements of lenders and expectations of owners.

Think about Procter & Gamble taking the money from lenders and owners and investing in Crest. Think about the additional cash, accounts receivable, inventory, land, and equipment Procter & Gamble needed to make and sell Crest.

Fourth, having made the investments in people and assets, a business operates or executes its plan by its employees using its assets. Businesses must make sales, incur operating costs, and generate an operating profit.

Close your eyes and think about Procter & Gamble making and selling Crest. Can you see a factory where the ingredients are mixed and packaged? Can you see warehouses where Crest is stored? Can you see salespeople selling Crest? Can you see delivery trucks delivering Crest to customers? Can you understand that because its operations have grown, Procter & Gamble needs more cash? If so, you can see Procter & Gamble's employees and assets at work. Procter & Gamble is executing and operating the business. If done right, Procter & Gamble is making an operating profit where sales exceed operating costs.

Fifth, businesses distribute this operating profit in the form of return to the providers of the money. Lenders come first and receive their required return called interest. After a business satisfies lenders with interest, what remains is net income. Net income is the reward or return to owners for providing ownership money. Ideally the business is able to generate an operating profit that meets the required return of lenders and expected return of owners.

Now think of Procter & Gamble using the operating profit to first pay its lenders interest and then reward its owners with net income. If done right, this operating profit is sufficient to pay Procter & Gamble's lenders the required interest and provide its owners with net income that meets or exceeds the owners' expected rate of return. If done right, value is created because Procter & Gamble's investment generated an operating profit that exceeded its cost of money.

In planning and executing the plan, managers must manage a business as a portfolio. All parts are related and work together to produce value. This process of obtaining money, investing money, and operating a business are all interrelated.

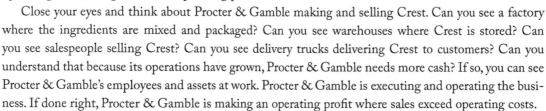

LEARNING OBJECTIVE 2
. . . .
OBTAINING MONEY

So how does a business convince lenders and owners to provide money? How does a business determine how much money should come from debt and how much money should come from owners? Let's look at these questions.

BORROWING MONEY FROM LENDERS

Businesses obtain loans by showing lenders that they can repay the loans with interest. Lenders often ask the following questions:

1. Why is the borrower borrowing?

2. How much does the borrower need?

3. How is the borrower going to repay the loan, or what are the sources of repayment?

4. When will the borrower pay the loan back?

5. Does it make sense to lend to the borrower?

The Hyundai Sonata.

Let's look at an example. You want to buy an auto. You go to the bank, fill out a loan application, and explain you want $20,000 to buy a car. You'd like to pay the money back, plus interest, in forty-eight monthly installments. You read in the newspaper that the bank is offering auto loans at 8% compounded monthly. You figure your monthly payment will be $488. The bank asks you how you plan to make the monthly payments. You explain that you are employed with a local business. You've been employed by that business for less than one year and currently earn $4,000 per month. After taxes, your take-home pay is $3,000. Your apartment rent and utilities are $1,000 per month. Your food and other living expenses are $700 a month. That leaves you $1,300 a month to pay the loan. The bank verifies the information and decides to approve your loan with conditions. Given that you just started a new job, the bank feels you are more risky than the average borrower. It requires a 9% interest rate, compounded monthly, making your monthly payment $498. The bank also wants your auto as collateral in case you do not repay the loan.

What has the bank done? First the bank asked "Why are you borrowing?" The answer is to buy an auto, which is a valid and legal use of money. Second, the bank asked "How much do you need?" The answer is $20,000, which appears reasonable. Third, the bank asked "How are you going to pay the loan back?" The answer is by going to work. Your paycheck is the primary source of repayment and appears ample to cover your living expenses and loan payment. However, the bank does not feel your new job is stable enough to provide ample security. So the bank asked for a secondary source of repayment in case

BUSINESS SENSE

M&M: IT'S MORE THAN CANDY; IT'S A NOBEL IDEA

In the 1950s, Professors Franco Modigliani and Merton Miller wrote a series of very famous articles. The articles looked at the impact of using debt or equity on the value of the business. They initially postulated that, in a perfect world, it did not matter how a business was financed. The value of the business was only a function of the benefits coming from the investment in and use of the assets. However they quickly recognized the world was not perfect. The world was full of imperfections such as risk and taxes. When these imperfections were considered, they realized it did matter how a business was financed. A business, striving to maximize its value, should choose that combination of debt and equity that creates the lowest weighted average cost of capital (WACC). For this and other work, Franco Modigliani received the 1985 Nobel Prize in Economics. Today, the business world refers to Modigliani and Miller's proposition simply as "M&M."

something bad happens and you lose your job and your paycheck. That secondary source of repayment is the auto. If you fail to work for whatever reason, the bank can seize and sell your auto. Fourth, the bank asked "When will you pay the loan back?" You said in forty-eight monthly installments, which appears reasonable. Fifth, the bank asked itself "Does it make sense to lend to this borrower?" The answer is yes, but with a higher interest rate to compensate for your higher-than-average risk.

When a business borrows money, it goes through a similar process. The business must show why it need the money and how it will be used. The business then needs to show that the amount of money requested is neither too large nor too small to meet this need. Next, the business must show that the loan can be paid back with the primary source of repayment, typically operating profit. If there is significant risk with the operating profit, the lender will often require the business to provide a secondary source of repayment, such as collateral. Then the business must show that the funds to repay the loan will be available when the loan payments are due. Structuring the loan with the right timing is critical. Last, the lender must determine if the business is trustworthy, the appropriate interest rate to charge, and other conditions needed for the lender to approve the loan.

Lenders lend money because they expect to be repaid the amount loaned, called the **loan principal**. Lenders also expect to be paid **interest**, the cost the business must pay to use the lender's money for a period of time. Lenders will not lend if they do not believe they will be repaid. However, all loans have some risk because nobody can perfectly see the future. If the lender approves the loan, the lender will require an interest rate that compensates the lender for 1) the rent on the money, assuming no risk, and 2) the risk of not being paid back (**default risk**). Remember Equation 9.1 from Chapter 09? Let's restate it in terms of the required return on debt (interest rate) called the **cost of debt**.

DIFFERENT LOANS AND DIFFERENT INTEREST RATES

All loans are not equal. As such, different loans have different interest rates. Why? The answer is risk. Let's look at some different loans.

You go to the bank and make a deposit into your checking account. What are you doing? You are loaning the bank your money. Does your deposit earn you a high or low interest rate? It earns you a low interest rate. Why? The answer is your loan to the bank is a very low-risk loan. You know you'll get your money back with interest. Why? The answer is your deposit is insured by the US Government's Federal Deposit Insurance Company (FDIC). Your deposit earns a low interest rate because the default risk is zero.

Now let's look at an auto loan. You go to the bank to borrow money to buy a new auto. Even using the auto as collateral, the interest rate the bank will charge is significantly higher than the interest rate the bank pays you on your deposit. Why? The answer is your auto loan has significantly higher default risk. Think about it. If you lose your job, you may not be able to pay the loan back. The bank will seize your auto and sell it to repay the loan. But can the bank sell the auto at a price that can repay the loan? The answer is maybe not. Why? What happens to the value of a new auto? It rapidly decreases. The bank may lose money when it sells your auto. Even with collateral, the bank is accepting significant default risk. The bank charges a higher interest rate because of the higher risk.

Let's look at your credit card loan. The bank that issues you the credit card is making you a loan and charges you a very high interest rate. Why? The answer is that the bank is accepting a very high level of default risk. If you cannot pay the loan, the bank has no collateral. The credit card loan is unsecured. The loan is very risky, requiring a very high interest rate.

EQUATION 10.1: The Pre-Tax Cost of Debt

$$Rd = R_f + Risk\ Premium$$

Where

Rd	The interest rate charged on the loan
R_f	Risk-free rate of return in the economy
Risk Premium	The additional required return to compensate for lender's risk

The interest charged by the lender is the business's cost of using debt financing. The nice thing about debt is that interest expense is tax deductible in the US. What that means is businesses get to deduct interest from operating income before they compute their taxes. Businesses pay less tax because of interest, thus reducing the after-tax cost of debt. The net impact of interest on net income is called the **after-tax cost of debt**. The after-tax cost of debt is

EQUATION 10.2: The After-Tax Cost of Debt

$$R_D = R_d\ (1 - Tx)$$

Where

R_D	After-tax cost of debt
R_d	The interest rate charged on the loan
Tx	The business's tax rate

OBTAINING MONEY FROM OWNERS

Businesses obtain money from owners by showing the business will produce a net income. However, this net income is only expected. There is no guarantee or legal requirement as in the case of debt. Owners provide money to businesses hoping for the best but willing to accept the worst. Their return is net income, which is the residual of everything a business does. As such, owners are the last to expect any benefit from the business. Their return is the least certain and thus at the highest risk. Because owners accept higher risks, owners have an expected rate of return that is higher than that of lenders. If the business earns an operating profit, lenders get their required return or interest before owners get their net income. If the business fails and goes into bankruptcy, lenders get their money before owners because of the priority of claims, as noted in Chapter 07.

What does this mean for the business? Owners expect the highest return because owners bear the highest risk. If a business does not meet this expected return, owners will no longer provide their money and the business will cease to exist. Business managers need to understand what owners expect. The return owners expect is the cost of the money owners provide. Let's restate Equation 9.1 in terms of the expected return on owners' equity or the **cost of equity**.

EQUATION 10.3: The Cost of Equity

$$R_E = R_f + Risk\ Premium$$

INVESTING IN OWNERSHIP

...y in assets. Owners provide much of that money. In the business world it is often said that owners ...iness "invests" the owners' money in people and assets. The term "investing" is used in many ...ring of something of value. When owners invest in a business, they are buying a business. When ...ss is buying assets. When a business invests in a person, the business may not own the person but is acquiring the labor of that person. The term investing is used in a lot of different ways but always represents buying or acquiring something of value.

Where

R_E	Expected rate of return on owners' equity
R_f	Risk-free rate of return in the economy
Risk Premium	The additional return owners expect due to risk

The expected return on owners' equity is the business's implied cost of the owner financing. (Note that the business cannot deduct net income or dividends in computing its taxable income. Thus, there is no tax adjustment as there is with debt.)

FINDING THE RIGHT MIX OF DEBT AND EQUITY

How a business is financed is critical and does impact value. In a perfect world where there is no uncertainty, it would not matter how a business is financed. But we do not live in a perfect world. How a business is financed does matter.

So how should a business be financed? What is the optimal mix of debt and owners' equity? The answer is that mix which produces the greatest value or the lowest average cost of money, called the **weighted average cost of capital (WACC)**. A business wants its cost of money to be as low as possible.

Remember a business is a portfolio. As a portfolio, financial capital is a blend of debt and owners' equity. Financial capital is a pool of money. The cost of that pool of money is a weighted average of its parts. The weighted average cost of capital (WACC) is calculated as:

Google offices, Haifa, Israel.

EQUATION 10.4: The Weighted Cost of Capital (WACC)

$$\text{WACC} = (\% \text{ of Debt})(R_d)(1 - Tx) + (\% \text{ of Equity})(R_E)$$

Where

WACC	Weighted average cost of capital
% of Debt	The amount of debt/(the amount of debt + the amount of owners' equity)

R_d	Cost of debt
Tx	Effective tax rate
% of Equity	The amount of equity/(the amount of debt + the amount of owners' equity)
R_E	Cost of equity

The WACC is the after-tax cost of the average dollar of financing used by the business.[1]

Now remember our example in Chapter 02? We borrowed $1,000 at 6% and invested it at 5%, destroying $10 in value. The cost of financing (6%) was greater than the return from investing (5%). However, we acknowledged that it could have been a poor investing decision or a poor financing decision. We could have created value if our financing had cost us 4%. The cost of financing (4%) would be lower than the return from investing (5%). To maximize the value of a business, we need to maximize the return on investing and minimize the cost of financing. We need to minimize the WACC. But how do we do that?

Let's look at certain truths.

1. Debt is very attractive. Why? Debt is cheaper than owners' equity. The required rate of return on debt is lower than the expected rate of return on owners' equity. This is because lenders assume less risk than owners do. What makes debt even more attractive is that interest is tax deductible.

2. Too much debt can force the business into bankruptcy. There is a point where businesses cannot afford to borrow more money. Why? The answer is too much debt could put the business out of business.

3. Putting points one and two together, a business will minimize its WACC by borrowing all the money that it can afford. Beyond that point, all additional financing should be with owners' money.

So the question is how much debt can a business afford? The answer is "it depends." It depends on the source of the repayment of the debt. It depends on the benefits and risk from hiring people, investing in assets, and operating the business.

Let's go back to our example of you buying an auto with a $20,000 loan. What would happen if you were a salesperson working for a commission? Last year you made $4,000 a month. But this year sales are down by 50%, and your monthly income is down to $2,000. Your income is volatile. Would you want to borrow the $20,000? Could you be sure that you could repay the loan in good and bad times? The answer is probably not.

The same principle applies to business. Debt is repaid from operating the business. If the operating profit is volatile and risky, then managers must worry about defaulting on the business's debt. Managers will typically use less debt and more owners' equity to finance the business. If the operating income is stable and predictable, then managers can feel good about borrowing. They feel confident that the operating income will be available to make the debt payments. Managers typically will use more debt and less owners' equity to finance the business.

Let's look at two good examples, Procter & Gamble and Google. Procter & Gamble knows its products like Crest have been, are, and should be very profitable. The operating profits from products like Crest are stable and predictable, which is why Procter & Gamble uses a lot of debt to finance its operations. Next is Google. Google competes in an ever-changing and very competitive marketplace. New products are introduced daily. As such, Google is less certain of its operating profit. That is why Google uses a lot of owners' equity to finance its operations.

FINANCING THE BUSINESS AND CREATING VALUE: DEBT VERSUS OWNERS' EQUITY

So a business will use less debt and more owners' money when the business is uncertain about the business's operating profit. If the business is certain about its operating profit, the business will use more debt and less owners' money. How does this affect a business's average cost of money, or WACC? Let's see.

Exhibit 10.1 depicts what happens to the cost of debt (R_D), the cost of equity (R_E), and the average cost of all funds (WACC) as a business uses more debt and less owners' equity. The optimal financial structure is that blend of debt and owners' equity that minimizes the WACC. That point coincides with the point that managers, lenders, and owners begin to worry about the business's ability to repay the debt. That point is where default risk becomes significant.

EXHIBIT 10.1: Optimal Financing Structure

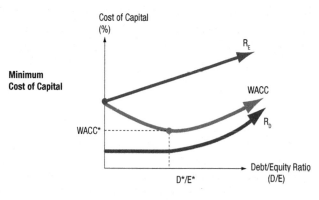

*The Optimal Debt/Equity Ratio

BUSINESS SENSE

JUNK

What comes to mind when you think of the word "junk"? Most people would say something of little value that very few people want. The financial world uses the word junk in a similar way.

In the financial world the word junk means debt that has a very high probability of default. Junk debt has high default risk and thus a high required rate of return, which is used to discount the interest and principal of the debt. The junk debt has a low value because it has high risk and thus a high discount rate.

When a business uses too much debt and not enough equity, the WACC will rise. The debt has a high probability of default. It is using "junk debt."

When people talk about the objective of business, some talk about maximizing the value of the whole firm (debt plus owners' equity), while others talk about maximizing the value of owners' equity. The goals are the same. Why? The answer is that the correct use of financial leverage enhances the value of both debt and owner's equity, and the incorrect use of financial leverage hurts both lenders and owners. So what is **financial leverage**? Financial leverage relates to the use of debt in place of owners' equity.

As can be seen in Exhibit 10.1, initially the cost of debt does not increase significantly as more debt or financial leverage is used. Why? Default risk does not initially change. It is assumed the business has the capacity to repay the debt up to a certain point. Beyond that point, default risk becomes significant and the cost of debt increases from the increased risk.

Exhibit 10.1 also shows that the cost of equity increases with every increase in debt. Why? The answer is financial leverage. The more debt a business uses, the more interest a business must pay. The higher the interest cost, the less certain owners are they will receive net income. The decrease of certainty means risk, which means a higher cost of owners' equity.

So the conclusion is that the providers of money, both lenders and owners, need to work together to provide the right financial leverage that minimizes the WACC. Lenders and owners both benefit when the business is correctly financed and they suffer when the business is not correctly financed. But to figure out the correct blend of debt and equity, lenders and owners need to understand how the money will be used to hire people and invest in assets. Lenders and owners must understand how the business will use their funds to operate a business, generate an operating profit, and create value.

LEARNING OBJECTIVE 3

INVESTING MONEY IN PEOPLE AND ASSETS

Businesses hire people and invest in assets. A business takes the money received from lenders and owners and invests it in assets such as cash, receivables, inventory, buildings, and intangible assets such as patents. The business also hires managers and employees to operate the business.

The assets and people of a business comprise a portfolio that is used to operate the business. The result of investing and operating activities is an operating profit. Our goal is to create an operating profit, after taxes, which meets or exceeds the after-tax average cost of the money lenders and owners provide the business (WACC).

AN EXAMPLE

Let's look at an investment decision in a wholesale auto parts company and see if it creates value. (A wholesale auto parts company buys auto parts in large quantities and sells the auto parts to retail stores and auto repair shops.) Let's assume we create a plan and show it to our lenders and owners. The lenders lend us $1,000,000 for five years at an annual interest rate of 10%, computed monthly ($8,333 interest per month). The owners provide us $1,000,000 and expect a 15% return. Our business will pay taxes at a 50% rate. We now have $2,000,000 in cash. Our WACC is 10%, computed as

$$\text{WACC} = (\% \text{ of Debt})(R_d)(1 - Tx) + (\% \text{ of Equity})(R_E)$$
$$\text{WACC} = (\$1,000,000/\$2,000,000)(.10)(1 - .50) + (\$1,000,000/\$2,000,000)(.15)$$
$$\text{WACC} = .10.$$

So what have we done? Look at Exhibit 10.2. Economically we have raised $2,000,000 in financial capital at a WACC of 10%. But all we've got is cash. We need to invest the cash to create value.

EXHIBIT 10.2: Initial Balance Sheet for Example

BALANCE SHEET AFTER FINANCING OBTAINED			
Assets		**Liabilities**	
Cash	$2,000,000	Debt	$1,000,000
		Owners' Equity	
		Stock	$1,000,000
Total Assets	**$2,000,000**	**Total Liabilities and Owners' Equity**	**$2,000,000**

Cash does not create an operating profit, so managers must use the cash to purchase a building in which to operate the business. Let's assume managers spend $1,000,000 in cash to purchase a building and $300,000 in cash to purchase several delivery trucks and other needed equipment. Next managers must purchase the auto parts, or inventory, to be sold to their customers. Let's assume managers buy $400,000 of inventory. They purchase the inventory with $100,000 in cash and promise to pay their suppliers the remaining $300,000 at the end of the month (short-term liability). The agreement to pay suppliers at a later date is called an account payable. So we've got our financing, building, equipment, and inventory. So what have we done? Look at Exhibit 10.3. We've invested the $2,000,000 provided by lenders and owners in a $1,000,000 building, $300,000 in equipment, and $100,000 in inventory. That leaves us with $600,000 in cash. We used accounts payable to acquire an additional $300,000 in inventory.

Inventory at a Serbian manufacturing company.

EXHIBIT 10.3: Evolving Balance Sheet for Example

BALANCE SHEET AT THE BEGINNING OF THE MONTH			
Assets		**Liabilities**	
Cash	$600,000	Accounts Payable	$300,000
Inventory	$400,000	Debt	$1,000,000
Building	$1,000,000	Total Liabilities	$1,300,000
Equipment	$300,000		
		Owners' Equity	
		Stock	$1,000,000
Total Assets	**$2,300,000**	**Total Liabilities and Owners' Equity**	**$2,300,000**

Now it's time to operate our business. Managers must now hire the employees needed to sell the inventory and operate the business. To hire the employees, we agree to pay them $25,000 per month in cash. The employees come together and use the building and equipment to provide and sell the inventory.

Let's look at our first month of operations. Our salespeople sell auto parts for $400,000. What did we get for the sales? Our customers gave us $200,000 in cash and a $200,000 promise to pay in the future. This promise is $200,000 in accounts receivable. The auto parts we sold cost our business $300,000. We sold $300,000 in inventory. We made a gross profit of $100,000. We also paid our employees $25,000 in cash. Our other operating costs were $25,000. We paid our taxes using a rate of 50%. So what have we done? Look at Exhibit 10.4. We earned a pre-tax operating profit of $50,000, paid interest of $8,333, paid taxes of $20,833, and earned net income after taxes of $20,834.

(Because different transactions are often taxed differently, we model transactions as after-tax transactions. Notice we earned a pre-tax operating profit of $50,000. If we applied the 50% tax rate, our after-tax operating profit is $25,000. Our pre-tax interest expense was $8,333. If we applied our 50% tax rate to the interest expense, our after-tax interest expense was $4,167. Subtracting the $4,167 after-tax interest expense from the $25,000 after-tax operating profit gives us the after-tax net income of $20,834.)[2]

A manager and his team in their daily staff meeting.

So what have we done? We obtained $2,000,000 in financial capital with an average cost, or WACC, of 10%. We earned an after-tax operating profit of $25,000. That after-tax operating profit provided the money to 1) pay the after-tax cost of debt (interest) of $4,167 and 2) leave net income of $20,834 for owners. If the owners were expecting a 15% annual return on their $1,000,000, the business needed to produce net income of $12,500 per month ($1,000,000 × .15/12 = $12,500). The business produced more than $12,500 in net income and thus created value.

INVESTING FOR VALUE—ADDING VALUE

Business is more complicated than the above example. The above example assumed our business operated only for one month and was not significantly impacted by time. However, our example demonstrates that the investment decision must produce an operating profit that meets, and ideally exceeds, the WACC. If it does, value is created. If it does not, value is destroyed.

When time and risk are injected into long-term investment decisions, the business must incorporate the time value of money. Managers ask, "Is the investment worth making? Is the business more valuable with the investment or without the investment? Does the investment create enough value to cover the cost of the investment?"

To answer these questions, managers must forecast the amount and timing of the after-tax operating profit from investing in assets. Managers often use operating cash flow, versus accrual operating profit, as the measure of benefits. Why? The answer is businesses invest cash and expect cash in return. Accrual income is based on many assumptions and can take time to turn into cash. (Suggestion: Look back on Chapter 08, to make sure you understand the difference between accrual and cash-basis accounting.)

Next managers must discount these benefits, over time, using the WACC as the discount factor. Sometimes managers will adjust the WACC to reflect special circumstances. But the WACC is the benchmark return the investment must earn to create value.

BALANCE SHEET AT THE END OF THE MONTH

Assets		Liabilities	
Cash	$420,834	Debt	$1,000,000
Accounts Receivable	$200,000		
Inventory	$100,000	**Owners' Equity**	
		Stock	$1,000,000
Building	$1,000,000	Retained Earnings	$20,834
Equipment	$300,000	Total Owners' Equity	$1,020,834
Total Assets	**$2,020,834**	**Total Liabilities and Owners' Equity**	**$2,020,834**

MONTHLY INCOME STATEMENT

Revenue	$400,000
Cost of Goods Sold	$300,000
Gross Profit	$100,000
Salaries and Operating Costs	$50,000
Earning Before Interest and Taxes (Pre-Tax Operating Profits)	$50,000
Interest	$8,333
Net Income Before Taxes (Taxable Income)	$41,667
Tax -50%	$20,833
Net Income	**$20,834**

BUSINESS SENSE

PERCEPTIONS COUNT

Have you ever been scared because you just didn't understand what was happening? Not understanding something is worrisome and makes us more cautious in how we proceed. Not understanding something is a source of risk and often leads to bad decisions and/or higher required rates of return.

When owners provide money to a business, they want to understand how the business will use the money. In big corporations, owners often have limited information to do this. They must use accrual financial statements that do not always provide the information they need.

First, financial statements report the past not the future. When lenders and owners provide money, they want to know about the business's plans for the future. Second, most financial statements use US GAAP, which uses accrual accounting. Owners provide cash to the business and want detailed insights into a business's cash flow.

To meet this challenge, businesses often provide supplemental information. Managers make press releases and provide additional insights to go along with published financial statements. The group within a business that provides this information is often called "investor relations." It's this group's job to provide quality, consistent information, in conformity with the law.

What results is a measure that reflects the value of the investment to the business. That value is the present value of the benefits the firm expects to receive if it invests in the chosen assets and/or people. The benefits include those from operating and liquidating the investment. That value is compared to the cost of the investment and the net reflects the projected value added or destroyed by the investment. The value of the investment less the cost of the investment is called the investment's **net present value (NPV)**. If the investment's NPV is positive, it is projected to increase the value of the business. If the investment's NPV is negative, it is projected to decrease the value of the business. Businesses should invest in positive NPV projects and not invest in negative NPV projects.

OTHER TOOLS OF INVESTING

Net present value is the primary tool used to evaluate investment decisions. However, businesses supplement NPV with other tools to help make the investment decision. First, businesses often rephrase NPV by looking at the **internal rate of return (IRR)** of a project. An investment's IRR is that discount rate that equates the benefits projected over time with the cost of the investment. It is computed using the equations in Chapter 09. The IRR is the effective rate of return on the investment and is compared to the WACC. If the IRR is greater than the WACC, the investment increases value and should be made. If the IRR is less than the WACC, the investment decreases value and should not be made. Would you acquire money that costs 6% to invest in an asset that will only earn you a 5% return? The answer is no.

Another tool sometimes used by business is the **accounting rate of return (ARR)**. The ARR is the net income produced by an investment, divided by the cost of that investment. ARR does not deal with time or risk. It also reflects accrual accounting and not cash flow. However, businesses often consider ARR in making an investment decision because it is what is reflected on financial statements. Lenders and owners often judge a business by looking at financial statements.

RAMON W. BREEDEN, JR.

With hard work, a focus on excellence, and a determination to compete, Ramon W. Breeden, Jr. (Ray) is a person who has made a difference. Ray started his business career by building a single house. He started with very little. He had to dig his first foundation by hand. However he had a dream. He worked hard. He worked smart. He focused on understanding the needs of his customers, attracting and retaining talented employees, and carefully taking risk. Today Ray's company specializes in single- and multi-family residences, commercial real estate, construction, property management, and much more. He built the Breeden Company into a world class enterprise by investing in projects that generated a risk-adjusted return that exceeded the cost of his money. Today Ray Breeden is one of the most successful real estate developers in the world. His wealth is measured in billions. But he also made sure, as he climbed the ladder of success, to create value for his customers, his employees, his investors, and his communities.

The last tool businesses sometimes use is the payback period. The **payback period** is the time it takes the business to recover its investment. An example is an investment that requires $10,000 in cash today, but will generate $2,000 in cash benefits for each of the next ten years. It will take five years for the business to recover its investment. The investment has a five-year payback. Although payback is measured in time, businesses often use it as a measure of risk. The longer it takes for an investment to pay back, the more risk is in the investment.

LEARNING OBJECTIVE 4
. . . .
RELATING THE FINANCING AND INVESTING DECISIONS

In a perfect world of certainty, the value of a business would be determined solely by the operating profit produced by hiring people and investing in assets. It would not matter how the business is financed. However, we do not live in a perfect world. Our imperfect world produces risk. Remember that risk is the uncertainty that could result in an outcome we do not desire. Risk is the uncertainty of receiving benefits that are lower in amount and/or later in time than we expect.

Risk is a reality in creating business value. Because of risk, the value of the business is determined by the investment decision, the financing decision, and the interaction of the two decisions. How a business is financed affects what a business invests in. The WACC from financing impacts the estimated value from investing. Yet what a business invests in affects how a business is financed. The volatility or risk of the operating profit, produced by the investing decision, affects how much debt and owners' equity the business should use. The investment decision thus affects the mix of debt and equity and a business's WACC.

Operating a business is about taking risk and being compensated for taking risk. Risk management is a very important part of managing any business. Risk comes from everything a business does. From within the business, risk comes from: hiring people and investing in assets, how the business is financed, and how the business is operated. Risk also comes from the external environment in which the business operates. Risk is everywhere and is a crucial part of a manager's planning, executing, and reviewing.

CHAPTER SUMMARY

So a business acquires money. It then hires people and invests in assets. If done right, value is created.

In this chapter we've explored financing and investing decisions. We've looked at how each contributes to the creation of value. We've also looked at how these decisions are related. To create value, the benefit from investing should meet, and ideally exceed, the cost of financing.

After reading this chapter, you should be able to:

1. Appreciate how the source and use of money impacts the value of a business (Learning Objective 1): To create value, a business must strive to earn an operating profit that exceeds the cost of its financing.
2. Appreciate how a business obtains money (Learning Objective 2): To maximize value, a business should strive to create the lowest weighted average cost of capital (WACC). A business's WACC is a function of its cost of debt, tax rate, cost of owners' equity, and the relative weight of debt and equity used.
3. Understand how a business invests money in assets (Learning Objective 3): To maximize value, a business should strive to invest in assets that earn an operating profit that exceeds its WACC.
4. Understand how a business's financing and investing decisions are related (Learning Objective 4): Because we live in a world of risk, the investing and financing decisions are not independent. The investment decision affects the financing decision and the financing decision affects the investing decision.

In this chapter we've seen how financing and investing are key factors in "How Business Works." Next, we need to explore how a business deals with risk. We'll explore how businesses recognize, measure, manage, and price risk.

KEYWORDS

accounting rate of return (ARR) 228

after-tax cost of debt 220

cost of debt 219

cost of equity 220

default risk 219

financial leverage 224

interest 219

internal rate of return (IRR) 228

junk 223

loan principal 219

net present value (NPV) 228

payback period 229

weighted average cost of capital (WACC) 221

SHORT-ANSWER QUESTIONS

1. What is meant by the financing decision?
2. What is meant by the investing decision?
3. What is meant by the operating decision?
4. Define the following terms:
   a. Default risk
   b. Cost of debt
   c. After-tax cost of debt
   d. Cost of equity
   e. Weighted average cost of capital (WACC)
   f. Financial leverage
   g. Junk
   h. Net present value (NPV)
   i. Internal rate of return (IRR)
   j. Accounting rate of return (ARR)
   k. Payback period
   l. Investor relations department

CRITICAL-THINKING QUESTIONS

1. What is the objective of the investment decision?
2. What is the objective of the financing decision?
3. How are the financing and investing decisions related?
4. How does risk affect the investing and the financing decisions?

PROBLEM

Your business has $500,000 of debt that has a cost of 8%. Your business also has $1,000,000 in owners' equity. Owners expect a return on their equity of 14%. You are looking at an investment that could earn you an after-tax operating profit over time that generates a return of 12% per year. Your tax rate is 50%. Answer the following questions:

1. What is your after-tax WACC? Show your computation.
2. Should you invest in this opportunity? Explain your answer.

ENDNOTES

1. When businesses compute their WACC, they are maximizing long-term value and typically use only long-term debt. They do not include short-term debt. Why? The answer is short-term debt is often used to finance short-term or temporary investments in assets. An example of a short-term or temporary investment in assets is a toy store that temporarily increases its inventory to meet its seasonal demand.

2. Because tax law is different from US GAAP, the impact of taxes must be made on an item-by-item basis. The income statement shows taxable income as operating income less interest. However, businesses look at the impact of taxes on each decision separately. This includes revenue, operating costs, and interest.

CHAPTER

11

UNDERSTANDING RISK

Introduction: Let's Talk About Risk

Understanding risk is very important. To create value a business needs to do more than generate benefits for ownership. But what is risk? Where does risk comes from? How do managers recognize and measure risk? What do managers do after they recognize and measure risk? Can risk be managed? If so, how can it be managed? What do managers do when risk cannot be managed?

In this chapter we'll explore these questions and issues. We'll explore the concepts and issues that frame the challenge of risk management. We'll explore how risk management is an important part of "How Businesses Works."

WHY RISK MATTERS

Think about any aspect of your life. Now ask yourself, "Is there anything certain in life?" The answer is "no." We are never 100% certain of what will happen when we cross a street, buy a product, or engage in a conversation with someone. Uncertainty and risk are a natural part of life. But there are outcomes of which we are more certain and outcomes of which we are less than certain. Some things inherently have more risk and others less risk. And how do we react? We typically do not like risk and, therefore, expect to receive compensation for taking risk. The higher the risk, the higher the compensation we expect. Risk matters in our personal lives as well as in business.

LEARNING OBJECTIVE 1
. . . .
RISK AND VALUE

In Chapter 01, risk was defined as the uncertainty that could result in an undesirable outcome. Risk is the uncertainty of receiving benefits that are lower in amount and/or later in time than we expect. We don't like risk. To take risk, we require higher benefits because having higher levels of risk without higher benefits lowers value. Having lower levels of risk, all other things remaining the same, increases value. We're risk-averse. To accept risk, we need to expect to receive higher benefits to compensate for taking risk. To take risk, we require higher return.

As an example, let's play a simplified game of roulette. We have a wheel that spins, the wheel has thirty-six holes, we have a board with thirty-six numbers, and we'll put a small marble in our wheel and spin the wheel. The ball will go round and round as the wheel spins. When the wheel stops spinning, the ball will come to rest in one of the thirty-six holes. You guess or bet on which number the ball will come to rest. You win if the ball comes to rest on the number you chose. You lose if the ball comes to rest on any other number. In which hole the ball will rest is in a random event, with each hole having a 1/36th chance of being the destination. The operator of the roulette game looks at you and asks, "Do you want to gamble?" You reply, "What are the opportunities?" The operator indicates that you have two options. First, you can wager that the ball will come to rest in an even or odd number. If you select an even, you win if the ball comes to rest in any even-numbered hole (2, 4, 6, 8, etc.). You lose if the ball comes to rest in any odd-numbered hole (1, 3, 5, 7, etc.). If you choose an odd number, you win with the odd numbers and lose with the even numbers. Second, you can wager the ball will come to rest in a specific number (e.g., 17). You will win if the ball comes to rest in that chosen number and lose if the ball comes to rest in any other number (5, 12, 27, etc.).

You then ask the operator, "What are the odds? How much will I win or lose if I wager $100?" The operator indicates you will win $200 if you win by choosing even/odds in option one (e.g., your original $100 wager plus $100 profit). You will lose your original $100 if you do not win. If you select a specific number by choosing option two, you will receive $3,600 (e.g., your original $100 wager plus $3,500 profit) if you win. In option two, you will also lose your original $100 if you do not win.

You ask, "Why is there less profit in option one?" You could lose your $100 in either option. So what's the difference? The difference is risk and return. You have a greater chance of losing in option two. In option one, you'll typically win eighteen out of every thirty-six spins and lose eighteen out of every thirty-six spins. In option two, you'll typically win one out of every thirty-six spins and lose thirty-five out of every thirty-six spins.

The probability of losing is much greater in option two. To entice you to play option two, the game rewards you with higher compensation for winning. Given you have a higher probability of losing, you require a higher benefit if you win.

So how does risk impact the value equation? Let's look at the value equation from Chapter 09.

EQUATION 11.1: The Value of a Business

$$V = \sum\nolimits_t^T FV_t / (1 + r)^t$$

Where

V	Value of the business
Σ	Summation sign
t	The number of time periods (t to T)
FV	After-tax operating earnings expected to be received in the future
r	Weighted average cost of capital (WACC)

Providers of money, both lenders and owners, expect higher operating profits if their money is to be used to fund risky investments. This increases the average cost of the money, or WACC. But where does risk come from? The answer is everywhere.

THE SOURCES OF RISK

Risk comes from everywhere. First, risk comes from outside the business, or its external environment. Examples include economic cycles, competitors, and changing customer needs or preferences. Second, risk comes from within the business, or internal environment. Examples include the way managers make decisions about the investing, financing, and operating activities. Third, risk comes from the interaction of the business's internal and external environments.

EXHIBIT 11.1: Business Environment

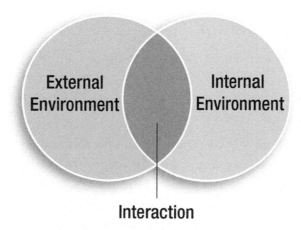

Now let's look at some common sources of risk that managers face.

INVESTING RISKS

Investing risks relate to the allocation of money (called financial capital) to hiring employees and investing in assets. There are many risks associated with this task, including:

1. Does your investment plan reflect what will happen in the economy and marketplace? Can you imagine expecting good economic times and getting bad economic times? If you expected good economic times you would purchase or produce a lot of inventory to sell. However, if you experienced bad economic times, you may not be able to sell the inventory at a profit. If you can't sell the inventory, you may not be able to pay your debts. If you cannot pay your debts your business may fail.

2. Does your investment plan reflect what your competitors are likely to do? Can you imagine expecting your competitor to create an inferior product, but realizing you have no sales because your competitor has a superior product?

3. Does your investment plan have the right blend of assets? Remember the people and assets of a business are a portfolio of economic resources. What happens if you have too many of one type of resource and not enough of another? Can you imagine selling more than you expected? Is this good? The answer is maybe and maybe not. What happens if you grow faster than was forecast? Your inventory and accounts receivables become larger than was forecast. You have not made arrangements to borrow the needed money or to receive it from your owners. Remember that assets equal liabilities plus owners' equity. Just because you are making a profit does not mean you can pay your debts. All your money is tied up in unexpected inventory and receivables, thus causing cash problems. You may not be able to pay your debts. Once again your business may fail.

4. Do you have a contingency plan if the unexpected occurs? What happens if a key piece of machinery breaks down? Your investment is no longer productive. Do you have a plan?

BUSINESS SENSE

GRASPING THE IMPACT OF UNCERTAINTY

Sometimes people feel confident and sometimes people feel unconfident. Why? The answer is risk. When people are scared and uncertain, they lack confidence and fear the worst. They change their behavior. Although fear hurts significant parts of the economy, it actually helps some parts.

Let's look at an example. You own a restaurant and you worry that the upcoming recession may hurt your business. But will it? It actually may help your business. If you own an expensive restaurant, it will probably hurt your business. Customers in a recession may not be able to afford eating at your restaurant. But where will they eat? All people need food. Given that they like to go to restaurants, they may go to a less expensive restaurant. If you own a less expensive restaurant, your business may actually increase during a recession. Bad economic times may actually lower your business's risk.

Think about it. Risk varies from one business to another because business models and strategies differ.

FINANCING RISKS

Financing risks relate to the acquisition of money from lenders and owners. As seen in Chapter 10, the way businesses are financed is dependent on the business's investing and operating decisions. Too much or too little debt, compared with owners' equity, can hurt value. There are many risks associated with financing, including:

1. Does the business have the correct amount of debt and owners' equity? Can you imagine expecting good economic times and financing with debt? What would happen if you experienced bad economic times? In good economic times, your customers would be buying your products and paying their debts. Your sales and accounts receivable would be turning into cash. With the cash you could easily meet your contractual debt obligations. In bad economic times, however, your customers would not be able to buy your products or pay their debts. You would have a cash problem and could not pay your debts. You would wish you had used owners' equity, not debt, to finance your business.

2. All debt is not the same. Lenders and borrowers must agree upon loan structure. Loan structure deals with when the loan will be repaid and what conditions the borrower must fulfill. Can you imagine using a one-year loan to finance a building that you expect to use for thirty years? Will the cash flow from using this building be sufficient to repay the loan in one year or should the loan be structured over a period greater than one year? Loan structure is critical to the success of the business.

3. What about where we borrow money? Let's look at an example. You own a shoe store. You buy shoes in Italy for 100,000 euros, payable in ninety days. One euro is equal to one US dollar in today's market. You sell the shoes in ninety days for $150,000 in the US. You go to convert your US dollars to pay your supplier, but the foreign exchange rate has changed. Now one euro is equal to two US dollars. You convert your $150,000 into 75,000 euros. You realize that you need another 25,000 euros, costing you $50,000. You have lost $50,000 because you financed your US sales with euros. You took foreign exchange risk and lost.

4. What do you think happens when your lenders and owners are not adequately informed? They get concerned. Ignorance creates risk. Doing something major and not informing the providers of money can create a lot of risk, which in turn hurts the business.

Currency		Buying		Selling
		Notes	T/C	Notes
USA	USD	35.03	35.60	36.10
EURO	EUR	45.72	45.97	46.86
ENGLAND	GBP	68.96	69.66	70.90
JAPAN	JPY	0.2879	0.2912	0.2971
SINGAPORE	SGD	22.89	22.99	23.56
HONG KONG	HKD	4.47	4.50	4.66
AUSTRALIA	AUD	27.08	27.36	27.97
NEW ZEALAND	NZD	24.18	24.32	25.31
SWITZERLAND	CHF	27.99	28.32	28.81
SWEDEN	SEK	4.89	5.03	5.19
DENMARK	DKK	5.94	6.13	6.26
CANADA	CAD	29.65	29.98	30.66
NORWAY	NOK	5.43	5.60	5.76
BRUNEI	BRD	22.10	-	23.50
INDONESIA	IDR	0.0025	-	0.005
MALAYSIA	MYR	8.53	-	10.76
CHINA	CNY	3.70	-	4.97
KOREA	KRW	0.029	-	0.043
TAIWAN	TWD	0.88	-	1.18
UAE	AED	7.75	-	10.20
BAHRAIN	BHD	59.63	-	96.33
OMAN	OMR	59.41	-	94.21
QATAR	QAR	7.67	-	10.22
SAUDI ARABIA	SAR	7.58	-	10.19
SOUTH AFRICA	ZAR	3.65	-	5.45

An exchange rates display.

OPERATING RISKS

Operating risks are the risks of executing plans. Even the best investing and financing plans can have problems with they are put into action. Such risks include:

1. What happens if a customer is hurt by your product? What happens if an employee is hurt on the job? Remember you may be liable under the law.

2. What happens if a key supplier goes out of business? You've got a problem that could cause your operations to cease. Have you got a contingency or backup plan?

3. Do you have the right people, both managers and employees? It takes people to manage assets, financing, customers, and other stakeholders. Having the right quantity and quality of people is critical. How many times have you walked out of a business because of poor service? How many times have you bought something because of superior service?

4. Are you complying with government regulations and operating the business in a legal, ethical, and socially responsible manner? Are you concerned about creating value for all stakeholders? In managing the short-term operations of the business, are you maintaining a long-term value perspective? The business's short-term operations must line up with the long-term objectives of the business. If not, problems will occur. What would you do if you had additional regulations or restrictions placed on you?

ADDRESSING RISK

Risk comes from everywhere. Everything a business does has an element of risk. Why? Because we are dealing with the future and nothing is certain regarding the future. Risk comes from outside and inside the business. It comes from investing, financing, and operating activities.

So if risk is everywhere, what do good managers do with risk? The answer is they manage and price risk. To do so, good managers create a comprehensive process to:

Recognize risk
Understand risk
Measure risk
Manage risk
Price risk

To recognize, understand, measure, manage, and price risk, managers need tools. Risk tools start with statistics.

LEARNING OBJECTIVE 2

UNDERSTANDING AND MEASURING RISK WITH STATISTICS

To work with risk, managers must first understand and measure what has occurred and is occurring. Then managers must project change and forecast the future. Managers use statistics to assist with this process of understanding and measuring the past and present and projecting the future. Statistics is the science of collecting, analyzing, summarizing, and presenting mass amounts of information. This science can be divided into descriptive statistics and inferential statistics.

DESCRIPTIVE STATISTICS

Descriptive statistics is the process of communicating the frequency and characteristics of an event or events within a population. Let's look at an example. We ask the question, "Why do some customers buy our product and some do not?" We first want to describe the total market for our own products and others' similar products. The market for these products is the population. Second, we need to determine what percentage of this market buys our product and what percentage of the population buys a competing product. We then need to analyze the characteristics of our and our competitors' products that determine who buys what.

To describe this information we use distributions. **Distributions** summarize the frequency of events. Let's go back to our example. You manufacture and sell clothing to undergraduate college students. You want to know why some customers buy your clothing and some do not. The market for your and similar products is 1 million customers. The age distribution of the total market is described in Exhibit 11.2.

EXHIBIT 11.2: Example: Age Distribution of Market

The Total Market—All Customers		
Age	**Number of Customers**	**Percentage**
19	550,000	0.55
20	50,000	0.05
21	100,000	0.1
22	250,000	0.25
23	50,000	0.05
Total	1,000,000	1.00

You sell to 300,000 customers, or 30% of the total market, and your competitors sell to the remaining 700,000 customers, or 70% of the total market. You ask, "Who is buying our clothing?" You determine the age distribution depicted in Exhibit 11.3.

EXHIBIT 11.3: Example: Age Distribution of Your Customers

Your Customers		
Age	**Number of Customers**	**Percentage**
19	0	0
20	0	0
21	50,000	0.166667
22	200,000	0.666667
23	50,000	0.166667
Total	300,000	1.00

You then ask who buys your competitors' clothing. You redefine the population as only customers buying products sold by your competitors. You determine the age distribution depicted in Exhibit 11.4.

EXHIBIT 11.4: Example: Age Distribution of Competitor

Competitor Customers		
Age	Number of Customers	Percentage
19	550,000	0.785714
20	50,000	0.071429
21	50,000	0.071429
22	50,000	0.071429
23	0	0
Total	700,000	1.00

So what did you learn? It appears that the distribution of your customers is different from the distribution of your competitors' customers.

STATISTICAL MEASURES

So how would you describe the above distributions? You have options. First you could describe the distributions like we did in Exhibits 11.2, 11.3, and 11.4. However, statisticians have more concise ways to describe distributions. They use summary measures to describe the central point of a distribution and the dispersion around that central point.

The first group of summary measures describes the midpoint or central tendency of the distribution. The most-used measure is a weighted average of all the data, called a mean. A **mean** is the average of all observations. Mathematically the mean is defined as:

EQUATION 11.2: Mean

$$Mean = \frac{\Sigma (X_1 + X_2 + X_3 + \dots X_N)}{N}$$

Where

Mean	The mean of the distribution
Σ	Summation
X	The value of individual observations
N	The number of observations

When looking at large number of observations, the mean can also be defined as:

EQUATION 11.3: Mean

$$Mean = \Sigma (X * P_x)$$

Where

Mean	The mean of the distribution
Σ	Summation
X	The value of individual observations
P_x	The relative frequency or percentage of observation X in the population

In our examples the mean ages after rounding are (see endnote 1 for computation of mean for the total market):

Your customers	22.0 years
Competitors' customers	19.4 years
Total market	20.2 years

Another measure of the midpoint is called the **median**. A median is that point where 50% of the distribution is above that number and 50% is below that number. It is the halfway point of the distribution.

In our examples the median ages are:

Your customers	22 years
Competitors' customers	19 years
Total market	19 years

A third measure of central tendency is called the **mode**. The mode of a distribution is the most frequent value in the distribution. In our examples the modes are:

Your customers	22 years
Competitors' customers	19 years
Total market	19 years

Now look back at our measures of mean, median, and mode. What do you see? You see your customers on average are older and your competitors' customers are younger.

The second group of summary measures describes the dispersion or variability around the measure of central tendency, or mean. The first measure of dispersion is called variance. Mathematically **variance** is defined as:

EQUATION 11.4: Variance

$$\text{Variance} = \Sigma \ (X_n - Mean)^2(P_x)$$

Where

Variance	The variance of the distribution
Σ	Summation
Mean	The mean of the distribution
X	The value of individual observations
P_x	The relative frequency or percentage of observation X in the population

In our examples the rounded variances are (see endnote 2 for computation of variance for the total market):

Your customers	.3 years
Competitors' customers	.8 years
Total market	2.1 years

A second measure of dispersion is standard deviation. The **standard deviation** of a distribution is the square root of the variance of the distribution.

In our examples the rounded standard deviations are

Your customers	.6 years
Competitors' customers	.9 years
Total market	1.4 years

Now look back at our measures of variance and standard deviation. What do you see? You see your customers are concentrated around the mean; there is less dispersion or variance compared to your competitors. Your competitors sell to a wider range of ages.

So statisticians use descriptive statistics to help managers understand what happened. In our example we clearly saw that your customers were older on average and varied less in age. The customers of your competitors were younger on average and varied more in age. But are descriptive statistics limited to looking at one variable or dimension? The answer is no. When we look at one variable or dimension we are using **univariate statistics**. Our example of customer age is an example of univariate statistics. When statisticians look at how multiple factors or dimensions relate to one another, we are using **multivariate statistics**. An example may be asking the question, "Why do older customers buy our products and younger customers buy the products of our competitors?" Maybe the color of your product appeals to older customers. When we look at the relationship of age and color we are using multivariate statistics.

To describe how one dimension relates to another dimension, statisticians have many measures and tools. One important tool is covariance. **Covariance** measures how two or more variables co-vary or move together. When covariance is standardized, the measure is called **correlation**. In our example, it would be very important to see if color and age co-vary and correlate. Maybe older customers like darker colors and dislike lighter colors. Maybe younger customers like lighter colors and dislike darker colors.

SAMPLING

Often businesses find it impossible to analyze the entire population. To help, businesses will **sample** the population to gain insights into the population. Businesses will use the data from sampling to infer the characteristics of the population. Sampling is tricky. If poorly done, samples will not reveal the information needed and inferences may be incorrect.

INFERENTIAL STATISTICS

Inferential statistics are statistics used to reach conclusions about a population. Although our example was using descriptive statistics, we began to use these statistics to infer relationships and cause and effect. Inferential statistics are the foundation of understanding the impact of decisions and forecasting

THE CHALLENGES OF SAMPLING

You want to know what type of automobiles customers buy in the US. Can you imagine trying to canvass every US driver to determine what he or she drives? It would be very hard, time-consuming, and expensive. So what do you do? The answer is you sample.

However, sampling is not as easy as it may appear. First, you need to make sure your sample represents your population. In the US there are drivers of almost all ages who purchase cars. If you take your sample at a college, your sample would not be representative of all drivers. Your sample would be biased to younger drivers. Your conclusions from sampling could cause you to produce the wrong automobile.

Second, your sample must be constructed correctly. You want to understand the buying habits of US drivers. You ask the question, "What automobile would you like to drive?" You've got problems with your sample. The automobiles that customers would like to drive and actually drive may be different. Why? Customers may not be able to afford the car they prefer and have to buy another car. Your poorly constructed sample can create problems for your business.

Sampling is a critical part of business that helps businesses understand what has happened, what is happening, and what will happen. Sampling is used when the population is too large to analyze. However, sampling must be done correctly or problems will occur.

the future. Let's look at our example and ask the question, "If older customers like darker colors and younger customers like lighter colors, could you increase your sales if you offered customers a choice between darker and lighter colors?" Inferential statistics look at how variables co-vary.

Using inferential statistics, managers can begin to plan and estimate the impact of decisions. They can forecast the wide range of possible outcomes and the probability of each outcome. This range of possible outcomes creates a probability distribution. Managers then look at the mean, median, and/or mode of this distribution as the expected value of the decision. Managers compute the variance and/or standard deviation of their projected distribution to forecast the upside and downside of the decision. Variance and standard deviation are measures of dispersion or variability. These measures are used to measure the uncertainty or risk in a decision.

MANAGING, RISKS, AND MAKING DECISIONS

Managing risk starts with:

- · What do I expect to happen if I decide to take certain actions?
- · Given what I expect, what else could happen? How good and how bad could things get?
- · What will happen if the expected and unexpected happens?

These questions are answered by using descriptive and inferential statistics. These questions are answered with measures such as mean, median, mode, variance, standard deviation, covariance, and correlation. These measures help managers forecast what to expect when they plan, execute, and review.

However, these measures also help managers forecast what could happen if the unexpected occurs. Let's look at several examples.

Example One—Inventory Management: A business wants to make sure it has enough but not too much inventory. The need for inventory is a function of forecasted sales. Using statistics, the business realizes its sales co-vary with the overall income level of the economy. When the income in the economy increases, the business's sales increase. When income in the economy decreases, the business's sales decrease. The business's sales and the income of the economy are positively correlated. The economy is forecast to grow. What should the business's managers do? One of the things managers should do is prepare for greater sales by buying more inventory.

Example Two—Financing the Business: A business does not know whether the economy will expand or contract. After analyzing the past, the business realizes its sales are positively correlated with the overall economy. The business expects the economy to expand and has the inventory and other resources needed to meet the increasing needs of customers. However, the business is concerned about the possibility of an unexpected downturn in the economy. If the business cannot sell its inventory, the business will not have the cash to pay its bills. The business could fail. So what can management do? Management can use statistics to estimate the impact of a bad economy on the business's sales and inventory. It can then arrange financing, debt, or owners' equity, in case the unexpected downturn occurs.

Interior of the Boeing factory, Seattle, Washington. Managing inventory, financing the business, and forecasting staffing needs are crucial to a business's success.

Example Three—Forecasting the Need for Employees: A business wants to have enough employees to produce and sell its products, but it does not want too many employees. Too many employees will hurt the business's operating profit and net income. Using statistics, the business analyzes past sales and estimates it needs ten employees to produce and sell every 1,000 units of product. Using statistics, the business estimates it sells one unit of product for every 10,000 people living in its market. The question becomes how many people are forecasted to live in the business's market?

The answer will tell managers how many employees to hire. Statistics helped managers reduce the uncertainty of hiring too few or too many employees.

LEARNING OBJECTIVE 3

. . . .

MANAGING AND PRICING RISK

Given that risk comes from everything a business does, risk management can be complicated and overwhelming. A business needs to systematically manage its risk.

THE PROCESS OF RISK MANAGEMENT

The **process of risk management** is the process of:

Given that risk comes from everything a business does, risk management must be involved in everything a business does. Risk management is a comprehensive program that looks at every part of a business and how those parts come together.

The current phrase for such a program is "**Enterprise Risk Management (ERM)**."[3] ERM is the process of identifying, analyzing, and addressing current and future risks. ERM is a management function and thus involves planning, executing, and reviewing.

The four principles of ERM are:

- · Establishment of risk tolerances

- · Programs to assess risk

- · Programs to monitor risk

- · Programs to continuously evaluate risk

Dealing with Risk

Recognize Risk

↓

Understand Risk

↓

Measure Risk

↓

Manage Risk

↓

Price Risk

Risk tolerance is about determining how much risk a business can and should accept. Risk tolerance refers to the willingness and/or ability to assume risk in any given activity and the business as a whole. Risk tolerance is about asking questions such as, "How much risk can a business accept and still survive?"

Risk assessment is about recognizing, analyzing, understanding, and measuring the significant risks associated with a business's investing, financing, and operating activities. Risk assessment looks at every part of the business and how those parts fit together in the business's model and strategy. A business should estimate and assess the magnitude and probability of potential losses from decisions and activities. This is done with sensitivity analysis. **Sensitivity analysis** is the process of estimating the impact of unexpected events. Risk assessment is about asking questions such as, "How bad can things get and will we be okay if they get that bad?"

Monitoring risk is about creating and implementing adequate controls to manage the risk accepted by the business. A part of risk monitoring is contingency planning. **Contingency planning** refers to management's plans to handle unexpected events. Also a part of risk monitoring is determining which risks a business can and cannot accept. If a business cannot accept a risk, then the business must find a way to eliminate or reduce the risk to an acceptable level. If the business cannot do so, the business must not go forward with the decision or activity.

Risk evaluation is the continuous examination of the risk management process and determining whether or not it is effective. If the process is not adequately managing risk, then changes must be made to the process of setting risk tolerances, assessing risk, and monitoring risk.

ALTERNATIVES TO HELP MANAGE RISK

First, managers must determine a business's risk tolerance. Managers must decide what risks can and cannot be accepted. If a risk is unacceptable, managers then must decide whether the risk can be eliminated or reduced.

To eliminate or reduce risk, managers have several alternatives. However, risk reduction often has a price. The old saying is true, "There is no free lunch." The cost versus the benefits of these alternatives must be evaluated. These alternatives include:

1. Risk management programs targeted at a specific risk

2. Insurance

3. Diversification

4. Hedging

Risk Management Programs

Businesses that recognize and understand risk can often create programs that eliminate or reduce those risks.

An example is a company that creates and produces a product. Such businesses must carefully design and test their products to ensure these products are safe to use. Businesses must design operating and manufacturing systems that ensure products will meet required specifications. This is often referred to as **quality control**.

Another example is risks of using a product. Customers must be informed of such risks. Have you ever listened to commercials trying to sell pharmaceutical products? How many times have you heard advertisements talk about possible side effects?

One last example is employee safety. Businesses must make sure that they produce their product in a safe environment. Precautions must be made to ensure employee welfare. This includes adequate training and supervision.

Insurance

A business can eliminate or reduce many risks by buying an **insurance policy** from an insurance company. Such insurance has a cost called an **insurance premium**. Insurance companies are willing to sell policies to businesses to cover such things as:

- Property damage from a fire, wind, or other physical events

- Loss of business income from catastrophic events such as hurricanes

- Work-related injuries to employees

- The death of key employees

- Liability and damages incurred by customers buying and using faulty products

Often you will hear the phrase, "The business is **self-insured**." When a business self-insures, the business is accepting the risk and pays for any losses.

Diversification

A business is a portfolio. As such, all things come together to create one unified risk profile for the company. Sometimes a company can reduce risk by diversification. Diversification is the process of combining different activities that co-vary but do not perfectly move together. Remember the old saying, "Don't put all your eggs in one basket."

Let's look at an example. Remember our Belgian chocolate example in Chapter 05? Remember how we lost money because we bought Belgian chocolates in euros and sold the chocolates in US dollars? In doing so we were taking foreign exchange risk. We accepted the uncertainty that we could lose money if the US dollar depreciated and the euro appreciated. But what if we simultaneously entered into a second contract to offset this risk? What would happen if we simultaneously agreed to buy wheat in the US and sell it in France? If we bought the wheat in US dollars and sold the wheat in euros, we would make money if the US dollar depreciated and the euro appreciated. The gain from this second contract (wheat), if properly structured, could offset the loss on the first contract (chocolate). We could eliminate the foreign exchange risk by diversifying our business.

A chocolate shop in Antwerp, Belgium.

Hedging Risk

Hedging risk is a term used in many ways. Sometimes people use the word "hedge" to mean using insurance or diversification. However, hedging often relates to using derivatives.

A **derivative** is any instrument that derives its value from something else. Derivatives come in many forms, the most common of which are 1) swaps, 2) futures and forwards, and 3) options.

Swaps

A **swap** is a financial agreement where two parties agree to swap something of value at a future date. Swaps are usually done with the help of an intermediary who specializes in such transactions. Banks often act as such an intermediary. The financial world uses swaps a lot to help with interest rates, foreign exchange, and other risks associated with acquiring and using money.

Let's go back and look at our example of buying the Belgian chocolates in euros and selling the chocolates in US dollars. The business could enter into a swap where the business promises to exchange a given quantity of US dollars for euros at a future date. The business would enter into a contract to swap US dollars for euros. The business would be guaranteed how many euros it would receive in the future and thus eliminate the foreign exchange risk. However, to eliminate this risk, the business would pay a fee to the intermediary.

A bakery in Oslo, Norway.

Futures and Forwards

A **future** is similar to a swap. A future is an agreement by two or more parties to buy and sell a specific item at a future price and date. Let's look at an example. You own a bakery and a large chain of grocery stores comes to you asking for a guaranteed price for bread during the next six months. You want the business but are scared of the risk. You could lose a lot of money if you guarantee the price of your bread and the cost of wheat goes up. Your business could fail. You cannot take the risk, but you want the business. To guarantee the price of wheat you could enter into a futures contract. You could agree to buy a given quantity of wheat at a specified price at a specified time in the future. You could guarantee the price of your wheat and thus guarantee that, if properly priced, your sale of bread will create a profit. The challenge is you have entered into a contract for the wheat regardless of whether the price of wheat goes up or down in the future. If the price of wheat goes up in the future, you are protected. If the price of wheat goes down, you still must purchase the wheat at the agreed-upon price. You may wish to buy the wheat at the lower price and not honor your futures contract. You have a contract, however, and you must fulfill your obligation.

A future is a standardized contract that is traded on public exchanges. (An example of a public exchange is the New York Stock Exchange.) Standardization means the contract has standard terms regarding the quantity of the item to be exchanged and the time of the exchange. Future contracts are written on such things as agricultural products, oil, copper, gold, and foreign exchange. Future contracts are even written on the price of money, where lenders and borrowers enter into a debt contract for a given quantity of money, at a specified price (interest), for a specified future time.

A **forward** contract is the same as a future contract with one exception. A forward contract is a customized, not standardized, contract. Forwards are not traded on a public exchange. Forward contracts

BUSINESS SENSE

SPECULATING WITH DERIVATIVES

Derivatives are often misunderstood. As the examples of swaps, futures, and options show, risk can be reduced by using derivatives. Derivatives can also create risk.

Let's look at the wheat farmer example. The farmer buys a put option from a seller. The seller receives an option premium. The seller is hoping that the price of wheat goes up, and the farmer does not exercise the option. If the seller of the put option was eliminating his or her risk, he or she would make sure he or she had a place to sell the wheat in case the price of wheat went down and the farmer exercised the option. If the option seller had a guaranteed market and price for the wheat, the option would be covered. If the seller did not have a guaranteed market and price for the wheat, the option would be naked or uncovered. With the naked or uncovered option, the seller is speculating and could lose a lot of money if the price of wheat goes down. The seller of the put option would have to buy the wheat from the farmer at a higher price and then sell the wheat in the market at a lower price. The seller of the naked or uncovered put option would be taking a lot of risk.

are usually created by intermediaries who customize the agreement to meet the specific needs of the buyers and sellers. Our bakery may go to a brokerage business that specializes in the buying of wheat from farmers and selling of wheat to businesses like our bakery. This brokering business would act as an intermediary and create the forward contract.

Options

An **option** is an instrument, sold by a seller to a buyer, which gives the buyer the right to do something. The buyer is the owner of the option contract. This option has a cost the buyer must pay to the seller, called an **option premium**. The owner of the option has the right to do something, but not the obligation to do it. If the owner does not want to fulfill the contract, the owner can let it lapse or expire. All that happens is the owner loses the option premium. So how are options used?

There are two types of options, calls and puts. A **call option** gives the option owner the right to buy from the option seller an item at a specified price at or during a specified time in the future. If the option owner exercises the call option, the owner buys or "calls out" the item from the option seller. A **put option** gives the option owner the right to sell the item to the option seller at a specified price at or during a specified time in the future. If the option owner exercises the put option, the option owner sells or "puts" the item on the seller.

Let's look back at our bakery example. You are concerned that the price of wheat could go up, but you are not sure. You do not want to lose money if the price of wheat goes up, but you would like to make the extra money if the price of wheat goes down. What to do? You could buy a call option on wheat. You could guarantee the price you pay for wheat in the future will not exceed the agreed-upon price. If the price of wheat goes up, you will exercise your call option and make the option seller sell you the wheat at the agreed-upon price. If the price of wheat goes down, you will buy your wheat in the market at the lower price. You will not exercise your call option. You will lose your premium, but you will also make more profit from the lower cost of wheat.

Now let's look at another example. You are the farmer producing the wheat. You know the cost to produce the wheat, such as seed and fertilizer. What you do not know is the price you will receive for the wheat when you sell it in the market. You hope the price of wheat will go up, but you are scared that the price of wheat might go down. If the price of wheat goes down, you could lose a lot of money. What to do? You could buy a put option on wheat. You could guarantee the minimum price you will receive for your wheat. If the price of wheat goes down, you will exercise your put option and sell the wheat to the option seller for the agreed-upon price. If the price of wheat goes up, you will not exercise your put option and sell your wheat in the market for the higher price. You will lose your premium but you will also make more profit from the higher price of wheat.

THE TOTAL FIRM PERSPECTIVE

In managing risk, managers must look at every part of the business. Why? The answer is risk comes from everything a business does. However, managers must never forget the value of the business is a function of the business's total risk. The question managers must ultimately ask is, "How does a decision affect the risk borne by lenders and owners?"

Let's look at an example in the financing, investing, and operating decisions. When a business hires employees and invests in assets that produce a stable, predictable operating income, then that business has low **operating risk**. Operating income is relatively certain and stable. Because of this low operating risk, the firm can use more debt and less equity. The firm can borrow money that "requires" it to pay interest and principal. The failure to do so could mean the failure of the business. In financing with debt, the business is using financial leverage and accepting higher **financial risk**. The high financial risk is offset by low operating risk. The overall risk in the business is manageable.

PRICING RISK

Managers should attempt to eliminate or reduce risk when possible and financially feasible. But businesses cannot eliminate all risks. The risk a business accepts is the risk the business's lenders and owners must bear. To compensate lenders and owners, managers must price this risk.

Let's look at an example. You operate a pharmaceutical company that provides critical, but very risky medication. Many of your customers are at risk. You understand the situation and inform your customers of the risk they assume when taking your medication. You try to buy product insurance but no insurance company will assume the risk. You face a dilemma. Do you produce the medication and assume the risks? Do you not produce the medication and deny your customers the chance for a better life? What do you do? If you produce the product and assume the risk, you must price the risk.

What does it mean to price the risk? The answer is charging a higher price for your product because of risk. The higher price will create higher operating income. The higher operating income will compensate the business's lenders and owners for the increased risk. Failure to compensate lenders and owners for risk will destroy value. Why? The answer is that lenders and owners will not provide money if they are not compensated for risk.

CHAPTER SUMMARY

Managing risk is a very important part of creating business value. Risk is everywhere and affects everything a manager does. The trick of successful risk management is recognizing the risk, understanding the risk, measuring the risk, managing the risk, and pricing the risk.

In this chapter we've explored risk. We've looked at how risk impacts the creation of value. After reading this chapter, you should be able to:

1. Appreciate risk and how risk affects value (Learning Objective 1): Risk is the uncertainty of an undesirable outcome. The higher the risk, the greater the return we expect.
2. Appreciate the use of statistics in understanding and measuring risk (Learning Objective 2): Statistics is the science of collecting, analyzing, summarizing, and presenting mass amounts of numerical information. Statistics can be divided into descriptive statistics and inferential statistics.
3. Appreciate how risk is managed (Learning Objective 3): Risk management is the process of recognizing risk, understanding risk, measuring risk, managing risk, and pricing risk.

In this chapter we've seen how risk management is an important part of "How Business Works."

KEYWORDS

call option 249

contingency planning 245

correlation 242

covariance 242

derivative 247

descriptive statistics 238

distributions 239

enterprise risk management
  (ERM) 245

financial risk 250

forward 248

future 248

inferential statistics 242

insurance policy 246

insurance premium 246

mean 240

median 241

mode 241

monitoring risk 245

multivariate statistics 242

operating risk 249

option 249

option premium 249

process of risk management 245

put option 249

quality control 246

risk 234

risk assessment 245

risk evaluation 245

risk tolerance 245

sample 242

self-insured 247

sensitivity analysis 245

standard deviation 242

statistics 238

swap 247

univariate statistics 242

variance 241

SHORT-ANSWER QUESTIONS

1. What is risk and where does it come from?
2. How does risk affect the value of a business?
3. What is the role of statistics in managing risk?
4. What does the process of risk management entail?
5. Define the following terms:
   a. Descriptive statistics
   b. Distribution
   c. Mean
   d. Median
   e. Mode
   f. Variance
   g. Standard deviation
   h. Univariate statistics
   i. Multivariate statistics
   j. Covariance
   k. Correlation
   l. Sampling and sample
   m. Inferential statistics
   n. Enterprise Risk Management (ERM)
   o. Risk tolerance
   p. Risk assessment
   q. Sensitivity analysis

   r. Risk monitoring
   s. Contingency planning
   t. Risk evaluation
   u. Quality control
   v. Insurance policy
   w. Insurance premium
   x. Insurance
   y. Self-insured
   z. Diversification
   aa. Hedging risk
   ab. Derivative
   ac. Swap
   ad. Future
   ae. Forward
   af. Option
   ag. Option premium
   ah. Call option
   ai. Put option
   aj. Covered option
   ak. Naked or uncovered option
   al. Speculating
   am. Operating risk
   an. Financial risk

PROBLEMS

Use the following information for questions 1 through 3.

You own a bicycle shop. You analyze your market and realize there are 600,000 customers of bicycles and one competitor. On average, a customer buys a new bicycle every three years, creating sales of 200,000 bicycles per year. You sample the population and your customers. You project the following for your customers:

Average Income Level of Customer	Number of Customers
Level 1 - $10,000	0
Level 2 - $30,000	5,000
Level 3 - $50,000	10,000
Level 4 - $70,000	20,000
Level 5 - $90,000	25,000
Level 6 - $110,000	40,000
Total	100,000

You project the following for all customers in your market:

Average Income Level of Customer	Number of Customers
Level 1 - $10,000	0
Level 2 - $30,000	15,000
Level 3 - $50,000	20,000
Level 4 - $70,000	30,000
Level 5 - $90,000	25,000
Level 6 - $110,000	110,000
Total	200,000

1. Compute the mean, median, and mode for:
   a. Your customers
   b. The total market
   c. Your competitors

2. Compute the variance for:
   a. Your customers
   b. The total market
   c. Your competitors

3. Compute the standard deviation for: a. Your customers b. The total market c. Your competitors.
4. What do your answers to questions 1, 2, and 3 tell you?

EXPLORING REAL BUSINESS

Go to the websites of Google, Target, Hyundai, and Procter & Gamble. The websites are

Google:	http://investor.google.com
Target:	http://www.target.com
Hyundai:	http://worldwide.hyundai.com/company-overview
Procter & Gamble:	http://www.pg.com

1. Describe the risks that you think each company has.
2. Look over each company's website and see what they are doing to manage risk.

ENDNOTES

1. The mean of total market is computed as 19(550,000/1,000,000) + 20(50,000/1,000,000) + 21(100,000/1,000,000) + 22(250,000/1,000,000) + 23(50,000/1,000,000) = 20.2

2. The variance of total market is computed as $(19 - 20.2)^2$(550,000/1,000,000) + $(20 - 20.2)^2$(50,000/1,000,000) + $(21 - 20.2)^2$(100,000/1,000,000) + $(22 - 20.2)^2$(250,000/1,000,000) + $(23 - 20.2)^2$(50,000/1,000,000) = 2.06

3. The phrase Enterprise Risk Management (ERM) and processes of ERM are the work of many professionals such as the members of the Casualty Actuarial Society. The organization, however, that is credited with being a pioneer in the area of ERM is the Committee of Sponsoring Organizations of the Treadway Commission (COSO), and is sponsored by the American Institute of Certified Public Accountants, the American Accounting Association, the Financial Executives International, the Institute of Managerial Accountants, and the Institute of Internal Auditors.

SECTION 4

MEETING THE NEEDS OF CUSTOMERS

In this section, you will read and review the following chapters:

CHAPTER

12

MARKETING

Introduction: Let's Talk About Marketing and Markets

What do customers buy and why do they buy it? How do customers make choices? How does a business determine what to sell, what price to charge, and how to distribute its products? How is a business affected by competition? How do managers create a sustainable competitive advantage that creates value? What is marketing and how do managers manage the marketing function?

In this chapter we'll explore these questions and issues. We'll explore the concepts and issues that frame the opportunities and challenges of marketing. We'll explore how understanding and meeting customers' needs is at the heart of "How Business Works." We'll start talking about creating customer value.

WHY MARKETING MATTERS

Have you ever walked into a store to buy an item and walked out having bought a lot more than you originally planned? Have you ever gone to the Internet to make a major purchase and compared one product to another to find the best value? Have you ever gotten excited about a product after seeing it on television? Have you ever taken a survey from a marketing research firm and wondered what was happening? If so you are experiencing the world of marketing. And why does marketing matter? It matters because marketing is all about making a sale, the first necessary step in creating value. Without a sale, there is nothing a business can do to create value for any stakeholder, particularly owners. A business must first create customer value.

EXHIBIT 12.1: The Marketing Process

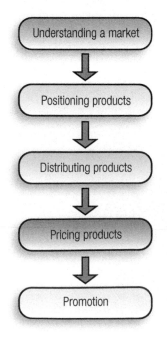

LEARNING OBJECTIVE 1

THE NATURE OF MARKETING

The objective of marketing is to create a successful sale. A **sale** is an exchange between a business and its customers. For a sale to be successful, both parties, the business and customer, must perceive that the sale creates value. The customer must believe that the value he or she receives from the product exceeds the cost or price of the product. The business must believe that the price it receives for the product compensates it for the cost and risk of acquiring (or producing), distributing, promoting, and financing the product.

There are many functions within a business. Each function should contribute to the creation of business value. Marketing contributes to business value by understanding and communicating with product markets. Successful businesses are focused on these markets. It is the responsibility of the marketing function to understand and guide the business regarding the needs and capabilities of the market for its product. This is often referred to as the **marketing concept**. However, it should be recognized that in doing so, marketing plays a unique and critical role in the success of any business. There is no function more important than the marketing function. Without a sale, nothing matters. The process of creating business value starts with a sale. Ultimately the existence of a business rests on whether or not it can convince the customer that the business's product provides the best value offered in a market.

THE MARKETING FUNCTION

In Chapter 01 **marketing** was defined as the process of understanding a market, positioning products to meet customer needs, distributing products, pricing products, and communicating product attributes to customers (promotion). Let's dissect the **marketing process**.

A business must first understand the market. A **market** is the collection of all 1) current and potential customers and 2) competitors seeking to satisfy the wants and needs of those customers. Markets are composed of customers and competitors. Before a business can create and sell a product, the business must first estimate whether or not customers will have the desire and ability to purchase the product. The business must also determine what alternatives competitors will provide customers.

Second is positioning a product within a market. A business must estimate if it can convince the customer to choose its product and not the product of its competitors. Can the business position its product in the market to achieve a sale? Can the business differentiate its product so the customer believes the business's product is preferable? Can the business create a competitive advantage that ideally is sustainable over long periods?

Third, a business must select the most effective mode of distributing the product. The business must choose the best way to bring its products to market at a cost low enough to maximize value.

Fourth, a business must determine the price it must and can charge for the product. The price it *must* charge is a function of a business's cost and risk. Over the long term, what must the business charge the customer so the sale of the product creates value for the business? The price it *can* charge is a function of the market. What will the customer pay for the business's product given the competition? If the price a business can charge is equal to or exceeds the price it must charge, then the business has the opportunity to create value.

Advertising in Shibuya, Tokyo, Japan.

Fifth, a business must promote the product. The business must convince the customer that its product is what the customer wants. The business must convince the customer that its product is superior to the products of its competitors. Customers will buy that product which they perceive gives them the greatest value. Advertising is a significant part of promotion. Promotion is about communication.

The output of the marketing process is often called the **marketing mix**. Many marketers break the marketing mix into four components called the **Four "P's" of marketing**. The four P's are product, place, price, and promotion. **Product** is the good or service to be exchanged. **Place** is the location and means of distributing the product. **Price** is the amount the customer pays the business for the sale. **Promotion** is the communication by the business to customers, designed to inform the customer of product attributes and persuade the customer to purchase the product. Although often discussed separately, good marketers know that product, place, price, and promotion are not independent. When customers enter into a sale, they buy more than a product. Customers buy a marketing mix.

Think about needing toothpaste such as P&G's Crest. Then think about shopping at Target. What are you buying when you visit a Target store? You buy the product, such as Crest toothpaste. You buy the place, Target's store location. The sale is measured by the price you pay Target for the toothpaste. How did you know that Target and Crest would meet your needs? The answer is promotion.

UNDERSTANDING THE MARKETING MIX

Have you ever stopped to think exactly what you are buying when you buy a product? Whether a good or a service, customers often do not recognize the complete package they buy. Let's look at a couple of examples.

Maid-Rite sandwich shop. This store housed the USA's first drive-thru window (est. 1927). It is on the National Register of Historic Places.

BUSINESS SENSE

WHAT DO COFFEE SHOPS SELL?

You walk into a coffee shop such as Starbucks. What do you see? Do you see customers coming and going only to purchase coffee? Is the price of coffee in a coffeehouse cheap? The answers to these questions are probably no.

Coffee shops sell much more than coffee. Besides coffee, most coffee shops sell a place to network, both physically and technologically. Look around. You'll see people meeting, talking, socializing, and networking in a comfortable environment. You see people using wireless access to do work. Although coffeehouses sell a lot of coffee, coffeehouses sell much more than coffee. That's why the price of a cup of coffee at a coffeehouse is high.

First, you are driving down a highway and become hungry. You have a lot of alternatives. Your alternatives range from nationally advertised (promoted) restaurants to local restaurants, from relatively fast service to service that takes longer due to food preparation, and from very inexpensive food to more expensive food. Your alternatives include restaurants that you must leave your automobile to be served or restaurants that you do not need to leave your automobile to be served (drive-through restaurants). So what do you choose? You choose that restaurant that provides you the best value. You compare the benefits each restaurant provides versus the price each restaurant charges.

On the surface you are merely buying food. In reality you are buying food, distributed through a physical asset and system, operated by people providing service, at a specific location. You are buying, at a price, a mixture of product, place, and promotion. You are buying a lot more than food.

Let's look at a second example. You have a cold. You are sick with sneezing, a mild cough, and congestion. Your doctor tells you the cold will pass with bed rest, fluids, etc. Your doctor tells you to go to the pharmacy and get a non-prescription cold remedy. You visit your local pharmacy and see numerous alternatives from which to choose. Which one product do you decide to buy? After reading the labels of your alternatives, you realize that the chemical composition of the products is similar. So what is the key determinant in your selection? Typically it's safety. You do not want to risk your health by taking the wrong product. You want the product to ease your pain, but you are very concerned about the safety of the product. You go to the pharmacy because you trust the pharmacy to sell only safe products. You look at the product's packaging to make sure that it is safe. You read the labels on the product to determine if it is safe. You think about the product's advertisements and brand to reduce your uncertainty.

What are you buying? You are buying much more than the mere chemicals that comprise the product. Product, place, and promotion focus on safety, a significant factor on what you, the customer, want.

When a business analyzes the market, it must have a clear understanding of what customers want, what the business can offer, and what the business's competitors can and will offer. The business must look beyond the basic product. The business must look at the marketing mix. But how does a business figure out what the customer wants? How does the business figure out the right marketing mix to entice the customer to buy? The answer is marketing research.

MARKETING RESEARCH

Producing and marketing a product is risky. Why? The answer is that a business produces and markets a product expecting customers will buy the product, and business value will be created. However, the business does not know this will occur; it only expects a sale and value creation.

To reduce this risk, businesses conduct marketing research. **Marketing research** is the process of collecting and analyzing data regarding current and potential customers and competitors. As such, like most processes designed to understand and manage risk, marketing research is based on statistics. Sampling, estimating expected outcomes, and recognizing that outcomes may vary are critical to assessing the probability of having a successful sale and creating business value. As such a typical **marketing research process** would entail the following steps:

Step 1: Define the research question.
Step 2: Design the research so the question can be answered.
Step 3: Collect the needed data.
Step 4: Analyze the data.
Step 5: Make strategic decisions based on the analyzed data.

This looks straightforward, but it can be challenging. Let's look at an example. A food manufacturer wants to sell a new food product. It wants to sell its new product to a chain of grocery stores. It discusses the product with the chain of grocery stores. The chain says it will purchase the product only if it is convinced its customers want it. The food manufacturer decides to conduct marketing research. It takes product samples to selected grocery stores and offers customers free samples. After tasting the free samples, customers are asked if they liked the product, would purchase the product, and how much they would pay. Customers indicate they like the product, would purchase the product, and pay a given price. The food manufacturer produces the product, and the grocery store chain makes an initial purchase. The projected sales, however, do not occur. Why? Why did customer behavior differ from the research findings? It could be the research design, data collection, or data analysis was flawed. Maybe the customers taking the food samples were not representative of all customers. Maybe the person handing out the samples and asking the questions coerced customers to say they liked and would purchase the product. Maybe the business failed to look at competitor information that indicated competitors were creating a superior product.

The methods used to conduct marketing research are varied. Marketing research can use **primary marketing data** created for the sole

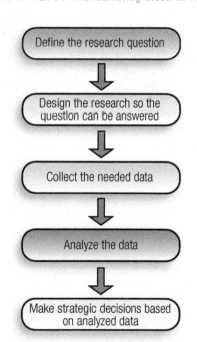

EXHIBIT 12.3: The Marketing Research Process

purpose of answering the marketing question. The data in the above grocery store example was primary data obtained from a survey. Marketing research can also use **secondary marketing data**. Secondary data already exists. An example of secondary data is information from the census. The Internet is a growing source of secondary data.

Marketing research is very important, but very challenging. To help businesses understand how markets behave, businesses often look outside their organization to specialists. There is a growing industry of businesses that specialize in marketing research. These marketing research businesses charge a fee to help other businesses determine how customers and competitors behave.

THE BEHAVIOR OF MARKETS—CUSTOMERS AND COMPETITORS

So how do markets behave? How do customers decide what to buy and what not to buy? How do competitors act and react? What motivates customers and competitors? Let's look at customers first.

CUSTOMERS

Customers are the people and organizations that buy a business's product. All customers typically go through a process to make their decision to buy or not to buy.

The Customer's Buying Decision

A customer's **buying decision** involves the following steps: recognizing a need or want; seeking information on which to base his or her buying decision; evaluating and comparing his or her alternatives; making the decision of what to buy or not to buy based on perceived value; and after the purchase—evaluating his or her buying decision and taking actions based on his or her satisfaction level.

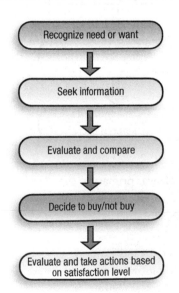

Customers holiday shopping at a mall in San Antonio, Texas.

EXHIBIT 12.4: The Buying Decision

- Recognize need or want
- Seek information
- Evaluate and compare
- Decide to buy/not buy
- Evaluate and take actions based on satisfaction level

Think about the earlier example of driving down a highway and needing to eat. What did you do? You recognized you had a need. You were hungry. You determined your alternatives by looking around at nearby restaurants. You evaluated the characteristics of your alternatives regarding type of food, type of service, brand, and price. You made your selection and purchased food from one restaurant. After the purchase and consuming the product, you evaluated your decision. Were you satisfied with the sale and product? If not, what would you do? Would you complain to the restaurant's management, recommend a friend never eat at the restaurant, and/or refuse to eat at the restaurant in the future? If you were satisfied with the sale and product, would you recommend the restaurant to a friend and/or eat at the restaurant in the future?

Customers go through the buying process so often that it often becomes habitual. For many items, customers instinctively go through the buying process without thinking about it, such as always buying Crest when they need toothpaste. For major purchases, however, customers go through the buying process carefully and methodically. Think about your decision to buy an automobile such as Hyundai's Elantra. Regardless of whether a customer goes through the process instinctively or methodically, certain factors affect this process. The factors are different for different types of customers.

The factors that affect a customer's buying process depend on the type of customer. Customers can be categorized as either consumers or businesses. A consumer is a person or household that buys a product for final consumption. The consumer market is often called the **B2C market**, or business-to-consumer market. When you buy an automobile from an automobile dealership, the sale occurs in the B2C market. A business is an organization that buys a product for resale or uses it to produce another product. When a business sells to another business, the market is often called the **B2B market**, or business-to-business market. When an automobile dealership buys an Elantra automobile from Hyundai, the sale occurs in the B2B market.

Consumer Behavior

Consumer behavior is complex. Why? The answer is that people's behavior is a function of numerous factors and how those factors interrelate. Consumer behavior is a function of cultural factors, social factors, economic factors, psychological factors, and individual factors.

Cultural factors relate to the factors consumers learn. Consumers learn what is acceptable and desirable regarding housing, food, clothing, transportation, and other products. Geography, gender, ethnicity, and other influences affect cultural factors. Does where you live affect the clothes you buy? The answer is probably yes.

Social factors relate to how consumers are affected by group behavior. A society is a grouping of people, and groups impact how group members behave. This is particularly true about what group members buy or do not buy. Groups may be formal such as a family or a college graduating class. Groups may also be informal such as social networking groups formed through the Internet. Within a group, different members assume different roles, such as opinion leader. Do your peers affect what you buy, such as clothing? The answer is probably yes.

Economic factors relate to a consumer's level of income and wealth. What a consumer buys is dependent on how much that consumer can spend. As noted in Chapter 04, consumer behavior (consumption) is directly impacted by where the overall economy is in the economic cycle. When the economy is growing, consumers spend more money and buy things. When the economy is not growing, consumers spend less money. Consumers save their money. Does your level of income affect what clothes you buy? The answer is probably yes.

Psychological factors relate to a consumer's motivation, perceptions, beliefs, and knowledge. These factors determine how a consumer prioritizes the decision on what to buy. Many people use **Maslow's Hierarchy of Needs** to visualize how consumers prioritize the buying decision[1]. At the top of Maslow's Hierarchy of Needs are psychological needs. Does how you feel, good or bad, affect your decision to buy clothes? The answer is probably yes.

As can be seen in Exhibit 12.5, in order to exist, consumers must first satisfy their most basic needs. These are called physiological needs. Food and water are examples of these needs. After a consumer satisfies his or her physiological needs, he or she proceeds to address his or her needs for safety. Beyond safety, consumers progress through social, esteem, and self-actualization needs. Self-actualization needs are the highest level of needs and the last to be fulfilled.

Individual factors relate to factors such as age, health, occupation, lifestyle, and personality. Not everyone wants to or can ride a motorcycle; some consumers do and some consumers do not. Not everyone wants a leather briefcase or business suit; some consumers do and some consumers do not. Not everyone wants to visit a disco; some consumers do and some do not. Such factors are individual. Do you think women and men buy the same items, or younger and older individuals buy the same items? The answer is probably no.

Business Behavior

Consumer behavior is complex; business behavior is also complex. Why? The answer is that business behavior is ultimately derived from consumer behavior. A business buys products for resale or use in producing another product. In doing so a business that sells to another business must recognize that the buyer is attempting to compete, has customers, and desires to create value. The seller is a supplier and an input into its customer's value chain.

Businesses are complex. A seller must appreciate this complexity when attempting to sell a product to a business. The seller must first consider the person or group of people who make the buying decision. Second, the seller must consider the people or groups who influence those making the buying decision. Last, the seller must consider the ultimate consumer of the buyer's product. The factors that affect a business's decision to buy include internal and external environments.

How a business makes a purchasing decision is affected by its **internal environment**. A business's internal environment includes the people, systems, and values used in making the purchase decision. An example of this is the formality of purchase decisions. Some businesses use a formal process where the business issues a **Request for Proposal (RFP)**. Potential suppliers must submit formal bids and hope that their bid is the most competitive. Other businesses have more informal processes, relying on less documentation.

A business's purchase decision is also impacted by its **external environment**. Factors that comprise a business's external environment include general economic conditions, government regulations, customer needs, and competitor actions.

Let's look at an example. You want to sell office supplies to a business. You do your research and determine you have a superior product at a lower price. You request a meeting with the purchasing agent of your prospective customer. You demonstrate your products with prices. First, the purchasing agent says she is pleased with your product and prices. Your products and prices are indeed superior to those of its current supplier, but you are not on the approved vendor list. You must fill out the needed forms and the business will do a background check. It wants to make sure you are a financially viable business that will be able to supply it with office supplies in the foreseeable future. After several weeks

EXHIBIT 12.5: *Maslow's Hierarchy of Needs with Examples*

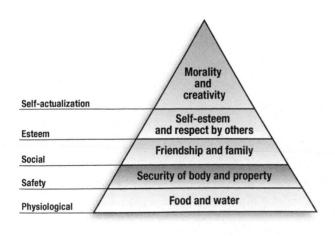

WHAT'S A NEED AND WHAT'S A WANT?

Have you ever met someone who had everything? Have you ever met someone who had no wants? The answer is probably not. Why do people have unmet wants? The answer is that people typically have limited income and wealth. So how do people decide how to spend their limited income and wealth? People usually categorize their desires as needs and wants.

Climb Maslow's Hierarchy of Needs. What do you see? You see a steady progression from needs, such as food, to wants, such as lavish vacations. Next time you buy something, ask yourself, "Is this a need or a want?" When you do, you are working with Maslow's Hierarchy of Needs.[1]

you are informed your business is now on the list of approved vendors. You are asked to submit your proposal in writing. You do so, only to learn that your prospective customer has been buying office supplies from your competitor supplier for over ten years. Your prospective customer has decided to inform its current supplier of your bid and ask if your competitor can match it. If it can, you will not get the business. When asked if this is fair, your prospective customer says it's legal and based on a long-standing, trusted, and successful relationship. Economic times are tough. Your competitor meets your bid and you lose the business. You ask your prospective customer what else you could have done. The buyer's internal and external environments have affected the outcome. Competing is tough.

COMPETITORS

To understand a market, a business must understand its customers and competitors. A **competitor** is a business that is attempting to sell a similar product to your current or prospective customer. A business must do research to determine who its competitors are, how these competitors operate, and how customers perceive the products of its competitors. This research is called **competitor analysis**. So how do competitors compete?

Competitors compete based on their products' marketing mix. Competitors compete by differentiating their products on marketing's four P's of product, place (distribution), price, and promotion. Like all businesses, competitors seek to use a winning strategy.

LEARNING OBJECTIVE 3

STRATEGIC MARKETING

Strategic marketing is a management function that entails planning, executing, and reviewing. Strategic marketing attempts to create business value by creating and sustaining a competitive advantage for the business. To achieve this advantage, businesses must first target the customer it wants to serve and then decide how it will provide value to that customer. A business attempts to create value for its customer with product features, distribution, price, and promotion.

Strategic marketing is about creating and implementing a strategy that creates value for the total business. To do so, the marketing of products must be managed as a portfolio. First, all the products a business sell comprise the business's portfolio of products. As such, a business must recognize that the marketing and sale of one product may affect the marketing and sale of other of its products. Second, the marketing function is one part of the business and must be coordinated with the other parts. These other functions include research and development, production, and finance. Marketing cannot sell a product a business cannot produce. A business cannot produce a product it cannot finance.

SEGMENTING THE MARKET AND TARGETING THE CUSTOMER

To effectively select a marketing strategy, a business must understand the market for its products. To do so, a business must segment the market (**market segmentation**). In competitive markets, being able to provide customers greater value is first about understanding the different needs of different customers in a market. However, it is also about understanding the capabilities of competitors.

Based on marketing research, businesses need to segment the market into subgroups or submarkets and analyze each. Such groupings may be based on characteristics like geography, age, gender, education, lifestyle, and/or ethnicity. Can you imagine selling snow tires in tropical climates, retirement housing to college students, or expensive automobiles to low-income families? It's important a business understand its customers. This starts with market segmentation.

After a business segments the market, the business must select or **target** that segment for which it believes it can create a competitive advantage. This is done by narrowing focus and analyzing customers and competitors.

Let's look at an example. Next time you look at television, think about the program you are watching. Then look at the advertising that comes with the program. What do you see? You see market segmentation and targeting. Programs that appeal to young viewers have advertising for stylish clothing, sports cars, and dating services. Programs that appeal to older viewers have advertising for medical procedures, life insurance, and retirement facilities.

DIFFERENTIATING: A PERSONAL THING

You want a job and you've identified the perfect position, but there is a lot of competition. There are a lot of qualified candidates for the job you want. What do you do? You analyze the customer, your prospective employer. You do your market research. You determine the employer's needs and value system. You try to promote yourself through your resume, emails, and personal interviews. You package yourself in the appropriate clothing. What are you doing? You are creating a competitive advantage by differentiating yourself from your competition.

CREATING A COMPETITIVE ADVANTAGE

To create a competitive advantage, a business must differentiate and position its product in the targeted market segment. The customer must perceive that a business's product provides the greatest value among the customer's alternatives. **Product differentiation** deals with creating a product that is different and possesses unique qualities that make it the most desirable among customer alternatives. **Product positioning** deals with getting the customer to perceive that the product is different and provides more value compared to competing products. Product positioning is about creating a perception that a product occupies a clear, distinct, and desirable place in the market. A business has several options in attempting to create a competitive advantage. These include:

> Product development
> Market development
> Market penetration

A strategy that focuses on product development attempts to develop and introduce a new product to an existing market. An example is when Procter & Gamble develops a new cosmetic for the changing US market. A strategy that focuses on market development attempts to get new customers to buy existing products. An example is when General Motors introduced Buick automobiles into China. A strategy that focuses on market penetration attempts to increase an existing product's share of existing markets. An example is a fast-food restaurant, such as McDonald's, lowering the price of its products (discounting) to attract customers from its competitors.

So how does a business decide what strategy to use at what time? It depends on the market. So let's look at how typical markets evolve. Let's use the Boston Consulting Group's analysis of product life cycles.[2]

PRODUCT LIFE CYCLES

Products evolve through a life cycle. Products are first introduced. If customers buy the product and are satisfied, the demand for the product grows. However, eventually the demand for the product does stop growing and ultimately declines. The demand for products evolves through stages of introduction, growth, maturity, and decline. In response to this demand, the supply of the product also evolves. Exhibit 12.6 depicts the life cycle of a successful product.

EXHIBIT 12.6: Product Life Cycle Analysis

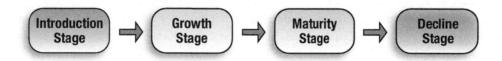

Introduction Stage

A business segments and targets a market. It believes that it has a competitive advantage. It believes it can use that competitive advantage to create value by introducing a new product in a new or existing

market or by introducing an existing product in a new market. It does so at great expense to create and promote the product. The business is assuming a lot of risk in hope of a big return. At first the demand for the product is low, but if the business is able to successfully differentiate and position the product, sales begin to increase. The business tries to promote the product with its unique and superior qualities including place or distribution. To introduce the product, however, businesses often offer the product at a reduced price. The net result is low sales and high expenses, resulting in losses. This life cycle stage is often described as the **opportunity stage**.

Growth Stage

If the business is successful in getting customers to accept its product, demand begins to grow. The business continues to promote the product but does not need to rely on a low price to create demand. Sales increase. With increased sales, a business is able to produce a growing net income. Risk is decreasing as customers embrace and buy the products. As sales and net income increase, competitors begin to enter the market. At first competitors try to differentiate their products. If unable to differentiate their products, competitors begin to lower prices. This stage is often described as the **star stage**.

Maturity Stage

If competitors are unable to attract customers by differentiation, competitors lower prices to attract sales. If the business cannot differentiate its product from competitor products, the business must also lower prices. Sales no longer grow. Competitors try to maintain market share. Net income begins to decrease with lower prices. Competition becomes fierce and some competitors begin to withdraw from the market. Risk increases. This stage is often described as the **cash cow stage**.

Decline Stage

Competitors struggle to attract sales. Sales continue to decrease as customers find better and more valuable alternative products. Prices continue to decrease. Eventually businesses begin to experience losses. Risk is once again very high. Competitors continue to withdraw from the market. Eventually there is insufficient demand to produce and sell the product. All competitors eventually withdraw from the market. This stage is often described as the **dog stage**.

Look around you. Think about the products you buy. Think about computers, cell phones, automobiles, newspapers, clothing styles, and restaurants. Think about department stores, discount stores, and Internet retailers. Think about traveling on trains, airplanes, and other modes of transportation. What do you see? You see products that come, grow, mature, and decline. You see products evolving through a life cycle.

LEARNING OBJECTIVE 4

THE LEGAL AND ETHICAL ISSUES OF MARKETING

Marketing is full of opportunities to defraud or act unethically. To gain a competitive advantage, businesses are often challenged to do the right thing. Competition creates both opportunities and challenges.

THE EIGHTY-TWENTY RULE

Businesses that introduce products into a market assume a lot of risk. Businesses that wait to enter a market until the market is growing assume lower risk. Remember risk and return? For that reason, businesses that introduce a product are called market leaders. Market leaders reap most of the profits but also suffer most of the losses.

There is an old adage in business that states, "Eighty percent of the profits go to the first twenty percent in the market, and twenty percent of the profits go to the last eighty percent in the market." The flip side of the eighty-twenty rule is ,"Eighty percent of the losses go to the first twenty percent in the market, and twenty percent of the losses go to the last eighty percent in the market." It's all about risk and return.

IMPACT OF COMPETITION

Is competition good? In a free market, competition is the heart of getting superior products at superior prices to market. There are winners and losers in competition. Ideally the customer and whole of society benefit from competition, but competition must be conducted fairly. In Chapter 04 the issue of monopolies and oligopolies was explored. It was noted that without guidance, competition can be destructive. Thus, there is a need for laws governing competition and marketing. Managers must comply with the laws governing the marketing of products. In addition, managers must act ethically.

MARKETING AND THE LAW

Look back on Chapter 07. Look at some of the laws and agencies that exist to protect the customer. Most times the seller knows more about the product than the customer. Remember the old adage, "Let the buyer beware." Laws are designed to:

1. Protect the customer from buying unsafe products

2. Inform the buyer what she or he is buying and not buying, including the rights and responsibilities of both the seller and buyer

3. Protect customers from sellers who unfairly manipulate the market by making false claims, withholding information, or engaging in discriminatory pricing practices.

   In a perfect world there would be perfect information and no uncertainty. However, we live in an imperfect world. The exchange created by marketing ideally creates seller and buyer value, although sometimes an exchange does not create value for both parties. Because sellers and buyers do have risk, the law tries to create an exchange that is fair and not based on misunderstandings and misrepresentations.

That task is the responsibility of government agencies such as the **Federal Trade Commission (FTC)**, **Consumer Protection Safety Commission (CPSC)**, and state and federal law enforcement agencies.

Markets constantly evolve. Marketing and the practice of business thus evolve. So too must the laws that create a safe and fair marketplace. Examples of this are the "Do Not Call Implementation Act of 2003" and the "Do Not Call Improvement Act of 2007." However, simply complying with the law does not relieve a business from the responsibility of acting ethically.

MARKETING AND ETHICS

The law defines the minimum level of acceptable behavior within a society. Law controls how people and businesses act. Law is how we require people and businesses to behave; ethical behavior is how we expect people and businesses to behave. Chapter 07 explores business ethics. Nowhere are business ethics more visible or challenged than in the world of marketing.

Marketing ethics deal with the behavior of producing, distributing, pricing, and promoting products in a fair and equitable manner. Businesses are often criticized for their marketing practices which may raise ethical questions. Examples of such criticism are:

- Businesses charge prices that overcompensate them for their costs and risks.

- Businesses often do not disclose enough information for the buyer to make an informed decision.

- Businesses often use pressure tactics in selling products.

- Businesses create products that appear safe and valuable when in fact the products are unsafe and/or of poor quality.

- Businesses discriminate on price and service when dealing with low-income and/or minority consumers.

- Businesses design and produce products to become obsolete and/or unusable, requiring consumers to purchase replacement products in the future.

Businesses have an ethical responsibility to all their stakeholders throughout society. In marketing, this ethical standard attempts to do the following:

- To provide value, fairly priced to all customers

- To provide sufficient information as to the origin and content of products, and what products can and cannot do

- To be socially responsible and recognize the legitimate needs of all current and future stakeholders in the business

Business ethics evolve and, ideally, improve over time. An example is sustainability. In the past, marketing ethics have centered on being fair and informative to current stakeholders, particularly current customers. However, the marketing world is embracing the concept of sustainable marketing. **Sustainable marketing** addresses the need for products to meet the current and future needs of customers.

Sustainable marketing attempts to meet the needs of current customers without infringing on society's ability to meet the needs of future customers. An example of sustainable marketing is creating and promoting products that do not hurt the environment or waste precious natural resources.

CREATING A SUSTAINABLE COMPETITIVE ADVANTAGE WITH MARKETING

The objective of the business is to create long-term value. To do so, businesses must create a sustainable competitive advantage. The sustainability of a business's competitive advantage starts with sales, over time.

Businesses must comply with the law; however, businesses do not always comply with the ethical standards of society. This is often seen in marketing. An example is "bait and switch" promotions. Such advertisements attract customers by offering great products at low prices. When the customer tries to buy the item, the business informs the customer it had a limited supply of the product. This is typically stated in the "fine print" of the advertisement. The business tries to sell the customer a similar product at a significantly higher price.

Marketing affects short-term sales as well as long-term sales. Often called **relationship marketing**, marketers recognize that buyers and sellers create relationships over time. Sometimes such relationships are positive and sometimes negative. Think about your buying decisions. Are there businesses you prefer and others you will not visit? The answer is probably yes. Now think about why you prefer certain businesses over other businesses. Some part of your preference is probably about trust. Now look back to the mission statement (also called its statement of purpose) of Target found at Target.com. Focus on the word "consistency." Target understands that it needs customers to have a great experience and return time and again. This is relationship marketing.

Creating business value starts with creating trusted relationships between the business and its customers. Ethical marketing is where such trusted relationships begin.

LEGAL VERSUS ETHICAL

You have a small and struggling automobile dealership. You need to sell an automobile soon or you will not be able to pay the rent. A prospective buyer comes to your business and looks at a used automobile. The automobile is running fine, but your mechanic informs you that the automobile will be inoperable in the next 10,000 miles unless expensive repairs are made. What do you do? The prospective buyer drives the automobile and does not detect the problem. The prospective buyer asks you if the automobile has any problems. What do you say? Do you decline to answer, telling him that the automobile has been and is running well? You could not warrant the automobile's future, only the automobile's past and present. Or do you tell the buyer the truth, that your mechanic believes the automobile will need significant repairs within the next 10,000 miles?

Being ethical is not easy. Ethics is often hard. But ask yourself, "How would you feel if you were the prospective buyer?"

CHAPTER SUMMARY

In this chapter we've introduced the nature and importance of marketing. We've explored the process of marketing products, competing in a market, and creating value for both the customer and business. After reading this chapter, you should be able to:

1. Appreciate the nature of marketing and the importance of the marketing in creating a sustainable competitive advantage (Learning Objective 1): Marketing is the process of understanding a market, positioning products to meet customer needs, distributing products, pricing products, and communicating product attributes to customers (promotion). The objective of marketing is to create a successful sale. For a sale to be successful, both parties, the business and customer, must perceive that the sale creates value.
2. Appreciate how markets behave (Learning Objective 2): Markets are composed of customers and competitors. Customers, whether consumers or businesses, go through a decision process when buying products. The process and ultimate decision to buy or not to buy is a function of many factors.
3. Appreciate marketing strategy (Learning Objective 3): Marketing strategy is about creating a successful sale. Different products in different markets at different times require different strategies. Successful products evolve over time through a life cycle.
4. Appreciate the legal and ethical dimensions of marketing (Learning Objective 4): Acting legally and ethically is critical to successful marketing that creates long-term value.

Marketing is critical to the success of any business. The value of a business is based on providing value to customers. Creating a competitive advantage is the heart of a business. But how does marketing create a competitive advantage? Product qualities are important, but many products with superior features fail. So what makes products successful in the market? How do all the elements of the marketing mix affect the success of a product? How do product, place (distribution), price, and promotion affect the success of marketing efforts? These are important questions in "How Business Works" and the subject of our next chapter, Chapter 13—The Marketing Mix: Product, Place, Promotion, and Price.

KEYWORDS

B2B market (business-to-business) 263

B2C market (business-to-consumer) 262

buying decision 262

C2C market (consumer-to-consumer) 263

cash cow stage 268

competition 268

competitor 265

competitor analysis 265

Consumer Protection Safety Commission (CPSC) 270

cultural factors 263

dog stage 268

economic factors 263

external environment 264

Federal Trade Commission (FTC) 270

individual factors 264

internal environment 264

market 258

market development 267

marketing 258

marketing concept 258

marketing mix 259

marketing process 258

marketing research 261

market penetration 267

Maslow's Hierarchy of Needs 263

opportunity stage 268

place 259

price 259

primary marketing data 261

product 259

product development 267

product differentiation 267

product positioning 267

promotion 259

psychological factors 263

relationship marketing 271

Request for Proposal (RFP) 264

sale 258

secondary marketing data 261

segment the market 266

social factors 263

star stage 268

strategic marketing 265

sustainable marketing 270

target segment of market 266

SHORT-ANSWER QUESTIONS

1. What is marketing and why is it important?
2. What processes do customers go through in making a decision to buy or not to buy a product?
3. What factors affect consumer behavior?
4. Define the following terms:
    a. Sale
    b. Marketing process
    c. Marketing concept
    d. Four P's of marketing
    e. Product
    f. Good
    g. Service
    h. Market research
    i. Marketing research
    j. Market research process
    k. Primary marketing data
    l. Secondary marketing data
    m. B2C market
    n. B2B market
    o. Maslow's Hierarchy of Needs
    p. Request for Proposal (RFP)
    q. Competitor
    r. Competitor analysis
    s. Product development
    t. Market development
    u. Market penetration
    v. Segmenting the market
    w. Targeting
    x. Product differentiation
    y. Product positioning
    z. Sustainable marketing
    aa. Relationship marketing
    ab. C2C market

CRITICAL-THINKING QUESTIONS

1. What does life cycle analysis tell us about how products evolve?
2. Can you think of examples of businesses acting ethically and unethically in marketing matters? List and describe these ethical and unethical practices.
3. What is marketing research and why is it important?

4. You are about to buy a book. You can buy it online from Amazon.com or a bookstore such as Barnes & Noble. Answer these questions:
   a. What are the four P's of each alternative?
   b. Why would you choose to buy a book at Amazon.com instead of Barnes & Noble, or Barnes & Noble instead of Amazon.com?

EXPLORING REAL BUSINESS

Go to the websites of Google, Target, Hyundai, and Procter & Gamble. The websites are

Google: http://investor.google.com

Target: http://www.target.com

Hyundai: http://worldwide.hyundai.com/company-overview

Procter & Gamble: http://www.pg.com

Look at the products each sells. Pick one or two products sold by each company. Answer the following questions for each product:

1. In what phase of the life cycle is the product?
2. Why is the product in that phase of its life cycle?
3. How would the answers to questions 1 and 2 above affect the way the product is marketed? Think about the 4 P's of each product.

ENDNOTES

1. Maslow, Abraham H., Maslow's Hierarchy of Needs, "A Theory of Human Motivation," Psychological Review 50 (1943):370–396. Print.
2. Per Boston Consulting Group, http://www.bcg.com/

THE MARKETING MIX: PRODUCT, PLACE, PROMOTION, AND PRICE

Introduction: Let's Talk About the Marketing Mix

How does a business determine what product to sell, how to distribute its product, and what price to charge for its product? How does a business promote and sell products? How does a business create value through the marketing function?

In this chapter we'll build on Chapter 12. We'll explore these questions and issues. We'll explore how a business's marketing mix is critical for "How Business Works."

WHY THE MARKETING MIX MATTERS

The objective of marketing is to create a successful sale. In a successful sale, both the business and customer perceive they are maximizing their value. To do so, a business must find that blend of product, place, price, and promotion that creates the highest value for both the business and its customer. So how does a business do that? The answer starts with a product that meets the needs and wants of the customer.

LEARNING OBJECTIVE 1

PRODUCTS

A product is a good or service. Businesses rarely sell one product; they typically sell multiple products. A business's portfolio of product lines is called its **product mix**. Procter & Gamble's product mix includes product lines for hair care, baby and child care, oral care, cosmetics, shaving, and pet nutrition. A **product line** is a group of similar products. P&G's product line of cosmetics includes CoverGirl products and Max Factor products. Look at Exhibit 13.1 to see P&G's complete product mix and product lines.

EXHIBIT 13.1: Procter & Gamble's Product Mix and Product Lines

So how does a business determine what products to sell? It starts with understanding the customer. Products must meet the needs and wants of customers. Products differ because customers differ. Because customers differ, businesses must position their product mix and product lines with different attributes.

POSITIONING PRODUCTS AND PRODUCT LINES BY TYPE OF CUSTOMER

Marketers initially position products and product lines by the type of customer, either consumer or business.

Consumer Products

For marketing purposes, a **consumer** is a person or household that buys a product for final consumption. **Consumer products** are products that are sold to consumers. Consumer products are typically categorized by how consumers perceive and purchase such products. A common way to classify consumer products is 1) convenience products, 2) shopping products, 3) specialty products, and 4) unsought products.

Convenience products are products that consumers buy frequently, instinctually, with minimum thought. Convenience products usually have a low price and are consumed in large quantities. Examples of convenience products are gasoline, detergent, and fast food. P&G's Cheer detergent is a convenience product.

Shopping products are products that consumers buy carefully and less frequently. Shopping products usually cost more and are consumed less frequently. Examples of shopping products are furniture, clothes, and airfare. Apple's iPhone is a shopping product.

Specialty products are products that consumers buy infrequently with a deliberate thought process. Specialty products are unique. Examples of specialty products are automobiles, jewelry, and computers. Hyundai's Kia is a specialty product.

The 2015 Kia Sportage.

Unsought products are products consumers do not initially or readily recognize they need or want. Consumers buy unsought products only after they are shown a need or want exists. Examples of unsought products are insurance, medical procedures, and legal services. Think about getting a notice from your college that to attend class you need to go to your doctor and receive the immunization. That is an unsought product.

Business Products

For marketing purposes, a **business** is an organization that buys a product for resale or use in producing another product. **Business products** are products sold to businesses. Business products are typically categorized by the product's purpose. A common way to classify business products is 1) materials and parts, 2) capital items, and 3) supplies and services.

Materials and parts are products businesses resell or use to create other products. Examples of materials and parts are clothing sold by a department store, steel used to manufacture automobiles, and wheat used to produce bread. Target's inventory is composed of materials and parts.

Capital items are products businesses buy that have a life longer than one year and are used in the acquiring, manufacturing, and selling of products and services. Examples of capital items are buildings, equipment, and intangible assets such as patents. P&G's buildings and equipment are capital items.

Supplies and services are products businesses buy to operate the business that are not classified as materials and parts or capital items. Supplies and services typically have short lives. Examples of supplies and services are office supplies, repair and maintenance items, and air travel. Google has a lot of such supplies.

Yet understanding products is more than understanding the type of customers. Products must deliver the desired attributes to create customer value.

CREATING CUSTOMER VALUE WITH PRODUCT ATTRIBUTES

Marketers position products and product lines to create customer value. To create customer value, marketers try to match product attributes with customer needs and wants. These attributes include features, quality, branding, packaging, labeling, warranties and guarantees, and support services.

Product features relate to the physical and mental attributes that provide customers satisfaction when they use the product. Why do some drivers buy convertible automobiles and other drivers buy automobiles with hard tops? The answer is satisfaction.

Product quality relates to a product's lack of defects. Does the product deliver the desired value by predictably satisfying the need or want of the customer? An example is the durability of clothing, comfort of furniture, and a patient's response to medical treatment. Think about buying a Duracell battery because it is dependable.

Branding relates to a business's attempt to differentiate its product from the product of competitors with a brand. A **brand** is a name, term, symbol, design, or combination thereof that identifies a product or business. A business owns a **trademark** when it registers its brand with the law. The law gives the business the exclusive right to use its trademark. Examples of branded names protected by trademarks are Google, CoverGirl, and Kia. An example of a branded symbol protected by a trademark is McDonald's golden arches or the Kia symbol you see on Kia cars. Branding ideally creates value by reducing customer uncertainty and risk associated with their buying decision. **Brand equity** is the term used to describe the ability of the brand to create value. Unbranded products are often called **generic products**. Think about buying CoverGirl cosmetics versus a generic brand.

BUSINESS SENSE

WHAT'S A GENERIC PRODUCT WORTH?

You go to the grocery store to buy packaged food or to a pharmacy to buy a cold remedy. What do you see? You see a lot of branded products. You also see a lot of generic products or products with store brands. You read the labels. The contents and packaging of the products are the same. The products are being distributed through the same store. Yet the prices of the generic products are below the branded products. Why? What are you buying in the branded product that you are not buying in the unbranded or generic product? The answer is simply the brand and brand equity. But why pay extra for the brand? Branding creates value by increasing the certainty about the product's attributes and lowering the risk to the consumer, for which customers pay more.

Packaging relates to designing and producing the container in which a product is sold or delivered. Packaging promotes and protects the product. However, packaging can also create value by creating benefits such as convenience and storage. A good example is food packaging. Does the packaging of a food item affect your decision to buy that food item? The answer is yes for most people. Think about the packaging of Pringles snacks.

Labeling entails a business attaching printed words or graphics to its products to educate the customer. Labels identify, describe, and/or inform the customer about the content, benefits, dangers, and proper use of the product. Labels often attempt to reduce the risk to the buyer and seller. Go to a grocery store, pick a product, and read the label. What do you think? At the very least you now know a lot more about what you are buying. However, the seller is also reducing the risk of the customer improperly using the product. Walk into Target, go to the pharmacy, pick up a container of P&G's Vicks, and read the label.

Warranties can be expressed or implied (see Chapter 07). A **warranty** is a seller's promise regarding the property's quantity and quality. Think about the importance of warranties the next time you purchase an automobile, television, or cell phone. Similar, but not identical, are guarantees. A **guarantee** is a promise, by the business to the customer, that the customer will be satisfied with the product. If the

Have you ever looked at a product and noticed the bar code on the label? Have you ever gone to a retailer that scans these bar codes to determine the price you must pay? These bar codes are called Uniform Product Codes or UPCs. Introduced in 1974, these bar codes contain the information needed to identify brand names, package sizes, and price. Today, most mass-produced products have such bar codes. UPCs have become an important part of identifying, distributing, pricing, and promoting products. UPCs help businesses better manage their sales and the inventory they sell.

customer is not satisfied with the product, then the customer has certain rights. Think about buying a television at Target. What happens if the television does not fit the space in your home? You return the television for a refund. You use your customer satisfaction guarantee. Warranties and guarantees reduce the risk of purchasing the product. Thus, customer value is increased.

Support services relate to the at-sale or post-sale services that a seller promises the buyer. Examples of support services are training and repair. Next time you buy a cell phone or computer, look at all the support services the seller offers. Such services reduce the buyer's risk and thus create customer value. Google understands this when it produces and sells its Android phone. Hyundai understands this when it produces and sells its automobiles.

Product is only one part of the marketing mix. Yet it is the most visible part. Creating customer value by segmenting the market, targeting the correct customer, and meeting the needs and wants of those customers is at the heart of the business's ability to create value for itself and its customer. But having a great product that adds value is only part of the marketing mix. It's time to look at the other parts of the marketing mix. Next it's time to explore how a business distributes a product.

LEARNING OBJECTIVE 2
· ·
DISTRIBUTION (PLACE)

Place is the location and means of distributing the product. Examples of place are buying a product in a discount store, buying a product over the Internet, and buying a product from a vending machine. The discount store, the Internet, and the vending machine are the means of distributing the product or place. To have a sale, a business must be able to get its product to the customer at the right time and in the right place. **Distribution** is how and when a business delivers its product to its customer. Distribution is often a critical factor in creating customer value and a sale. Think about buying a soda from a vending machine. What were you buying? A lot of what you purchased was the use of the vending machine or the means of distribution.

Yet distribution is more than the physical means used to deliver a product. Distribution is about distribution channels, often referred to as marketing channels.

MARKETING CHANNELS

A **marketing channel**, or **distribution channel**, is composed of the organizations that help the business make its product available for ultimate consumption. Organizations that help the business promote, finance, and distribute its product are part of the business's marketing channel. Members of the marketing channel are called **marketing intermediaries**.

Marketing channels are classified as either direct or indirect. A **direct marketing channel** is where the business does not use a marketing intermediary. An **indirect marketing channel** is where the business uses one or more marketing intermediaries.

Let's look at an example of a direct marketing channel that does not use marketing intermediaries. You are Google. You provide computer services to consumers. You have a varied product mix, but your primary product is a computer search engine that is free to users. So how does Google create a sale for itself? Google sells advertising directly to other businesses. Google's sales force sells Google's services directly to advertisers. In doing so, Google does not use a marketing intermediary. Google's marketing channel is a direct marketing channel.

Let's look at an example of an indirect marketing channel that uses marketing intermediaries. You are Procter & Gamble. You make great consumer products. But do you sell these products directly to consumers? The answer is no. You sell your products to a wholesaler in large quantities. A **wholesaler** is defined as an organization that buys products for resale to retailers. A **retailer** is defined as an organization that sells products to the ultimate consumer of the product. The wholesaler and retailer are marketing intermediaries and a significant part of P&G's marketing channel.

Retailers and Wholesalers

Retailers are businesses that sell products to the final consumer. Some retailers target markets based on product lines and brand. A Hyundai dealership is an example of this strategy. Hyundai dealerships buy automobiles from Hyundai for resale to consumers. Some retailers target markets based on price. A retailer such as Tiffany & Co is an example of this strategy. Tiffany & Co sells very expensive jewelry. Some retailers target markets based on product assortment and variety. A store such as Target is an example of this strategy. Some retailers target markets based on convenience. A retailer that sells sodas through a vending machine is an example of this strategy.

Retailers are often categorized as specialty stores, department stores, supermarkets, department stores, convenience stores, discount stores, deep discount stores, and non-store retailers. A **specialty store** carries a limited product line. Examples of a specialty store are Gap, Dick's Sporting Goods, and Brooks Brothers. A **department store** carries several product lines. Examples are Sears, Macy's, and J C Penney. **Supermarkets** carry numerous lines of food and household products. Examples are Publix, Safeway, and Giant. **Convenience stores** are relatively small retailers, located in easily acces-

sible places, which sell a limited number of products used in everyday life. Examples are 7-Eleven, Sheetz, and Circle K. **Discount stores** sell numerous product lines of household products to price-conscious customers. Examples are Target, Walmart, and Kmart. **Deep discount stores** sell product lines at very low prices. Costco, Sam's Club, and BJ's are examples of deep discount retailers. **Non-store retailers** are retailers that have limited or no physical presence. Non-store retailers use distribution channels such as vending machines, kiosks, home shopping networks, and the Internet. When someone buys an application for a cell phone over the Internet, he or she is using a non-store retailer.

A Hyundai dealership in Sapporo City, Japan.

Wholesalers are businesses that sell products to businesses for resale or business use. Wholesalers typically buy from producers and sell to retailers. The two most common types of wholesalers are 1) merchant wholesalers and 2) brokers and agents. **Merchant wholesalers** buy and resell products. Think about the produce you buy at a local grocery store. Where did the grocery buy the produce? The answer is not from the farmer but from a merchant whole-saler. Merchant wholesalers take ownership of the products and create value by providing warehousing, inventory, and transportation services. Brokers and agents facilitate the buying and selling of products without taking ownership. Brokers and agents are compensated with fees or commissions. A **broker** brings the buyer and seller together, helping both the buyer and seller in negotiating the deal. Think about a real estate broker, helping the buyer and seller complete the transaction. An **agent** represents either a buyer or seller. Think about an agent for a professional baseball player. The agent negotiates the contract on behalf of the baseball player.

CHOOSING THE CORRECT MARKETING CHANNEL: CREATING VALUE

So why would a business use indirect marketing channels and marketing intermediaries? The answer is they create value. Marketing intermediaries create value by providing efficiency, convenience, and cost savings. A marketing intermediary is a part of a business's value chain. Such businesses facilitate the producer in supplying products to the consumer. As such the choice to use marketing intermediaries is about creating value for the business and customer.

Let's go back to our example of P&G. Can you imagine P&G using its own stores to exclusively sell its branded products? Why does P&G use supermarkets in its marketing channel? The answer is customers want choices, efficiency, and convenience. Supermarkets, pharmacies, department stores, and other intermediaries provide a distribution process that efficiently, conveniently, and inexpensively provides a choice to customers. These marketing intermediaries add value to the customer and to P&G.

Let's look at another example, Google. Why doesn't Google use marketing intermediaries for its search engine product? The answer is that such intermediaries do not add convenience, efficiency, or cost savings. Such marketing intermediaries would not add value.

So when a customer buys a product, the customer is also buying distribution and a marketing channel. The value the customer receives is more than the attributes of the product. The price the customer pays compensates the business for more than acquiring or producing a product.

LEARNING OBJECTIVE 3

PRICE

Price is the amount the customer pays the business for the sale. Price is the value exchanged by the customer to receive the value of the product. Price is also the value received by the business for delivering or exchanging the value of the product.

But how does a business determine the price it will charge for the product? The business wants to charge the highest price possible. In doing so, the business will maximize its operating profit and value. The customer wants the business to charge the lowest price possible. The customer wants to receive the

Zukkie's Bike Shop in Brooklyn, New York City, New York.

product's benefits at the lowest cost. In doing so, the customer will maximize its value. So where do the wants and needs of the business and customer meet?

The answer in a free market is demand and supply. Remember demand and supply in Chapter 04? It's time to use these insights.

THE WANTS AND NEEDS OF THE BUSINESS

A business wants to create a sale by supplying a product to the market. Why? The answer is the business seeks an operating profit from a sale. That operating profit compensates the providers of the money (debt and owner's equity) for the use of their money. So how does a business determine whether or not a sale provides the needed operating profit? It must first look at the cost the business incurs from the acquisition or production of the product, the delivery of the product, the sale or promotion of the product, and operating the business. Remember operating profit is sales less operating costs such as cost of goods sold, salaries, rent, advertising, and utilities.

So what does it cost to produce or acquire a product, deliver the product, promote the product, and operate the business? In Chapter 08 the challenge of managerial accounting was introduced. A part of that challenge is determining the cost of products. Basically costs can be divided into two types, variable costs and fixed costs. **Variable costs** vary directly with the amount sold. **Fixed costs** are costs that do not vary with the amount sold.

Let's look at the bicycle store example from Chapter 08. You sell 120 bicycles at an average price of $200. You paid $100 for each bicycle sold and incurred $8,000 in other operating costs for employees, rent, advertising, and utilities. Your income statement looks like:

EXHIBIT 13.2: Income Statement (120 bicycles sold at $200)

Sales	$24,000	(120 bicycles at $200 each)
Cost of Goods Sold	12,000	(120 bicycles at $100 each)
Gross Profit	$12,000	
Other Operating Costs	8,000	
Operating Profit	$4,000	

Your variable costs were $100 per bicycle. Your fixed costs were $8,000.

Now what did the sale of each bicycle contribute to the business? The business received $200 for each bicycle sold. Each bicycle cost the business $100. So the sale of each bicycle contributed $100 to the business ($200 – $100). Each bicycle sold contributed $100 to pay for the fixed expenses. After the fixed expenses are paid, then the $100 from each sale goes to operating profit. The remainder represents the contribution margin each sale provides. The **contribution margin** is defined as the amount the business earns from each sale after paying its variable costs.

EQUATION 13.1: Contribution Margin

$$CM = P - VC$$

Where

CM	Contribution margin per unit of sales
P	Price per unit of sales
VC	Variable cost per unit of sales

So how can we use this insight? We can first compute the product's break-even sales.

BREAK-EVEN ANALYSIS

Ask yourself how many sales does it take to pay the fixed expenses? When a business asks this question, it is looking at the break-even point or break-even sales. The break-even point is the number of sales a business must achieve to generate a zero operating profit. The **break-even point** is calculated as:

EQUATION 13.2: Break-Even Point

$$BE = FC/CM$$

Where

BE	Break-even point
FC	Fixed costs
CM	Contribution margin

In the bicycle store, the break-even point would be computed as:

$$BE = \$8,000/\$100 = 80 \text{ bicycles}$$

If the business sold 80 bicycles, the income statement would look like:

EXHIBIT 13.3: Income Statement (80 bicycles sold at $200)

Sales	$16,000 (80 bicycles at $200 each)
Cost of Goods Sold	8,000 (80 bicycles at $100 each)
Gross Profit	$8,000
Other Operating Costs	8,000
Operating Profit	$0

Note that each sale contributes $100, the contribution margin, to paying the fixed costs. If the business's sales are below its break-even point, then the business has an operating loss equal to the contribution margin times the number of sales below its break-even sales level. Let's look at our example. Let's assume our bicycle store only sells 60 bicycles. The income statement would look like:

EXHIBIT 13.4: Income Statement (60 bicycles sold at $200)

Sales	$12,000 (60 bicycles at $200 each)
Cost of Goods Sold	6,000 (60 bicycles at $100 each)
Gross Profit	$6,000
Other Operating Costs	8,000
Operating Loss	($2,000)

We lost $2,000 because we failed to sell the required number of bicycles. We failed to sell 20 bicycles (60 versus 80 bicycles). Each of the 20 sales that did not materialize lost the business $100 (contribution margin), for a total of $2,000 (20 bicycles * $100 per bicycle contribution margin).

Also note that each sale above the break-even point creates an operating profit equal to the contribution margin times the number of sales above its break-even sales level. Let's assume the bicycle store sells 120 bicycles. Look back at Exhibit 13.2. The business had an operating profit of $4,000. The business sold 40 more bicycles than it needed to break even (120 bicycles versus 80 bicycles). Each of those 40 sales contributed $100 to the operating profit. Combined, the sale of the 40 extra bicycles created a $4,000 operating profit (40 bicycles * $100 per bicycle contribution margin).

So how does break-even analysis help price products?

PRICING PRODUCTS WITH BREAK-EVEN ANALYSIS

Let's look at our bicycle example. The business needs $1,000 to pay the interest expense, $1,000 to pay taxes, and $2,000 to provide owners an adequate profit. The business needs an operating profit of $4,000. If the business believes it can sell 120 bicycles at $200 per bicycle, will it achieve this $4,000 operating profit? The answer is yes. Look at Exhibit 13.2. The sale of the first 80 bicycles paid for the fixed cost of operating the business. The sale of the last 40 bicycles produced an operating profit of $4,000, or $100 contribution per 40 bicycles sold.

But what happens if the business sells each bicycle for more or less than $200? If the price is lower, then the number of bicycles sold could be higher. If the price is higher, then the number of bicycles sold could be lower.

Let's extend our example. The business conducts market research and finds it would only sell 100 bicycles if the price of each bicycle is $225. It would sell fewer bicycles but the contribution margin would increase to $125 ($225 less $100 variable costs). The break-even point would be 64 bicycles ($8,000/$125 = 64 bicycles). The operating profit would be $4,500 (36 bicycles above the break-even point * $125 per bicycle). The income statement would look like:

EXHIBIT 13.5: Income Statement (100 bicycles sold at $225)

Sales	$22,500 (100 bicycles at $225 each)
Cost of Goods Sold	10,000 (100 bicycles at $100 each)
Gross Profit	$12,500
Other Operating Costs	8,000
Operating Profit	$4,500

The business also found from its marketing research that it would sell 150 bicycles if the price of each bicycle were $180. It would sell more bicycles but the contribution margin would decrease to $80 ($180 less $100 variable costs). The break-even point would be 100 bicycles ($8,000/$80 = 100 bicycles). The operating profit would be $4,000 (50 bicycles above the break-even point * $80 per bicycle). The income statement would look like:

EXHIBIT 13.6: Income Statement (150 bicycles sold at $180)

Sales	$27,000 (150 bicycles at $180 each)
Cost of Goods Sold	15,000 (150 bicycles at $100 each)
Gross Profit	$12,000
Other Operating Costs	8,000
Operating Profit	$4,000

A bicycle shop interior.

So what price should the business choose? Ideally the business would choose to sell 100 bicycles at $225 per bicycle. This maximizes the operating profit. If risk and time do not change, selling 100 bicycles at $225 each maximizes the operating profit and value of the business. The analysis of different pricing alternatives on the business's profitability is often called **cost-volume-profit analysis**.

So a business wants to be able to pay its costs and provide, and ideally maximize, operating profit and thus value. But how do businesses do this?

COST-PLUS PRICING

When a business prices its products based on costs and desired profit, the business is using cost-plus pricing. **Cost-plus pricing** is designed to provide the business sufficient sales revenue to 1) pay its costs and 2) create a sufficient operating profit. But the challenge of cost-plus pricing is determining and allocating the cost of acquiring or producing a product, delivering the product, selling the product, and operating the business.

Let's look at variable and fixed costs. Variable costs are easy to allocate to products. Sometimes fixed costs are not as easy to allocate to products. The reason is businesses often have multiple products that share the fixed costs. When fixed costs are not easy to allocate to a product, managers often price the product on the margin. When a business focuses only on variable costs, often called **marginal costs**, it is said to be **pricing-on-the-margin**. The price per sale, often called the **marginal revenue**, less the marginal or variable costs, produces the contribution margin. Businesses that price products on the margin require a higher contribution margin to cover the unallocated fixed costs.

Ideally businesses can allocate fixed costs to products. When the business can allocate fixed costs to products, the business is able to price on the **total costs** (variable costs plus fixed costs) of the product. When the business divides the total costs by the number of sales, it computes the average cost of a sale. The business can then use the average cost to price its products. The **average cost** of a sale is computed as:

EQUATION 13.3: Average Costs per Sale

$$AC = TC/Sales$$

Where

AC	Average cost per sale
TC	Total cost (variable costs plus fixed costs)
Sales	Number of sales

A business that can allocate fixed costs to a product can price on average cost.

Let's look at our original example as depicted in Exhibit 13.2. First is pricing-on-the-margin. The marginal revenue per sale was $200 per bicycle, the marginal or variable cost of each sale was $100, and the contribution margin (marginal revenue less marginal cost) was $100 ($200 − $100). This contribution margin must pay for the unallocated fixed costs plus provide an adequate operating profit.

Now let's assume we can allocate the fixed costs. The total cost for sales of 120 bicycles was $20,000 ($12,000 variable costs plus $8,000 fixed costs). What was the average cost per sale at the sales level of 120 bicycles? It was $166.67 ($20,000 total costs/120 bicycles). Assuming the bicycle store will sell 120 bicycles, the store must price each bicycle at $166.67 to obtain a zero operating profit, or break even. Everything over $166.67 will create an operating profit.

Ideally a business prices it products using total costs plus a desired operating profit. However, unless a business is using special promotional pricing, it does not want to charge a price below the product's marginal or variable cost. Is this easy? The answer is not always. Why? The market and customer ultimately determine the price. The only decision the business has is whether to sell the product at the market price or not.

THE WANTS AND NEEDS OF THE CUSTOMER

What the business wants or needs must be tempered by market realities. Ultimately it is the customer and the market that jointly determine the price of a product. The customer, or buyer, demands the product and the business supplies the product. In a free market, a sale occurs when the price reflects that demand equals supply.

Price, however, enters into a buyer's decision differently, depending on the demand for the product.

PRICE AND PRODUCT DEMAND

Sometimes price affects a customer's decision to buy or not to buy a product. Sometimes price does not affect a customer's decision to buy or not to buy a product. When price does matter, higher prices mean customers will buy less of the product and lower prices mean customers will buy more of the product. It is said that the product is **price elastic**. Price elasticity refers to the impact of price on the buyer's decision to buy or not to buy the product. When prices do not matter, customers will buy the product regardless of price. It is said that the product is **price inelastic**.

So what products are price elastic and what products are price inelastic? Go back to Chapter 12. Look at Exhibit 12.4: Maslow's Hierarchy of Needs. Think about what products are needs and what products are wants. How many times have you complained about the price of gasoline or prescription drugs, yet paid the price charged? If you are like most people, the answer is a lot. Your demand for such products is price inelastic. Yet have you ever gone into a store, found a piece of clothing you want, but decided the price was too high? You did not buy the clothes because price mattered. Your demand for such products is price elastic.

Yet within Maslow's Hierarchy of Needs[1], the needs and wants for products shift. Demand, supply, and thus prices, do change over time. Three forces act to shift the demand and supply of products. The first of these forces is cyclicality. The second of these forces is seasonality. The third force is the evolution of customer tastes, needs, and options.

Cyclicality deals with the overall state of an economy. Remember Chapter 04? Economies go through cycles. When the economy is strong and growing, customers feel good and buy products more easily. Price is important, but not as important as when the economy is not strong and not growing.

In bad economic times customers save and buy less. Price becomes very important in their decision to buy or not to buy.

A product is said to be a **cyclical product** when the state of the economy affects the demand for the product. Examples of cyclical products are automobiles, housing, and designer clothes. A product is said to be a **non-cyclical product** if the state of the economy does not affect the demand for the product. Examples of non-cyclical products are food and prescription drugs.

If a product is cyclical, the state of the economy may directly or inversely affect the demand for a product. Most people appreciate that a strong economy typically creates a strong demand for most cyclical products and a weak economy typically creates a weak demand for most cyclical products. But have you ever thought about good times hurting the demand for products and bad times helping the demand for products? Such products are called **counter-cyclical products**. Let's look at an example. Regardless of the state of an economy, people must eat food. The question is what food do they eat? In good times, people like to buy expensive food like lobster. In bad times a lot of people cannot afford lobster. Lobster is a cyclical product that is directly affected by the economy. So what do people eat in bad times? In bad times, people buy inexpensive food like hamburger and chicken. Think about it. Hamburger and chicken are counter-cyclical products. In bad times people eat more hamburger and chicken than in good times.

The second force is seasonality. **Seasonality** deals with the time of year a product is produced and sold. **Seasonal products** are products that are affected by the seasons of the year. Examples are bathing suits, snow mobiles, and lawn mowers. Walk into Target and see how its inventory changes over a year. **Non-seasonal products** are products that are not affected by seasonality. Examples are medical services, computers, and cell phones.

Seasonality affects price because it affects demand. Have you ever noticed how expensive summer clothes are in April but how inexpensive those same clothes are in September? Have you ever noticed how expensive back-to-school supplies are in August but how inexpensive those same supplies are in May? It's all about seasonality.

The third force is the natural evolution of customer needs and wants. Lifestyles change. New and better products are introduced. Demand, supply, and thus the price of products evolve. Let's look at two examples. First is transportation. In the early 1900s, owning an automobile was a luxury only the wealthy could afford. Most people used horses to travel from one place to another. Today, automobiles are often a necessity, not a luxury item. Horses are no longer a necessity, but a luxury item. Let's look at a second example. In the early 1900s, telephones were a luxury item that only the wealthy could afford. Most people used physical letters and the mail to communicate. Today, telephones are often considered a necessity, not a luxury item. The use of physical letters and the mail service is decreasing. Cell phones, email, and related technology are quickly making traditional mail service obsolete.

So prices reflect demand. But how does a customer react to price? How does a customer use price in deciding whether to buy or not to buy a product?

PRICE AND THE DECISION TO BUY

Customers seek the greatest value at the lowest cost. Customers look at price in two ways. First, customers compare price with their perceived absolute value of the product. Second, customers compare price with the perceived relative value of the product.

First is the **perceived *absolute* value of the product**. Customers create a perception of a product's value based on perceived benefits from owning the product. Customers then compare this perceived value with the product's price. If customers believe the price is greater than the value they will receive from the product, they do not buy the product. If customers believe the price is lower than the value they will receive from the product, they will consider buying the product.

Second is the **perceived *relative* value of the product**. Given customers perceive a product has absolute value, customers then compare the benefits and costs of that product with the benefits and costs of alternative or competing products. Customers then choose that alternative which provides them the best value. As competition and substitutes enter into a customer's decision on what product to buy, value becomes relative.

So businesses and customers both want to create value. But how do the wants and needs of the business and its customers come together?

The Realities of Managing Price

If a business prices a product too high, customers will typically not buy it. To buy a product, customers must first perceive the product's absolute and relative values are greater than the product's price. If the customer does not buy the business's product, the business will fail due to the lack of sales.

On the other hand a business has problems when it prices its product too low. Customers may buy the product, but the business could lose money or fail to make a sufficient operating profit. Charging too low a price could also cause the business to fail.

So pricing products is a challenge. It is a challenge for two reasons. First, as noted earlier, a business must determine its costs and required operating profit. Second, a business must determine the demand for the product and the impact of price on the customer's decision to buy. Both are difficult. Both require marketing managers to understand their business, understand the market, and create a pricing strategy that creates value for both the business and customer. Marketing managers must constantly plan, execute, and review pricing strategy.

Marketing managers must determine what price to charge, when to charge the price, and how to charge the price. There are long-term and short-term pricing issues. Sometimes a business will want to set a price that may not create a sufficient contribution margin or operating profit in the short-term. Such a situation may arise due to difficult economic times, new competition, or the introduction of a new product. Businesses may use discounts, rebates, and coupons to temporarily adjust prices. Likewise businesses may temporarily price products as a bundle to create the perception of greater value. Examples of bundling are a department store that offers a collection of individual cosmetic products. The price of the collection is lower than the price of the individual products combined. Another example is when an automobile dealership offers a bundle or package of maintenance services at a discounted price.

No matter what the price scheme a marketing manager chooses, it must be integrated into the product mix. Pricing is simply charging the customer for the product and product distribution. But for a price to be accepted by the market, the customers must perceive that the price creates value for them. Creating this perception is the job of promotion.

LEARNING OBJECTIVE 4

PROMOTION

So what is promotion and what is the role of promotion in creating a sale? Promotion is the process of communicating to customers the absolute and relative values of the product. The ultimate goal of promotion is to create a successful sale. Remember a successful sale creates perceived value for both the customer and business. As such, promotion informs, persuades, and reminds customers of the value that a product creates in the customer's life.

MARKETING COMMUNICATION

Promotion is first and foremost a communication process. As all communications processes, promotion involves a sender of information, a message, a communication medium, noise, a receiver, and a feedback process. The sender creates a message and sends or encodes the message through a medium. As the message goes through the medium, the message is affected by noise. Noise is anything that interferes with the receiver clearly understanding the message. Ultimately the message is received by the receiver who decodes or interprets the message. The receiver then provides the sender feedback with actions or lack of actions. Look at Exhibit 13.7: **The Communication Process.**

EXHIBIT 13.7: The Communication Process

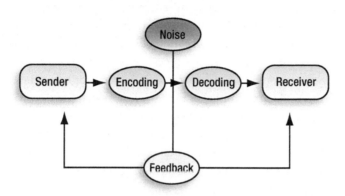

Let's look at the example of P&G selling its Gillette razors. P&G wants to inform, convince, and constantly remind potential buyers of razors that P&G's razors create absolute and relative value. The message is P&G's razors are more than a great buy; the razors are the best buy for a buyer of razors. P&G chooses a medium to send this message such as television advertising. However, as the advertising is being aired on the television, P&G must recognize potential customers may encounter noise. An example of noise is a potential customer not listening to the advertising due to distractions. Another example of noise is potential customers having preconceived ideas about P&G or its Gillette razors. After the customer receives the message, the customer interprets the message. How a customer interprets a message is affected by such forces as culture, income, and lifestyle. Next, no matter what message the potential customer receives and interprets, actions result. Either the customer buys the Gillette razor proving the promotion was successful, or the customer does not buy the Gillette razor proving the promotion was unsuccessful. The sale, or lack of, is both the action and feedback. If the promotion was successful, a sale occurs. If the promotion failed, a sale does not occur.

EXHIBIT 13.8: The Promotion Process

THE PROMOTION PROCESS

Marketers attempt to create a sale by using the following **promotion process**:

```
┌──────────────────────┐
│    Target Market     │
└──────────────────────┘
          ↓
┌──────────────────────┐
│ Determine Objectives │
└──────────────────────┘
          ↓
┌──────────────────────┐
│    Design Message    │
└──────────────────────┘
          ↓
┌──────────────────────┐
│    Choose Medium     │
└──────────────────────┘
          ↓
┌──────────────────────┐
│       Execute        │
└──────────────────────┘
          ↓
┌──────────────────────┐
│   Collect Feedback   │
│  and Make Adjustments│
└──────────────────────┘
```

1. Target a market segment and customer

2. Determine the communication objective

3. Design the message to be communicated

4. Choose a medium to communicate the message

5. Execute by delivering the designed message through the selected medium

6. Collect feedback, review the feedback, and make adjustments as needed

First, a business must clearly segment the market and target the desired customer. The business must understand the customer and the competition.

Second, the business must determine the objective of the communication. Marketers understand that buyers go through a process in deciding to buy or not to buy a product. Look back in Chapter 12. Remember the buying process? Buyers often go through this process in steps or stages. Customers first become aware of a product. Customers then progress from awareness to understanding the product, to preferring the product, to wanting or needing the product, and to purchasing the product. In determining the objective of the communication, marketers must focus on one or more of these steps.

Third, the message must be designed. Often referred to as the **AIDA model**, the message should focus on customer *attention*, *interest*, *desire*, and *act*. The message should first get the attention of the customer, then hold the customer's interest, then create a desire in the customer to buy the product, and last motivate the customer to act or buy the product.

Fourth, the business must select the medium or media to be used in communicating the message. This decision is about choosing the best promotional mix to effectively deliver the message. The promotion mix includes advertising, sales promotion, personal selling, direct-marketing tools, and public relations.

Fifth and sixth are the steps of execution and feedback. Steps one through four are about planning. Step five, execution, is about putting the marketing plans into action. Step six is about comparing plans to actual results, or reviewing. Marketers must understand the past to make future marketing more effective. Step six is about learning from marketing's successes and failures.

BUSINESS SENSE

INFOMERCIALS

Have you ever turned on your television, found a really interesting and entertaining program, and realized that the program's focus was not just informing and entertaining but also selling you a product? Examples of such products are vacations, health care products, and financial services. That's the world of infomercials. Infomercials are typically 30-minute programs that provide knowledge, entertain, and target a customer for a sale.

THE PROMOTIONAL MIX

The **promotional or marketing communications mix** is the mix of advertising, sales promotion, personal selling, direct-marketing techniques, and public relations used by a business to communicate a marketing message.

Advertising is defined as any non-personal presentation of ideas about a product or product line. Advertising is delivered through media such as newspapers, magazines, radio, television, outdoor signage, and the Internet. Look around you. Advertising is everywhere, sometimes using some of the most unexpected media. Next time you go to a sporting event and buy a drink, look at the container. It could have advertising on it. Next time you go to a grocery store look down at the shopping cart. It could have advertising on it. Next time you ride public transportation, look at the bus or train car. It could have advertising on it.

Sales promotions are techniques used to encourage the customer to buy the product in the short-term. Businesses use sales promotions to create an immediate sale. Examples of sales promotions are coupons, refunds and rebates, free samples, product demonstrations, in-store displays, and event sponsorships. Open up a typical newspaper on Sunday and look at all the coupons and special offers. Walk into a department store and see the displays, often referred to as point-of-purchase displays. Walk into a grocery store and see the free samples. These are sales promotions.

Personal selling is defined as the personal interaction, intended to create a sale, between a business's sales force and potential customers. Personal selling often involves a process of prospecting and qualifying potential customers, researching and understanding how to approach targeted customers, approaching targeted customers and beginning the seller–buyer relationship, presenting and demonstrating the product, dealing with customer concerns, completing or closing the sale, and finally following up the sale to ensure the customer perceives the sale created value and the seller–buyer relationship is positive. Exhibit 13.9 depicts the **personal selling process.**

An example of personal selling is a real estate agent. First the real estate agent must segment the market, prospect the market, and then target the customer. Second the real estate agent must research what the customer wants, needs, and values. Third, the real estate agent must meet and get acceptance by the potential customer. Fourth the real estate agent must show the potential customer properties that meet the customer's wants, needs, and values. Fifth the real estate agent must assist the customer in buying the real estate. Last, the real estate agent must follow up the sale by making sure the customer is happy. Ideally the real estate agent follows up on the sale to make sure the customer will 1) use the real estate agent in the future and 2) refer other customers to the real estate agent.

Direct marketing refers to techniques used to get customers to purchase products from their home, office, or other non-retail settings. Direct marketing techniques include direct mail, catalogues, mail order, telemarketing, and online promotions through the Internet. Next time you pick up the telephone and hear a telemarketer, that's direct marketing. Next time you collect your mail and see a catalogue, that's direct marketing.

Public Relations refers to the process of communicating to the public that the business creates value for the public as a whole. Businesses use public relations to create a positive image. Public relations attempt to create publicity. **Publicity** is information that creates an image of a business and its products; ideally publicity is positive. Examples of public relations are when a newspaper publishes an

Personal Selling

Prospecting and qualifying potential customers

↓

Researching and understanding how to approach targeted customers

↓

Approaching targeted customers

↓

Presenting and demonstrating the product

↓

Dealing with customer concerns

↓

Completing or closing the sale

↓

Following up the sale to ensure customer satisfaction

A historic telephone advertisement.

Coca-Cola promotions staff preparing a booth at a computer applications show in Taipei.

article about a business contributing money to a charity, a local sport team wears uniforms with the business's name or logo, or a business is awarded a commendation for doing a socially responsible act.

CHOOSING THE BEST PROMOTIONAL MIX

Choosing the most effective mix of promotional techniques is not easy. Marketers must carefully conduct research into customer needs and responses. Competitor actions must also be considered. Then there is always the issue of cost versus benefits.

Likewise how to use the promotional mix is also a challenge. Who will be the lead in promoting a product is important. There are two common strategies regarding who will lead promotional efforts. There is a pull strategy and a push strategy.

A **promotional pull strategy** is where the product producer uses a lot of advertising focused on the ultimate consumer. A pull strategy creates a demand in the consumer that *pulls* retailers and other marketing channel members into offering the product. An example of a pull strategy is a soda manufacturer such as Coke. Coke advertises its product, convincing the customer to go to the retailer and purchase the soda.

A **promotional push strategy** is where the producer's promotional efforts are focused on retailers and other channel members. These marketing channel members then promote the product to the ultimate consumer. The promotional efforts *push* the product from the producer, through the retailer, to the ultimate consumer. An example of a push strategy is where a producer of a generic product, such as unbranded food product, promotes its product to a retailer, such as a grocery store. The retailer in turn advertises the product to the consumer.

LEARNING OBJECTIVE 5

THE MARKETING MIX–LIFE CYCLE SUMMARY

Managing the marketing function and the marketing mix is a challenge, full of risk but also the potential for return. Finding the correct blend of product, place, price, and promotion that creates a successful sale is not easy. Simultaneously creating customer and business value is difficult, particularly in a competitive world that is constantly changing.

Look back into Chapter 12. Think about the product life cycle in Exhibit 12.6: Product Life Cycles. Think how product attributes, distribution channels, price, and promotion evolve. What is successful in one stage may not be successful in another stage. Let's refine Exhibit 12.6 by adding the different parts of the marketing mix.

EXHIBIT 13.10: Product Life Cycles

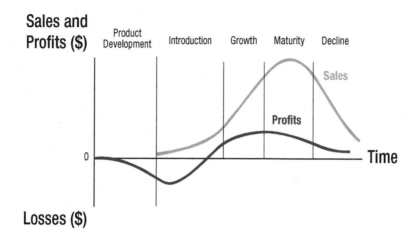

First, think about the different types of products. Think how those products evolve through a life cycle. Today, cell phones quickly go through a life cycle, while automobiles go through a life cycle more slowly.

Second, think about how products are distributed. Often the means of distributing a product changes as it evolves through a life cycle. An example is clothing. Sometimes clothing is introduced through exclusive specialty retailers. As products evolve, they are next sold in department stores and ultimately in discount stores.

Third, think about how a product's price changes as it evolves through a life cycle. An example is computers. Think about demand and supply changing through time. Think about demand exceeding supply in the growth phase of a computer model's life cycle, creating a high price. Then think about competition entering the market, increasing supply and driving down the price.

Last, think about choosing the right way to promote a product. Think how the promotion mix changes as a product evolves through a life cycle. Would you promote a new soft drink the same way you'd promote a mature and well-established alternative such as Coke or Pepsi? The answer is probably not.

CHAPTER SUMMARY

In this chapter we've explored the marketing mix, which is the mixture of product, place, price, and promotion. We've looked at how marketing attempts to create a successful sale, creating perceived value for the customer and business.

After reading this chapter, you should be able to:

1. Understand how a business positions its product (Learning Objective 1): A product is a good or service. There are many types of customers and there are many types of products. Matching the product to customer wants and needs is a goal of marketing.

2. Understand how a business distributes its product (Learning Objective 2): Place is the location and means of distributing the product. A business uses marketing channels to distribute its products. Marketing channels are composed of marketing intermediaries that move the product to the ultimate consumer.

3. Understand how a business prices its product (Learning Objective 3): Price is the amount the customer pays the business for the sale. The objective of pricing is to create value for both the business and customer. Pricing is complicated and must take into consideration costs, competitors, and other factors.

4. Understand how a business promotes its product (Learning Objective 4): Promotion is the process of communicating to customers the absolute and relative values of the product. The promotional or marketing communications mix is the mix of advertising, sales promotion, personal selling, direct-marketing techniques, and public relations used by a business to communicate a marketing message.

5. Appreciate how a product's marketing mix evolves through the product's life cycle (Learning Objective 5): Products evolve through a life cycle, moving from introduction, to growth, to maturity, to decline. As such, the product's marketing mix evolves.

So marketing and the marketing mix are critical to the success of any business. The business must have a competitive advantage in order to create value. The competitive advantage originates in the business's product. Getting the customer to perceive that competitive advantage is the role of marketing. However, for marketing to fulfill this role, the business must first have a competitive product. To have such a product, the business must innovate. Innovation, entrepreneurship, and small business are our next topics in "How Business Works."

KEYWORDS

advertising 291
agent 281
AIDA model 290
average cost 285
brand 278
brand equity 278
branding 278
break-even point 283
broker 281
business 277
business products 277
capital items 277
Communication Process 289
consumer 276
consumer products 276
contribution margin 282
convenience products 277
convenience stores 280
cost-plus pricing 285
cost-volume-profit analysis 285
counter-cyclical products 287
cyclicality 286
cyclical product 287
deep discount stores 280
department store 280
direct marketing 291
direct marketing channel 280
discount stores 280

distribution channel 279
distribution 279
fixed costs 282
generic products 278
guarantee 278
indirect marketing channel 280
labeling 278
marginal costs 285
marginal revenue 285
marketing channel 279
marketing intermediaries 280
materials and parts 277
merchant wholesalers 281
non-cyclical product 287
non-seasonal products 287
non-store retailers 280
packaging 278
perceived absolute value of the
    product 287
perceived relative value of the
    product 288
personal selling 291
personal selling process 291
price elastic 286
price inelastic 286
pricing-on-the-margin 285
product 276
product features 277

product line 276
product mix 276
product quality 278
promotion 288
promotional or marketing
    communications mix 291
promotional pull strategy 292
promotional push strategy 292
promotion process 290
publicity 291
public relations 291
retailer 280
sales promotions 291
seasonality 287
seasonal products 287
shopping products 277
specialty products 277
specialty store 280
supermarkets 280
supplies and services 277
support services 279
total costs 285
trademark 278
unsought products 277
variable costs 282
warranty 278
wholesaler 280

SHORT-ANSWER QUESTIONS

1. What is the marketing mix? Define each part of the marketing mix.
2. What is a product mix? What is a product line? Give examples of each.
3. What are the different types of products? Give examples of each.
4. What are marketing channels? What role do marketing intermediaries play in the marketing process?
5. What is a promotional mix? What are the different types of promotion?

6. Define the following terms:
   a. Product
   b. Product mix
   c. Product line
   d. Consumer
   e. Consumer products
   f. Convenience products
   g. Shopping products
   h. Specialty products
   i. Business products
   j. Materials and parts

k. Capital items
l. Supplies and services
m. Product features
n. Product quality
o. Branding
p. Brand
q. Trademark
r. Brand equity
s. Generic products
t. Packaging
u. Labeling
v. UPC codes
w. Warranties
x. Guarantees
y. Support services
z. Place
aa. Distribution
ab. Marketing channels or distribution channels
ac. Marketing intermediaries
ad. Direct marketing channel
ae. Indirect marketing channel
af. Retailer
ag. Specialty store
ah. Department store
ai. Supermarket
aj. Convenience store
ak. Discount store
al. Deep discount store
am. Non-store retailer
an. Wholesaler
ao. Merchant wholesaler
ap. Broker
aq. Agent

ar. Price
as. Variable cost
at. Fixed cost
au. Contribution margin
av. Break-even point
aw. Cost-volume-profit analysis
ax. Cost-plus pricing
ay. Marginal cost
az. Pricing-on-the-margin
ba. Marginal revenue
bb. Total cost
bc. Average cost
bd. Price elastic
be. Price inelastic
bf. Cyclicality
bg. Cyclical products
bh. Non-cyclical products
bi. Counter-cyclical products
bj. Seasonality
bk. Seasonal products
bl. Non-seasonal products
bm. Promotion
bn. The promotion process
bo. AIDA model
bp. Advertising
bq. Infomercials
br. Sales promotion
bs. Personal selling
bt. Personal selling process
bu. Direct marketing
bv. Indirect marketing
bw. Public relations
bx. Promotional pull strategy
by. Promotional push strategy

PROBLEMS

Use the following information to answer the questions:

Bill's Used Cars (BUC) sells cars. Each month BUC pays rent, salaries, and other fixed costs to operate the business, totaling $10,000 per month. The average price BUC pays for its cars is $5,000. The average price for which BUC sells its cars is $7,500.

1. What is BUC's
   a. Sale price or marginal revenue per car?
   b. Variable costs, also called marginal cost, per car?
   c. Fixed operating costs per month?
   d. Contribution margin per sale?
   e. Break-even sales volume?

2. If BUC sells 10 cars per month, what is the average total cost of each car sold?

3. How much operating profit would BUC earn if BUC sold:
   a. 0 cars per month?
   b. 2 cars per month?
   c. 4 cars per month?
   d. 6 cars per month?
   e. 10 cars per month?

4. BUC just hired a new salesman, Tom, who has an idea. Tom believes that BUC should have a sale. BUC should lower the average price of its cars to $7,000. He believes that sales will increase from 10 cars per month to 15 cars per month. However, to have this sale, BUC will need to spend an additional $4,000 to advertise and market the great deals. What will happen to the:
   a. Contribution margin?
   b. Fixed costs?
   c. Operating profit?

5. Based on your answers in question 4, should BUC hold the sale?

EXPLORING REAL BUSINESS

Go to the websites of Google, Target, Hyundai, and Procter & Gamble. The websites are

Google:	http://investor.google.com
Target:	http://www.target.com
Hyundai:	http://worldwide.hyundai.com/company-overview
Procter & Gamble:	http://www.pg.com

Look at the products each sells. Pick one or two products sold by each company. Answer the following questions for each product.

1. What attributes does the product have?
2. Who buys the product and what are the attributes of these customers?
3. How does the company distribute, price, and promote the product?

ENDNOTE

1. Maslow, Abraham H., Maslow's Hierarchy of Needs, "A Theory of Human Motivation," *Psychological Review* 50 (1943):370–396. Print.

CHAPTER

14

ENTREPRENEURSHIP AND SMALL BUSINESS

Introduction: Let's Talk About Starting Something New

How do businesses create and develop products that deliver greater value? What are entrepreneurs and what makes them special? How does someone start a new business?

In this chapter we'll explore these questions and issues. We'll examine how change can create business value. We'll explore how innovation, product development, and entrepreneurship are very important parts of "How Business Works."

LEARNING OBJECTIVES

After reading Chapter 14, you should be able to meet the following learning objectives:

1. Appreciate the role of innovation in business
2. Appreciate the opportunities and challenges of entrepreneurship
3. Explore the world of starting and operating a small business

Hippies at a Grateful Dead concert at Red Rocks Amphitheater, Colorado.

WHY INNOVATION AND ENTREPRENEURSHIP MATTER

When we look at old movies or look at new movies about earlier times, it's natural to think about living in that time period. We wonder what it would be like to live in the American West during the 1800s, or in Europe during the Middle Ages, or in the 1960s with hippies and social unrest. But can you imagine actually walking or riding in a covered wagon to go everywhere? In the 1800s there were no automobiles or airplanes. Can you imagine living in thatched huts or stone castles with no plumbing or electricity? In the Middle Ages that's what people did. Or can you imagine living in a world that had no cell phones, personal computers, or the Internet? That's what the world looked like until the mid-1980s. The world has changed a lot. Why? The world changes because of innovation. Entrepreneurs seek to use innovation to create value and make the world better. The world without innovation and entrepreneurs would be a vastly different place. Innovation and entrepreneurship matter.

LEARNING OBJECTIVE 1
. . . .
INNOVATION

THE NATURE OF INNOVATION

Have you ever walked into a store, seen a new product, and asked yourself, "Why didn't I think of that?" That's innovation. Have you ever looked at the ways businesses change and ideally improve their distribution, pricing, and promotional activities? That's innovation. Have you ever tried to figure out how to create or produce a product more efficiently? That's also innovation. Innovation is everywhere. Innovation is that process that looks at what is and asks the question, "How do I make what is even better?" Innovation is at the heart of progress and making our world better. It is one of the most important economic drivers of a free market economy. Innovation creates growth and prosperity, and enhances our standard of living.

Innovation is the successful application of new products and/or processes. Note that innovation is not invention. Invention relates to the creation of new products and/or processes. What is the difference? The difference is innovation requires successful application. What is a successful application? A successful application creates value. Examples of business innovations are:

1. Introduction of a new product into existing or new markets

2. Changing an existing product to meet new needs of existing or new markets

3. Introduction of a new process to manufacture, sell, or finance a new or existing product

THE PROCESS OF INNOVATION

Innovation is all about change. Change is never easy as change creates risk. However, doing nothing in a competitive and evolving market is also risky. Businesses that fail to innovate ultimately fail to survive.

Innovation is about constantly striving to acquire a competitive advantage, and in doing so, create value for both the customer and business.

Look around you. Examples of innovation are everywhere. Think about Procter & Gamble constantly reengineering and improving its product line for Gillette razors. Think about Hyundai constantly reengineering and improving its automobiles and introducing new automobiles that better meet customer needs. Think about Google creating the Android phone and constantly upgrading its search engine. Think about Target redesigning its stores to enhance customer shopping and introducing new products such as fresh groceries.

Innovation can be radical or subtle. Most innovation is small and incremental. Yet regardless of whether innovation is radical or small, the goal of innovation is positive change that creates value. So how does innovation occur? Exhibit 14.1 shows the Innovation Process.

First is the recognition of an opportunity. Some people, through training or natural instinct, have the ability to vision or see opportunities. They are not confined by conventional thinking and possess a special creativity. Think about it. Someone had to envision using the internal combustion engine to permit people to travel from one place to another. Someone had to envision having phones that did not use wires. Someone had to envision an Internet site that enabled people and organizations to research any topic.

Second is researching the feasibility of a product and/or process. There are a lot of good ideas that ultimately are impractical, too expensive, or the market will not accept. Did you know the first FAX machines were produced before World War II? The problem was that the market was not ready for the technology. Fifty years later the world was ready and the successful application of the FAX technology and innovation occurred.

Third is creating and testing the product and/or process. The third stage is about creating the invention—and seeing if the product or process works. Innovation is risky, but not testing the invention creates unnecessary risk.

EXHIBIT 14.1: The Process of Innovation

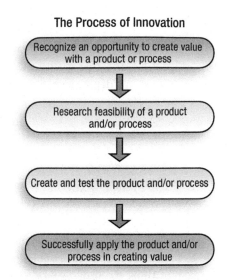

The Process of Innovation

Recognize an opportunity to create value with a product or process

↓

Research feasibility of a product and/or process

↓

Create and test the product and/or process

↓

Successfully apply the product and/or process in creating value

HENRY FORD — THE INNOVATOR

Henry Ford is recognized as a giant in the automotive world. In the early part of the twentieth century, he created and built Ford Motor Company into a global giant. But think about it. Did Henry Ford create the automobile? The answer is no. Did Henry Ford create the process to efficiently and inexpensively produce items? The answer is no. So what did Henry Ford do? He innovated. Henry Ford saw the opportunity to use the emerging technology of the day and apply it to automobile manufacturing. Before Henry Ford, each automobile was built individually. Automobiles were expensive and considered a luxury. Henry Ford used assembly-line technology to produce automobiles that were standardized. This efficiency lowered the cost of automobiles and made automobiles affordable. Henry Ford's innovation brought the automobile to the masses.

Fourth is the successful application of the product and/or process. If done right, the first three steps of the innovation process should maximize the chance that the invention will be successfully used and innovation will occur. The fourth step is doing it.

So who is responsible for the innovation process? It varies. Innovation starts with the recognition of an opportunity to create value. Within a business, it is everyone's responsibility to look for ways to create value. In larger businesses, however, the research, development, and successful application of ideas often rest in a department or function called research and development.

THE ROLE OF RESEARCH AND DEVELOPMENT

A **research and development (R&D)** department or function is responsible for acquiring and applying new knowledge to create new products and processes, refine existing products and processes, and ultimately decide whether or not new or existing products and processes can create value. R&D is a function that works closely with the other parts of a business to foster innovation and thus create value.

Why do many companies have a separate R&D department? The answer is cost and efficiency. Think about Procter & Gamble and its constant drive to create better products, such as cosmetics, at lower costs. Think about the expertise needed to conduct the marketing research, design of production processes, and testing of products and processes. In reality, creating and developing products and processes is a constant challenge, often requiring special expertise.

CONSTANT INNOVATION: CREATING AND DEVELOPING PRODUCTS AND PROCESSES

To create a sustainable competitive advantage, businesses must constantly innovate.

Innovation is more than creating new products. Innovation can take many forms: creating new products; altering existing products to meet the changing needs of the market; and finding better ways to produce, distribute, or market products. Innovation is a business's ability to create value by successfully responding to the ever-changing needs of the market.

This change can be seen in the product life cycle. Look at Exhibit 14.2: Product Life Cycle. Look over the life cycle insights introduced in Chapters Twelve and Thirteen. Now think about how a business must innovate in order to create value for its customers and owners.

First is the introduction stage. In this stage innovation is about creating and introducing a new product or introducing an existing product to a new market. Sales are low. Price, after considering sales promotions such as discounting, is typically low. The average cost of each unit sold is high. The business is incurring an operating loss. Risk is very high. So why would a business knowingly incur such losses and risk? The answer is the future. The business seeks to move out of the introduction stage into the growth stage as quickly as possible. How does it do that? It needs customer acceptance of the product. To achieve customer acceptance, the

EXHIBIT 14.2: Innovation and Product Life Cycles

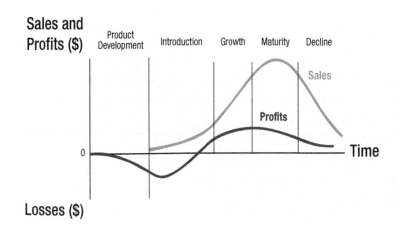

BUSINESS SENSE

ECONOMIES OF SCALE

Think about the total cost of producing an item. Look back to Chapter 13 and remember that total cost is the sum of variable and fixed costs. As the number of units produced increases, what happens to the average cost of each unit? It goes down. When this happens, economists and business people say they are experiencing "economies of scale."

So what do economies of scale mean to a business? As the average cost of a product decreases, the business can lower the price it charges for the product without incurring a loss. If properly managed, being bigger can create a competitive advantage, particularly when the business is competing on price and needs to be the low-cost provider.

business first needs a product that has a competitive advantage. Second, the business must get targeted customers to try the product. Promotion is intense and focused on product acceptance. But if successful, the product is accepted by the market and sales begin to grow.

Second is the growth stage. Here the demand for the product grows because customers accept and desire the product. The competitive advantage of the product is clearly established. Sales increase because of the product's attributes. Price increases. The business no longer needs sales promotions such as discounts. The product is now produced in mass quantities, creating efficiencies and driving the average cost per unit down. The business is creating a strong and growing operating profit. Risk is decreasing, but the business must still innovate. Why? The answer is competition. Competitors see the success of the product and try to duplicate it. First, competitors will try to create a superior product. If competitors cannot create a superior product, then competitors will try to replicate the existing product. Either way the business must constantly innovate to sustain its competitive advantage. To do so the business must innovate to differentiate its products as superior. Promotion must focus on both acquiring new customers and maintaining existing customers. If it cannot, the product will mature.

Third is the mature stage. If the business can no longer differentiate its product with innovation, the business faces a severe challenge from competition. Customers, seeking the greatest value, no longer demand the product because of the product's unique benefits. The product may still have absolute value, but it has lost its relative value. The business will be forced to compete on price to maintain demand. Price drops but costs do not drop. Operating profits decrease. Risk once again increases. Promotion focuses on maintaining existing customers. In order to maximize operating profits, businesses must try to lower costs. Businesses innovate to try to be the **low-cost provider**.

The fourth and final stage of the product life cycle is decline. Here the demand for the product declines. Businesses lower price to try to attract customers. Businesses attempt to lower costs through innovation and by reducing promotion costs. Risk once again is high. Eventually the product becomes unprofitable and the business must face the reality of discontinuing the product. Innovation, regarding both product and related processes, cannot save the product at this point.

Shoppers in Chennai, India.

INNOVATION, VISION, AND FOSTERING CHANGE

So innovation is everywhere in successful businesses. In a competitive market, constant innovation is critical to create value. But how does a business foster innovation? What qualities are critical for the successful application of new products and/or processes? It's time to talk about entrepreneurship.

LEARNING OBJECTIVE 2

ENTREPRENEURSHIP

When people talk about innovation, they often think about entrepreneurship and entrepreneurs. Why? The answer is **entrepreneurship** is the process of attempting to convert an invention into a successful innovation. **Entrepreneurs** are individuals who lead the process of entrepreneurship.

Entrepreneurs are special people because they are the driving force behind innovation. A free market economy will not grow without entrepreneurs. Entrepreneurs are people who are willing to take high risks with the expectation of high returns. Besides providing and risking money, entrepreneurs are willing to invest and risk their time and talents in hopes of creating a successful business.

So are all entrepreneurs the same? The answer is no. There are different types of entrepreneurs.

TYPES OF ENTREPRENEURS

When most people hear the term *entrepreneur*, they think of a single individual who owns and operates an independent small business, often hoping to build his or her small business into a large business. However, there are many different types of entrepreneurs.

Entrepreneurs are often not individuals, but teams of people. These **entrepreneurial teams** are composed of individuals with different talents and abilities. Although a person may have a vision, he or she may recognize he or she does not have the ability to design a product, to market the product, to produce the product, or to finance the business. He or she needs a team to successfully apply his or her ideas.

Micropreneurs are entrepreneurs who have a vision limited in size. Often called **home-based businesses**, these businesses typically provide services such as legal, accounting, and technology assistance.

Intrapreneurs are entrepreneurs who work for and in large businesses. Large businesses often recognize the need for innovation and hire select employees who share that vision and can help the business innovate.

But whatever the type of entrepreneur, are there qualities that make some entrepreneurs successful and some not successful? Most people believe the answer is yes.

A woman working at her home-based business.

SUCCESSFUL ENTREPRENEURS

Being an entrepreneur is neither easy nor ideal for many people. The words passionate, tough, independent, cunning, optimistic, positive, focused, and determined are often used to describe entrepreneurs. However, successful entrepreneurs typically have four qualities. These qualities are vision, knowledge, managerial and personal skills, and drive.

First is vision. Successful entrepreneurs have vision, which turns into a dream. Successful entrepreneurs have the ability to recognize an opportunity to create value. Creative and often unconventional, they see opportunities that others do not see. Think of the vision of Google's founders, Larry Page and Sergey Brin. As the first sentence of Google's mission states: "Our mission is to organize the world's information and make it universally accessible and useful" (www.google.com). Page and Brin had vision that they converted into a dream.

Second is knowledge. Successful entrepreneurs have or acquire the knowledge to determine whether or not their vision is feasible. Successful entrepreneurs know what to do with their vision. They do their research, test their ideas, and become informed. Successful entrepreneurs are realists who acknowledge the challenges of converting their vision into reality. Google's Larry Page and Sergey Brin applied their knowledge in deciding to move forward with their vision.

Third, successful entrepreneurs have strong managerial and personal skills. They understand the need to plan, execute, and review. Successful entrepreneurs are positive, prudent, disciplined, hard-working individuals who are committed to converting their vision into reality. They are typically leaders with good organizational and communication skills. They have the ability to work independently as well as in teams. Larry Page and Sergey Brin put together a great team that could manage.

Fourth, successful entrepreneurs have drive. Drive has many dimensions. First, because of their strong belief in their vision, they are willing to take high levels of risk. Second, the success of their idea becomes very personal. They are willing to take personal responsibility for the success or failure of their vision. Third, they show passion for their vision and work long hours, doing whatever it takes to achieve success. Successful entrepreneurs take ownership of their vision and do not easily accept failure. Can you imagine Larry Page and Sergey Brin creating Google in 1998? Google was unlike any other company, and creating it was risky. But Page and Brin had drive, worked hard, and had passion about their vision.

So if successful entrepreneurs have these qualities, what causes entrepreneurs to fail?

EXHIBIT 14.3: The Qualities of Successful Entrepreneurs

Google's Sergey Brin.

BUSINESS SENSE

E-COMMERCE

So where are today's opportunities to take invention and innovation to entrepreneurship and beyond? The answer is frequently in the world of technology. E-commerce is changing the world. **E-commerce, or electronic commerce,** is the buying and selling of products over the Internet or other computer software. Because of E-commerce, business models and strategy are being reinvented. E-commerce is opening up new ways of doing business.

Think about it. Think of all the products you buy over the Internet. Think about the possibilities of selling products over the Internet. Think about how the Internet is creating more educated customers. Think about what the future holds for E-commerce. That's innovation.

THE CHALLENGES OF ENTREPRENEURS

Most entrepreneurs fail. If Innovation is the successful application of new products and/or processes, then most entrepreneurs fail at innovation. No entrepreneur starts a business believing he or she will fail. So what are the common errors that many entrepreneurs make?

Common errors that entrepreneurs often make fall into two groups. First there are the errors of creating the business. Second are the errors of operating and growing the business.

It is a difficult task with many dynamic parts, each bringing opportunities to fail with it. Some common errors entrepreneurs make in creating the business are:

1. Lack of personal commitment in all phases of the business.

2. Failure to be patient.

3. Failure to conduct adequate research into the market for the product and/or process.

4. Failure to plan, including contingency planning.

5. Failure to communicate to all stakeholders the potential value and risk the product and/or process could create.

6. Failure to obtain adequate financing to sustain the development and offering of the product and/or process.

If an entrepreneur is successful in creating a business, he or she often has problems with managing the business. Some common errors in managing the business are:

1. Failure to personally control the execution of the plan.

2. Failure to review the execution and make needed adjustments to the business's operations, including how the business is financed.

3. Failure to acquire and train competent employees.

4. Failure to delegate authority and responsibility to trusted employees as the business grows.

5. Focusing on one aspect of the business and neglecting other critical aspects of the business. An example is focusing on sales and not managing costs.

So entrepreneurs face numerous challenges. Yet they are very important to an economy. Are there any resources provided by government to help entrepreneurs become successful? The answer in the US is yes.

SUPPORT FOR ENTREPRENEURS

Entrepreneurs create jobs, income, and growth. To attract entrepreneurs, state and local governments often provide incentives and support to help entrepreneurs. Examples of this support are incubators and enterprise zones.

An **incubator** is a place, provided by state or local governments or other organizations, where facilities and professional services are provided at a low cost. Universities and colleges often create incubators in the areas of science and technology. In return for inexpensive access to expensive resources, the entrepreneur is often required to pay for these facilities and services when the product and/ or process become profitable.

Enterprise zones are special geographic areas that governments create to attract and support entrepreneurs. Governments attract entrepreneurs with low taxes and other special services such as utilities. Check out **www.ezec. gov** to explore enterprise zones near you.

Incubators and enterprise zones are created to assist entrepreneurs. But there are also resources available to entrepreneurs that are small businesses. So let's talk small business.

An economic development zone in the Philippines.

LEARNING OBJECTIVE 3

SMALL BUSINESS

So what is a small business? What's the difference between an entrepreneur and small business person? Many small business owners are entrepreneurs. Yet not all small business owners are entrepreneurs. There can be a difference regarding size and nature.

First is size. Typically size is used to define a small business. A common definition of a **small business** is an independent business with fewer than 500 employees. Per the US Small Business Administration's Office of Advocacy, there are approximately 28.2 million businesses in the US that meet the size criteria. Sometimes entrepreneurial ventures are small businesses, but other times such entrepreneurial ventures are large in scale and do not meet the size criteria.

Second is the nature of the business. Entrepreneurs try to successfully convert invention into innovation. Owners and managers of small businesses may or may not do that. Some small businesses are not innovators themselves, but follow innovators. In doing so, the businesses provide products that are valuable, but not unique or innovative. Think about it. Doctors who own and operate their own practices are small business owners. Yet do they innovate? The answer is probably not.

Yet whether entrepreneurs or not, small businesses are critical to the success of the US economy. Let's look at some facts about the US private sector (non-government)[1]:

1. Small businesses account for over 99.7 percent of the number of all proprietorships, partnerships, and corporations.

2. Small businesses account for approximately half of all employees of private businesses.

3. Small businesses pay approximately 42 percent of all business private-sector payrolls.

4. Small businesses generated 67 percent of all new jobs created since mid-2009.

5. Small businesses created 46 percent of the non-farm gross domestic product in the private sector.

6. Small businesses produced between 16 times the number of patents per employee than large firms filing for patents.

7. Home-based businesses account for over 50 percent of small businesses. A home business is any business where the owner uses his or her home as his or her office.

Small business is so important to the US economy that the US federal government has created a special agency to assist small businesses. That agency is the **Small Business Administration (SBA)**.

It's hard to debate the importance of small business to the US economy. But why do so many people want to become a small business owner?

THE OPPORTUNITIES AND CHALLENGES OF SMALL BUSINESS

Owning a small business and being your own boss can be invigorating and fulfilling. It can also be frustrating and problematic. What are the opportunities and challenges of starting and operating a small business?

Opportunities

Look around you. What do you see? You probably see small businesses everywhere. Your doctor, your lawyer, and your barber or beautician are probably in small businesses. Opportunities are everywhere to start a small business, buy a small business, or franchise a business. So why do people take the risk of owning their own business?

Small businesses line the main street in Salinas, California.

When asked, owners of small businesses often say the biggest benefit of owning and operating a small business is the self-satisfaction of creating value for themselves and those who are important to them. The benefits can be financial. Yet the psychic income of making all the critical decisions and seeing the results of those decisions is often cited as a major motivator for owners of small businesses. To own and operate a successful business is very special.

Yet the benefits are not without costs and challenges.

Challenges

Owners of small businesses have many challenges. The major challenges are centered on knowledge, management skills, risk, and responsibility.

First is the challenge of knowledge. Owners of a small business must manage all critical functions within the business. Unlike a large business, small businesses typically have no departments for marketing, research and development, human resources, production, accounting, or finance. Small businesses may have employees who perform such functions, but ultimately the owner must make almost all critical decisions. This challenge is about more than time, it is also about knowledge and expertise.

The second challenge is the ability to be a good manager. Look back to Chapter 03 at the traits of successful managers. Successful small business owners know how to communicate, lead teams, organize, and be effective managers.

The third challenge is risk. Small business owners often assume a lot of risk. Lenders often require small business owners to pledge their personal assets to secure business loans. If the business fails, it's more than losing one's job. The owner can lose his or her personal wealth.

The fourth challenge is responsibility. People often dream of being their own boss. People like the idea of being responsible to nobody except themselves. Yet successful small business owners will tell you they have the toughest boss of all, the customer. Most owners of small businesses will tell you that the customer ultimately pays the bills and thus must be satisfied.

So how does a small business owner meet these challenges? He or she must be an effective manager.

TIP-TOP VALUE

Leaving his native country Greece, Terry Vassalos came to the United States in 1974 with nothing more than a dream and strong work ethic. His hard work and attention to detail created one of the most popular restaurants in all of Central Virginia. It's the Tip Top Restaurant.

So what is Terry's secret? It's a focus on value. Terry understands that customers come to his restaurant because he delivers superior value. His customers praise the food and service. But to do that, Terry understands that delivering quality food and service starts with attracting and retaining the best wait-staff, cooks, and managers. It's about creating a team that focuses on value.

The result is a win-win-win-win. Customers win, employees win, the community wins, and Terry wins. Terry took risks, worked hard, and created a very successful business. His success is all about creating value for his customers, his team, and himself.

MANAGING A SMALL BUSINESS

What do effective managers do? They plan, execute, and review.

Planning

Every business needs an integrated plan. It's the road map that guides the business and communicates to all stakeholders how the business will create value. However, planning is one of the most difficult tasks faced by small business owners. To assist small business owners, the US government's **Small Business Administration (SBA) (www.sba.gov)** has created guidance on what should be included in a plan.

The SBA recommends a business plan include three sections. The first section deals with the business, the second with financial data, and the third with critical documents.

The Business

The first section of the plan describes in detail the business model and strategy. In doing so, the business plan should clearly state the reason the business exists. The plan should show the business's product and the customers the business will target. The business should address its competition and how it plans to create a competitive advantage.

The first section should then show how owner(s) plans to operate the business, including procedures and controls. The plan should show how the business will acquire or produce the product, and then how the business plans to market the product. In doing so, the plan must show the employees and assets the business will need. The plan should demonstrate the value chain of the business.

The Financial Plan

The second section details the financial plan of the business. This section should include past, present, and projected financial statements for the business and owner(s). These statements include a balance sheet, income statement, and cash flow statement. Simply put, the financial plan should show how the business will raise the financial capital (money) to hire the employees and acquire the assets. In doing so, the financial plan should also show how the business will generate an operating profit to repay lenders and provide owners an adequate return.

Any financial plan should address risk. The projected financial statements, or **pro-forma financial statements**, deal with the future and are thus based on assumptions. Examples of such assumptions are sales, costs, needed employees, and needed assets. These assumptions should be clearly stated and justified by market research. But because the future is uncertain, sensitivity analysis should be conducted to look at different assumptions. The small business owner should be ready to show what actions he or she would take if sales did not materialize, costs were higher, customers did not pay as agreed, or other unfavorable events. In doing so, the small business owner should address the risk of the operating the business. How the business will deal with this risk is an important part of the financial plan. Insurance, diversification, and other techniques to be used should be shown. Break-even analysis is also helpful.

Critical Documents

The third section includes the documents needed to support the business and financial parts of the business plan. Such documents include the resumes of owners, loan applications and agreements, tax returns, contracts, and other legal documents supporting the formation of the business, licenses, and ownership of assets.

Execution

Planning is a challenge. Putting the plan into action is another challenge. Besides managing the day-to-day functions of the small business, owners must face four, often critical, execution issues. The first is finding competent and trustworthy advisors. The second is financing. The third is managing growth. The fourth is exiting the business.

Finding Competent and Trustworthy Advisors

Large businesses typically have employees who handle legal, accounting, and other professional services. Small businesses do not have the size or funds available for such employees. For such insights, small

business owners must go outside their business and find competent and trustworthy professionals to advise and assist them in achieving their goals.

Let's look at three examples. First, small business owners must find a competent and trustworthy lawyer to assist in choosing the correct form of the business (sole proprietorship, partnership, or corporation). Second, small business owners must find a competent and trustworthy accounting firm to help design the business's accounting system, compile financial statements, and prepare tax returns. Third, small business owners must find a competent real estate professional to find the best location for their business.

Financing the Small Business

Small business is often risky business, which means acquiring financing is always a challenge. Uncertain sales and costs mean that generating an operating profit can be very uncertain. Often small business owners must provide all the needed money in the form of equity.

To lend money to small businesses, many lenders ask for guarantees or collateral. Often such guarantees and collateral come from the personal wealth of the owner. However, as noted later, the Small Business Administration has a program where the federal government insures some small business loans.

In addition to personal funding and the SBA, there are investors who specialize in lending to new and growing businesses. These groups understand the high risk of such businesses and structure financing that meets their special needs. Such financing may be in the form of debt and/or owners' equity. The first group is referred to as venture capitalists or VCs. A **venture capitalist (VC)** is an organization that pays cash for the debt and stock of selected new businesses. Venture capitalists look for businesses that have the potential to grow rapidly. The goal of most venture capitalists is to help the business grow, and eventually sell or divest of the business's debt and/or stock within five to seven years.

Angels are the second group and similar to venture capitalist. An **angel** is a wealthy individual who buys the stock of selected new businesses. Angels are also attracted to businesses that have the potential for high growth. Angels may or may not desire to be long-term investors.

Managing Growth

Small business owners often face a challenge regarding growth. If their business succeeds, what do they do next? Do they maintain the business at its current size or do they grow their business?

Many small business owners grow their business without having the adequate resources to do so. As a business grows, it takes more people, assets, and financing. Plans must be adjusted to reflect a bigger and more complex business. This is particularly true regarding management. Owners of successful small businesses must initially take direct control of every major part of their business. However, as the business grows, owners must begin to delegate responsibility and authority for making decisions. This is often hard for small business owners and can cause significant problems. There is a difference between managing small businesses and businesses that are not small.

Exiting a Small Business

So what does the owner of a successful small business do when he or she wants to leave the business for retirement or other ventures? The owner needs to either close the business or sell the business. Small business owners often experience problems because they fail to plan how they will exit their business. Small business owners should think about this when forming their business.

A vacant pub in England is shuttered and has for-sale signs posted.

In closing a business, the small business owner must terminate his or her employees, sell the business's assets, pay all debts, and receive what remains. This is often hard on the owners, employees, customers, vendors, and other stakeholders. However, finding the right person to succeed the owners is also hard. Often small business owners use business brokers to assist in selling their small business. A **business broker** is an individual or organization that brings together those interested in buying a small business and sellers of small businesses.

Review

Like all businesses, small businesses must learn from both their successes and failures. Small businesses must adapt to the changing needs of the market. Failure to do so will ultimately cause the small business to fail. Review often results in changing plans. Given planning is a challenge, review is also a challenge. All too often small business owners concentrate on execution and neglect planning and review.

So managing a small business is not always easy. There are a lot of challenges. Are there any resources to help and assist small business owners? The answer is yes.

RESOURCES OF SMALL BUSINESS

Small business owners have numerous challenges. But even with such challenges, the joys of entrepreneurship and small business ownership are real. Entrepreneurs and small business are very important to the health of a free market economy. So to assist the creation and development of these ventures, special resources are available. Let's look at some of these resources in the US.

The Small Business Administration (SBA) is an agency of the US federal government that provides support to small businesses. Visit and explore the website of the SBA (www.sba.gov). It shows that the SBA's mission is to "to aid, counsel, assist and protect the interests of small business concerns, to preserve free competitive enterprise and to maintain and strengthen the overall economy of our nation." SBA programs fall into three categories: first are programs to assist small businesses in acquiring financing; second are programs to educate small business owners; and third are programs to assist and counsel small business in acquiring government contracts.

First are financing programs. If a small business has a strong business plan and meets the SBA's criteria, the SBA can assist a small business with obtaining debt and/or owners' equity. Regarding debt, the SBA can guarantee loans made by banks to small businesses. The SBA can also directly loan government funds to small businesses in the case of disasters. Regarding owners' equity, the SBA helps small businesses acquire owners' equity by licensing Small Business Investment Companies. A **Small Business Investment Company (SBIC)** is a private venture capital business that provides owners' equity funding to small businesses. The benefit of being a licensed SBIC is such businesses can borrow money from the government.

Second the SBA offers programs to educate and counsel small business owners. Within the SBA are Small Business Development Centers. **Small Business Development Centers (SBDCs)** are nonprofit agencies created to educate, assist, and advise small businesses. SBDCs bring together private individuals and businesses; local, state, and federal governments; and educational institutions to help small businesses.

SCORE is a nonprofit organization that uses retired business executives to assist and counsel small businesses. SCORE is a resource partner of the SBA and is called the "Counselors of America's Small Business." SCORE volunteers often mentor and coach small business owners.

The SBA has a special office to help women become successful owners of small businesses. The **Office of Women's Business Ownership (OWBO)** oversees a network of **Women's Business Centers (WBCs)** that help educate socially and economically disadvantaged women.

Third the SBA offers programs to assist and counsel small business in acquiring government contracts and business opportunities. An example is helping small businesses overcome problems after a natural disaster. Another example is providing surety bonds for small minority contractors trying to do business with the government. Such businesses must guarantee or ensure the government they will successfully complete the contract. A **surety bond** is a form of insurance policy that does this.

CHAPTER SUMMARY

In this chapter we've explored the nature and importance of innovation in business. We looked at the important role entrepreneurs and small business play in a free market economy. We've also looked at the benefits received and challenges faced by entrepreneurs and owners of small businesses.

After reading this chapter, you should be able to:

1. Appreciate the role of innovation in business (Learning Objective 1): Innovation is the successful application of new products and/or processes. Innovation must be constant to remain competitive in the ever-changing world of business.
2. Appreciate the opportunities and challenges of entrepreneurship (Learning Objective 2): Entrepreneurship is the process of attempting to convert an invention into a successful innovation. There are many types of entrepreneurs.
3. Appreciate the world of starting and operating a small business (Learning Objective 3): Small business is the heart of US business. Although challenging, there are great rewards for owning and operating your own business.

In this chapter we've explored these questions and issues. Now it's time to look at the systems and processes needed to produce products that meet customer needs. Products are at the heart of creating customer and business value. As such, products are at the heart of "How Business Works."

KEYWORDS

angel 311
business broker 311
E-commerce or electronic
   commerce 304
enterprise zones 307
entrepreneurial teams 304
entrepreneurs 304
entrepreneurship 304
home-based businesses 304
incubator 306
innovation 300

intrapreneurs 304
invention 300
low-cost provider 303
micropreneurs 304
Office of Women's Business
   Ownership (OWBO) 312
pro-forma financial statements
   310
research and development (R&D)
   302
SCORE 312

small business 307
Small Business Administration
   (SBA) 307
Small Business Development
   Centers (SBDCs) 312
Small Business Investment
   Company (SBIC) 312
surety bond 312
venture capitalist (VC) 311
Women's Business Centers
   (WBCs) 312

SHORT-ANSWER QUESTIONS

1. Why is innovation so important?
2. What is entrepreneurship?
3. What is a small business?
4. Define the following terms:
    a. Innovation
    b. Invention
    c. Process of innovation
    d. Research and Development (R&D)
    e. Economies of scale
    f. Low-cost provider
    g. Entrepreneurship
    h. Entrepreneur
    i. Entrepreneurial team
    j. Micropreneurs
    k. Home-based business
    l. Intrapreneurs
    m. E-commerce or electronic commerce
    n. Incubator
    o. Enterprise zones
    p. Small business
    q. US Small Business Administration (SBA)
    r. Pro-forma financial statements
    s. Venture capitalist
    t. Angel financing
    u. Business broker
    v. Small Business Investment Center (SBIC)
    w. Small Business Development Center (SBDC)
    x. SCORE
    y. Office of Women's Business Ownership (OWBO)
    z. Women's Business Centers (WBCs)
    aa. Surety bond

CRITICAL-THINKING QUESTIONS

1. Describe and discuss the process of successful innovation.
2. What qualities do you need to be a successful entrepreneur?
3. What's the difference between being an entrepreneur and a small business owner?
4. What resources does the US government provide small business owners? List and describe these resources.

SPECIAL ASSIGNMENT—STARTING YOUR OWN BUSINESS

Think of a business you'd like to start in the future. Dream a little. Think about what it would take to start and operate that business. Now go to the website of the US Small Business Administration (www.sba.gov) and read over the section on creating a business plan. Now create a business plan for your dream business.

ENDNOTE

1. See www.sba.gov

PRODUCING PRODUCTS AND VALUE CHAINS

Introduction: Let's Talk About Making Something Special

How do businesses make or produce products? How do businesses create and sustain a competitive advantage and create value with production? How do businesses balance the need for producing quantity and quality?

In this chapter we'll explore these questions and issues. We'll explore the opportunities and challenges in producing products that add value to the customer and business. We'll explore how production is critical in "How Business Works."

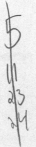

WHY PRODUCING THE RIGHT PRODUCT MATTERS

You walk into a store and find a product that appears to meet your needs. It looks good. You question whether you should buy it or not. You begin to question how it is made. Are you sure that you'll be satisfied? Are you sure you'll receive the value you expect and need? How, when, and where was the product produced? You realize the product you might buy is the result of a production process and that production process does matter. The chain of activities used to produce the product impacts the value of the product.

LEARNING OBJECTIVE 1
VALUE CHAINS AND PRODUCING PRODUCTS

Businesses produce products, both goods and services. But how do they produce products? The answer is value chains. Remember value chains in Chapter 02? It's time to take a closer look at value chains.

In Chapter 02 a **value chain** was defined as how a business converts inputs into outputs that create value for its stakeholders.[1] It is a mapping of how the system that takes inputs (people, assets, and money) combines those inputs and produces outputs that create value for customers, owners, and other important groups. Remember that a business model and strategy are all about inputs and outputs, and a value chain is a description of the systems that comprise the business's model and strategy. Exhibit 15.1 shows an example of a value chain.

EXHIBIT 15.1: The Value Chain

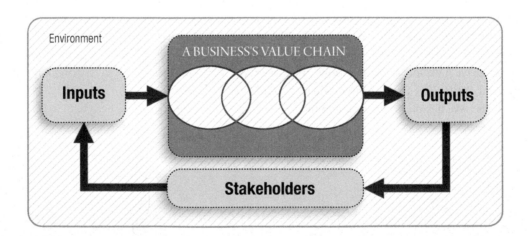

In Chapter 02, value chains were introduced using Procter & Gamble. Let's look at three more examples. First is Hyundai, a manufacturer of automobiles. Second is Target, a business that buys and resells goods. Third is Google, a business that produces intangible products (Internet search engine) plus tangible products (Android phone). We'll focus on the value chain used by Google to produce its search engine. We all know what a finished automobile looks like, we all shop for goods in retailers, and we all use the Internet to search for information (search engine). But have you ever thought about the inputs, systems, and decisions used to create these products?

EXAMPLE 1: HYUNDAI

First, Hyundai must use information from market research to estimate *what* customers want in an automobile and *when* customers want it. Based on marketing research, Hyundai must design an automobile that meets customer needs. With this insight, Hyundai must estimate the quantity of automobiles that will be sold and when the automobiles will be sold.

Second, Hyundai must figure out *how* to meet customer demand. Hyundai wants to produce the right product at the right time. To do this, Hyundai must estimate its need for assets, people, and systems needed to produce the automobiles.

Let's start with the assets Hyundai will need. These assets include the manufacturing facility and equipment, often called the **plant** or **fixed assets**. But Hyundai will need more than long-term assets to produce the automobiles. (Remember "long term" means the assets are expected to be used for a period greater than one year.) Hyundai also needs short-term assets, called **working capital**, such as inventory, receivables, and cash. Hyundai must project the long- and short-term assets it will need to produce the automobiles.

Next Hyundai must address the need for people or employees. Hyundai needs to employ workers to produce the automobiles and others to manage the workers and systems used to produce the automobiles. Yet any person will not do. Hyundai must first determine the skill set it needs from both the workers and managers. Second, Hyundai must decide the quantity of workers and managers it will need to produce the automobiles during each time period.

Third, Hyundai must determine the systems it will use to integrate the people and assets to produce the automobiles. What type of processes will Hyundai use to produce the automobiles? How will Hyundai's employees use its assets to build the automobiles?

Now close your eyes and think about a Hyundai plant in Montgomery, Alabama. Can you see an orchestrated flow of people and assets, using an assembly line that takes metal, plastic, and other materials to systematically create a finished automobile? That's Hyundai's value chain. That's production.

Hyundai car assembly line.

EXAMPLE 2: TARGET

First, Target must use information from market research to estimate what the customer wants from a general merchandise retailer in the targeted market. With this insight, Target must estimate the products customers will buy, how much of the products it will buy, and when it will buy the products.

Second, Target must figure out how to meet customer demand. To do this, Target must estimate its need for assets, people, and systems needed to buy and sell the products.

Let's start with the assets Target will need. These assets include the building and equipment. But Target will need more than buildings and equipment to operate. Target also needs working capital such as inventory and cash. Target must project the long- and short-term assets it will need to sell its products.

Shopping at Target.

Next Target must address the need for people. Target needs workers to operate the store and others to manage the workers and systems used to operate the store. Yet any person will not do. Target must first determine the skill set it needs from both workers and managers. Second, Target must decide the quantity of workers and managers it needs to operate the store during each time period.

Third, Target must determine the systems it will use to integrate the people and assets to operate the store. What type of processes will Target use to operate the store? How will Target's employees use its assets to operate the store?

Now close your eyes and think about walking into a Target in Florida. Can you see an orchestrated flow of people and assets used to create a pleasant and satisfying experience for customers? That's Target's value chain. That's production.

EXAMPLE 3: GOOGLE

Google offices, Spain.

First, Google must use information from market research to estimate what customers want in a search engine and when customers want it. From that Google must design a search engine that meets the customers' needs. With this insight, Google must estimate the number of customers who will use its search engine and when the customers will use its search engine.

Second, Google must figure out how to meet customer demand. Google wants to produce the right product at the right time. To do this, Google must estimate its need for assets, people, and systems needed to provide the search engine.

Once again, let's start with assets. These assets include the facility (building), equipment (servers), and working capital such as cash. (Think about Google's business model. Google's search engine business has no physical inventory.) But Google will also need intangible assets such as computer software. Google must project the tangible and intangible assets it will need to produce the search engine.

Next, Google needs workers to create and maintain the search engine and others to manage the workers and systems used to create and operate the search engine. Once again skills and knowledge are critical. Google must first determine the skill set it needs from both the workers and managers. Second, Google must decide the quantity of workers and managers it will need to create and operate the search engine for each time period.

Third, Google must determine the systems it will use to integrate the people and assets to produce and operate the search engine. How will Google's employees use its assets to create and operate the search engine?

Now close your eyes and think about Google. Think about turning on your computer and using the services of Google at your home, school, or even your local coffee shop. Think about what is happening at Google to produce the service you are using. Can you see an orchestrated flow of people and assets that gives you the ability to ask questions, find information, and go places using the Internet? That's Google's value chain. That's production.

COMPARING BUSINESSES AND THEIR VALUE CHAINS

Think about the value chains for Procter & Gamble, Hyundai, Target, and Google. What do you see? You see that all businesses have a system of converting inputs into outputs. Yet each of these four businesses has a different value chain. The reason is that business models and strategies are different. Buying and selling clothes (Target) is different from manufacturing cosmetics (P&G). Providing an Internet search engine (Google) is different from producing an automobile (Hyundai).

Value chains are different between businesses because of their business models. However, value chains can also be different because of each business's strategy. In an attempt to create a competitive advantage, businesses examine how they convert inputs into outputs that customers buy. Businesses attempt to create and produce a better product at a lower price. A business, in order to compete, must carefully manage every aspect of its operations. Kmart, Walmart, and Target are all discount retailers of general merchandise. All have the same or a similar business model. However, they have strategies that differentiate them. These strategies focus on using their value chains (people, assets, money, and systems) to create more value for the customer and business.

Hyundai Sonata.

Grape harvesting and processing at an Oregon winery.

MANAGING PRODUCTION AND OPERATIONS

Production is the creation or making of products. **Production management** is a term used to describe all the activities needed to create or make a product. With the increased importance of producing services, the term "production management" has been replaced with the term **operations management**. Thus, the terms "operations management" and "production management" are interchangeable in today's business world.

CREATING VALUE WITH VALUE CHAINS

Have you ever had to choose between products that had the same features and price, but one was higher quality because it was made better? You probably bought the higher-quality product. Have you ever had to choose between similar products with similar quality, but one had a lower price? You probably bought the less-expensive product. So how does a business produce a higher-quality product at a lower cost? The business may do this with production. Companies can create a competitive advantage with operations.

Too often people think businesses create a competitive advantage by introducing new products. However, businesses can also create a competitive advantage by making products better or cheaper. Think about buying a cell phone. Features are important. But how about quality? How about price?

Managers who plan and execute production efficiently (low cost) and effectively (desired quality) add as much value to the customer and business as managers responsible for creating new products. Innovation is important in every part of a business, including production and operations.

Operations management is the management of the value chain. Operations managers manage the inputs and systems used to make finished products that customers will buy. As such operations managers are responsible for acquiring the inputs, moving these inputs through a system of conversion, and ultimately creating a finished product.

Operations managers should manage production with a focus on value for both the customer and business. An operations manager wants to create value for the business by keeping the product's cost to the business as low as possible. However, an operations manager also wants to produce a product that creates value for the customer. To do this, an operations manager must manage both the quantity and quality of the product produced.

To achieve the balance between business and customer value, operations managers must plan, execute, and review inputs and systems.

LEARNING OBJECTIVE 2
· · · · · · · · · · · · · · · · · · · ·
PRODUCTION INPUTS AND SYSTEMS

Different businesses have different business models and strategies. As such, different businesses have different value chains. A business must carefully plan how it will produce its product. There is a difference between a manufacturing business like Hyundai, a retailing business like Target, and a service business like Google. Yet regardless of the business's model, strategy, and value chain, all businesses must first decide the inputs and systems to be used. Then the business must acquire the inputs and manage the systems. The process of planning production inputs and systems is often called **Enterprise Resource Planning (ERP)**. To understand ERP, let's first look at production inputs. Second, we'll look at production systems.

PRODUCTION INPUTS

There are three types of inputs. First are assets, second are people, and third are data (information).

Assets

A business must determine the assets it will need. A business may need long-term assets called facilities. However, a business also may need short-term assets, often referred to as working capital.

Let's look at the assets involved in Hyundai's producing an automobile. First, Hyundai has a facility, a building full of equipment. With the facility it will produce the automobile. To produce the automobile it needs an inventory of engines, body frames, transmissions, and other parts. Hyundai purchases these parts from suppliers. Hyundai then stores these parts in warehouses. At the designated time, Hyundai uses labor and assembly-line systems to convert the inventory of parts into an inventory of finished automobiles. Hyundai then sells the automobiles to its dealers. Hyundai typically does not receive cash immediately from the dealers. It receives a promise to pay in the future, or an accounts receivable. When the dealers pay the receivable, Hyundai receives cash. Hyundai uses the cash to pay for the parts, labor, and other costs it incurs in operating the business.

Now as Hyundai produces more automobiles, it needs more inventory, accounts receivables, and cash. It may need more facilities.

Facilities

Facilities are long-term assets such as land, building, and equipment. Planning facilities deals with determining 1) the location or site of the facilities, 2) the size of the facilities, and 3) the layout of the facilities.

Facilities should be located in areas where the other inputs to production are easily obtained and economical. An example is locating an automobile manufacturing facility in an area that has an ample supply of qualified labor. Also an automobile manufacturing facility should be located in an area with excellent transportation for receiving and shipping inventory. When choosing Montgomery, Alabama, as a manufacturing location, Hyundai looked at both labor and transportation.

London's city skyline as seen from the Thames (photograph by David Iliff, http://commons.wikimedia.org).

In addition to location, the size and design (layout) of the facility is critical. Facilities are significant investments. Increasing, decreasing, or altering facilities is not easy; these changes are costly after the facilities are acquired. Managers should be careful to make sure that a business has sufficient facilities to meet customer demand for the product now and in the foreseeable future. Yet, because facilities are costly, a business does not want too many facilities.

Working Capital

Working capital is the name given to short-term assets that are an integral part of the operating cycle of the business. A business's **operating cycle** is defined as the time that elapses between the acquisition of inventory and the receipt of cash from the sale of inventory. Working capital includes inventory, cash, and accounts receivable. Although financial managers often manage accounts receivable and cash, operation managers must understand the flow of the operating cycle and the impact of their actions. Having too little or too much working capital can cause problems for the business and hurt its value.

Chapter Seventeen explores managing assets. But assets without people do not produce products. The most critical production input is people.

People

A business must have workers and managers to produce a product. Employees are the most important resource in any business. To produce a product, a business must first decide the qualities it needs in its employees. Second, a business must estimate the number of employees it needs to produce its products.

Like assets, a business may have too few or too many people. Too few or too many people can hurt a business's value, but the quantity of employees is not the only issue. The quality of a business's employees is also critical. Do the employees have the technical and personal skills needed to produce the business's product? Employees who do not have the needed skills and qualities can hurt the value of business.

Chapter Sixteen explores the challenges of hiring, training, and supervising employees. But for employees to create value, they need to be informed.

Data and Information

Data are the facts that are input into a system. Among other things, data capture what customers want, what products are produced, and what products cost. **Information** is the knowledge derived from data. Data are converted or transformed into information with **analytics**. Relevant, accurate, and timely information is critical to the successful production of a product.

Let's look at an example. P&G wants to create and produce a line of cosmetics that meets the needs of women under the age of 30. Price is a major concern for the targeted market. P&G samples potential customers under the age of 30 and acquires large amounts of data, which must be analyzed and synthesized. By converting the data into information, P&G can gain knowledge about how much the targeted market will pay for cosmetics. With this knowledge P&G can design and produce cosmetics that customers will buy and will generate business profits.

Chapter Eighteen explores the management of raw data and subsequent transformation into useful information. But assets, people, and information must come together. There need to be systems that integrate assets, people, and data. Without good systems, the best assets, people, and data will not produce the best products.

How does P&G ensure this group of women will like its new cosmetics line?

EXHIBIT 15.2: The Transformation of Data into Information

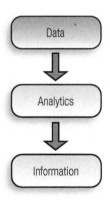

PRODUCTION SYSTEMS

In Chapter 02 a business system was defined as the processes a business uses to operate. Using people, data, and processes, businesses create, produce, and sell a product. Thus, **production or operations systems** are the means of converting inputs into outputs.

Systems are the means of integrating assets, people, and information into a productive process. (Remember that data are transformed into information with analytics.) Nowhere is this more obvious than in producing a product. Production systems use information to get the right people, doing the right thing, with the right assets, at the right time.

Systems can be very simple or complex. Systems can be high tech or low tech. (Chapter Eighteen explores the technology used in production and operations.) Systems can be very rigid or flexible. Why so much variety? Different businesses have different business models and strategies, which are reflected in the different types of production systems.

So what are different types of production systems?

EXHIBIT 15.3: The Components of Business Systems

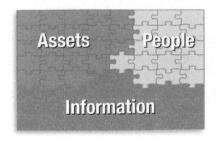

The Types of Production Systems

There are many different ways to produce a product. Managers have many options from which to choose. To be efficient and effective, operations managers use different techniques and processes to produce different products. So what are some of the options operations managers use?

First, production processes are typically analytical or synthetic. An **analytical process** is a production process that breaks a product into parts. The resulting products are often called **by-products**. An example of an analytical process is using harvested corn to create products. The harvested corn is separated into parts, with each part used to create value. The kernels of corn can be used to produce food for people, while the dried husks that surround the kernels can be used to produce food for cattle and other farm animals. A **synthetic process** is the opposite of an analytical process. A synthetic process combines inputs or products to create another product. An example of a synthetic process is P&G's CoverGirl cosmetics. Can you envision all the different ingredients coming together to create CoverGirl cosmetics? That's a synthetic process.

Second, production processes can be designed to create standardized or custom products. **Mass production** is the process of producing standardized products in large quantities. Mass production is usually cost efficient because

Operations at a vehicle assembly line in Ukraine, 2010.

it uses an assembly line. An **assembly line** is where workers do a limited number of tasks on products that move through a process. Each worker has an assigned task. When a worker completes his or her assigned task on a product, the product moves to another worker, who completes another task on that product. An example of mass production is the production of engines for Hyundai. Engines are typically standardized. Standardized products move through a process that assembles component parts into a finished product.

Customized mass production is a mass-production process that permits limited customization of the product. An example is automobile production at Hyundai. Hyundai uses assembly lines to mass-assemble cars. However, at critical points, the assembly line permits limited customization with select options such as sound systems, color, and type of engine.

Customized production is the process of producing a unique product that meets the unique needs of a customer. An example is a customized piece of jewelry or a customized home. Customers of customized products often do not consider price to be as important as the product's unique qualities. However, to lower costs, customized production is often designed around a modular process. A **modular process** is one that is subdivided into parts, called modules. Each module can be independently created and

BUSINESS SENSE

AUTOMATION AND ROBOTS

Think about being a production manager for Hyundai. You want to maximize the quantity and quality of products produced while minimizing the cost per unit. So how do you do it?

In the world today, more and more businesses are turning to computer-driven production systems and automation. Why? The answer is increased quantity and quality produced at lower costs. Think about it. Computer-directed robots now play a major role in building products such as automobiles, which means the automobiles are of higher quality. But the cost of producing automobiles is also lower. Robots and automated systems are expensive, but humans are also expensive. Think about the cost of producing products that are inconsistent. Robots can repeat the same task over and over again with less variation than a human can.

Computers, robotics, and automation are the wave of the future because they help produce value for both the customer and business.

used in multiple and different processes. Think of building a customized home. You sit down with the builder and design your home. However, the builder will use standardized elements for heating, electrical, plumbing, and other components.

Third, production processes can be continuous or intermittent. A **continuous process** is a production process that operates continuously, without interruption, for long periods of time. An example of a continuous process is P&G manufacturing Tide detergent. When P&G makes Tide, it makes a lot of Tide at one time using a continuous process. An **intermittent process** is a production process that frequently starts and stops. The frequency of starting and stopping is due to the limited number of customers or the need to adjust the production process. An example of an intermittent process is the medical profession. Doctors and nurses must constantly stop and start delivering their product to meet the different needs of their patients.

Fourth, operations managers often need to be able to switch from one type of process to another. **Flexible production** relates to a production process that can be easily changed. An example is P&G producing Crest toothpaste in different flavors.

So operation managers have a lot of options in choosing the systems to be used. But are there tools that help managers figure out which process is best? The answer is yes.

The Tools of Managing Operations

Operations managers often use two tools to help manage production processes. The two tools are Gantt Charts and PERT Charts.

A **Gantt chart**, named for Henry L. Gantt, is a graph that depicts how a product is produced over time. A Gantt chart depicts how and when a product progresses through the production process. Exhibit 15.4 is an example of a Gantt Chart.

EXHIBIT 15.4: Gantt Chart

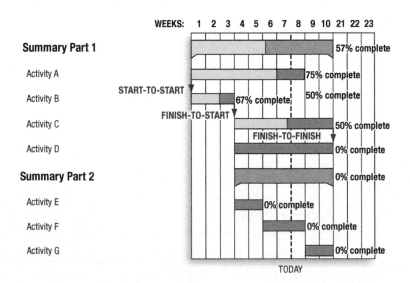

A similar but more complex technique is a **PERT chart**. PERT is the acronym that stands for "program evaluation review technique." A PERT chart depicts the tasks or activities needed to produce a product. A PERT chart also shows the timing or sequence of each task or activity. PERT charts emphasize the critical path embedded in the production process. A **critical path** is that sequence of events that takes the longest time to complete. As such, the activities that comprise the critical path determine the minimum time it will take to produce the product. Exhibit 15.5 is an example of a PERT chart.

EXHIBIT 15.5: PERT Chart

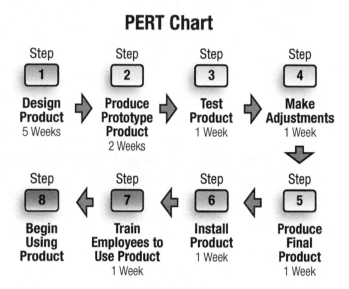

Gantt, PERT, and similar techniques help managers manage operations. Think about how useful such techniques are in managing the production of Hyundai's Kia automobile or Diamond Foods Pringle snacks. Such techniques are an important part of managers' planning, executing, and reviewing.

LEARNING OBJECTIVE 3

· · · · · · · · · · · · · · · · · · · ·

PLANNING, EXECUTING, AND REVIEWING—
PRODUCING QUALITY PRODUCTS THAT ADD VALUE

PLANNING PRODUCTION

Production or operations managers first figure out how much product must be produced at what time. They then plan by routing, scheduling, and budgeting activities. **Routing** refers to planning the sequence of tasks that will take place to produce a product. Look back at the earlier discussion of PERT charts and see how managers must figure the sequence and critical path of the production process.

Next production managers must schedule. **Scheduling** refers to assigning tasks to specific people, machines, processes, or even departments. Scheduling is about what will happen, who will do it, how it will be done, and when it will be done.

Last is budgeting. **Budgeting** refers to putting numbers to the plan. A budget shows what will be produced, when it will be produced, and what it will cost. From budgets come standards. **Standards** relate to goals a business desires to meet regarding how much will be produced, when it will be produced, and how much each unit produced will cost. An important part of setting standards is recognizing what costs are controllable and non-controllable. A **controllable cost** is a cost that employees and managers can affect. An example is waste caused by inefficiency. A **non-controllable cost** is a cost that employees or managers cannot affect. An example is the cost of a kilowatt hour of electricity.

Often a business will not have one plan or budget but a series of budgets and standards. Together they create a flexible budget. A **flexible budget** recognizes that certain parts of production may not be controllable. Thus, these non-controllable events may produce different outcomes. The business must concentrate on the controllable events and be flexible enough to adapt to the unexpected. A flexible budget is a form of contingency planning, making sure the business maximizes its chances of succeeding in all situations.

EXECUTING PRODUCTION

Execution is putting the plan into action and producing the product. As the product is being produced, systems must be in place to control production. **Control** is the process that monitors activities to ensure that the plan is being adhered to and making corrections if needed. The goal of the production process is to create the desired quantity and quality of the product, at the desired time, at the desired cost. Control systems help achieve this goal.

EXHIBIT 15.6: Control Steps

A good control system provides accurate and timely information on any variation from a budget or a standard. But management must also recognize that the standards are based on estimates. Control systems should quickly and efficiently get to why standards are or are not being achieved. Exhibit 15.6 is an example of a control system.

As a part of the control process, a business's accounting department should collect production data, convert these data into usable information, and provide management with timely knowledge about production activities. To do this, the accounting department creates a cost accounting system. **Cost accounting systems** are accounting systems that report to management the quantity, quality, and cost of production in a given time period.

Cost accounting systems are typically either job-order systems or process systems. A **job-order cost system** allocates costs to individual or groups of products. An example of a business that uses a job-order system is Hyundai. Each automobile is given a number that identifies it as it goes through the production process. Costs are allocated to the automobile, or job, as the automobile is converted from parts into a finished product ready to sell.

A **process cost system** averages costs over large numbers of nearly identical products. An example of a process cost system is P&G's manufacturing Tide detergent. Costs are incurred but hard to allocate to individual boxes of Tide. So P&G allocates the costs to the total number of units produced in a given period. It then divides the total costs by the number of units produced, determining the average cost per unit.

REVIEWING PRODUCTION

Review starts by comparing planned and actual events. Review is the process of learning from the past to make the future better. A business cannot change the past, good or bad. All that it can change is the present and future. An example of this is when the cost of a product exceeds budget. The cost overruns

OPERATIONAL RISKS: FIXED COSTS, VARIABLE COSTS, AND FLEXIBILITY TO ADAPT

In Chapter 11 risk was defined as the uncertainty that could result in an undesirable outcome. Undesirable outcomes can come from anywhere in a business, including production. Think about it. Investing a lot of money in a building and equipment is risky. Entering into long-term contracts with labor, guaranteeing employment regardless of output is risky. Production managers must constantly manage risk.

Production managers must worry about what is expected and unexpected. As the probability of the unexpected increases, managers may want a production process that is more flexible. Even if the total cost of production is higher on average, managers may want a production process where costs are controllable. As the probability of the unexpected decreases, businesses may want a production process that is more standardized. Although costs may be non-controllable in a standardized process, the average cost per unit could be lower.

Now think about Procter & Gamble producing Crest toothpaste. Marketing research can forecast the demand for Crest with high precision. Crest is produced with large, automated systems using fixed assets. The costs of using these assets are non-controllable after acquisition. P&G uses low levels of labor, which is controllable.

Now think about Target selling electronics, clothes, and merchandise. Marketing research tries to forecast the demand for such products, but recognizes that market conditions may change. The demand for such products may be high or low depending on numerous factors. To cope with this uncertainty, Target uses a lot of temporary or part-time labor. As customers buy more merchandise, Target hires more employees. As customers buy fewer products, Target hires fewer employees. Labor is controllable.

cannot be recovered or recouped. Costs that cannot be recovered are called **sunk costs**. However, a good business can learn from such experiences and make the present and future better.

A business must look at the past and strive to perpetuate the good things (favorable variances) and correct the bad things (unfavorable variances). Successful businesses understand change is constantly occurring. Successful businesses understand that change is an opportunity to continuously improve.

In review, the role of a cost accounting system is to quickly and efficiently show management if execution is going according to plan. Variances are used to help with this task. Look back at Chapter 08. A **variance** is the difference between actual and budgeted amounts. Variances are computed for the 1) quantity of products produced (assuming acceptable quality) and 2) the cost of the products produced. Variances can be favorable or unfavorable.

The key to review is quickly assessing responsibility and being able to take appropriate action. Product testing is a big part of this task. Sampling and testing products is important to make sure that the customer will receive his or her expected value. But when problems occur, the business must act promptly. Can you imagine the millions of dollars that it costs an automobile manufacturer to recall defective automobiles? Somehow standards were not met and timely corrective action not taken.

This brings us to two very special challenges in production. The first challenge is managing the productivity and cost of assets, people, and systems used in production. The second challenge is producing and managing quality.

MANAGING THE PRODUCTIVITY AND COSTS OF ASSETS, PEOPLE, AND SYSTEMS USED IN PRODUCTION

The goal of production is to produce the quantity and quality of products customers want and will buy. However, the goal of production is also to produce products at the lowest cost. This drive for lowering cost is often called **lean operations**, or attempting to be the **low-cost-producer**. Balancing these goals is not always easy. It's a matter of balancing productivity and costs.

Productivity is a measure of output per unit of input. An example is the number of customer inquiries Google's search engine can conduct per hour. Google can estimate the cost of each inquiry by dividing this number into the cost of operating the search engine per hour. The lower the cost per inquiry means Google is managing its inputs more efficiently and enhancing its operating profit.

To manage productivity, production managers must carefully and prudently manage the quantity, quality, and cost of assets, people, and systems.

Managing Assets and Related Costs

First, let's look at assets. It has been noted that assets, such as facilities and working capital, can be significant investments. Managers must be careful to make sure that a business has sufficient assets to meet customer demand now and in the foreseeable future. For example, if Hyundai has too small a facility or too little inventory, it cannot build the automobiles to meet customer demand.

Yet assets are costly and a business does not want too many. Remember that assets must be financed with financial capital, money provided by lenders and owners. Financial capital is not free. Lenders and owners expect a return that rewards them for the use of their money. Assets that are not needed and unproductive pull the value of the business down.

A modern warehouse with a pallet rack storage system to manage the business's inventory.

An example of this challenge is managing supply chains. **Supply chain management** deals with managing the interface between a business and its suppliers. How and when a supplier delivers inventory to a business is important. Holding, warehousing, and handling inventory are expensive activities. Many manufacturing and retail businesses are moving to just-in-time inventory. **Just-in-time inventory** is when a business works with its supply chain to minimize the raw materials on hand without causing production problems. Using information and technology, purchasing agents work with suppliers to make sure the business has the amount of inputs or inventory it needs at the exact time it needs them. The purchasing business tries to minimize the amount and costs of inventory it must hold.

Managing People and Related Costs

Hiring, training, and managing people are a challenge. A business wants enough employees to meet the needs of its customers. If Target does not have a sufficient number of trained employees, customers will not get the service they want. Customers will no longer shop at Target, hurting Target's value. However, too many people can also hurt Target's value. People, like assets, must be productive. Have you ever walked into a store and seen employees with nothing to do? That hurts the business's value.

To cope with this challenge, some businesses are outsourcing certain activities. **Outsourcing** occurs when a business uses sources outside its organization to provide production or professional services. An example is when you have problems with your computer. You call the computer company's help desk or technical services. Are you getting help from employees of the computer company or employees of a company hired by the computer company to service its customers? If the employee doesn't work directly for the computer company, then that's outsourcing.

Managing Systems and Related Costs

Systems, like assets and people, are not free. Systems are expensive and must produce benefits to justify the related costs. This is best seen in accounting systems that provide information. The goal of an accounting system is not to provide more information, but to provide information that managers can and will use to manage. If managers cannot or will not use the information, the cost of the information system does not add value to the business. The cost hurts the value of the business.

PRODUCING AND MANAGING THE QUALITY OF PRODUCTS

Quality is the second special challenge faced by production or operations managers. **Quality** is how well a product meets customer expectations. Thus, quality is a function of customer expectations regarding their perception of the product's value. What is a high quality for one customer may be a low quality for another customer. Thus, understanding customer expectations is the first step in creating a quality product. An example is when you go to a restaurant. When you go to a fast-food restaurant and spend $10 on a meal, your expectations are different from what they'd be if you went to a very upscale, expensive restaurant where you'd spend $100 on a meal.

The goal of the business is to consistently produce quality products that meet customer expectations. But producing quality products has its benefits and its costs. Quality must be managed so the benefits from producing quality products exceed the costs of producing quality products. So what are the benefits and costs of producing quality products?

A McDonald's restaurant in Japan.

The Benefits and Costs of Quality

What happens when a customer expects a product to have certain qualities, buys that product, and discovers the product meets her or his expectations? She or he is a satisfied customer. The value the customer received from buying the product justifies the price paid. The customer may return to buy more products. The customer may encourage her or his friends and colleagues to buy the product. The business that sold the product gets future sales, which increases its value.

What happens when a customer expects a product to have certain qualities, buys that product, and discovers the product does not meet her or his expectations? She or he is a dissatisfied customer. The value the customer received from buying the product does not justify the price paid. The customer may return the product to the business. This costs the business money immediately, and the customer probably will not buy more products from the business. The customer may discourage her or his friends and colleagues from buying the product. The business that sold the product does not get future sales, which hurts its value.

Yet there are other costs associated with producing quality. Systems to control and ensure quality are costly. Inspections, sampling, and other quality-producing activities have a cost. Yet not inspecting, sampling, and taking corrective action is also expensive. What do you think it would cost P&G to recall a defective product? How would it hurt the value of the product's brand?

So producing quality products maximizes benefits and minimizes costs. A business must weigh the costs and benefits of quality. So are there programs and techniques to help manage quality and produce benefits that exceed costs? The answer is yes.

Programs to Produce and Manage Quality

Total Quality Management (TQM) is the philosophy that producing quality products is an essential part of all aspects of a business. Customer satisfaction is necessary for a business to achieve long-term success. TQM is about meeting customer expectations, maximizing the benefits from meeting customer expectations, and minimizing the costs of not meeting customer expectations. Often called **quality assurance**, TQM deals with designing products, marketing products, producing products, and supporting customers with services such as guarantees, repairs, and education.

The key to TQM is a business's workers and managers. Everyone in a business must understand and work toward quality. To assist in this, some businesses use quality circles. A **quality circle** is a team of employees that works with each of the parts of a business to address opportunities and challenges regarding quality.

But systems are also important. Often special systems are created to monitor and control quality. Such systems typically use statistics to help sample 1) the quality of products as they are being produced and 2) ultimate customer satisfaction. The systems to collect and analyze these data are often referred to as **statistical process control (SPC)**.

But what happens with the information from such systems? What do managers do to create quality? The answer is programs such as Six Sigma, ISO programs, and actions needed for Baldrige Awards.

Six Sigma is a process developed in the early 1980s by Motorola that is now used by hundreds of businesses. To create a quality output, Six Sigma focuses on the inputs and systems. The focus of Six Sigma is design, measurement, analysis, and control of inputs and systems. The goal of Six Sigma is to produce products with no more than 3.4 defects per million parts or actions. That is a success rate of 99.999%.

Another set of programs is that of the **International Standards Organization (ISO)**. ISO is a non-government federation of standard-setting groups throughout the world. Based on independent audits, ISO certifies that a business meets strict standards regarding quality. ISOs' most notable programs are ISO 9000 and ISO 14000. **ISO 9000** is the current set of standards for understanding and meeting customer needs. **ISO 14000** is the current program to help businesses manage their impact on the environment. ISO 14000 is a program designed to recognize businesses that protect and enhance the environment. It benchmarks best practices and is not a set of strict standards.

The **Baldrige Awards** are another program to enhance quality in the United States. The National Baldrige Awards Program was created by Congress in 1987. Each year the President awards the Baldrige Award to businesses that show outstanding performance in obtaining quality. Firms compete for the prestigious Baldrige Award by submitting to evaluation. Businesses are evaluated on their leadership; strategic planning; customer and market orientation; measurement, analysis, and knowledge management; focus on human resources; process and systems management; and success or results.

CHAPTER SUMMARY

In this chapter we've explored how a business uses its value chain to produce a product. We've examined the techniques and tools used by businesses to create value through production and operations.
After reading this chapter, you should be able to:

1. Understand the nature of value chains used to produce products (Learning Objective 1): A value chain is how a business converts inputs into outputs that create value for its stakeholders. It is a mapping of how the system that takes inputs (people, assets, and money), combines those inputs, and produces outputs that create value for customers, owners, and other important groups.
2. Appreciate the role of inputs and systems in production (Learning Objective 2): The process of planning production inputs and systems is often called Enterprise Resource Planning (ERP). Inputs include assets, people, data, and the money to finance the inputs. The systems used for the inputs to produce outputs vary depending on the desired outcome.
3. Understand the challenges and opportunities in managing production, including quality (Learning Objective 3): Managing operations and production is about planning, executing, and reviewing. There are numerous techniques and systems that successful managers use to create value through operations and production.

In this chapter we've explored these questions and issues. Now it's time to look at the people, both workers and managers, a business hires. Above all else, a successful business must hire, train, and reward the right employees. Employees are a key to "How Business Works."

KEYWORDS

analytical process 324
analytics 324
assembly line 325
Baldrige Awards 332
budgeting 327
by-products 324
continuous process 326
control 328
controllable cost 327
cost accounting systems 328
critical path 327
customized mass production 325
customized production 325
data 324
enterprise resource planning (ERP) 322
facilities 323
fixed assets 319
flexible budget 328
flexible production 326

Gantt chart 326
information 324
intermittent process 326
International Standards Organization (ISO) 332
ISO 9000 332
ISO 14000 332
job-order cost system 328
just-in-time inventory 330
lean operations 330
low-cost-producer 330
mass production 325
modular process 325
non-controllable cost 328
operating cycle 323
operations management 321
outsourcing 330
PERT chart 326
plant 319
process cost system 328
production 321

production management 321
production or operations systems 324
productivity 330
quality 331
quality assurance 332
quality circle 332
routing 327
scheduling 327
Six Sigma 332
standards 327
statistical process control (SPC) 332
sunk costs 329
supply chain management 330
synthetic process 325
Total Quality Management (TQM) 332
value chain 318
variance 329
working capital 319

SHORT-ANSWER QUESTIONS

1. What is a value chain? Why do value chains differ between businesses?
2. What programs encourage quality in the US? Describe each.
3. What is a cost accounting system and how does it help production?
4. What role does quality play in producing a product?
5. Define the following terms:
   a. Value chain
   b. Plant or fixed assets
   c. Working capital
   d. Production
   e. Production management
   f. Operations management
   g. Enterprise resource planning (ERP)
   h. Facilities
   i. Operating cycle
   j. Data
   k. Information
   l. Analytics
   m. Production or operations systems
   n. Analytical process
   o. By-products
   p. Synthetic process
   q. Mass production
   r. Assembly line
   s. Customized mass production
   t. Customized production
   u. Modular process
   v. Continuous process
   w. Intermittent process
   x. Flexible production
   y. Gantt chart
   z. PERT chart
   aa. Critical path

ab. Routing

ac. Scheduling

ad. Budgeting

ae. Standards

af. Controllable cost

ag. Non-controllable cost

ah. Flexible budget

ai. Control

aj. Cost accounting system

ak. Job-order cost system

al. Process cost system

am. Sunk cost

an. Variance

ao. Lean operations

ap. Low-cost producer

aq. Productivity

ar. Supply chain management

as. Just-in-time inventory

at. Outsourcing

au. Quality

av. Total quality management (TQM)

aw. Quality assurance

ax. Quality circle

ay. Statistical process control (SPC)

az. Six Sigma

ba. ISO 9000

bb. ISO 14000

bc. Baldrige Awards

CRITICAL-THINKING QUESTIONS

1. How does production, often called operations, create value?

2. Discuss the challenges of managing production regarding
   a. Planning
   b. Execution
   c. Review

3. Can you think of products where a business's production process created value? Describe how this happened for each of these products.

4. Think about being a production manager. Can you think of any of the challenges you may face when working with 1) marketing and 2) research and development? Can you describe them? What would you do to address these challenges?

5. Think about the value chain for producing a book, such as this book. Can you describe it?

EXPLORING REAL BUSINESS

Go to the websites of Google, Target, Hyundai, and Procter & Gamble. The websites are

Google:	http://investor.google.com
Target:	http://www.target.com
Hyundai:	http://worldwide.hyundai.com/company-overview
Procter & Gamble:	http://www.pg.com

Look at the products each sells. Pick one or two products sold by each company. Answer the following questions for each product.

1. Does the product have a competitive advantage? List competing products. Which product creates the best value and why?
2. How important is the value chain in achieving the competitive advantage noted in question 1 above? Explain why.

ENDNOTE

1. The term "value chain" is attributed to Michael Porter. See Porter, Michael. *Competitive Advantage: Creating and Sustaining Superior Performance.* New York: Free Press, 1998. Print.

SECTION 5

MANAGING ECONOMIC RESOURCES

In this section, you will read and review the following chapters:

CHAPTER

OPPORTUNITIES AND CHALLENGES IN MANAGING INFORMATION, TECHNOLOGY, AND E-BUSINESS

Introduction: Let's Talk About Information, Technology, and E-Business

What's the role of information in creating value? How is technology changing the way we do business? What are E-business and E-commerce, and what is their impact on the world of business?

In this chapter we'll explore these questions and issues. We'll explore the opportunities and challenges in using information, technology, and E-business. We'll explore how these topics can help create value and are important in "How Business Works."

WHY INFORMATION MATTERS

It is often said that information is power. In a business, information is the power to create a strategic competitive advantage and thus value. Knowing or seeing something that others do not know or see is the first step in being able to innovate, to produce, and to market products that deliver more value to the customer and the business. Good and timely information creates greater benefits, more timely benefits, and benefits that come with lower risk. Information matters.

LEARNING OBJECTIVE 1

THE NATURE AND IMPORTANCE OF INFORMATION AND INFORMATION SYSTEMS

So what is information? Data are facts. Data are useless unless they are transformed into information. **Analytics** is the process a person or organization uses to convert data into information. **Information** is knowledge that a person or organization can use to make decisions. See Exhibit 16.1.

EXHIBIT 16.1: Creating Information

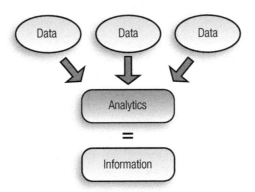

Analytics or analytical processes can be simple or complex. They can be basic decision rules or highly sophisticated systems and processes used to filter and integrate data for decision making. Think about it. Let's look at a rather simple but personal example. You go to the grocery store and read the data on the box of cereal. The data reflect the product's contents and nutritional value. However, that's data, not information. You analyze the data and convert the data into information by using decision rules such as more sugar makes the cereal taste better, but it may be harmful to your body in other ways. What's happening? You are using analytics to convert data to information, which you can then use to make a buying decision.

Business analytics serve the same purpose as personal analytics. Business analytics can also be simple. Let's look at a simple example. You do a background search on a potential supplier. You receive data that the supplier delivers late one out of five times on average. You convert the data into information that the supplier is unreliable. You decide that you cannot use an unreliable supplier.

Yet business analytics can be very complex. How does a business such as Procter & Gamble decide what products to produce, when to produce them, how to produce them, how to market them, and how to price them? Such decisions are based on a lot of data, transformed into information, and used as inputs into the decision processes.

THE NATURE OF INFORMATION

Good information empowers a manager to make good decisions that create value. Bad information or lack of information is a barrier to making good decisions. To add value, information ideally should possess five qualities. Information should be pertinent, correct, complete, timely, and cost effective. See Exhibit 16.2: The Qualities of Valuable Information.

EXHIBIT 16.2: The Qualities of Valuable Information

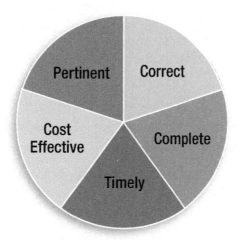

Information should first be as pertinent as possible. Information is pertinent if it helps the manager make a decision. The decision maker should clearly define what information is needed and what information is not needed. All too often managers must make decisions without the information they need. This causes bad decisions or decisions that create unnecessary uncertainty and risk. However, managers often have more information than they need, causing confusion. This is often called **information overload**. Managers must define what information they need to make a decision.

CASE STUDY

IMPROVING THE WORLD WITH TECHNOLOGY: E-COMMERCE AT WORK

Pictured (center) with his management team and shareholders at NASDAQ stock exchange in New York in October 2005.

Trip Davis was an entrepreneur and executive in travel technology and data services. Noted as a visionary and driving force in the travel industry, he built two successful technology services firms which have been enablers of online travel, now the largest E-commerce category, and fundamental changes in travel marketing and distribution. In 2002 and 2007, he was named one of the top 25 most influential executives in the travel industry by Business Travel News. Davis was the non-executive co-founder and chairman of TRX, Inc., a global leader in travel technology and data services. Serving as CEO for nine years through 2008, he led the company to revenue of over $120 million and completed a successful IPO in 2005. In 2013 TRX was acquired by Concur Technologies. TRX processes approximately $400 billion per year in travel volume on behalf of its clients, including transaction data from over 400 sources in 50 countries. Clients include travel agencies, travel web sites, corporations, travel suppliers, government agencies, and credit card companies.

THE VALUE OF INFORMATION

What would you pay for information? Think about it. Although we sometimes view information as free, it really has a cost. Sometimes we pay the cost directly. An example is when we pay to use the Internet. We pay a fee to our internet service provider to use the Internet to acquire information. Sometimes we pay the cost indirectly. When we use Google to research a product, the businesses that own the listed website pay Google a fee depending where they are listed. Businesses pay a lot of money to Google to be listed first. And who ultimately must pay the cost of that fee? That cost or fee is passed on to the customers when they buy the product. It's a cost of doing business like any other marketing expense.

So what is information worth? Information is like any other product. Information has a price that is a function of the demand and supply for that information. The market sets the price for information based on the perceived quantity, timing, and risk of the benefits the information provides. The more valuable the information, the higher the price. The less valuable the information, the lower the price.

Let's look at an example. You are about to make an offer to buy a house. The house looks great, but you are not an expert on construction. You want information about the house's parts and components. You worry that you may be buying a house with hidden problems. You worry about the risk of buying the house. So what do you do? You hire an expert to inspect the house, provide you information, and reduce your risk. You hire an expert to tell you whether the house has or does not have plumbing, electrical, structural, and other problems. Do you have alternatives in choosing an inspector? The answer is yes. Not all inspectors charge the same price. The experts with proven track records demand a higher fee than those with less proven expertise. You ask yourself, "What's the information from a good inspection worth?"

Information has a cost. The question is whether or not the price of information adds value. That's a question we all must face every day.

Information should be as correct as possible. Information is correct if it is accurate and reliable. Can the manager depend on the information to provide him or her a clear picture of what has happened or what the situation is? Managers need information that is valid and dependable.

Information should also be as complete as possible. For information to be complete, it should be thorough. Complete information gives the manager all the insights the manager needs to make a correct decision. Completeness deals with empowering the manager to see the situation in its totality. Have you ever hear people say they were "blind-sided" because they didn't see something they needed to see? Managers can be blind-sided because they were not informed of all the dimensions of their decision.

Information should be as timely as possible. For information to be timely, the information should be able to affect the manager's decision. Managers must make decisions at the correct point in time to ensure the decisions have the desired impact. Being late often destroys the positive impact of decisions. Information that is not timely can delay a manager's decision and thus destroy any positive impact of the decision.

Information should be cost effective. Information is not free—it is expensive. The benefits of information must be weighed against the cost of the information. The benefits from better information must exceed the cost of the information. What are the benefits of information? Information should help the manager create profits that are higher, quicker, and with lower risk.

Let's look at P&G as an example. P&G must decide what products it will produce. So how does it decide? It does market research. P&G weighs the cost and benefits of gathering data and transforming those data into information. P&G designs a market research program that efficiently and cost effectively samples potential buyers in the targeted market segment. It then collects the appropriate data, converts the data into information, and gives the decision maker the information to use. Ideally the information the manager receives is pertinent, correct, complete, and timely. It helps him or her make the best decision. However, the manager must still accept there are risks in designing and producing the products. Why? Because after the decision is made to produce a given product, it still will take two years to create a production process to produce the product. Customer preferences can change in two years. However, to wait until P&G is certain means that P&G could miss the opportunity.

So if a business wants information that is pertinent, correct, complete, timely, and cost effective, how does it do it? The answer is information systems.

INFORMATION SYSTEMS

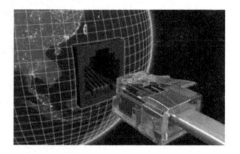

Look back at Chapter 02. A business system uses people, data, and processes to create and sell a product. An **information system (IS)** is a system that uses people and processes to convert data into information with analytics. The **management of information systems** is called **MIS**.

The design and structure of an information system is called its **information architecture**. The goal of information architecture is to create an information system that adds value to a business. As such, information architecture is built on understanding the ultimate user of the information system, the decision maker.

Information architecture recognizes that an information system has three major elements. First are inputs. The inputs are data. Second are processes (analytics) to convert the data into information. Processes are designed using people, software, and hardware. Third are outputs, the information and decisions that result from the inputs and processes. Exhibit 16.1 depicts an information system.

First is data. An effective information system must be designed to acquire and record data so that data can be easily converted into information that is pertinent, correct, complete, timely, and cost effective. When data are acquired and entered into the information system, the data become part of a database. A **database** is the collection of data that are deposited in the information system. It all begins with obtaining and entering the right data, at the right place, at the right time, in an efficient and cost-effective manner.

Second are the processes or analytics used to convert the data into information. People, software, and hardware comprise these processes. **Software** is the term used to describe the instructions, programs, and rules used to process the data into information. **Hardware** is the term used to describe the physical assets used to assist in converting the data into information. In today's world of computers, software is the computer programs and hardware is the computers. Using hardware and software, computers are able to retrieve the required data. This retrieval is often called **data mining**, where data are analyzed to provide answers to questions. With the requested data, data can be converted into information and output created.

Third are outputs. Outputs are the information and decisions that result from converting the data into information. Outputs ultimately determine the value an information system provides a business. Although data, software, and hardware are important parts of any information system, the most visible part of any information system is the outputs.

Today is often called the "Information Revolution." Why? The answer is that information is transforming the way people live and businesses operate. Information and information systems are changing business models and strategies everywhere. Today the world of business is based on information technology.

BUSINESS ANALYTICS

Today technology is changing the world of business like never before. Technology and systems are now capable of gathering huge amounts of data and converting that data into information. This information is empowering businesses to better understand and create value for all its stakeholders.

Business Analytics is the ongoing, methodological exploration of an organization's data to gain new insight to help solve business problems and identify opportunities to create value for the organization's stakeholders. Business analytics is about using data and statistical tools to help understand and predict behavior. With this prediction, a business can operate more efficiently in its drive to create value.

Examples of business analytics are everywhere it the world of business. Think about a retailer's need to understand a customer's wants and needs. With the data, business analytics attempts to predict the customer's future wants and needs. The retailer's marketing mix (product, distribution, price, and promotion) can better focus on the customer. Think about a business' need for good, productive employees. With the data, business analytics can be used to better understand prospective employees and predict which will be most productive. Last, think about a lenders need to better understand a prospective borrower's ability to repay a loan. Once again, business analytics can help model and predict the outcome of this decision.

LEARNING OBJECTIVE 2
. . . .
INFORMATION TECHNOLOGY AND BUSINESS

Information technology (IT) is the term used to describe information systems and how information systems are used. Today, information technology is everywhere. It is transforming how every aspect of business is conducted. Research, marketing, production, accounting, finance, and all other parts of the business world are becoming more efficient and effective because of today's information technologies.

TODAY'S INFORMATION TECHNOLOGIES

At the heart of the evolution of information technology is telecommunications. **Telecommunications** is the term used for transmitting information over distance. Today, the term telecommunications is used to describe computerized information networks. A **network** is a process or system used to transmit and communicate data and information between people and/or organizations. Transmission of data and information can be through telephone wires (**digital subscriber line or DSL**), high-speed fiber-optic lines (**broadband**), or airwaves (**wireless**). Computers and transmission technology have enabled networks to evolve so they now provide large amounts of data and information efficiently and at relatively low cost.

The biggest example of evolution is internets and intranets. An **internet** is an information system between independent organizations. An **intranet** is an information system within an organization. An intranet is often described as a **virtual private network (VPN)**. An **extranet** is an intranet that allows users outside the organization limited access to inside information.

Information networks have created a new way to conduct work. No longer is work confined to a physical space such as a building. Work can now be performed in cyberspace. **Cyberspace** is the term used to describe the flow of information through a network, including the hardware, software, and means of transmitting data. A critical part of today's cyberspace is "the internet."

The Internet

The **Internet**, starting with a capital "I," is the largest public internet. Often called the **NET**, the Internet enables millions of users to provide and access large amounts of data and information. Originally created by the US Department of Defense for military use, the Internet has become a global phenomenon.

Individuals businesses, individuals, and governments cannot access the Internet without the help of an **internet service provider (ISP)**. An ISP is a commercial business or government with permanent access to the Internet. It sells temporary Internet access to the customer for a fee.

The **World Wide Web (www)** is the system used to access the Internet. Anyone who has permanent access or presence on the World Wide Web must provide a **portal**, or point of entry to and exit from the World Wide Web. This portal is often called a **website**. Every website is identified with a unique address, or **Uniform Resource Locator (URL)**. Under this address or URL, a business can store and display information. Typically a business will introduce a user to its website with a **home page**. A home page informs the user what data and information are available and how to retrieve the data and information.

An example is P&G's website, www.pg.com. When you visit P&G's website you start with the company's home page. From there you can navigate to other pages that provide data and information such as a description of the company, a list of its products, and financial information.

The Internet has become an integral part of doing business because of the development of servers and browsers. Servers are computers that provide a service. In the case of the Internet, a **server** contains the information that a business provides through its website. A **browser** is a computer or computer program that permits someone to gain access to the data and information found on websites. Let's look at Google. You turn on your computer and use an ISP to gain access to the Internet. You use a browser such as Internet Explorer to browse the Internet. You then type in www.google.com. What do you see? There is Google's website, located on Google's server.

However, networks are not the only information technology that is transforming how business operates. Decisions once made exclusively by people are now often made or enhanced by various types of information systems throughout the business.

Design and Manufacturing Systems

Think about Hyundai designing and manufacturing an automobile in 1960 versus today. In 1960, Hyundai used state-of-the-art technology. However, it was very labor intensive. Think of a room full of tables with engineers manually drawing designs. Think of craftsmen building prototypes of cars. Think of technicians testing the prototypes for fuel economy, comfort, and other attributes. Then think of an assembly line that produces the automobiles. Think of laborers carefully placing parts together, testing products, and making critical decisions about quality. Now think of today. Today labor is still important, but robots and information systems have taken over.

Today, **computer-aided design (CAD)** is being used to design and test products quickly and efficiently. **Computer-aided manufacturing (CAM)** is being used to plan

Examples of robot-aided manufacturing processes.

and control manufacturing processes. **Computer-integrated manufacturing (CIM)** is combining CAD and CAM to create totally integrated manufacturing processes. Think about how Hyundai uses the output of its CAD as input into its CAM. That's automation today. Today CIMs are increasing the quality of products, lowering the cost of products, and shortening the time needed for production.

Marketing Systems

Think about P&G's Gillette product line. Think about making razor blades in 1950 and today. In 1950, Gillette used state-of-the art technology to estimate what product the market wanted, how to promote the product, how to price the product, and how to distribute or sell the product. However, it was very labor intensive. People gathered the data, recorded the data, analyzed the data, and interpreted the data. People used personal contact, phones, and mail to communicate. Advertising was done with the radio, newspapers, billboards, and a new technology called television.

Today, P&G uses information systems called **Customer Relationship Management (CRM)** systems to provide its sales force timely information on customer needs, product availability, pricing alternatives, and promotion options. Sales personnel stay in constant contact with their business and customers with instant messaging and other technologies. Technology has permitted businesses like P&G to understand and target markets more precisely and efficiently.

Advertising and marketing strategies have changed. New and evolving technologies developed by Google and other businesses have provided more focused outlets for advertising. Likewise the Internet has become the focal point of viral marketing. **Viral marketing** is where a business attempts to get customers to tell friends and family about the business's product. Although not new, viral marketing has boomed with Internet chat rooms and other social networking software.

BUSINESS SENSE

OUTSOURCING

Outsourcing is defined as subcontracting a service to an outside party. There are many pros and cons to outsourcing. However, outsourcing has become a significant practice in today's business world.

Outsourcing is prevalent in the area of information technology. Have you ever bought a product where the manufacturer or retailer promises to provide technical support? Think about buying computer hardware or software. Think about buying electronics. Think about buying products that require assembly. Now think about having problems and calling or emailing for help. Many times the party helping you is not an employee of the business that made or sold the product. That business has outsourced the technical support to another business. The manufacturer or retailer has paid a fee to another business to help with product support. That's outsourcing.

Why has outsourcing become a widespread practice today? The answer is technology. Technology has enabled businesses to outsource services. Why has outsourcing become a global phenomenon? Once again, technology is the answer. The evolution of information systems is a global phenomenon. Information technology has brought the world closer together.

Human Resource Systems

Think about running a retail business such as Target in 1960 and today. In 1960, a retailer would need a human resource department that advertised for, hired, and trained people. The human resource department would then need to schedule the people and coordinate their activities. It would need to manage these people and make sure the right people, were doing the right thing, at the right place, at the right time. It took a lot of people to operate the human resource function.

Now think about the human resource function today at a company like Target. Think about hiring people. Think about efficiently advertising positions, receiving applications over the Internet, and screening which applicants are acceptable and which are not. Think about training and how people can learn more using web-based technologies. Think about **expert systems** that artificially make decisions based on proven rules and logic. Think about using expert systems to decide how many employees should work at a given time and what each employee should do. Think about using computer software called **collaborative learning systems** to help employees work together to solve problems.

Accounting Systems

Per Chapter 08, accounting is the area within a business that recognizes, measures, records, and reports information about a business's transactions. It's hard to imagine that in 1960 businesses such as Target and P&G had to use hundreds of people and millions of sheets of paper to account for transactions.

Today, we're moving to a paperless society where information is more useful. Information is more accurate, complete, and timely. Accountants can create more flexible accounting systems that quickly adapt to the changing needs of all stakeholders, including managers and providers of financial capital. Why? The answer is technology.

Finance Systems

Walk into the offices of the finance department of Target. What do you expect to see? Today, businesses are better able to work with the providers of financial capital (debt and equity). Why? The answer is technology.

Think about working with lenders and shareholders in 1960. It was a long and challenging process to acquire their money and properly use their money to create value. Today, although still challenging, this task has been made easier by information technology. Today, finance departments can instantaneously see how financial markets change. Look at the desk of senior financial managers and see the computer screens that track the price and cost of a business's stock and debt.

Likewise a business can better communicate with investors and thus reduce the risk investors assume by lending to the business or buying its stock. What does that mean? It means investors do not have as high a risk premium and thus charge the business a lower cost of capital. How is this done? Go look at the website of a business like Target and click on "Investor Relations." What do you see? You see a lot of information that investors want and need.

TRANSFORMATION AND EMERGING TECHNOLOGIES

Technology is constantly transforming the world of business. This transformation is the direct result of trying to create value by achieving a competitive advantage. Technology has permitted businesses to create, produce, and market better products at lower costs. Technology is transforming business models and strategies. Think about it. Could Google exist today without today's technology? The answer is no.

Yet transforming business is about change. Change can create great opportunities and great challenges. New or emerging technologies can be disruptive, creating unforeseen problems and risk.

Problems with Transformational and Emerging Technologies

An example of a transformational technology is the Internet. The Internet has permitted people to access large quantities of data and information easily, quickly, and at low cost; it has also destroyed communication barriers. Yet in doing so, problems occur. See Exhibit 16.3.

EXHIBIT 16.3: Some Challenges with Transformational Technology

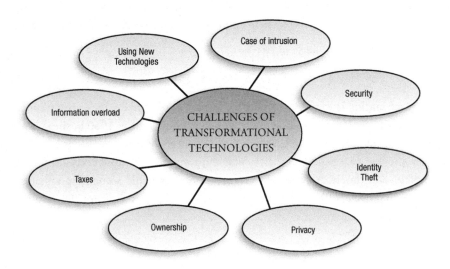

First is information overload. As noted earlier, information overload is where the user has too much information. Too much information can confuse the decision maker. The decision maker must filter the information.

Second is the ease that others can intrude on others. Such intrusive behavior can cause problems. Cookies, adware, and spam are examples of problems caused by the lack of a barrier. **Cookies** are files that permit someone to track what websites a user visits. **Adware** is programs that permit advertisers to send computer users advertisements without the user's permission. **Spam** is unsolicited emails.

Third is security. Spyware, viruses, and hackers are examples of problems caused by the lack of security. **Spyware** is programs that show to outsiders what a computer is doing without the permission of the user of the computer. **Viruses** are computer programs that destroy other computer programs without the consent of the computer user. **Hackers** are outsiders who obtain access to, and thus control of, a computer without the permission of the owner of the computer.

Fourth is identity theft. **Identity theft** is where, using technology such as the Internet, someone can steal another's identity. **Phishing** is a scam where spam emails are sent asking for personal information. The sender impersonates a bank or other trusted relationship seeking the receiver to disclose

An example of a phishing alert on a web browser

information that permits the sender to steal the receiver's identity. That theft permits the sender to go into the receiver's bank accounts, make illegal purchases, and conduct other fraudulent activities.

Fifth is privacy. Privacy deals with an individual's or business's right to withhold information. What should a business or person know about you? What shouldn't a business or person know about you? Should a business be able to track everything you buy, when you buy it, where you buy it, and how you pay for it? Should anyone be able to look at personal emails?

Sixth is ownership of intellectual property such as computer software. Look back at Chapter 07, then look at Chapter 17. A business can own patents, copyrights, and trademarks, often called intellectual property. An example is the proprietary computer software developed by Google used in its Android phones. After you buy an Android phone, do you own or does Google own the software?

Seventh are taxes. When a transaction occurs using the Internet, should it be taxed like similar transactions that do not use the Internet? If so, who should pay the tax, how much tax should be paid, and to whom should the tax be paid?

Eighth is using new technologies, such as the Internet, to conduct illegal acts such as false advertising. Accountability is often hard when buyers and sellers have no physical contact.

Legal and Ethical Issues with Emerging Technologies

It is difficult for business and society to deal with the above problems. Why? First, the problems are global. Without international cooperation, often laws in one country have little impact on the problem. Second, the problems are constantly evolving. As new technologies emerge, new opportunities are created to disrupt and defraud.

Regardless of how difficult, there is always a need to address the abuse of technology. Let's look at some examples.

First is security. Most networks require some form of identification for use. Only approved users can use a network. Approved users are required to have **passwords** and/or **personal identification numbers (PINs)** to enter and use an information system. **Firewalls**, programs on computers that limit access, are often needed to protect computers and computer users from spyware, viruses, and hackers. Last, businesses often use encryption to protect data and information. **Encryption** is the process of transforming easily understood data and information into coded and unintelligible data. Only with the code can someone use the original data and information.

Second is privacy. Privacy starts with security. However, even if security is breached, are there limits to what someone can and cannot do with information? Recently, the US courts found that the Fourth Amendment of the US Constitution protected emails from unlawful search.

Third is ownership of intellectual property. The US Patent and Trademark Office enforces laws that protect trademarks, copyrights, and patents on information systems and other technologies. Trademarks, copyrights, and patents are explored in Chapter 17.

Fourth is using technology, such as the Internet, to conduct illegal activities. The US Federal Trade Commission (FTC) is charged with regulating business conducted on the Internet. The FTC enforces laws regarding false advertising and laws that prohibit senders of spam from sending spam to recipients who have requested not to receive such emails **(CAN-SPAM Act of 2003)**.

ETHICS AND THE INTERNET

Ethics is about trust. Can we trust each other to do what is right? Can we trust ourselves to do what is right? Although the answer should be yes, in practice this is often a challenge that technology has made more difficult. Why? The answer is the lack of human contact makes unethical behavior easier.

Let's look at a personal example. Let's look at using a chat room or some other technology that connects people without personal contact. Someone asks you to describe yourself. Do you tell him or her only the good and flattering things? Or do you give him or her a complete picture of your strengths and weaknesses? Do you fully recognize and accept the consequences for half-truths or little white lies? Do you rationalize that it's okay to be deceptive because everyone does it? Do you stretch the truth because you probably will never see the other party in person? What's ethical?

Let's look at a business example. Is it ethical for an employee to use a business's computer and ISP to surf the Internet during his or her lunch hour? How about emailing friends and family using a business's computer? Does an employee have the right to get upset when a business censors his or her personal emails sent using the business's computer? Think about it. These are questions of ethics.

Fifth are taxes. In the US, profits are taxed by the federal and state governments. The tax is paid where the taxed is deemed to have been earned. But what about sales? Each state has its own set of rules for applying sales tax. Whether or not sales tax applies to a sale conducted over the internet depends in most cases on the seller's presence in the state.

So the law is trying to catch up to emerging technologies. As noted in Chapter 07, laws are only the lowest level of acceptable behavior within a society. But do our laws reflect how we expect responsible members of society to act? Remember that ethical behavior is how we expect people and businesses to behave. Law is how we require people and businesses to behave.

Today, information systems and other technologies are an integral and necessary part of the business world. Yet, because of identity theft, hackers, and other noted challenges, billions of dollars are wasted each year because users cannot trust such systems and technologies. Today, businesses are making the use of systems and technologies a significant part of their code of ethics. Whether based on principles, rules, or a combination, a business's code of ethics cannot avoid addressing ethics regarding the use of technology.

So business is changing. Information systems and new technologies have revolutionized business. How business creates, produces, and markets products has changed.

LEARNING OBJECTIVE 3
. . . .
E-BUSINESS

How a business acquires and manages its assets, people, and money has changed. Many of today's businesses have become E-businesses. **E-business,** or electronic business, is the term used to describe businesses that use information and communication technologies to support marketing, production, finance, and the other functions of business. In E-business, information systems are integral parts of a business's model and strategy, as well as its value chain and competitive advantage.

A good example of an E-business is Google. Look at Google's business model and strategy. Google's model, strategy, product, and value chain center on information systems. In fact, Google's competitive advantage is that it has become an integral part of the information systems of others. How often do you hear people who are seeking information say, "Just Google it"?

E-business involves every aspect of the business. However, the most visible part of E-business is the generation of revenue or sales. This brings us to E-commerce.

E-COMMERCE AND E-TAILING

E-commerce is the term used for the buying and selling of products over networks such as the Internet. Retailers that sell over the Internet are often called E-tailers.

When you think of Target, what do you envision? We probably envision a retailer that sells products in buildings. Now go to Target's website. What do you see? You see the traditional retailer that advertises its locations. But you also see an E-tailer that sells products over the Internet. All you need to do is search through Target's product line, click your selection, pay, and Target will deliver the product to your address.

Traditional modes of selling products are often called high-touch modes; Target uses the high-touch mode in its traditional stores. E-commerce modes are often called high-tech. Target's website facilitates its high-tech alternative. Today, the world is gradually moving from high-touch to high-tech modes. However, the movement has not been easy or revolutionary. It's been and will continue to be gradual and evolutionary. During the late 1990s companies that bought and sold products on the Internet blossomed. However, many failed because customers were not ready to change their buying habits from 100% high-touch to 100% high-tech. The failure of these businesses was called the "dot-com bust."

Today, E-commerce is everywhere. E-commerce facilitates sales between business and consumers (B2C), between businesses (B2B), between business and government (B2G), and even between consumers (C2C).

CHAPTER SUMMARY

In this chapter we've explored how information and technology are changing the world of business. We've explored the opportunities and challenges created by emerging and evolving technologies.

After reading this chapter, you should be able to:

1. Understand the nature and importance of information and information systems in operating a business (Learning Objective 1): An information system (IS) is a system that uses people and processes to convert data into information with analytics.
2. Appreciate the role of information technology in operating a business (Learning Objective 2): Information systems and technology are transforming every aspect of business. The information revolution is creating opportunities and challenges for the world of business.
3. Appreciate the evolutionary changes in business called E-business and E-commerce (Learning Objective 3): E-business, or electronic business, is the term used to describe businesses that use information and communication technologies to support marketing, production, finance, and the other functions of business. E-commerce is the term used for the buying and selling of products over networks such as the Internet.

In this chapter we've explored these questions and issues. Now it's time to look at the how a business acquires its money through both debt and equity. Technology, along with people and assets, are not cheap. It takes money to acquire resources. Money is a significant part of "How Business Works."

KEYWORDS

adware 348
analytics 340
broadband 344
browser 345
Business Analytics 344
CAN-SPAM Act of 2003 349
collaborative learning systems 347
Computer-Aided Design (CAD) 345
Computer-Aided Manufacturing (CAM) 345
Computer-Integrated Manufacturing (CIM) 346
cookies 348
Customer Relationship Management (CRM) 346
cyberspace 345
data 340
data mining 343
database 343

digital subscriber line (DSL) 344
E-business 350
E-commerce 351
encryption 349
E-tailers 351
expert systems 347
extranet 344
firewalls 349
hackers 348
hardware 343
home page 345
identity theft 348
information 340
information architecture 343
information overload 341
Information Systems (IS) 343
Information Technology (IT) 344
internet service provider (ISP) 345
intranet 344

management information systems (MIS) 343
network 344
passwords 349
personal identification numbers (PINs) 349
phishing 348
portal 345
server 345
software 343
spam 348
spyware 348
telecommunications 344
Uniform Resource Locator (URL) 345
viral marketing 346
virtual private network (VPN) 344
viruses 348
website 345
World Wide Web (www) 345

SHORT-ANSWER QUESTIONS

1. What are data, analytics, and information? How do data become information?
2. What are information systems? What comprises an information system?
3. What makes information valuable?
4. Define the following terms:
   a. Data
   b. Analytics
   c. Information
   d. Information overload
   e. Information systems (IS)
   f. Management of information systems (MIS)
   g. Information architecture
   h. Database
   i. Software
   j. Hardware
   k. Data mining
   l. Business Analytics
   m. Information technology (IT)
   n. Telecommunications
   o. Network
   p. Digital subscriber line (DSL)
   q. Broadband
   r. Wireless
   s. Internet
   t. Intranet
   u. Virtual private network (VPN)
   v. Extranet
   w. Cyberspace
   x. Internet (NET)
   y. Internet service provider (ISP)
   z. World wide web (www)
   aa. Portal

ab. Website
ac. Uniform resource locator (URL)
ad. Home page
ae. Server
af. Browser
ag. Computer-aided design (CAD)
ah. Computer-aided manufacturing (CAM)
ai. Computer-integrated manufacturing (CIM)
aj. Customer relationship management (CRM)
ak. Viral marketing
al. Outsourcing
am. Expert system
an. Collaborative learning system
ao. Cookies
ap. Adware

aq. Spam
ar. Spyware
as. Viruses
at. Hacker
au. Identity theft
av. Phishing
aw. Password
ax. Private identification number (PIN)
ay. Firewall
az. Encryption
ba. CAN-SPAM Act of 2003
bb. E-business
bc. E-commerce
bd. E-tailers

CRITICAL-THINKING QUESTIONS

1. How has the information revolution affected what you buy and how you buy it? Give examples and explain.
2. What are the legal and ethical issues facing E-business and E-commerce? Give examples and explain.
3. How has the information revolution lowered and increased risk?
4. Dream about the future. What technology innovations do you see in the future? How will these innovations affect business?

EXPLORING REAL BUSINESS

Go to the websites of Google, Target, Hyundai, and Procter & Gamble. The websites are

Google:	http://investor.google.com
Target:	http://www.target.com
Hyundai:	http://worldwide.hyundai.com/company-overview
Procter & Gamble:	http://www.pg.com

1. How do you think information systems and technologies impact each company? Give examples and explain your answers.
2. Describe how E-business and E-commerce are impacting each company.

CHAPTER

17

OPPORTUNITIES AND CHALLENGES IN MANAGING PEOPLE

Introduction: Let's Talk About People

People are ultimately what make a business work and as such, are at the heart of any successful business. Yet managing people is not easy. So how does a business use people to create value? How does a business determine who to hire, train, and retain? How does a business motivate employees to be productive?

In this chapter we'll explore these questions and issues. We'll explore the critical opportunities and challenges in managing the human capital of a business. We'll explore how these topics are key considerations in "How Business Works."

LEARNING OBJECTIVES

After reading Chapter 17, you should be able to meet the following learning objectives:

1. Appreciate the nature and importance of the human resource function
2. Appreciate the challenges and techniques of motivating employees
3. Appreciate the different means of compensating employees
4. Appreciate the challenges and opportunities in employer-employee relationships

WHY PEOPLE MATTER

People are the heart of any business. A business needs assets and money. But above all else, it needs good people to manage and work in the business. People ultimately make and implement the decisions of what the business will produce, what people the business will employ, what assets the business will acquire and use, and how to finance the business. The employees of a business are its most important resource. A business is only as good as its people. Creating value is first about people. People matter.

LEARNING OBJECTIVE 1
. . . .
HUMAN RESOURCES: THE HEART OF THE BUSINESS

Hiring, training, motivating, and retaining good employees is the single most important decision and opportunity a business faces. Yet hiring, training, motivating, and retaining employees are also a big challenge. It is often said that managing people is the most challenging aspect of managing any business. Why? The answer is that people are complex and people are different. Close your eyes and think about yourself. Are you simple to understand? The answer for most people is no.

A good manager must first clearly define the job his or her employees need to do. But a good manager must also work hard to motivate his or her employees to do the right thing at the right time. This task starts with understanding people. This task is the responsibility of the human resource department or function.

THE HUMAN RESOURCE FUNCTION

A business's **human resource function (HR)** is responsible for the business's employees. This includes assessing the needs of the business for employees, recruiting and hiring the right employees, training employees, evaluating employees, motivating employees, and compensating employees. Some businesses have a single HR department while other businesses have an HR function within each department of the business.

EXHIBIT 17.1: The Human Resource Function

Assessing the Needs of the Business

HR must first understand the business. That starts with understanding the business's model and strategy and how the business is organized to compete and create value. Look back into Chapter 03.

HR must then work with the other parts of the business or departments to understand the needs of each part. The needs include the quantity of people, the skills each person needs, and the timing of when people are needed. The task is often called a **job analysis** or **staffing analysis**.

Besides analyzing current needs, HR must also look at the business's future needs. HR must estimate how employees will progress through the organization. Some employees will remain with the business at their current position. Some employees will move to other positions, either as lateral moves or a promotions. Some employees will leave the organization. This future perspective is often called **succession planning**. HR must ensure the business has the correct number and quality of people now and in the future.

Next, HR must prepare a job description and job specification. A **job description** is what the employee is expected to do. A job description details the employee's responsibilities. A **job specification** lists the qualities the employee must possess to be considered for the job. Such qualities include personal qualities, work experience, and education.

Finding and Recruiting the Right Employees

After developing a job description and specification, HR must then advertise that the business is in need of employees. HR must recruit an applicant pool of prospective employees. This pool may be internal (current employees) or external to the business. HR must advertise the job position using the job description and job specifications. HR may choose to use newspapers, radio, television, emails, or on-line services.

HR may also use businesses and governmental agencies that specialize in finding employees for others. These businesses are called **employment agencies**. Employment agencies that specialize in finding applicants for management positions are often called **executive search firms**. Slang for an executive search firm is a **head hunter**.

Hiring the Right Employees

To apply for a job, applicants must complete an application and/or provide a resume. An **employment application** is a document, created by the business, which the applicant completes to provide information requested by the business. This information includes addresses, work experience, education, and special talents or abilities. Applications typically request references, both personal and work related. A **resume** is a document created by the applicant that lists his or her current address and contact information, work experience and history, education, and special talents or abilities.

HR then reviews the applications and/or resumes, eliminating applicants who do not meet the job specifications. HR then selects those applicants who best meet the needs of the business. Applicants are notified and interviews arranged.

During the interview, the interviewer wants to make sure the applicant fully understands the expectations of the business. The interviewer then needs to assess whether or not the applicant can meet those expectations. Does the applicant have the needed technical skills? In addition, does the applicant have the needed personal skills? Such skills include communication, team orientation, personal appearance, time management, organization, dependability, and trustworthiness. Interviewing prospective

MONSTER.COM AND SUCH

Where do businesses go to find employees today? Where do prospective employees go to find jobs? Today, more and more employers and applicants are using Internet services that quickly and efficiently communicate and match employer and employee needs. Such a service is provided by businesses like Monster.com.

Think about the benefits that technology provides for both employers and employees. Such services reduce time, uncertainty, and cost. Such services add value.

employees is challenging. Look at the following website for tips on how to be a good interviewer: (http://www.ehow.com/how_2091029_interview-prospective-employee.html).

Different businesses use different techniques during an interview. Some businesses like structured interviews with a well-scripted process. Some businesses prefer a less structured and more informal interview. Some businesses structure the interview as a question-and-answer period. Some businesses like a situational interview where the applicant is put into situations to see if he or she can perform the needed tasks.

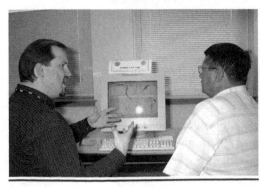

A recent college graduate in a job interview.

In addition to the interview or set of interviews, applicants are often tested. Tests can be technical or behavioral. Technical skills relate to doing specific tasks the employee must perform. Examples are math skills, computer skills, and manual skills such as operating equipment. Behavioral skills relate to how an employee will act in certain situations. Examples of behavioral skills are decision-making in uncertain times, managing stress during conflicts, and working with others in teams.

Last, businesses often conduct background checks to make sure the applicant is truthful and meets the requirements of the job. Such background checks include contacting references and former employers and may also include contacting law enforcement agencies, credit agencies, and agencies that specialize in investigating an applicant's past.

HR then selects the best applicant for the job. The decision must be communicated to the applicant and all others within the business who are affected by the decision. The applicant is made an offer of employment, clearly communicating the terms and expectations for employment. The terms of employment include job requirements, starting date, salary, benefits such as health care, and when the applicant must accept or decline the offer of employment.

A manager training a new employee.

Hiring the right employee is critical. The business and employee must both feel that each is receiving value. Creating value for the business is dependent on having the right person, doing the right thing, at the right time. Hiring the wrong person can be destructive to an organization's productivity. However, hiring the wrong employee is also costly. Why? Think of all the money that is spent on advertising, interviewing, and selecting the right person. Then think about the money that the business will spend on training the employee. Last, if needed, think of all the money the business must spend to terminate an employee. Hiring the wrong employee hurts productivity and is very expensive. Businesses must be very careful in hiring employees.

Training Employees

Training is critical. First, it ensures employees understand what is expected. Second, it provides employees the skills needed to be successful. Third, it provides a basis of evaluating the employee's performance.

Training can take many forms. Training may occur in formal, classroom settings. Training may occur using printed materials, webcasts, and videos. Training may occur through mentoring by senior employees. A **mentor** is an experienced employee who becomes a coach or advisor to a new or subordinate employee. Last, training may occur by experiencing the job, or **on-the-job training**. Such training entails a manager or co-worker showing the employee what to do in the actual work setting.

Training begins with orientation. **Orientation** is where the employee is instructed in the business's policies and procedures. Training then progresses to technical or skill-based training. Often this is called **employee training**. Training of management is often called management development. **Management development training** deals with the business' policies and procedures for planning, executing, and reviewing.

Evaluating Employees

Evaluating employees is an important part of the HR function. First, employees should always understand if they are meeting expectations. How can employees improve if they are not informed? Second, as noted later, evaluation is a major employee motivator. It is a time to address employee uncertainty, which can detract from their productivity. Third, evaluation permits the business to assess the employee's contribution to value. It is a time to reward good performance and correct problems. If change is needed, evaluation gives the business the opportunity to make such changes.

The typical process of evaluating an employee entails five steps, all revolving around the management process of planning, executing, and reviewing. First, the criteria for performance must be established. This should be done and communicated to the employee before the employee starts to work. Second, information is gathered on whether or not the employee is meeting the established criteria. Third, the information is analyzed. Fourth, the employee's supervisor or superior communicates the findings

EXHIBIT 17.2: The Evaluation Process

360-DEGREE EVALUATIONS

When most people think about an evaluation, they think of a supervisor, sitting down with a subordinate, judging performance in a confrontational manner. The supervisor compares the desired performance with the actual performance and makes critical decisions such as pay, promotion, or termination. Yet the ultimate reason for evaluation is to help an employee perform better in the future. The past is over and cannot be changed. What can be changed is the future.

Understanding this, many businesses use a process called a 360-degree evaluation. A 360-degree evaluation is where the employee is evaluated by subordinates, coworkers, and superiors. A 360-degree evaluation may even include customers and suppliers with whom the employee works. Think of the geometry of a circle. A circle has 360 degrees. A 360-degree evaluation gives employees insight in how they are perceived by everyone with whom they work. It enables the employees to see how they can enhance their performance in every aspect of their job. The final evaluation is presented to the employee by his or her supervisor, but the evaluation is based on input from all parties with whom the employee interacts.

to the employee, verbally and/or in writing. Fifth, the employee and supervisor must then use the performance appraisal to establish future plans.

Evaluating employees is difficult. How does someone assess whether someone else is doing a good or bad job? First, performance criteria should be objective and measurable when possible. Such measures include sales, customer surveys, profits, production quotas, and number of defects. Second, the method for gathering information and measuring performance should be unbiased and consistent. Information should be gathered to create a fair and complete picture of the employee's performance. Performance criteria and measures of performance should not change from one period to another without a good reason. Third, performance evaluations should be timely. Employees are owed timely evaluations. Last, employees should clearly understand the criteria and methods used to evaluate their performance. How can employees be held accountable if they do not understand the ramifications of their actions?

The methods used to gather data, analyze data, and assess employee performance vary. Some methods rely on subjective information such as interviews and observations. Some methods rely on objective information such as surveys, recorded sales, products rejected due to inadequate quality, or customer complaints. Some methods use a single evaluator. Some methods use multiple evaluators.

LEARNING OBJECTIVE 2
. . . .
MOTIVATING EMPLOYEES

Motivating employees is an important part of any business. Have you ever gone into a business where employees seem happy to be at work? You see productive people making great products and delivering great service. Have you ever gone into a business where employees are not happy? When you see people who dread coming to work, you often find poor products and service.

So how do you motivate high performance? Why do people work, and what motivates them to perform to the best of their ability? The answer is complex because people are complex. Before we look at key motivators such as compensation, let's look at the behavioral theories used in business.

THEORIES OF EMPLOYEE BEHAVIOR

Understanding employee behavior is based in psychology. Theories have evolved as the study of psychology has evolved.

Expectancy Theory

Expectancy Theory[1] states that employees are motivated by the expectation of reward. If an employee works hard and performs well, then the employee expects to be rewarded. To motivate an employee to perform, a business must clearly communicate how performance will be measured and rewarded. If the employee performs at the specified level, then the business must reward the employee.

Think about it. You go to work. Your supervisor tells you you'll get a raise if you work hard and do a great job. You work hard and outperform every measure given you. However your supervisor informs you will not get a raise or promotion. You ask why. Your supervisor tells you there were other criteria, not told to you, that were used to determine raises and promotions. How would you feel? Could you trust your employer in the future? Would you be motivated to work hard in the future? The answer is probably not.

Equity Theory

Equity Theory[2] states that employees are motivated to perform only if they believe the value they receive is fair compensation compared to the compensation of others. Equity theory states that employees compare compensation and rewards, and expect equal pay for equal work. If they do not receive equal compensation and/or rewards, they are not motivated. It's a matter of perceived fairness.

Think about it. You go to work. However, you find out that you are paid less than someone who is doing the same job or less. How do you feel? Are you motivated to work hard and perform to your best? The answer is probably not.

Maslow's Hierarchy of Needs

Remember **Maslow's Hierarchy of Needs**[3] in Chapter 12? Employees are people too. Review Exhibit 12.5 and think how employees have different needs. Think how businesses motivate employees by meeting the physiological needs first, safety needs second, social needs third, esteem needs fourth, and self-actualization needs last. Salary helps an employee meet his or her physical needs such as food and shelter. Salary and other benefits, such as health care, provide the employee financial security and safety. But after those needs are met, what counts? Does the work environment provide employees a place to meet their social needs? Do employees like where they work because of the culture, physical environment, and other colleagues? Are employees proud of where they work? Last, do employees feel they are a valued part of the business?

A productive team working in an open office environment.

Think about it. Ideally all jobs would meet all the needs of every employee. However employees and businesses must recognize that employees prioritize their needs. Different employees are motivated by different needs. Whether or not a job helps an employee's esteem is not very relevant if the employee does not earn enough money to eat. Yet a highly paid manager may deem a large office, an impressive title, or longer vacations to be more of a motivator than an increase in salary.

Herzberg's Two-Factor Theory of Motivation

Fredrick Herzberg[4], a psychologist, conducted studies and found motivators that affect employee performance fall into two groups, motivational factors and hygiene factors. Hygiene factors, often called maintenance factors, include pay, job security, and interpersonal relationships. The absence of hygiene factors causes problems and job dissatisfaction. The presence of these factors, however, did not ensure job satisfaction. So what motivates job satisfaction? Herzberg believes it is motivational factors. Motivational factors include the work itself, the sense of achievement, recognition, a feeling of growth, and responsibility.

In comparing Maslow's Hierarchy of Needs and Herzberg's Two-Factor Theory of Motivation, certain similarities appear. Both theories view physical, safety, and social needs to be important and necessary for motivating an employee to perform. However, the existence of such hygiene factors is not sufficient to produce highly productive employees. Esteem and self-actualization are needed to motivate an employee to excel. Business needs to meet the hygiene needs of its employees. However to compete at the highest level, businesses must also meet the motivational needs of its employees.

Think about it. A miner wants to be safe and will not work in an unsafe mine. Safety is necessary. But is that all a miner expects? How about being recognized for high performance? How about feeling important and valued? How about the prospect of being promoted?

McGregor's Theory X and Theory Y

Douglas McGregor[5] observed that managers manage employees under one of two groups of assumptions. The first group of assumptions is called Theory X. Theory X managers assume:

1. Employees typically dislike work.

2. To get employees to work, they must be forced, controlled, and often threatened with punishment.

3. Employees typically prefer to be directed and controlled, as they avoid responsibility.

4. Employees are motivated primarily with fear and money.

The second group of assumptions is called Theory Y. Theory Y managers assume:

1. Employees like to work.

2. Employees work best with they are committed to the goals of the work.

3. Employees' commitment to work is a function of the rewards they perceive from doing the work.

4. Employees often seek responsibility.

5. Employees are capable of being creative and imaginative in solving problems and making decisions.

6. Most businesses realize only a part of an employee's potential value.

7. Different employees are motivated by different rewards.

Theory X managers create an organization that controls employees. Strict and rigid rules are important to Theory X managers. Creativity is not rewarded. In contrast, Theory Y managers are more flexible, seeking input from employees to opportunities and challenges.

Think about it. Do you think that some organizations work better with strict control, requiring employees perform certain tasks, at certain times, and not to show initiative? How about working on an assembly line? Do you think some organizations need employees to take initiative and use creativity to deliver valued products? How about an art gallery? Do you think there are businesses that need a blend of Theory X and Theory Y?

A SUMMARY VIEW OF MOTIVATION

People are complex. Business is complex. This complexity makes motivating employees a significant challenge. Different people, in different situations, are motivated by different things. That's why managing people is a big challenge for any business. Regardless of what theory a manager uses, there is one consistent factor that is important. That's compensation.

LEARNING OBJECTIVE 3
. . . .
COMPENSATING EMPLOYEES

Compensating employees is critical. Employees need to feel the labor they give to a business is being fairly compensated. The most visible measure of value received by an employee is compensation. Yet the business must also feel the value of the employee's labor is worth the cost of the compensation. So what is compensation? Compensation is more than a paycheck. Compensation deals with benefits paid directly to the employee in cash, fringe benefits, work–life arrangements, and non-cash compensation.

CASH COMPENSATION

Cash compensation can come in different forms, including salary, commission, and profit sharing.

Salary

Salary is the cash payment employees receive for their labor, from their employer. **Gross pay** is the compensation the business agrees to pay employees for their work. **Net pay** is the amount received by the employee, and is gross pay less deductions for taxes and other items.

Salary may be fixed or hourly. A **fixed salary** is paid on a fixed basis, where the employee is paid a stated amount per pay period, regardless of the hours worked. An **hourly salary** is paid based on the hours worked by the employee. The employee is paid a fixed rate per hour, but her or his salary is a function of the hours she or he works. The more hours the employee works, the more salary he or she receives. It is said the employee is an hourly employee.

Commissions and Similar Pay Arrangements

Commissions are another form of cash compensation. Some businesses pay employees based on physical output such as sales or units produced. A **commission** is where a person is paid a percentage of sales. When employees are paid per units produced, it is often referred to as **piece-goods work**.

Profit Sharing

Cash compensation may also be paid in the form of a profit-sharing plan. **Profit sharing** is where an employee is paid a percentage of the business's profits. Profits may be computed using the profits of the total business or part of a business such as a division.

FRINGE BENEFITS

Fringe benefits relate to employee benefits such as sick pay, vacation pay, maternity or paternity leave, health insurance, life insurance, and retirement benefits. Such benefits can be important to employees but are also expensive for businesses to provide. Think about it. When a business pays an employee on vacation, it costs the business money. When a business pays an employee who is out sick or on leave to have a new child, it costs the business money. When a business provides health care, retirement programs, and other fringe benefits, it costs the business money. Per the US Labor Department, fringe benefits accounted for over 30% of the total compensation earned by US workers. Let's look at several typical and important fringe benefits.

Health Care

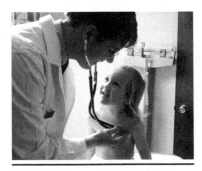

Family health care benefits are often available through employers.

Health care benefits pay selected medical costs. Not all businesses provide health care to their employees. Why? The answer is that health care is expensive. Treating medical conditions is costly. If the business provides health care benefits, it can either purchase health care insurance or pay for health care benefits directly.

In 2010 the US passed a law requiring that everyone have access to basic, affordable health care. The law is the **Patient Protection and Affordable Care Act of 2010**. The law requires businesses that employ more than 50 permanent employees to provide basic health benefits to its current employees. The law also requires that all low income individuals, regardless of employment status, have access to affordable health insurance.

The extent and terms of health care coverage differ between employers. Each business sets the benefits to which employees are entitled. The more extensive the coverage, the greater the costs. That's why different health plans at different businesses cover different illnesses and conditions, have different limits, and require employees to pay differing parts of the cost of the insurance. Some health plans cover the basics such as access to doctors when ill, hospitalization in case of major illness or injury, and life sustaining prescriptions and require employees to pay differing costs. Some health care plans go beyond the basics to include elective surgery, wellness programs such as gym membership, and preventive programs, such as annual check-ups with doctors.

A business may choose not to provide health care benefits to its retirees by buying health insurance or paying benefits directly. If it does not choose to do so, retirees are eligible for health care benefits provided by Medicare or Medicaid. Retirees are entitled to Medicare when they reach the age of 65. **Medicare** is a health insurance program provided by the US government for retirees that have sufficient money to pay for part of their health care costs. **Medicaid** is a health insurance program provided by the US government for retirees and others that do not have sufficient money to pay for part of their health care costs. The US government gets the money to fund Medicare and Medicaid through a tax on employers.

Retirement Programs

Next are retirement programs. There are two basic types of retirement programs that directly affect a business and its employees.

First is **Social Security**, a US government-sponsored plan. (Social Security taxes are withheld from the employee's paycheck.) Employees and employers pay a percentage of the employee's gross salary to the government. In return, employees receive a calculated payment when they retire at the age of 62 or after. The higher an employee's salary, the more social security tax the employee and employer pay, and the more the US government pays the employee when the employee retires.

Second, there are employer-sponsored retirement programs. Most employer-sponsored plans are regulated by the US government under the **Employment Retirement Income Security Act of 1974 (ERISA)**. Employer-sponsored plans are either defined contribution plans or defined benefit plans.

A **defined contribution plan** is a company-sponsored retirement plan where the business and/or employees contribute money to a special fund each pay period. The money is invested at the direction of the employee and earns a return. Amounts contributed and earned are the property of the employee and can be used when the employee retires. Have you ever heard of 401K plans? A 401K plan is a defined contribution plan.

A **defined benefit plan** is a company-sponsored retirement plan that guarantees the retiree a monthly income, every month, for the rest of his or her life. The business must estimate when the employee will retire, how long the retired employee will live, and how much the retiree will receive during each year of his or her retirement. The business must then contribute adequate money to a retirement fund that will pay the retirement benefits.

Unemployment Compensation

Businesses in the US pay a tax, based on an employee's compensation, to the US government to provide unemployment benefits. When an employee is dismissed because of lack of work, at no fault of the employee, the employee can apply for and receive **unemployment benefits** for a designated number of weeks. Unemployment compensation is paid for 26 weeks but can be extended up to an additional 20 weeks. Although limited, these benefits are intended to help the unemployed employee during the period he or she is seeking another job.

WORK–LIFE ARRANGEMENTS

Employers often provide employees special work–life benefits. These benefits include:

- Job sharing
- Flex time
- Dependent care
- Educational benefits
- Telecommuting

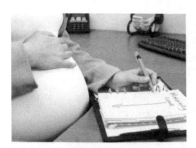

- Vacation pay

- Maternity or paternity leave

- Sick pay

- Sick leave

Job sharing occurs when two or more employees do the work of one full-time employee. **Flex time** occurs when an employee can determine his or her own work schedule. **Dependent care** is when the business provides care for children, elderly parents, or other dependents of the employee. **Educational benefits** are when a business provides employees training or pays for outside education such as college and technical schools. **Telecommuting** is when an employee can use technology to work at home. **Vacation pay** occurs when an employee is paid for days that the employee is relaxing and enjoying pursuits other than work. **Maternity or paternity leave** is when a business permits an employee to not work because of a baby. Maternity or paternity leave may or may not be compensated. **Sick pay** occurs when an employee is paid for days an employee is ill and cannot work. **Sick leave** is the time an employee is not required to work due to an illness. However sick leave may or may not be compensated.

PAYING FOR PERFORMANCE, EXECUTIVE COMPENSATION, AND EXCESS

Think about an ideal compensation system. Such a system would first measure the value an employee contributes to the business. Second, such a system would compensate the employee based on this value. The higher the value contributed to the business, the higher the business would compensate the employee. Such a system is often called performance pay.

Now think if such a system is possible or easy. The answer is sometimes yes and sometimes no. Why? The answer is that the value of an employee to the business is sometimes easy to measure and sometimes hard to measure. An example where it is easy to measure an employee's value is with a commissioned salesperson. The more sales the person makes, the greater the value he or she is to the business and the higher his or her compensation. An example where it is not easy to measure an employee's value is with an accountant. An accountant adds critical value, but that value is hard to measure directly.

So how would you compensate a senior executive such as the president of a business? Is performance pay possible? How would you measure his or her performance? Let's start with his or her job description. As an agent of the business's owners, his or her job is run the entire business in such a way that increases owners' value. If he or she does a good job, the value will increase. If he or she does a bad job, the value will decrease. So doesn't it make sense that a senior executive would be compensated on the performance of a business's stock? That's the reason so many executives of large, publicly traded businesses receive stock options. It's performance pay. The more value they create for owners, the more compensation they receive.

Yet is there a limit on how much a senior executive should receive in compensation? There is a debate on this issue. The debate is all about performance pay. Should an executive receive high levels of compensation when the business he or she manages is not creating value? Is there a limit to how much any executive is worth? Can executives be overcompensated?

NON-CASH COMPENSATION

Two common examples of **non-cash compensation** are employee stock options and golden parachutes.

Employee Stock Options

Businesses can compensate employees by giving employees the ability to buy the stock of the business at reduced prices; this is known as stock options. Stock options are a popular way of compensating senior management for increasing the value of the business. Look back to Chapter 11. Employee stock options are call options.

Golden Parachutes

Golden parachutes are payments made as part of termination agreements. Per the agreement, the business pays the manager a given sum of money if the manager is dismissed.

DESIGNING A COMPENSATION PACKAGE

Compensating employees is about motivating employees to provide value to the business. First, the compensation should cost the business less than the value provided by the employee. Second, the employee should believe her or his compensation is fair and meets her or his needs better than any other alternative. The compensation should motivate the employee to do her or his best.

Sometimes it's difficult to simultaneously achieve these two objectives. Different employees have different needs. Think about it. Wouldn't you expect that a single salesperson, age 25, would seek a different compensation package from a married accountant, age 45, with two children in high school?

To help with this challenge, businesses sometimes provide employees options regarding cash compensation, fringe benefits, work–life arrangements, and non-cash compensation. Employees are given limits and choose from an assortment of alternatives. Such compensation plans are called **cafeteria plans** because employees can select items to create a package that best meets their needs.

LEARNING OBJECTIVE 4
. . . .
EMPLOYER-EMPLOYEE RELATIONSHIPS

Managing people is important. Nothing in a business is more important than people. Yet managing people can also be challenging due to several factors. Three particular areas of interest are relations with organized labor, laws affecting employment, and terminating employees.

ORGANIZED LABOR

Employees have often sought to organize so they can collectively bargain with a business for compensation, working conditions, job security, and other related issues. A **union** is a legal organization that employees join and empower to represent them in negotiating with an employer. When the supply of labor exceeds the demand for labor, employees often feel helpless as individuals. So what do they do? They organize so their individual voices can come together and exert power in negotiating with employers. As can be imagined, unions can sometimes be a challenge for business. However unions can also be a means for a business to create strong employer–employee relationships.

EXHIBIT 17.3: 2014 Membership in the Major Unions of the US – 2015

Members	Union
2,952,972	National Education Association of the United States
1,613,448	American Federation of Teachers
1,305,128	American Federation of State, County, and Municipal Employees
1,271,150	United Food and Commercial Workers International Union
662,175	International Brotherhood of Electrical Workers
628,413	Communications Workers of America
536,787	Laborers' International Union of North America
330,556	United Association of Journeymen and Apprentices of the Plumbing and Pipe-Fitting Industry of the U.S. and Canada
298,765	International Association of Fire Fighters
291,278	Maritime Trades Department
278,297	National Association of Letter Carriers
237,561	Screen Actors Guild – American Federation of Television and Radio Artists
192,601	Amalgamated Transit Union
128,314	International Association of Bridge, Structural, Ornamental and Reinforcing Iron Workers
122,139	International Alliance of Theatrical Stage Employees
116,691	Transport Workers Union of America
107,067	International Union of Painters and Allied Trades
105,620	National Rural Letter Carriers Association
104,975	Office and Professional Employees International Union
60,303	International Federation of Professional & Technical Engineers

Source: http://kcerds.dol-esa.gov/query/getOrgQry.do

The History of Unions

Unions are not new. Unions in the US have been around since the mid-nineteenth century. The earliest significant labor union was called the **Knights of Labor**. Founded in 1869, the Knights of Labor sought to improve society by making businesses and employees behave in a more moral and responsible fashion. In 1886, Samuel Gompers and several leaders of the Knights of Labor created a new organization called the **American Federation of Labor (AFL)**. The AFL sought to improve working conditions and the standard of living for workers. The AFL embraced the practice of strikes to accomplish its goals. A **strike** is where union members refuse to work until their demands are met or an agreement is reached.

Samuel Gompers in the office of the American Federation of Labor, 1887.

During the 1930s, many unions were created that focused on the needs of workers in specific industries, such as steel, mining, communications, and manufacturing. Often called industrial unions, these unions eventually joined together to form the **Congress of Industrial Organizations (CIO)**. In 1955, the AFL and CIO merged to become the **AFL-CIO**.

Today, the power of unions is real, but diminishing. US businesses are using less union labor today because of many factors. These factors include a shift to a service-based economy from a manufacturing-based economy, improved working conditions, and better compensation. Look at Exhibits 17.4 and 17.5. Look at some of the unions that exist today in the US. See how union membership in the US has evolved over time.

EXHIBIT 17.4: The Number of Union Members in the US Over Time

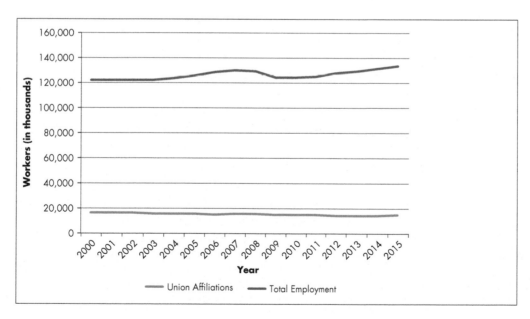

Source: http://www.bls.gov/webapps/legacy/cpslutap1.htm

The Power and Organization of Unions

Unions can be a very powerful force in business. Why? The answer is that unions represent employees and a business needs employees.

A Teamsters labor union gathering in 2007.

When employees feel that they need the power of a union, they can seek membership in an existing union or create a new union. If the majority of a business's employees vote to join a union, the business becomes a **union shop**. The employees join the union, pay dues to fund union activities, vote on matters of interest, and must abide by the decisions of the union's membership and elected officers. If a business becomes a union shop, the union notifies the business and the **National Labor Relations Board (NLRB)** that the union is now the official agent that represents the employees. The National Labor Relations Board (NRLB) is the US government agency that is charged with enforcing the laws regarding unions.

A union shop can take various forms. A **closed shop** is where all employees must join the union. The Taft-Hartley Act, noted later, made closed shops illegal in the US. An agency shop is where employees can choose to join or not to join the union. Because all employees receive the benefits of the union, all employees of an agency shop must pay union dues. A maintenance shop is where all union members must remain union members as long as they are employed by the business.

Union members elect local representatives, called **shop stewards**, and senior union officers such as union president, secretary, and treasurer. Senior union officers negotiate a labor contract with a business. Contracts typically deal with compensation, job security, and working conditions. Negotiating these contracts is called **collective bargaining**. The members of the union then vote to approve or reject the contract. If the contract is approved by the majority of the membership, the contract is ratified (**ratified contract**).

A ratified labor contract is like any other legal contract. If either party does not abide by the terms of the contract, legal action can be taken. However before legal action is taken, most union contracts provide a grievance and/or mediation procedure. A **grievance procedure** is a formal process, agreed upon in the union contract, designed to fairly resolve differences. An example is a union contract that specifies that an employee may be dismissed for being late to work. Before the business could dismiss the employee, it would submit the problem to a grievance committee. Most grievance committees are composed of union members and representatives of the business. The committee would hear evidence and determine if the employee was late and should be dismissed. A **mediation procedure** is where a neutral third party tries to get the business and union to resolve their differences through negotiation. Often this procedure includes **arbitration**, where a neutral third party decides how the grievance will be resolved. If the arbitration is binding (**binding arbitration**), the decision of the neutral third party is final. The union and the business must abide by the decision. If the arbitration is non-binding, then the union and business may take future actions.

Union and Employer Tactics

Unions negotiate with a business on compensation, job security, and working conditions. If a union and business cannot agree on the terms of a contract, each can take actions.

Union members can stop work and strike. A strike officially endorsed by a union is called an **authorized strike**. A strike that is not approved by the union is called an **unauthorized** or **wildcat strike**. Union members cannot physically harm non-union employees or stop the other functions of the business. However union employees can picket. **Picketing**

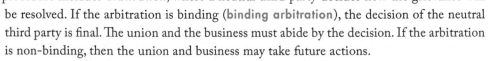

is where striking union members march outside the business with signs communicating their position. Union members can also boycott a business. **Boycotting** is where union members and those sympathetic to union members refuse to buy a business's product, sell to the business, or accept employment at the business.

In response to a strike, a business can create a lockout. A **lockout** is where the business refuses to permit employees to enter the business. A business may also try to hire strikebreakers. A **strikebreaker** is a non-union employee hired to replace striking employees. If a US business believes it is critical to the nation's welfare, the business can also ask the President of the United States to issue a temporary injunction. A **temporary injunction** is where a US federal court requires striking employees to return to work for a given period of time. This period of time is often called a **cooling-off period**. What is a critical industry? Think about it. What would happen if the members of a railroad union decided to call a strike that would stop the flow of food and other critical resources throughout the economy? Railroads are an example of a critical industry.

Laws Dealing with Unions and Collective Bargaining

Laws governing unions and collective bargaining have evolved over time. The intent of these laws is to ensure that union members and business are treated fairly.

In 1932, the **Norris-LaGuardia Act** was enacted to make it easier for employees to create, join, or operate a union. The Norris-LaGuardia Act sets clear standards for courts to follow in issuing injunctions that stop employees from organizing, striking, picketing, and boycotting.

In 1935, the **Wagner Act** required business to negotiate with union officials who are elected by union employees. The Wagner Act also prohibits businesses from firing or discriminating against employees who favor or join a union. Last, the Wagner Act established the National Labor Relations Board (NLRB) to oversee the creation of unions and enforce laws dealing with union–employer relationships.

In 1947, the **Taft-Hartley Act** prohibited unions from using unfair tactics. Unions must negotiate with business in full faith, cannot charge excessive union dues, harass non-union workers, or coerce employers. As noted earlier, the Taft-Hartley Act made closed shops illegal.

In 1959, the **Landrum-Griffin Act** regulated the internal operations of unions. The Landrum-Griffin Act requires unions to operate as a democracy, where members vote for the union's senior management. The Landrum-Griffin Act also prohibits unions from engaging in racketeering and other illegal activities.

EMPLOYMENT LAWS

In addition to laws governing the relationships of unions and business, there are laws that govern employment. In the US, the **Department of Labor (DOL)** and its agencies are empowered to enforce employment law.

Minimum Wages

In 1938, the **Fair Labor Standards Act (FLSA)** empowered the federal government to set a minimum wage that all employers must pay. The Fair Labor Standards Act also required employers to pay higher compensation for working overtime if you are an hourly employee. See Exhibit 17.5.

EXHIBIT 17.5: US Minimum Wages Through Time

Year	Value of the Minimum Wage in Current Dollars	Year	Value of the Minimum Wage in Current Dollars
1955	$0.75	1985	$3.35
1956	$1.00	1986	$3.35
1957	$1.00	1987	$3.35
1958	$1.00	1988	$3.35
1959	$1.00	1989	$3.35
1960	$1.00	1990	$3.80
1961	$1.15	1991	$4.25
1962	$1.15	1992	$4.25
1963	$1.25	1993	$4.25
1964	$1.25	1994	$4.25
1965	$1.25	1995	$4.25
1966	$1.25	1996	$4.75
1967	$1.40	1997	$5.15
1968	$1.60	1998	$5.15
1969	$1.60	1999	$5.15
1970	$1.60	2000	$5.15
1971	$1.60	2001	$5.15
1972	$1.60	2002	$5.15
1973	$1.60	2003	$5.15
1974	$2.00	2004	$5.15
1975	$2.10	2005	$5.15
1976	$2.30	2006	$5.15
1977	$2.30	2007	$5.85
1978	$2.65	2008	$6.55
1979	$2.90	2009	$7.25
1980	$3.10	2010	$7.25
1981	$3.35	2011	$7.25
1982	$3.35	2012	$7.25
1983	$3.35	2013	$7.25
1984	$3.35	2014	$7.25
		2015	$7.25

http://www.infoplease.com/ipa/A0774473.html

Discrimination

The Civil Rights Act of 1964 was landmark legislation and significantly changed human resource management in US businesses. Title VII of the Civil Rights Act of 1964 prohibits discrimination in hiring, firing, compensating, training, terms, conditions, or privileges of employment. Discrimination is defined as an employment act based on race, religion, creed, sex, or national origin. Title VII was later amended to include age (Age Discrimination in Employment Act of 1967 [ADEA]). The Civil Rights Act of 1964 also created the Equal Employment Opportunity Commission (EEOC) to discourage discrimination. The Equal Employment Opportunity Act of 1972 (EEOA) strengthened the powers of EEOC and empowered the EEOC to enforce anti-discrimination laws.

After its creation, the EEOC initiated strong actions to correct past and current practices of discrimination. Such actions were called affirmative action. Affirmative action often forced businesses to give preference to underrepresented minorities in hiring and promotions. Such practices were challenged in federal court. The US Supreme Court found that Title VII was not intended to create reverse discrimination. Reverse discrimination is where an applicant or employee was denied equal treatment because they were not a member of an underrepresented minority.

The Civil Rights Act of 1991 amended Title VII to provide victims of discrimination the right to a jury trial. The Civil Rights Act of 1991 also permitted victims to seek punitive damages.

The Americans with Disabilities Act of 1990 (ADA) prohibits a business from discriminating against applicants and employees who have disabilities that will not affect their job performance. ADA also requires businesses to make reasonable accommodations to assist disabled applicants or employees. An example of reasonable accommodations is providing wheelchair-accessible facilities.

Employee Safety

The Occupational Safety and Health Act of 1970 (OSH ACT) requires businesses to provide employees a safe place to work. To enforce this law, the Occupational Safety and Health Act of 1970 created a US government agency to set standards, enforce the law, and oversee employee safety. This agency is called the Occupational Safety and Health Administration (OSHA).

Sexual Harassment

Employees should expect a safe workplace, free from physical harm from an employer or fellow workers. However employees should also expect a workplace free from sexual harassment. Amendments to Title VII of the Civil Rights Act of 1964 make sexual harassment illegal. Title VII defines sexual harassment as, "Unwelcomed sexual advances, requests for sexual favors, and other verbal or physical conduct of a sexual nature that explicitly or implicitly affects an individual's employment, unreasonably interferes with an individual's work performance, or creates an intimidating, hostile, or offensive work environment."

Family and Medical Leave

Family and Medical Leave Act of 1993 (FMLA) requires employers to guarantee a job to employees who need medical or sick leave to start a family with children, take care of family members because of illness, or recover from a personal illness. Employers must provide twelve weeks in a twelve month period. The leave can be paid or unpaid.

Employees Who Are Non-US Citizens (Immigration)

The **Immigration and Nationality Act (INA)** requires employers to employ only US citizens or nationals, and non-US citizens who have been authorized to work in the US. Authorization to work in the US must be granted by the US government. Authorization can be short- or long-term, depending on the situation.

Child and Youth Labor

A "Tube boy" in the mule room of the Richmond Spinning Mill in Chattanooga, Tennessee, in 1910.

The Fair Labor Standards Act (FLSA) has special provisions for hiring employees under the age of 18, called **minors**. The FLSA prohibits employers from hiring employees under the age of 14, and sets special restrictions for employees under the age of 18. On behalf of these minors, the FLSA also regulates the salary, working conditions, and maximum hours permitted per week.

DECIDING TO END THE EMPLOYEE–EMPLOYER RELATIONSHIP—TERMINATION

There are times when a business must accept the fact that an employee does not add value to the business. There are two causes for this situation. First, the employee does not perform as required. Second, the employee's services are no longer needed.

Terminating an employee is a challenge. It is typically demoralizing to both the employee and business. It is also expensive. However, to succeed, businesses must embrace the fact that business models and strategies must evolve to meet the changing needs of the marketplace. As such, the contribution of all resources, including people, must be constantly evaluated. The benefit of an employee must be compared with the cost of that employee, and a decision to retain or terminate the employee made.

A business should always be careful in terminating an employee. First, the reasons should be legal. Businesses must be careful not to discriminate or do other illegal acts in terminating an employee.

Second, the reasons for terminating an employee should be valid and well documented. Sometimes such documentation may be easy. An example is terminating an employee because he or she did not meet an agreed-upon quota. Another example is when the demand for a business's product decreases, deeming the services of an employee unneeded. However sometimes documenting problems may not be easy. An example is terminating an employee because he or she is destructive to the overall output of the team. Businesses must be careful in terminating employees because unsupported actions may be viewed as discriminatory and unjust.

Third, terminating an employee can be expensive. Businesses must be careful to meet agreed-upon obligations regarding termination payments. Such payments include compensation and fringe benefits. Payments after termination are referred to as **severance pay**.

CHAPTER SUMMARY

In this chapter we've explored the nature and importance of the human resource function. After reading this chapter, you should be able to:

1. Understand the nature and importance of the human resource function (Learning Objective 1): A business's human resource function (HR) is responsible for assessing the need for employees, recruiting and hiring employees, training employees, evaluating employees, motivating employees, and compensating employees.

2. Appreciate the challenges and techniques of motivating employees (Learning Objective 2): Motivating employees to perform is critical to a successful business. However motivating employees is complicated because people are complicated.

3. Appreciate the different means of compensating employees (Learning Objective 3): Compensation deals with salary, fringe benefits, work–life arrangements, and non-cash compensation.

4. Appreciate the challenges and opportunities in employer–employee relationships (Learning Objective 4): Businesses must be very sensitive to relations with organized labor, laws affecting employment, and terminating employees.

In this chapter we've explored these questions and issues. Now it's time to look at the opportunities and challenges in managing a business's other resource, assets. "How Business Works" is about people using assets to create value.

KEYWORDS

affirmative action 373

AFL-CIO 369

Age Discrimination in
  Employment Act of 1967
  (ADEA) 373

agency shop 370

Americans with Disabilities Act
  of 1990 (ADA) 373

arbitration 370

authorized strike 370

binding arbitration 370

boycotting 371

cafeteria plans 367

Civil Rights Act of 1964, Title
  VII 373

Civil Rights Act of 1991, Title
  VII 373

closed shop 370

collective bargaining 370

commission 364

Congress of Industrial
  Organizations (CIO) 369

cooling-off-period 371

defined benefit plan 365

defined contribution plan 365

Department of Labor (DOL)
  371

dependent care 366

discrimination 373

educational benefits 366

employee training 359

employment agencies 357

employment application 357

Employment Retirement Income
  Security Act of 1974 (ERISA)
  365

Equal Employment Opportunity
  Act (EEOA) 373

Equal Employment Opportunity
  Commission (EEOC) 373

Equity Theory 361

executive search firms 357

Expectancy Theory 361

Fair Labor Standards Act
  (FLSA) 371

Family and Medical Leave Act of
  1993 (FMLA) 373

fixed salary 363

flex time 366

fringe benefits 364

golden parachutes 367

grievance procedure 370

gross pay 363

head hunter 357

health care benefits 364

human resource function (HR)
  356

Immigration and Nationality Act
  (INA) 374

job description 357

job sharing 366

job specification 357

Knights of Labor 369

Landrum-Griffin Act 371

lockout 371

maintenance shop 370

management development
  training 359

Maslow's Hierarchy of Needs
  361

maternity or paternity
  leave 366

mediation procedure 370

Medicaid 365

Medicare 364

mentor 359

minors 374

National Labor Relations Board
  (NLRB) 370

net pay 363

non-cash compensation, employees 367

Norris-LaGuardia Act 371

Occupational Safety and Health
  Act of 1970 (OSH ACT) 373

Occupational Safety and Health
  Administration (OSHA) 373

on-the-job training 359

orientation 359

paternity leave 366

Patient Protection and Affordable
  Care Act of 2010 364

picketing 370

piece-goods work 364

profit sharing 364

ratified contract 370

resume 357

reverse discrimination 373

salary 363

severance pay 374

sexual harassment 373

shop stewards 370

sick leave 366

sick pay 366

Social Security 365

staffing analysis 357

strike 369

strikebreaker 371

succession planning 357

Taft-Hartley Act 371

telecommuting 366

temporary injunction 371

unauthorized strike 370

unemployment benefits 365

unions 367

union shop 370

vacation pay 366

Wagner Act 371

wildcat strike 370

SHORT-ANSWER QUESTIONS

1. What is the job of a business's human relations department or function?
2. If a union and business disagree, what can the union do? What can the business do?
3. What acts of discrimination by employers are illegal in the US?
4. What is sexual harassment?
5. Define the following terms:
   a. Human resource function (HR)
   b. Job or staffing notice
   c. Succession planning
   d. Job description
   e. Job specification
   f. Employment agencies
   g. Executive search firms
   h. Head hunters
   i. Employment application
   j. Resume
   k. Orientation
   l. Mentor
   m. On-the-job training
   n. Employee training
   o. Management development
   p. 360-degree evaluation
   q. Expectancy Theory
   r. Equity Theory
   s. Maslow's Hierarchy of Needs
   t. Herzberg's Two-Factor Theory of Motivation
   u. McGregor's Theory X and Theory Y
   v. Salary
   w. Gross pay
   x. Net pay
   y. Fixed salary
   z. Hourly salary
   aa. Commission
   ab. Piece-goods work
   ac. Profit-sharing plan
   ad. Health care benefits
   ae. Patient Protection and Affordable Care Act of 2010
   af. Medicare
   ag. Medicaid
   ah. Social Security
   ai. Employment Retirement Income Security Act of 1974 (ERISA)
   aj. Defined contribution plan
   ak. Defined benefit plan
   al. Unemployment benefits
   am. Job sharing
   an. Dependent care
   ao. Flex time
   ap. Educational benefits
   aq. Telecommuting
   ar. Vacation pay
   as. Maternity or paternity leave
   at. Sick pay
   au. Sick leave
   av. Employee stock options
   aw. Golden parachutes
   ax. Cafeteria plan
   ay. Performance pay
   az. Union
   ba. Knights of Labor
   bb. American Federation of Labor (AFL)
   bc. Strike
   bd. Congress of Industrial Organizations (CIO)
   be. AFL-CIO
   bf. Union shop
   bg. National Labor Relations Board (NLRB)
   bh. Closed shop
   bi. Agency shop
   bj. Maintenance shop
   bk. Shop steward
   bl. Collective bargaining
   bm. Ratified contract
   bn. Mediation procedure
   bo. Grievance procedure
   bp. Arbitration
   bq. Binding arbitration
   br. Authorized strike
   bs. Unauthorized or wildcat strike
   bt. Picketing
   bu. Boycotting
   bv. Lockout
   bw. Strikebreaker
   bx. Temporary injunction

by. Cooling-off period

bz. Norris-LaGuardia Act

ca. Wagner Act

cb. Taft-Hartley Act

cc. Landrum-Griffin Act

cd. Department of Labor (DOL)

ce. Fair Labor Standards Act (FLSA)

cf. Title VII of the Civil Rights Act of 1964

cg. Discrimination

ch. Age Discrimination in Employment Act of 1967 (ADEA)

ci. Equal Employment Opportunity Commission (EEOC)

cj. Equal Employment Opportunity Act (EEOA)

ck. Affirmative Action

cl. Reverse discrimination

cm. Civil Rights Act of 1991

cn. Americans with Disabilities Act of 1990 (ADA)

co. Occupational Safety and Health Act of 1970 (OSH)

cp. Occupational Safety and Health Administration (OSHA)

cq. Sexual harassment

cr. Family and Medical Leave Act of 1993 (FMLA)

cs. Immigration and Nationality Act (INA)

ct. Minor

cu. Severance pay

CRITICAL-THINKING QUESTIONS

1. Think about yourself. Write a resume that reflects who you are today. Then write a resume that reflects who you want to be in ten years.

2. How do you feel about being managed using:
    a. Expectancy Theory
    b. Equity Theory
    c. Maslow's Hierarchy of Needs
    d. Herzberg's Two-Factor Theory
    e. Theory X and Theory Y?

3. Look at the different forms of compensation and relate them to Maslow's Hierarchy of Needs.

4. Think about being terminated. How do you think the employee being terminated feels? Imagine you are the employee's supervisor who will inform the employee that he or she is terminated. What's important for you to do and not do?

EXPLORING REAL BUSINESS

Go to the websites of Google, Target, Hyundai, and Procter & Gamble. The websites are

Google:	http://investor.google.com
Target:	http://www.target.com
Hyundai:	http://worldwide.hyundai.com/company-overview
Procter & Gamble:	http://www.pg.com

Go to the section regarding employment and human resources. Answer the following questions:

1. What are the policies and procedures the company has regarding applying for employment?
2. What is the company's policy regarding discrimination and sexual harassment?

ENDNOTES

1. Vroom, Victor and Philip W. Yetton. *Work and Motivation*. Pittsburgh: University of Pittsburgh Press, 1973. Print.
2. Adams, John Stacey. "Inequity in Social Exchange" *Advances in Experimental Social Psychology* vol. 2 (1965): 267–299. Print.
3. Maslow, Abraham. "A Theory of Human Motivation." *Psychological Review* 50:4 (1943): 370–396. Print.
4. Herzberg, Frederick. *The Motivation to Work*. 1959. Reprint: New Brunswick, NJ: Transaction Publishers, 1993. Print.
5. McGregor, Douglas. *The Human Side of Enterprise*. New York: McGraw Hill, Print. 1960.

18

OPPORTUNITIES AND CHALLENGES IN MANAGING ASSETS

LEARNING OBJECTIVES

After reading Chapter 18, you should be able to meet the following learning objectives:

1. Appreciate the nature and importance of managing assets
2. Appreciate how assets are used in a business
3. Appreciate how a business manages assets

Introduction: Let's Talk About Assets

People are the heart of any business, but people use assets to create value. Often called real capital, what are assets? What assets are needed for a business to create value? How does a business use assets to create value? What principles govern the investment of money in assets?

In this chapter we'll explore these questions and issues. We'll explore the critical opportunities and challenges in managing the assets of a business. We'll explore the role of assets in "How Business Works."

WHY ASSETS MATTER

People are the most valuable resources of any business. But people need assets to create value. Can you imagine the people of Google delivering an Internet search engine without computers? Can you imagine Hyundai building an automobile without a factory? Can you imagine Procter & Gamble creating Tide detergent without chemicals and other ingredients? Can you imagine Target operating without products to sell? The answer to all of these questions is no. All businesses need assets to operate. Assets matter.

LEARNING OBJECTIVE 1
. . . .
APPRECIATING THE NATURE AND IMPORTANCE OF ASSETS

A business acquires financial capital, called money. The business then uses the money to hire employees who then acquire and use assets to create value. To create value, the operating profit from hiring people and investing in assets must exceed the cost of the money. So what is an asset? An **asset** is defined as an economic resource that the business owns and uses to make an operating profit and create value.

People are often called assets. Why? The answer is that people are an economic resource that a business uses to make an operating profit. However a business does not own people. Employees are free to leave the business any time they desire. A business cannot assume employees will remain with the business in the future. Thus, the cost of people is an expense or cost of the period in which they are employed.

So how are assets used in a business? The answer is it depends. It depends on the business's model and strategy. Think about it. Assets are the things people need to use to make a business valuable. Assets are resources used to operate the business. Assets are the things that a business needs to create, produce, and sell a product. So what determines the assets a specific business needs? Does Google need the same assets as Procter & Gamble? Does Target need the same assets as Hyundai? The answer is no. Each has a different business model and strategy and thus different needs for assets.

An electronics factory in Shenzhen, China.

VARIOUS TYPES OF ASSETS

Assets come in many different forms. Let's look at some of the assets used by many businesses. Many businesses own:

Cash

Marketable securities

Accounts receivable

Inventory

Prepaid expense

Property, plant, and equipment

Patents, copyrights, and trademarks

Goodwill

Assets are often classified as either short-term or long-term assets. A short-term asset, often called a **current asset**, is an asset that is cash or expected to be turned into cash within one year. Cash, marketable securities, accounts receivable, inventory, and prepaid expense are typically classified as current assets. A long-term asset, often called a **non-current asset**, is an asset that is not expected to be turned into cash within one year. It will take more than one year to convert long-term assets into cash. Property, plant, equipment, patents, copyrights, trademarks, and goodwill are typically classified as non-current assets.

So how does a business operate with assets?

ASSETS AND OPERATING A BUSINESS

Let's look at an example. Think about opening a new store for Target. Marketing research shows that a location is perfect for a new store. Based on estimates, the finance department determines that the store should create value. The store's operating profit should exceed the cost of money. So what does Target do? First, it plans. It figures out what people and assets it will need. It then sets in motion a series of events to acquire the needed resources. As noted in Chapter 16, Target's human resource (HR) function is charged with assessing and filling the need for employees. But that still leaves the assets. Target must forecast the types and amount of assets it will need to open and operate the store.

So what are the assets Target will need? Let's look at Target's operations and business model. First, it must acquire the land, building, and equipment for the store. Hopefully these physical assets will produce a lot of profits and cash for many years in the future. As such, these assets are long-term or non-current assets. Given that these are long-term assets, the business will probably use long-term debt and/or equity to finance these assets.

Next, the business will need inventory, or something to sell to its customers. It contacts its suppliers and orders inventory. When the inventory is delivered to the store, the manager accepts delivery and takes ownership of the inventory. Target now has an asset called inventory. However, does the manager pay cash for the inventory? The answer is probably no. The manager signs a receipt indicating Target now owns the inventory but owes the suppliers money at a future date. The inventory is a current asset because Target hopes to sell the inventory quickly.

Target now has a store and inventory, and with the assistance of HR, it has its employees. What else does Target need? It also needs some cash to put in the cash registers at each check-out counter. Target must have cash.

Now we're ready to open the store. The employees come to work. The customers come into the store and shop. And our business is operating. Customers select the merchandise, or inventory, they want. They then go to the check-out counter. There the customer pays for the inventory. Target's inventory goes down. It has incurred a cost of goods that it sold. However, Target also has a sale and receives payment of either cash or a promise to pay cash in the future. When a customer uses his or her credit card, he or she promises to pay the issuer of the credit card, such as a bank, in the future. The issuer of the credit card promises to pay cash to the store in two to three days, depending how long it takes to process the credit card transaction. Target has an accounts receivable from the issuer of the credit card. The hope is that the net result is a sale where the money received is greater than the cost of the inventory sold. Target loses one asset called inventory. Target receives another asset called cash or accounts receivable.

Third, if the customer used a credit card, Target will receive the cash from the credit card issuer in about three days. So what does Target do with the cash provided by the cash or credit card sale? It pays the employees for their work. Target's cash goes down but its payable to its employees also goes down. Next, Target will use the cash to pay the money it owes to the suppliers of inventory. Once again Target's cash goes down but its accounts payable also go down. If done right, the net result is the cash received, less the cash paid, is positive. The net cash is then used to pay the interest and principal of Target's long-term debt. What cash remains

Shoppers at a Target in San Bruno, California.

belongs to the owners. (Note: Look back in Chapter 08. Remember that accrual profit and cash profit are ultimately the same. The only difference is time. Accrual accounting recognizes transactions when the transaction occurs. Cash accounting only recognizes transactions when the cash is incurred.)

Our example is far simpler than the reality of opening and operating a Target store, but it does provide basic insights into the need for and use of assets. A business needs assets to operate. A business needs assets that are short-term or current in nature. Target needed cash, accounts receivable, and inventory. However the business also needs long-term or non-current assets. Target needed land, buildings, and equipment.

LEARNING OBJECTIVE 2

HOW ASSETS ARE USED IN A BUSINESS

A business needs current and non-current assets that can be tangible or intangible. Let's look at why a business needs these assets.

WORKING CAPITAL AND CURRENT ASSETS

A business needs **working capital**, or current assets, to operate. Current assets are an integral part of a business's operating cycle. An **operating cycle** is the time that elapses between the time the inventory is purchased and the time the cash is collected from the customer. Current assets include cash, marketable securities, inventory, and prepaid expenses.

A business finances its working capital or current assets with 1) current liabilities or 2) long-term financing in the form of debt or equity. **Current liabilities** are accounts payable and other debts a business must pay within one year. **Net working capital** is current assets less current liabilities. Net working capital measures the amount of current assets financed with long-term debt or equity. The amount of a business's net working capital is a function of its business model and strategy and is addressed in Chapter 19.

Cash

Cash includes currency and money a business has in its checking and other bank accounts. Cash is the most liquid investment. But why does a business have cash?

In the early 1900s, a famous economist named John Maynard Keynes said a business needs cash for three reasons1. First, a business needs cash to pay its bills. Keynes called this the **transaction demand for money**. A business cannot operate if it cannot pay its bills. Second, a business needs cash in case bad and unexpected events happen. What happens if a business expects sales that do not materialize? It is left with inventory and no cash. It needs some extra cash to help it through such times. Keynes called this the **precautionary demand for money**. Third, a business needs cash to be able to take advantage of unique opportunities. Keynes called this the **speculative demand for money**.

Marketable Securities

Marketable securities are short-term investments a business makes in financial securities, which are low risk. These investments are low risk because they have low default risk and are easy to sell or turn into cash. An asset is said to be **liquid** if it can be easily sold and turned into cash. Marketable securities typically include government and corporate debt traded in a public market.

RAINY DAYS AND DAYS WHERE CASH IS KING

Sometimes bad things happen that are unexpected, which can result in businesses having a hard time paying their bills. Such businesses become distressed. They must sell inventory and other valuable assets to acquire cash and survive. But who buys this inventory or other assets? Often other businesses want to take advantage of another business's misfortune. Such "rainy days" are opportunities to buy valuable assets at low prices. But where do purchasing businesses get the cash? Sometimes the purchasing business must act quickly and does not have time to borrow the money. Sometimes, when the economy is in a recession, it's hard to borrow the money or sell equity. So what happens? The businesses that have extra cash are able to take advantage of the situation and buy valuable assets at low prices. During these times it is often said, "Cash is King." Businesses that have extra cash can take advantage of the distressed situation and rule the day.

Why would a business invest cash in such securities? First, cash earns no return. Marketable securities do yield a business some return. Because of the low risk, marketable securities do not typically yield the business a high return, but some return is better than no return. Second, given marketable securities are liquid, a business can use marketable securities to meet the precautionary and speculative demand for money noted earlier.

Accounts Receivable

A **receivable** is a claim on another person or business. Receivables typically come from selling to customers. The customer does not pay cash but promises to pay the business at a later date. The business has a receivable from the customer. So why would a business permit a customer to defer payment for the sale? A business would prefer a cash sale. The reason is marketing. When a business grants a customer the ability to buy the business's product but pay later, the business is financing the customer's sale. The customer has an account payable to the business that corresponds to the business's account receivable.

When a business offers to finance a customer's purchase, it becomes part of the customer's decision to buy. Think about the earlier example of Target. If Target did not accept credit cards, what would happen to its sales? The sales would go down. Target needs to accept credit cards because customers require it. If Target did not accept credit cards, many of its customers would shop at other stores. Because other stores accept credit cards, they would have a competitive advantage over Target.

The challenge with accounts receivable is determining whether or not the receivable will ultimately turn into cash. Will the customer honor his or her obligation and pay the business the cash that he or she owes? The business hopes the answer is yes, but it does not always know. To get a sale, a business may take a risk on a customer knowing the customer may or may not pay. If this is the case, a business must estimate the cash the business will and will not receive. The business must recognize that some of its customers will not pay their receivables. This amount is called an **allowance for bad debts**. Accounts receivable, less allowance for bad debts, is called **net receivables**  and represents the amount of money the business expects to receive from its customers. Besides affecting the value of the accounts receivable asset, the amounts a business does not collect is also a cost of doing business, called **bad-debt expense**.

To provide customers the incentive to pay earlier versus later, sometimes a business will provide a customer a discount for paying cash. The business may also offer a customer a discount for paying his or her debt to the business early. This is called a **trade discount**. An example is when a business gives a discount of 2/10, net 30. What that phrase means is the customer will receive a 2% discount if he or she pays within 10 days. If the customer does not pay within 10 days, the full amount is due in 30 days.

Inventory

Inventory is the store of goods that a business owns and sells to customers. Inventory can be of two types, purchased or produced. **Purchased inventory** are goods that are purchased by a business, to be resold without modification, as is. The inventory Target purchases from its suppliers is purchased inventory. Target buys the inventory and puts the inventory in its stores as is. Accounting for purchased inventory is not always easy, particularly when the volume of inventory is high. Accountants have different methods to account for such inventory, including first-in-first-out (FIFO) and last-in-first-out (LIFO). This issue is best explored in accounting courses.

Produced inventory are goods that are purchased by a business to be modified and converted into another good. Hyundai's inventory is produced inventory. Hyundai purchases inputs like steel, plastic, and other items needed to build an automobile. These inputs are called **raw materials**. Hyundai then combines the raw materials with labor and begins creating an automobile. During the transformation of the raw materials into a finished automobile, the inventory is called **work-in-process**. When the transformation process is complete, a finished automobile appears. The automobile is ready to sell. The inventory of finished automobiles is called **finished goods**. Accounting for produced inventory is not always easy. Accountants make a lot of assumptions about what it costs to produce a product (example: What is a fixed versus a variable cost?). This issue is also best explored in accounting courses.

Typically a business owns its inventory. It has legal title to its inventory. However, sometimes a business holds for sale inventory that it does not own. A business holds inventory on consignment. **Consignment** is where a business holds and sells inventory that is owned by another business or person. Because the business does not own the inventory, it is not an asset of the business. When the business sells the consigned inventory, most of the proceeds from the sale go to the owner of the inventory. The business receives a part of the sales price as a commission.

So why would a business own inventory? Why would a business allocate its resources to inventory? The answer is marketing. A business needs something to sell.

Prepaid Expenses

A **prepaid expense** is a cost paid by the business prior to receiving the benefit from the cost. Most costs are paid at the time or after a business receives the benefit from the cost. Employees are paid after they work. Utilities are paid after the business uses the electricity, gas, or water. The cost of advertising is typically paid after the advertising appears. Yet businesses must prepay some expenses such as insurance and rent.

When P&G purchases insurance, it must prepay the cost. This is an asset because the business would get a refund if it canceled the insurance. But after the period of coverage is finished, the insurance is used up. There is no asset. So the business acquires an asset when it pays for the insurance. During the period of insurance coverage, the asset goes away and the business incurs a cost or expense for insurance.

So why do businesses have prepaid expenses? The answer is convention. Some businesses require its customers to prepay before they deliver their product. Typically this asset is not large, but it is a part of operating a business.

NON-CURRENT ASSETS

Non-current assets, often called long-term assets, are assets that are expected to benefit the business for a period greater than one year. The business pays money for these assets. The assets are used over their useful life to create value for the business. Most of these assets are used over long periods of time. As the assets are used, the value of these assets decline. This loss of value is a cost to the business.

Non-current assets are typically divided into two groups, tangible and intangible assets. **Tangible assets** are assets that can be touched such as property, plant, and equipment. **Intangible assets** are assets that can't be touched. Patents, copyrights, and goodwill are traditionally called intangible assets.

Tangible Assets

Property, plant, and equipment (PP&E) are the physical assets most people associate with a business beyond the business's product. The terms **facilities** or **fixed assets** are often used to describe PP&E. Target has its stores. P&G and Hyundai have their factories. Google has its computers. The purpose of PP&E is to provide the business the needed long-term physical assets to operate.

Land

Land is a part of the physical surface of the Earth. Stores, factories, and offices must sit on land. Land has an infinite life. Land can be used over and over again for many different things. Thus, unless something drastic happens that diminishes or impairs the value of the land, we assume the value of the land does not decline. The value of the business's original investment in land does not decrease over time.

Buildings

Buildings are another part of PP&E. A **building** is a physical structure attached to land. Businesses need buildings and invest money to build or acquire stores, factories, storage and distribution facilities, and offices. But unlike land, buildings do deteriorate in value as they are used. Think about a Target store, a factory for P&G or Hyundai, and an office building for Google. These businesses use their buildings to create, produce, and sell their product. But as the buildings are used, they become worn, obsolete, and lose value. The decline of this value is called depreciation. **Depreciation** is an estimate of how much a non-current, tangible asset declines in value in a given period. Buildings are assumed to depreciate with use. The value of the building is the

original cost of the building less the depreciation that has accumulated since the business acquired the building. The value of the building is the building's original cost, less its **accumulated depreciation**. This net amount is often called the building's **net book value**. The estimated decrease in value of the building each period is a cost of that period and called **depreciation expense**. Estimating how a building depreciates in a period is sometimes hard and based on numerous assumptions. Accountants can use different methods to recognize depreciation. Some of these methods are straight-line depreciation, double-declining balance depreciation, and sum-of-the-years depreciation. These methods are explored in accounting courses.

Equipment

A piece of **equipment** is a physical, non-current asset that a business uses that is not considered land or buildings. Go into a Target store and look at the cash registers, shelving, and display cases. These are equipment. Think of a factory for P&G or Hyundai. The assembly lines, the systems, and trucks are equipment. Think about Google and what it takes for it to operate. Google's computers are equipment.

Equipment is like a building. It is assumed to depreciate over time with use. Thus, equipment has an original cost, an accumulated depreciation, a net book value, and a period of depreciation expense. Like buildings, how a business recognizes depreciation is based on numerous assumptions.

Leased Property

An interesting questions arises when one is asked, "What does it take to own land, a building, or equipment?" Typically we say that you must have legal title to the asset. But what happens when you pay to use the asset but do not legally own the asset?

When a business pays to use an asset but does not own the asset, it is called leasing. **Leasing** is where one party (called the **lessee**) pays the owner of the property (called the **lessor**) a fee to use the property for a specific time period. The fee is called **rent**. The contract between the lessor and lessee is called a **lease**.

In most situations, the lease is for a short period of time. An example is when you go to the airport and lease an automobile for a week. A week is a very small part of the automobile's estimated life. Leases for a small part of the asset's useful life are called **operating leases**. The rent is an expense or cost of doing business. But what if the lease is for a longer period of time? Such a lease is called a **capital** or **capitalized lease**. The lessor recognizes the value of the lease as a long-term asset. It then depreciates this value over the term of the lease. The lessor also recognizes this value as a lease obligation. A lease obligation is a form of long-term debt. As the lessor makes lease payments, this debt is reduced. A lease is a contract between a lessor and lessee; defaulting on such contracts has legal implications. (See Chapter 07.)

Intangible Assets

Intangible assets include patents, copyrights, trademarks, and goodwill. These assets cannot be touched but are very important in the business world.

Intangible assets typically have a useful or legal life. As such, the value of these assets declines over time. When a business invests in an intangible asset, the cost of the asset is recognized as a long-term investment. However, this asset will decline in value over its useful or legal life. Thus, like a building, the asset's value must be decreased over time. Long-term tangible assets are depreciated. Long-term intangible assets are amortized. Each period an estimate is made of the decline in the value of the intangible asset. This decrease is recognized as a cost or expense of that period, called **amortization expense**. The value of the intangible assets at a particular time is the cost of the asset less the amortization that has accumulated since the business acquired the asset. Thus, similar to a tangible asset, the intangible asset has a cost, less the **accumulated amortization**, equaling the asset's net book value.

Patents

When a business, or person, invents something that is novel, useful, and non-obvious, it can ask the US federal government for a patent. A **patent** gives the owner the exclusive right to use the patented idea, process, or product. If granted by the government, the patent protects the business from anyone using its invention without the business's permission. Patents are granted for such things as a machine, process, or design for the manufacture of a product. The legal life of a patent is 20 years. The current law that governs patents is called the **Federal Patent Statute of 1952**. The government agency that oversees the granting of patents is called the **United States Patent and Trademark Office (PTO)**. When the owner of a patent feels that another business or person is illegally using his or her patented idea, product, or process, he or she can file a lawsuit against the accused body for **patent infringement**. The **US Court of Appeal for the Federal Circuit**, in Washington DC, was created in 1982 to judge patent lawsuits.

Copyrights

When an author or artist produces a unique work, he or she can seek a copyright for that work from the US federal government. A **copyright** gives the author the exclusive right to use that work. Examples of items that can be copyrighted are books, periodicals, poems, short stories, sermons, newspapers, motion pictures, entertainment productions, works of art, architectural drawings and designs, and music.

The legal life of a copyright varies. If a person owns a copyright, the copyright has a life of 70 years beyond the life of the author or artist. If a business owns a copyright, the copyright has a life equal to the shorter of 1) 95 years after the first publication or 2) 120 years from the year of creation. After the copyright period ends, the work enters the **public domain** and can be used by anyone. The law that currently governs copyrights is the **Copyright**

Old Patent Office Building in Washington, D.C.

Act of 1976. The government agency that oversees the granting of copyrights is called the **United States Copyright Office**. When the owner of a copyright feels that another business or person is illegally using his or her copyright, the owner can file a lawsuit against the accused body for **copyright infringement**.

Trademarks

A business often creates a company name or logo with which it wants to be identified. An example is the name Hyundai and its brand name Kia. A **trademark** is defined as a distinctive mark, symbol, name, word, motto, or device that identifies the products of a business. A business can apply for exclusive use of a trademark with the US federal government office **United States Patent and Trademark Office (PTO)**. If granted, the business is given exclusive rights to the trademark for 10 years. However the business can renew the trademark for an unlimited number of times. Each renewal is for 10 years.

The law that currently governs copyrights is the **Federal Lanham Trademark Act of 1946**. The government agency that oversees the granting of patents is called the **United States Patent and Trademark Office (PTO)**. When the owner of a trademark feels that another business or person is illegally using his or her trademark, the owner can file a lawsuit against the accused body for **trademark infringement**.

A McDonald's ice cream kiosk in Shanghai, China. The golden arches trademark is recognized around the world.

It should be noted that trademarks can become so used that the trademark becomes generic. A **generic name** is a name that becomes a common name for a product line. If a trademark becomes a generic name, it loses its trademark protection. Examples of trademarks that became generic names are Laser, Nylon, Frisbee, and Kerosene.

Goodwill

Often a successful business creates an intangible asset called goodwill. **Goodwill** is the value of the business that exceeds the value of its tangible and intangible assets other than goodwill. Where does goodwill come from? It comes from the business creating a competitive advantage. Some people attribute a business's goodwill to its brand, some to its people, and some to its customers. In reality, goodwill comes from all those places. A business should always seek to create goodwill. Target, P&G, Google, and Hyundai all have created goodwill.

Goodwill is real. However, recognizing that goodwill exists is easier than measuring goodwill. For that reason, a business in the US does not recognize goodwill on its financial statements unless it buys the goodwill. An example of buying goodwill is when one business buys another business. If the purchasing business pays a price that exceeds the value of the acquired business's tangible and intangible assets, it will recognize an asset called goodwill or the difference. If this asset is recognized, it is not amortized. The value of the goodwill asset may be adjusted downward if the business loses the goodwill in subsequent years.

LEARNING OBJECTIVE 3
. . . .
HOW BUSINESS MANAGES ASSETS TO CREATE VALUE

So assets are critical to creating business value. A business needs assets to create value. But how does a business determine how much or how little of an asset is needed? How does a business manage its assets? The answer is that the business should compare the cost and benefits from each asset and make sure the asset is contributing to the business's value.

Three important principles should never be forgotten. First, assets are a critical part of the business's ability to create an operating profit that impacts value. Second, **investing in assets is risky—that risk impacts value.** Third, assets are not independent. A business is a portfolio where success requires that all parts work together.

THE VALUE OF ASSETS

First, remember a business acquires money and uses the money to hire people and invest in assets. By hiring people and investing in assets, a business is able to generate an operating profit that compensates the providers of the money. Ideally the operating profit from hiring people and investing in assets exceeds the cost of the money. If that happens, value is created. If the cost of the money exceeds the operating profit, then value is destroyed. So when a business hires people and invests in assets it must ask the question, "What is the benefit we expect to receive from these expenditures and investments?" Next, the business must ask, given the cost of the money, "Do these expenditures and investments in people and assets justify the use of the money?" A business does not want to invest money in assets that are not productive.

NURSERY RHYMES AND ASSETS

There is a famous children's story about Goldilocks and the three bears. Goldilocks realizes that the best porridge is not too hot or too cold, it's just right. Goldilocks also realizes that chairs can be too big or too small and should be just right. Last, Goldilocks realizes that beds can be too hard or too soft and should be just right.

Managing assets is a lot like Goldilocks's choice of porridge, chair, and bed. A business can have too much of an asset. A business needs just the right amount of an asset to maximize its value. That amount is a function of the business's model and strategy. It's a matter of finding just the right fit.

Recognize, however, that too little investment in assets also hurts value. To pay its bills, a business needs adequate levels of cash or marketable securities. A business may lose customers, and the profit from sales, if it is does not finance its customers with accounts receivable. A business may lose sales and profits with too little inventory or PP&E.

The job of management is to make sure the business has enough, but not too many, assets. Too many or too few assets will hurt the value of the business.

Investing in Assets Is Risky

Investing in assets is risky. Think about it. Will a business collect its accounts receivable? Will a customer buy a business's inventory? Will a business be able to produce a desirable product with its property, plant, and equipment? Will a business be able to use its intangible assets to create a competitive advantage? These are difficult questions. Investing in assets is a risky decision.

The Interdependence of Assets

Assets must work together. A business cannot create value with only property, plant, and equipment. It needs inventory. A business cannot create value with only inventory. It needs cash. A business cannot create value with only cash. The assets of a business must work together. Look at the earlier example using Target. Think of the interdependence of assets through the operating cycle. Think about how current and non-current assets work together to create value. Managers cannot evaluate the contribution of an asset without appreciating the role of the asset in the business's total operations.

INVESTING IN AND MANAGING ASSETS

The decision to invest in an asset or groups of assets is like all management functions. It entails planning, executing, and reviewing. When a business decides to invest in an asset, it must first look at the role of the asset in creating value. Second, it must decide how it will measure the asset's contribution to value. Third, it must forecast the benefits and cost of the assets, ultimately deciding the amount to be invested. Fourth, it must monitor the use and productivity of the asset. Last, it must continuously evaluate the investment and make adjustments as needed. Let's look at some examples.[2]

Cash and Marketable Securities

Remember the purpose of cash and marketable securities? Cash and marketable securities provide the business with needed liquidity to pay its bills. A business that cannot pay its bills, in good or bad economic times, faces bankruptcy. Next cash and marketable securities provide funds in case of an emergency and for unexpected opportunities.

A business must look at its business model and strategy and determine how much cash and marketable securities it needs. A business that is very cyclical and seasonal may face a lot of uncertainty. It must look at its expected cash inflows from sales and other sources and its cash outflows from paying bills and other needs. But it must also realize that these cash flows are expected and that the unexpected can easily occur. Thus, it may want to hold a large amount of cash and marketable securities. It may decide to hold cash and marketable securities equal to 90 days' worth of bills. That way it is sure it can pay its bills in good or bad times.

A business that is less volatile and is able to forecast its cash flow might not hold a lot of cash and marketable securities. It may decide to hold cash and marketable securities equal to 30 days' worth of bills. If a business does not need the liquidity, then it does not want to hold the cash or marketable securities. Remember the money that is financing the investment in cash requires a return. Holding cash that is not needed means the business is incurring an unneeded financing cost.

A common measure to help manage a business's liquidity is **cash-to-expense ratio**. This ratio measures how many days of operating expenses a business holds in cash and marketable securities.

EQUATION 18.1: Cash-to-Expense Ratio

$$L = (C + MS)/E$$

Where
	L	Cash-to-expense ratio
	C	Investment in cash
	MS	Investment in marketable securities
	E	Annual operating expenses/365 days

Accounts Receivable

Remember the purpose of accounts receivable? A business has accounts receivable to entice the customer to buy its products. Accounts receivable are customers' accounts payable and are a form of loan to the customer. So which customers does a business permit to pay later? What payment terms should a business set for its customers regarding when an accounts receivable should be paid?

First, a business does not want to sell to a customer when there is a high probability the customer will not pay as agreed. If the business cannot collect payment for the sale, then it loses money. Businesses often look at a customer's creditworthiness by using references, agencies that report a customer's financial condition called credit bureaus, and past experiences with the customer.

Second, a business must give terms that entice a customer to buy the business's product. However, terms that are too generous often provide no extra profit and are costly. Let's look at an example. If a business's competitor is offering customers the ability to pay for purchases 30 days after a sale, then the business may need to match these terms. If the customer does not pay the receivable for 60 days, the business has twice as many receivables as needed to compete. The business does not get any additional operating profit from carrying the receivable for 60 days versus 30 days. However, the business does incur additional financing cost to finance the extra receivables.

Two common measures used to help manage this issue are 1) **accounts receivable turnover** and 2) **accounts receivable collection period**. These measurements can help managers project or estimate the business's available cash. Accounts receivable turnover measures how many times a year a business collects it accounts receivables.

EQUATION 18.2: Accounts Receivable Turnover

$$ARTO = S/AR$$

Where   ARTO   Accounts receivable turnover ratio
         S   Annual sales
         AR   Investment in accounts receivable

The accounts receivable collection period measures how many days it takes to collect accounts receivable.

EQUATION 18.3: Accounts Receivable Collection Period

$$ARCP = AR/DS$$

Where   ARCP   Collection period
         AR   Investment in accounts receivable
         DS   Daily sales (annual sales/365 days)

Inventory

Remember the purpose of inventory? A business has inventory to provide customers something to buy. If a business does not have enough inventory, then it loses sales and profits. But if a business has too much inventory, it does not gain any additional sales and incurs extra financing costs.

Depending on a business's model and strategy, it may be easy or it may be hard to forecast sales. What will customers buy and when will they buy it? These may be hard questions to answer. If a business is concerned that the demand for its product may exceed its forecast, the business may want to have extra inventory called **safety stock**. However if a business is concerned that the demand for its product may be less than forecast, it may want to create a pricing plan that offers discounts for any unsold inventory.

Two common measures used to help manage inventory are 1) inventory turnover and 2) days' sales in inventory. Inventory turnover measures how many times a year a business converts its inventory into sales.

EQUATION 18.4: Inventory Turnover

$$ITO = COGS/I$$

Where   ITO   Inventory turnover ratio
         COGS   Annual cost of goods sold
         I   Investment in inventory

Days' sales in inventory compares the level of inventory to the inventory sold per day.

$$DSI = AI/DCGS$$

Where	DSI	Days' sales in inventory
	I	Investment in inventory
	DCGS	Cost of daily sales (annual cost of goods sold/365 days)

Property, Plant, and Equipment (PP&E)

Remember the purpose of PP&E? The purpose of PP&E is to provide the business with the physical assets it needs to operate. A business needs PP&E to create, produce, and market its products. A business wants to maximize the productivity of PP&E.

A common measure of the productivity of PP&E is called **fixed-asset turnover**. The fixed-asset turnover ratio measures the relationship between a business's investment in PP&E versus the business's sales.

EQUATION 18.6: Fixed-Asset Turnover

$$FATO = S/PPE$$

Where	FATO	Fixed-asset turnover
	S	Annual sales
	PPE	Investment in property, plant, and equipment

Like all assets, a business does not want too little or too much PP&E. Yet, unlike current assets, PP&E is a long-term asset that is often not flexible. A business cannot quickly adapt PP&E. It takes time to build a factory, or store, or office building. And after it is built, it is hard to alter these assets. As such, investments in PP&E are usually riskier than investments in current assets.

To assist in making decisions about PP&E, businesses use tools that incorporate the long-term benefits of these assets and the long-term cost of financing these assets. Three examples are net present value, internal rate of return, and payback. (Note: Look back to Chapter 10 for a discussion of these tools.)

Net present value (NPV) measures the expected long-term value of investing in PP&E and related working capital versus the cost of investing in PP&E. NPV incorporates the time value of money since a business typically invests in PP&E for a long time. If the expected value from investing in PP&E is greater than the cost of PP&E, the investment has a positive NPV. The business should invest in PP&E because the investment creates value. If the expected value from investing in PP&E is less than the cost of PP&E, the investment has a negative NPV. The business should not invest in PP&E because the investment destroys value. To determine the expected value of the investment, the business uses its weighted average cost of financing.

A technique similar to NPV is the **internal rate of return (IRR)**. IRR is the rate of return an investment in PP&E and related working capital earns over time. A business then compares the IRR with its weighted cost of capital. If the IRR exceeds the business's weighted cost of capital, then the business should make the investment. The investment will create value. If the IRR is below the business's weighted cost of capital, then the business should not make the investment because the investment will destroy value.

Payback is the amount of time it takes for the business to receive cash that is equal to the cost of the PP&E. Payback has many drawbacks because it does not directly deal with the time value of money, a business's weighted average cost of capital, and thus value. However, payback is a measure of risk often used by business. The longer it takes for a business to recover its investment in PP&E, the riskier the investment. Payback helps in assessing the risk of an investment.

DIVESTING ASSETS

Managing assets is like any other management function. Managing assets entails planning, executing, and reviewing. Sometimes a business invests in assets expecting the assets to create value. After executing the asset plan, the business may discover that the assets do not create value. The assets destroy value. Forecast conditions may not materialize. Conditions may change. For whatever reason, the business discovers that its investment of money in assets is not producing value.

A business uses the same principles noted above to decide to eliminate or divest of assets. It is hard and often disruptive to sell a factory or discontinue selling a product line. Yet to remain competitive, businesses must be prepared to make such decisions. All assets must contribute to creating value. Assets that do not contribute value should be sold, eliminated, and divested.

MANAGING ASSETS—PUTTING IT ALL TOGETHER

So how does someone evaluate a business's total portfolio of assets? There are two critical questions used to evaluate a business's investment in total assets. First, does the investment in and use of the business's assets permit a business to pay its liabilities? If a business cannot pay its bills, it will fail. Second, do the assets create sufficient net income to justify the investment?

Paying Liabilities

In the earlier discussion of cash and marketable securities, the cash-to-expense ratio was reviewed to help measure a business's liquidity. Other common measures used to look at a business's ability to pay its liabilities are the **current ratio** and **quick ratio**. When you look at these ratios you assume the business's operating cycle will continue to function, where inventory will be sold and accounts receivable collected.

The current ratio is computed as:

EQUATION 18.7: Current Ratio

$$CR = CA/CL$$

Where CR   Current Ratio
       CA   Current Assets
       CL   Current Liabilities

Remember current assets are cash, marketable securities, accounts receivable, inventory, and prepaid expenses. Current liabilities are accounts payable and other liabilities due to be paid within the next year.

The quick ratio is computed as:

$$QR = QA/CL$$

Where   QR   Quick Ratio
         CA   Quick Assets
         CL   Current Liabilities

Quick assets are cash, marketable securities, and accounts receivable. Current liabilities are accounts payable and other liabilities due to be paid within the next year.

Total Asset Productivity

So assets work together to create net income. It takes cash, accounts receivable, inventory, plant, and other assets working together to create value. A common measure used to evaluate the investment in total assets is the **return on assets (ROA)**.

ROA is computed as:

$$ROA = NI/TA$$

Where   ROA   Return on Assets
              NI   Net Income
              TA   Total Assets

ANALYZING ASSETS: AN EXAMPLE

Let's look at an example in Conley Enterprises (CE). Conley Enterprises buys handmade crafts from artists around the world and then sells these crafts to specialty stores. The financial statements for CE are shown in Exhibits 18.1 and 18.2. Now let's compute the ratios above for year 2015.

Cash-to-Expense Ratio

Cash-to-Expense Ratio = (Cash + Marketable Securities)/(Total Expenses/365 days) = ($50,000 + $30,000)/(($120,000 + $40,000 + $20,000)/365) = 162 days

CE has cash and marketable securities equal to 162 days of its expenses. That's a lot of cash or near cash (marketable securities). It shows the business should be able to pay its liabilities in the next year regardless of whether sales are good or bad.

EXHIBIT 18.1: Example — Conley Enterprises Balance Sheet

CONLEY ENTERPRISES
BALANCE SHEET AT DECEMBER 31, 2015
(in US Dollars)

Assets		Liabilities	
Cash	$50,000	Accounts Payable	$30,000
Marketable Securities	$30,000	Accrued Liabilities	$10,000
Accounts Receivable	$20,000	Loans Due in Less Than One Year	$20,000
Inventory	$20,000	Total Current Liabilities	$60,000
Total Current Assets	$120,000	Long-Term Liabilities	$140,000
Property, Plant, & Equipment	$300,000	Total Liabilities	$200,000
Less Accumulated Depreciation	$100,000	**Owners' Equity**	
Net	$200,000	Stock	$100,000
		Retained Earnings	$100,000
Intangible Assets	$80,000	Total Owners' Equity	$200,000
Total Assets	$400,000	Total Liabilities and Owners' Equity	$400,000

Accounts-Receivable Turnover Ratio

$$\text{Accounts-Receivable Turnover Ratio} = \text{Sales/Accounts Receivables}$$
$$= \$240,000/\$20,000$$
$$= 12 \text{ times a year}$$

CE turns its accounts receivable over 12 times a year. CE collects its receivables quickly for this type of business.

Accounts-Receivable Collection Period

$$\text{Accounts-Receivable Collection Period} = \text{Accounts Receivable/}$$
$$(\text{Sales/365 days}) = \$20,000/(\$240,000/365)$$
$$= 30 \text{ days}$$

It takes CE 30 days to collect its average receivable. CE collects its receivables quickly for this type of business.

EXHIBIT 18.2: Example—Conley Enterprises Income Statement

CONLEY ENTERPRISES
INCOME STATEMENT FOR YEAR ENDING DECEMBER 31, 2015
(in US Dollars)

Sales	$240,000
Cost of Goods Sold	$120,000
Gross Profit	$120,000
Operating Expenses	$40,000
Operating Profit (EBIT)	$80,000
Interest Expense	$20,000
Taxable Income	$60,000
Taxes	$20,000
Net Income	$40,000

Inventory-Turnover Ratio

$$\text{Inventory-Turnover Ratio} = \text{Cost of Goods Sold}/\text{Inventory}$$
$$= \$120,000/\$20,000$$
$$= 6 \text{ times a year}$$

CE turns its inventory over 6 times a year. This is good for this type of business.

Days'-Sales-in-Inventory Ratio

$$\text{Days'-Sales-in-Inventory Ratio} = \text{Inventory}/(\text{Cost of Goods Sold}/365 \text{ days}) = \$20,000/(\$120,000/365)$$
$$= 61 \text{ days}$$

It takes CE 61 days to sell its inventory. This is good for this type of business.

Fixed-Asset Turnover Ratio

$$\text{Fixed-Asset Turnover Ratio} = \text{Sales}/\text{Fixed Assets}$$
$$= \$240,000/\$200,000$$
$$= 1.2 \text{ times a year}$$

CE turns its fixed assets over 1.2 times a year. This is good for this type of business.

Current Ratio

$$\text{Current Ratio} = \text{Current Assets/Current Liabilities}$$
$$= \$120,000/\$60,000$$
$$= 2$$

CE's current assets are cash, marketable securities, accounts receivable, and inventory; its current liabilities are accounts payable, accrued liabilities, and short-term loans.

For every current liability, CE has 2 times that amount in current assets. This is a lot, but understandable when you realize that CE wants to make sure it can pay its liabilities.

Quick Ratio

$$\text{Quick Ratio} = \text{Quick Assets/Current Liabilities}$$
$$= \$100,000/\$60,000$$
$$= 1.67$$

CE's quick assets are cash, marketable securities and accounts receivable; its current liabilities are accounts payable, accrued liabilities, and short-term loans.

For every current liability, CE has 1.67 times that amount in quick assets. This is a lot, but understandable when you realize that CE wants to make sure it can pay its liabilities.

Return on Assets (ROA)

$$\text{ROA} = \text{Net Income/Total Assets}$$
$$= \$40,000/\$400,000$$
$$= .10$$

CE earns a $.10 return in net income for every dollar invested in assets. Whether this is good or bad depends on how the owners feel. That depends on how the business is financed, a topic for Chapter 19.

CHAPTER SUMMARY

In this chapter we've explored the nature and importance of the assets.
After reading this chapter, you should be able to:

1. Understand the nature and importance of managing assets (Learning Objective 1): An asset is an economic resource that the business owns and uses to make an operating profit. Assets and people produce the operating profit that drives the value of the business.
2. Appreciate how assets are used in a business (Learning Objective 2): There are many types of assets, each with a purpose in creating business value. Different businesses have different assets and combinations of assets because they have different business models and strategies.
3. Appreciate how a business manages assets to create value (Learning Objective 3): Managing assets is a challenge. Businesses need enough assets but do not want too many assets. The benefit from investing in assets must exceed the cost of investing in the assets.

Now that we've explored these questions and issues, it's time to look at the opportunities and challenges in managing a business's information technology and E-commerce. In the business world of today, information, technology, and E-commerce are key parts of "How Business Works."

KEYWORDS

SHORT-ANSWER QUESTIONS

1. What role do assets play in creating business value?
2. What is the difference between current and non-current assets? What is the difference between tangible and intangible assets?
3. Define the following terms:
   a. Asset
   b. Tangible asset
   c. Intangible asset
   d. Current asset
   e. Non-current asset
   f. Working capital
   g. Operating cycle
   h. Current liability
   i. Net working capital
   j. Cash
   k. Transaction demand for money
   l. Precautionary demand for money
   m. Speculative demand for money
   n. Marketable securities
   o. Liquid assets and liquidity
   p. Accounts receivable
   q. Allowance for bad debts
   r. Net receivables
   s. Bad-debt expense
   t. Trade discount
   u. Inventory
   v. Purchased inventory
   w. Produced inventory
   x. Raw materials
   y. Work-in-process
   z. Finished goods
   aa. Consignment
   ab. Prepaid expense
   ac. Property, plant, and equipment (PP&E)
   ad. Fixed asset
   ae. Facilities
   af. Land
   ag. Building
   ah. Depreciation
   ai. Accumulated depreciation
   aj. Net book value
   ak. Depreciation expense
   al. Lessee
   am. Lessor
   an. Rent
   ao. Lease
   ap. Operating lease
   aq. Capital or capitalized lease
   ar. Accumulated amortization
   as. Amortization expense
   at. Patent
   au. Federal Patent Statute of 1957
   av. Patent infringement
   aw. US Court of Appeal for the Federal Circuit
   ax. Copyright
   ay. Revision Act of 1976
   az. Public domain
   ba. United States Copyright Office
   bb. Copyright infringement
   bc. Trademark
   bd. Federal Lanham Trademark Act of 1946
   be. United States Patent and Trademark Office (PTO)
   bf. Trademark infringement
   bg. Generic name
   bh. Goodwill
   bi. Cash-to-expenses ratio
   bj. Accounts-receivable turnover
   bk. Accounts-receivable collection period
   bl. Safety stock
   bm. Inventory turnover
   bn. Days' sales in inventory
   bo. Fixed-asset turnover
   bp. Net present value
   bq. Internal rate of return
   br. Payback
   bs. Current ratio
   bt. Quick ratio
   bu. Return on assets

CRITICAL-THINKING QUESTIONS

1. When does it make sense for a business to invest in assets? When does it not make sense for a business to invest in assets?
2. Why do different businesses have different assets?
3. Think of a business you'd like to own. Answer the following questions:

    a. What assets would you need to operate the business?
    b. How would you manage each asset?

4. Do you think that the productivity of assets is based on the productivity of the people using the assets? Explain.

EXPLORING REAL BUSINESS

Go to the websites of Google, Target, Hyundai, and Procter & Gamble. The websites are

Google:	http://investor.google.com
Target:	http://www.target.com
Hyundai:	http://worldwide.hyundai.com/company-overview
Procter & Gamble:	http://www.pg.com

1. Describe the business model of each company.
2. Compute the following:
    a. Cash-to-expenses ratio
    b. Accounts-receivable turnover
    c. Accounts-receivable collection period
    d. Inventory turnover
    e. Days' sales in inventory
    f. Fixed-asset turnover
    g. Current ratio
    h. Quick ratio
    i. Return on assets
3. Do you think the company is doing a good or bad job managing its assets?

ENDNOTES

1. Keynes, John Maynard. *The General Theory of Employment, Interest and Money*, 1936. Print.
2. How people analyze assets varies. Sometimes people use ratios with average numbers instead of waiting on ending numbers. They'll use average accounts receivable, average inventory, and average fixed assets. Sometimes people use ratios with operating income or cash flow instead of net income. It all depends on the analysts and what they are looking for.

19

CHAPTER

OPPORTUNITIES AND CHALLENGES IN MANAGING FINANCIAL CAPITAL (DEBT AND EQUITY)

Introduction: Let's Talk About Money

It takes money to operate a business. Referred to as financial capital, money is what a business uses to hire people and invest in assets. But how does a business get money? What are the different options available to a business in acquiring financing? How does a business decide what option is best? How does financial capital impact the value of the business?

In this chapter we'll explore these questions and issues. We'll explore the critical opportunities and challenges in managing the financial capital of a business. We'll explore acquiring money and how it is an important part of "How Business Works."

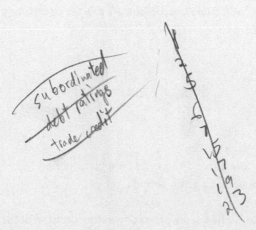

WHY MONEY MATTERS

There is an old saying, "It takes money to make money." Why? The answer is it takes money to hire people and acquire assets. Money is the medium of exchange we use to operate a business and measure value. Money matters because it is what people use to make business work.

LEARNING OBJECTIVE 1

APPRECIATING THE NATURE AND IMPORTANCE OF FINANCIAL CAPITAL

Value is created by people using assets. But it takes money to hire the people and acquire the assets. So a business needs money. But does it really matter how a business acquires the money? In a perfect world where there is no risk, the answer is no, it doesn't matter. However, it does matter in an imperfect world full of risk. The value created by people and assets can be enhanced or destroyed by how the business acquires its money or financial capital.

Let's apply the principles noted in earlier chapters and look at a simple example of creating value. You start a business and plan to operate the business for one year, at which time you will dissolve the business. You acquire $10,000 for one year at a cost of 6%. You invest the $10,000 and earn an operating profit of $500. You make and sell a product. The revenue from these sales exceeds the cost of these sales by $500. You now have the original $10,000 plus the $500 profit from operating the business. However, the providers of your money are expecting a 6% return or an operating profit of $600. You destroyed value. Simply put, the cost of the money ($600) is greater than the operating profit ($500) you generated from investing in people and assets. However, was value destroyed because you made a poor investing decision or a poor financing decision? If you acquired the $10,000 at a cost of 4%, you would have created value. Thus,creating value is about comparing the benefits from investing versus the cost of financing. The financing decision does matter.

The financing decision is about acquiring the right amount of money at the lowest possible price. Now look back at Chapter 10. Remember the weighted average cost of capital? Remember we want that blend of **debt** and equity that minimizes the weighted average cost of capital. Given that debt is less expensive than equity, the business wants to borrow all the money it can afford. The rest of the money a business needs should be acquired as equity.

But how does a business determine how much it can afford? Often a business will look at its coverage ratio. A **coverage ratio** compares a business's earnings before interest and taxes (EBIT) to the cost of its debt. An **interest coverage ratio** compares a business's pre-tax operating profit with the interest a business owes in a given period.[1]

EQUATION 19.1: Interest Coverage Ratio

$$ICR = EBIT/I$$

Where

ICR	Interest Coverage Ratio
EBIT	Earnings before interest and taxes for a given period
I	Interest expense for a given period

A **debt coverage ratio** compares a business's pre-tax operating profit with the interest and principal a business owes in a given period.

EQUATION 19.2: Debt Coverage Ratio

$$DCR = EBIT/(I + D)$$

Where

DCR	Debt Coverage Ratio
EBIT	Earnings before interest and taxes for a given period
I	Interest expense for a given period
D	Principal payments on debt for a given period

Let's look at an example of computing the interest coverage ratio and debt coverage ratio. During a year, Cameron Corporation has an operating profit (EBIT) of $100,000. The business has interest expense of $5,000 and debt principal payments of $25,000. Cameron Corporation's interest coverage ratio is 20 ($100,000/$5,000). Cameron Corporation earns an operating profit twenty times the amount it owes in interest expense. Cameron Corporation's debt coverage ratio is 3.33 ($100,000/($5,000 + $25,000)). Cameron Corporation earns an operating profit 3.33 times the amount it owes in interest expense plus debt principal payments.

A higher coverage ratio implies the business is using less debt and more equity. A lower coverage ratio implies the business is using more debt and less equity. So how much coverage should a business have? When a business is uncertain of its EBIT or pre-tax operating profit, it will use less debt and more equity. It will have a high coverage ratio. Why? The answer is that the business wants to make sure that its operating profit is always sufficient to cover or pay the cost of its debt. In contrast, if a business is certain of its EBIT or pre-tax operating profit, it will have a low coverage ratio. Why? The answer is that the business is confident that its operating profit will be sufficient to cover or pay the cost of debt. The business can be financed with a lot of debt.

Now think about it. If a business is investing the money in a venture that is risky, then it needs financing that is flexible. Debt requires repayment at specific times and under specific conditions. If the

BUSINESS SENSE

AFFORDING DEBT

How much debt can a business afford? Figuring that out is a lot like figuring out how much debt you can afford.

Think about it. You want to buy a new television to replace your old television. You find one that is perfect. It costs $500, and you have $200 in the bank. But you also have a personal line of credit called a credit card. You have a credit limit of $2,000. You can buy the television, but you'll need to charge between $300 and $500, depending on how much cash you want to keep. You think about it. The credit card is a loan that must be repaid. Plus it is an expensive loan that costs you 18% per year, or 1.5% per month. You calculate your monthly payment if you borrow $300. It's approximately $30 per month. You ask yourself two questions. First, does the new television give you added enjoyment worth $30 per month? Does it add $30 in value? Second, can you afford to pay $30 a month? Will you have the cash to pay off the debt?

A business must ask the same two questions when it borrows money. First, will the money be used to create value? Do the benefits of spending or investing the money outweigh the cost of the money? Second, can the business repay the loan given the terms of the loan?

business fails to meet those terms and conditions, the business could fail. Instead of using debt, the business wants to finance risky investments with equity. Remember equity is not as restrictive as debt. Owners expect a return. However, owners are not guaranteed anything. Owners accept higher risk than lenders. Owners are compensated for this higher risk with higher expected returns.

Conversely if a business is investing the money in a venture that is not risky, then it should use debt. Debt is cheaper than equity and lowers the business's weighted average cost of capital. The business can feel good about borrowing money. It can guarantee that it will be able to pay the debt at the specified times and under the specified terms.

Analysts use ratios to look at the amount of debt and equity a business uses to finance its assets. A common measure is the debt ratio. The **debt ratio** is the percentage of debt used to finance assets.

EQUATION 19.3: Debt Ratio

$$DR = TD/TA$$

Where

DR	Debt ratio
TD	Total debt
TA	Total assets

Let's look at an example of computing the debt ratio. Addie Industries has total assets of $1,000,000. These assets are financed with $300,000 in debt and $700,000 in owners' equity. Addie Industries has a debt ratio of 30% ($300,000/$1,000,000).

So what are the options in acquiring money with debt and equity?

LEARNING OBJECTIVE 2

. . . .

ACQUIRING MONEY WITH DEBT

A debt is a contractual loan agreement between the provider of money, called the lender, and the user of the money, called the borrower. There are three major sources of debt. First is trade credit. Second are financial intermediaries such as banks. Third is the capital market.

USING TRADE CREDIT

The term **trade credit** relates to money that a business owes to its suppliers. When a business buys goods or services, it typically pays for these products after the products are delivered. During the time between delivery and payment, the business is indebted to the supplier. A business and its suppliers agree on when the business will pay the debt before the product is delivered.

Most trade credit is called accounts payable. **Accounts payable** is trade credit that is documented with a bill. When a business does not receive a bill at the time the product is received, the business estimates the amount of the debt. Such debts are called **accrued liabilities**. Fees to lawyers, accountants, and other professionals are often accrued. Salaries and other compensation earned by and owed to employees are also accrued.

Typically suppliers of trade credit do not charge interest. However, suppliers may give a discount if the business pays early. Look back at Chapter 17. Look over the discussion about trade discounts in the section on working capital and current assets—accounts receivable. A supplier's accounts receivable is the accounts payable of the business purchasing the product.

BORROWING FROM FINANCIAL INTERMEDIARIES

What is a financial intermediary? A **financial intermediary** is a business that acquires money from one source and then provides it to others. Banks, savings institutions, and credit unions are examples of financial intermediaries. Let's see how financial intermediaries operate by looking at a bank. Depositors deposit money in a bank expecting the bank to repay the money. The bank then lends the money to individuals and businesses. The bank pays the depositor a lower rate of interest than it charges its loan customers. The difference in interest rates enables the bank to pay its other operating costs and provide a profit to the bank's owners.

Because financial intermediaries are a critical part of the US economy, they are regulated. The **US Federal Reserve (the Fed)** and the **US Federal Deposit Insurance Company (FDIC)** are the primary regulators of banks in the United States. The Fed sets guidelines for lending, operating, accepting risk, and minimum levels of equity. The FDIC insures bank deposits. The standard deposit insurance amount is $250,000 per depositor, per bank.

Financial intermediaries lend money to businesses in the form of loans. A loan agreement is a financial contract. The document that details the terms of the agreement is called the **indenture**. These specific terms must be met, or the lender

THE BUSINESS OF BANKING

Think about it. How does a bank operate? Banks make net income by obtaining funds and then lending and investing these funds. In the United States, banks acquire approximately 92% of their funds with deposits (liabilities). That means banks have approximately 8% stockholders' equity. To attract deposits, banks pay depositors interest. On average, 80% of U.S. bank assets are loans or investments. A bank makes net income only when the interest it earns on loans and investments exceeds the interest it pays on deposits plus other operating expenses.

Most people think the business of banking is about earning a return on loans and investments that is greater than the cost of their deposits. That's important. But operating a bank is also about risk management. First there is default risk. Depositors do not accept default risk in loaning a bank money. However the bank takes default risk when lending out the money. Second is liquidity risk. Think about using a depositor's checking account to fund a 30 year mortgage. What happens when the depositor demands their money and the bank does not have it? The bank will not be repaid by the borrower for years. Third is interest rate risk. Think about a depositor agreeing to lend money to the bank for one year at a fixed interest rate (e.g., certificate of deposit). Now think about the bank using this money to fund a five year car loan at a fixed interest rate. What happens when the depositor comes to the bank in one year and demands a higher interest rate because the economy is doing better? The interest earned on the loan does not change, but the cost of the money that funds the loan goes up. The bank could lose money. Fourth is operating risk. Can you imagine the billions of transactions that a big bank processes each year? Think about the risk of incorrectly processing each transaction.

Risk is everywhere in a bank. Banks are highly leveraged businesses that operate in very competitive markets. That's why banks are regulated. When a bank takes on more risk, regulators require the bank to have more stockholders' equity. Safety and soundness are important to every good banker. Risk management is critical for a bank to survive and prosper.

can use the court system to make the borrower repay or force the borrower into bankruptcy. The loan agreement specifics the following:

- The amount of money borrowed and owed to the lender. This is called the **loan principal**.

- The periodic cost of the loan, or **interest rate**. Interest rates are typically stated in annual terms although they may be computed in periods less than one year.

- The timing of the loan. The loan contract specifies when the borrower will repay the principal and interest to the lender. The loan contract also specifies when the loan will be completely repaid. This point in time is called the loan's **maturity**.

- The special conditions to which the borrower and lender agree. Often called **loan covenants**, these conditions include what the borrower can and cannot do. Examples include maintaining a given level of cash or working capital, not paying dividends, providing collateral, or not borrowing any additional money.

- The rights of the lender and borrower. The loan agreement specifies what happens if the other party fails to fulfill the loan contract.

Loans from financial intermediaries can take different forms. Short-term loans are loans that must be repaid within one year. Such loans are often called **working-capital loans** and help finance temporary increases in accounts receivable and inventory. A special type of short-term loan is a line of credit. A **line of credit** is an agreement between a business and financial intermediary that gives the business the right to borrow a given amount of money, under agreed-upon conditions, during a specified period of time. The business is not required to borrow the money but has the ability to borrow the money any time it needs it during the specified period. Note the business has the right, not the obligation, to borrow the money. For this right, the business typically pays a fee to the financial intermediary, in addition to any interest and principal on money actually borrowed.

Long-term loans finance the long-term needs of the business, including the acquisition of land, building, and equipment. Many long-term loans, called **mortgages**, are collateralized by selected assets such as land, building, or equipment. In case the business fails to repay the loan as agreed, the financial intermediary can seize and sell the assets.

BORROWING IN CAPITAL MARKETS

Financial intermediaries borrow money (e.g., deposits) and lend that money to others. Financial intermediaries bring together the people and organizations that have the money (e.g., depositors) and those that need the money (e.g., loan customers). To demonstrate, let's look at a bank. The depositor provides the money to the bank. The bank lends the money to a loan customer who needs a loan to buy a car, buy a home, or other need. This loan customer does not owe the depositor. The loan customer owes the bank and the bank owes the depositor. Thus, the bank is an intermediary.

Capital markets also bring together the people and organizations that have and need money. However, capital markets are the place where the providers and users of money come together directly. Lenders who have money lend directly to borrowers. A **capital market** is defined as a market where debt and equity are traded. Capital markets are often called **securities markets** because such markets are a place where debt and equity securities are sold and bought. Acquiring equity is discussed in more depth later.

Like a loan from a financial intermediary, a loan issued in a capital market has an indenture. The indenture specifies the principal, interest rate, maturity, covenants, and rights of all parties.

Businesses use capital markets to borrow short-term and long-term money. **Commercial paper** is short-term, unsecured loans issued in a capital market, by large, low-risk businesses. Commercial paper is used to finance short-term and working-capital needs of a business. When a business uses commercial paper, it is said to acquire the money in a special part of the capital market called the **Money Market**.

A **bond** is a long-term loan that is issued in a capital market. There are many types of bonds. Bonds are typically issued for periods greater than one year. Many bonds have maturities of ten years, twenty years, thirty years, or even longer. Borrowers may agree to pledge assets to lower the risk to lenders. Such bonds are called **collateralized or secured bonds**. Bonds that are not backed by collateral are called unsecured bonds. Bonds that have low priority of claims in bankruptcy are called **subordinated bonds**. Unsecured subordinated bonds are called **debentures**. Look at the Chapter 07. Remember bankruptcy? Unsecured or subordinated debt has a lower priority of claims in bankruptcy. Thus, such debt is subordinated to secured debt backed with collateral.

THE COST OF DEBT

Lenders, whether a financial intermediary or participant in a capital market, require borrowers to pay for the use of their money. This cost is called interest. Look back into Chapter 10. The interest rate is a function of a risk-free rate and a risk premium. Look at Equation 19.4 and Exhibit 19.1.

EQUATION 19.4: The Required Rate of Return for Debt

$$Rd = Rf + Risk\ Premium$$

Where

Rd	Required rate of return on the debt
R_f	Risk-free rate of return in the economy
Risk Premium	The additional required return to compensate for lenders' risk

EXHIBIT 19.1: Risk and Return

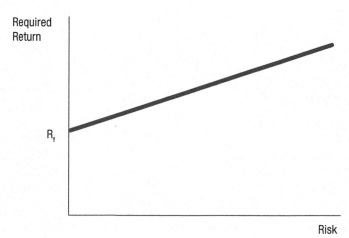

The Risk-Free Rate

Remember, the risk-free rate is a short-term rate where lenders are certain the borrower will repay the loan as agreed. In reality there is no perfect measure of the risk-free rate because there is no loan where lenders are 100% certain of repayment. However, lenders often use the interest rate the US government pays on its short-term borrowing, such as the interest rate on 90-day US Treasury Bills. This rate is called the **90-day T-bill** rate.[2]

Standard & Poor's Headquarters in Lower Manhattan, New York City, New York.

As noted in Chapter 04, the economy expands and contracts through cycles. As such, the demand and supply of money expands and contracts, causing the cost of money to go up and down. Thus, the risk-free rate is not constant, but changes through time.

Risk Premium

The risk premium lenders charge is the compensation the lender requires for accepting risk. The primary risk the lender accepts is the risk of not being paid as agreed upon. This is called default risk. Like the risk-free rate, risk premiums are

EXHIBIT 19.2: Debt Ratings

Moody's		S&P		Fitch		
Long-term	Short-term	Long-term	Short-term	Long-term	Short-term	
Aaa		AAA		AAA		Prime
Aa1		AA+	A-1+	AA+	F1+	
Aa2	P-1	AA		AA		High grade
Aa3		AA-		AA-		
A1		A+	A-1	A+	F1	
A2		A		A		Upper medium grade
A3	P-2	A-	A-2	A-	F2	
Baa1		BBB+		BBB+		
Baa2	P-3	BBB	A-3	BBB	F3	Lower medium grade
Baa3		BBB-		BBB-		
Ba1		BB+		BB+		Non-investment grade speculative
Ba2		BB		BB		
Ba3		BB-	B	BB-	B	
B1		B+		B+		
B2		B		B		Highly speculative
B3		B-		B-		
Caa1	Not prime	CCC+				Substantial risks
Caa2		CCC				Extremely speculative
Caa3		CCC-	C	CCC	C	In default with little prospect for recovery
Ca		CC				
		C				
C				DDD		
/		D	/	D	/	In default
/				D		

WHAT'S UP WITH INTEREST RATES

When people talk about loans, you often hear terms such as prime, subprime, or LIBOR? These terms all relate to loans and interest rates. Remember interest is the price of borrowed money called debt, liabilities, or loans. Given debt comes in many forms, different terms are used.

First is the risk free rate. In the US, many use the US 90 Day Treasury Bill rate as the risk free rate. These Treasury Bills are often referred to as "T Bills." However many people around the world do not use the US Treasury Bill rate as a risk free rate. They use the London Interbank Offered Rate, referred to as "LIBOR." LIBOR is the interest rate that high quality international banks charge one another for short-term interbank loans.

Second, are terms used to address risk and interest rates. The term "Prime Rate" is used to indicate the lender sees the borrower as a low risk borrower. The loan is a "Prime Loan." The lender charges the borrower the lowest rate feasible, often called the lender's prime rate. If the lender see the borrower as a high risk, the lender will charge the borrower a higher rate to compensate for the higher risk. The loan is called a "Sub Prime Loan," as its quality is less than a prime loan. The interest rate charged on subprime loans depends on the degree of risk the lender perceives.

also a function of the demand and supply of money. As such, the risk premium lenders charge borrowers changes over time.

To measure the risk premium at a specific time, financial intermediaries use research to analyze a borrower's past and present. The financial intermediary then forecasts the borrower's future. In the process of this analysis, the financial intermediary will categorize the loan from very low risk to very high risk. If the financial intermediary agrees to lend to the borrower, the financial intermediary will charge a higher interest rate for higher risk.

In capital markets, lenders often use rating agencies to help analyze the default risk in a loan. Examples of credit rating agencies include Moody's, Standard & Poors (S&P), and Fitch. These agencies rate a debt issue and provide a debt rating. The higher the rating, the less the perceived default risk. Less risk means less risk premium, which means the cost of the debt is lower. The lower the rating, the more the perceived default risk. More risk means more risk premium, which means the cost of the debt is higher. Look at Exhibit 19.2 and see the criteria used by agencies that rate debt.

Fixed and Variable Rate Loans

A **fixed-rate loan** specifies the interest rate as a specific rate that does not change over the life of the loan. However, because interest rates change over time, some lenders and borrowers prefer to specify the interest rate as a variable rate. A **variable-rate loan**, often called a **floating-rate** or **adjustable-rate** loan, is a loan where the interest rate changes over time. An example would be a loan where the borrower is charged an interest rate equal to the current 90-day T-bill rate plus 2%. As the 90-day T-bill rate changes, so does the interest rate on the loan. As interest rates in the economy drop, the borrower pays less interest. As interest rates in the economy increase, the borrower pays more interest.

ACQUIRING MONEY WITH EQUITY

Owners provide money to businesses. Owners' money is called owners' equity. The reward for owning a business is the net income (or loss) that a business earns and the value the profit creates. For this net income, owners must bear the highest level of risk in a business.

BUSINESS SENSE

WHAT'S UP WITH DIVIDENDS?

Have you ever wondered what cash dividends, stock dividends, and stock splits are? Have you ever wondered why and when a company may pay a cash dividend, or issue a stock dividend, or split its stock?

First, let's look at cash dividends. A cash dividend is a payment, in cash, of retained earnings. Although many people look at a company's current dividend versus its current net income, dividends paid in a given year are not paid from the net income of that year. Often people will compute a dividend-payout ratio. A dividend-payout ratio is a company's current dividends divided by its current net income. However, many businesses pay dividends in years they are unprofitable. Likewise many businesses that are profitable do not pay dividends. But why is this so?

A business pays cash dividends because it cannot use the cash to create value. When a business pays cash dividends, it is reducing an asset called cash. It is also reducing its retained earnings and thus owners' equity. The business is doing so because it cannot use the cash to create value. The business cannot use the cash to earn a return that exceeds the cost of equity, the return owners require. The owners are better off because the business does not hold onto excess cash that does not create value. The owners can take their cash dividends and find better, more valuable uses outside the business. On the other hand, if the business can use the cash and earn a return that is greater than the owners' required rate of return, then the business should keep the cash and not pay cash dividends. In doing so, they are creating value for the owners by giving the owners a return that is greater than they require.

So cash dividends are a distribution of retained earnings that a business cannot use to create value. But what are stock dividends and stock splits? A stock dividend occurs when a company issues new shares of stock to existing stockholders, without the stockholders paying the company for those shares. An example is when a company declares a 1-for-10 stock dividend. If you own 10 shares of a company, the company will give you an 11th share free. A stock split is merely a large stock dividend, where the number of shares outstanding changes by greater than 25%. An example is a 2-for-1 stock split. If you currently own 1 share of a company, you will own 2 shares of the company after the split. The number of shares outstanding after the stock split is 100% greater than it was before the stock split.

Stock dividends and stock splits do not increase or decrease cash or owners' equity. Stock dividends and splits only change the number of shares outstanding. So why does a business have a stock dividend or split? Sometimes a business uses stock dividends and splits to signal good things or upcoming events. Let's look at an example. A business's stock price is $100 per share. The business realizes that good things are going to happen in the future that will increase its value. Although the business is happy with its increasing value (called Market Cap), it is concerned that some potential stockholders may not be able to purchase its stock if the price increases beyond $100. So the business declares a 2-for-1 stock split. After the split, the number of shares outstanding doubles and price per share drops to around $50. Yet the Market Cap does not decrease. The value of the business is maintained, yet the price per share is lowered.

There are two ways in which an owner provides money to a business. First, an owner can contribute money. For that contribution an owner receives the right to select the management, make critical decisions, and control the business. Second, an owner can decide to let the business keep or retain the net income (loss) the business earns. Businesses retain earnings because they need the funds to grow or meet other needs.

A proprietorship has an owners' equity account called **proprietorship capital**. Proprietorship capital is a combination of money an owner has contributed and the net income (or loss) the owner has retained in the business. A partnership has individual accounts for each partner. These accounts sum to be owners' equity and are called **partnership capital**. Partnership capital reflects what each partner contributed to the business and each partner's share of the net income or loss in the business.

Corporations have **stock**. When a business is a corporation, it sells or issues stock to its owners called **stockholders** or **shareholders**. The documents that show a person or organization owns a share of a corporation are called **stock certificates**. The owners pay the business for the stock. The amount the business receives is reflected in two owners' equity accounts. The first account is the par account. **Par** is the official stated value of the stock, often called the **face value** of the stock. Second is an account called **capital surplus**, sometimes called **paid-in-capital in excess of par**. All amounts, received from stockholders, greater than par are recorded in this account. The two accounts, par and capital surplus, sum to the amount the stockholders paid the company when the stock was issued by the company.

Owners control the business by voting. An owner of a sole proprietorship owns all of the business and thus makes all owner decisions. Partners own part of a partnership, and vote according to the partnership agreement. Look back to Chapter 06. Note that there are different types of partners and partnerships, including general and limited. Stockholders vote according to rights outlined in their stock certificate.

THE TYPES OF CORPORATE STOCK

To sell stock, a business must get permission from its existing stockholders. When stockholders approve of selling stock, the stock is said to be **authorized**. When the business sells the stock, the stock is issued. The stock is said to be **authorized**, **issued**, and **outstanding**. If the business decides to buy the stock back from stockholders, this repurchase is called **Treasury Stock**. The repurchased stock is said to be **authorized**, **issued**, **but not outstanding**. If the existing stockholders decide that the repurchased stock cannot be sold again, the stock is no longer authorized and is **retired**.

In addition to the stock accounts, corporations have an account called **retained earnings**. Retained earnings are the accumulated profits (losses) that have remained in the business that have not been paid to owners in the form of dividends. Retained earnings are the property of owners and thus a part of owners' equity. When a business no longer needs to retain the profits, the business pays the profits to its owners. In a corporation, these payments of profits are called **cash dividends**.

There are two basic types of stock, common and preferred. All corporations have common stock. Some corporations choose to issue preferred stock.

Common stock represents the ownership of the business. Common stockholders elect the business's Board of Directors. The Board of Directors hires the business's management. Common stockholders thus directly or indirectly control the business. The power and responsibility of governing a corporation rests in its common stockholders. Dividends paid to common stockholders are called **common dividends**.

Preferred stock represents a group of owners that have special rights or preference. When a business issues preferred stock, it promises to pay the preferred stockholders a stipulated amount of dividends each period. Dividends paid to preferred stockholders are called **preferred dividends**. An example is a corporation that issues 6% preferred stock, with a par of $100. The corporation promises

to pay the holder of each share of preferred stock a preferred dividend of $6 per year (6% times $100 par) before it pays a dividend to its common stockholders. If a corporation does not pay these preferred dividends, the business cannot pay dividends to its common stockholders. For these special rights, a preferred stockholder's dividends are limited to the amount specified in the preferred stock certificate. Preferred stockholders typically do not vote on critical matters such as the selection of the Board of Directors. Although preferred regarding dividends, preferred stockholders have limited power in directing company decisions.

ACQUIRING EQUITY USING CAPITAL MARKETS

Equity, as well as some debt, is sold through capital markets. Capital markets can be public or private. A **public capital market** is a capital market where anyone can buy the debt or equity issued by a business. The New York Stock Exchange is an example of a public capital market. In the US, public capital markets are regulated by the **Securities and Exchange Commission (SEC)** and other government agencies. A **private capital market** is a capital market that is not open to everyone. Only selected people or organizations can buy debt or equity in a private capital market. As such, private capital markets are less regulated than public capital markets. When a business sells debt or equity through a private capital market, it is often called a **private placement**.

When a company issues stock in a public capital market for the first time, the issue is called an **initial public offering (IPO)**. When the same business sells subsequent stock issues, these stock issues are called **secondary stock offerings (SPO)**.

Capital markets use brokers and agents who help investors and lenders find businesses that need their money. Such brokers help negotiate the deal and are called **investment bankers**. For their services, an investment banker is paid a fee based on the size and complexity of the deal. An investment banker helps the borrower create and sell the debt or equity contract in a capital market. The selling of debt and equity in a capital market is called **issuing the debt or equity**. Finding a buyer for the debt or equity is often called **placing the debt or equity**. If an investment banker guarantees the business issuing the debt or equity a specific amount of money, it is said the investment banker is **underwriting** the debt or equity issue.

The U.S. Securities and Exchange Commission headquarters located in Washington, D.C.

THE COST OF EQUITY

After a business pays its operating costs and the cost of its debt, what results is net income. This net income or loss belongs to the owners of the business. Businesses compute the net income per share of stock by dividing net income, less preferred dividends, by the number of common shares outstanding. This is called **earning per share (EPS)**.

Net income of loss is a residual and can be great or small. Everyone else in a business gets paid before owners. As such, owners accept the highest risk in a business and expect to receive the highest return. Look at back at Exhibit 19.1: Risk and Return. The higher the risk owners accept, the higher the return they expect. So how much return do owners expect or require? Look at Equation 19.5.

EQUATION 19.5: The Required Rate of Return for Equity

$$Re = R_f + Risk\ Premium$$

Where

Re	Required rate of return on equity
R_f	Risk-free rate of return in the economy
Risk Premium	The additional required return to compensate for owner's risk

The risk-free rate of return is the same risk-free rate of return discussed in the cost of debt. However, the risk premium is different because the risk accepted by an owner is different from the risk of a lender. First, lenders get their interest before stockholders get their net income. Second, if a business is liquidated, lenders have a higher priority of claim than owners. Lenders get their money before owners. Thus, lenders are more certain than owners in receiving their money. Lenders have risk, but less risk than owners. Owners have the highest risk of anyone in a business.

So how do owners determine how much risk they are accepting and how much risk premium to require? Measuring the risk of ownership is a challenge. First, a business is not legally bound to earn net income or pay a dividend. A business does its best, but unlike debt, is not contractually obligated to provide a return. Second, risk deals with the future. The business's past performance may or may not be a good indicator of the business's future.

Owners use different ways to estimate their risk. Some are quantifiable and some are subjective. The most-used measure builds on the concept of diversification. Owners are expected to diversify their risk by using a portfolio of stocks. As such, the risk that should be rewarded is the risk that cannot be diversified. This risk is measured by a term called Beta. **Beta** measures how the return from a business is correlated to the return earned from investing in the overall market for stocks. Beta measures the **non-diversifiable** or **systematic risk** in an investment. (Note: Look back at Chapter 11 for a discussion of diversification.)

THE VALUE OF OWNERSHIP—MEASURING RETURN (ROE)

The cost of equity is real. However, it is also a challenge to measure because it is subjective. A measure often used to evaluate the return an owner earns is called return on equity (ROE). **Return on equity** is the ratio of a business's net income divided by its owners' equity.

EQUATION 19.6: Return on Equity (ROE)

$$ROE = NI/OE$$

Where	ROE	Return on Equity
	NI	Net Income
	OE	Owners' Equity

Now think about how a business creates net income. A business acquires money with debt and equity. It hires people and invests the money in assets. The people use the assets and operate the business, creating an operating profit. The business uses the operating profit to first pay interest to the providers of debt. What remains is net income. Now let's decompose return on equity (ROE) into these three components. First is acquiring money with debt and owners' equity. Second is the investing of money in assets. Third is using the assets to create a net income. Return on equity (ROE) can be decomposed as follows:

EQUATION 19.7: Return on Equity (ROE) Decomposed

$$ROE = NI/S * S/TA * TA/OE$$

Where   ROE   Return on Equity
           NI   Net Income
           S   Sales
           TA   Total Assets
           OE   Owners' Equity

The ratio of net income to sales (NI/S) is called the **net income percentage** or **profit margin**. This ratio measures how the business operates. The ratio of sales to total assets (S/TA) is called **total-asset turnover**. This ratio measures the productivity of investing in assets. The ratio of total assets to owners' equity (TA/OE) is called **financial leverage**. This ratio measures how a business finances it assets.

Let's look at an example. In a given year, Golden Bears, Inc. earns net income of $100,000. It has sales of $1,000,000, total assets of $500,000, and owners' equity of $200,000. The ROE for Golden Bears, Inc. is 50% ($100,000/$200,000). Now decompose ROE into the profit margin, total-asset turnover, and financial leverage. What you see is the profit margin is 10% ($100,000/$1,000,000). Total-asset turnover is 2 ($1,000,000/$500,000). Financial leverage is 2.5 ($500,000/$200,000). Return on equity can be decomposed as:

$$ROE = .10 * 2 * 2.5$$
$$ROE = .50 \text{ or } 50\%$$

THE VALUE OF OWNERSHIP—SOME SUMMARY THOUGHTS

Remember the value of owning a business is a function of the net income an owner expects to receive, the timing of the expected net income, and an opportunity cost called the expected or required rate of return. This required rate of return for owners, called the cost of equity, is a function of risk. The value of a business to its owners is created and maximized by producing timely net income that is the highest in quantity and lowest in risk. This is a challenge. To meet this challenge, owners and managers must recognize that a business is a well-crafted portfolio of people, assets, and money. When properly managed, a business creates value for its owners by creating value for its customers, employees, suppliers, and society. It's about teamwork.

In summary, a **business** is an organization, recognized under the law, which attempts to create value by exchanging products with customers for money or money substitutes. How business works is about creating value by acquiring money, using the money to hire people and invest in assets, and operating in such a way as to create a sustainable competitive advantage. In a free market economy, how business works is about competing to win.

BOOK AND MARKET VALUE

Look back at Chapter 08—Financial Reporting and Accounting. Think about the challenge of reporting value. Does a business use historical values or current market values in its balance sheet? Does the value of owners' equity reflect what has happened (historical value) or what owners expect to happen in the future (current market value)?

Look back to the discussion of conservatism in Chapter 08. US accounting standards are conservative and use historical values. US standards are designed not to overstate value even if it means value is understated. What does that mean for owners' equity? It means that the accounting value (referred to as "book value") of a business may not be the market value of the business.

The book value of a business is the owners' equity value reported in its financial statements. In the US, book value is a conservative measure of the value of a business. Book value of a business reflects what owners paid for the business in the past and retained earnings. Does the book value reflect what someone would pay to buy the business now? The answer is not always. The current market value of a business is a function of the future earnings that owners and prospective owners think they will receive. The current value of the business is often called the market capitalization (Market Cap) of a business. The market capitalization of a business is the current price of each share of stock multiplied by the number of shares outstanding.

Let's look at some examples of this issue. First, look at Google, Procter & Gamble, Target, and Hyundai. Look at the financial statements of each company. Look at the value of owners' equity. What do you see? You see the book value of each of these companies. Second, look at the current stock price and shares outstanding of each of the companies. Multiply the current stock price per share and the shares outstanding to compute the company's Market Cap. What have you done? You've determined what the current market is saying the company is worth. Now compare the book value and Market Cap of each company. What do you see? You see the Market Cap, or current market value, of each company is greater than its book value. Why? US accounting standards are conservative. People who analyze a company must understand that a business's financial statements may not always reflect everything they need to know.

CHAPTER SUMMARY

In this chapter we've explored the nature and importance of the money provided by lenders and owners. After reading this chapter, you should be able to:

1. Understand the nature and importance of financial capital (Learning Objective 1): Financial capital is the money a business receives from debt and owners' equity. Financial capital has a cost. The providers of the debt and owners' equity require an operating profit that compensates them for the use of their money over time and accepting risk. A business tries to minimize the cost of financial capital by having the right amount of debt and owners' equity.
2. Appreciate the types, benefits, and costs of debt (Learning Objective 2): A debt is a contractual loan agreement between the provider of money, called the lender, and the user of the money, called the borrower. There are three major sources of debt: trade credit, financial intermediaries, and capital markets.
3. Appreciate the types, benefits, and costs of equity (Learning Objective 3): There are two ways in which owners provide money to a business: contributed capital and retained earnings. Contributed capital is acquired in the capital market.

In this chapter we've explored these questions and issues. We've explored the critical opportunities and challenges in managing the financial capital of a business.

KEYWORDS

90-day T-bill 412

accounts payable 408

accrued liabilities 408

adjustable-rate loan 413

authorized, issued, but not
    outstanding 415

beta 417

bond 411

borrower 408

business 418

capital market 410

capital surplus 415

cash dividends 415

collateralized or secured bonds
    411

commercial paper 411

common dividends 415

common stock 415

coverage ratio 406

debentures 411

debt 406

debt coverage ratio 406

debt rating 412

debt ratio 408

default risk 412

earning per share (EPS) 416

face value 415

financial intermediary 409

financial leverage 418

fixed-rate loan 413

floating-rate loan 413

indenture 409

initial public offering (IPO) 416

interest coverage ratio 406

interest rate 409

investment bankers 416

issuing the debt or equity 416

lender 408

line of credit 410

loan covenants 410

loan principal 410

London Interbank Offered Rate
    (LIBOR) 413

maturity 410

Money Market 411

mortgages 410

net income percentage 418

non-diversifiable or systematic
    risk 417

paid-in-capital in excess of par
    415

partnership capital 415

placing the debt or equity 416

preferred dividends 416

preferred stock 415

prime loan 413

prime rate 413

private capital market 416

private placement 416

profit margin 418

proprietorship capital 415

public capital market 416

retained earnings 415

return on equity 417

secondary stock offerings (SPO)
    416

Securities and Exchange
    Commission (SEC) 416

securities markets 410

shareholders 415

stock 415

stock certificates 415

stockholders 415

subordinated bonds 411

subprime loan 413

total-asset turnover 418

trade credit 408

Treasury Stock 415

underwriting 416

unsecured bonds 411

US Federal Deposit Insurance
    Company (FDIC) 409

US Federal Reserve (the Fed) 409

variable-rate loan 413

working-capital loans 410

SHORT-ANSWER QUESTIONS

1. What role does financing play in creating business value?
2. Why is debt less expensive to use than owners' equity?
3. What are debt ratings and what do they measure?
4. Define the following terms:
   a. Coverage ratio
   b. Interest-coverage ratio
   c. Debt-coverage ratio
   d. Debt ratio
   e. Debt
   f. Lender
   g. Borrower
   h. Indenture
   i. Loan principal
   j. Interest rate
   k. Maturity
   l. Loan covenant
   m. Trade credit
   n. Accounts payable
   o. Accrued liabilities
   p. Financial intermediary
   q. US Federal Reserve (FED)
   r. US Federal Deposit Insurance Company (FDIC)
   s. Working capital loan
   t. Line of credit
   u. Mortgage
   v. Capital market
   w. Securities market
   x. Commercial paper
   y. Money market
   z. Bond
   aa. Collateralized or secured bond
   ab. Unsecured bonds
   ac. Subordinated bonds
   ad. Debentures
   ae. Capital lease
   af. Cost of debt
   ag. 90-day T-bill rate
   ah. Default risk
   ai. Fixed-rate loan
   aj. Variable-rate loan
   ak. Floating-rate loan
   al. Adjustable-rate loan
   am. Debt rating
   an. Proprietorship capital
   ao. Partnership capital
   ap. Stock
   aq. Stockholders or shareholders
   ar. Stock certificate
   as. Par
   at. Capital surplus or paid-in-capital in excess of par
   au. Book value
   av. Market capitalization (Market Cap)
   aw. Authorized stock
   ax. Issued stock
   ay. Outstanding stock
   az. Treasury stock
   ba. Retired stock
   bb. Retained earnings
   bc. Dividend
   bd. Cash dividends
   be. Stock dividends
   bf. Stock splits
   bg. Common stock
   bh. Common dividends
   bi. Preferred stock
   bj. Preferred dividends
   bk. Public capital market
   bl. US Securities and Exchange Commission (SEC)
   bm. Private capital market
   bn. Initial public offering (IPO)
   bo. Secondary public offering (SPO)
   bp. Investment banker
   bq. Issuing the debt or stock
   br. Placing the debt or stock
   bs. Underwriting
   bt. Earnings per share (EPS)
   bu. Beta
   bv. Non-diversifiable or systematic risk
   bw. Return on equity (ROE)
   bx. Net income percentage or profit margin
   by. Total-asset turnover
   bz. Financial leverage
   ca. Business

CRITICAL-THINKING QUESTIONS

1. When does it make sense for a business to finance with debt and when does it make sense for a company to finance with owners' equity?
2. Why is the cost of equity so hard to measure?
3. How does return on equity reflect the acquiring and using of money?

4. How does the productivity of assets affect how a business should be financed? Explain.
5. Think of a business you'd like to own. Answer the following questions:
   a. How would you finance the business?
   b. Why would you finance the business that way?

EXPLORING REAL BUSINESS

Go to the websites of Google, Target, Hyundai, and Procter & Gamble. The websites are

Google:	http://investor.google.com
Target:	http://www.target.com
Hyundai:	http://worldwide.hyundai.com/company-overview
Procter & Gamble:	http://www.pg.com

1. Describe the business model of each company.
2. Compute the following:
   a. Interest coverage ratio
   b. Debt ratio
   c. Return on equity
   d. Net income percentage or profit margin
   e. Total-asset turnover ratio
   f. Financial leverage
3. Do you think the company is doing a good or bad job financing its assets?

ENDNOTES

1. How people analyze the way a business is financed varies. Sometimes people use ratios with average numbers instead of using ending numbers. They'll use average debt and average owners' equity. Sometimes people use ratios with operating income or cash flow instead of net income. It all depends on the analysts and what they are looking for.
2. Many banks and other financial institutions use the London Interbank Offered Rate (LIBOR) instead of the 90-day T-bill rate. LIBOR is the interest rate that international banks charge one another for very short-term, unsecured loans. LIBOR changes as the demand and supply of money changes throughout the world.

APPENDIX

FINANCIAL ANALYSIS

Introduction to Financial Analysis

So how does someone analyze a business to determine whether it is doing well or doing badly? How does someone methodically look at a business to see if it is creating value? This analysis is called financial analysis. It's the process of using a business's financial statements and other related information to evaluate a business. Financial analysis is using the reports accountants and others provide to evaluate the past and current performance of a business. With this evaluation, analysts can then begin to predict the future of the business and its value.

THE PROCESS OF FINANCIAL ANALYSIS

Is there a logical process that analysts, stockholders, and other decision makers use to conduct financial analysis? The answer is yes. That logical way is to first figure out the forces that affect a business. Then someone can look at the financial information to determine whether or not a business is successfully operating within these forces.

The process of financial analysis typically has five steps. These steps are:

1. Understand a business's model and strategy

2. Understand the environment in which the business operates

3. Analyze the content of the financial statements and other information, making adjustments if desired

4. Analyze the business's operations

5. Use the financial analysis to make decisions

Let's look at each step.

STEP 1. UNDERSTAND A BUSINESS' MODEL AND STRATEGY

Look back at Chapter 02. A business model describes how a business creates and delivers value. A business model describes the inputs, processes, and outputs of a business. A business strategy is how a business tries to compete against similar businesses with similar business models and win the competition to create value. A business's value chain is a mapping of a business's model and strategy, showing how a business converts inputs (people, assets, and money) into outputs that create value for customers, owners, and other stakeholders.

Before looking at the numbers and other financial information, analysts try to understand a business's model, strategy, and thus value chain. Different businesses have different inputs, processes, and outputs. Different businesses try to differentiate their business and successfully create a competitive advantage by using these inputs, processes, and outputs differently.

STEP 2. UNDERSTAND THE ENVIRONMENT IN WHICH THE BUSINESS OPERATES

After analysts understand a business's model and strategy, the analysts then try to understand the environment in which the business operates. The environment has two major dimensions. First is the nature of the business and how it reacts to macroeconomic forces. Per Chapter 04, economic or business cycles affect different businesses in different ways. Second is the competitive environment. Who are the business's competitors and what are their strategies? Often analysts will benchmark competitors with competitor analysis, sometimes called industry analysis. Look back through Chapters Twelve through Fourteen about innovation, marketing, and production. Think about how a business creates a competitive advantage.

STEP 3. ANALYZE THE CONTENT OF THE FINANCIAL STATEMENTS ANDOTHER INFORMATION, MAKING ADJUSTMENTS IF DESIRED

Before using information, analysts must determine if information is reliable and reflects the operations of the business. How does an analyst do this? He or she first looks at the audit opinion.

Next, analysts must read the financial statements and notes that explain the accounting methods and assumptions used by the business. If the analyst believes that adjustments should be made to reflect their perceived economic reality, then the analyst will make the desired adjustments. An example of such adjustments is changing the method to compute inventory and cost of goods sold. Another example is adjusting the allowance for bad debts and bad-debt expense. A final example is changing the reported value of fixed assets or intangible assets based on perceived market conditions, depreciation, or amortization.

(Note: Before using financial statements, make sure you are comfortable with what the financial statements are telling you and what the financial statements are not telling you. Look back at Chapter 08 and make sure you appreciate the nature of financial statements.)

STEP 4. ANALYZE THE BUSINESS'S OPERATIONS[1]

To analyze the operations of a business, using the business's financial statements, analysts typically ask the following:

- Question 1: Is the business a going concern? In others words, will the business exist in the near future? Is the business sufficiently liquid and can it pay its short-term obligations?

- Question 2: How is the business earning a net income or loss?

- Question 3: Where is the business getting its money and can it pay its obligations, both short-term and long-term debt?

- Question 4: How is the business investing its money and is it using these assets efficiently?

- Question 5: Is the business generating enough net income to reward its owners for the use of their money?

To answer these questions, analysts look at numbers, relationships, and trends over time. Analysts often benchmark competitors to see how their numbers, relationships, and trends compare to the business being examined.

Look at the exhibit in this appendix to see commonly used ratios and how they help answer the above questions. Look back at the chapters referenced in this exhibit and think about the business transactions and economic factors being recognized, measured, and reported.

STEP 5. USE THE FINANCIAL ANALYSIS TO MAKE DECISIONS

After all that work, the analysts must make decisions. How is the business performing? What's the business's value or worth? What would you pay for the business? Can the business operate more efficiently and improve its value?

---

1   When a ratio is computed using a balance sheet number, analysts sometimes use averages for these balance sheets numbers. Examples of such balance sheet numbers are accounts receivable, inventory, total assets, debt, and owners' equity. Analysts use averages when there are large differences between years. An example would be Return on Assets being computed by dividing Net Income by Average Total Assets for the year.

APPENDIX EXHIBIT: Ratios Used in Financial Analysis

Question	Chapter Reference	Ratio
Is the business a going concern (liquidity)	16	Net Working Capital = Current Assets − Current Liabilities
	16	Current Ratio = Current Assets/Current Liabilities
	16	Quick Ratio = Quick Assets / Current Liabilities
	16	Cash-to-Expense Ratio = (Cash + Marketable Securities)/ Daily Operating Expenses
How is the business earning a net income or loss?	8	Gross Profit Margin Percentage = Gross Profit/Sales
	8	Net Income Percentage = Net Income/Sales
	8	Common sizing where each item on the income statement, both income and expense, is divided by sales or revenue. The result is percentages that sum to 100%, of revenue, reflecting the relationship of costs, revenue, and net income or loss.
Where is the business getting its money, and can it pay its debt obligations?	19	Debt Ratio = Total Debt/Total Assets
	19	Interest Coverage Ratio = EBIT/Interest Expense for a Year
	19	Debt Cover Ratio = EBIT/(Interest Expense + Principal Payments for a Year)
	8	Common sizing where each type of liability and equity is divided by total assets. The result is percentages that sum to 100%, reflecting the percentage of each type of financial capital in a business financial structure.
How is the business investing its money, and is it using its assets efficiently?	16	Accounts Receivable Turnover Ratio = Sales/Accounts Receivable
	16	Inventory Turnover Ratio = Cost of Goods Sold/Inventory
	16	Fixed Asset Turnover Ratio = Sales/Fixed Assets
	16	Return on Assets = Net Income/Total Assets
	16	Total Asset Turnover = Sales/Total Assets
	8	Common sizing where each type of asset is divided by total assets. The result is percentages that sum to 100%, reflecting the percentage of each type of asset in a business' asset mix.
Is the business generating enough net income to reward its owners?	8	Earnings per Share (EPS) = Net Income/Average Number of Common Shares Outstanding (See note below.)
	8	Dividends Per Share (DPS) = Dividends/Average Number of Common Shares Outstanding
	8	Dividend Payout Ratio = Dividends/Net Income (See note below.)
	8 and 19	Return on Equity (ROE) = Net Income/Owners' Equity
	19	Return on Equity (ROE) = Net Income/Sales * Sales/Total Assets * Total Assets/Owners' Equity
	9	Price Earnings Ratio (PE) = Price Per Share of Stock/ Earnings Per Share
Note: This assumes the business only has common stock outstanding.		

PROBLEM

Addie Enterprises, Inc. (AE) is a company that services fire and police equipment in Central Ohio. The economic environment is challenging, as the economy is beginning to start to recover from a deep recession. Governments that hire AE to maintain and repair equipment are demanding. Likewise AE has several significant competitors. AE's management believes it is successful and that success is founded on quality service and competitive prices.

Below are AE's financial statements and related information for 2016.

BALANCE SHEET AT DECEMBER 31, 2016
(in US Dollars, all numbers are in 000s)

Assets		Liabilities	
Cash	$80	Accounts Payable	$460
Marketable Securities	$175	Accrued Liabilities	$480
Accounts Receivable	$650	Total Current Liabilities	$940
Inventory	$645	**Long-Term Liabilities**	
Total Current Assets	$1750	Loans	$1520
Fixed Assets		Long-Term Liabilities	$550
Property, Plant, & Equipment	$6400	Total Long-Term Liabilities	$2070
Less Accumulated Depreciation	$1250	Total Liabilities	$3010
Net Property	$5150	**Owners' Equity**	
		Common Stock ($1 par)	$550
Other Assets		Retained Earnings	$5340
Other Assets	$2000	Total Owners' Equity	$5890
Total Assets	$8900	Total Liabilities and Owners' Equity	$8900

INCOME STATEMENT FOR YEAR ENDING
DECEMBER 31, 2016
(in US Dollars, all numbers are in 000s)

Sales	$9045
Cost of Goods Sold	$3240
Gross Profit	$5805
Operating Expenses	$2380
Earnings Before Interest and Taxes	$3425
Interest Expense	$200
Taxable Income	$3225
Taxes	$1130
Net Income	$2095

Look at the above information provided by Addie Enterprises, Inc. Now ask yourself the following questions:

1. What is Addie Enterprises, Inc.'s business model and strategy?

2. What is the environment in which Addie Enterprises, Inc. operates?

3. Look over Addie Enterprises, Inc.'s 2016 financial statements. Look at the company's assets, liabilities, owners' equity, revenue, expense, and other information.

4. Analyze the business operations of Addie Enterprises, Inc. Compute the ratios found in the exhibit in this appendix. (Note: Round to 2 decimal points.) Answer the following questions:

5. What do you think about Addie Enterprises, Inc.'s financial performance? Would you like to own Addie Enterprises, Inc.? If so, why? If not, why not?

   · Do you think the business a going concern?

   · How is the business earning a net income or loss?

   · Where is the business getting its money and can it pay its debt obligations?

   · How is the business investing its money and is it using it assets efficiently?

   · Is the business generating enough net income to reward its owners?

Dividends	$250
Stock Price at January 1, 2016	$500
Stock Price at December 31, 2016	$30
Current Portion of Long-term Debt at December 31, 2016	$165
Average Number of Shares Outstanding in 2016	$525
Debt Principal Payments	$165

APPENDIX B

DOING BUSINESS AROUND THE WORLD

Doing business in different countries can be challenging as well as rewarding. Understanding a country's laws and culture is not easy. Below are selected references for understanding the laws and culture of different countries.

World Bank: Economy Rankings Based on Ease of Doing Business

http://www.doingbusiness.org/rankings

US State Department: Doing Business in Other Countries

http://www.state.gov/e/eb/cba/

Kwintessential: Global Guide to Customs, Culture, and Etiquette

http://www.kwintessential.co.uk/resources/country-profiles.html

Accounting and Consulting Firms

The four largest, global accounting firms are Ernst & Young (E&Y), PricewaterhouseCoopers (PwC), Detloitte, and KMPG. These firms provide a large quantity of reference materials on doing business in various countries. An example of materials provided by these firms are:

KPMG – Doing Business in China

http://www.state.gov/e/eb/cba/

A

Account—a summary of the transactions of a particular type, such as cash, accounts receivable, accounts payable or sales

Accountability—holding managers responsible for meeting standards by rewarding managers for exceeding them and correcting managers for failing to meet them

Accountants—people who work with the accounting department and carry out the accounting function

Accounting—the function within a business that recognizes, measures, records and reports information about a business's transactions

Accounting department—function responsible for recognizing, measuring, recording and reporting the value of the assets, borrowed money, money provided by owners, revenue and costs; creates value by providing accurate and timely financial information to managers

Accounting rate of return (ARR)—a tool to evaluate investment decisions calculated by net income produced by the investment, divided by the cost of that investment but does not factor time and risk into its calculations

Accounts payable—the amount that a business owes to its suppliers that requires formal documentation that the money is owed

Accounts receivable—a transaction in which a business does not receive cash when it sells its product, but instead agrees to accept a customer's promise to pay in the future; represented on a business's balance sheet as an asset

Accounts receivable collection period—measures how many days it takes to collect accounts receivable; calculated by investment in accounts receivable divided by daily sales, which is annual sales divided by 365 days in a year

Accounts receivable turnover—measures how many times a year a business converts its accounts receivable to cash; calculated by annual sales divided by invent in accounts receivable

Accrual basis of accounting—a basis of accounting that recognizes business transactions when they occur, regardless of whether or not the transaction immediately affects cash

Accrued liabilities—the amount that a business owes to its suppliers that does not require formal documentation, such as wages, rent, interest and utilities

Accumulated amortization—the amortization, or annual decline in value of an intangible asset, that is aggregated to show the total decline in value over the intangible asset's life

Accumulated depreciation—the depreciation, or annual decline in value of a tangible asset, that is aggregated to show the total decline in value over the tangible asset's life

Acquisition—occurs when a company buys the assets of another company, but may not assume the debts

Adjustable-rate loan—see *variable-rate loan*

Administrative rules and decisions—laws developed by individuals or agencies, empowered by the government

Adverse audit opinion—one of the four types of audit opinions that states auditors do not believe the financial statements fairly present the business's operations and activities

Advertising—one of the aspects of promotional or marketing communications mix that is any non-personal presentation of ideas about a product or product line that can be delivered through media such as newspaper, magazines, radio, television, outdoor signage and the Internet

Adware—programs that permit advisers to send computer users advertisement without the user's permission

Affirmative action—actions initiated by the Equal Employment Opportunity Commission (EEOC) to correct past and current actions of discrimination by forcing businesses to give preference to underrepresented minorities in hiring and promotion

AFL-CIO—the merger between the American Federation of Labor (AFL) and the Congress of Industrial Organizations (CIO) that occurred in 1955

After-tax cost of debt—the net impact of interest on net income, which is the interest rate charged on the loan, or cost of debt, minus the portion of the interest expense that reduces the taxes paid because interest is tax deductible

Age Discrimination in Employment Act of 1967 (ADEA)—the act that amended Title VII to include age in the definition of discrimination

Agency shop—a business where employees can choose to join or not to join the union, but all members must still pay dues

Agent—a person or organization that acts for the benefit of another person, called the principle; often the Board of Directors for an organization

AIDA model—the third step of the promotion process in which marketers design the message that indicates the message should focus on customer *attention, interest, desire,* and act to get the customer's attention, hold the customer's interest, create a desire in the customer to buy the product, and motivate the customer to act or buy the product

Allowance for bad debts—the amount that a business recognizes that some of its customers will not pay their receivables

American Federation of Labor (AFL)—a new labor organization founded after the Knights of Labor in 1886 to improve working conditions and standards of living for workers by embracing the practice of strikes to achieve their goals

Americans with Disabilities Act of 1990—laws that prohibit discrimination based on physical and mental handicaps that will not affect their job performance and require businesses to make reasonable accommodations to assist disabled applicants or employees

Amortization—the loss of value of an asset over time, which similar to depreciation, except that it is reserved for intangible—not fixed—assets except goodwill

Amortization expense—a recognized cost or expense for the decrease in value of a long-term intangible asset

Analytical process—a production process that breaks a product into parts called by-products

Analytics—the process a person or organization uses to convert or transform data into information

Angel—a wealthy individual who buys the stock of selected new businesses; attracted to businesses that have the potential for high growth, but may or may not desire to be long-term investors

Annual Percentage Rate (APR)—the actual rate earned over a year; if the compounding periods are more than once a year, the APR will be greater than the simple interest, and it will be less than the simple interest if the compounding periods are longer than one year; see also *effective rate of return*

Annuities due—an annuity where the payments are received at the beginning, as opposed to end, of the period

Annuity—a stream of equal payments made at equal time intervals

Appeals—see *appellate courts*

Appellate courts—the courts to which a party appeals a decision that the lower courts made that they do not agree with

Appreciating currency—when the value of one country's currency has increased in value, meaning it takes less of that currency to equal another country's currency

Arbitration—the act utilizing an independent individual to review the facts of a disputed situation and to make a decision

Arbitrator—the independent individual who reviews the facts and makes the decision for two disputing parties in arbitration

Articles of Incorporation—a part of the corporate charter contract that establishes a business as a corporation

Assembly line—the production system where workers do a limited number of tasks on products that move through a process; a worker has one assigned task and, when completed, the product moves to another worker, who completes another task on the product

Asset—an economic resource that the business owns and can use to operate a business; ex: building, cash, and equipment

Association of Southeast Asian Nations (ASEAN)—an economic agreement between Indonesia, Malaysia, the Philippines, Singapore, Thailand, Brunei, Vietnam, Cambodia, Laos, and Myanmar

Audit—the activity of an accounting firm, independent of the business, coming into a business and reviewing the business's internal controls, and how the transactions are being recognized, measured, recorded and reported

Audit opinion—the opinion that auditors use to attest to the fairness of the reports that a business issues

Auditors—the accountants that work on audits

Authorized stock—stock that is approved to be sold by the existing stockholders of a business

Authorized, issued, and outstanding stock—stock that has been sold by a business in the market; it was approved to be sold by existing stockholders of the business, sold into the market, and still exists circulating through the market because it was not repurchased by the issuing business

Authorized, issued, but not outstanding stock—stock, in particular Treasury Stock, that has been authorized for sale by the existing shareholders, issued because it was sold on the market but is not still circulating in the market because it was repurchased by the issuing business

Authorized strike—a strike endorsed by the union

Autocratic leader—leaders who make decisions without seeking the input of others

Average cost—the total costs of business products divided by the number of sales; only calculable when a business can allocate its fixed costs to a product

Average tax rate—the total tax divided by the taxable income

B

B2B market—the name for the resale market, or business-to-business market, which occurs when a consumer is a business that buys a product from another business for resale

B2C market—the name for the consumer market, or business-to-consumer market, which occurs when a consumer is a person or household that buys a product for final consumption

Bad debt expense—the amount that a business does not collect

Balance of payments—a summary of the economic transactions in a period between that country and other countries; divided into three main parts: current account capital account and financial account

Balance of trade—the exports of a company minus its imports

Balance sheet—a financial statement of a business that tells what economic resources a business owns or controls (assets) and the sources of funds the business uses to finance those economic resources (debt and owner's equity) at a point in time, such as the last day of a year

Baldrige Awards—another program, besides the International Standards Organization (ISO), that is designed to enhance quality in the United States by allowing the President to give the award to businesses that show outstanding performance in obtaining quality

Bank of International Settlements (BIS)—a membership group that facilitates banking between its member companies

Bankruptcy—regress for the honest debtor

Bankruptcy Act—the act that classifies bankruptcy as either straight bankruptcy or liquidation, or reorganization

Barriers to entry—one of Porters's Five Forces that refers to the difficulty new businesses may have in entering the market

Bartering—the act of exchanging one product for another product without the use of currency

Beta—measures how the return from a business is correlated to the return earned from investing in the overall market for stocks to show the non-diversifiable, or systematic, risk in an investment

Binding arbitration—the decision of the neutral third party, or arbitrator, is final

Board—see *Board of Directors*

Board of Directors—a group of directors elected by the owners to make critical decisions and serve on a business's governing body on their behalf

Bond—a long-term loan that is typically issued for periods greater than one year

Borrower—one who becomes indebted to a lender

Boycotting—action union members and those sympathetic to the union members when they refuse to buy a business's product, sell to abusiness, or accept employment at a business

Brand—the name, term, symbol, design or combination thereof that identifies a product or business

Brand equity—the ability of a brand to create value, as opposed to an unbranded, generic product

Branding—a business's attempt to differentiate its product from the product of competitors with a brand, or name, term, symbol, design or combination thereof that identifies a product or business

Break-even point—the number of sales a business must achieve to generate a zero operating profit calculated by the fixed costs divided by the contribution margin

Broadband—transmission of data and information through high-speed fiber-optics lines

Broker—an individual who brings the buyer and seller together, helping both the buyer and seller in negotiating the deal

Browser—a computer or computer program that permits someone to gain access to information found on websites

Budget—a financial plan that shows the projected sales and costs that result from management's decisions; also show the assets and people needed to produce the sales and expense, as well as the source of money to finance the decisions

Budgeting—adding numbers to a plan to show what will be produced, when it will be produced, and what it will cost

Building—a physical structure attached to land; deteriorates in value as it is used

Business—an organization, recognized under law, which attempts to create value by exchanging products with customers for money or money substitutes like a credit card; for marketing, an organization that buys a product for resale or use in producing another product

Business Analytics—is the ongoing, methodological exploration of an organization's data to gain new insight to help solve business problems and identify opportunities to create value for the organization's stakeholders.

Business broker—an individual or organization that brings together those interested in buying a small business and sellers of small businesses

Business cycle—see *economic cycle*

Business laws—rules that society has created to govern what is acceptable and not acceptable behavior for businesses

Business model—the description the system a business uses to create and deliver value. It is comprised of several parts focuses on a business's customers and what a business does to meet its customers' needs, and the inputs, processes and outputs that create value.

Business products—products sold to businesses that are typically categorized by the product's purpose, such as materials and parts, capital items, and supplies and services

Business strategy—the differentiation a business uses to try to compete against businesses with similar business models and win the competition to create value for stakeholders, including customers

Business systems—the processes that a business uses to operate, often composed of numerous systems and subsystems

Buying decisions—the process a customer goes through to make a decision to buy an item, which includes: customers recognize a need or want; customers seek information on which to base their buying decision; customers evaluate and compare their alternatives; customers make the decision of what to buy or not to buy based on perceived value; after the purchase, customers evaluate their buying decision and take actions based on their satisfaction level

By-products—the products that result from the analytical process that breaks a product into parts

C

C2C Market—market where consumers sell to consumers without the use of a marketing intermediary

C Corporations—the type of corporation that represents most corporations, called conventional corporation

Cafeteria plans—compensation plans that a business provides that allow each employee to choose between options regarding cash compensation, fringe benefits, work-life arrangements, and non-cash compensation to select the package that best meets his or her needs

Call option—an option that gives the option owner the right to buy from the option seller an item at a specified price at or during a specified time in the future

CAN-SPAM Act of 2003—laws that the US Federal Trade Commission (FTC) enforce regarding false advertising and prohibit senders of spam from sending spam to recipients who have requested not to receive such emails

Capital account—part of the balance of payments that is comprised of the financial assets transferred from one country to another because the owner moves from one country to another, and the transfer of ownership of intangible assets (such as patents, trademarks and copyrights) from one country to another

Capital items—a category of business products that businesses buy that have a longer life than one year and are used in the acquiring, manufacturing, and selling of products and services, such as buildings, equipment, and intangible assets like parents

Capital market—where the provider of the money lends the money directly to the borrower and does not use an intermediary; a market where debt and equity are traded

Capital surplus—one owner's equity account that reflects the amount of money owner's pay that is greater than the par value, or stated value of the stock

Capitalistic economies—an economy where individuals and businesses are free to compete and to receive the benefits from winning the competition

Capitalized lease—a lease that is for most or all of an asset's useful life where the lessor recognized the value of the lease as a long-term asset and depreciates it over the life of the asset, and recognizes the lease obligation as long-term debt

Cash—the currency that a business owns; the most liquid asset on a business's balance sheet

Cash basis of accounting—a basis for accounting that recognizes a business transaction only when it affects the business's cash, when it is a received or when it is paid out

Cash cow stage of life cycle—another name for the maturity stage in the product life cycle that is characterized by lowering prices, stagnant sales, decreased net income, fierce competition, and rising risk, as business's compete for customers

Cash dividend—the payment of cash that a corporation pays its owners when the owners decide they do not want to leave the cash in the business as retained earnings

Cash flow statement—a financial statement of a business that shows how the cash account, in the balance sheet, changed during a given period from operating, investing and financing activities; reflects beginning cash, plus sources of cash, less uses of cash, netted to be ending cash

Cash-to-expense ratio—ratio that measures how many days of operating expenses a business holds in cash and marketable securities; measures a business's liquidity

Central American Free Trade Agreement (CAFTA)—an economic agreement between the United States, El Salvador, Guatemala, Honduras, Nicaragua and the Dominican Republic

Centralized organization—a group in which the authority to make decisions rests on a few senior managers; characteristics of these organizations include consistency and standardization

Certified Public Accountant (CPA)—the accountants, licensed by a state through a set of stringent education and practice requirements, that are the only parties that may issue an audit opinion

Change management—the managerial trait that relates to a manager's ability to deal with change in an effective and positive manner; this involves the knowledge of understanding opportunities and challenges and knowing when to be flexible and when not to be

Chief executive officer (CEO)—a highest senior manager of a company, often called the President of the Company

Chief financial officer (CFO)—a key senior manager that reports to the CEO or President, often called the Treasurer or Vice President of Finance

Chief information officer (CIO)—a key senior manager that reports to the CEO or President, often called the Vice President of Technology

Chief marketing officer (CMO)—a key senior manager that reports to the CEO or President, often called Vice President of Marketing

Chief operating officer (COO)—a key senior manager that reports to the CEO or President, often called Vice President of Operations

Civil law—a breach of duty between two parties, such as a businesses or people

Civil Rights Act—the act that prohibits discrimination in hiring and compensating employees based on race, color, religion, sex, marital status, and age

Civil Rights Act of 1991—amended Title VII to provide victims of discrimination the right to a jury trial and permitted victims to seek punitive damages

Claims for unemployment benefits—a leading economic indicator that foretells future employment levels by examining the number of new people claiming unemployment benefits

Clayton Act—a doctrine passed by the US government that, along with the Sherman Antitrust and Robinson-Patman Acts, intended to foster competition by preventing a business or businesses from restraining and thus controlling trade

Closed shop—a business where all employees must join the union; made illegal in the US by the Taft-Hartley Act

Closing the accounting records—the process accountants perform of ending one period and starting another period

Closing the books—see *closing the accounting records*

Collaborative learning systems—computer software that helps employees work together to solve problems

Collateral—an asset used to secure a loan, such as land, building or intangible property

Collateralized or secured bonds—bonds in which borrows agree to pledge assets to back the bond to lower the risk to lenders

Collective bargaining—the negotiation process in which members of the union approve or reject the contract through a majority vote

Collusion—occurs when competing businesses get together and set prices

Commercial paper—a type of short-term, unsecured loan issued in a capital market by large, row-risk businesses; considered a financial substitute for money, per the law

Commission—compensation where a person is paid a percentage or as a function of the amount of sales in a given period

Common dividends—dividends that are paid to common shareholders

Common law—laws created through the court system by interpreting other laws or settling disputes

Common Market of the Southern Cone (MERCOSUR)—an economic agreement among Argentina, Brazil, Paraguay, Columbia, Ecuador, Peru, Bolivia, and Chile

Common stock—one type of stock that represents ownership of the business that allows stockholders to elect the business's Board of Directors and gives them the power and responsibility to govern the corporation

Commonwealth of Independent States (CIS)—an economic agreement between the 11 republics that formerly composed the Soviet Union—Armenia, Azerbaijan, Belarus, Kazakhstan, Kyrgyzstan, Moldova, Tajikistan, Turkmenistan, Ukraine, and Uzbekistan

Communication process—the process that information takes to get from the sender to the receiver; begins by the sender creating a message and sending it to the receiver through a medium for the receiver to receive and decode or interpret the message and ends with the receiver giving feedback to the sender by either taking action or not taking action; the process can be affected by noise, which interferes with the receiver clearly understanding and

Communism—a political and economic system in which there is no private ownership; all things, including businesses, are collectively owned by everyone, but the government operates the businesses and decides what will be produced and how it will be priced, as well as what jobs the citizens will do and how they are paid

Comparative advantage—businesses in different countries have an advantage in producing certain products over others; this can be countries with lower costs in inputs than other countries

Compensatory damages—damages that are used to compensate the plaintiff for his or her injury related to his or her loss in value

Competitive advantage—a business's ability to do something that allows it to outperform its competitors

Competitor—a business that is attempting to sell a similar product to the same customers (current or potential) as another business

Competitor analysis—the research that a business does to determine who its competitors are, how these competitors operate, and how customers perceive the products of competitors

Compounding—earning interest for more than one period; see *interest-on-interest*

Comptroller—see *controller*

Computer-aided design (CAD)—a computer program that is used to design and test products quickly and efficiently

Computer-aided manufacturing (CAM)—a computer program that is used to plan and control manufacturing processes

Computer-integrated manufacturing (CIM)—combines computer-aided design (CAD) and computer-aided manufacturing (CAM) to create totally integrated manufacturing processes to increase the quality of products, lowering the costs of products, and shortening the time needed for production

Conglomerate—a combination of unrelated businesses

Congress of Industrial Organizations (CIO)—the organization that occurred after many specific industrial unions came together to focus on workers' needs in specific industries, such as steel, mining, communications, and manufacturing

Conservatism—the main underlying principle of US GAAP that governs accountant's conduct to not overstate the value of an asset, or understate the value of a liability or debt

Consignment—occurs when a business holds and sells inventory that is owned by another business or person

Consolidated—occurs when a wholly owned subsidiary is combined into the parent company

Consumer—a person or household that buys a product for final consumption

Consumer Price Index (CPI)—an estimate of how the average price of consumer goods has changed over time

Consumer products—products that are sold to consumers, typically categorized by how consumers perceive and purchase products, such as convenience products, shopping products, specialty products, and unsought products

Consumer Protection Safety Act—the act that created the Consumer Protection Safety Commission (CPSC)

Consumer Protection Safety Commission (CPSC)—a government agency that sets product safety standards and requires the disclosure of information regarding the content, operation, and safety of products

Consumer sentiment—a leading economic indicator that is a measure that tells managers how consumers feel

Consumption—one of the sources or uses of the GDP that occurs when individuals buy products (goods and services) that are manufactured in their home country; consumption is a source of GDP or the individual receiving the income and a use of GDP for the individual buying (or using) the item

Contingency plan—plans developed by all managers that detail what course of action a company should take in case the unexpected occurs

Contingency planning—a tool of monitoring risk in enterprise risk management that is management's plan to handle unexpected events

Continuous process—a production process that operates continuously, without interruption, for long periods of time

Contract—occurs when two or more parties enter into an agreement

Contribution margin—the amount that is contributed to the operating profit of the business, calculated as price of the unit less the variable cost per unit

Control—using systems to monitor execution and attempt to ensure that execution meets the goal of planning, beginning with managers setting clear and reasonable goals

Controllable cost—a cost that employees and managers can affect

Controlled or regulated economy—an economy in which businesses are privately owned and heavily regulated by the government; the government tells businesses what they can and cannot do, but businesses still keep their profits

Controller—the chief accountant in a business

Convenience products—a category of consumer products with a low price, consumed in large quantities that consumers buy frequently, instinctually, with minimal thought, such gasoline, detergent, and fast food

Convenience stores—stores that are small, located in easily accessible places, and sell a limited number of products used in everyday life, such as 7-Eleven, Sheets, and Circle K

Cookies—files that permit someone to track what websites a user visits

Cooling-off period—the period of time over which striking employees are required by the US federal court to return to work

Cooperative—a business, formed either as a partnership or corporation, for the benefit of customers

Copyright—the exclusive right to publish a work, such as a book, periodical, poem, short story, sermon, newspaper, motion picture, entertainment production, works of art, architectural drawings and designs, and music

Copyright infringement—the lawsuit that can be filed against a person or business for illegally using another business or person's copyright

Copyright Revision Act of 1976—the law that currently governs copyrights

Corp.—the abbreviation attached to a company's name that shows it is a corporation

Corporate charter—the contract with a state government that makes the corporation a separate legal entity with the ability to enter into contracts, own property, incur liabilities, and earn net income or loss in and of itself

Corporate officers—the senior managers of an organization such as the President, Vice Presidents, Treasurer, and Secretary

Corporation—a form of business that is viewed by the law as an entity different from its owners

Correlation—a measure of how one dimension relates to another dimension when covariance is standardized that shows two variables move together, or in the opposite direction

Cosigner—another individual signs the loan along with the person seeking the money to agree to pay the loan

Cosigns—occurs when another individual, a cosigner, signs the loan along with the person seeking the money

Cost—the price that a business incurs when it buys or makes products, also known as expense

Cost accounting systems—accounting systems that report to management the quantity, quality, and cost of production in a given time period

Cost of debt—the required return on debt, or interest rate, which includes the risk-free rate of return in the economy and the risk premium, or the additional required return to compensate for lender's risks

Cost of equity—the return owners expect to compensate them for the use of their money, which is calculated by the risk-free rate of return in the economy, and the additional risk owners expect due to risk without adjusting

for taxes because dividends are not deductible for tax purposes

Cost of Goods Sold—the expense related to a product sold

Cost-plus pricing—a business practice of pricing products based on costs and desired profit that provides sufficient sales revenue to pay a business's costs and create a sufficient operating profit

Cost-push inflation—one type of inflation that occurs when the cost of an item goes up without an increase in demand

Cost-volume-profit analysis—the analysis of the impact of different pricing alternatives on the business's profitability

Counter-cyclical products—a product that has its demand affected by the state of the economy in an inverse relationship, meaning that a strong economy decreases demand and a weak economy increases demand; occurs in products such as inexpensive foods and generic brands

Court—a place, designated by the government, where it is decided if an illegal act occurred

Court of Appeals—the designated court that disputing parties go to when one of the parties disagrees with a judgment made in a lower court

Covariance—covariance is the measure of how closely two or more variables co-vary, or move together

Coverage ratio—ratio that compares a business's earnings before interest and taxes (EBIT) to the cost of debt

Criminal law—the breaches of duty to society such as theft or murder

Critical path—the sequence of events that takes the longest time to complete, and, as such, determine the minimum time it will take to produce the product

Cultural factors—the factors heavily influenced by geography, gender, ethnicity, and other influences that customers learn, such as what is acceptable and desirable regarding housing, food, clothing, transportation, and other products

Culture—the beliefs and norms of a society that is created as a function of geography, religion, social values, standard of livings, and education levels

Currency—a country's money

Current Account—one aspect of the balance of payments that is composed of exports and imports, factor payments, and transfer payments

Current Assets—cash or assets expected to convert to cash within the next year, such as cash, accounts receivable and inventory; also called short-term assets

Current liabilities—liabilities that are due to be repaid in one year or less, such as accounts payable, estimated liabilities called accrued liabilities, and short-term debt from banks or other lenders; also called short-term liabilities

Current ratio—a common measure used to look at a business's ability to pay its liabilities by dividing the current assets by the current liabilities

Customer power—one of Porter's Five Forces that refers to the power customers have in the business' value chain

Customer Relationship Management (CRM)—an information system that provides a sales force timely information on customer needs, product availability, pricing alternatives, and promotion options

Customers—people or organization that buy a business's products

Customized mass production—a mass-production process that permits limited customization of the product such as selecting certain options in a product

Customized production—the process of producing a unique product that meets the unique needs of a customer

Cyberspace—the flow of information through a network, including the hardware, software, and means of transmitting data

Cyclical product—a product that sees its demand affected by the state of the economy such as automobiles, housing, and designer clothes

Cyclical unemployment—a state of economy when the market for one person's labor is temporarily low; examples include an economic downturns

Cyclicality—one of the three forces that shifts supply and demand; refers to the overall state of the economy

D

Data—the facts about everything a business does that are input into the system

Database—a collection of data that are deposited in the information system

Data mining—the retrieval and analysis of data using hardware and software to provide answers to questions

Days' sales in inventory—compares the level of inventory to the inventory sold per day; calculated by the average inventory divided by the cost of daily sales, which is the annual cost of goods sold divided by 365 days

Debentures—unsecured, subordinated bonds

Debt—see *liabilities*

Debt coverage ratio—ratio that compares a business's pre-tax operating profit (EBIT) with the interest and principle a business owes in a given period (I+D); calculated by EBIT/(I+D)

Debt rating—a rating provided by one of the three debt rating agencies—Moody's, Standard & Poors (S&P), and Fitch—that helps lenders analyze the default risk of a loan; a higher rating indicates a lower default risk and a lower rating indicates a higher default risk

Debt ratio—percentage of debt used to finance assets; calculated by total debt (TD)/total assets (TA)

Decentralized organization—a group in which the authority to make and implement decisions rests in many managers, often junior and middle managers; characteristics of these organizations include flexibility, adaptively and creativity

Decline stage of life cycle—another name for the dog stage in the product life cycle that is characterized by declining sale, prices, and demand, and increased risk, which often result in losses, as customers search to find better and more valuable alternative products until all businesses have withdrawn from the market due to insufficient demand

Deep discount stores—stores that sell products lines at very low prices such as Costco, Sam's Club, and BJ's

Default risk—the risk that the borrower will not repay the lender the money he or she borrowed; compensated for in the interest rate assigned to the loan

Defendant—the party accused of a crime that is brought to court by the prosecutors

Deficit—occurs when government spending is greater than tax revenue and means that the government must borrow the extra funds it needs

Defined benefit plan—a company-sponsored retirement plan that guarantees the retiree a monthly income, every month, for the rest of his or her life; the business must estimate when the employee will retire, how long the employee will live, and how much the retiree will receive during each year of his or her retirement

Defined contribution plan—a company-sponsored retirement plan where the business and/or employees contribute money to a special fund each pay period, and then invest the money at the direction of the employee and earns a return

Deflation—occurs when the prices of items go down from their present prices; occurs when the supply for a product exceeds the demand for the product

Demand—one aspect of the economic supply and demand model that refers to individuals and businesses that have something they want to buy products; buyers are also called consumers

Demand curve—the model that depicts the relationship of price and quantity that faces consumers; when prices for products are low, then consumers have an incentive to purchase more, and when the prices are high, consumers have less of an incentive to purchase

Demand-pull inflation—one type of inflation that occurs when demand for a product exceeds the available supply of the product

Department of Labor (DOL)—government agencies empowered to enforce employment law

Department store—a store that carries several product lines, such as Sears, Macy's, and JC Penney

Dependent care—a service in which the business provides care for children, elderly parents, and other dependents of an employee

Depreciating currency—when the value of one country's currency has declined in value, meaning it takes more of that currency to equal another country's currency

Depreciation—the decrease in an asset's value as a result of usage or age that is shown on a business's balance sheet as a decrease in the asset's value on the balance sheet

Depreciation expense—the estimated decrease in value of the building each period; a cost that is recorded as an expense on the income statement

Depression—occurs when the economy contracts and shrinks into very long and severe recession

Derivative—a risk management tool that is any instrument that derives its value from something else, such as a swap, futures and forwards, and options

Descriptive statistics—one of the two forms of statistics that is the process of communicating the frequency and characteristics of an event or events within a population

Digital subscriber line (DSL)—transmission of data and information through telephone wires

Direct foreign investment—occurs when a business directly invests money in assets to conduct business in a different country, which can include starting a new business, expanding a current business, or buying an existing business; the riskiest form of global business but holds the greatest potential for profit

Direct marketing—one of the aspects of promotional or marketing communications mix that are techniques including direct mailing, catalogues, mail order, telemarketing, and online promotions through the Internet used to get customers to purchase products from their home, office, or other non-retail settings

Direct marketing channel—a marketing channel where businesses do not use a marketing intermediary

Disclaimer—one of the four types of audit opinions that states that auditors are not issuing an opinion on whether or not the financial statements fairly present the business's operations and activities

Discount stores—stores that sell numerous product lines of household products to price-conscious customers, such as Target, Walmart, and Kmart

Discrimination—an employment act based on race, religion, creed, sex, or national origin

Disposable income—the income earned by an individual that remains after taxes are paid

Distribution—a summary of the frequency of events used to describe the total market, or population, and to determine what percentage of the market buys the product we are investigating and what percentage buys a competing product; also how and when a business delivers its product to its customer

Distribution channel—see *marketing channel*

District court—a federal court where disputes are initially tried.

Diversification—occurs when unrelated businesses come together in such a way that the overall risk of a company is reduced

Dividend—a corporate distribution of income to its owners

Divisional managers—see *operational manager*

Divisional organization—a group in which the business is divided into certain market, geographic, or product-based divisions

Dog stage of life cycle—another name for the decline stage in the product life cycle that is characterized by declining sale, prices, and demand, and increased risk, which often result in losses, as customers search to find better and more valuable alternative products until all businesses have withdrawn from the market due to insufficient demand

Domestic business—a business with a totally domestic (meaning within a single country) value chain

Double taxation—occurs when the corporation pays taxes on its income and the owner pays taxes when the income is distributed as a dividend

Dumping—occurs when countries sell products to other countries below the cost incurred to produce those products to foster exports

Durable goods—goods that have long lives, such as cars, washing machines, and computers

E

E-business—businesses that use information and communication technologies to support marketing, production, finance, and the other functions of business and uses information systems as an integral part of a business's model and strategy, as well as its value chain and competitive advantage; also called electronic business

E-commerce or electronic commerce—buying and selling of products over networks such as the Internet

E-tailers—retailers that sell over the Internet

Earning per share (EPS)—calculated by dividing net income, less preferred dividends by the number of common shares outstanding to show the net income available to each share of stock

Earnings before interest and taxes (EBIT)—sales less all of the operating expense that a business incurs in the specified period, such as cost of good sold, salaries, rent, depreciation, utilities, and advertising; can also be stated as gross profit less operating expenses, which would exclude cost of goods sold from the list above; see also *operating profit*

Economic cycle—the ups and downs an economy experiences as it hits peaks, contracts to fall to troughs and then again expands back to peaks

Economic factor—the factors that relate to a consumer's level of income and wealth that are directly impacted by where the overall economy is in the economic cycle; what a consumer buys depends on how much a consumer can spend

Economic index—measures the relative change of an economic factor over time; includes three main measures: Consumer Price Index, Producers Price Index and GDP deflator

Economics—the study of the financial welfare of an economy and how an economy operates

Economists—the individuals who study the economy

Economy—a way of describing the financial state of society

Educational benefits—services a business provides to employees in which the business provides training or pays for outside education such as college or technical schools

Effective rate of return—see *annual percentage rate (APR)*

Embargo—a trade barrier that does not permit the importing and/or exporting of a product within its borders

Eminent domain—the doctrine that states that an individual must surrender property, for reasonable compensation, to a government if the government needs the property for public use

Employee training—the training step, following orientation, in which the employee is instructed on the technical or skill-based training

Employees—people hired by a business to manage and operate it

Employment agencies—business and governmental agencies that specialize in finding employees for others

Employment application—a document, created by the business, which the applicant completes to provide information requested by the business such as address, work experience, education, special talents or abilities

Employment Retirement Income Security Act of 1974 (ERISA)—the US government act that regulates employer-sponsored defined benefit and defined contribution retirement programs

Encryption—the process of transforming easily understood data and information into coded and unintelligible data so that only those

with the code can use the original data and information

Enterprise Resource Planning (ERP)—the process of planning production inputs, (assets, facilities and working capital) and systems, which integrate assets, people, and information into a productive process

Enterprise Risk Management (ERM)—the process of identifying, analyzing, and addressing current and future risks by using the four principles: establishment of risk tolerances, programs to assess risk, programs to monitor risk, programs to continuously evaluate risk

Enterprise zones—special geographic areas that governments create to attract and support entrepreneurs; often governments use low taxes and other special services like utilities to attract entrepreneurs

Entrepreneurial teams—one type of entrepreneur that is composed of individuals with different talents and abilities that combine these to market, produce, or finance their product and successfully apply their ideas

Entrepreneurs—the individuals who lead the process of entrepreneurship

Entrepreneurship—the process of attempting to convert an invention into a successful innovation

Environmental Protection Agency (EPA)—the agency responsible for administering the federal laws dealing with the environment, including water quality, air quality, and waste disposal

Equal Employment Opportunity Act (EEOA)—enacted in 1972 to strengthen the powers of Equal Employment Opportunity Commission (EEOC) and to empower the EEOC to enforce anti-discrimination laws

Equal Employment Opportunity Commission (EEOC)—created by the Civil Rights Act of 1964 to encourage anti-discrimination

Equal Opportunity Act—the act that prohibits lenders from discriminating based on race, color, religion, sex, marital status, national origin, or age

Equal Pay Act—the act that prohibits discrimination in hiring and compensating employees based on race, color, religion, sex, marital status, and age

Equilibrium point—the price at which buyers (the demand) and sellers (the supply) agree to make an exchange, which determines the quantity and price products will be bought and sold in the market; also called the market price

Equipment—a physical, non-current asset that a business uses that is not considered land or buildings

Equity—money contributed by the owners of a business

Equity theory—theory that states that employees are motivated to perform only if they believe the value they receive is fair compensation compared to the compensation of others and expect equal pay for equal work

Ethics—the codes and standards we live by that govern our behavior

European Union (EU)—an economic trading unit that consists of 27 countries in Europe; agreed to one currency, eliminated tariffs and restrictions between member countries, and act as one unit in dealing with non-EU countries

Excise tax—a tax that a government assesses on the manufacture, sale, or consumption of a product

Execute—part of the management process that involves using systems to operate the business, according to plans to achieve desired goals

Execution—see *execute*

Executive search firms—employment agencies that specialize in finding applicants for management positions

Exemplary damages—see *punitive damages*

Expectancy theory—theory that employees are motivated by the expectation of reward; if an employee works hard and performs well, then the employee expects to be rewarded, so the business must clearly communicate how performance will be measured and rewarded

Expected return—see *required rate of return*

Expense—the cost or value surrendered to create a sale and operate a business during a period of time

Expert systems—a system that artificially makes decisions based on proven rules and logic

such as how many employees should work at a given time and what each employee should do

Export-Import Bank (Ex-Im Bank)—a US government agency that facilitates exports by directly loaning money to foreign companies that import US products and guaranteeing loans from private lenders to such importers

Exports—one source of GDP that occurs when goods and services produced in a home country are sold to buyers in another country

Expressed contracts—occurs when the details of the contract are clearly stated and agreed upon by all parties

Expressed warranty—occurs when the seller explicitly makes statements to the buyer that become a part of the bargaining and sales transaction

External environment—the important factors that a business does not directly control, which include the overall economy, customer desires, and competitor actions

Extranet—an intranet that allows users outside the organization limited access to information

F

Face value—see *par*

Facilities—see *fixed assets*

Factor payments—a component of the current account that includes payments of interest and dividends

Factors of production—the resources that an economy needs to operate and prosper; includes labor, natural resources, money, and knowledge

Fair Credit Reporting Act—the act that ensures credit information is accurate

Fair Debt Collection Practices Act—the act that prohibits lenders from using abusive collection tactics like harassment

Fair Labor Standards Act (FLSA)—the act that requires employers to pay employees no less than minimum wage and to pay higher compensation for working overtime

Fair value—the reporting of assets and liabilities at their current value, as used under IFRS

Family and Medical Leave Act of 1993—the law that requires businesses to ensure job security for those who need medical or sick leave to start a family with children, take care of family members because of illness, or recover from personal illness for a period of twelve months and can be paid or unpaid

Federal Aviation Administration (FAA)—one regulator of selected industries and business relationships that are critical to welfare of society

Federal courts—courts with jurisdiction to hear disputes regarding federal laws or disputes involving parties from multiple states; divided into district, Court of Appeals, and US Supreme Court

Federal Deposit Insurance Corporation (FDIC)—one regulator of selected industries and business relationships that are critical to welfare of society such as banks; insures bank deposits up to a maximum of $250,000

Federal Food and Drug Administration (FDA)—one regulator of selected industries and business relationships that are critical to welfare of society

Federal Lanham Trademark Act of 1946—the law that currently governs trademarks

Federal Patent Statute of 1952—the current law that governs patent

Federal Reserve (the Fed)—the central bank of the United States that holds the responsibility of determining the money supply within the economy

Federal Trade Commission (FTC)—the organization responsible for administering laws designated to protect customers

Fiduciary—one who is entrusted with responsibilities and expected to act in the business's best interest

Finance (or treasury) department—function responsible for acquiring and managing financial resources (money); creates value by working with lenders and owners to acquire money and making sure the money is wisely invested in assets and people

Financial account—a component of the balance of payments that is composed of direct foreign investment, buying and selling long-term financial assets (debt and stock), and buying and selling short-term financial assets (debt)

Financial accounting—the accounting rules used to report to owners and lenders about the performance of a business

Financial Accounting Standards Boards (FASB)—the governmental board that is made up of accounting a business professions to set rules, or standards, that companies must follow in providing information to lenders and stockholders

Financial activities—one receipt or use of cash on the cash flow statement that shows the cash provided by or used for financing activities, such as long-term debt and owner's equity

Financial analysis—the process of analyzing a business's operations to see how it creates value by looking at the operating profit produced by investing in assets and people, how the business is financed, debt or owner's equity, and how it pays its debts; common measurements include Return on Equity (ROE), Return on Assets (ROA), and financial leverage

Financial capital—the process of acquiring money for a business; comes from borrowed funds (debt) or from owners (equity)

Financial instruments—documents that represent debt and equity

Financial intermediary—a middleman between the ultimate provider of the money (depositor) and the user of the money (loan customer)

Financial leverage—one tool in financial analysis that determines how the business financed its assets; computed by Total Assets/Total Owner's Equity

Financial risk—the risk that arises from financing assets with debt, or increasing financial leverage; higher financial leverages means higher financial risk

Finished goods—the inventory that is completely transformed from raw goods; completed inventory

Finished goods inventory—the finished, produced inventory that is ready for sale

Firewalls—programs on computers that limit access to protect computers and computer users from spyware, viruses, and hackers

Fiscal policy—government spending and taxation

Fixed asset—the buildings, land, and/or equipment that a business owns (not rents) used to conduct business

Fixed-asset turnover—measures the relationship between a business's investment in PP&E versus the business's sales; calculated by the annual sales divided by the investment in property, plant, and equipment

Fixed costs—costs incurred by a business that do not vary with the amount sold and will be incurred regardless of whether or not the business has sales, such as rent expense

Fixed exchange rate system—a system where the government fixes, or pegs, the exchange rate of its currency to another country's currency

Fixed-rate loan—a loan in which the interest rate remains constant at a specific rate over the life of the loan

Fixed salary—a salary paid on a fixed basis, where the employee is paid a stated amount per pay period, regardless of the hours worked

Flat tax—a method of taxation where the tax rates do not vary

Flex time—a work schedule where an employee can determine his or her own schedule

Flexible budget—a form of contingency planning in which there are a series of budgets and standards to recognize that certain parts of production may not be controllable; a form of contingency planning to make sure the business succeeds in all situations

Flexible production—a production process that can easily be changed

Floating exchange rate system—a system where the government permits the price of its currency be determined by a free market

Floating-rate loan—see *variable-rate loan*

Foreign exchange—the act of exchanging one country's currency for another

Foreign exchange rates—the rate used to convert one country's currency into another currency

Formal leader—leaders that have formal authority based on the position they hold in the company, yet are still empowered by team members to act as leaders; managers are often formal leaders

For-profit business—a business that attempts to create an exchange between the business and a customer that results in a profit

Formal networks—the communication process adopted by senior management that brings a business organization together

Forward—a type of derivative that is, similar to a future contract, an agreement by two or more parties to buy and sell a specific item at a future price and date, but dissimilar from a future a forward is customized, not standardized, to fit a business's needs

Four "P's" of marketing—comprised of product, place, price, and promotion

Four types of audit opinions—these are: unqualified or clean opinion, qualified or subject-to opinion, adverse opinion, and disclaimer

Franchise agreement—an agreement between the franchisor and franchisee

Franchisee—the business that buys the rights to use the franchisor's name for a fee and the a percentage of sales

Franchising—the sale of the use of a business's, called a franchisor, name, processes, and products to another business, the franchisee, in exchange for a fee and royalties on sale; reduces the investment and risk franchisor must make to enter the market but also limits the profits a franchisor can make

Franchisor—the business that owns and sells the rights to use its name, processes. and products

Fraud—an example of an intentional tort that is the act of misrepresenting facts

Free market economy—an economy like the United States where buyers and sellers are free to buy and sell what they want, at a price they choose

Free market system—see *free market economy*

Free trade—the buying and selling of products in markets that are free from government intervention

Fringe benefits—employee benefits provided by employers such as sick pay, vacation pay, maternity or paternity leave, health insurance, life insurance, and retirement benefits

Full employment—an economic state where everyone who wants and needs a job has one

Functional manager—see *operational manager*

Functional organization—a group in which the business is organized by line or staff functions

Future—a type of derivative that is, similar to a swap, a standardized agreement by two or more parties to buy and sell a specific item at a future price and date to alleviate the risk of changes in prices at a future date

Future value—the amount of money expected to be received at a future date

G

Gantt chart—a graph that depicts how a product is produced over time to show how and when a product progresses through the production process

GDP deflator—an estimate of how the prices of all items have changed in a given period

General Agreement on Tariffs and Trade (GATT)—the beginnings of international trade guidelines that eventually transformed into the World Trade Organization (WTO)

General creditor—a lender of unsecured debt

General partner—the owners of a general partnership; general partnership interest in a limited partnership

General partnership—a collection of individuals who sign into agreement to jointly become owners of a business

Generally Accepted Accounting Practices (GAAP)—the set of standards set by the Financial Accounting Standards Board (FASB) that business must follow in providing information to their lenders and stockholders

Generic name—a name that becomes a common name for a product line

Generic products—unbranded products that do not use their brand to create value

Global businesses—businesses where the inputs, processes, and outputs come from, are in, and go to markets throughout the world; inputs

and processes include assets, people, and money, and the outputs are the products

Globalization—the breakdown of barrers—from geography, language and cultural misunderstandings—enabling businesses to compete in global markets

Golden parachutes—termination agreements between a business and selected senior managers to pay the manager a given sum of money if the manager is dismissed

Goods—physical items we can touch or feel; e.g., food, cars, and clothing

Goodwill—an intangible asset that reflects the special value that some business's have created due to marketing, research, or other factors that makes the value of the business exceed the value of its tangible and other intangible assets; only recognized when goodwill is purchased

Government regulation—one major part in selecting the method of doing business in different countries; examples of this include trade barriers, protectionism, embargos, quotas and tariffs

Government Spending—a source of GDP that occurs when governments spend money on things such as national defense, roads and services

Graduated tax—a method of taxation where the tax rate varies depending on the level of income

Gramm-Leach-Bliley Act—the act that protects a borrower's privacy

Grievance procedure—a formal process, agreed upon in the union contract, designed to fairly resolve differences

Gross domestic product (GDP)—the value of the goods and services produced in an economy in a given year;

Gross pay—the compensation the business agrees to pay the employee for his or her work

Gross profit—sales less costs of good sold

Growth stage of life cycle—another name for the star stage in the product life cycle that is characterized by growing demand, decreased risk, and increased sales, which result in growing net income, as the market begins to accept the business's product

Guarantee—an agreement that the guarantor will repay the loan if the original person fails to repay it; also a promise, by a business to a customer, that the customer will be satisfied with the product, or, if he or she is not satisfied, the customer has certain rights

Guarantor—the individual that agrees to repay the loan if the original person fails to repay it

H

Hackers—outsiders who obtain access to, and thus control of, a computer without the permission of the owner of the computer

Hardware—the physical assets used to assist in converting the data into information

Hart-Scott-Rodino Antitrust Improvements Act—A doctrine passed by the US government intended to foster competition by preventing a business or businesses from restraining and thus controlling trade

Headhunter—the slang term for executive search firms; see *executive search firms*

Health care benefits—the benefits a business provides to current or retired employees by paying selected medical costs

Home-based businesses—see *micropreneurs*

Home page—the introduction to a website that a user first sees and that informs him or her what data are available and how to retrieve those data

Horizontal integration—occurs when a business buys another business that is a competitor or similar company

Hourly salary—a salary paid based on the hours worked by the employee; the rate per hour is fixed, but the salary is a function of the number of hours worked

Housing starts—one of the leading economic indicators that measures the number of permits issued to construction companies to build new houses

Human capital—term used to describe the people of a business; used to create value

Human resource (HR) department or function—function responsible for the company's employees; creates value by understanding the organization's need for employees, finding the right employees, and motivating, training, evaluating, rewarding, and compensating them

I

Identity theft—the theft or stealing of another's identity by using technology such as the Internet

Immigration and Nationality Act (INA)—requires employers to employ only US citizens or nationals, and non-US citizens who have been authorized by the US government to work in the US

Impairment—the expense that records the loss of value for goodwill on a company's balance sheet; all other intangible assets except for goodwill use amortization to record losses in value

Implied contract—occurs when the circumstances and facts imply that a contract exists, such as with an auto mechanic to repair your car

Implied warranty—a warranty that exists but is not explicitly stated

Imports—a use of GDP that relates to the products purchased from sources outside the home country

Inc.—the abbreviation attached to a company's name that shows it is a corporation

Income statement—a financial statement of a business that communicates how the business has performed during a period, such as the entire year.

Income taxes—taxes a government assesses on a business's net income before taxes, or taxable income

Incubator—a place, provided by state or local government or other organizations, where facilities and professional services are provided at a low cost; often entrepreneurs must pay for the inexpensive access to the expensive facilities and services when the product and/or process become profitable

Indemnified employee—an employee that the business agrees to defend for any accused wrongdoings

Indenture—the document that details the terms of a loan agreement between a financial intermediary and the business that receives the money

Indirect marketing channel—a marketing channel where businesses use one or more marketing intermediaries

Individual factors—the factors, such as age, health, occupation, lifestyle, and personality that affect how different individuals respond to their needs

Inferential statistics—a type of statistics that is used to reach conclusions about a population used to help understand the impact of decisions and forecasting the future by examining how variable co-vary

Inferior courts—the first level of the states' court system in which a judge hears the facts and makes a decision or judgment; examples include municipal, small claims, and justice of the peace courts

Inflation—occurs when the prices of items go up from their present prices

Informal leader—leaders who do not have formal authority within the company but are still empowered by team members to act as leaders

Informal networks—a communication process not formally established by senior management that creates opportunities and challenges in a business through trusted colleague connections; also called a social network

Information—the knowledge derived from data; data are converted to information through an analytical process

Information architecture—the design and structure of an information system to create an information system that adds value to the business

Information overload—the state when managers have more information than they need to make a decision, which causes confusion

Information revolution—the influx of knowledge and information from the Internet, technology, and other information innovations that shifted the way businesses created value away from relying on customer's lack of knowledge to increased transparency

Information system (IS)—a system that uses people and processes to convert data into information with analytics

Information technology (IT) department—function responsible for managing the technology used throughout a business; provides value by managing data, computer hardware, and computer software the company needs, staying on top of current technology, and educating the users of technology

Initial public offering (IPO)—the issuance of stock by a business on a public capital market for the first time

Innovation—finding new ways to think and do things that create value for customers and the business; the successful application of new products and/or processes

Insider trading—occurs when someone buys or sells financial securities based on nonpublic or preferential information

Insurance policy—tool businesses can use to eliminate or reduce many risks by transferring the risk to the insurance company that the business buys the policy from

Insurance premium—the periodic cost that a business pays to obtain an insurance policy from the insurance company

Intangible assets—property other than physical assets of a business that help create operating profit

Intangible property—property that is not tangible, such as copyrights, patents, trademarks, and financial securities

Intellectual property—intangible assets of a business that help create an operating profit, including copyrights, trademarks and patents

Interest—cost or expense a business must pay to borrow money or incur debt

Interest coverage ratio—ratio that compares a business's pre-tax operating profit (EBIT) with the interest (I) a business owes in a given period; calculated by EBIT/I

Interest-on-interest—the additional interest earned for multiple periods of compounding from the value of money earning interest on the interest earned in earlier periods

Interest rates—a leading economic indicator that is the price or cost of borrowed money

Intermediaries—a person or organization that facilitates an exchange

Intermittent process—the production process that frequently starts and stops due to a limited number of customers or the need to adjust the production process

Internal controls—the ability of the accounting system to capture all business transactions, and detect and prevent fraud

Internal environment—factors that a business can control, including products the business sells, where it will conduct business and how it will manage employees

Internal rate of return (IRR)—a tool to evaluate investment decisions that is the discount rate that equates the benefits projected over time with the cost of the investment; compared to a business's Weighted Average Cost of Capital (WACC) to determine whether the investment will increase value

International Accounting Standards Board (IASB)—the board that sets the International Financial Reporting Standards (IFRS) for the international community, similarly to the Financial Accounting Standards Board of the United States and US GAAP

International businesses—businesses whose value chains have evolved to include selected international inputs, processes, and outputs

International Financial Reporting Standards (IFRS)—the set of standards that governs international financial reporting but is less conservative than US GAAP,

International Monetary Fund (IMF)—an organization created to promote international trade and help countries create and maintain stable economies by helping member countries with exchange-rate problems

International Standards Organization (ISO)—non-government federation of standard-setting groups throughout the world that certifies

a business meets strict standards regarding quality; uses ISO 9000 and ISO 14000

internet—(written with a little 'i') an information system between independent organizations

Internet—(written with a capital "I") the largest public internet that enables millions of users to provide and access large amounts of data and information; see also *NET*

Internet service provider (ISP)—a commercial business or government with permanent access to the Internet, to which it temporarily sells access to a customer for a fee

Interstate Commerce Commission (ICC)—one regulator of selected industries and business relationships that are critical to welfare of society

Interstate issues—a dispute involving parties in multiple states

Intranet—an information system within an organization; see also *virtual private network (VPN)*

Intrapreneurs—one type of entrepreneurs who work for and in large businesses; large businesses often recognize the need for innovation and hire select employees who share that vision and can help the business innovate

Intrastate—occurring within a state

Intrastate issues—a dispute involving parties of the same state

Introduction stage of life cycle—another name for the opportunity stage in the product life cycle that is characterized by high risk, low sales, and high expenses, which often result in losses, as a business tries to introduce a new product into a new or existing market by promoting the product's unique and superior qualities

Invention—the creation of new products and/or processes

Inventory—the supply of goods, purchased or produced, that a business (if in the business of selling a good) sells in the normal course of business; represented on a business's balance sheet as an asset; also serves as a leading economic indicator

Inventory turnover—measures how many times a year a business converts its inventory into sales; calculated by annual cost of goods sold divided by the investment in inventory

Investing activities—one receipt or use of cash on the cash flow statement that shows the cash provided by or used in buying and selling long-term assets

Investment—one source of GDP that occurs when individuals or businesses spend money on capital items, such as buildings and equipment

Investment bankers—brokers and agents who help investors negotiate a deal between investors and lenders for a fee based on the size and complexity of the dear

Involuntary bankruptcy—when the business's creditors put the business in bankruptcy by petitioning the bankruptcy court

ISO 9000—one of the International Standards Organization's (ISO) current set of standards for understanding and meeting customer needs

ISO 14000—one of the International Standards Organization's (ISO) current set of standards to help businesses manage their impact on the environment and to recognize businesses that protect and enhance the environment that benchmarks best practices

Issued stock—see *authorized, issued, and outstanding stock*

Issuing the debt or equity—the selling of debt and equity in a capital market

J

Job analysis—see *staffing analysis*

Job description—the description of what the employee is expected to do to outline its responsibilities

Job-order cost system—one type of cost accounting system that allocates costs to individual or groups of products

Job sharing—when two or more employees do the work of one full-time employee

Job specification—a list of the qualities the employee must possess to be considered for the job such as personal qualities, work experience, and education

Joint ventures (JV)—occurs when two or more parties, typically businesses, enter into a business relationship for a single enterprise or transaction to share the investments, risk, profits and losses; requires each party to make a significant investment, but one that is lower than if a single company were to conduct the business alone

Jointly Liable—the general partners of a partnership are, together, responsible for the debts of the partnership

Judges—the individuals who manage and oversee courts; they can be elected or appointed by elected officials

Junk—a term to describe debt that has a very high probability of defaulting and requires a high rate of return, which couples together to give the debt a very low value; often results from a business financing with too much debt and not enough equity, which causes the WACC to rise

Juries—a group of citizens selected to decide whether an individual is guilty or innocent

Jurisdiction—the factor that decides to which court a dispute will be referred by determining if that court has the authority to decide on that issue

Just-in-time inventory—occurs when a business works with its supply chain to minimize the raw materials on hand, without causing production problems, by ensuring the business has the amount of inputs or inventory it needs at the exact time it needs them

K

Knights of Labor—the earliest significant labor union, founded in 1869, to improve society by making business and employees behave in a more moral and responsible fashion

Knowledge—one of the factors of production that is insight and expertise of the people

L

Labeling—a business attaching printed words or graphics to its products to educate the customer to identify, describe, and/or inform the customer about the content, benefits, dangers, and proper use of the product to reduce the risk to the buyer and seller

Labor—one of the factors of production that is the people in an economy or organization who operate a business

Laissez-faire leader—a leader who sets the overall direction and guidelines but permits others to make decisions about implementation

Land—part of the physical surface of the Earth; has an infinite life and is assumed that the value does not decline over time, as a building would

Landrum-Griffin Act—regulates the internal operations of unions by requiring unions to operate as a democracy, where members vote for their union's senior management, and prohibits unions from engaging in racketeering and other illegal activities

Laws—rules that a society accepts as the minimum acceptable behavior; they govern what is and what isn't acceptable behavior

Lawsuit—the disputed situation between a plaintiff and a defendant that is settled in court

Leader—people empowered by a team who motivate team members to collectively achieve a goal; may or may not be leaders

Leading economic indicators—economic indicators that precede a peak, contraction, trough, or expansion, which managers can use to predict the future state of the economy

Lean operations—the drive to lower costs in production without sacrificing quality; see also *low-cost-producer*

Lease—an agreement or contract between the owner of the property and another party where the owner gives the other party the right to use the property

Leasing—where one party, the lessee, pays the owner of the property, lessor, a fee to use the property for a specific time

Lender—a person or organization that provides money to a borrower

Lessee—the party that pays rent on the property in a lease

Lessor—the owner of the property in a lease

Leveraged buyout (LBO)—occurs when a company uses high levels of debt to buy another company

Liabilities or liability—money borrowed with a promise of paying it back in the future; an individual or organization's obligation or promise of repayment that comes about because of a transaction or event

License—occurs when two businesses enter into a legal agreement that grants one business the right to use another company's intellectual property for a fee

Licensee—the business that owns the license

Licensing—a company that owns intellectual property, called a licensor, grants another company, called a licensee, the right to use that property, typically for a fee

Licensor—a business that owns intellectual property and grants or sells the license

Lien—a legal document that gives the borrower the right to seize and sell the collateral if the borrower does not pay the loan

Limited liability—the owner of the corporation can only lose the amount that he or she paid for his or her stock

Limited Liability Corporation (LLC)—a type of corporation that can elect to be taxed as a partnership or corporation without the restrictive ownership of an S Corp; however, the ownership cannot be sold or transferred

Limited Liability Partnership (LLP)—similar to a general partnership with the exception that some partners can be designated as limited partners

Limited partners—a partner in a Limited Liability Partnership that puts money into a partnership and receives an agreed-upon share of the profits or loss, but cannot actively manage the partnership but also cannot lose more than his or her investment

Line functions—functions directly involved in a company's value chain, specifically inputs, the process(es) used to convert the inputs to outputs and the outputs sold to customers; these include purchases, production and marketing

Line of credit—an agreement between a business and a financial intermediary that gives the business the right to borrow a given amount of money, under agreed-upon conditions, during a specific period of time; this type of loan is not a requirement but gives the business the option and ability to borrow money it needs during the specified time

Liquid—an asset that can be sold easily and turned into cash

Loan covenants—the special conditions to which the borrower and lender agree that outlines what the borrower can and cannot do such as maintaining a given level of cash or working capital, not paying dividends, providing collateral, or not borrowing additional money

Loan principal—the amount of money that has been loaned and is expected to be repaid to the lender

Loans—money that a lender provides a borrower

Lockout—action a business takes against employees by refusing to permit employees to enter the business

London Interbank Offered Rate (LIBOR)—The interest rate that high quality international banks charge one another for interbank loans

Long-term assets—assets that are not short-term assets and have an economic life greater than one year, including land, buildings, equipment, and intangible assets, such as patents, copyrights and trademarks

Long-term liabilities—liabilities that are due to be paid in periods beyond one year, such as loans due in a period longer than one year, retirement benefits, long-term taxes, contingent debts from lawsuits, and other actions

Loss—when the revenue the business receives is less than the cost of the product

Low-cost-producer—the drive for producing quality products at the lowest cost possible; see also *lean operations*

Low-cost provider—the business strategy utilized in the maturity stage of the life cycle analysis in which businesses innovate to lower costs and maximize operating profit

M

Macroeconomics—the study of how an overall society behaves financially

Maintenance shop—a business where all union members must remain union members as long as they remain employed by the business

Majority interest or majority stockholder—name to represent an entity that holds control (51% of ownership) of a company

Managed floating exchange rate system—a system where a government takes action to prevent its currency from appreciating or depreciating

Management—process of making decisions that affect the value of a business; the process is a cycle of planning, executing, and reviewing

Management development training—training that focuses on managers to help deal with the functions of planning, executing, and reviewing

Management of information systems (MIS)—managing the systems that use people and processes to convert data into information with analytics

Manager—an individual who is responsible for looking after the interests of the business's owners and other stakeholders and creating value

Managerial accounting—a type of accounting that attempts to meet the information needs of a business's managers by looking at the details of a business transaction so that managers can understand what is happening in the transaction to plan, execute, and review

Marginal costs—see *variable costs*

Marginal propensity to consume—the tendency of an individual to spend disposable income

Marginal propensity to save—the tendency of an individual to save disposable income

Marginal revenue—the price that a business gets for every sale

Marginal tax rate—the tax rate that a business or individual will pay on the next dollar of taxable income

Market—a place, either physical or not, where people and organizations exchange products or other things of value, such as money; also defined as the collection of all current and potential customers and competitors seeking to satisfy the wants and needs of those customers

Market price—see *equilibrium point*

Market development—one aspect of creating a competitive advantage that attempts to get new customers to buy existing products, such as by introducing an existing product into a new market where it was not previously sold

Market penetration—one aspect of creating a competitive advantage that attempts to increase an existing product's share of existing market, such as by lowering the price of the product to encourage more buyers

Marketable securities—short-term investments a business makes in financial securities, which are low risk because they have low default and easy to sell to turn into cash

Marketing—the process of understanding a market, positioning products to meet customer needs, distributing products, pricing products, and communicating product attributes to customers (promotion)

Marketing channel—organizations that help the business make its product available for ultimate consumption that can either be direct or indirect; see also *distribution channel*

Marketing concept—the responsibility of marketing to understand and guide the business regarding the needs and capabilities of the market for its products

Marketing department—function responsible for understanding the market (positional customers and competitors), making sure products will meet customer needs, pricing the product, trying to show the customer why the product adds superior value, and distributing the product; adds value by helping the business create, distribute. and sell products that customers want and will buy

Marketing intermediaries—comprised of members of the marketing channel that are organizations that help the business promote, finance, and distribute its products

Marketing mix—the output of the marketing process; can be summarized as the "Four P's of marketing," which are product, place, price, and promotion

Marketing process—includes: understanding a market, positioning products, distributing products, pricing products, and promotion

Marketing research—the process of collecting and analyzing data regarding current and potential customers and competitors

Marketing research process—the statistical process that defines the research question, designs the research so the question can be answered, collects the needed data, analyzes the data, and makes strategic decisions based on analyzed data to create business value

Marx, Karl—the man who formulated the idea of communism as a political and economic system in which there is no private ownership

Maslow's Hierarchy of Needs—a tool used to visualize how consumers prioritize the buying decisions that is topped by psychological needs; include—from bottom to top—physiological, safety, social, esteem, and self-actualization needs

Mass production—the process of producing standardized products in large quantities

Master Limited Partnership (MLP)—a limited partnership that can be traded in a public market

Matching concept—the principle that accountants follow to try and match sales and the expenses incurred to generate those sales

Materials and parts—a category of business product that are products businesses resell or use to create other products, such as clothing sold in a department store, steel used to manufacture automobiles, and wheat to produce bread

Maternity leave—leave from work a business permits its maternal employees to take to care for a baby

Matrix organization—a group organized in a combination of a divisional model and a functional model in attempt to capture the benefits of both divisional and functional models

Maturity—the point of time in which the loan must be completely repaid

Maturity stage of life cycle—another name for the cash cow stage in the product life cycle that is characterized by lowering prices, stagnant sales, decreased net income, fierce competition, and rising risk, as business's compete for customers

Mean—a statistical measure of the average of all observations, where 50% of the distribution is above the number and 50% is below that number, or the halfway point

Median—a statistical measure of the midpoint of all observations

Mediation—the act of negotiating a settlement between two parties

Mediation procedure—the process in which a neutral third party tries to get a business and union to reconcile their differences through negotiation

Mediator—an individual assigned to help negotiate a settlement between two parties

Medicaid—a health insurance program provided by the US government for older Americans who do not have sufficient money to pay for part of their health care costs

Medicare—a health insurance program provided by the US government for older Americans who have sufficient money to pay for part of their health care costs

Mentor—a form of training that involves an experienced employee who becomes a coach or advisor to a new or subordinate employee

Merchant wholesalers—retailers who buy and resell products, such as grocery stores

Merger—occurs when a company buys another company and assumes all assets and all debts

Microeconomics—the study of how individual people and organizations behave financially

Micropreneurs—one type of entrepreneurs that have a vision limited in size and typically provide services such as legal, accounting, and technology assistance; see also *home-based businesses*

Minority interest—the name to describe the owners of a business that do not have control

Minority stockholders—see *minority interest*

Minors—individuals under the age of 18

MIS—see *management of information systems*

Mission statement—a description of a business's business model, strategy, and operating values to show why it exists and how it operates

Mixed economics—a free market that is modified with regulation and socialism

Mode—a statistical measure of the central tendency, or the most frequent value in the distribution

Modular process—a process that uses teams, where team members do multiple tasks in the production of the product such as the heating, electrical, and plumbing in a custom home

Monetary policy—the government's management of the supply of money to help the economy grow faster or slower

Money—one of the factors of production (called financial capital) that is the medium of exchange, used to buy, sell, pay, and operate in the economy

Money market—a special part of the capital market where businesses use commercial paper to acquire money

Money supply—the amount of money in an economy; used to determine GDP

Monitoring risk—one of the principles in enterprise risk management (ERM) that creates and implements adequate controls to manage the risk accepting by the business through contingency plans and determining which risks a business can and cannot accept

Monopoly—an economic situation when one business controls the entire supply of a product; the supplier is able to set the price as high or low as it desires because the buyer has no alternatives

Mortgages—long-term loans collateralized by selected assets such as land, building, or equipment that allows the financial intermediary to seize and sell the assets if the business fails to repay the loan

Multinational businesses—businesses that are international or global

Multiplier effect—economic concept that states that when you spend money, you create income for someone else that allows that person to spend his or her money and create income for you

Multivariate statistics—a measure of descriptive statistics that examines multiple factors or dimensions, and how they relate to each other

N

National Labor Relations Board (NLRB)—the US government agency that is charged with enforcing the laws regarding agencies; notified by the union that a business has become a union shop, and the union is now the official agent that represents the employees

Nationalized—occurs when a government owns a business

Natural resources—one of the factors of production that includes minerals, water, land, and all other elements found in nature

Negative trade balance—occurs when a country imports more than it exports; also called a *trade deficit*

Negligence—an example of an unintentional tort that is the act of not using reasonable care in the conduct of their affairs

Negotiable commercial paper—the owner of the commercial paper can sell it without the consent of the borrower, such as when a bank can sell a business's loan to another bank without its consent

NET—see *Internet*

Net book value—the value of the building is the building's original cost, less the accumulated depreciation

Net income—the amount left for the owners of a business get after the business pays all of its expenses; (revenue—operating expense—interest)

Net income before taxes—earnings before interest and taxes minus interest; see also *taxable income (or loss)*

Net income or loss—taxable income less tax expense; the amount that belongs to the owners of a business

Net income percentage—the ratio of net income to sales (NI/S) to measure how a business operates; see also *profit margin*

Net pay—the amount received by the employee, and is gross pay less deductions for taxes and other items

Net present value (NPV)—one method of evaluating whether the investment will add or destroy value by measuring the value of the investment, adjusted for time, less the cost of the investment; if the NPV is positive, the investment adds value, and if negative, NPV destroys value

Net profit—see *net income*

Net receivables—accounts receivables, less allowance for bad debts; represents the amount of money the business expects to receive from its customers

Net working capital—a business's current assets less current liabilities; used to measure the amount of current assets financed with long-term debt or equity

Networks—with people, a communication process that brings people and organizations together for a common purpose; networks can include suppliers, competitors, employees, and even the government; with technology, a process or system used to transmit and communicate data and information between people and/or organizations

Ninety-day (90) T-bill—the short-term government bond that lenders often use as the risk-free rate in determining short-term borrowing rates

Nominal GDP—the price component of the GDP at the current price of goods and services produced

Nominal income—the measure of the income of individuals, businesses, and nations in current-year dollars that are not adjusted for changing prices caused by inflation or deflation

Non-controllable cost—a cost that employees or managers cannot affect such as the cost of a kilowatt-hour of electricity

Non-current assets—see *long-term asset*

Non-cyclical product—a product that does not see its demand affected by the state of the economy such as prescription drugs and food

Non-diversifiable risk—risk that cannot be diversified out of a business's portfolio through a collection of unrelated investments; measured by beta

Non-negotiable commercial paper—the owner of the commercial paper cannot sell the commercial paper without the consent of the business, such as when a bank cannot sell a business's loan to another bank without the consent of the borrower

Non-seasonal products—products that are not affected by the seasons of the year such as medical services, computers, and cell phones

Non-store retailers—retailers that have limited or no physical presence and use distribution channels such as vending machines, kiosks, home shopping networks, and the Internet

Nondurable goods—goods that have relatively short lives such as food, clothing, and utilities

Norris-LaGuardia Act—enacted in 1932 to make it easier for employees to create, join, or operate a union by setting clear standards for courts to follow in issuing injunctions that stop employees from organizing, striking, picketing, and boycotting

North American Free Trade Agreement (NAFTA)—an agreement joining the United States, Canada, and Mexico into one economic unit; removed barriers to trade such as tariffs, quotas, and other restrictions

Not-for-profit—when a business attempts to balance revenue and costs; create an exchange with an objective other than profit

Notes—see *financial instruments*

O

Occupational Safety and Health Act of 1970 (OSH Act)—the law that requires businesses to provide a safe workplace and established the Occupational Safety and Heath Administration to oversee that this took affect

Occupational Safety and Health Administration (OSHA)—the US government agency, created by the Occupational Safety and Health Act of 1970, to set standards, enforce the law, and oversee employee safety

Off-shoring—a business that uses foreign factors of production instead of or in addition to domestic factors of production because the business needs to stay price competitive or gain a comparative advantage

Office of Women's Business Ownership (OWBO)—a special office to help women become successful owners of small businesses; oversees the Women's Business Centers (WBCs)

Oligopoly—an economic situation where a few businesses control the supply of a product; issues occur when these business get together and set prices

On-the-job training—a form of training that involves the employee gaining experience by performing the job such as a manager or co-worker showing the employee what to do in the actual work setting

Operating activities—one receipt or use of cash on the cash flow statement that shows the cash provided by or used in generating net income

Operating cycle—the time that elapses between the production of inventory and the receipt of cash from the sale of inventory

Operating leases—a lease that is for a small part of the asset's useful life

Operating profit—the money left for a business after deducting expenses of operating the business (revenue— operating expenses); e.g., cost of products sold and cost of employee salaries; see also *earnings before interest and taxes*

Operating risk—the risk associated with the operating income of a business; a more stable, predictable operating income reduces operating risk, while sporadic, less predictable operating income increases operating risk

Operational managers—a manager that specializes in a functional area; e.g., plant manager

Operational plans—a plan middle and junior managers use to break down tactical plans into very specific activities and standards to show details of how actions are to be performed and goals reached

Operations department—function responsible for making the product; adds value by producing products customers want at a price they are willing to pay that creates net income for the business

Operations management—see *production management*

Opportunities—an aspect of SWOT analysis that is external to the business that a business cannot control; these include entering a new market, acquiring new technology, and improving market conditions

Opportunity cost—also known as the rate of return; the amount of value foregone in one exchange to pursue another opportunity; a function of the risk-free rate of return and of risk premium

Opportunity stage of life cycle—another name for the introduction stage in the product life cycle that is characterized by high risk, low sales, and high expenses, which often result in losses, as a business tries to introduce a new product into a new or existing market by promoting the product's unique and superior qualities

Option—a type of derivative that is an instrument sold by a seller to a buyer that gives the buyer the right—not obligation—to do something

Option premium—the price that the buyer must pay to the seller for an option

Oral contracts—occurs when the parties agree verbally without recording their agreement in a written document

Organization of Economic Cooperation and Development (OECD)—an organization that promotes free trade between member countries, which include 30 countries in North America, Europe, East Asia, and the South Pacific

Organization of Petroleum Exporting Countries (OPEC)—an economic agreement between member countries regarding the production of crude oil that created a trading bloc that impacts its pricing; current member companies include Algeria, Iran, Iraq, Kuwait, Libya, Nigeria, Qatar, United Arab Emirates, Venezuela, and Saudi Arabia

Orientation—the first stage of training where the employee is instructed in the business's policies and procedures

Outsourcing—a business that uses another business to build or service all or part of its products because the other business can create or deliver something better or at a lower cost

Outstanding stock—see *authorized, issued, and outstanding stock*

Overseas Private Investment Corporation (OPIC)—a US government agency that encourages US companies to invest in foreign countries by ensuring that the companies will not lose money from foreign currency devaluation or foreign government takeover

Owner's capital—the amount of money that an owner contributes to a sole proprietorship or partnership; a form of owner's equity for businesses that do not have stock

Owner's equity—the money that the owners of a business contribute; can be represented by owner's capital or stock

P

Packaging—designing and producing the container in which a product is sold or delivered to promote and protect a product; can also create value by creating benefits such as convenience and storage

Paid-in-capital in excess of par—see *capital surplus*

Par—the official stated value of stock; also called face value

Parent company—a company that owns a separate entity, called a subsidiary

Participative leader—leaders who attempt to involve as many people as possible in decision making; also known as democratic leaders

Partnership agreement—the legal document that outlines the rights and responsibilities of each general partner

Partnership capital—the amount of capital, or money, that each partner in a partnership has contributed to a business and each partner's share in the net income or loss in the business; the sum of partnership capital equals the owner's equity for the business

Passwords—a form of identification that improves security by only allowing approved users to enter and use an information system

Patent—the exclusive rights to a use of the patented idea, process, or product

Patent infringement—the lawsuit that can be filed against a person or business for illegally using another business's or person's patented idea, product, or process

Paternity leave—leave from work a business permits its paternal employees to take to care for a baby

Patient Protection and Affordable Care Act of 2010—a US law intended to make health care affordable and accessible to all people. The law requires businesses that employ more than 50 permanent employees to provide basic health benefits to its current employees.

Payback period—a tool to determine how long it will take to recover the cost of an investment by dividing the cash benefits per period by the total investment to determine the number of periods

Perceived absolute value of the product—the perception of a product that customers create about the value of perceived benefits from owning the product, and then compare the perceived value to the product's price; customers purchase goods that have a perceived value greater than the price, and do not purchase goods that have a perceived value lower than the price

Perceived relative value of the product—the perception of a product that customers create about the value of perceived benefits from owning the product, and then compare the perceived value to the perceived value of *alternative* or *competing* products; customers purchase goods that have a perceived value greater than alternative or competing products, and do not purchase goods that have a perceived value lower than alternative or competing goods

Perfect competition—economic situation where there are numerous buyers and sellers all with equal economic power; buyers have alternatives and sellers must supply to the buyers with the best products at the lowest prices to compete for buyers

Perpetuity—a special type of annuity, which pays a future amount forever; present value of a perpetuity is calculated by dividing the periodic perpetuity by the rate of return

Personal identification numbers (PINs)—a form of identification that improves security by only allowing approved users to enter and use an information system

Personal property—property that is not classified as real property, such as cars, moveable machines, and inventory

Personal selling—one of the aspects of promotional or marketing communications mix that is the personal interaction, intended to create a sale, between a business's sales force and potential customers; usually includes using the personal selling process

Personal selling process—the process of prospecting and qualifying potential customers, researching and understanding how to approach targeted customers, approaching targeted customers and beginning the seller-buyer relationship, presenting and demonstrating the product, dealing with customer concerns, completing or closing the sale, and following up with the sale to ensure the customer perceives the sale created value and the seller-buyer relationship is positive

PERT chart—a chart that depicts the tasks or activities needed to produce a product, or shows the timing or sequence of each task activity by emphasizing the critical path embedded in the process; acronym stands for "program evolution review technique"

Phishing—a scam where spam emails are sent asking for personal information which allows the sender to steal the receiver's identity

Picketing—the action striking union members take by marching outside a business with signs communicating their position

Piece-goods work—compensation where employees are paid per units produced in a given period

Place—one of the Four "P's" of marketing that is defined as the location and means of distributing the product

Placing the debt or equity—the process of finding a buyer for the debt or equity

Plaintiff—the party harmed in a civil lawsuit that brings the defendant to court

Planning—part of the management process that involves envisioning the future, finding opportunities, setting goals and determining the best alternative(s) to achieve these goals, and developing systems that will enable the business to execute the selected alternatives Plant—see *fixed assets*

Portal—a point of entry to and exit from the World Wide Web

Porter's Five Forces—a model to help determine the external environment surrounding a business; includes examining 1) supplier power, 2) barriers to entry, 3) customer power, 4) threat of substitute products, and 5) rivalry

Portfolio—the pool or mix of different resources that comprises a business

Precautionary demand for money—one of the three reasons, as defined by economist John Maynard Keyes, that a business needs cash defined as a business's need to hold cash for bad and unexpected events that may happen

Preferred dividends—dividends paid to preferred shareholders; usually guaranteed to be paid at a stipend amount and receives preference over common shareholders

Preferred stock—one type of stockholders in a business that represents a group of owners that have special rights or preferences such as giving these stockholders a guarantee that they will pay a specified amount of dividends each period

Prepaid expense—a cost paid by the business prior to receiving the business from the cost

Present value—the value of money today

President—see *Chief Operating Officer (CEO)*

Price—one of the Four "P's" of marketing that is defined as the amount the customer pays the business for the sale

Price discrimination—one way that a business or businesses restrain and control trade by charging similar customers different prices to manipulate competition

Price-Earnings Ratio (PE)—one method of valuing a business that shows a company's future versus its present earnings; the ratio of the current price of a share of stock divided by the business's current earnings per share (which is net income divided by the number of shares outstanding)

Price elastic—the condition that occurs when demand and supply react to price changes; typically occurs when consumers can defer purchasing the product or have lots of alternatives or choices

Price fixing—one way that a business or businesses restrain and control trade by one or a group of businesses setting the price of an item, as opposed to the market

Price inelastic—the condition that occurs when demand and supply do not react to price changes; typically occurs when consumers must have the product and have no other alternatives or choices

Pricing-on-the-margin—the business practice of pricing its products by focusing on the variable, or marginal, costs

Primary market—the market, on which a corporation sells stock, receives the money, and the buyer receives the stock

Primary marketing data—a method of marketing research that uses data created for the sole purpose of answering the marketing question

Prime loan— A high quality loan with low perceived risk of default

Prime rate—The interest rate charged on prime loans

Principal—an individual that empowers another to represent him or her, such as the stockholders of an organization

Principle-based ethics—one form of ethical standards based on principles

Priority of claims—the determination of preferential treatment given to different types of financial capital

Private capital market—a capital market that is not open to everyone but only for selected people or organizations to buy debt or equity

Private Export Funding Corporation (PEFCO)—owned by a group of private US banks that lend money to foreign companies that import US products

Private market—a market that is not open to everyone

Private placement—a private market sale of debt or equity

Private property—property owned by individuals and businesses

Pro-forma financial statements—the projected financial statements that address a business's financial risk by constructing financial statements based on assumptions such as sales, costs, needed employees, and needed assets; assumptions must be clearly stated and justified by market research, and sensitivity analysis should be conducted to look at different assumptions

Process cost system—one type of cost accounting systems average costs over large numbers of nearly identical products to determine the average cost per unit

Process of risk management—the process that a business uses to systematically manage its risk by: recognizing, understanding, measuring, managing, and pricing risk

Produced inventory—the inventory that a business has for sale that it has produced rather than purchased

Producers Price Index (PPI)—an estimate of how the price of products sold between businesses has changed in a given period

Product—one of the Four "P's" of marketing that is defined as goods or service to be exchanged; see *goods* or *service*

Product development—one aspect of creating a competitive advantage that attempts to develop and introduce a new product to an existing market

Product differentiation—the creation of a product that is different and possesses unique qualities that make it the most desirable among customer alternatives

Product features—relates to the physical and mental attributes that provide customers satisfaction when they use a product

Product life cycle—the cycle in which a successful product evolves; comprised of introduction stage (also called opportunity stage), growth stage (also called star stage), maturity stage (also called cash cow stage), and decline stage (also called dog stage)

Product line—a group of similar products in a business that, across the business, make up the business's product mix

Product mix—a business's portfolio of product lines

Product positioning—the process of creating a customer perception that the business's product is different, occupies a clear, distinct, and desirable place in the market, and provides more value compared to competing products

Product quality—relates to a product's lack of defects, such as the durability of clothing, comfort of furniture, and patient's response to medical treatment

Production department—see *operations department*

Production management—the activities needed to create or make a product

Production or operations systems—the means of converting inputs into outputs

Productivity—the use of resource to create income; includes getting the most output from the resources in the economy by measuring the output per unit of input

Profit—occurs when the revenue from the exchange exceeds the cost incurred from the exchange (revenue—cost)

Profit margin—see *net income percentage*

Profit sharing—compensation where an employee is paid as a percentage of profits; may be computed using the profits of a total business or part of the business such as a division

Progressive tax—a method of taxation where the rate of taxation goes up as the level of income goes up

Promotion—one of the Four "P's" of marketing that is defined as the communication by the business to customers, designed to inform the customer of product attributes and persuade the customer to purchase the product; also defined as the process of communicating to customers the absolute and relative values of the product

Promotional or marketing communications mix—the mix of advertising, sales promotion, personal selling, direct-marketing techniques, and public relations used by a business to communicate a marketing message

Promotional pull strategy—a strategy that the product producer uses a lot of advertising focused on the ultimate consumer to create demand in the consumer that pulls retailers and other marketing channel members into offering the product because consumers demand it

Promotional push strategy—a strategy that the product producer's promotional efforts are focused on retailers and other channel members, who then promote the product to the ultimate consumer

Promotional process—the six-step process used to create a sale by targeting a market segment and customer, determining the communication objective, designing the message to be communicated, choosing a medium to communicate the message, executing by delivering the designed message to the selected medium and collecting feedback, reviewing feedback, and making adjustments as needed

Property—an item of value that a person or businesses owns

Property, plant, and equipment (PP&E)—see *fixed assets*; represented on a business's balance sheet as an asset

Property taxes—periodic taxes assessed by governments on the value of property

Proprietorship capital—an owner's equity account that is a combination of money an owner has contributed and the net income (or loss) the owner has retained in the business

Prosecutors—government lawyers that charge the accused with their crime and bring them to court

Protectionism—the actions a government takes to protect domestic businesses by limiting the operations of foreign businesses

Psychological factors—the factors that relate to a consumer's motivation, perceptions, beliefs, and knowledge that determine how a consumer prioritizes the decision on what to buy

Public capital market—a market where anyone can buy or sell a financial security

Public Company Accounting Oversight Board (PCAOB)—the governmental body that oversees and approves the rules set by the Financial Accounting Standards Board (FASB)

Public domain—the end of the life of a copyright when it becomes public and can be used by anyone

Public market—a market where anyone can buy all or part of a business

Public property—property owned by the government

Public relations—one of the aspects of promotional or marketing communications mix that is the process of communicating to a business's public that the business creates value for the public as a whole to create a positive image

Publicity—the information that creates an image of a business and its products

Publicly traded—describes a company's stock and debt that are traded in a public capital market

Punitive damages—damages awarded to the plaintiff in excess of his or her compensatory damages that work to punish the defendant for outrageous acts

Purchased inventory—inventory that a business has to sell that it has purchased rather than produced

Purchasing power parity—a theory that states inflation in a country hurts the value of that country's currency; also states that the same item in two different countries should have the same "real" cost, where real cost adjusts for inflation, and if price is not the same, consumers buy the lower-cost alternative

Put option—an option that gives the option owner the right to sell the item to the option seller at a specific price at or during a specified time in the future

Q

Qualified or subject-to audit opinion—one of the four types of audit opinions that states that auditors believe the financial statements fairly present the business's operations and activities except for select items

Quality—producing products that meet customer expectations regarding the perception of the product's value

Quality assurance—another name for Total Quality Management (TQM); see also *Total Quality Management (TQM)*

Quality circle—a team of employees that works with the parts of a business to address opportunities and challenges regarding quality

Quality control—the process that a business must go through to design operating and manufacturing systems that ensure products meet required specifications

Quick ratio—a common measure used to look at a business's ability to pay its liabilities, which is calculated by dividing quick assets by the current liabilities where quick assets are cash, marketable securities, and accounts receivable

Quota—a trade barrier that permits selected products to be imported and/or exported but limits the amount

R

Rate of return—the rate of change that will be received over a time period, usually given in as an annual rate

Ratified contract—describes a contract that is approved by the majority of the membership of a union and now governs the workers' employment

Raw materials—the inputs purchased by a business that are used in the production of goods

Raw materials inventory—the materials used to build produced inventory but are not yet completed

Real capital—term used to describe assets; used to create value

Real GDP—the price component of the GDP as the current price of goods and services produced adjusted to remove the impact of price changes by adjusting for the GDP deflator

Real income—the measure of income of individuals, businesses, and nations in current-year dollars that are adjusted for inflation or deflation

Real property—land and items permanently attached to the land

Receivable—a claim on another person or business

Recession—two consecutive quarters of negative growth in real GDP

Regular annuities—annuity payments made or received at the end of the period, as opposed to the beginning

Relationship marketing—a form of marketing that recognizes that buyers and sellers create relationships, positive or negative, over both the short and long term time periods

Rent—the periodic fee a lessee pays to a lessor to use property

Reorganization—Chapter 11 of the Bankruptcy Act

Request for Proposal (RFP)—a formal process that a business uses to alert potential suppliers that the business has a need, and the suppliers should submit formal bids

Required rate of return—the return expected by those that provide money; mathematically stated, it is the risk free rate plus the risk premium

Research and development (R&D) department (pg 14, 324)— function is responsible for acquiring and applying new knowledge to create new products, to refine existing products, and to decide whether or not existing products can create value; adds value by helping the business create products that customers want and will buy

Resume—a document created by applicants that lists their address, contact information, work experience and history, education, and special talents or abilities that the human resource department uses to screen applicants and assess whether they meet job specifications

Retail prices—the average price of consumer goods

Retailer—an organization that sells products to the ultimate consumer of the products

Retained earnings—the business's accumulated net income and losses that the owner's have left in the business, as opposed to taken out in the form of cash dividends

Retired stock—stock that has been repurchased from stockholders by a business, but then the existing stockholders decide the stock cannot be sold again; the stock is no longer authorized

Return—a percentage relating what the lender or owner received from a business relative to what they put in the business during that period

Return on Assets (ROA)—one tool in financial analysis that determines how the business used its assets to generate net income; computed by Net Income/Total Assets

Return on Equity (ROE)—one tool in financial analysis that determines the return the business generated for its owners; computed by Net Income/Total Owner's Equity

Revenue—the money or money substitutes a business receives for a product, also known as sales

Reverse discrimination—discrimination in which an applicant or employee is denied equal treatment because he or she was not a member of an underrepresented minority

Review—part of the management process that involves using systems to compare the desired outcomes to the actual results

Risk—the uncertainty of receiving benefits that are lower in amount and/or later in time than expected; higher risks decrease value and require a higher return

Risk-free rate of return—the cost of money dictated by the economy to compensate for time, assuming no risk

Risk assessment—one of the principles in enterprise risk management (ERM) that is about recognizing, analyzing, understanding, and measuring the significant risks associated with a business's investing, financing, and operating activities by looking at every part of the business, and how those parts fit together in the business model and strategy

Risk evaluation—one of the principles in enterprise risk management (ERM) that is a continuous examination of the risk management process and determining whether or not it is effective and that makes changes to the process of setting risk tolerances, assessing, and monitoring risks

Risk premium—the additional cost of money to compensate for uncertainty and risk; higher risk requires higher return to the money providers

Risk tolerance—one of the principles in enterprise risk management (ERM) that determines how much risk a business can and should accept; defined as a business's willingness and/or ability to assume risk in any given activity and the business as a whole

Rivalry—one of Porter's Five Forces that relates to the intensity of the competition in the industry

Robinson-Patman Act—a doctrine passed by the US government that, along with the Sherman Antitrust and Clayton Acts, intended to foster competition by preventing a business or businesses from restraining and thus controlling trade

Routing—the discussion of PERT charts and see how managers must figure the sequence and critical path of the production process

Rule-based ethics—one form of ethical standards based on rules

S

S Corporations—a corporation that can be formed if certain criteria are met to have the liability of a corporation but taxed as a corporation

Safety stock—extra inventory that a business holds in excess of its forecasted demand so that the business does not run out of inventory if demand is higher than anticipated

Salary—the cash payment the employee receives for his or her labor, from His or her employer

Sale—an exchange between a business and a customer that transfers ownership of the property

Sales promotions—one of the aspects of promotional or marketing communications mix that is the techniques used to encourage the customer to buy the product in the short term such as coupons, refunds, rebates, free samples, product demonstrations, in-store displays, and event sponsorship

Sales tax—a type of excise that on the purchase, sale and consumption

Sample—a smaller portion of the entire population used to infer the characteristics of the population

Sarbanes-Oxley (SOX)—a United States law that requires management to disclose the significant risks faced by a business, and places more personal responsibility on management to provide fair and complete financial statements

Savings—a use of GDP that refers to the money an individual sets aside for the future, such as a savings account, a retirement fund, or investments

Scheduling—assigning tasks to specific people, machines, processes, or even departments; refers to what will happen, who will do it, how it will be done, and when it will be done

SCORE—a nonprofit organization that uses retired business executives to assist and counsel small businesses; a resource partner of the SBA, called the "Counselors of America's Small Business," that often mentors and coaches small business owners

Seasonal products—products affected by the seasons of the year such as bathing suits, snowmobiles, and lawn mowers

Seasonal unemployment—an economic state when the demand for employees varies depending on the time of year; examples include holiday periods or weather changes

Seasonality—one of the three forces that shifts supply and demand; refers to the time of year a product is produced and sold

Secondary market—the market on which a stockholder sells his or her stock to anyone other than the issuing company

Secondary marketing data—a method of marketing research that uses data that already exists

Secondary stock offerings (SPO)—a subsequent offering of stock by a business that has already issued stock at least once on a public capital market

Secured debt/creditor—a loan that is guaranteed with collateral

Securities and Exchange Commission (SEC)—the government regulator of public markets where financial instruments are bought and sold to ensure that market participants are well informed and the market is not unfairly manipulated

Securities markets—another name for capital markets because debt and equity securities are bought and sold; see also *capital markets*

Segment the market—the process of breaking the market into subgroups or submarkets based on certain characteristics, such as geography, age, gender, education, lifestyle, and/or ethnicity, to effectively select a marketing strategy that allows the business to provide customers greater value

Self-insured—the phrase for a business's risk management process that does not involve the purchase of an insurance policy, but rather the business accepts the risk and pays for any losses

Senior managers—a level of manager hired by the Board of Directors that directs and coordinates the overall business organization; e.g., chief executive officer (CEO); see also *manager*

Seniority—a loan that has a higher priority of claim

Sensitivity analysis—the process of estimating the impact of unexpected events through assessing the magnitude and probability of potential losses from decisions and activities

Server—contains the information that a business provides through its website

Services—intangible activities that we know exist but cannot touch and feel; e.g., haircuts and education

Severance pay—pay received by an employee after termination

Sexual harassment—unwelcomed sexual advances, requests for sexual favors, and other verbal or physical conduct of a sexual nature that explicitly or implicitly affects an individual's employment, unreasonably interferes with an individual's work performance, or creates an intimidating, hostile, or offensive work environment; made illegal by Title VII of the Civil Rights Act of 1964

Shareholders—see *stockholders*

Sherman Antitrust Act—the original doctrine intended to foster competition by preventing a business or businesses from restraining and thus controlling trade; amended by the Clayton and Robinson-Patman Acts.

Shop stewards—the individual elected by the union members to be the local representative for a union

Shopping products—a category of consumer product that costs more and that consumers buy carefully and less frequently, such as furniture, clothes, and airfare

Short-term borrowing—loans from banks and other lenders that a business must pay within the next year

Sick leave—time an employee is not required to work due to an illness but may or may not be compensated

Sick pay—payment an employee receives for days an employee is ill and cannot work

Simple interest—the rate of return for one year without within-year compounding

Single taxation—occurs when the income of a business is taxed only once, as in a sole proprietorship

Six Sigma—a process developed in the early 1980s by Motorola that focuses on the inputs and systems to produce products with no more than 3.4 defects per million parts or actions for a success rate of 99.999%.

Small business—an independent business with fewer than 500 employees

Small Business Administration (SBA)—the government agency that the United States has established to assist small businesses, including managing a small business and what should be included in the integrated plan that guides the business and communicates to all stakeholders how the business will create value

Small Business Development Centers (SBDCs)—nonprofit agencies created to educate, assist, and counsel small business by bringing together private individuals and businesses

Small Business Investment Company (SBIC)—a private venture capital business that provides owners' equity funding to small businesses and can borrow money from the government

Smith, Adam—a Scottish philosopher who wrote *An Inquiry into the Nature and Causes of the Wealth in Nations*; he believed in competition and that an "invisible hand," called the multiplier effect, guides the economy

Social factors—the factors that relate to how consumers are affected by group behavior, such as society, family, or a college graduating class where different members assume different roles to influence what group members buy or do not buy

Social networks—see *informal network*

Social responsibility—how the business relates to society, including customers, employees, and suppliers by seeking to improve the quality and quantity of life for all of its stakeholders

Social Security—a US government-sponsored plan retirement program where employees and employers pay a percentage of the employee's gross salary to the government and in return, receive a calculated payment when they retire at the age of 62 or after

Socialism—an economic system in which the government owns selected businesses, typically those that are most critical to the welfare of the society; the government makes the decisions on what is produced, how it is priced, and who can or cannot purchase the items

Software—the instructions, programs, and rules used to process the data into information

Sole proprietorship—one person owns and controls the business with no legal action to start or close the enterprise

Spam—unsolicited emails

Span of influence—the scope of responsibilities that a particular manager has, increasing as managers move up the management hierarchy

Special or administrative court—see *district courts*

Specialty products—a category of consumer products that are unique that consumers buy infrequently with deliberate thought process, such as automobiles, jewelry, and computers

Specialty store—a store that carries a limited product line, such as Gap, Dick's Sporting Goods, and Brooks Brothers

Speculative demand for money—one of the three reasons, as defined by economist John Maynard Keyes, that a business needs cash defined as a business's need to be able to take advantage of unique opportunities

Spyware—programs that show to outsiders what a computer is doing, without the permission of the user of the computer

Staff functions—functions indirectly involved in a company's value chain that support activities of the line functions; examples include accounting, finance and information systems

Staffing analysis—the understanding, often done by the human resource department, of the quantity of people, skills each person needs, and timing of when people are needed for the business to compete and create value

State courts—courts that deal with all intrastate disputes and are not handled by the federal courts

Stakeholders—parties who require that a business offer value greater than the value they give up; e.g., owners, employees, suppliers, customers, lenders or society

Standard deviation—the statistical measure of dispersion around the mean by square rooting the variance

Standard of living—the income or quality of life of a person

Standards (pg 199, 350)—benchmarks or goals that businesses use to determine if budgeted transactions are being achieved; also goals a business desires to meet regarding how much will be produced, when it will be produced, and how much each unit produced will cost

Star stage of life cycle—another name for the growth stage in the product life cycle that is characterized by growing demand, decreased risk, and increased sales, which result in growing net income, as the market begins to accept the business's product

Statement of retained earnings—a financial statement of a business that shows how the retained earnings account, in the owner's equity section of the balance sheet, changed during a given period; reflects the beginning retained earnings in the period, plus the net income earned in the period, less the dividend declared during the period

State Supreme Court—the highest court of appeals at the state level; operates much like the US Supreme Court in federal cases

Statistical process control (SPC)—the systems to collect and analyze the data about the sample of the quality products as they are being produced, and ultimate customer satisfaction

Statistics—the science of collecting, analyzing, summarizing and presenting mass amounts of information in two main ways: descriptive statistics and inferential statistics

Statute of limitations—the stated period of time in which certain wrongful acts must be proven

Statutes of frauds—the statute that each state has that clearly states what contracts must be in writing to be enforceable in that particular state

Statutory law—laws enacted by votes of the people, or by representatives elected by the people

Stock—a representation of a part of the ownership in a business

Stock certificate—the documents that owners, called stockholders or shareholders, hold to show their ownership

Stock swap—occurs when a company buys another company with stock

Stockholders—the owners of a corporation who buy shares of stock that represent their ownership

Straight bankruptcy or liquidation—Chapter 7 of the bankruptcy act

Strategic alliance—occurs when businesses in different countries agree to help each other produce and/or sell multiple products over time, which often centers around the marketing of a company's product by a foreign country; diminishes the risk of entering an unknown market but reduces potential profit

Strategic plans—the plan used by senior management to set and communicate the business' broad goals and long term objectives but does not provide specific details

Strengths—an aspect of SWOT analysis that is internal to a business that a business can control; examples include holding a patent

Strict liability—a doctrine that holds the seller liable for damages, incurred by the buyer or other parties, when the product was unreasonably unsafe. The plaintiff does not have to show intent or negligence, just that an injury occurred and that the defendant's actions or product caused the injury.

Strike—a practice used by union members in which they refuse to work until their employers meet their demands

Strikebreakers—non-union employees hired to replace striking employees

Structural unemployment—an economic state when there are structural barriers preventing employers and employees from coming together; examples include geography and education

Subordinated loan—the second loan on a loan using the same collateral as another

Subordinated bonds—bonds that have low priority of claims in bankruptcy

Subprime Loan—A loan that has significant default risk

Subsidiary—occurs when a purchased company remains a separate company from its purchaser, the parent company

Succession planning—the human resource department's estimation of how employees will progress throughout the organization in planning for the future

Sunk costs—costs that cannot be recovered once spent

Supermarkets—stores that carry numerous lines of food and household products such as Publix, Safeway, and Giant

Supplier power—one of Porter's Five Forces that refers to the power that suppliers have in a business's value chain

Supplies and services—a category of business products that businesses buy to operate the business that are not classified as materials and parts or capital items, and typically have a short life, such as office supplies, repair and maintenance items, and air travel

Supply—one aspect of the economic supply and demand model that refers to individuals and businesses that have something they want to sell or supply to buyers; sellers seek the highest price possible

Supply chain management—managing the interface between a business and its suppliers

Supply curve—the model that depicts the relationship of price and quantity that faces suppliers; suppliers able to charge higher prices for the products, then they have an incentive to produce more, and when there are lower prices, suppliers have less of an incentive to produce

Support service—the services at-sale or post-sale that a seller promises a buyer, such as training and repair

Surety—an individual willing to cosign a loan with another person

Surety bond—an example of a program offered by the SBA that assists and counsels small businesses that is a form of insurance policy that ensures that the small business will guarantee the government that it will successfully complete its contract

Sustainable competitive advantage—a business's ability continue to do something that allows it to outperform its competitors over the long term as a truly successful company

Sustainable marketing—a form of marketing that addresses the need for products to meet the current and future needs of customers without infringing on society's ability to meet the needs of future customers

Swap—one type of a derivative that is a financial agreement where two parties agree to swap something of value at a future date to alleviate the risks associated with the value

SWOT analysis—an analogy for "strengths, weaknesses, opportunity, and threats" that managers must recognize within their company; strengths and weaknesses are internal to the business, whereas opportunities and threats are external to the business

Synthetic process—a process that combines inputs or products to create another product

Systematic risk—see *non-diversifiable risk*

T

Tactical plans—a plan that functional managers use to breakdown broad goals and long-term objectives into more precise goals and actions

Taft-Hartley Act—prohibits unions from using unfair tactics and forcing them to negotiate with a business in full faith, to not charge excessive union dues, to prohibit harassing non-union workers, and to refrain from coercing employers; made closed shops illegal

Tangible assets—see *tangible property*

Tangible property—property that can be seen and touched because it physically exists

Target—a business's selection of the segment in its market for which it believes it can create a competitive advantage, and on which it begins to focus its marketing efforts

Tariffs—a tax on foreign businesses that is at a higher rate than domestic businesses

Tax planning and strategy—management decisions to ensure that a business complies with the law and to minimize or defer the payment of taxes

Taxable income (or loss)—net income (revenue minus costs) before taxes; see also *net income before taxes*

Taxes—a use of GDP that is a required payment made to the government as the cost to live in a society; used to pay for roads, public servants, and military

Team—cohesive groups of people who focus on an objective

Teamwork—the steps members take to achieve their objectives

Technology—the devices and systems used in a business and society

Telecommunications—technology that transmits information over distance through computerized information networks

Telecommuting—technology that allows an employee to work from home

Temporary injunction—action the US federal court takes to require striking employees to return to work for a given period of time; granted when the President of the United states, or other such government officials, believes that the business is critical to the nation's welfare

Threat of substitute products one of Porter's Five Forces that refers to the availability of products that the customer can substitute for the business's products

Threats—an aspect of SWOT analysis that is external to the business that a business cannot control; examples include new competitors, deteriorating economic conditions, and changing customer tastes

Title VII of the Civil Rights Act of 1964—prohibits discrimination in hiring, firing, compensating, training, terms, conditions, or privileges of employment

Time period—the amount of time between today's present value and the amount expected to be received at the future value

Tort—a wrongful act that injures another person; falls into two categories—intentional and unintentional torts

Total Asset Turnover (TAT)—the ratio of sales to total assets (S/TA) to measure the productivity of investing in assets

Total costs—the variable costs plus fixed costs of a product; calculable when a business can allocate fixed costs to its products

Total Quality Management (TQM)—the philosophy that producing quality products is an essential part of all aspects of a business by meeting customer expectations, maximizing the benefits from meeting customer expectations, and minimizing the costs of not meeting customer expectations; deals with designing products, marketing products, producing products, and supporting customers with services such as guarantees, repairs, and education

Trade account—the money a business owes to its suppliers; see *balance of trade*

Trade barriers—a way in which a government is trying to protect domestic business by employing options to limit the operations of foreign business; these include embargoes, quotas, and tariffs

Trade credit—the money that a business owes to its suppliers

Trade deficit—see *negative balance of trade*

Trade discount—the discount a business may offer to a customer to incentivize a business to pay their debt to a business early

Trade Surplus—see *positive balance of trade*

Trademark—the right to own a symbol or a word or words registered with the law to represent an exclusive right to a product or business

Trademark infringement—the lawsuit that can be filed against a person or business for illegally using another business's or person's trademark

Traits of successful managers—the combination of ten managerial skills that allow one manager to succeed more than another

Transaction demand for money—one of the three reasons, as defined by economist John Maynard Keyes, that a business needs cash defined as a business's need to pay its bills

Transactional leader—a leader who helps a team reach a clearly defined, desired objective

Transformational leader—a leader who helps his or her team envision possibilities and the need to change

Transitional unemployment—a state of economy when an employee or employer desires to make a change; examples include leaving one job for another or being dismissed

Treasury Bills—the name for short-term Treasury Securities

Treasury Securities—the name for United States government loans; their short-term rate charged is often used by lenders of money as the risk-free rate because it is assumed to be safer to loan money for a short period of time to the US government is safer and thus, less risky, than loaning money to any other group or for longer periods of time

Treasury stock—stock that has been repurchased back from stockholders by the issuing business

Trial courts—courts that have jurisdiction over the matters not covered in inferior courts where judges and juries are both used to decide disputes

Truth-in-lending laws—laws that require lenders to inform a borrower of all the terms of the debt, including the effective interest rate being charged

U

Unauthorized strike—a strike that is not approved by the union; see also *wildcat strike*

Underemployment—occurs when an individual is overqualified to do the work they are performing

Underwriting—the guarantee by investment bankers to a business issuing debt or equity that the business will receive a specific amount of money

Unemployment—an economic state when full employment does not occur and individuals who want and need work cannot find it

Unemployment benefits—benefits an employee can receive for a designated number of weeks when an employee is dismissed because of a lack of work, at no fault of the employee; intended to help the unemployed employee during the period he or she is seeking employment

Uniform Commercial Code (UCC)—the code adopted by all states that governs most contract law; requires five things for a contract to exist

Uniform Resource Locator (URL)—the unique address that identifies a website that allows a business or person to store and display information

Union—a legal organization that employees join and empower to represent them in negotiating with an employer to collectively bargain with the employer for issues such as compensation, working conditions, or job security

Union shop—used to describe a business that has had the majority of its employees vote to join a union

United Nations (UN)—an organization formed after World War II to foster world peace and cooperation

United States Copyright Office—the government agency that oversees the granting of patents

United States Patent and Trademark Office (PTO)—the government agency that oversees the granting of patents and trademarks

Univariate statistics—a measure of descriptive statistics that examines one variable or dimension

Unlimited liability—the owner of a business is personally responsible for the debts of the business

Unqualified or clean opinion—one of the four types of audit opinions that states that the auditors believe the financial statements fairly present the business's operations and activities

Unsecured bonds—bonds that are not backed by collateral

Unsecured debt/creditor—a loan that is not guaranteed with collateral

Unsought products—a category of consumer product that consumers do not initially or readily recognize they need or want and only buy them after they are shown a need or want exists, such as insurance, medical procedures, and legal services

US Court of Appeals for the Federal Circuit—the federal court created in 1982 to judge patent lawsuits

US Federal Deposit Insurance Company (FDIC)—US federal agency that insures bank deposits and regulates banks

US Federal Reserve (the Fed)—one of the primary regulators of banks in the United States; sets up guidelines for lending, operating, accepting risk, and maximum levels of equity

US Supreme Court—the highest level of federal courts, and the highest federal court of appeals; can choose whether or not to hear and rule on a case

Utility—a measure of satisfaction or benefits gained from the purchase of a product

V

Vacation pay—payment an employee receives for days that the employee is relaxing and enjoying pursuits other than work

Value—a combination of the quantity or amount of the benefits expected to receive, the expected timing of the benefits expected to receive, and the opportunity costs and risks involved. Value is higher when 1) the benefits are higher, 2) the quicker the benefits are received, and 3) the risks are lower. Value incorporates the present and the future expectations.

Value-added tax (VAT)—an imbedded tax ultimately paid by the consumer that is assessed at each stage of converting the inputs into outputs as a product move through its value chain

Value chain—the system defined in a business model that maps how the business converts inputs, such as people, assets, and money, into outputs that create value for customers, owners and other stakeholders

Variable costs—costs incurred by the business that will vary directly with the amount sold, such as cost of goods sold

Variable-rate loan—a loan in which the interest rate changes over time, forcing the borrower to pay more interest as rates rise and less interest when the rates fall; also called floating-rate or adjustable-rate loans

Variance—in accounting, the difference between actual and budgeted (standard) amounts to compute the quantity of products produced, and the cost of the products produced; in statistics, the measure of dispersion between the mean of the distribution and the value of the individual observation

Velocity—the number of times money is used in a given period; used to measure GDP

Venture capitalist (VC)—an organization that pays cash for the debt and stock of selected new businesses; looks for businesses that have the potential to grow rapidly so that the venture capitalist can help the business grow, and eventually sells or divests of the business's debt and/or stock within five to seven years

Vertical integration—occurs when a business buys another business that is a part of the business's value chain

Vice presidents—senior managers who report to the president or chief operating officer; vice presidents include chief financial officers, chief operating officers, chief information officers, and chief marketing officers

Viral marketing—marketing in which a business attempts to get customers to tell friends and family about the business's product

Virtual private network (VPN)—see *intranet*

Viruses—computer programs that destroy other computer programs without the consent of the computer user

Visioning—the process of looking at the past and present, embracing the forces of change, and forecasting the future; typically the overall direction of a business is the responsibility of top management

Voluntary bankruptcy—when a business puts itself into bankruptcy by petitioning the bankruptcy court

W

Wagner Act—enacted in 1935 to require businesses to negotiate with union officials who are elected by the union and employees and to prohibit businesses from firing or discriminating against employees who favor or join a union; also established the National Labor Relations Board (NLRB) to oversee the creation of unions and enforce laws dealing with union-employer relationships

Warranty—a seller's promise or guarantee regarding the property's quantity and quality; can be either expressed or implied

Weaknesses—an aspect of SWOT analysis that is internal to the business that a business can control; examples include a lack of trained employees

Website—one form of a portal that allows entry to and exit from the World Wide Web

Weighted average cost of capital (WACC)—a measure of the mix of debt and equity that produces the greatest value and lowest average cost of money measured by the weighted average after-tax cost of debt and cost of equity

Wholesale prices—the prices of products sold between businesses

Wholesaler—an organization that buys products for resale to retailers

Wholesalers—businesses that buy products from produces and sell products to businesses for resale or business uses; divided into merchant wholesalers, and brokers and agents

Wholly owned—occurs when a company buys all of another company

Wildcat strike—see *unauthorized strike*

Wireless—transmission of data and information through airwaves

Women's Business Centers (WBC)—a center that helps educate socially and economically disadvantaged women; overseen by the Office of Women's Business Ownership (OWBO)

Work-in-process—the inventory that is in the process of transformation from raw goods into a finished product

Work-in-process inventory—the partially finished produced inventory that a company holds

Workers' compensation—the law that requires businesses to pay employees injured on the job

Working capital—short-term assets such as inventory, receivables, and cash

Working capital loans—short term loans that must be repaid within one year; often used to help finance temporary increases in accounts receivable and inventory

World Bank—an organization created after World War II owned by countries throughout the world to make loans to countries to help develop their economies

World Trade Organization (WTO—an organization that attempts to break down economic barriers and mediate trade disagreements between member countries

World wide web (www)—the system used to access the Internet

Written contract—occurs when the parties record their agreement in a written document

CREDITS

INDEX

CPSIA information can be obtained
at www.ICGtesting.com
Printed in the USA
LVOW02s1837120816

500035LV00005B/23/P